THE ECONOMICS
OF THE
ENTERPRISE
FOR
ASEAN INITIATIVE

The **Institute of Southeast Asian Studies (ISEAS)** was established as an autonomous organization in 1968. It is a regional centre dedicated to the study of socio-political, security and economic trends and developments in Southeast Asia and its wider geostrategic and economic environment.

The Institute's research programmes are the Regional Economic Studies (RES, including ASEAN and APEC), Regional Strategic and Political Studies (RSPS), and Regional Social and Cultural Studies (RSCS).

ISEAS Publications, an established academic press, has issued more than 1,000 books and journals. It is the largest scholarly publisher of research about Southeast Asia from within the region. ISEAS Publications works with many other academic and trade publishers and distributors to disseminate important research and analyses from and about Southeast Asia to the rest of the world.

East-West Center Studies

Books bearing the imprint "East-West Center Studies" are works developed with substantial support from the East-West Center. The East-West Center is an education and research organization established by the U.S. Congress in 1960 to strengthen relations and understanding among the peoples and nations of Asia, the Pacific, and the United States. The Center contributes to a peaceful, prosperous, and just Asia Pacific community by serving as a vigorous hub for cooperative research, education, and dialogue on critical issues of common concern to the Asia Pacific region and the United States. Funding for the Center comes from the U.S. government, with additional support provided by private agencies, individuals, foundations, corporations, and the governments of the region. For more information, visit the Center's web site at www.EastWestCenter.org.

THE ECONOMICS

OF THE

ENTERPRISE

FOR

ASEAN INITIATIVE

Seiji F. Naya
Michael G. Plummer

ISEAS Institute of Southeast Asian Studies
Singapore

First published in Singapore in 2005 by
ISEAS Publications
Institute of Southeast Asian Studies
30 Heng Mui Keng Terrace
Pasir Panjang
Singapore 119614

E-mail: publish@iseas.edu.sg
Website: http://bookshop.iseas.edu.sg

The responsibility for facts and opinions in this publication rests exclusively with the authors and their interpretations do not necessarily reflect the views or the policy of the publisher or its supporters.

ISEAS Library Cataloguing-in-Publication Data

The Economics of the Enterprise for ASEAN Initiative / edited by Seiji F. Naya and Michael G. Plummer.
1. Free trade—ASEAN countries.
2. Free trade—United States.
3. United States—Foreign economic relations—ASEAN countries.
4. ASEAN countries—Foreign economic relations—United States.
5. ASEAN countries—Commerce—United States.
6. United States—Commerce—ASEAN countries.
7. Southeast Asia—Economic integration
I. Naya, Seiji Finch.
II. Plummer, Michael G., 1959-
HF1717 A9E19   2005

ISBN 981-230-335-9 (soft cover)

Typeset by International Typesetters Pte Ltd, Singapore
Printed in Singapore by Utopia Press Pte Ltd

SFN: *To my wife, Jane, who has been so supportive throughout the project.*

MGP: *In loving memory of my mother-in-law, Rosella Speranza, "... ci mancherai infinitamente ..."*

Contents

List of Tables

List of Appendix Tables

List of Figures

Acknowledgements

A study of this sort requires the participation of many different individuals and institutes and, hence, the authors would like to acknowledge our friends and colleagues to whom we are most indebted. First, we would like to thank Barbara Weisel of the Office for the US Trade Representative for her encouragement and moral support throughout the project. Second, the project would not have been possible without the financial, administrative, and research support of the East-West Center. In particular, we would like to thank its President, Charles Morrison, Nancy Lewis, Ralph Carvalho and Carolyn Eguchi. Craig Guzinsky of the University of Hawaii and the East-West Center offered superb research assistance in all phases of the project; without his help, this study would have been much diminished in terms of form and substance. Third, Teri Simpson Lojewski, of the State Department/USAID Technical Assistance and Training Facility at the ASEAN Secretariat in Jakarta, offered highly-useful recommendations regarding this project. Fourth, the Bologna Center of the Johns Hopkins University contributed significantly in terms of its support and encouragement from day one. We would especially like to thank its Director, Amb. Marisa Lino, and Barbara Wiza. Moreover, we received excellent research assistance, in particular in terms of the quantitative aspects of the project, from Steven Wendel, and in terms of data gathering and other research-related activities from Stephanie Law, Michael Waldron, and Sara Giannozzi. Fifth, as we note in both Chapters 1 and Chapter 4, our research partners in the region were critical to the project, both in terms of their contributions to Chapter 4 and in giving input to other aspects of the project. These include: Hadi Soesastro (CSIS); Robert Severino and Federico Macaranas (AIM); Mohammad Ariff (MIER); Chia Siow Yue (Global Development Network); and Wisarn Pupphavesa (NIDA). Sixth, the results of this study were presented at a variety of forums. The Ford Foundation provided funding for us to organize a conference around this study in September 2004 in Bangkok, Thailand, at which we received excellent comments, including from Wisarn Pupphavesa, who helped us organize the conference, William E. James, Dean DeRosa, Narongchai Akrasanee, and Stephen Parker. Other presentations were made to the American Economic Association's 2005 Annual Meeting, Johns Hopkins University SAIS-DC (October 2004), an INR/State Department Workshop in March 2005 (for which we are highly indebted to Patricia Scroggs, Cora Foley, and James Dorian), and the 2005 ASEAN-AUSTR Senior Economic Officials Meeting (Manila, March 2005). We benefited from the comments of participants at each of these presentations. Last but not least, we are grateful to the staff of the Institute of Southeast Asian Studies (ISEAS), especially Mrs. Triena Ong and Ms Dayaneetha De Silva, for their generous help in making this publication a reality.

It should be added, of course, that the ideas expressed in this study are those of the authors alone.

Glossary

ADB	Asian Development Bank
AEC	ASEAN Economic Cooperation
AFTA	ASEAN Free Trade Area
AIA	ASEAN Investment Area
AIJV	ASEAN Industrial Joint Ventures
ANZCERTA	Australia, New Zealand Closer Economic Relation Trade Agreement
APEC	Asia Pacific Economic Cooperation
APT	ASEAN Plus Three
ASEAN	Association of Southeast Asian Nations
ASEM	Asia Europe Meeting
AUI	ASEAN-U.S. Initiative
BBC	Brand-to-Brand Complementation
BTA	bilateral trade agreement
CAFTA	Central American Free Trade Agreement
CEPT	Common Effective Preferential Tariff
CGE	computational general equilibrium
CMLV	Cambodia, Myanmar, Laos and Vietnam
CPO	crude palm oil
CU	customs unions
DWE	detention without examination
EAI	Enterprise for ASEAN Initiative
ECIG	export credit and insurance guarantee
EFTA	European Free Trade Association
EU	European Union
FDI	foreign direct investment
FTA	free trade agreement
FTAA	Free Trade Area of the Americas
GATS	General Agreement on Trade in Services

GATT	General Agreement on Tariffs and Trade
GDP	gross domestic product
GPA	WTO Government Procurement Agreement
GSP	Generalized System of Preferences
GTAP	Global Trade Analysis Project
ICT	information communication technology
ILO	International Labour Organization
IPR	intellectual property rights
ISI	Integrated Sourcing Initiative
MERCOSUR	Southern Common Market (Argentina, Brazil, Paraguay and Uruguay)
MFA	Multi-Fibre Agreement
MFN	most-favoured nation
MRA	mutual recognition agreements
NAFTA	North American Free Trade Area
NTB	non-tariff barrier
OECD	Organization for Economic Cooperation and Development
PAFTAD	Pacific Area Trade and Development Forum
PBEC	Pacific Basin Economic Council
PECC	Pacific Economic Cooperation Council
PTA	Preferential Trade Agreement
RTA	regional trade agreements
SITC	Standard International Trade Classification
SPS	sanitary and phytosanitary measures
SRCC	Spearman Rank Correlation Coefficient
TIFA	Trade and Investment and Facilitation Agreement
TIFL	Trade and Investment Facilitation and Liberalization
TRIMS	Trade-related Investment Measures
TRIPS	Trade-related Aspects of Intellectual Property Rights
UNDP	United Nations Development Program
URAA	Uruguay Round of Agricultural Agreement
USSFTA	U.S.-Singapore Free Trade Agreement
USTR	U.S. Trade Representative
WIPO	World Intellectual Property Organization
WTO	World Trade Organization

1

Introduction and Overview

I.   Introduction

During the APEC Annual Summit in October 2002, President Bush announced his desire to pursue a series of bilateral free-trade areas (FTAs) under the rubric of the "Enterprise for ASEAN Initiative" (EAI). There were only two conditions for being included under the EAI: (1) Association of Southeast Asian Nations (ASEAN) members needed to be a member of the World Trade Organization (WTO); and (2) they had to have in place a Trade and Investment Facilitation and Liberalization (TIFL) agreement with the United States. This effectively posed no problem for the original ASEAN member-states (Indonesia, Malaysia, the Philippines, Thailand and Singapore) and Brunei Darussalam but could impede negotiations with the new members, i.e., Cambodia, Laos, Myanmar, and Vietnam ("CLMV"), all of which are transitional economies. Of this group, only Cambodia is now a WTO member-state (as of September 2004). Still, Vietnam has normal trade relations with the United States and a Bilateral Trading Agreement (BTA) and could join the WTO in 2005. Laos and the United States have already negotiated a BTA, similar to the U.S.-Vietnam accord, which was put into place in 2005 when the U.S. Congress granted normal trade relations status to Laos. Only Myanmar is likely to be left on the sidelines.

Background

In many ways, the EAI did not come as a surprise to most observers for a number of reasons. First, the Bush administration had been actively pursuing FTAs with partners throughout the developing world. The U.S. policy of merely supporting multilateral liberalization under the GATT/WTO framework changed in the 1980s, first with an FTA (in manufactures) with Israel and followed by an FTA-like agreement with the Caribbean Basin (1986), the U.S.-Canada FTA (1989), and NAFTA (1994). When the Bush administration received Trade Promotion Authority in 2002, it wasted no time in negotiating a number of bilateral FTAs with countries throughout the world.

One of these FTAs was with Singapore, which leads us to our second reason why the EAI was expected: Singapore is a key member of ASEAN and it was believed that after cementing an agreement with Singapore, it would only make sense—from both the U.S. and ASEAN points of view—to consider an accord with the other ASEAN member-states. The U.S.-Singapore FTA (USSFTA) is one of the most modern FTAs in the world today; it was explicitly mentioned in the EAI announcement that the USSFTA, finalized in 2003, would be used as a "model" for the other bilateral U.S.-ASEAN FTA accords. While the EAI framework would no doubt require diversity in substance given the diversity of ASEAN—and the fact that Singapore was an "easy" partner in that it is rich, developed, has no agricultural sector, and is uncompetitive in other "sensitive" areas, unlike most of the rest of ASEAN—the USSFTA did mark which areas and sectors would be included in the U.S.-ASEAN FTAs.

Third, given the regionalism *zeitgeist*, ASEAN is a natural priority "target". As can be seen in Table 1.1, ASEAN countries differ considerably in terms of size, per capita income, and openness. In fact, the coefficient of variation of per capita incomes in ASEAN, which is an indication of how diverse the region is, comes to 1.6, among the highest of any economic grouping in the Asia-Pacific region and, indeed, the world.[1] Nevertheless, they are all important and—for most countries—growing trading partners of the United States. If one controls for their size, as discussed below, the U.S. trade with these countries is several *times* more than one would expect if they were randomly selected partners. Also, the ASEAN countries play host to a more than proportionate share of U.S. multinational investment and have become key to the

Table 1.1
Economic Characteristics of the ASEAN and Selected Asia-Pacific Economies

	Population	GDP	Per Capita GNI		Goods		Goods	
			$ dollars	PPP	Exports	Imports	Export	Imports
	$ millions	$ billions			$ millions		percentage of GDP	
Developed Countries								
United States	288	10,383.1	35,400	36,110	693,860	1,202,430	6.7	11.6
Canada	31	714.3	22,390	28,930	252,394	227,463	35.3	31.8
Japan	127	3,993.4	34,010	27,380	416,726	337,194	10.4	8.4
Australia	20	409.4	19,530	27,440	65,034	72,689	15.9	17.8
New Zealand	4	58.6	13,260	20,550	14,363	15,077	24.5	25.7
China	1,280	1,266.0	960	4,520	325,565	295,203	25.7	23.3
NIEs								
Hong Kong	7	161.5	24,690	27,490	201,150	207,168	124.5	128.3
Korea	48	476.7	9,930	16,960	162,470	152,126	34.1	31.9
Singapore	4	87.0	20,690	23,730	125,177	116,441	143.9	133.9
Taiwan	19	290.6	13,420		135,065	112,602		
ASEAN								
Brunei[2]	370			18,600				
Cambodia	12	4.0	300	1,970	1,500	1,989	37.5	49.7
Indonesia	212	172.9	710	3,070	57,130	31,288	33.0	18.1
Laos	6	1.7	310	1,660	298	431	17.7	25.7
Malaysia	24	94.9	3,540	8,500	93,265	79,869	98.3	84.2
Myanmar	49				3,015	2,324		
Philippines	80	78.0	1,030	4,450	36,265	35,229	46.5	45.2
Thailand	62	126.9	2,000	6,890	68,853	64,721	54.3	51.0
Vietnam	80	35.0	430	2,300	16,530	19,000	47.1	54.2
South Asia								
Bangladesh	136	47.6	380	1,770	6,093	7,914	12.8	16.6
India	1,049	510.2	470	2,650	49,251	56,595	9.7	11.1
Nepal	24	5.5	230	1,370	568	1,419	10.2	25.6
Pakistan	145	59.1	420	1,960	9,913	11,233	16.8	19.0
Sri Lanka	19	16.6	850	3,510	4,699	6,140	28.4	37.1
World	6,199	32,312.1	5,120	7,820	6,454,929	6,590,272	20.0	20.4

TABLE 1.1 (continued)

	Services ($ millions)		Services (% GDP)		Good and Services (% GDP)		Inv't % GDP	Saving % GDP	GDP Growth Rate % 2003	GDP Growth Rate % 2004
	Exports	Imports	Export	Imports	Exports	Imports				
Developed Countries										
United States	272,630	205,580	2.6	2.0	9.3	13.6	18	14	3.0	4.3
Canada	36,272	41,932	5.1	5.9	40.4	37.7	20	25		4.0
Japan	64,909	106,612	1.6	2.7	12.1	11.1	26	26	2.4	
Australia	17,443	17,740	4.3	4.3	20.1	22.1	24	22		
New Zealand	5,041	4,682	8.6	8.0	33.1	33.7	20	22		
China	39,381	46,080	3.1	3.6	28.8	27.0	40	43	9.1	8.8
NICs										
Hong Kong	43,333	24,800	26.8	15.4	151.4	143.6	23	32	3.2	7.5
Korea	27,080	35,145	5.7	7.4	39.8	39.3	26	27	3.1	4.4
Singapore	29,599	27,155	34.0	31.2	178.0	165.1		45	1.1	8.1
Taiwan					50.5	44.7			3.3	6.0
ASEAN										
Brunei²					52.9	25.1				
Cambodia	593	372	14.8	9.3	52.3	59.0	8	14	5.2	4.5
Indonesia	6,517	16,779	3.8	9.7	36.8	27.8	14	21	4.5	4.8
Laos	127	5	7.6	0.3	25.3	26.0	22		5.8	6.5
Malaysia	14,753	16,248	15.5	17.1	113.8	101.3	32	42	5.3	6.8
Myanmar	405	364					13	12		
Philippines	3,029	4,311	3.9	5.5	50.4	50.7	19	19	4.7	5.5
Thailand	15,232	16,573	12.0	13.1	66.3	64.1	24	31	6.8	6.4
Vietnam	2,948	3,698	8.4	10.5	55.5	64.7	56	28	7.1	7.5
South Asia										
Bangladesh	305	1,391	0.6	2.9	13.5	19.6	23	22	5.3	5.5
India	24,553	18,464	4.8	3.6	14.5	14.7	25	12	8.2	6.5
Nepal	303	205	5.5	3.7	15.7	29.3	15	14	2.7	3.6
Pakistan	1,536	2,093	2.6	3.5	19.4	22.6	21	14	5.1	6.4
Sri Lanka	1,247	966	7.5	5.8	35.9	42.9	15	14	5.9	5.0
World	1,511,226	1,475,405	4.7	4.6	24.7	25.0	20	20		

Notes: ¹ GNI PPP

² www.cia.gov/cia/publications/factbook

Source: World Bank, *World Economic Indicators 2004*

trade and investment strategies of many American companies. The major push towards greater economic integration in ASEAN over the past decade and a half—from the ASEAN Free Trade Area, or AFTA, to the decision in October 2003 to create an "ASEAN Economic Community", a commitment which was re-dedicated at the November 2004 Summit—makes it an even more attractive region.

Finally, the United States has long pondered a series of FTAs with the ASEAN countries. In the late 1980s, the authors of this study were asked to lead a group of both ASEAN and American scholars to study the growing importance of ASEAN-U.S. economic relations and to recommend means of strengthening bilateral and regional relations. This study was titled the *ASEAN-U.S. Initiative* (AUI), funded by the State Department and United Nations Development Programme (UNDP) and published by the Institute of Southeast Asian Studies (Singapore) in late 1989 (Naya et al. 1989). The most salient conclusion of this study was that, in order to promote closer relations, a framework agreement should be developed under which the United States and ASEAN could eventually form an FTA. However, it noted that before an FTA could be negotiated, ASEAN needed to deepen economic integration significantly, which it subsequently did (see Chapter 5). Coupled with the new U.S. interest in bilateralism, "supply" and "demand" appear to be in place, making the moment propitious.

Why Bilaterals rather than a Regional Agreement?
While the motivations for U.S.-ASEAN FTAs are evident, it is less clear why the United States would choose to negotiate with ASEAN countries on a *bilateral* level, rather than as a *group*. The AUI considered a framework agreement that would be ASEAN-wide, though it recognized the need to compensate for regional diversity. The 2004 China-ASEAN FTA includes ASEAN as a region. Although certain Japanese regional initiatives in terms of finance, e.g., the Chiang Mai Initiative, include a regional framework based on bilateral accords, Japan is choosing to negotiate with ASEAN on a regional basis, and ASEAN+3 initiatives are also regionally-oriented. While the EU has not launched any FTA initiatives with Asian countries yet, it tends to prefer regional accords as well. For example, it had originally negotiated a series of Association Agreements with North African countries using a bilateral approach, but discovered that a region-wide policy would create fewer problems and

would be more consistent. Hence the creation of its Global Mediterranean Policy. Why is the United States, then, intent on negotiating its FTAs with ASEAN on a bilateral basis?

Briefly, there are at least several reasons for this. First, technically the United States could not negotiate with ASEAN as a region due to membership problems related to the CMLV members: it has imposed strict economic sanctions on Myanmar, and Laos and Vietnam are not yet members of the WTO (as mentioned above, the United States does not even have normal trade relations with Laos yet). Any such agreement, therefore, could not be entirely regional, but rather of the "10-X" sort. Second, even the AUI acknowledged with respect to the ASEAN-6 (the original ASEAN members plus Brunei) that the tremendous diversity of ASEAN posed a great challenge to a U.S.-ASEAN regional accord. ASEAN includes a developed, rich, and resource-poor Singapore; an extremely small, rich, resource (energy) dependent Brunei; middle- to high-middle income, resource-rich Indonesia, the Philippines, Thailand and Malaysia; and, of course, the CMLV, which are still building market economies, not to mention being among the Least Developed Countries (see Table 1.1). Cultural and political diversity also complicate matters. Coupled with the diverse needs and sensitive industries of the ASEAN countries, how could a regional agreement be possible? The CMLV countries were not members of ASEAN when the AUI recommendations were tabled.

This diversity has always dogged ASEAN cooperation at Asia-Pacific and other international forums, as no common positions were easy to take with such a diverse membership. Now, a loose FTA—like the Chinese-ASEAN FTA or arguably even AFTA itself—could accommodate these problems, but as we argue in this study, the United States does not agree to "loose", "flexible" FTAs: they are all legally binding and precise. And, frankly, ASEAN does not need another "loose" agreement. We believe this is why the United States will be such a good partner in these agreements: it will force structural policy reform in such a way that will reinforce the competitiveness of the ASEAN countries in ways that have proven extremely difficult in the current political environment.

Third, the United States wanted to move forward quickly with its FTA agenda and it knew that an FTA with Singapore would be relatively easy and would allow the United States to fashion a basic model for the other ASEAN countries. As is discussed in Chapter 4, Singapore was highly motivated to form an FTA with the United States, and the structure of the Singapore economy made it an easy sell (from political and economic points of view) in the United States, with strong support from the business community. While the decision to go ahead with this bilateral agreement briefly strained relations with the other ASEAN member states who saw it as a dilution of ASEAN solidarity, it was later accepted. Moreover, through this process, the United States has been able to show that it still intends to be highly engaged in Asia, despite its well-publicized initiatives elsewhere (particularly in Latin America and the Middle East but also in Africa).

A fourth potential motivation—offered by U.S. commercial policy cynics—relates to a criticism that the United States is now turning its back on the WTO and is "going bilateral" because it is easier to dominate bilateral accords (the "divide and conquer" argument). But this suggests a misunderstanding of the recent evolution of U.S. commercial policy. First, the United States continues to be active at the WTO and, in effect, it has been really the Europeans, implicitly supported by the Japanese, that have been the most reticent in pushing forward "Single Undertakings" at the GATT/WTO, particularly with respect to agriculture. Suggesting that the Europeans—the most active supporters of regionalism in the world—and the Japanese are doing this just so that they can dominate partners at the bilateral level would be to misunderstand what is driving the process. The same is true of the United States; the Bush administration's support of FTAs finds its roots in a frustration with where the WTO Single Undertaking can go, as opposed to what it can achieve in terms of market access and economic integration in FTAs (we discuss this at length in Chapter 5). And it has not always chosen to go bilateral; the Free Trade Area of the Americas (FTAA) was always the biggest FTA priority of the first Bush administration. An FTA with Central America (CAFTA) has been negotiated and is currently being debated in the U.S. Congress.

Second, if it were true that the United States wanted to maximize its economic benefits through asymmetric power-plays in bilateral FTAs, why has it chosen so many FTAs with countries having little economic importance to the United States? Was the U.S.-Jordan accord, the U.S.-Moroccan accord, or the U.S.-Bahrain accord due to economics? No, and neither was CAFTA. These were part of a new diplomatic and commercial policy strategy that is being integrated with the same goals in mind.

In sum, there are some strong arguments in favor of bilateral FTAs.

However, given that ASEAN itself has an "FTA plus" in place (AFTA, plus many industrial and other accords, as discussed in Chapter 5) and is working toward the ASEAN Economic Community (AEC), having a common framework for these accords with the ASEAN member-states would make a great deal of sense, as it would ensure consistency, minimize policy discrepancies, and actually make it easier for ASEAN to promote intra-regional cooperation in the future (e.g., within the framework of the AEC) due to certain necessary policy harmonization and adoption of "best practices". Thus, bilateral FTAs under a regional EAI framework could be advantageous from both the U.S. and ASEAN perspectives.

The EAI Study

This study has been conducted under the auspices and the financial support of the East West Center with the recommendation and encouragement of the Office of the U.S. Trade Representative. We also received partial financial support from the U.S.-ASEAN Business Council and the ASEAN-U.S. Technical Assistance and Training Facility. The study is in some ways a modern follow-up to the AUI. It is designed to analyse issues related to the economics and political economy of the EAI in terms of its potential benefits and costs, as well as from the perspective of U.S. and ASEAN trade policy. In brief, the data and economic analysis of our study suggest that the United States is in many ways the region's most important economic partner in terms of trade and investment and will continue to play a key role in the economic future of all ASEAN countries. Closer economic cooperation with the United States also holds the most hope for expediting necessary structural change in the region, as well as having numerous inherent benefits. Moreover, we note that, while FTAs may not be optimal in a pure economic sense, the current general trend in regionalism increases the potential costs of remaining outside regional networks. Further, given that the United States is the region's most important strategic partner and the EAI reinforces the long-term interest and commitment of the United States to engage in Southeast Asia, our economic results strongly support bilateral strategic interests as well.

The study itself is organized in six chapters, with this Chapter 1 being an overview of the main results of the composite chapters. Chapter 2 gives a detailed analysis of the U.S.-ASEAN economic relationship. It begins with a review of U.S.-ASEAN trade in goods in a global context, followed by in-depth analysis of the changing structure of bilateral trade at various levels of disaggregation. It then repeats this review for trade in services, though data restrictions render the analysis less rich than in the case of trade in goods. Next, the chapter considers U.S. foreign direct investment (FDI) to the ASEAN region, again in a comparative context. This analysis is undertaken with respect to both other OECD source-country outflows to ASEAN as well as U.S. (and other) OECD outflows to ASEAN relative to China. Moreover, it gives a detailed analysis of U.S. FDI in ASEAN at the sectoral level over the 1993–2003 period.

Chapter 3 considers explicitly the economics of the EAI, that is, bilateral FTAs between the United States and ASEAN member-states. It begins with an extensive review of modern theories of the economics of FTAs, including "static" (that is, one time changes in tariffs or non-tariff barriers inherent in an FTA), "dynamic" (e.g, the effects of an FTA on FDI, economies of scale, technology transfer, and the like), and economic policy. This is followed by a series of empirical tests of the economics of the EAI using three techniques: (1) a large econometric gravity model, in order to capture the degree of trade bias in the U.S.-ASEAN economic relationship, with a view to ascertaining if these agreements would be characterized as "natural" economic blocs; (2) a review of economy-wide estimates of these FTAs based on the work of Gilbert (2003); and (3) a disaggregated technique to identify the sectors that will be most significantly affected by the EAI.

Chapter 4, which identifies the "special bilateral issues" that will likely be involved in the EAI FTA negotiations, was based on reports prepared for this study by a consortium of researchers from throughout the region, including Hadi Soesastro (CSI, Indonesia); Mohamad Ariff (MIER, Malaysia); Federico Macaranas (AIM, the Philippines); and Wisarn Pupphavesa, Yuthana Sethapramote and Niramol Ariyaarpakamol (NIDA, Thailand). The Report for Brunei Darussalam was written by Seiji Naya and Michael Plummer. Moreover, given that Singapore is meant to be a "model" for the EAI FTAs, we thought it would be useful to include an ex-post evaluation of the USSFTA. This is undertaken by Professor Chia Siow Yue.[2] In this chapter, we review not only the critical economic and policy-related elements that exist in the bilateral relationships but also where the stumbling blocs will be in the negotiations, as well as how the United States and ASEAN might overcome them. In sum, while it would appear that there will be many difficult issues to tackle in all the remaining FTAs (save, perhaps, a U.S.-Brunei agreement), we argue that the negotiations are well worth the effort, as it will help structural reform in ASEAN and the United States, as well as inducing the ASEAN countries to adopt certain policies that have not yet been properly articulated (for example, with respect to competition policy, government procurement, intellectual property protection, and the like).

We consider the EAI in the context of a changing global, Asia-Pacific, and subregional environment in Chapter 5. Given the regionalism *zeitgeist* that has transformed FTAs from an *"exception"* to the GATT/WTO principle of non-discriminatory, "most-favoured-nation" trade relationships into the *"rule"*, it is important to consider the EAI in light of these new developments. We do this first for the "Triad" countries (Europe, Japan, and the United States) before analysing EAI as part of the process of the general trend of Asia-Pacific economic cooperation, i.e., under APEC and ASEAN itself. As part of this discussion, we also consider the emergence of China as a competitive "threat" to ASEAN in terms of economics, and to the United States with respect to strategic economic policy in the region. The chapter also features a chronology of ASEAN- and ASEAN+3-related economic initiatives.

Finally, Chapter 6 makes the case for the EAI, summarizing the major economic considerations put forth in the earlier chapters. In addition to these economic arguments, it focuses on policy motivations, that is, the EAI as a defensive strategy for ASEAN; a proactive commercial policy approach for the United States; and a strategic imperative for both.

Overview of Chapter 1

In this Chapter 1, we give a summary of the main analysis and conclusions of the study. We begin with a discussion of various FTA-related issues in Section II, followed by an analysis of bilateral trade and investment links in Section III (overall flows) and Section IV (interdependence at the disaggregated level). Next, the chapter reviews the results of our econometric ("gravity") model, which focuses on capturing the changing trade relationship between the U.S. and ASEAN (Section V); existing economy-wide estimates of the effects of a series of U.S.-ASEAN bilateral FTAs (Section VI); and our own disaggregated technique to identify the actual commodity groups that will be most affected by the EAI FTAs (Section VII). Section VIII considers relevant emerging trends in the global marketplace and the Asia-Pacific in particular and their relevance for the EAI. Section IX gives some concluding remarks.

II. FTA Issues

The effect of integration is generally measured in terms of trade creation and trade diversion when tariffs and other trade barriers are eliminated. This measurement is obviously too narrow in terms of actual reality. If the driving force behind policy change is merely reducing tariffs to zero, and tariffs are already fairly close to zero, the net effect cannot be large. But modern FTAs, at least with the United States, go far beyond trade and trade barriers to span issues and concessions affecting foreign investment, e-commerce, intellectual property rights, telecom services, information communication technology, various key services—such as banking, consulting, and legal services—foreign investment laws, and other areas.

Modern FTAs address many non-border issues that not only tend to increase flows of FDI but also reduce many transactions costs associated with multinational business. As was clearly demonstrated in the case of EU integration with the creation of the Single Market, a key area relates to harmonization of product standards, mutual recognition of product testing, mutual recognition of professional certifications and qualifications, and the like. Many of these areas are covered in the U.S.-Singapore agreement and will likely be an important part of the EAI. Now, it is important to underscore that these areas generally imply the adoption of "best practices", reducing unnecessary costs, and bolstering competition, rather than creating a "fortress".

In the case of most recent FTAs, trade and investment in goods and services are affected in various ways (expounded at length in Chapter 3), giving rise to income and employment changes and economic growth, lowering transactions costs and stimulating FDI inflows, particularly from outside the region. Increasing FDI inflows from the United States—and from other countries wishing to have duty-free access to the U.S. market—constitutes a prominent incentive for the ASEAN countries. This is especially important in the current ASEAN economic context, as a number of member-states have had particularly disappointing inflows of FDI in recent years (noted later). Enhancing FDI should be a major benefit of EAI FTAs. These changes are expected to lead to considerable gains in efficiency and productivity, as well as provide for the necessary groundwork to facilitate technology transfer. Most of these areas are already priorities of the various ASEAN governments. *In many ways, modern FTAs will complement government efforts to restructure the economy to enhance its competitiveness and upgrade the industrial base to higher value added sectors.*

As ASEAN countries move up the development ladder, they will be competing increasingly in areas in which economies of scale matter, including electronics, chemicals, and auto-related production. They are currently restricted by the small size of each ASEAN market. As ASEAN integration proceeds apace, exports will have duty-free (or close to duty-free) access to a regional market, but once again, the combined ASEAN market is not that big relative to the domestic markets of the United States, Japan and the EU. Hence, the EAI—as well as ASEAN+3 initiatives—could help competitiveness in these areas.

Moreover, the non-border issues that are covered in the agreement tend to make frequent reference to WTO protocols, disciplines and agreements, e.g., in the area of services, government procurement, and intellectual property. In this sense, the forced-efficiency related areas are clearly "building blocs" to multilateral cooperation.

III. Trade of Goods and Services and Foreign Investment

In order to assess the potential economic impact of the EAI for both the United States and ASEAN member-states, we first examine trade of goods and services and FDI flows (in Chapter 2). We note that exports and imports have grown substantially between the two regions. Two-way trade from 1990 to 2003 rose from US$51 billion to US$118 billion, or 2.3 times (Tables 1.2 and 1.3). The United States is the largest export market for ASEAN as a whole and for most individual countries (with the notable exception of Indonesia). Exports to the United States comprised 16 per cent of total ASEAN exports in 2003, though this share is lower than the 20 per cent share recorded in 1990. ASEAN imports from the U.S. in 2003 were 12.3 per cent of its total, declining from 14.7 per cent. ASEAN imports with Japan have declined from 23.6 per cent in

TABLE 1.2
Exports of ASEAN, China, Japan and the United States
(in % of world total)

TO	Exports of				
	ASEAN	**JA**	**CH**	**U.S.**	**DA**
Japan					
1990	18.5	–	14.1	12.4	14.4
2003	12.1	–	13.6	7.2	10.1
U.S.					
1990	20	32	11	–	22
2003	16	25	21	–	18
China					
1990	1.8	2.1	–	1.2	5.1
2003	6.7	12.1	–	3.9	12.0
ASEAN					
1990	19.1	11.5	5.8	4.8	10.9
2003	20.4	12.3	6.0	6.1	10.7
Dev. Asia					
1990	35.1	31.3	48.3	15.5	33.3
2003	36.3	39.7	42.8	16.4	42.1
World[1]					
1990	138,813	287,678	69,478	393,106	451,900
2003	426,636	473,911	438,250	723,611	1,562,727

Note: [1] in US$ millions
Source: IMF, *Direction of Trade Statistics, 2004*

1990 to 16.1 per cent in 2003. Likewise, exports declined from 18.5 per cent to 12.1 per cent. On the other hand, ASEAN trade with China has been rising rapidly. For example, ASEAN exports to China rose 6.7 per cent in 2003 from 1.8 per cent in 1990 while imports rose 8.1 per cent from 2.9 per cent over the same period. This rapid increase in trade with China underscores the growing importance of the Chinese market to the ASEAN countries and a significant economic motivation for the FTA agreed to in November 2004. Intra-ASEAN trade has been rising more in imports than exports. Intra-ASEAN exports rose slightly to 20.4 per cent in 2003 from 19.1 per cent in 1990, but intra-ASEAN imports increased 23.5 per cent from 15.4 per cent over the same period.

TABLE 1.3
Imports of ASEAN, China, Japan and the United States
(in % of world total)

FROM		Imports of				
		ASEAN	**JA**	**CH**	**U.S.**	**DA**
Japan						
	1990	23.6	–	13.4	18.0	21.0
	2003	16.1	–	18.0	9.3	16.4
US						
	1990	14.7	22.5	10.7	–	15.2
	2003	12.3	15.6	8.2	–	9.9
China						
	1990	2.9	5.1	–	3.2	7.7
	2003	8.1	19.7	–	12.5	12.1
ASEAN						
	1990	15.4	11.9	5.5	5.6	9.8
	2003	23.5	13.9	11.0	6.0	13.9
Dev Asia						
	1990	29.9	28.9	35.1	20.2	30.7
	2003	40.9	40.4	26.3	24.4	42.7
World						
	1990	158,870	235,307	58,632	517,020	467,800
	2003	393,621	382,922	412,836	1,305,220	1,455,220

Source: IMF, Direction of Trade Statistics, 2004

The ASEAN countries do constitute an important market particularly for certain U.S. exports, although obviously a fairly even distribution of U.S. trade destinations across Europe, the Americas, and Asia, and the relatively small size of the ASEAN markets, naturally result in relatively low trade shares. Nevertheless, ASEAN's share of U.S. exports has gone up to 6.1 per cent in 2003 from 4.8 per cent in 1990, while the ASEAN share of U.S. imports also rose slightly from 5.6 per cent to 6.0 per cent during the same period. In sum, the United States is trading more with ASEAN and while the percentages are small, they derive from very large numbers.

In terms of trade balances, the United States has a merchandise trade deficit with the EAI countries, which rose from US$10 billion in 1990 to US$35 billion in 2003 (6 per cent of the total U.S. deficit of US$581 billion). However, it is important to stress that (as shown in Table 1.4) the United States has a significant trade surplus in the area of services. The growth rate of U.S. exports of services to the EAI countries were higher than the global average. Likewise the U.S. had a surplus in services trade with ASEAN (US$5.65 billion in 2002).

TABLE 1.4

a: Trade in Commercial Services:
U.S., ASEAN, and Selected Other Countries, 2002
(US$ millions)

	Exports	Imports	Balance
World	1,570,100	1,545,500	24,600
U.S.	272,630	205,580	67,050
Japan	64,909	106,612	(41,703)
Indonesia	5,369	15,950	(10,581)
Malaysia	14,753	16,248	(1,495)
Philippines	3,029	4,225	(1,196)
Singapore	26,946	20,551	6,395
Thailand	15,232	16,573	(1,341)
ASEAN-5	65,329	73,547	(8,218)
China	39,381	46,080	(6,699)

b: U.S. Trade in Private Services with ASEAN-5, 2002 (US$ millions)

	Exports	Imports	Balance
World	279,495	205,234	74,261
Japan	29,688	17,312	12,376
Indonesia	1,021	285	737
Malaysia	1,142	498	644
Philippines	1,514	1,274	240
Singapore	5,766	2,070	3,697
Thailand	1,139	810	329
ASEAN-5	10,582	4,937	5,645
China	6,073	4,136	1,937

Source: U.S. Department of Commerce, Bureau of Economic Analysis

We should note that the surplus in services is not sufficient to balance the deficit in the merchandise account but the origins of the trade deficit in the United States—or any country for that matter—are macroeconomic in nature; the United States had more than half-trillion dollar overall merchandise trade deficit, essentially because of insufficient net private savings in the United States to cover the huge increase in the U.S. government's need to borrow (i.e., the budget deficit). The figure for 2004 will exceed that; it is projected to be over US$600 billion, or about 6 per cent of GDP.

Nevertheless, rapid economic growth in ASEAN (pre- and post-Crisis) has provided myriad new market opportunities for U.S. exports and investors abroad. ASEAN countries have not yet reverted to the pre-Crisis growth trend, but the economic expansion over the past five years has been far greater than the global average, and future prospects are bright.[3] These trends would suggest that ASEAN will play an increasing role in U.S. global economic interaction in the future. Moreover, as ASEAN lies in the heart of one of the most dynamic regions of the world, it will continue to be an attractive place for U.S. multinationals.

However we might also point out that in addition to potential "growth effect", ASEAN could easily become an even more attractive destination for U.S. FDI in the short- and medium-term for other reasons, such as AFTA, which reduces considerably transactions costs associated with using ASEAN as a production hub. The same can be said for the ASEAN Economic Community (AEC) agreement to create a region in which trade in goods and services, capital, and skilled labour would flow freely. While the deadline for the implementation of the AEC is in 2020, the process will be one of continual liberalization, which is in line with the current policy thrusts of the ASEAN countries anyway.

Over the years, American firms have invested a substantial amount, second only to Japan, in ASEAN. The U.S. FDI stock in ASEAN countries came to approximately US$87.7 billion in 2003, substantially higher than the U.S. FDI stock of $11.9 billion in China (Table 1.5). However, total FDI *inflows* into ASEAN from the United States as well as other investing countries has declined sharply from US$23 billion in 1997 to US$5.7 billion in 2002 (Table 1.6). Indonesia, in particular, has had a substantial and continuous negative inflow of FDI since 1998.

Often, this shift in FDI priority on the part of U.S. and other OECD investors has been due to the huge inflow into China, US$49 billion

TABLE 1.5
U.S. FDI Outward Position in and Outflows to ASEAN and China
(US$ million)

	U.S. FDI Stock					U.S. Outflows				
	1990	1993	2001	2002	2003	1990	1993	2001	2002	2003
Indonesia	3,207	4,864	10,551	10,341	10,387	691	475	985	1,207	72
Malaysia	1,466	1,975	7,489	6,954	7,580	175	377	17	(609)	763
Philippines	1,355	1,953	5,436	4,642	4,700	177	369	970	(597)	(325)
Singapore[1]	3,975	8,875	40,746	52,449	57,589	620	1,743	5,593	4,377	5,699
Thailand	1,790	2,943	6,176	7,608	7,393	316	285	1,286	1,501	(560)
ASEAN-5	11,793	20,610	70,398	81,994	87,649	1,979		8,851	5,879	5,649
China	354	916	12,081	10,254	11,877	30	556	1,912	924	1,540

Notes: [1] 2002 Singapore is from 2001 data
For explanation of differences between calculations of U.S. FDI position and U.S. FDI outflows, see Chapter 2.
Source: http://www.bea.doc.gov/bea/di/1001serv/intlserv.htm

in contrast to US$5.7 billion for ASEAN-5 in 2002. In other words, the FDI has been "diverted" in favour of China. However, as we stress in Chapter 5, while it may be true that China is becoming an increasing competitor in terms of trade, there is no evidence to suggest that FDI in China has inordinately been at the expense of ASEAN.[4] In fact, the problems associated with attractive FDI flows to ASEAN are more "home grown"; policies needed to rectify the situation would be the same even if China had not experienced its tremendous boom in FDI in recent years.

IV. Commodity Trade Patterns and the EAI

In terms of commodity trade patterns, ASEAN countries have achieved remarkable success in increasing their respective shares of manufactured goods in total exports. The United States has been a major catalyst in this process. Manufacture exports as a percentage of total exports in the ASEAN countries vary from 69 per cent (Indonesia) to over 90 per cent (Singapore and Malaysia). Electronics and electronic machinery have emerged as the dominant sector for the exports of Malaysia, the Philippines, and Thailand, as well as being the most dynamic area in Indonesia. This has resulted in the role of the United States becoming even more pronounced. Our research (and that of others) shows that

TABLE 1.6

OECD FDI Outflows to ASEAN, Selected Years 1985–2000

(US$ million)

Inflows Reported by ASEAN Country:	1995	1997	1998	1999	2000	2001	2002
ASEAN-5							
Indonesia	4,346.0	4,677.0	(356.0)	(2,745.0)	(4,550.0)	(3,278.0)	(1,513.4)
Malaysia	4,178.2	5,136.5	2,163.4	3,895.3	3,787.6	553.9	3,203.4
Philippines	1,478.0	1,222.0	2,287.0	1,725.0	1,345.0	982.0	1,111.0
Singapore	7,206.4	8,085.2	5,492.9	8,550.6	11,919.1	(2,025.1)	2,030.5
Thailand	2,068.0	3,894.7	7,315.0	6,102.7	3,366.0	3,820.1	900.2
ASEAN-5 Total	19,276.6	23,015.4	16,902.3	17,528.6	15,867.7	52.9	5,731.7
New ASEAN							
Cambodia	150.8	204.0	242.9	230.3	148.5	148.1	53.8
Lao PDR	95.1	–	–	–	33.9	23.9	25.4
Myanmar	279.2	390.8	317.8	255.6	258.3	210.3	128.7
Vietnam	1,780.4	2,220.0	1,671.0	1,412.0	1,298.0	1,300.0	1,400.0
New ASEAN Total	2,305.5	2,814.8	2,231.7	1,897.9	1,738.7	1,682.3	1,607.9
ASEAN-10 Total	21,582.0	25,830.2	19,134.0	19,426.5	17,606.4	1,735.2	7,339.6
China	35,849.2	44,237.0	43,751.0	38,753.0	38,399.0	44,241.0	49,308.0

Note: 1996 data are not included for reasons of space.

Source: Asian Development Bank, *Key Economic Indicators*, Table 33, http://www.adb.org.

FDI has been the key protagonist of electronics exports for all of these countries, and the United States has been the leader in this process. Hence, the U.S. market will likely be more important in the future as the ASEAN economies mature and diversify. *In essence, the United States is playing an essential role in facilitating structural change in the region, towards medium-sophisticated production of electronics and electronic machinery, areas where its comparative advantage has been "revealed " to lie* (and in face of stiff Chinese competition).

In Chapter 2, we endeavour to capture the dynamics of changing patterns of EAI trade by examining the extent to which commodity composition or make-up changed between the United States and ASEAN countries. Using the Spearman Rank Correlation Coefficient (SRCC) technique, we find that U.S. imports from Indonesia, Malaysia, the Philippines, Singapore and Thailand changed significantly over the 1990s; SRCC's estimates are 0.307, 0.382, 0.301, 0.547, and 0.400.[5] Hence, for example, when ranking the exports of Indonesia to the United States in 1990 and 1999, we find that the correlation comes to only about 30 per cent, suggesting considerable change (i.e., the ranking of export items is quite different). In fact, this change is even more pronounced than in the case of any other Asian country included in the sample with the exception of Vietnam, with which the United States was just beginning to establish a normal diplomatic relationship (normal trade relations were only formalized in 2001).

Regarding the change in structure of U.S. exports to the ASEAN countries, one derives far less change. To some degree this is to be expected; as noted above, the United States is an advanced industrial country and one would expect its comparative advantage to be fairly stable. However, one could not say that the structure of U.S. exports to the EAI countries was stagnant, as the SRCC's are estimated to be 0.524, 0.614, 0.592 and 0.638 for Indonesia, Malaysia, the Philippines, and Thailand, respectively, over the 1990s, lower than for other Asian countries with the exception (once again) of Vietnam and, to some extent, China.

Since the EAI negotiations are being done bilaterally and not with ASEAN as a whole, there is a possibility of facing negative effects of export diversion for those countries which are excluded from an FTA. The degree to which such countries are affected will depend critically on how much overlap there is between their exports and those of the countries that succeeded in obtaining preferential treatment through an FTA (and of course, the level of commodity-level protection in the export market).

We have attempted in our calculations (Chapter 2) to determine the extent to which EAI exports are similar to each other, using two techniques. The first is the SRCC technique described above, but instead of ranking the structure of exports of the same country between two years, we rank the structure of exports of two countries (to a specific market) for the same year. A high estimated SRCC value would, therefore, suggest significant export overlap, whereas low values would mean not much competition at all. We do this at the 5-digit Standard International Trade Classification (SITC) level (2,881 commodities) for the exports of Indonesia, Malaysia, the Philippines and Thailand to the U.S. market for the years 1995 and 1999.[6] The SRCCs fall in the negative range for Singaporean competition with all but Malaysia and fairly positive for the others, up to 0.277 in the case of Indonesia-Thailand, 1995.[7] While we have no yardstick by which to deem what constitutes a "high" SRCC and a "low" SRCC, these values suggest that there is not a great deal of overlap across countries. However, it is noteworthy that competition between Malaysia and the Philippines in the U.S. market has been rising over time, while there has been less overlap between the Philippines and Indonesia. Competition between Thailand and the Philippines has risen and is relatively high, but it has fallen with respect to Malaysia and Indonesia. This is an important consideration given that the United States began free-trade-area negotiations with Thailand in July 2004. *Using this methodology, it would seem that Singapore's partners have little to fear from the U.S.-Singapore FTA (USSFTA), with the possible exception of Malaysia.*

In sum, the SRCC calculations suggest that some but not a considerable degree of export overlap exists between the EAI countries—and, hence, the risk of trade diversion due to being left out of a free-trade area world not be particularly high. We have also compared ASEAN and Chinese exports to the United States (as well as other OECD countries, reported in Chapter 2). If there is considerable overlap, then the EAI might even make more sense to ASEAN, that is, as a means of gaining a preferential edge over China's exports in the U.S. market. Our results suggest that China is consistently a greater competitor in the U.S. market with individual ASEAN countries than they are with themselves; SRCCs in 1999 for Chinese exports competing with Indonesia (0.30), Malaysia (0.279), the Philippines (0.362) and Thailand (0.40) are always higher than the corresponding numbers derived for intra-ASEAN competition.

We repeat these correlation exercises using a separate and equally popular export similarity technique, known as the Finger-Kreinin Index (FK Index), as a check for the strength of these results. The FK Index endeavours to estimate export similarity by calculating the relative importance of various commodities in the export structure of pairs of countries, and then using a filtering technique. These results (and the FK Index approach) are also presented in Chapter 2. Suffice it to note here that the general conclusions are robust; that is, intra-ASEAN competition is not high for most pairs of countries in U.S. and other OECD markets (though the FK Index estimates are higher than the SRCC calculations) but is rising, and overlap with China tends to be considerably higher than intra-ASEAN competition.

V.   U.S.-ASEAN Links: Application of a Gravity Model

In the economics literature, the two most widely-used "classes" of empirical approaches are the "gravity model" and Computational General Equilibrium (CGE) models. In our applied statistical research, we use a large gravity model to assess closely the determinants of the U.S.-ASEAN economic relationship and review and critique various CGE approaches to the economic effects of possible EAI FTAs that already exist.

Our model is based on a database made publicly available at the Andrew Rose website (University of California, Berkeley)[8] and includes trade between 178 different countries for as many years as is statistically tractable, with more than forty years for countries like the United States and most other European countries. A full description of the model is offered in Chapter 3. Here, we note that the model posits trade between countries as a function of traditional factors, such as the size of GDP of the trading countries, the relative wealth, the distance between them, relative factor endowments, and a variety of non-traditional factors, such as if the countries are island states, whether or not the countries share a common language, if they share a common border, etc. We also include a "binary" (dummy) variety for whether or not a regional trading arrangement exists between the member states, such as ASEAN. In our results, we are mostly concerned with whether or not ASEAN has a "special" role to play in U.S. trade, that is, does any special bias exist in favour of trade with ASEAN, and has this bias been getting stronger or weaker? Our discussion above regarding trade shares would suggest that, while ASEAN is small, it seems to have been more important in U.S. trade than would be suggested by its size, relative wealth, distance, etc. But we had no solid statistical support for that notion. In this exercise, we test for it using a comprehensive econometric model.

In short, if the ASEAN binary or "dummy" variable is positive and statistically significant, it means that there is a trade bias in favour of trade with ASEAN. If this binary variable is rising (falling) over time, it means that the trade bias is increasing (decreasing). We run our entire gravity model for U.S. trade with ASEAN, as well as for EU trade with ASEAN as a "control country".

In Figure 1.1, we report the magnitude of the coefficient estimates for each year and denote those that are statistically significant as a "dot". Given that the gravity models are log linear in general but the binaries cannot be logged, the meaning of the coefficients have to be treated with care. For example, an estimated coefficient equal to 1.5 would suggest that U.S. trade with the ASEAN countries is 165 per cent higher than one would expect, given the effects of all the other variables controlled for in the model.

After controlling for the usual factors, such as size, wealth, and distance, etc., Figure 1.1 reveals that there exists a bias toward bilateral trade in U.S.-ASEAN trade patterns. Indeed, we find that the U.S.-ASEAN relationship is special, in that the partnership adds extra explanatory power to the determinants of trade flows. This would confirm our hypothesis above.

However, separating out individual ASEAN country regressions in Chapter 3, we discover this special relationship does not quite materialize in the case of Indonesia (except for a few years); exists only to some degree in the case of Malaysia but appears to be declining over time and with a good deal of volatility; and is most notable in the cases of Thailand, the Philippines, and Singapore but, again, the magnitudes and, in the case of the Philippines, statistical significance, decreases over time. We suggest that this decrease in bias toward bilateral trade could be a result of the fact that the United States (and the EU) has been creating FTAs and other bilateral accords with ASEAN's competitors. This might, therefore, be due to trade diversion. Or it could be that

ASEAN countries have been losing competitiveness for other reasons, e.g., the emergence of China and India as major competitors, or local structural factors. *In any event, the EAI would certainly help remove any associated trade diversion from regional agreements, give the region a level playing field in the U.S. market, and even give it a competitive edge over such formidable competitors as China.*

FIGURE 1.1
ASEAN Gravity Regression, Original ASEAN Countries

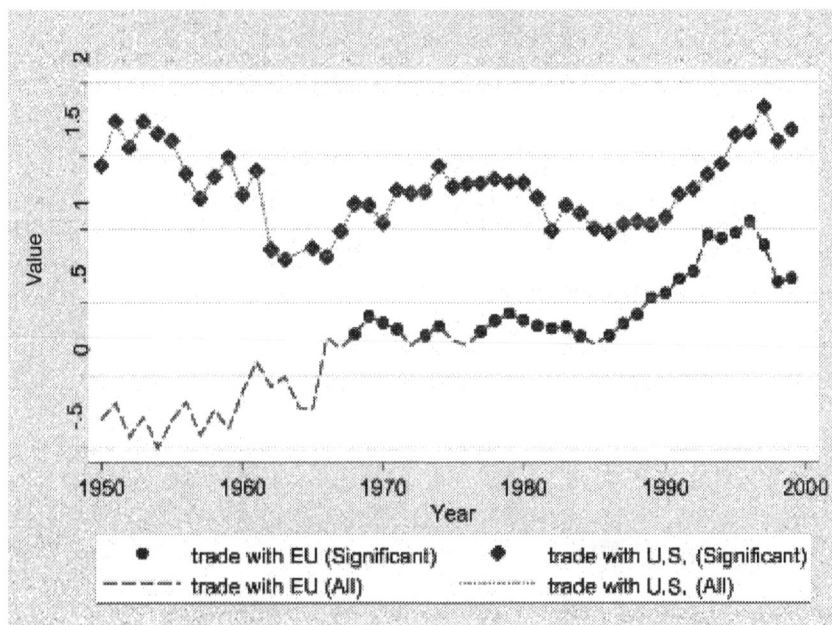

VI. CGE Estimates of Economic Impact of the FTAs

The above analysis would suggest that a series of FTAs between the United States and ASEAN under the rubric of the EAI would be advantageous to bilateral trade and investment and, hence, would seem to make sense from this perspective. A natural question to ask, however, regards the likely overall economic effects of the EAI: How large will the associated gains and costs be? Such an assessment is not a simple task. In order to assess the impact of an FTA, partial equilibrium analysis does not

TABLE 1.7

Effects of Various FTAs on EAI Countries

(Equivalent variation basis; per cent of GDP)

FTAs:	Indonesia	Malaysia	Philippines	Thailand	Singapore	U.S.	Japan
Singapore-U.S.	-0.02	-0.04	-0.05	-0.01	0.66	0.00	0.00
Singapore-Japan	-0.02	-0.35	-0.08	-0.09	4.06	0.00	0.00
Japan-South Korea	-0.01	-0.07	-0.05	-0.03	-0.07	-0.01	0.01
Japan-SK-China	-0.15	-0.70	-0.35	-0.21	-0.87	-0.02	0.25
ASEAN+3	0.69	1.24	-0.19	1.00	4.12	-0.03	0.34
Pacific 5 (1)	-0.02	-0.13	-0.06	-0.02	0.92	0.02	-0.01
Global Free Trade	1.31	6.05	3.42	2.57	6.94	-0.05	0.98

Notes: [1] Pacific 5 = FTA between Australia, Chile, New Zealand, Singapore and the United States

Source: Scollay, Robert and John P. Gilbert, *New Regional Trading Arrangements in the Asia Pacific* (Washington, D.C.: IIE, May 2001).

appear appropriate, though it is useful in evaluating individual sectors (discussed below). The gravity model merely focused on trade flows and their determinants, rather than explicit ramifications of a bilateral FTA for the overall economy. To estimate the direct and indirect impact of an FTA for aggregate welfare, GDP, and trade patterns, one needs an open economy, multi-sector general equilibrium model. In fact the CGE model has become a standard tool in estimating the FTA impact. Revolutions in computer technologies have made undertaking such modelling far easier, and one model, employed by Gilbert (2003), is devoted to the analysis of bilateral U.S.-ASEAN FTAs using a CGE model based on the Global Trade Analysis Project (GTAP) of Purdue University. Details of the model are outlined in Chapter 3. CGE estimates of the impact of various existing and potential FTAs with important implications for ASEAN are summarized in Table 1.7, and the overall economic effects of U.S.-ASEAN bilateral FTAs are presented in Table 1.8.

From these tables, several observations are worth noting. First, excluded ASEAN countries from various FTAs invariably suffer a decline in GDP, probably resulting from trade diversion. For example, the Singapore-U.S. FTA yields a positive effect on GDP for Singapore, but a negative effect on all excluded ASEAN countries. The same result holds for the Singapore-Japan FTA. A large impact in relative terms comes from a Northeast Asian FTA. In other words, if an FTA involving China, South Korea and Japan is formed, it will have a significant negative impact on all ASEAN countries. Second, one striking feature of the FTA results regards how small the GDP gains are for almost all countries and cases. While the signs might be correct in the sense that they are consistent with our expectations, the magnitudes are consistently small and even in some instances insignificant. In the case of the ASEAN countries, this

TABLE 1.8
CGE Estimates of Nominal GDP Changes by Bilateral FTAs between the U.S. and ASEAN countries (%)

	Indonesia	Malaysia	Philippines	Singapore	Thailand
ASEAN	2.75	0.46	3.1	0.66	0.72
U.S.	−0.02	0.03	0.01	−0.01	0.07

Source: Gilbert, John, 2003, "CGE Simulations of US Bilateral Free Trade Agreements", (Washington, D.C.: IIE, as cited in DeRosa 2003.

is especially strange, considering that outward-oriented policy reform over the past two decades has been associated with a strong positive effect on growth and development. In the case of the United States, it is understandable that given the size of the U.S. economy and the fact that the United States is the most open large economy in the world, the impact is not going to be significant. But it is somewhat surprising that the impact on the United States is either zero or negative. Only in the cases of a Pacific-5 FTA and a U.S.-Thai FTA is there a GDP gain, i.e., of 0.02 per cent and 0.07 per cent, respectively.

There are a few exceptions, especially in the case of global free trade, in which Malaysia and Singapore would have a growth effect greater than 6 per cent. But the CGE model used reflects instant and automatic adjustment when FTAs go into effect. In practice, it may take a few years, or even longer, for the adjustment to be completed when FTAs are instituted and prices are adjusted accordingly. Therefore, the growth rate shown in tables may have to be divided by a few years to generate the appropriate annual increase.

In view of such a small gain or even loss estimated by this model, one might question whether it is worth the time and energy of engaging in the difficult processes of FTA negotiations and the reforms and structural adjustments a country must make. Indeed, CGE estimates of global free-trade tend to also be very small, or at least far smaller than one would expect, given the strong case for free trade made by economists and the clearly superior performance of outward-oriented economies.

As is discussed at length in Chapter 3, a major shortcoming associated with CGE models in general and when applied to the impact of FTAs in particular is that they fail to take into account sufficiently (if at all) "dynamic" economic effects, such as changes in investment flows, particularly FDI; technology transfer; liberalization of various transactions costs associated with non-tariff and non-border obstacles to interchange; (indirectly and directly) forced "best practices" in terms of management, governance, and bookkeeping; and other policy-related issues. Also, trade in services, an increasingly large part of total trade, is not incorporated into many of these models, and for those that do include trade in services, liberalization benefits are difficult to capture due to paucity of data in terms of disaggregated trade flows and quantification of barriers to trade. In fact, these models generally focus on the one-time effect of a price change induced by an FTA; such a scenario would no doubt have limited long-run effects on associated economies, especially since the economies we are focusing on are already very liberal on average (e.g., the average U.S. tariff is approximately 5 per cent and the ASEAN countries are among the most open economies in the developing world). However, policy changes and dynamic benefits of regionalism have long-run effects that build up over time and tend to be "path dependent".

In sum, it is likely that these static CGE estimates are gross understatements of what we really could expect from a series of EAI-based FTAs. Our review of empirical work on CGE models finds that trade creation tends to dominate trade diversion for just about all FTAs and customs unions. Also, welfare gains are sometimes many times larger when models incorporate such items as increasing returns, imperfect competition, technology transfer, and dynamic effects, e.g. capital accumulation and total factor productivity improvements.

VII. A Disaggregated Look at the Effects of the EAI FTAs

The gravity model works with overall trade flows, and CGE models tend to be fairly aggregate in nature. But the business community is far more interested in the economics of the EAI at a practical level, that is, as disaggregated as possible, preferring effects on *products* rather than *sectors*. U.S. and ASEAN exporters are no doubt interested in what the overall effects of the EAI FTAs would be on partner economies, and how overall sectors would be affected. Yet, they are far more concerned with the effects on their own individual commodity lines. In other words, it is interesting to learn that the effects of a U.S.-Thai FTA will be positive and that the U.S. electronics sector will gain. But if my business deals with a certain type of video recorder, *that* is what is of most concern to me.

We develop our own approach to address this question. We devise a highly-disaggregated approach to "matching" 5- digit SITC commodities (approximately 3,000 items) to protection applied on export of various markets and then estimate potential trade expansion, which allows us to underscore the key product groups that would be affected (in both the United States and ASEAN). Our results are reported in Chapter 3 and its appendix. We find that the top few exports of every EAI country (with the possible exceptions of Thailand and Brunei) tend to dominate their exports to the United States. Moreover, as would be expected, these commodities generally fall in the electronics-related category, with a few exceptions. However, protection tends to be low in electronics in the United States; therefore, the estimated trade expansion potential is limited (in many cases, the U.S. MFN-applied or GSP-applied tariff is even zero, implying zero trade expansion potential).

Nevertheless, it is important to note that these estimates are merely extrapolations based on a partial, static methodology; we stress that the dynamic effects of the EAI could actually make these sectors by far the chief benefactors. Other top product groups where protection is high would not only generate the greatest degree of trade but also would help facilitate structural change in partner countries.

We did not do similar estimates for the services sector, due to lack of disaggregated data on services trade and, of course, difficulties associated with quantifying estimates of protection. However, given the growing importance of trade in services to the U.S. and EAI economies, it is likely that this is an area that will be heavily influenced by the EAI. As is clear from the U.S.-Singapore FTA (and the United States has said explicitly that it intends to use this agreement as a model for the EAI FTAs), services will be a key negotiating area in all bilateral FTAs. Our analysis strongly suggests that an FTA with the United States could also go a long way in helping the ASEAN countries push their own economic reform agenda in these areas. The financial sector and ICT are the most salient sectors in this regard.

VIII. Policy Perspectives

Every major FTA or customs union in the world has arguably been more of a political, political economy, and/or diplomatic tool than an economic one. This is true of the creation of the EEC and its expansion; NAFTA; even APEC. Hence, there are many policy-related considerations that need to be addressed in considering the economics of the EAI. Based on our analysis in Chapter 5, some of the main issues in the context of the global economy in general and the Asia-Pacific in particular would be:

1. While the United States continues to be a key market for ASEAN countries, intra-regional economic integration in East Asia has been increasing substantially. Moreover, this trend is market-driven,

rather than policy-driven, as was arguably the case in the early years of EU integration. Hence, regional initiatives such as AFTA tend to be of the "flag following trade" variety.

2. ASEAN economic cooperation, though in the form of a preferential trading agreement, has unambiguously embraced an outward-oriented approach to trade and investment with other countries and regions. This "open regionalism" will tend to be welfare enhancing and meets the "qualitative dependency" criteria, which is developed in Chapter 3.

3. Intra-ASEAN economic integration is being driven by a desire to increase regional economic efficiency in order to increase efficiency and competitiveness at the *global* level, rather than to increase intra-regional trade as a goal in and of itself (as is the case with many other FTAs in the developing world, which are driven more by politics than economics).

4. Economic integration within ASEAN—and with the world in general—is also being used as a means of promoting needed domestic economic reform, in much the same as regional initiatives enabled countries in the EU and NAFTA to undertake reforms that would otherwise have been difficult or impossible. In this sense, we argue that the United States will be the best possible FTA partner for the ASEAN countries.

5. Many of the initiatives that are being developed within ASEAN and between ASEAN member-states and other partners, such as the United States, could also have been accomplished under the WTO, at least in theory. However, the WTO process is currently experiencing considerable difficulties and, besides, in some areas much more can be done within a regional framework.

Implications of regionalism in Japan, the EU, and the United States

1. Japan has made an important and obvious shift toward embracing FTAs only over the past few years. Its first FTA was with Singapore, finalized in November 2002.

2. As noted above, the estimated effects of Japan's existing and regional initiatives are almost uniformly negative for the ASEAN countries (when they are excluded). Malaysia is the most vulnerable to these accords. While the effects are not estimated to be large relative to GDP, the downward bias of CGE models,

plus the usual disproportionate sectoral effects, suggest that the real implications for the respective ASEAN countries could be more drastic.

3. Hence, given the importance of Japan as a trading partner and source of FDI, ASEAN countries have a strong incentive to link up with Japan. However, such an FTA will be more difficult than in the case of the EAI, mainly due to agriculture. But the United States should anticipate a Japan-ASEAN accord in the future, particularly given the newly-formed China-ASEAN FTA commitment.

4. The EU is a less important economic partner and, relative to Japan and the United States, has not done much in terms of promoting economic cooperation accords with the region. Its most important initiative to date is Asia Europe Meeting (ASEM). But unlike, say, APEC, ASEM has no specific economic agenda or liberalization vision.

5. ASEAN countries suffer from the loss of MFN status created by the EU's complicated "pyramid of preferences", in which all (original) ASEAN countries find themselves among the lowest preferential rankings (along with other WTO members). ASEAN has also been negatively affected by the Single Market Program, which created a common market in Europe, and will be hurt (though marginally) by the Fifth Enlargement of the EU, which began on 1 May, 2004.

6. Hence, ASEAN countries do have an incentive to develop closer economic ties with the EU. However, no such initiatives are in the offing. Moreover, the agricultural question will be an important one once the EU and ASEAN sit down at the negotiating table, given the highly-protectionist Common Agricultural Policy of the EU. For example, agriculture is the reason why the EU-MERCOSUR (Southern Common Market) agreement has not yet been concluded. Labour-intensive sectors like textiles and clothing will also cause difficulties, as they will within the EAI context.

7. Nevertheless, it is likely that the EU will soon realize its strong interest in staying engaged in East Asia, particularly as the EAI and Japanese initiatives develop, given the fact that Asia is the most exciting region in the world. After all, the EU is the most unrepentant regionalist in the world.

8. With respect to the United States, the Bush administration has been far more aggressive than its predecessors in pursuing FTAs. Many of these are already being undertaken with EAI-country competitors. The EAI is an important part of this process and will likely receive a priority in the near future; the U.S. Trade Representative (USTR) is already in the first phase of negotiations with Thailand over a bilateral FTA.

9. The most significant FTA that the United States currently has is NAFTA, and it is a bit too early to gauge just how much trade diversion the region has suffered due to preferential treatment in favour of Mexico. One study actually has estimated a positive effect. However, certain key sectors are no doubt being negatively affected, and there is strong anecdotal evidence that ASEAN is suffering from investment diversion in favour of Mexico. The EAI would allow ASEAN to redeem its most-favoured-nation treatment in the U.S. market and could give it a competitive edge over other competitors, most notably China.

Asia-Pacific Economic Cooperation

1. There is actually a long history of cooperation at the Asia-Pacific level, including Pacific Area Trade and Development Forum (PAFTAD), Pacific Basin Economic Council (PBEC) and Pacific Economic Cooperation Council (PECC). However, APEC, launched in 1989, was the first government-related form of cooperation initiated at the region-wide level.

2. In a way, the establishment of APEC reflects the recognition by the Asia-Pacific countries of the importance of the United States as a major market for their goods and as a source for investment. Because of this, many countries believe that the United States cannot be left out of any meaningful cooperation effort in the region.

3. APEC is unique internationally for a variety of regions. For example, rather than being a tightly knit regional grouping, APEC embraces "open regionalism" whereby whatever preferences are negotiated among the APEC members are also given to a third party so that there is no trade diversion effect (though it is not clear if countries outside the region would have to reciprocate or not). Moreover, it does not negotiate formal reductions in trade and investment barriers. All liberalization within APEC is

voluntary; no sanctions or penalties exist for countries that miss agreed-upon targets.

4. By just about any measure, the "value added" of APEC is quite low. However, some progress is being made. For example, extensive work is being undertaken by APEC working groups on improving customs clearance procedures, including the creation of a businessperson's "smart card", investment agreements, exploration of means to facilitate technology transfer, cooperation in infrastructure, standards and conformance, harmonization of product standards, enhanced dialogue on trade and investment facilitation, and development cooperation.

5. It is likely that economic integration along the lines of the ASEAN+3 will continue, particularly since the gains to the member-states would be large (though, obviously, negotiations will continue to be difficult in sensitive sectors). While there is little reason to believe that ASEAN+3 initiatives will end up being inward-looking—quite the contrary—the United States will still suffer from a loss of competitiveness in these markets if it is locked out of the ASEAN-3 accords. Hence, it is in the U.S. interest, as well as those of the EAI countries, to keep the United States actively engaged in the region.

ASEAN and the "Chinese Competitive Threat"

1. As China has become a major international powerhouse, it has been perceived as a threat by both developed and developing countries. This is particularly true of the ASEAN countries, whose exports are increasingly similar to China's in the U.S. and other OECD markets.

2. Moreover, as discussed above, there is a perception in ASEAN that FDI has been diverted to China. The fact that FDI inflows to the EAI countries have been generally disappointing while Chinese inflows have been booming has been used to support this argument.

3. However, our statistical work shows that China is not necessarily "special"; as the world becomes more closely integrated, competition rises. China is just an important part of this process.

4. Hence, while the Chinese threat is real in this sense, the policy

prescriptions for ASEAN are essentially the same as they would have been without the spectacular emergence of China in the international marketplace: ASEAN countries need to concentrate on lowering the costs of doing business, improving productivity, and facilitating market-consistent structural change.

5. In addition, China will likely be a key economic partner, as well as competitor, in the future. China does have a huge trade surplus but its import growth has been extremely strong. This will likely continue as the economy continues to overheat. Regional initiatives with China might be embraced with this goal in mind: China is, after all, an important part of the ASEAN+3.

6. Finally, the Chinese Threat strengthens the case for the EAI. The ASEAN countries have the incentive to obtain a competitive edge over China in the U.S. market, and the United States needs to avoid being locked out of the East Asian integration process, of which China will ultimately be a key protagonist.

IX. Conclusion

In sum, we would argue that the EAI makes sense for both the United States and ASEAN in terms of economics and other variables. However, we have not yet stressed that the process of negotiations will be difficult, especially in certain sectors. In Chapter 4, we consider what the "special issues" will be in terms of negotiations that will be forthcoming for each bilateral FTA.

As is clear from a perusal of that chapter, there will be many obstacles to overcome if an agreement is to be reached. And this is true for both sides. Since the USSFTA will be used as a model for these negotiations, the ASEAN member-states will find themselves having to adopt policies that are cutting-edge, and given that economic reform still has a considerable way to go in a number of sectors in all ASEAN countries, this will pose a great challenge. On the other hand, the United States will face liberalization of sensitive areas as well, including agriculture and labour-intensive sectors.

But putting controversial issues on the table is not such a bad thing. If the EAI forces the United States to open up its protected sectors, we would argue that this is in the long-run interest of the U.S. economy. The same is true of the Malaysian, Philippine, and, of course,

Thai auto industries. Moreover, most ASEAN countries do not have a competition policy in place and, yet, it is clear that they need one: The EAI will help produce domestic regulation in this regard. Intellectual property protection in ASEAN tends to be strong on the books, but weak in implementation. The EAI will help here, too. It will also assist modernization of the financial sectors of the region—an important area, as the Crisis-induced reforms in ASEAN lost momentum with economic recovery—and create greater transparency in government procurement and corporate governance. It will no doubt lead to greater degrees of national treatment in the area of FDI, which is widely recognized to be an important obstacle to certain FDI flows.

The "conflict management" field is based on the premise that conflict is good in the sense that it allows serious issues to be tackled. This is an excellent example of this process. Hence, the difficult negotiations ahead, might be considered a positive rather than a negative aspect of the EAI.

Notes

[1]   Asian Development Bank (2002). The coefficient of variation is calculated as the standard deviation divided by the mean.
[2]   We are grateful to the Ford Foundation for funding a conference in Bangkok, 27–28 September, 2004, hosted by NIDA, at which each of these researchers were able to present their findings.
[3]   According to the ADB's *Asian Economic Monitor*, December 2004 (http://www.adb.org), growth in the first three quarters of 2004 was strong and the economic outlook for 2005 exceptionally bright, despite some potential risks. Its December 2004 estimates of GDP growth in the EAI countries in 2004 and 2005 (respectively) are: Indonesia: 4.9 per cent and 5.3 per cent; Malaysia: 7.1 per cent and 5.4 per cent; the Philippines: 5.9 per cent and 4.7 per cent; Singapore: 8.3 per cent and 4.4 per cent; and Thailand: 6.1 per cent and 5.7 per cent.
[4]   Lee and Plummer (forthcoming), for example, try to test for this effect using a gravity model and reject the hypothesis that FDI to China has been at the expense of ASEAN.
[5]   See Table 2.5.
[6]   We also calculate SRCCs for ASEAN exports to the OECD as a whole and other individual OECD markets (these are given in Chapter 2). However, the overall basic conclusions do not change with respect to export competition.

[7] See Table 2.6.
[8] http://faculty.haas.berkeley.edu/arose/RecRes.htm#GATTWTO.

References

Asian Development Bank. *Asian Development Outlook.* Manila: ADB, 2002.

Naya, S., M. Plummer, S. Sandhu, and N. Akrasanee, 1989. *ASEAN-U.S. Initiative.* Singapore: ISEAS, 1989.

2

Introduction to the U.S.-ASEAN Economic Relationship

I.   Introduction

As noted in Chapter 1, the goal of this second chapter is to give an analytical overview of the U.S.-ASEAN economic relationship in terms of trade in goods (Section III), trade in services (Section IV), and foreign direct investment, or FDI (Section V). Section VI summarizes the main points of the review. While we do touch to some degree on economic incentives for the creation of bilateral U.S.-ASEAN country free-trade areas, we will focus on the economics of the EAI in the next chapter.

II.   Trade in Goods

It is uncontroversial to assert that exports have been an important engine of growth in Asia over the past three decades.[1] The Asian crisis of 1997–98 may have expelled the myth that, somehow, Asian economic growth defied economic gravity, but it did nothing to reduce the strong empirical evidence that exports have played a critical role in regional growth. In fact, the slowdown in export growth in ASEAN prior to 1997 no doubt contributed to the financial meltdown that began in July 1997.

Das (2001) gives an important historical perspective to the remarkable export performance of Asia over the past three decades.[2] His data show that the developing-Asia share of world exports grew from 7 per cent in 1965 to 19 per cent in 1997 (a total of US$1.009 trillion), with the NIEs leading the way (from 1.6 per cent to 10.4) followed by the ASEAN-4 (1.9 per cent to 3.9 per cent) and China (1.5 per cent to 3.3 per cent).[3] This remarkable performance is especially impressive in light of the fact that global trade boomed over this period.

Bilateral Trade

Without doubt, the United States has been a key trading partner of the Enterprise for ASEAN (EAI) countries included in this study, that is, Brunei, Indonesia, Malaysia, the Philippines, and Thailand (EAI-5), as well as Singapore. Over the past two decades, the share of the United States in EAI-5 exports has grown for Indonesia and Malaysia and stayed fairly constant in the case of Thailand (at about one-fifth of total exports in 2002). While it has fallen in the case of the Philippines, the U.S. share of Philippine exports is the highest of any ASEAN country at one-fourth of total exports in the early 2000s (Table 2.1).

Tables 2.1 and 2.2 summarize the direction of exports and imports, respectively, of the United States, the EAI-5, the rest of ASEAN, and other selected Asian countries and country groupings in 2002. The United States was the destination of 13.2 per cent of Indonesian exports, in third place behind Japan (21.1 per cent) and the EU (13.9 per cent). It falls to fourth place in terms of imports, behind Japan (14.1), Singapore (13.1),[4] and the EU (12.4).

The United States plays a more prominent role as a trading partner in the cases of Malaysia, the Philippines and Thailand. It is the most important market for Malaysian exports (20 per cent of the total) and second to Japan in terms of imports (16.5 per cent), whereas it is number one for the Philippines in terms of both exports (24 per cent) and imports (20.6 percently, slightly above Japan's share of 20.4 per cent). It is also the largest market for Thailand with a 20 per cent share ot total exports, well ahead of the EU (14.8 per cent), Japan (14.5 per cent), and on par with the entire ASEAN-10. As a source of Thai imports, however, the United States is far less important; with only a 10 per cent share it is in fourth place behind Japan (23 per cent), the EU (11 per cent), and

TABLE 2.1
Bilateral Exports of U.S., ASEAN, and Selected Others: 2002
(per cent and US$ millions)

OF/TO	World (US$ mil)	IN	MA	PH	SI	TH	BR	ASEAN-6	ASEAN-10	CH	HK	KO	JA	APT[1]	DA[2]	CER	US	NAFTA	EU
Indonesia	57,144	–	3.55	1.36	9.36	2.15	0.06	16.48	17.33	5.08	2.17	7.19	21.08	52.85	39.06	3.63	13.25	13.95	13.87
Malaysia	93,265	1.93	–	1.43	17.11	4.26	0.28	25.01	25.76	5.63	5.69	3.37	11.29	51.74	47.53	2.61	20.19	21.40	12.40
Philippines	36,502	0.56	4.51	–	6.77	2.97	0.01	14.82	15.13	3.71	6.46	3.67	14.50	43.47	36.15	1.03	23.81	25.67	17.44
Singapore	125,087	3.28	17.43	2.43	–	4.56	0.36	28.07	30.09	5.49	9.17	4.16	7.14	56.06	54.96	3.03	15.27	16.17	12.53
Thailand	68,851	2.44	4.12	1.85	8.07	–	0.06	16.53	19.66	5.16	5.37	2.03	14.52	46.74	36.80	2.68	19.64	21.54	14.82
Brunei	2,109	1.50	0.20	0.02	9.21	19.58	–	30.51	19.58	10.42	0.03	19.92	65.29	115.25	60.92	18.30	13.20	13.38	3.02
ASEAN-6	382,958	2.03	7.39	1.68	7.66	3.13	0.21	22.10	23.77	5.26	6.29	4.08	12.58	51.98	45.75	2.85	17.75	18.97	13.53
Cambodia	2,476	0.03	0.74	0.07	3.10	0.41	0.00	4.36	5.47	0.90	0.33	0.11	2.75	9.57	7.06	0.08	42.08	42.62	16.77
Laos	298	0.05	0.12	0.01	0.15	28.55	–	28.88	51.44	2.95	0.02	0.03	2.05	56.49	55.59	0.11	0.89	1.61	38.09
Myanmar	2,629	1.09	2.65	0.06	3.70	31.61	0.01	39.12	39.25	4.73	0.85	1.94	3.80	50.58	56.80	0.40	13.13	14.26	13.67
Vietnam	15,713	1.50	1.89	1.63	5.43	1.39	0.01	11.85	13.33	6.45	1.50	2.72	7.46	31.45	27.07	15.78	14.96	16.11	24.20
ASEAN-10	404,074	1.99	7.10	1.65	7.51	3.25	0.20	21.71	23.38	5.28	6.03	3.98	12.26	50.92	44.87	3.32	17.75	18.96	13.98
China	325,711	1.05	1.53	0.63	2.14	0.91	0.01	6.26	7.23	–	17.96	4.76	14.89	44.83	33.99	1.59	21.51	23.71	14.81
Hong Kong	200,199	0.43	0.99	1.15	2.02	1.08	0.03	5.71	6.26	39.33	–	1.95	5.37	52.92	51.55	1.35	21.42	23.75	13.26
Korea	162,471	1.94	1.98	1.82	2.60	1.44	0.02	9.79	11.31	14.62	6.24	–	9.32	41.49	38.13	1.64	20.28	23.09	13.37
India	50,447	1.15	1.16	0.77	2.09	1.40	0.01	6.57	7.14	4.10	4.50	2.25	3.77	21.76	23.38	1.17	22.44	25.02	22.42
Japan	416,632	1.50	2.64	2.03	3.40	3.17	0.08	12.82	13.31	9.59	6.10	6.87	–	35.87	43.18	2.34	28.85	31.51	14.71
ASEAN+3[1]	1,509,087	1.44	3.31	1.49	3.96	2.24	0.08	12.52	13.54	10.85	7.85	4.25	8.21	44.70	42.21	2.23	22.39	24.53	14.20

TABLE 2.1 (continued)

OF/TO	World (US$ mill)	IN	MA	PH	SI	TH	BR	ASEAN-6	ASEAN-10	CH	HK	KO	JA	APT[1]	DA[2]	CER	US	NAFTA	EU
Devlp Asia[2]	1,299,000	1.08	3.29	1.24	3.96	1.86	0.07	11.50	12.80	10.53	9.77	3.15	10.77	47.02	41.25	2.02	20.25	22.23	14.54
Australia	65,159	2.60	1.91	0.96	4.05	2.10	0.04	11.67	12.10	6.95	2.93	8.33	18.49	48.80	39.32	6.51	9.59	11.49	12.32
New Zealand	14,159	1.47	1.94	1.50	1.25	1.16	0.01	7.33	7.79	4.63	2.03	4.39	11.49	30.32	25.34	20.31	15.53	19.15	14.96
ANZCERTA	79,318	2.40	1.91	1.06	3.55	1.94	0.04	10.90	11.33	6.53	2.77	7.62	17.24	45.50	36.83	8.97	10.65	12.86	12.79
United States	693,000	0.37	1.49	1.05	2.34	0.70	0.01	5.96	6.05	3.18	1.82	3.26	7.42	21.73	17.79	2.15	–	15.96	20.79
Canada	252,381	0.12	0.11	0.08	0.13	0.13	0.00	0.57	0.59	1.01	0.29	0.50	2.04	4.43	2.85	0.33	87.68	88.28	4.18
Mexico	160,038	0.01	0.05	0.01	0.19	0.03	–	0.27	0.27	0.28	0.12	0.13	0.29	1.10	1.17	0.07	89.38	91.14	3.26
NAFTA	1,105,419	0.26	0.97	0.68	1.52	0.47	0.00	3.91	3.97	2.27	1.23	2.18	5.16	14.79	11.97	1.43	32.96	43.36	14.46
EU	2,430,000	0.18	0.32	0.13	0.55	0.26	0.01	1.44	1.52	1.31	0.78	0.64	1.64	5.90	5.51	0.74	9.32	10.77	61.07

Source: IMF, *Direction of Trade Statistics, 2003.*
[1] ASEAN-10 plus China, Korea, Japan and Hong Kong
[2] Developing Asia refers to all Asia except for Japan

TABLE 2.2
Bilateral Imports of U.S., ASEAN, and Selected Others: 2002
(% and US$ millions)

OF/FROM	World (US$ mil)	IN	MA	PH	SI	TH	BR	ASEAN-6	ASEAN-10	CH	HK	KO	JA	APT¹	DA²	CER	US	NAFTA	EU
Indonesia	31,285	–	3.31	0.36	13.11	3.81	0.11	20.70	21.52	7.76	0.77	5.26	14.09	48.64	41.32	5.57	8.45	9.84	12.38
Malaysia	79,506	3.21	–	3.27	12.00	3.97	0.01	22.45	22.98	7.74	2.92	5.32	17.82	53.87	45.48	2.18	16.48	17.07	11.38
Philippines	35,397	2.16	3.62	–	6.53	2.97	0.07	15.35	16.09	3.54	4.47	7.78	20.43	47.85	38.34	2.25	20.59	21.40	7.78
Singapore	116,482	4.59	18.22	2.15	–	4.64	0.18	29.78	25.98	7.61	2.44	3.69	12.51	49.80	45.67	2.02	14.26	15.03	11.84
Thailand	64,721	2.41	5.62	1.67	4.49	–	0.70	14.89	16.14	7.61	1.41	3.90	23.02	50.68	35.94	2.62	9.57	10.44	10.98
Brunei	1,635	2.14	17.43	0.28	30.64	2.69	–	53.19	70.74	1.41	3.99	1.77	21.47	99.38	61.83	1.99	3.12	3.19	10.76
ASEAN-6	329,026	3.12	8.35	1.91	5.88	3.30	0.22	22.78	22.05	7.19	2.42	4.71	16.91	50.88	42.59	2.54	13.95	14.75	11.17
Cambodia	2,476	3.07	2.42	0.36	15.67	22.90	0.00	44.43	49.23	11.19	15.06	5.13	3.10	83.71	89.66	0.36	1.29	1.34	4.97
Laos	736	0.11	0.41	0.00	3.94	60.36	–	64.82	75.39	8.11	0.83	0.67	2.67	87.68	86.16	1.73	0.63	0.68	5.85
Myanmar	2,951	2.03	8.91	0.14	19.54	12.06	–	42.68	42.90	27.02	2.37	5.35	4.30	81.94	79.59	0.63	0.39	0.41	3.15
Vietnam	19,976	2.16	3.66	0.57	11.46	5.22	–	23.07	23.58	11.84	4.23	12.33	11.76	63.75	66.17	1.85	3.19	3.43	9.40
ASEAN-10	355,164	3.05	8.03	1.81	6.37	3.73	0.21	23.20	22.61	7.65	2.61	5.14	16.39	52.17	44.64	2.47	13.11	13.87	10.95
China	295,440	1.52	3.15	1.09	2.39	1.90	0.08	10.12	10.56	–	3.65	9.67	18.10	41.99	37.93	2.25	9.22	10.83	13.06
Hong Kong	207,761	0.72	2.45	1.30	4.68	1.83	–	10.98	11.12	44.30	–	4.70	11.30	71.42	68.93	0.92	5.69	6.31	8.50
Korea	152,123	3.10	2.66	1.23	2.25	1.12	0.30	10.67	11.01	11.44	1.11	–	19.63	43.19	27.85	4.42	15.19	16.60	11.25
India	64,960	2.20	2.98	0.15	4.49	0.70	–	10.52	10.93	4.53	2.44	2.34	3.17	23.41	22.37	2.44	6.94	8.07	21.96
Japan	337,194	4.20	3.31	1.93	1.48	3.12	0.45	14.49	15.30	18.33	0.42	4.60	–	38.64	43.61	4.71	17.38	20.03	13.00

TABLE 2.2 *(continued)*

OF/FROM	World (US$ mil)	IN	MA	PH	SI	TH	BR	ASEAN-6	ASEAN-10	CH	HK	KO	JA	APT[1]	DA	CER	US	NAFTA	EU
ASEAN+3[1]	1,347,682	2.65	4.31	1.54	3.55	2.59	0.22	14.86	15.06	14.72	1.72	5.35	12.25	48.51	44.76	2.96	12.42	13.89	11.58
Dvlp. Asia[2]	1,224,000	1.71	4.41	1.47	4.24	2.26	0.12	14.22	14.64	12.32	2.17	5.50	16.04	50.67	42.73	2.57	10.87	11.69	11.81
Australia	69,551	3.40	3.04	0.61	3.36	2.44	0.45	13.30	15.00	10.07	1.04	3.73	12.34	42.18	34.69	3.82	18.33	20.11	22.98
New Zealand	14,853	1.24	2.50	0.29	1.80	1.75	0.53	8.11	8.35	8.14	0.44	2.47	12.21	31.61	22.90	22.46	13.88	15.42	19.61
ANZCERTA	84,404	3.02	2.95	0.55	3.09	2.32	0.47	12.39	13.83	9.73	0.93	3.51	12.31	40.32	32.62	7.10	17.55	19.29	22.39
United States	1,202,000	0.86	2.06	0.95	1.26	1.31	0.03	6.46	6.80	11.11	0.81	3.07	10.37	32.16	26.35	0.77	–	29.13	19.32
Canada	221,981	0.28	0.58	0.32	0.28	0.51	0.00	1.97	2.07	4.59	0.29	1.40	4.42	12.76	10.14	0.65	62.65	66.28	11.13
Mexico	168,679	0.31	1.18	0.55	0.92	0.50	–	3.46	3.46	3.72	0.30	2.34	5.54	15.37	12.79	0.35	63.17	65.83	9.75
NAFTA	1,592,660	0.72	1.76	0.82	1.08	1.11	0.02	5.52	5.79	9.41	0.69	2.76	9.03	27.68	22.65	0.71	15.42	38.19	17.16
EU	2,321,900	0.42	0.60	0.29	0.58	0.47	0.00	2.37	2.59	3.12	0.68	0.95	2.89	10.24	9.13	0.48	7.29	8.23	58.62

Notes: [1] ASEAN-10 plus China, Korea, Japan and Hong Kong
[2] Developing Asia refers to all Asia except for Japan
Source: IMF, *Direction of Trade Statistics*, 2003

the ASEAN-10 (16 per cent). The United States is a fairly small market for the oil-dominated exports of Brunei Darussalam (13 per cent of the total) and as a source of imports (3 per cent).

The growth in trade of the EAI countries and ASEAN more generally is increasingly intra-regional in nature. The ASEAN Plus Three (APT) countries (ASEAN-10, China, South Korea, and Japan), which formed the core of the "East Asian Economic Bloc" proposed by Prime Minister Mahathir of Malaysia in December 1990, constituted in 2002 an overwhelming majority of Brunei exports and a majority of exports for Malaysia and Indonesia and a large share of Thai (47 per cent) and Philippine (43 per cent) exports. Moreover, this trend has been market-led, as preferential trading arrangements were not important in Asia over this period, with the possible exception of the ASEAN Free-Trade Area (AFTA), which was being implemented over this period. Numerous proposals for intra-regional trading arrangements in Asia suggest that the "flag is following trade", an important consideration for the United States, as we discuss at length in Chapter 5.

Given the size of the U.S. market and its fairly balanced trade between Asia, Europe, and the Americas, the EAI countries do not account for a large share of either U.S. exports or imports. However, this does not mean that the markets are insignificant. On the contrary, the United States exported approximately US$2.6 billion, US$10.3 billion, US$7.3 billion, and US$4.9 billion to Indonesia, Malaysia, the Philippines, and Thailand, respectively, in 2002 (Table 2.1). Together the ASEAN-6 countries constituted 6 per cent of total U.S. exports, almost double the share of China and slightly less than that of Japan (7.4 per cent). Thus, while the numbers are relatively unimpressive at the aggregate level given the size of the U.S. economy—one reason why our estimates of the economic effects of the EAI for the United States in Chapter 3 tend to be so small—at the microeconomic, sectoral level, they can be significant, as discussed below.

Regarding bilateral trade balances, using data from Table 2.1 we calculate that the United States reported an overall trade deficit of US$509 billion in 2002, on the order of 4 per cent of GDP. The APT countries accounted for 46 per cent of this total (US$236 billion), of which Japan constituted US$73 billion and China, US$111 billion. The EAI countries (based on U.S. data) each had a trade surplus with the United States, coming to US$7.8 billion, US$14.4 billion, US$4.1 billion, and US$10.8 billion for Indonesia, Malaysia, the Philippines, and Thailand respectively. The U.S. deficit with Brunei was much smaller at US$259 million. Of course, these data inflate the true deficit of the United States in several ways, including the fact that export prices are calculated on a free on board (f.o.b.) basis, whereas import values include the costs of customs, insurance, and freight (cif). Moreover, there are questions as to the origin of the goods in calculating imports, which has led to important trade disagreements particularly between the United States and China.[5] Nevertheless, even using reporting data from the EAI we find that these countries still report a trade-in-merchandise surplus (though with lower values).

Now, to an economist, bilateral trade balances are unimportant. What matters most is the overall trade balance, which in turn is determined by domestic macroeconomic fundamentals. A priori, we do not know if a trade surplus (deficit) is good or bad for the economy: it depends on many factors. For example, the Japanese and German economies have generally stagnated since the early 1990s (though there are some signs of sustainable growth in 2004, at least in Japan) while the U.S. economy boomed until 2001, but the former had huge trade surpluses and the latter a large (and increasing) trade deficit. In this sense, addressing the origins of a trade imbalance starts at home (e.g., an increase in net national savings in the United States). And, what really matters at the bilateral level is the quality and quantity of economic interchange. The EAI proposal for bilateral free-trade areas is designed to do just that, not merely in terms of trade in goods but also services, FDI, and other areas.

Nonetheless, with respect to *political* economy, trade imbalances *do* matter. Trade deficits have been frequently used as an excuse for populist protectionist measures, and a bilateral trade surplus can be used as a reason for closer integration (e.g., NAFTA was sold in part by the Clinton administration on the basis of the U.S. trade surplus with Mexico at the time). But there is no reason why a trade deficit cannot be used as a political selling point for a free-trade area. *For example, the barriers to trade in ASEAN—with certain sectoral exceptions—are generally much higher than is the case for the United States, suggesting, ceteris paribus, that U.S. exporters have more to gain than ASEAN exporters in terms of trade-barrier liberalization.* Besides, as we shall see below, the United States has a large bilateral surplus in trade in services with the EAI countries.

Change in the Structure of U.S.-EAI Trade

Perhaps even more important than the sheer magnitudes of international trade flows are the dynamic changes in the *structure* of EAI trade, arguably the reflection of a healthy development process. If the explosive growth in ASEAN trade were predominantly a function of changes in agricultural and national resource-intensive goods exports, as it was for some countries in the past, the trade numbers would be somewhat deceiving: economic growth and development can be very different things. For a variety of reasons, an increase in the share of manufactured exports relative to primary exports, as well as the progressive increase in the share of more sophisticated manufactured goods, constitutes an important part of the economic development process, as well as reducing the susceptibility of exports and, hence, economic growth to vicissitudes in the international marketplace (due to, for example, less volatile and better terms of trade, less exposure to natural shocks, and technology-related benefits that are generated more easily in higher-technology areas). Indeed, promotion of manufactures is a key motivation behind the outward-oriented development policies that East Asia—and, progressively, much of South Asia—has embraced.

Tables 2.3 and 2.4 reveal how U.S. trade with the EAI countries has changed since the early 1990s. For Singapore, Malaysia and the Philippines, electrical machinery and equipment are by far the most important export category for trade with the United States, accounting for over three-fourths and two-thirds of Malaysian and Philippine exports, respectively, in 2001. Over 80 per cent of Singapore exports fall in this category. The increase in the share of this category was especially impressive in the case of the Philippines, where the share of electrical machinery and equipment more than doubled.

Thailand's exports to the United States have followed a similar pattern but in a less pronounced way. Electrical machinery and equipment constituted 31 per cent of Thai exports to the United States at the beginning of the 1990s, a close second to miscellaneous manufactures (32 per cent) in the export rankings. Food was also an important export category, with an 18 per cent share of the total. By the end of the decade, electrical machinery and equipment was by far the most important export sector, rising to 45 per cent of the total (miscellaneous manufactures fell to 27 per cent and food to 14 per cent).

TABLE 2.3
Structure of EAI-5 Exports to the U.S., Selected Years, 1990–2001

Indonesia

		1990	1992	1994	1996	1997	1998	1999	2000	2001
1	Food	0.09	0.10	0.08	0.09	0.10	0.10	0.09	0.08	0.08
2	Bev/Tobacco	0.00	0.00	0.00	0.00	0.00	0.00	0.00	0.00	0.00
3	Crude Mat.	0.14	0.12	0.10	0.12	0.09	0.08	0.05	0.05	0.04
4	Mineral Fuels	0.27	0.11	0.12	0.07	0.05	0.05	0.06	0.06	0.04
5	Anim/Veg Oils	0.01	0.01	0.01	0.01	0.01	0.01	0.01	0.01	0.00
6	Chemicals	0.01	0.01	0.01	0.01	0.01	0.01	0.01	0.02	0.02
7	Manu Goods	0.16	0.15	0.14	0.11	0.12	0.14	0.13	0.12	0.11
8	Mach/Equip	0.01	0.08	0.14	0.18	0.20	0.21	0.24	0.24	0.25
9	Misc Manuf	0.30	0.41	0.39	0.40	0.41	0.38	0.39	0.41	0.44
10	Comm NES	0.00	0.00	0.00	0.01	0.00	0.01	0.01	0.01	0.01
Total	US$ millions	3,681.4	4,914.1	7,020.2	8,742.6	9,173.8	9,973.0	9,525.4	10,367.0	9,930.7

Malaysia

		1990	1992	1994	1996	1997	1998	1999	2000	2001
1	Food	0.02	0.02	0.01	0.00	0.01	0.01	0.01	0.00	0.00
2	Bev/Tobacco	0.00	0.00	0.00	0.00	0.00	0.00	0.00	0.00	0.00
3	Crude Mat.	0.04	0.02	0.02	0.02	0.01	0.01	0.01	0.01	0.00
4	Mineral Fuels	0.06	0.01	0.00	0.01	0.01	0.01	0.01	0.02	0.01
5	Anim/Veg Oils	0.02	0.02	0.01	0.01	0.01	0.01	0.01	0.01	0.01
6	Chemicals	0.01	0.01	0.01	0.02	0.02	0.02	0.01	0.01	0.02
7	Manu Goods	0.04	0.04	0.03	0.03	0.03	0.03	0.03	0.02	0.02
8	Mach/Equip	0.61	0.69	0.75	0.76	0.77	0.77	0.80	0.81	0.80
9	Misc Manuf	0.18	0.18	0.15	0.14	0.13	0.14	0.11	0.10	0.11
10	Comm NES	0.01	0.01	0.01	0.01	0.01	0.02	0.02	0.02	0.02
Total	US$ millions	5,496.1	8,594.7	14,418.6	18,330.7	18,016.9	19,518.8	21,424.3	25,568.2	22,227.8

TABLE 2.3 *(continued)*

Philippines

		1990	1992	1994	1996	1997	1998	1999	2000	2001
1	Food	0.11	0.09	0.06	0.05	0.04	0.04	0.04	0.03	0.03
2	Bev/Tobacco	0.00	0.00	0.00	0.00	0.00	0.00	0.00	0.00	0.00
3	Crude Mat.	0.01	0.01	0.01	0.00	0.00	0.00	0.00	0.00	0.00
4	Mineral Fuels	0.00	0.00	0.00	0.00	0.00	0.00	0.00	0.00	0.00
5	Anim/Veg Oils	0.04	0.06	0.03	0.04	0.03	0.03	0.01	0.01	0.01
6	Chemicals	0.01	0.01	0.01	0.00	0.00	0.00	0.00	0.00	0.00
7	Manu Goods	0.05	0.03	0.03	0.03	0.02	0.02	0.03	0.02	0.03
8	Mach/Equip	0.29	0.34	0.43	0.55	0.63	0.63	0.66	0.69	0.63
9	Misc Manuf	0.47	0.44	0.42	0.31	0.25	0.25	0.23	0.22	0.26
10	Comm NES	0.01	0.01	0.02	0.01	0.01	0.03	0.02	0.02	0.03
Total	US$ millions	3,622.5	4,623.0	6,025.1	8,496.4	10,435.5	12,334.7	12,352.8	13,934.7	11,307.2

Brunei

		1991	1992	1994	1996	1997	1998	1999	2000	2001
1	Food	1.62	0.00	0.00	0.00	0.00	0.00	0.00	0.00	0.00
2	Bev/Tobacco	0.00	0.00	0.00	0.00	0.00	0.00	0.00	0.00	0.00
3	Crude Mat.	0.00	0.00	0.00	0.00	0.00	0.00	0.00	0.00	0.31
4	Mineral Fuels	51.38	0.00	0.00	0.00	0.00	43.25	67.08	51.56	37.31
5	Anim/Veg Oils	0.00	0.00	0.00	0.00	0.00	0.00	0.00	0.00	0.00
6	Chemicals	0.00	0.00	0.00	0.00	0.00	0.00	0.00	0.00	1.91
7	Manu Goods	0.00	0.66	0.02	0.00	0.00	0.00	0.00	0.02	0.00
8	Mach/Equip	0.08	0.02	0.11	0.17	0.42	0.04	0.02	0.16	0.01
9	Misc Manuf	43.73	54.36	56.57	94.46	95.13	37.36	30.95	46.96	59.39
10	Comm NES	3.20	44.95	43.30	5.37	4.45	19.34	1.93	1.31	1.06
Total	US$ millions	28.5	30.3	47.2	50.5	55.8	224.0	388.7	383.8	357.6

TABLE 2.3 *(continued)*

Thailand

		1990	1992	1993	1994	1995	1996	1997	1998	1999
1	Food	0.18	0.18	0.17	0.17	0.15	0.14	0.13	0.14	0.14
2	Bev/Tobacco	0.00	0.01	0.00	0.00	0.00	0.00	0.00	0.00	0.00
3	Crude Mat.	0.02	0.02	0.02	0.03	0.04	0.03	0.03	0.02	0.02
4	Mineral Fuels	0.02	0.00	0.01	0.01	0.00	0.00	0.00	0.00	0.00
5	Anim/Veg Oils	0.00	0.00	0.00	0.00	0.00	0.00	0.00	0.00	0.00
6	Chemicals	0.00	0.00	0.00	0.00	0.01	0.01	0.01	0.01	0.01
7	Manu Goods	0.11	0.10	0.10	0.09	0.08	0.08	0.08	0.09	0.10
8	Mach/Equip	0.31	0.35	0.36	0.40	0.42	0.44	0.47	0.46	0.45
9	Misc Manuf	0.32	0.32	0.32	0.29	0.29	0.28	0.27	0.27	0.27
10	Comm NES	0.01	0.01	0.01	0.01	0.01	0.02	0.02	0.01	0.01
Total	US$ millions	5,588.85	7,926.80	8,982.30	10,799.18	11,854.39	11,798.40	12,595.02	13,970.54	14,329.88

Singapore

		1990	1992	1993	1994	1995	1996	1997	1998	1999
1	Food	0.01	0.01	0.01	0.01	0.01	0.01	0.01	0.01	0.01
2	Bev/Tobacco	0.00	0.00	0.00	0.00	0.00	0.00	0.00	0.00	0.00
3	Crude Mat.	0.00	0.00	0.00	0.00	0.00	0.00	0.00	0.00	0.00
4	Mineral Fuels	0.02	0.01	0.01	0.01	0.01	0.01	0.01	0.01	0.01
5	Anim/Veg Oils	0.00	0.00	0.00	0.00	0.00	0.00	0.00	0.00	0.00
6	Chemicals	0.04	0.05	0.04	0.04	0.03	0.03	0.04	0.02	0.03
7	Manu Goods	0.01	0.01	0.01	0.01	0.01	0.01	0.01	0.01	0.01
8	Mach/Equip	0.77	0.79	0.81	0.83	0.86	0.87	0.86	0.85	0.82
9	Misc Manuf	0.10	0.11	0.09	0.07	0.06	0.05	0.05	0.06	0.07
10	Comm NES	0.04	0.02	0.03	0.03	0.03	0.03	0.04	0.04	0.06
Total	US$ millions	10,095.28	11,560.70	13,049.16	15,656.27	18,897.17	20,648.26	20,067.14	18,653.95	18,191.20

Source: OECD

TABLE 2.4

Structure of US Exports to EAI-5, Selected Years 1990–2001

Indonesia

		1990	1992	1995	1997	1998	1999	2000	2001
1	Food	0.03	0.02	0.10	0.06	0.06	0.11	0.13	0.18
2	Bev/Tobacco	0.00	0.01	0.01	0.00	0.00	0.00	0.00	0.00
3	Crude Mat.	0.19	0.18	0.21	0.17	0.20	0.23	0.24	0.24
4	Mineral Fuels	0.01	0.01	0.01	0.01	0.01	0.02	0.01	0.01
5	Anim/Veg Oils	0.00	0.00	0.00	0.00	0.00	0.00	0.00	0.00
6	Chemicals	0.19	0.13	0.16	0.13	0.11	0.18	0.20	0.15
7	Manu Goods	0.07	0.05	0.07	0.07	0.08	0.09	0.07	0.06
8	Mach/Equip	0.47	0.55	0.39	0.52	0.49	0.32	0.30	0.30
9	Misc Manuf	0.03	0.03	0.03	0.03	0.03	0.03	0.03	0.04
10	Comm NES	0.02	0.02	0.02	0.01	0.02	0.02	0.01	0.01
Total	US$ millions	1,881.0	2,732.2	3,317.0	4,430.0	2,290.9	2,038.3	2,401.9	2,498.9

Malaysia

		1990	1992	1995	1997	1998	1999	2000	2001
1	Food	0.02	0.02	0.04	0.02	0.02	0.02	0.02	0.03
2	Bev/Tobacco	0.01	0.01	0.01	0.01	0.01	0.01	0.01	0.01
3	Crude Mat.	0.03	0.02	0.03	0.02	0.01	0.01	0.01	0.02
4	Mineral Fuels	0.00	0.00	0.00	0.00	0.00	0.00	0.00	0.00
5	Anim/Veg Oils	0.00	0.00	0.00	0.00	0.00	0.00	0.00	0.00
6	Chemicals	0.05	0.05	0.06	0.06	0.04	0.05	0.05	0.06
7	Manu Goods	0.05	0.05	0.06	0.06	0.05	0.04	0.04	0.04
8	Mach/Equip	0.77	0.75	0.70	0.72	0.77	0.76	0.77	0.75
9	Misc Manuf	0.04	0.05	0.07	0.09	0.08	0.07	0.09	0.07
10	Comm NES	0.03	0.03	0.03	0.02	0.02	0.02	0.02	0.02
Total	US$ millions	3,169.3	4,034.1	8,190.8	10,330.7	8,952.9	9,060.0	10,937.5	9,380.2

TABLE 2.4 *(continued)*

Philippines

		1990	1992	1995	1997	1998	1999	2000	2001
1	Food	0.13	0.16	0.12	0.10	0.09	0.09	0.08	0.09
2	Bev/Tobacco	0.01	0.01	0.01	0.01	0.00	0.00	0.00	0.00
3	Crude Mat.	0.05	0.05	0.05	0.02	0.02	0.03	0.02	0.02
4	Mineral Fuels	0.00	0.02	0.01	0.00	0.00	0.00	0.00	0.00
5	Anim/Veg Oils	0.00	0.00	0.00	0.00	0.00	0.00	0.00	0.00
6	Chemicals	0.10	0.10	0.07	0.05	0.04	0.04	0.04	0.04
7	Manu Goods	0.08	0.08	0.06	0.05	0.04	0.03	0.03	0.03
8	Mach/Equip	0.53	0.48	0.60	0.68	0.72	0.74	0.73	0.73
9	Misc Manuf	0.06	0.06	0.05	0.06	0.06	0.05	0.07	0.06
10	Comm NES	0.04	0.04	0.03	0.02	0.03	0.02	0.02	0.02
Total	US$ millions	2,435.1	2,679.4	5,071.8	7,137.1	6,736.2	7,222.1	8,799.1	7,664.5

Brunei

		1991	1992	1994	1996	1997	1998	1999	2000	2001
1	Food	0.12	0.35	0.71	0.32	0.73	0.64	1.48	0.62	1.17
2	Bev/Tobacco	1.70	0.66	1.22	0.74	0.74	0.00	0.00	0.04	0.02
3	Crude Mat.	0.09	0.01	0.10	0.02	0.49	0.17	0.87	0.94	0.58
4	Mineral Fuels	0.03	0.01	0.01	0.01	0.07	0.03	0.01	0.30	0.35
5	Anim/Veg Oils	0.00	0.00	0.30	0.00	0.00	0.01	0.02	0.00	0.01
6	Chemicals	0.76	0.13	0.32	0.52	1.89	1.64	3.49	2.00	2.21
7	Manu Goods	0.63	0.69	0.70	2.30	2.13	2.57	4.75	6.07	7.34
8	Mach/Equip	91.56	87.63	51.05	76.43	64.62	81.84	74.02	71.98	67.28
9	Misc Manuf	1.95	1.22	2.83	2.21	5.08	6.35	5.72	9.77	10.51
10	Comm NES	3.15	9.30	42.76	17.46	24.25	6.75	9.65	8.27	10.54
Total	(US$ millions)	162.0663	452.6829	370.9911	348.4381	176.7754	122.9067	66.7423	156.262	104.0177

TABLE 2.4 *(continued)*

Thailand

		1990	1992	1993	1994	1995	1996	1997	1998	1999
1	Food	0.03	0.04	0.05	0.04	0.04	0.04	0.03	0.03	0.04
2	Bev/Tobacco	0.02	0.02	0.02	0.02	0.01	0.01	0.01	0.01	0.01
3	Crude Mat.	0.07	0.06	0.05	0.06	0.09	0.06	0.05	0.05	0.06
4	Mineral Fuels	0.01	0.01	0.01	0.01	0.01	0.01	0.01	0.01	0.01
5	Anim/Veg Oils	0.00	0.00	0.00	0.00	0.00	0.00	0.00	0.00	0.00
6	Chemicals	0.11	0.10	0.11	0.11	0.10	0.10	0.09	0.10	0.11
7	Manu Goods	0.07	0.08	0.07	0.09	0.09	0.08	0.07	0.07	0.05
8	Mach/Equip	0.59	0.62	0.56	0.53	0.53	0.57	0.61	0.62	0.61
9	Misc Manuf	0.06	0.05	0.10	0.09	0.09	0.10	0.09	0.07	0.08
10	Comm NES	0.04	0.03	0.03	0.04	0.04	0.03	0.04	0.04	0.03
Total	(US$ millions)	2853.30	3769.91	3555.46	4624.00	6158.50	6934.91	7159.73	5233.36	4984.60

Singapore

		1990	1992	1993	1994	1995	1996	1997	1998	1999
1	Food	0.02	0.02	0.02	0.02	0.02	0.02	0.01	0.01	0.01
2	Bev/Tobacco	0.02	0.01	0.01	0.01	0.01	0.01	0.01	0.01	0.00
3	Crude Mat.	0.01	0.01	0.01	0.01	0.01	0.00	0.01	0.00	0.01
4	Mineral Fuels	0.02	0.03	0.03	0.04	0,02	0.02	0.01	0.01	0.02
5	Anim/Veg Oils	0.00	0.00	0.00	0.00	0.00	0.00	0.00	0.00	0.00
6	Chemicals	0.09	0.09	0.09	0.08	0.10	0.09	0.10	0.08	0.09
7	Manu Goods	0.05	0.05	0.04	0.04	0.05	0.05	0.05	0.04	0.04
8	Mach/Equip	0.62	0.59	0.62	0.64	0.63	0.63	0.63	0.69	0.66
9	Misc Manuf	0.13	0.15	0.12	0.12	0.13	0.15	0.14	0.13	0.13
10	Comm NES	0.05	0.05	0.05	0.04	0.03	0.03	0.03	0.03	0.04
Total	US$ millions	7,597.41	8,948.11	10,654.63	11,713.58	13,647.68	14,677.03	15,697.37	15,673.48	16,246.88

Source: OECD

Indonesia's trade with the United States has changed by even more than that of the previous three countries. The share of electrical machinery and equipment in total exports was less than that of Malaysia, the Philippines, or Thailand, at one-fourth of total exports in 2001. But this is up from only one per cent in 1990. Nevertheless, the biggest export category for Indonesia continues to be (labour- and natural resource-intensive) miscellaneous manufactures. It is interesting to note that, while each of these countries is resource rich, no agricultural or natural resource category accounts for an important share of the exports of EAI countries to the United States, though some of the manufactured exports are natural-resource intensive (especially for Indonesia) and the 14 per cent share of food in Thai exports to the United States is not insignificant.

This cannot be said of U.S. exports to the EAI (Table 2.4). Food exports constitute almost one-fifth of U.S. exports to Indonesia and almost one-tenth of exports to the Philippines (U.S. exports of food to Thailand represent only around 4 per cent of the total). However, as expected, electrical machinery and equipment is the most important U.S. export to all five original ASEAN countries; it is the single most important category for each country and dominant in the cases of Malaysia and the Philippines (three-fourths of total exports) and Singapore (two-thirds of total exports). The composition of U.S. exports to the EAI countries is much more stable than in the case of EAI exports to the United States, no doubt a reflection of the fact that the United States is an advanced, developed country.

Finally, U.S. trade with Brunei, which is far less important in terms of value and bilateral trade shares for both countries than is the case of the ASEAN-4 countries, is fairly straightforward, though trade has become more diversified over the past 10 years. In 1991, for example, approximately 92 per cent of U.S. exports to Brunei fell in the electrical machinery and equipment category, while 51 per cent of Brunei exports to the United States was in the area of mineral fuels (and miscellaneous manufactures accounted for an additional 44 per cent). By 2001, trade had changed fairly substantially: U.S. exports of electrical machinery and equipment continued to be the most important export sector but its share in the total had fallen to two-thirds, while miscellaneous manufactures and "commodities not elsewhere specified" each rose from trivial shares in 1991 to 11 per cent each.[6] Brunei exports to the United

States continued to be dominated by mineral fuels and miscellaneous manufactures, but the latter actually grew to account for a larger share than the (combined) former categories in 2001, i.e., 59 per cent versus 37 per cent. *Hence, it is not true that petroleum tells the whole story of Brunei exports to the United States; in fact, as we will see below and in Chapter 3, textiles and clothing have actually become relatively significant exports of Brunei to the United States.*

A higher level of disaggregation of the U.S.-EAI trade structure gives a better idea of the actual changes at the product level. This is done in Appendix Tables 2.1–2.8, based on data provided by the ASEAN Secretariat for selected years 1993–2002, in which bilateral trade is broken down into 100 different product groups, as opposed to the nine categories included in Tables 2.3–2.4.

With respect to disaggregated exports to the United States, only apparel (17 per cent) and electrical equipment (15 per cent) accounted for a greater than 10 per cent share of Indonesian exports to the United States in 2002. These shares are up from 12 per cent and 9 per cent, respectively, of total Indonesian exports in 1993. Malaysian exports show a far greater concentration in exports to the U.S. market, with computers and machinery (28 per cent) and electrical equipment (42 per cent) constituting almost three-fourths of all exports. Interestingly, while computers and machinery exports have increased their share from 13 per cent in 1993, electrical equipment is actually down considerably from 58 per cent of total Malaysian exports in 1993. The same two product groups stand out as key Philippine exports to the United States, with computers and machinery (17 per cent) and electrical equipment (42 per cent) comprising 60 per cent of the total. These two sectors have displayed impressive growth over time, increasing their shares of total Philippine exports from 4 per cent and 32 per cent, respectively, since 1993. With a 14 per cent share of the total, apparel is also an important export of the Philippines to the United States, although its share has fallen significantly from 21 per cent in 1993.

As was noted in the analysis of the more aggregated data above, Thai exports to the United States are less concentrated than is the case of the other EAI countries. The top two sectors continue to be computers and machinery and electrical equipment, but they only accounted for 15 per cent and 22 per cent, respectively, of total exports to the United States. Moreover, the exports of these categories tend to be far more stable over time; they accounted for an 11 per cent and 22 per cent share, respectively, in 1993. Fish (SITC 03) and preparations of meat and fish (SITC 16) were the only significant agriculture exports to the United States in 2003 at 5 per cent and 6 per cent of total exports, respectively, and apparel (SITC 61) was the only other Thai export category (6 per cent) comprising more than 5 per cent of the total.

Brunei exports to the United States, though more diversified than in the past, are still fairly insignificant. In fact, in terms of 5-digit SITC products, which is our level of analysis in Chapter 3, only 28 exported product categories (out of approximately 3,000 possible commodities) were valued at more than US$500,000. The top three exports were: shirts made of cotton for men (US$19 million), petroleum coke (US$17 million), and trousers (US$14 million).

Clearly, for the EAI countries (and ASEAN more generally), the electronics and machinery sector, which is category 7 of the SITC protocol, has become the key protagonist in export growth (with the exception of Brunei). Hence, in considering the determinants of EAI export growth and its dependence on external demand, one is led to focus on SITC 7, and on electronics-related exports in particular. A number of studies have focused on this sector. For example, Tamamura (2002) uses input–output analysis to capture the FDI-export link in East Asia, as well as decompose the effect of external demand (by country) on production, using electrical goods/electronics as a case study. He finds that, for 1995 (his latest year), in every country, external demand induced more production than domestic demand except in China and (marginally) Indonesia, where, however, domestic demand fell in 1985 from 94 per cent of total production to 66 per cent in the case of the former and from 87 per cent to 52 per cent in the case of the latter. Most countries followed a similar pattern of internationalization of electronics production. The most extreme cases were Malaysia and Taiwan, where domestic demand induced only 6 per cent and 10 per cent of production, respectively. The United States was the most important external source of induced demand in electronics in 1995 (often by a considerable margin), with a simple average share of approximately 25 per cent for the sample. In the key cases of Malaysia, the Philippines, and Taiwan, U.S. demand was even more important than domestic demand, and in the case of Thailand, they were about the same.

In sum, the electronics and machinery sector is leading the way in the restructuring of EAI exports, and the United States is a key protagonist in this process.[7]

In Chapter 3, we give detailed analysis and estimates of the effects of an FTA between the United States and the EAI countries at a highly-disaggregated level of analysis. However, it would be useful at this point to capture the true dynamics of the changing structure of U.S.-EAI trade in terms of the aggregate picture of changing exports and imports. One way to address this process would be to ask the question, "To what extent has the pattern of trade between the United States and the EAI countries changed over time?" We attempt to answer this question by ranking EAI country exports (imports) to the United States according to their importance in national export structures in 1990, 1995, and 1999, and then attempt to correlate how similar they are. We do this using the Spearman Rank Correlation Coefficient (SRCC) technique. The SRCC is a non-parametric estimate, showing how the rankings of two series (in our example, trade structure for different years) are correlated with each other. The estimates range from –1 to +1: perfect rank correlation would be unity in absolute value, while complete lack of correlation would be zero. For comparison purposes, we also estimate SRCCs for ASEAN trade with the EU,[8] and include additional ASEAN and other Asian countries in the exercise. All estimates were statistically significant at the 99 per cent level of confidence. The results are given in Table 2.5.

U.S. imports from Indonesia, Malaysia, the Philippines and Singapore changed significantly over the 1990s; SRCCs estimates are 0.307, 0.382, 0.301, and 0.400, respectively. Hence, when ranking the exports of Indonesia to the United States in 1990 and 1999, we find that the correlation comes to only about 30 per cent, suggesting considerable dynamism (i.e., the ranking of export items is quite different). In fact, this dynamism is even more pronounced than in the case of any other Asian country included in the sample with the exception of Vietnam, with which the United States was just beginning to establish normal diplomatic and, hence, a trade relationship. It is also worth noting, however, that most of this change in structure took place in the first half of the decade. The Asian Crisis could well have been responsible in part for this reduction in the rate of change, or it may just be a sign of increasing maturity (and, hence, less potential for change at the margin).

A possible exception to this dynamism would be Thailand, whose

TABLE 2.5
Structural Change of EAI and Other Asian Trade with U.S. and EU
(Spearman Rank Correlation Coefficients, 3-Digit SITC, 1990s)

	US Imports		US Exports		EU Imports	EU Exports
	1990–95	1990–99	1990–95	1990–99	1995–99	1995–99
EAI						
Indonesia	0.476	0.307	0.692	0.524	0.758	0.804
Malaysia	0.542	0.382	0.774	0.614	0.801	0.798
Philippines	0.474	0.301	0.751	0.592	0.672	0.799
Thailand	0.701	0.547	0.766	0.638	0.861	0.875
Singapore	0.620	0.400	0.857	0.741	0.829	0.911
Other ASEAN						
Vietnam[1]	na	0.097	na	0.366	0.503	0.770
Other Asia						
China	0.887	0.828	0.662	0.513	0.936	0.822
Hong Kong	0.764	0.597	0.858	0.769	0.842	0.921
Taiwan	0.895	0.831	0.833	0.747	0.921	0.910
South Korea	0.819	0.706	0.855	0.723	0.869	0.814

Note: [1]For U.S. trade with Vietnam, 1995–99.
Source: Plummer (2003).

SRCC comes to 0.547 over the 1990s. This comes as no surprise; our 1-digit and 2-digit SITC analyses above confirmed that Thai exports to the United States demonstrated less volatility. Nevertheless, the structural change in these exports was more dynamic than any of the "other Asian" countries.

Regarding the change in structure of U.S. exports to the EAI countries, one derives far less change. To some degree this is to be expected; as noted above, the United States is an advanced industrial country and one would expect its comparative advantage to be fairly stable. However, one could not say that the structure of U.S. exports to the EAI countries was stagnant, as the SRCCs are estimated to be 0.524, 0.614, 0.592 and 0.638 for Indonesia, Malaysia, the Philippines, and Thailand, respectively, over the 1990s, lower than for other Asian countries with the exception (once again) of Vietnam and, to some extent, China.

But perhaps the expectation of low SRCCs may be based on old-fashioned thinking in economics. A traditional explanation would be that the structure of exports and imports are both correlated with *per capita* income; the more developed the country, the greater the share of sophisticated exports generated from a more developed economy, and the more sophisticated are the tastes of the population (and, hence, imports tend to be more sophisticated). But with the increasing global division of labour, a country's imports may end up as its exports with a small amount of value-added. Foreign direct investment, discussed at length below, plays an important role in this process; indeed, as is well documented in the literature (e.g., Lee and Roland-Holst 1999), the trade-FDI link is not only important but in some cases dominant, a result that would be congruent with Tamamura (2002). In addition, the economics literature is increasingly respecting the important role that imports play in the process of technology transfer. In fact, the change in the structure of exports from the United States could likely be explained by both rising wealth in these countries (and, therefore, their respective consumer demand structures) and the need for more sophisticated intermediate inputs for their respective dynamic export regimes, rather than organic changes in the U.S. market.

C. EAI and Intra-Asian Competition in U.S. and OECD Markets

The above analysis was bilateral in nature. That is, we considered the U.S.-Brunei, U.S.-Indonesia, U.S.-Malaysia, U.S.-Philippines, U.S.-Sinagpore and U.S.-Thailand economic relationships. As the EAI is a framework under which FTAs will be developed, this was a deliberate organizational decision. *But it is important to note that the bilateral FTAs will not be negotiated in a vacuum.* An example might illustrate the point. Suppose that the United States fails to reach an FTA with one country, but succeeds in negotiating one with the other countries. The country without the FTA will now be at a disadvantage; it may believe that the failure merely perpetuates the status quo but in fact it will face negative effects of trade diversion (discussed in Chapter 3). The degree to which it will be hurt will depend critically on how much overlap there is between its exports and those of the countries that succeeded in obtaining preferential treatment through an FTA (and, of course, the level of commodity-level protection in the export market).

Thus, to what extent are EAI exports similar to each other? One way to answer this question is to use the SRCC technique described above, but instead of ranking the structure of exports of the same country between two years, we rank the structure of exports of two countries (to a specific market) for the same year. A high estimated SRCC value would, therefore, suggest significant export overlap, whereas low values would mean not much competition at all.

We do this at the 5-digit SITC level (2881 commodities) for the exports of Indonesia, Malaysia, the Philippines, Singapore and Thailand to the U.S. and OECD markets for the years 1995 and 1999. The results are presented in Table 2.6. Singapore has by far the lowest SRCCs, indicating that its export structure does not compete much with other ASEAN countries in the U.S. and OECD markets. This might suggest that the U.S.-Singapore FTA would not particularly put the rest of ASEAN at a disadvantage, as their exports diverge significantly from Singapore's exports. With respect to the other ASEAN countries, the SRCCs fall in the 0.17 (Malaysia-Philippines, 1995) to 0.277 (Indonesia-Thailand, 1999) range. While we have no yardstick by which to deem what constitutes a "high" SRCC and a "low" SRCC, these values suggest that there is not a great deal of overlap across countries. However, it is noteworthy that competition between Malaysia and the Philippines in the U.S. market has been rising over time, while there has been less overlap between the Philippines and Indonesia. Competition between Thailand and the Philippines has risen and is relatively high, but it has fallen with respect to Malaysia and Indonesia. This is an important consideration given that the United States began FTA negotiations with Thailand in July 2004.

Regarding EAI exports to the OECD as a whole, the same general picture emerges, with a few exceptions. First, Singapore continues to have the lowest SRCCs in ASEAN. Moreover, even for the other pairs of countries, the SRCCs tend to be even somewhat lower than in the U.S. case, with a range of 0.09 (Malaysia-Philippines, 1995) and 0.277 (Philippines-Thailand, 1995). Second, an upward trend in competition is more in evidence in the OECD market; with the exception of competition with Singapore and all its partners and between the Philippines and Thailand, all SRCCs actually rose over this time period for the EAI countries.

Thus, according to SRCC calculations, it does appear that there exists considerable overlap between the structure of EAI exports to their major trading partners. The only exception is Singapore, which, given its essentially developed-country level of economic sophistication, may not be surprising.

However, the SRCC only *ranks* exports; this statistical technique does

TABLE 2.6
Correlation of ASEAN-4 Exports to US, Japanese, and OECD Markets
(Spearman Rank Correlation Coefficients, 5-Digit SITC, Selected Years)

a. U.S. Market

	Indonesia	Malaysia	Philippines	Thailand	Singapore
Indonesia					
1999	–	0.2460	0.201	0.21	–0.112
1995	–	0.2128	0.268	0.277	–0.15
Malaysia					
1999	0.2460	–	0.191	0.187	0.174
1995	0.2128	–	0.174	0.199	0.203
Philippines					
1999	0.201	0.191	–	0.263	–0.105
1995	0.268	0.174	–	0.231	–0.081
Thailand					
1999	0.21	0.187	0.263	–	–0.024
1995	0.277	0.199	0.231	–	–0.006
Singapore					
1999	–0.112	0.174	–0.105	–0.024	–
1995	–0.15	0.203	–0.081	–0.006	–

b. OECD Market

	Indonesia	Malaysia	Philippines	Thailand	Singapore
Indonesia					
1999	–	0.151	0.128	0.2206	–0.172
1995	–	0.100	0.091	0.2093	–0.177
Malaysia					
1999	0.151	–	0.13	0.247	0.114
1995	0.100	–	0.092	0.229	0.162
Philippines					
1999	0.128	0.13	–	0.25	–0.123
1995	0.091	0.092	–	0.277	–0.094
Thailand					
1999	0.2206	0.247	0.25	–	–0.041
1995	0.2093	0.229	0.277	–	–0.229

Notes: [1] All SRCC estimates are statistically significant at the 99 level
   [2] Additional OECD markets are available from the authors upon request.
Source: OECD, *International Trade Statistics, 2003;* Authors' calculations.

not directly calculate the degree of overlap, which may suggest certain biases. Hence, we also consider an "export similarity" approach, the most popular being the Finger-Kreinin Index, or FK Index (Finger and Kreinin 1979). Lloyd (2005) offers an extensive review of the strengths and weaknesses of the FK Index, as well as its relationship with alternative approaches. In essence, the FK Index is calculated as follows:

$$S = \sum_i \min \left([X_{ia} / \sum X_{ia}], [X_{ib} / \sum X_{ib}] \right),$$

Where:
i=trade by disaggregated commodity
a, b=two countries

The first ratio is the share of product i in country a's total exports and the second ratio is the share of commodity i in country b's exports. If those shares are equal, then the ratio in the formula would sum to one, indicating perfect similarity. On the other hand, if they are totally different, the formula would be zero. Thus the index can range from 0 to 1. Like the SRCCs, this index is sensitive to the degree of disaggregation.

In Table 2.7, we present FK Index calculations for the same countries, with somewhat different results, particularly for Singapore. For the ASEAN-4, beginning with exports to the U.S. market we note first that the range of the export similarity calculations is higher than in the case of the SRCCs, falling between 0.261 (Philippines-Indonesia, 1995) and 0.53 (Philippines-Malaysia, 1999). Second, the FK Indices increase over time in the case of every country pair with the exception of Malaysia and Thailand. Once again, the same picture generally emerges in the case of exports to the OECD, where the FK Indices fall in a slightly broader range of 0.257 (Philippines-Indonesia, 1995) and 0.592 (Malaysia-Philippines, 1999). Moreover, the trend is upward in all cases except one, but this time it is the Philippines and Thailand experiencing a slight decline in the index.

While the SRCC rankings would have led us to believe that competition between Singapore and the rest of ASEAN was not very stiff, our export similarity indices present a different story. While the FK indices reveal only minor overlap between exports of Singapore and Indonesia and Thailand, Malaysia exports and, to a lesser degree, Philippine exports appear to compete significantly with Singapore in the U.S. and OECD markets. In fact, the export similarity between Malaysian and Singapore exports is the highest of any two pairs of

TABLE 2.7
Finger-Kreinin Measure of Export Similarity:
EAI Exports to U.S. and OECD Markets
(5-Digit SITC, Selected Years)

a. U.S. Market

	Indonesia	Malaysia	Philippines	Thailand	Singapore
Indonesia					
1999	–	0.3070	0.266	0.393	0.144
1995	–	0.2950	0.261	0.376	0.149
Malaysia					
1999	0.3070	–	0.530	0.347	0.585
1995	0.2950	–	0.451	0.356	0.499
Philippines					
1999	0.266	0.530	–	0.390	0.41
1995	0.261	0.451	–	0.382	0.356
Thailand					
1999	0.393	0.347	0.390	–	0.237
1995	0.376	0.356	0.382	–	0.261

b. OECD Market

	Indonesia	Malaysia	Philippines	Thailand	Singapore
Indonesia					
1999	–	0.3120	0.258	0.3860	0.148
1995	–	0.2680	0.257	0.3580	0.149
Malaysia					
1999	0.3120	–	0.592	0.370	0.605
1995	0.2680	–	0.449	0.363	0.512
Philippines					
1999	0.258	0.592	–	0.367	0.54
1995	0.257	0.449	–	0.383	0.395
Thailand					
1999	0.3860	0.370	0.367	–	0.26
1995	0.3580	0.363	0.383	–	0.29

Notes: [1] Additional OECD markets are available from the authors upon request.
Source: OECD, *International Trade Statistics, 2003*; Authors' calculations.

countries, coming to 0.585 and 0.605 in the U.S. and OECD markets, respectively.

In sum, while the SRCC calculations suggest that some but not a considerable degree of export overlap exists between the EAI countries—and, hence, the risk of trade diversion due to being left out of a free-trade area world not be particularly high—the Finger-Kreinin Index of export similarity, which is a more direct estimate of overlap, does not generally support this conclusion, particularly in the case of Singapore. Hence, based on these measures, a successful FTA under the EAI between the United States and the Philippines to the exclusion of Malaysia might pose a potential threat to Malaysia exports. To understand exactly which products would be at risk, we need to compare highly disaggregated (again, 5-digit SITC) values of exports, which is what we do in Chapter 3.

As a final point, the world in general and ASEAN countries in particular have been nervous regarding the potential threat of Chinese exports in the wake of China's accession to the WTO, its explosive economic growth, and its sheer size. To what degree do the ASEAN countries compete with China in key markets? If there is little export overlap, then it may well be that the "Chinese Threat" is exaggerated. On the other hand, if there is considerable overlap, then the EAI might even make more sense to ASEAN, that is, as a means of gaining a preferential edge in the U.S. market.

To answer this question, we once again perform SRCC calculations, comparing the rank structure of Chinese exports and that of the ASEAN countries to the U.S. and other key OECD markets. The results are presented in Table 2.8.

In many ways the results are surprising and do not assuage the ASEAN fears of the Chinese Threat. Relative to intra-ASEAN competition in OECD markets (Table 2.6), the SRCC values are high and tend to be growing over time in most markets. In fact, for the OECD as a whole, Chinese export overlap is rising for every country, while in the case of exports to the United States and other main OECD markets the picture is mixed. The only exception to this result is the case of Singapore, which has very low overlap with Chinese exports in the OECD markets.

Thus, the increasing competition from China might suggest another motivation for the EAI, that is, to create an edge over China in the U.S. market.

III. Trade in Services

In developed countries, services continue to constitute by far the

TABLE 2.8
Correlation of Chinese and Selected East Asian Exports
to OECD Markets
(Spearman Rank Correlation Coefficients, 5-Digit SITC, Selected Years)

	Thai	Singapore	Phil	Malay	Indo	Korea	Taiwan
OECD							
1999	0.446	0.254	0.443	0.355	0.363	0.349	0.473
1997	0.421	0.212	0.403	0.312	0.35	0.322	0.428
1995	0.379	0.189	0.369	0.276	0.337	0.318	0.408
US							
1999	0.400	0.107	0.362	0.279	0.3	0.227	0.438
1997	0.419	0.105	0.406	0.312	0.324	0.215	0.435
1995	0.401	0.101	0.369	0.317	0.404	0.268	0.427
EU							
1999	0.307	0.118	0.352	0.214	0.241	0.148	0.336
1997	0.305	0.077	0.318	0.198	0.236	0.131	0.296
1995	0.294	0.047	0.327	0.200	0.224	0.135	0.289
JAPAN							
1999	0.305	0.039	0.262	0.135	0.258	0.247	0.21
1997	0.300	0.065	0.308	0.187	0.312	0.235	0.214
1995	0.269	0.010	0.332	0.094	0.32	0.225	0.183
Korea							
1999	0.131	0.396	0.127	0.041	Insign	NA	Insign
1997	0.111	−0.079	0.181	0.02	0.144	NA	Insign
1995	Insign	−0.224	0.123	−0.159	Insign	NA	−0.138

Note: All coefficients are statistically significant at the 99 per cent level unless specified as insignificant (Insign).
Source: OECD, *International Trade Statistics, 2003*; Lee and Plummer (forthcoming)

largest share of national economies. For example, in the United States approximately 80 per cent of the economy falls under the general rubric of services. Services have also increased in importance as a share of total international trade: in 2000, the share of services in total exports came to approximately 28 per cent in the United States and 22 per cent in the EU, with an average for the entire OECD coming to about 19 per cent (OECD 2002, pp. 20–21).

The same trend is observable in developing countries. During the development process, it is typical that: (1) agriculture falls as a percentage of GDP; (2) manufacturing first rises and then falls as the economy matures; but (3) services continue to grow throughout the development process. As a percentage of trade, exports of services from developing countries have risen from 9 per cent in 1980 (approximately half the share of developed countries) to about 18 per cent in 2000, on a par with that of the developed countries (OECD op. cit.).

While this process has been constant throughout history, services take on a special importance in the 21st century. This is due to a number of factors, including: (a) consumer tastes have become increasingly sophisticated: a good share of the growth in consumer spending is in the general area of "high tech", including such services areas as computer software, Internet-related services, and telecommunications innovations; (b) production processes have become more complicated, sophisticated, and international in scope, with global competition increasing substantially; and (c) inputs under the general area of "services" tend to be essential to industrial and enterprise growth and competitiveness.[9] Indeed, businesspeople, scholars, and policymakers are increasingly recognizing the strong link between the competitiveness and efficiency of the services sectors and that of the economy as a whole.

Hence, it was a high priority of member-states to extend the auspices of the GATT to include services during the Uruguay Round, which led to the creation of the General Agreement on Trade in Services (GATS). GATS continues to take form, and issues such as market access in various commercial services will no doubt play a critical role in the Doha Trade Agenda.

Given the complicated and diverse nature of trade in services, liberalization at the global level can be more delicate and in many ways more difficult than trade in goods. Services can be high tech or low tech; inputs and/or final products; privately provided or publicly provided; and closely related to other areas, such as FDI. Trade in goods internationally tends to be almost always privately provided, with strong GATT/WTO controls on state intervention, including the technical prohibition against state subsidies and constraints in the form of state-owned enterprise's having to abide by market principles (GATT Article XVII). Many services areas, however, still include government involvement, and state prerogatives in certain areas are recognized by the GATS. Moreover, trade in goods tends to be separate from FDI, though clearly there are indirect links between trade and FDI (discussed later in the chapter). In the area of services, however, trade can be intricately linked to FDI; in some sectors, trade in services is impossible *without* FDI.

The OECD defines four "modes" of trade in services: (1) cross-border supply, in which a company exports the service from home, e.g. by fax or e-mail; (2) consumption abroad, in which the user of the service consumes it outside his/her home country, e.g. tourism; (3) commercial presence, in which a company directly supplies the service to foreign customers (this involves establishment of an affiliate abroad and constitutes over three-fourths of all trade in services); and (4) presence of natural persons, in which the service-exporting country sends personnel abroad to supply services.

In terms of global services trade, WTO data (Appendix Table 2.9) show that not much has changed in terms of developing–developed countries shares (North America and the EU continue to constitute almost two-thirds of global trade in services) but that the *distribution* between countries in the developing world has changed substantially, with the successful countries increasing their shares significantly. Africa and Latin America have seen their shares generally stagnate (or fall) to approximately 2 per cent and 4 per cent, respectively, whereas Asia increased its share from about 12 per cent to 16 per cent (excluding developed-country Japan, which actually saw its share drop). China, which achieved the highest real economic growth of major economies over this time-span, saw its share in trade in services expand the most rapidly, actually tripling over this period. It is no coincidence that China also received the most FDI in the developing world.

An association between rapid real economic growth and rapid growth in services trade does not mean that the latter caused the former. Such estimation is much more complicated; indeed, there exists a chicken-and-egg ("simultaneity") problem here. However, regardless of which causes which, the development of the services sector is clearly an important part of the development process. As noted by the OECD (2002), there is a very close relationship between the share of services in output and per capita GDP: the correlation coefficient is 0.80 (where 1.0 would imply a perfect correlation).

In this section, we first consider the overall patterns of trade in services of the United States and the ASEAN countries, followed by analysis of the bilateral trade in services relationship between the United States and individual EAI countries.

A. U.S. and EAI Countries' Trade in Services

Table 2.9 presents the share of world exports and imports of services by country and regional groups. It shows that global services trade has boomed internationally, from US$924 billion in 1992 to US$1.57 trillion in 2002. U.S. exports of services almost doubled over this period to US$273 billion, or 17 per cent of total world services exports, up from 11 per cent in 1992. The United States had a US$67 billion surplus in trade in services in 2002, one of the (few) bright spots in the U.S. current account (it will be recalled from Section II that its reported balances on trade in goods in 2002 was a deficit of US$509 billion).

Export growth of commercial services in the EAI countries has been volatile. The Asian Crisis hit commercial services exports hard in ASEAN. Only Malaysia saw significant growth from 1992 to 2002, with exports rising by an impressive 200 per cent. However, the value of Malaysian exports of services was less in 2002 than it was in 1997. Indonesian services exports rose from US$3.4 billion in 1992 to US$5.4 billion in 2002, but this latter figure is down 21 per cent from its peak in 1997. Philippines exports of commercial services actually were less in value in 2002 (US$3 billion) than in 1992 (US$4.6 billion). Thai exports of services grew from US$9.2 billion in 1992 to US$15.2 billion in 2002, an increase of two-thirds, but the 2002 figure is down by 9 per cent from its 1996 peak prior to the Asian Crisis (US$16.7 billion).

Growth in imports of commercial services in the EAI countries, however, outpaced global growth (65 per cent) significantly in Indonesia, Malaysia, and the Philippines, increasing by 100 per cent, 125 per cent, and 83 per cent, respectively, whereas Thai service import growth slightly underperformed (63 per cent) relative to the global average. All four had commercial services deficits, amounting to US$10.6 billion, US$1.5 billion, US$1.2 billion, and US$1.4 billion, respectively, for Indonesia, Malaysia, the Philippines and Thailand.

B. U.S.-EAI Relationship in Trade in Services

Table 2.10 gives a detailed breakdown of bilateral U.S. trade in "private services", which is a slightly more general definition than the commercial services definition used in Table 2.9 (and, hence, the values on total exports and imports are slightly different). The EU has been traditionally the largest export market for U.S. services, coming to US$96 billion,

TABLE 2.9
Trade in Commerical Services: U.S., ASEAN, and Selected Other Countries, 1992–2002
(US$ millions)

A. Exports of Commerical Services

	1992	1993	1994	1995	1996	1997	1998	1999	2000	2001	2002
World	924,200	941,800	1,037,800	1,188,900	1,274,700	1,326,700	1,340,500	1,391,100	1,475,700	1,478,100	1,570,100
US	158,707	165,871	180,645	197,839	215,928	232,285	237,907	258,638	277,324	269,114	272,630
EU (15)	431,900	411,900	443,600	506,000	531,900	537,600	575,800	597,800	606,200	625,700	686,100
Japan	47,622	51,611	56,776	63,966	66,375	68,137	61,795	60,313	68,303	63,671	64,909
Indo	3,391	3,878	4,680	5,342	6,462	6,792	4,340	4,453	5,060	5,361	5,369
Malay	4,880	6,294	9,200	11,438	14,966	15,569	11,400	11,800	13,812	14,331	14,753
Phil	4,565	4,617	6,749	9,323	12,929	15,130	7,465	4,778	3,935	3,112	3,029
Sing	16,102	18,498	22,939	29,556	29,741	30,778	18,028	23,609	26,682	26,092	26,946
Thai	9,162	10,877	11,425	14,652	16,704	15,619	13,074	14,542	13,785	12,932	15,232
China	9,108	10,992	16,354	18,430	20,567	24,504	23,879	26,165	30,146	32,901	39,381

B. Imports of Commercial Services

	1992	1993	1994	1995	1996	1997	1998	1999	2000	2001	2002
World	939,100	953,100	1,037,000	1,190,900	1,261,700	1,302,600	1,326,800	1,376,800	1,460,900	1,469,600	1,545,500
US	102,393	108,159	118,832	127,250	137,388	150,459	164,073	181,006	205,153	202,018	205,580
EU (15)	417,600	396,300	428,000	493,400	512,900	514,900	563,400	585,100	596,200	614,900	668,700
Japan	92,323	95,488	105,449	121,548	128,701	122,079	110,705	114,173	115,686	107,027	106,612
Indo	7,884	9,595	11,136	13,230	14,777	16,214	11,744	11,336	14,755	15,595	15,950
Malay	7,248	9,371	11,918	14,822	17,406	18,115	12,973	14,622	16,603	16,539	16,248
Phil	2,305	3,072	4,639	6,906	9,392	14,073	10,087	7,492	6,066	5,102	4,225
Sing	9,430	11,217	13,800	17,249	19,625	18,629	16,955	19,121	21,579	20,308	20,551
Thai	10,254	12,307	15,231	18,601	19,313	17,144	11,874	13,464	15,329	14,484	16,573
China	9,207	11,563	15,781	24,635	22,369	27,724	26,467	30,967	35,858	39,032	46,080

Source: WTO, *International Trade Statistics 2003*, Table A7

TABLE 2.10

U.S. Trade in Private Services, 1992–2002

(US$ millions)

A. Exports	1992	1993	1994	1995	1996	1997	1998	1999	2000	2001	2002
World	**163,596**	**171,079**	**186,089**	**203,060**	**221,390**	**237,877**	**243,811**	**264,695**	**283,484**	**275,498**	**279,495**
EU	51,594	52,460	55,850	63,797	70,051	74,783	81,941	88,796	94,004	90,665	95,670
Japan	25,399	26,596	28,713	33,029	33,274	33,731	29,687	30,810	33,147	30,053	29,688
ASEAN-5											
Indonesia	770	892	874	1,153	1,413	1,789	1,474	1,486	1,113	1,005	1,021
Malaysia	602	675	884	1,029	1,277	1,257	1,049	1,109	1,114	1,181	1,142
Philippines	967	1,240	1,181	1,055	1,233	1,499	1,319	1,652	1,609	1,605	1,514
Singapore	2,144	2,411	2,639	3,150	3,849	4,089	3,817	5,144	6,058	5,892	5,766
Thailand	748	1,013	1,014	1,183	1,213	1,238	1,160	1,134	1,171	1,075	1,139
China	1,569	1,916	2,050	2,509	3,166	3,610	3,957	4,027	5,199	5,650	6,073

B. Imports	1992	1993	1994	1995	1996	1997	1998	1999	2000	2001	2002
World	**102,014**	**107,808**	**118,344**	**126,754**	**136,885**	**149,966**	**163,565**	**180,531**	**204,665**	**201,615**	**205,234**
EU	34,747	36,583	40,175	44,804	46,289	52,671	60,165	66,640	76,624	76,178	77,205
Japan	10,514	11,747	12,667	13,361	12,940	13,521	13,358	15,969	17,329	16,557	17,312
ASEAN-5											
Indonesia	435	432	443	448	553	550	310	379	439	295	285
Malaysia	265	301	357	454	458	535	374	382	386	526	498
Philippines	788	852	1,039	1,124	1,363	1,463	1,244	1,197	1,534	1,485	1,274
Singapore	746	948	1,164	1,240	1,823	2,105	1,858	2,352	2,356	1,893	2,070
Thailand	393	379	478	678	803	760	800	924	928	869	810
China	1,054	1,306	1,476	1,683	1,937	2,225	2,302	2,683	3,257	3,654	4,136

Source: Department of Commerce, Bureau of Economic Analysis, http://www.bea.doc.gov/bea/di/1001serv/intlserv.htm.

or 34 per cent of total U.S. exports. This is up slightly from 32 per cent in 1992. Japan is second, with U.S. exports totalling US$30 billion in 2002, or 11 per cent of the total. Yet the Japanese market has been disappointing to U.S. services exporters; in 1992, Japan accounted for a greater percentage (16 per cent) and, in fact, the value of imports from the United States was considerably higher in nominal terms in 1997 (US$34 billion) than in 2002. This can be explained in part by Japanese economic stagnation in the 1990s and early 2000s. But it is also true that the 1990s saw considerable liberalization of services in the Japanese market, particularly in financial services in the late 1990s as part of the process known as the "Big Bang". On the other hand, U.S. exports of services to China almost tripled over this period, coming to US$6 billion in 2002.

Over the 1992–2002 period, U.S. services exports to Indonesia, Malaysia, the Philippines and Thailand have grown respectively by 75 per cent, 90 per cent, 57 per cent, and 52 per cent to total US$1 billion, US$1.1 billion, US$1.5 billion, and US$1.1 billion in 2002. These growth rates are higher than the overall private services export growth rate of the United States over the 1992–2002 period (71 per cent) for Indonesia and Malaysia, but lower for Thailand and the Philippines (which, in turn, is the largest EAI market for the United States).

The values underscore the fact that each EAI country was a larger export market in earlier years. For example, relative to 2002, U.S. services exports to Indonesia, Malaysia, and Thailand in 1997 were down by 28 per cent, 9 per cent, and 8 per cent, respectively, whereas the value of exports to the Philippines essentially went unchanged (but exports to the Philippines were actually higher for each year over the 1999–2001 period). Again, this no doubt reflects in part the negative growth effect of the Asian Crisis. Still, it is difficult to explain this stagnation merely through growth effects, as the values did not pick up with the economic rebound—especially in Malaysia—in the post-Crisis years.

U.S. services imports from the EAI display even greater volatility. While overall U.S. imports of services doubled over the 1992–2002 period to US$205 billion (the growth rate of EU exports to the United States was particularly impressive at 120 per cent), Indonesian exports actually fell from US$435 million to US$285 million. Malaysian, Philippine, and especially Thai exports fared much better, growing by 89 per cent, 62 per cent, and 106 per cent, respectively, over this period, even though these rates are below the global mean except in the case of Thailand. In 2002 the value of Malaysian exports came to US$498 million and that of the Philippines, US$1.3 billion.

With respect to the balances of trade in services in the current account, we noted above in the discussion of overall net exports that the United States had a relatively-large trade surplus and the EAI countries all had deficits. This same is true at the bilateral level: the United States had a surplus on this account with Indonesia, Malaysia, the Philippines, and Thailand to the tune of US$736 million, US$644 million, US$240 million, and US$329 million, respectively, in 2002. These surpluses for the United States are in each case higher than they were in 1992, with the exception of Thailand.

Regarding the structure of bilateral trade in services, reliable and disaggregated data are difficult to collect. However, according to DeRosa (2002, Table 5), the "travel and transport" sector dominates services exports of ASEAN, with this sector comprising 90 per cent, 80 per cent, and 86 per cent of the services exports of Indonesia, Malaysia, and the Philippines, respectively, in 2002. Thailand had an even higher concentration of exports in this area at 91 per cent. Interestingly, a significant share of these services exports were related to merchandise trade in Indonesia (14 per cent) and the Philippines (29 per cent), whereas only 2 per cent of Malaysia services exports were related to trade in goods.

With respect to EAI-country services imports from the United States, the structure is much more diversified. The travel and transportation sector continues to be the largest import sector in Indonesia (54 per cent of the total) and the Philippines (67 per cent), but "business and other services" is the largest import item for Malaysia (48 per cent) and is significant for both Indonesia (26 per cent) and the Philippines (27 per cent) as well. The third sector included in DeRosa (2002), "royalties and licensing fees", is the smallest in each country, coming to 20 per cent, 12 per cent, and 5 per cent for Indonesia, Malaysia and the Philippines, respectively.

The EAI countries represent an important services export market and source of imports for the United States. Nevertheless, the key point is that the value of bilateral trade in services between the United States and the EAI countries (as well as ASEAN more generally, with the exception of Singapore) has been expanding at less than the overall pace of global and U.S. growth, suggesting that specific policy remedies, some of which might be included in an FTA, would be in order.

IV. Foreign Direct Investment

Foreign direct investment (FDI) inflows are paramount to an outward-looking development strategy in the contemporary global economy. Foreign direct investment brings in new (risk sharing, non-debt creating) capital flows, foreign exchange, easy access to foreign markets, and technology transfer.

Increasingly, ASEAN countries have been placing a stronger emphasis on technology transfer in their multilateral and bilateral relationships. We will discuss the economics of FTAs at length in the next chapter; suffice to note here that regional economic integration accords such as FTAs can promote FDI inflows through reductions in transaction costs (be they border- or non-border in origin), as well as creating a more stable environment and internal "policy competition".[10] In doing so, they establish an attractive business environment within which multinationals can easily profit from a vertical division of labour and facilitate the emergence of multinationals within the developing region itself. In fact, a prime motivation for the creation of AFTA was its perceived positive effect on FDI inflows to the region at a time when competition for such flows was increasing. Indeed as ASEAN countries embraced more outward-oriented development strategies, they placed a higher emphasis on luring FDI inflows. This resulted in a greater perceived need for industrial cooperation schemes like Brand-to-Brand Complementation (BBC), ASEAN Industrial Joint Ventures (AIJV), and, most recently, the ASEAN Investment Area (AIA). We discuss these initiatives at length in Chapter 5.

In addition, the Asian Crisis underscored the risks associated with financing current account deficits through short-run capital as opposed to long-term flows such as FDI. Prior to the Asian Crisis, the ratio of short-term flows (mainly bank loans) to FDI increased rapidly, exposing the region to the possibility of capital flight in the case of a crisis.[11] FDI is far less footloose.

Below, we first give a brief review of the determinants of FDI. As the literature is vast, we constrain ourselves to consider major issues but, given the goals of this study, we will place special attention on trade-investment links. Next, we analyse the U.S.-EAI bilateral relationship, first in a global context and then at the bilateral level. Included in the analysis will be a careful delineation of the relationship at the sectoral level.

A. The Determinants of FDI and Trade-Investment Links

Why do firms invest abroad instead of, say, exporting or licensing? After all, setting up production facilities aboard is expensive; holding everything else constant, a firm might be better off just building its product at home, where its operational costs in terms of market information and the like would be lowest and where it could perhaps benefit from economies of scale, and then exporting it to foreign markets. Several theories focus on the factor endowment characteristics of the FDI host country—for example, cheap labour or plentiful resources of a particular type. And policies of the host country matter a great deal: the lower the trade barriers and costs associated with engaging in FDI, the more likely it is that a firm may prefer FDI over exports.

Moreover, "firm-specific advantages" (FSAs), e.g., in technology and manufacturing know-how, can sometimes be exploited through licensing rather than FDI. A theory of FDI, therefore, needs to be based on FSAs that are not easily commercialized through markets—such as knowledge of the final markets for the manufactured good. For the advanced, large-scale multinationals, Buckley and Casson (1976) argued that such firms rely on FSAs extensively by producing complex products requiring coordination of labour procurement and training, marketing, research and development, and so on.

Dunning's "eclectic approach" to FDI is probably the most comprehensive in dealing with the question of why firms engage in FDI. Dunning highlights three key requirements for direct investment: (1) The firm must possess "ownership advantages" over other firms (FSAs); (2) The firm must find it beneficial to utilize these advantages directly instead of selling or leasing them ("internalization" advantages); and (3) The firm must find it profitable to combine these advantages with at least one factor input abroad so that local production dominates exporting ("locational" advantages). Locational advantages include proximity to markets, specialized suppliers, evasion of protective barriers, and factor endowment advantages (Ramstetter 1993).

Within the general context of FDI theory, the relationship between trade and investment has received special attention in the analyses of Kojima (1973) and Vernon (1966).[12] Kojima distinguished between "trade-oriented" and "anti-trade oriented" FDI. Trade-oriented investment occurs when the source country has a comparative disadvantage in the industry of the investment, and so capital flows toward countries with a comparative advantage in the activity. This kind of investment leads to greater trade and greater worldwide efficiency. Anti-trade-oriented investment occurs in industries in which the source country has a comparative advantage, but investment nevertheless occurs, perhaps because of protection or oligopolistic competition. This kind of investment leads to diminished trade, market segmentation, and possibly reduced global welfare.

Vernon's "product life-cycle" hypothesis argues that FDI takes place as the production process of a new product in the innovating country (the United States) becomes standardized, making it more profitable to move production offshore, first to other developed countries and eventually to developing countries. In this model, the investment flow initially tends to diminish trade by replacing exports, but as the industry shifts entirely abroad, it tends to increase trade again.

By the 1970s, the accumulated investment experience of U.S. multinationals abroad had considerably foreshortened the linear progression suggested by the product-life cycle hypothesis. It was found that experience gained in the investment process reduced the costs of producing abroad so much that even relatively new products could now be located in the country with the optimal factor endowments. In this context, provided that location makes a difference, foreign investment is likely to lead to the concentration of production and to increased international trade.

This also calls attention to the powerful role of international experience in the investment process. The relatively limited role of FDI in most national economies suggests that foreign investment is costly, presumably because of the investing firm's inadequate knowledge of and experience in the foreign business environment. A history of successful investment and/or close contacts through trade and other economic linkages can substantially reduce this cost.

The Kojima-Vernon models form the basis of the oft-cited "trade-investment nexus". The principal connections between FDI and trade analysed in the literature run from FDI to trade. The Kojima and product life-cycle models, for example, suggest specifically what the impact of FDI on trade should be, depending critically on the investment's characteristics. The "time structure" of most models of the investment–trade relationship suggests that changes in FDI at a particular time cause changes in trade at a later time. Hence, there is a lag in the process.

Evidence that FDI causes trade would support the trade-oriented theories of Kojima, Vernon and others. For example, Brainard (1993) finds that US$1 of sales of U.S. foreign affiliates generates about US$0.13 of exports and US$0.15 of imports. Hufbauer, Lakdawalla and Malani (1994) estimate that a 1 per cent increase in outward FDI to a host country leads to a .25 per cent increase in exports to that country.

While economists suggest that the principal connections between FDI and trade run from FDI to trade, in fact trade can also cause FDI. This "simultaneity" is evident in the economic literature, with causality tests showing the relationship going both ways (see, for example, contributions in Lee and Roland-Horst 1999).

Thus, the theory of FDI underscores that the decision for investment abroad is complicated and based on many variables, but that policy is extremely important. Moreover, trade and FDI have been shown—both in theory and in empirical modelling—to be linked in a variety of ways. Hence, it is important to note that trade policies will affect FDI, and FDI policies will affect trade. Economic liberalization, therefore, needs to be "holistic" in nature.

B. The U.S.-EAI FDI Relationship: A Statistical Review

Table 2.11 summarizes the stock of U.S. FDI (on a historical-cost basis) and U.S. FDI outflows to the world, ASEAN, and China for selected years, 1989–2003. The U.S. FDI stock (or position) increased tremendously over this period, growing from US$382 billion to US$1.8 trillion. Moreover, U.S. outflows rose steadily and significantly each year as the 1990s progressed, peaking at US$209 billion in 1999 before settling in to an average of US$134 billion over the 2000–2003 period.

The dynamism of U.S. FDI abroad—and that of other OECD members—is a salient aspect of globalization; production undertaken by U.S. firms has been transpiring increasingly outside of the United States itself. This process has been used by the critics of globalization to claim that this internationalization of U.S. production is forcing the United States to lose employment positions to foreigners. However, the criticism ignores two critical facts: (1) if U.S. firms did not diversify abroad, their U.S. operations would be less competitive, which would have implications for job-creation locally; and (2) over this period, foreign investment into the United States grew at an even faster pace than U.S. investment abroad. For example, over the 1989–1994 period, U.S. FDI outflows slightly exceeded inflows on average by US$7 billion per year, but in 2000, U.S. FDI inflows exceeded U.S. outflows by US$42 billion (UN 2001).

Taking the region together, we find that the stock of U.S. investment in the EAI-5 countries came only to about US$30 billion in 2003, or about 1.7 per cent of the U.S. total. This value is only slightly more than half the stock of U.S. FDI in Singapore. In 2003 U.S. FDI in the ASEAN-4 was largest in Indonesia, where investment totalled $10.4 billion, followed by Malaysia (US$7.6 billion), Thailand (US$7.4 billion) and the Philippines ($4.7 billion).[13] Since the Asian Crisis U.S. FDI outflows to the EAI have varied considerably.

It should be noted at this point that one would think that changes in the U.S. FDI position in ASEAN over, say, a two-year time frame would be essentially equivalent to U.S. FDI outflows. From the figures included in Table 2.11, this does not always seem to be the case; in fact, in certain cases, the differences are substantial (compare, for example, changes in the U.S. FDI position in Singapore over 2000–2001 and net outflows to Singapore. The former are far greater than the latter). This inconsistency, according to the U.S. Commerce Bureau of Economic Analysis, is due to the way that U.S. FDI position abroad is calculated. Variations in this stock can be due to two changes: capital flows (which are recorded as net outflows in our case) *and* valuation adjustments. The two major categories of valuation adjustments are currency adjustments—i.e., changes in exchange rates and — "other" adjustments—e.g., differences in proceeds of asset sales and book values and various capital gains and losses.

It was noted in our review of trade that China is perceived as a "threat" to ASEAN's most important markets. Our statistical analysis confirmed the existence of a fairly high overlap between ASEAN and Chinese exports to the OECD and the United States in particular. We see that this Chinese competition also emerges in the context of FDI: while U.S. FDI outflows to the EAI have been volatile and fairly low, U.S. investment in China has been rising quite consistently (with some

TABLE 2.11
U.S. FDI Outward Position in and Outflows to ASEAN and Selected Asia, Selected Years 1989–2003

a: U.S. FDI Stock in ASEAN
(Historical-Cost Basis, US$ millions)

	1989	1990	1993	1996	1997	1998	1999	2000	2001	2002	2003
All countries	381,781	430,521	564,283	795,195	871,316	100,0703	1,215,960	1,316,247	1,460,352	1,601,414	1,788,911
EAI											
Indonesia	2,771	3,207	4,864	8,322	6,729	8,104	8,402	8,904	10,551	10,341	10,387
Malaysia	1,263	1,466	1,975	5,663	6,530	5,629	6,222	7,910	7,489	6,954	7,580
Philippines	1,107	1,355	1,953	3,541	3,219	3,931	3,517	3,638	5,436	4,642	4,700
Singapore	2,998	3,975	8,875	14,912	18,026	17,550	20,665	24,133	40,746	52,449	57,589
Thailand	1,511	1,790	2,943	5,000	4,332	5,209	5,500	5,824	6,176	7,608	7,393
Brunei	17	26	47	-18	10	62	21	-2	-17	-33	-28
Rest of ASEAN											
Burma	(D)	(D)	(D)	90	(D)	(D)	(D)	(D)	(D)	(D)	(D)
Cambodia	0	0	0	0	0	-1	-2	1	1	1	1
Laos	0	0	0	-2	-4	-6	(*)	(*)	(*)	(*)	(*)
Vietnam				24	15	(D)	168	141	172	222	222
China	436	354	916	3,848	5,150	6,350	9,401	11,140	12,081	10,499	11,877

b. U.S. FDI Outflows to ASEAN and Selected Asian Countries (US$ Millions)

	1989	1990	1993	1996	1997	1998	1999	2000	2001	2002	2003
All countries	37,604	30,982	77,247	84,426	95,769	131,004	209,392	142,627	124,873	115,340	151,884
EAI											
Indonesia	-65	691	475	956	21	461	505	683	985	1,207	72
Malaysia	50	175	377	1,298	733	-470	-250	1,787	17	-609	763
Philippines	49	177	369	738	107	287	-255	480	970	-597	-325
Singapore	165	620	1743	2,760	3,697	261	3,863	3,688	5,593	4,377	5,699
Thailand	384	316	285	849	-16	424	1,103	722	1,286	1,501	-560
Brunei	10	7	8	-57	25	-19	-20	-24	-15	-17	4
Rest of ASEAN											
Burma	(D)	(D)	(D)	29	(D)	(D)	(D)	(D)	(D)	(D)	(D)
Cambodia	0	0	0	0	0	-1	-1	1	(*)	(*)	(*)
Laos	0	0	0	-2	-2	-2	4	(*)	(*)	(*)	(*)
Vietnam				56	-10	(D)	122	-18	-1	26	-14
China	100	30	556	933	1,250	1,497	1,947	1,817	1,912	924	1,540

Source: U.S. Department of Commerce, Bureau of Economic Analysis website, "U.S. Direct Investment: Country Position on a Historical Cost Basis and Capital Flows".

Note: In this table, unlike in the international transaction accounts, capital outflows are shown without a current-cost adjustment.

bumps) and impressively, from a stock of only US$354 million in 1990 to US$11.9 billion in 2003.

This does not mean, however, that ASEAN's main problem is "investment diversion" to China. While competition does matter, multinational companies will continue to invest in countries where they can earn profits. Simply put, if they estimate that they can make a great deal of money in China but only a good return in ASEAN, multinationals—provided that they are not financially constrained—will invest in both markets. The big challenge to luring FDI to ASEAN lies in effective economic policies, including regional economic integration accords.

Table 2.12 presents U.S. FDI outflows to ASEAN from a comparative perspective. Table 2.12a presents FDI outflows from selected OECD

TABLE 2.12
OECD FDI Outflows to ASEAN, Selected Years 1985–2000

a. FDI Outflows from Selected OECD countries to ASEAN

	1985	1990	1995	1996	1997	1998	1999	2000
United States	−108	1979	3411	6657	4532	963	6075	4680
Major EU								
France	68.2	177	251.4	441.3	280.7	1338.8	1660.8	158
Germany	18.7	93.7	1128.4	1059.2	-224.9	395.1	1729.8	1804.2
Italy	..	..	13	76	120.5	26.7	16.1	8.4
UK	263	975	398.4	1988.1	2515.7	-3297.8	3791.6	6065.7
Japan	935	4082	4558	5888.8	7097.7	4404	4197.1	..

Sources: OECD, *International Direct Investment Statistics Yearbook 2001*, CD-ROM; author's calculations.

b. Inflows Reported by ASEAN Countries:

EAI	1989	1990	1995	1996	1997	1998	1999
Thailand	1775.5	2444.0	2068.0	2335.9	3894.7	7315.0	6213.0
Indonesia	682.0	1093.0	4346.0	6194.0	4677.0	−356.0	−2745.0
Malaysia	1667.9	2333.0	4178.2	5078.0	5136.5	2163.4	1552.9
Philippines	563.0	530.0	1478.0	1517.0	1222.0	2287.0	573.0
Singapore	2886.6	5574.7	7206.4	8984.1	8085.2	5492.9	6984.3
Myanmar	7.8	161.0	277.2	310.4	387.2	314.5	216.3
Lao PDR	4.0	6.0	95.4	160.0	86.0	45.0	79.0
Vietnam	4.0	16.0	2349.0	2455.0	2745.0	1972.0	1609.0
Cambodia	...	....	150.8	293.6	204.0	121.0	125.5
ASEAN Total	7590.8	12157.7	12146.7	14539.0	15402.1	15260.4	15227.1

Source: Asian Development Bank, *Key Economic Indicators*, Table 33, http://www.adb.org.

countries to ASEAN (based on OECD data) and Table 2.12b summarizes FDI inflows reported by the individual ASEAN countries themselves (based on Asian Development Bank data). From Table 2.12a we note that, as we saw in Table 2.11, there is no clear trend in U.S. FDI outflows to the region but, in general, they are usually only second to Japan. This would be the case even if the Big Four EU countries were aggregated. Table 2.12b confirms that Singapore has been by far the largest recipient of overall FDI flows to ASEAN.

Thailand's FDI inflows were also larger than any of the other EAI countries in the 1998–99 period (Singapore comes in a close second). If we consider the Asian Crisis to have lasted from July 1997 to August 1998, this period would be the first year and a half of the post-Crisis era. Prior to the Crisis, FDI inflows to Malaysia tended to be on par or higher than those of Thailand. While it is difficult to determine a trend in such a short period, this change is somewhat puzzling. One argument might be that there was (at least) a short-term cost associated with the imposition of capital controls targeted at short-term capital flows, that is, the (mostly temporary) restrictions on certain financial transactions of foreigners introduced on 1 September 1998 in Malaysia. These may have negatively affected long-term capital flows (like FDI), even if these latter flows were generally not affected by the package.

In short, U.S. investment in the EAI-5 countries has been disappointing to the region's officials in both relative and absolute contexts. *Given our discussion above regarding the inherent benefits of FDI, the priority placed by ASEAN countries on luring FDI to the region, and the critical role of policy in determining FDI, economic cooperation, by lowering transaction costs associated with FDI, could significantly improve incentives for U.S. FDI in the region.*

As in the case of trade, the sectoral distribution of FDI is an important indicator of the nature of any bilateral economic relationship. Table 2.13 gives the sectoral distribution of the stock of U.S. FDI in the EAI countries for selected years, 1993–03, and Table 2.14 summarizes U.S. FDI outflows to the region.[14] In Indonesia, investment in the mining sector—especially petroleum—dominates U.S. FDI, accounting for 79 per cent of the total stock in 2003. This share is slightly down from 89 per cent in 1993. Investment in manufacturing increased its share (slightly) from 4 per cent to 5 per cent of the total. Most of the U.S. manufacturing FDI in Indonesia, both in terms of stock and flows, is in

TABLE 2.13
Stock of U.S. FDI in EAI-3, Selected Years, 1990–2002
(US$millions)

	All industries	Mining	Utilities	Manufacturing Total	Of which: Food	Chemicals	Primary and fabricated metals	Machinery	Computer and electronic products	Electrical equipment, etc.	Transportation equipment
2003											
Indonesia	10,387	8,250	728	470	37	265	31	–6	6	13	(D)
Malaysia	7,580	733	0	4,706	–11	254	(D)	103	3,981	–1	–8
Philippines	4,700	329	187	2,144	259	197	21	23	799	2	(D)
Thailand	7,393	1,214	(*)	3,113	24	1,032	97	157	763	16	–49
2002											
Indonesia	10,341	7,280	591	536	17	361	27	–2	15	10	(D)
Malaysia	6,954	562	0	4,355	–11	195	15	86	3,683	(*)	7
Philippines	4,642	370	187	2,468	229	243	20	21	1,015	1	(D)
Thailand	7,608	1,060	32	2,807	35	969	90	95	638	13	–57
2000											
Indonesia	8,904	7,212	(D)	558	13	361	18	25	27	(D)	(D)
Malaysia	7,910	(D)	0	5,028	–8	250	15	52	4,385	(D)	(D)
Philippines	3,638	(D)	(D)	1,725	170	293	17	59	830	13	(D)
Thailand	5,824	1,111	(*)	2,627	39	991	87	52	1126	28	119

TABLE 2.13 (continued)

Older class system used pre-1999	All industries	Petroleum	NOT USED	Manufacturing Total	Of which: Food and Kindred Products	Chemicals and Allied Products	P&F Metals	Ind. Mach and Equip	Elect and Electric Equip	Transportation Equipment	Other Manufacturing
1998											
Indonesia	8,104	5,115		275	(D)	136	8	-17	31	(D)	(D)
Malaysia	5,629	1,048		3,679	3	291	6	546	2,623	0	210
Philippines	3,931	283		1,558	337	398	33	13	599	0	178
Thailand	5,209	1,209		2,313	109	306	70	1,093	219	(D)	(D)
1995											
Indonesia	6,777	4,449		289	19	156	9	-6	37	(D)	(D)
Malaysia	4,237	639		2,620	(D)	178	(D)	-139	2,290	0	264
Philippines	2,719	326		1,214	304	369	(D)	6	364	0	(D)
Thailand	4,283	1,374		1,525	121	351	77	(D)	352	-1	(D)
1993											
Indonesia	4,864	4,315		178	(D)	73	6	(D)	(D)	-1	(D)
Malaysia	1,975	309		1,287	(D)	53	-3	(D)	1,090	0	139
Philippines	1,953	(D)		934	269	366	26	-2	150	10	114
Thailand	2,943	1011		960	52	176	(D)	(D)	219	0	137
1990											
Indonesia	3,207	2,751		120	6	61	3	(D)	(D)	0	(D)
Malaysia	1,466	402		745	7	52	2	4	575	0	105
Philippines	1,355	(D)		675	235	215	16	-5	139	0	76
Thailand	1,790	626		768	38	121	30	(D)	237	0	(D)

Source: U.S. Department of Commerce, Bureau of Economic Analysis website, U.S. Direct Investment: Country position on a historical cost basis, detailed annual country by industry tables

TABLE 2.14
Outflows of US FDI to ASEAN, Selected Years, 1990–2003
(US$millions)

Older class system used pre-1999	All industries	Petroleum	NOT USED	Manufacturing Total	Of which: Food and Kindred Products	Chemicals and Allied Products	P&F Metals	Ind. Mach and Equip	Elect and Electric Equip	Transportation Equipment	Other Manufacturing
1998											
Indonesia	461	292		−46	(D)	20	−3	−9	7	(D)	(D)
Malaysia	−470	−190		−318	−2	−289	(*)	−176	135	0	14
Philippines	287	−40		−7	9	36	−4	8	−64	0	8
Thailand	424	−10		412	(D)	17	21	(D)	−30	(D)	(D)
1995											
Indonesia	519	842		8	2	21	(*)	−12	5	(D)	(D)
Malaysia	1,037	210		631	(D)	28	(D)	−70	610	0	56
Philippines	269	40		58	−81	98	(D)	1	23	0	(D)
Thailand	686	235		203	2	52	12	(D)	81	(D)	(D)
1990											
Indonesia	691	572		19	1	6	1	(D)	(D)	0	(D)
Malaysia	175	26		104	−3	7	(*)	−9	96	0	14
Philippines	177	(D)		87	13	40	−3	−2	24	0	16
Thailand	285	56		149	6	16	(D)	(D)	5	0	31)

*Less than $500,000 (+/−)

D Suppressed to avoid disclosure of data of individual countries

Source: U.S. Department of Commerce, Bureau of Economic Analysis.

TABLE 2.14 (continued)

	All industries	Mining	Utilities	Manufacturing Total	Of which: Food	Chemicals	Primary and fabricated metals	Machinery	Computer and electronic products	Electrical equipment, etc.	Transportation equipment
2003											
Indonesia	(D)	(D)	141	(D)	16	(D)	(D)	(D)	-7	1	(D)
Malaysia	503	-40	0	175	*	65	(D)	17	48	(D)	-3
Philippines	-488	(D)	-475	-43	46	-14	2	2	216	1	(D)
Thailand	-622	-21	-32	289	-4	7	3	56	202	3	-91
2002											
Indonesia	400	-42	(D)	51	11	57	5	-12	-13	-5	(D)
Malaysia	936	-50	0	890	5	-9	1	15	947	(D)	(D)
Philippines	722	74	30	658	36	6	2	4	324	-7	(D)
Thailand	880	373	(D)	-41	-25	20	1	(*)	-74	20	-75
2000											
Indonesia	683	733	(D)	31	2	21	5	-9	(D)	(D)	(D)
Malaysia	1,787	(D)	0	1,369	-15	66	1	13	1,259	(D)	(D)
Philippines	480	(D)	(D)	798	30	18	4	(D)	622	7	(D)
Thailand	772	-34	(*)	676	5	602	4	(D)	257	13	-65

the chemical sector. *Hence, U.S. multinationals have not been investing in labour-intensive sectors in Indonesia,* which is where they might well have the biggest economic impact in terms of job creation and technology transfer.

The story is different for Malaysia, the Philippines, and (to some extent) Thailand, where manufactures tend to account for most of U.S. FDI. Almost two-thirds of the stock of U.S. FDI in Malaysia was in manufactures in 2003, and the vast majority of this investment (85 per cent) is in the area of computer and electronic products. Hence, over half of the total stock of U.S. investment in Malaysia is in computer and electronics, almost on par with the bilateral trade share in this sector.

U.S. FDI in the Philippines is less concentrated; in 2003 somewhat more than one-half of the stock of U.S. investment in the Philippines was in manufactures, and 37 per cent of manufacturing FDI flows went to the computer and electronics sector. Over time, the share of U.S. manufacturing FDI in the Philippines has been roughly unchanged from one-half in 1993.

Thailand is somewhat of an intermediate case between Indonesia on the one hand and Malaysia-Philippines on the other. In 2003 slightly less than half (42 per cent) of U.S. FDI in Thailand was concentrated in manufactures. One-fourth of manufacturing FDI was in computers and electronics, while chemicals constituted approximately one-third of the total. However, it is interesting to note that U.S. FDI in the electronics sector actually grew faster than that in any other EAI country, increasing an impressive three-and-a-half fold from 1998.[15]

Hence, unlike the case of Indonesia, Malaysia, the Philippines and possibly Thailand may find the *distribution* of U.S. FDI flow to be satisfactory, for these latter three countries have placed a priority on developing the electronics sector and each appears to have a "revealed" comparative advantage in this sector, as it also dominates trade in goods of these countries. But the quantity of FDI inflows from the United States has been less than what policymakers in all three countries would have hoped.

V. Summary

Below, we delineate several salient points made in each of the above sections:

A. Trade in Goods

1. The U.S.-ASEAN trade relationship is important to all countries, though to various degrees. In particular, the United States constitutes a key market for Malaysia, the Philippines, and Thailand, with promises to be of even greater importance as Indonesian structural change proceeds apace.

2. While the United States is the most important market for exports for most EAI countries, ASEAN trade is increasingly intra-Asian in nature. This trend is being driven by the market and suggests that emerging free-trade areas being contemplated in Asia, while perhaps "natural blocs" as they reinforce market-driven tendencies, could work to the determinant of U.S. economic interests in the region. This "defensive" approach is certainly one U.S. motivation for the EAI.

3. Given the size of the U.S. market and its fairly even distribution of trade across Europe, Asia, and the Americas, it comes as no surprise that the EAI countries do not constitute a large share of U.S. exports. But together the ASEAN-6 countries constituted 6 per cent of total U.S. exports, almost double the share of China and slightly less than that of Japan (7.4 per cent).

4. At the disaggregated level, the most important component of bilateral trade tends to be in the general area of electronics and machinery (SITC 7) for all countries, with apparel being important also for Indonesia and the Philippines. These products are part of the "new economy", where hardware and software meet. Hence, policies geared toward trade in these goods will be increasingly interlinked with other areas, including intellectual property-related issues.

5. Electronics exports of the EAI are being driven to no small degree by external demand in the U.S. market, as well as U.S. FDI flows.

6. The structure of bilateral trade between the United States and the EAI countries has been impressive since 1990 and has changed significantly, as the ASEAN countries have matured themselves.

7. Statistical evidence would suggest that the EAI countries tend to compete with each other to various degrees in OECD markets, including the United States, though the extent of competition depends on the pairing of countries and the estimation technique

used. Still, it is likely that sufficient overlap exists such that a free-trade area with the United States concluded by one EAI to the exclusion of another could potentially lead to significant trade diversion in the case of the latter.

8. The EAI countries seem to compete even more with China in the United States (and other OECD markets) than they do with each other. In this sense, a free-trade area with the United States could give ASEAN a competitive edge over China in arguably its most important market.

B. Trade in Services

1. Trade in services has become increasingly important globally, a trend that will likely continue given the important role that trade in services plays in the modern economy and as an input to other areas of economic activity. It will likely continue to play a key role in determining competitiveness globally.

2. The United States has revealed itself to have a strong comparative advantage in trade in services, as indicated by its increasing share of the rapidly-growing global trade in services. It has a considerable surplus in this category of the current account.

3. As ASEAN countries mature and economic development proceeds apace, a strong, vibrant, efficient and flexible services trade sector will become of the essence. To date, the EAI countries have delivered varied performances in terms of exports of services, with the exception of Malaysia, which has seen its exports and imports more than double.

4. The growth rate of U.S. exports of services to the EAI countries was higher than the global average for all save the Philippines (which is the United States' most important EAI market), but the values in 2002 were down in all countries relative to the recent past. EAI services exports to the United States have been growing at less than the global average and in 2002 were also less than in earlier years.

5. Although data are hard to come by, it would appear that the structure of services exports from ASEAN to the United States is concentrated in travel and transportation, and a significant portion is related to trade in goods (save for Malaysia).

6. In short, the U.S.-EAI relationship in trade in services is somewhat disappointing, even though it has a great deal of potential. The United States is a global leader in services; the EAI countries are dynamic economies in which services trade will play an increasingly important role. Policy action, including with respect to economic cooperation in the form of a free-trade area, could help to strengthen the bilateral U.S.-EAI relationship, as well as giving a boost to U.S. and EAI overall trade in this area.

C. Foreign Direct Investment

1. Thus, the theory of FDI underscores that the decision for investment abroad is complicated and based on many variables, but that policy is extremely important. Moreover, trade and FDI are closely linked. Hence, it is important to note that trade policies will affect FDI, and FDI policies will affect trade. Economic liberalization, therefore, needs to be "holistic" in nature.
2. U.S. FDI outflows have been robust over the past 15 years. FDI inflows to the EAI countries were strong in the early 1990s but have been mixed since the mid-late 1990s. There has been some rebound but the performance continues to be erratic and below potential.
3. U.S. investment in the EAI-5 countries has been disappointing. We will be discussing in subsequent chapters policies that might be used to enhance U.S. FDI in the EAI countries, particularly in the context of EAI bilateral FTAs. By lower transaction costs associated with FDI, economic cooperation could significantly improve incentives for U.S. FDI in the region.
4. With respect to the sectoral distribution of U.S. FDI in the EAI countries, investment tends to be concentrated in the mining sector in Indonesia, followed by chemicals. These are not the type of sectors that are conducive to job creation and technology transfer, which are important benefits of FDI to the host economy. On the other hand, U.S. FDI in Malaysia and the Philippines tends to be concentrated in manufactures and, within this sector, computers and electronic equipment. Hence, for these latter two countries, the "quality" of FDI is good (these are promoted industries) even if the "quantity" is less than optimal.

Notes

[1] Naya (2002) and the World Bank (1993) provide extensive surveys of the role of exports in the Asian success story.

[2] This section borrows from Plummer (2002).

[3] The relatively closed South Asia-3 (Bangladesh, India and Pakistan) actually saw their share fall from 1.3 per cent to 0.9 per cent.

[4] Most of the trade between Singapore and Indonesia falls under the category of petroleum trade and, hence, "double counting" is as important issue.

[5] The differences in large part stem from entrepôt trade through Hong Kong.

[6] In some years over this period, the share of "commodities not elsewhere specified" actually jumped substantially, rivalling even electrical machinery and equipment in 1994 (though never surpassing it).

[7] This point is also made in Plummer (2002).

[8] We only include the years 1995 through 1999 for the EU, as the Fourth Enlargement of the EU to include Austria, Sweden, and Finland began in 1995.

[9] This subsection draws in part from Plummer (forthcoming 2005).

[10] By "policy competition" here we imply that countries within a free-trade area will have an incentive to adopt best practices, promote a low-cost business environment, and embrace greater transparency if they are to compete effectively for FDI flows within a given trade area.

[11] It is beyond the scope of this text to give a detailed analysis of the origins of the Asian Crisis. See, for example, Naya (2002).

[12] This review borrows from Petri and Plummer (1999).

[13] Brunei actually shows a negative U.S. stock position, but this is due to the way that the figures are calculated, e.g., with respect to the valuation adjustments and capital losses. Suffice to say that the U.S. position in Brunei is virtually nil.

[14] We are forced to exclude Brunei from this analysis, as the Department of Commerce, Bureau of Economic Analysis, which published the most comprehensive data on U.S. FDI, does not include Brunei in its sectoral breakdown.

[15] One needs to take account of the definitional change between 1998 and 2000/2002. However, computer and electronic products dominate the latter classification, making it a close match to the old definition. Adding in other electronics-related areas would not change the conclusion.

References

Brainard, S. Lael. "An Empirical Assessment of the Factor Proportions Explanation of Multinational Sales". NBER Working Paper No. 4583, December 1993.

Buckley, P.J. and M. Casson. *The Future of the Multinational Enterprise* London: Macmillan, 1976.

Das, Dilip K., 2000. "Asian Exports: The Present Predicament". In *Asian Exports* edited by D. Dilip. Oxford: Asian Development Bank/Oxford University Press.

Kojima, Kiyoshi. "A Macroeconomic Approach to Foreign Direct Investment", *Hitotsubashi Journal of Economics* 14 (June 1974).

Finger, J.M. and M.E. Kreinen. "A Measure of 'Export Similarity' and its Possible Uses". *Economic Journal* 89 (1979): 905–12.

Lee, Hiro and David Roland-Holst, eds., *Economic Development and Cooperation in the Pacific Basin: Trade, Investment, and Environmental Issues*. Cambridge: Cambridge University Press, 1999.

Lizondo, J. Saul. "Foreign Direct Investment". In *Determinants and Systemic Consequences of International Capital Flows*. Washington, D.C.: IMF, 1991.

Lloyd, Peter J., "Measures of Similarity and Matching in International Trade". In *Empirical Methods in International Trade: Essays in Honor of Mordechai Kreinin*, edited by M. Plummer. London: Edward Elgar, 2005.

Naya, Seiji. *The Asian Development Experience*. Manila: Asian Development Bank, 2002.

OECD. *GATS: The Case for Open Services Markets*. Paris: OECD, 2002.

Plummer, Michael G. "EU and ASEAN: Real Integration and Lessons in Financial Cooperation", *World Economy* 25, no. 10 (December 2002).

Plummer, Michael G. "Structural Change in a Globalized Asia: Macro Trends and U.S. Policy Challenges". *Journal of Asian Economics* 14, no. 2, April 2003: 243–81.

————. "Separating the Apples from the Oranges in the Doha Trade Agenda: The Case of Postal versus Express Delivery Services". In *The World Trade Organization: Legal, Economic, and Political Analysis*, edited by A. Appleton, P. Macrory, and M. Plummer, forthcoming.

Ramstetter, Eric D. "Foreign Direct Investment in the Asia-Pacific Region". monograph prepared for UNCTAD, 1993.

Tamamura, Chiharu. "Structural Changes in International Industrial Linkages and Export Competitiveness in the Asia-Pacific Region". *ASEAN Economic Bulletin*, 19, no. 1 (April 2002): 52–82.

United Nations. *World Investment Report 2001*. New York: UN, 2001.

Vernon, Raymond, "International Investment and International Trade in the Product Cycle". *Quarterly Journal of Economics* 80, 1966.

World Bank, 1993. *East Asian Miracle: Economic Growth and Public Policy*. Oxford: Oxford University Press.

Appendix Tables

APPENDIX TABLE 2.1
Disaggregated Indonesian Exports to U.S. by Product Chapter, 1993–2001

Chapter	Sector	1993	1995	1996	1998	1999	2000	2001
01	Live Animals	0.0001	0.0000	0.0000	0.0000	0.0000	0.0000	0.0001
02	Meat & Edible Meat Offal	0.0002	0.0001	0.0002	0.0002	0.0001	0.0001	0.0001
03	Fish	0.0219	0.0129	0.0176	0.0285	0.0311	0.0325	0.0346
04	Dairy Produce	0.0000	0.0000	0.0008	0.0002	0.0004	0.0004	0.0006
05	Other Animal Products	0.0001	0.0000	0.0001	0.0000	0.0000	0.0000	0.0000
06	Live Trees	0.0000	0.0000	0.0000	0.0000	0.0001	0.0001	0.0002
07	Edible Vegetables	0.0011	0.0008	0.0002	0.0000	0.0003	0.0004	0.0005
08	Edible Fruit & Nuts	0.0007	0.0002	0.0003	0.0010	0.0009	0.0007	0.0005
09	Coffee, Tea, Spices	0.0176	0.0261	0.0203	0.0302	0.0180	0.0176	0.0131
10	Cereals	0.0016	0.0000	0.0000	0.0002	0.0002	0.0000	0.0000
11	Malt & Wheat Gluten	0.0000	0.0000	0.0002	0.0000	0.0000	0.0000	0.0000
12	Seeds	0.0002	0.0004	0.0003	0.0001	0.0002	0.0001	0.0002
13	Lac, Gums & Resins	0.0002	0.0002	0.0000	0.0000	0.0001	0.0001	0.0001
14	Other Vegetable Products	0.0000	0.0000	0.0001	0.0000	0.0001	0.0000	0.0000
15	Fats & Oils	0.0105	0.0104	0.0089	0.0069	0.0113	0.0101	0.0011
16	Preparations Meat/Fish	0.0073	0.0079	0.0061	0.0063	0.0055	0.0053	0.0061
17	Sugars	0.0002	0.0001	0.0001	0.0003	0.0010	0.0007	0.0005
18	Cocoa	0.0123	0.0150	0.0182	0.0357	0.0275	0.0143	0.0198
19	Prep. Cereals/Flour/Milk	0.0005	0.0002	0.0002	0.0001	0.0004	0.0007	0.0012
20	Prep. Vegetables/Fruit/Nuts	0.0052	0.0083	0.0081	0.0018	0.0085	0.0060	0.0059
21	Misc. Edible Products	0.0000	0.0000	0.0001	0.0000	0.0001	0.0001	0.0001
22	Beverages	0.0000	0.0000	0.0000	0.0000	0.0000	0.0000	0.0000
23	Waste from Food Industry	0.0000	0.0000	0.0003	0.0002	0.0002	0.0003	0.0003
24	Tobacco	0.0027	0.0022	0.0019	0.0029	0.0017	0.0016	0.0015
25	Salt/Sulphur/Lime/Cement	0.0001	0.0000	0.0000	0.0001	0.0004	0.0008	0.0011
26	Ores	0.0101	0.0000	0.0000	0.0017	0.0000	0.0000	0.0020
27	Lubricants/Fuels/Oil	0.1213	0.1000	0.2752	0.0546	0.0762	0.0622	0.0571
28	Inorganic Chemicals	0.0000	0.0000	0.0001	0.0006	0.0001	0.0023	0.0019
29	Organic Chemicals	0.0013	0.0018	0.0026	0.0042	0.0043	0.0059	0.0075
30	Pharmaceutical Products	0.0000	0.0000	0.0000	0.0000	0.0000	0.0000	0.0000
31	Fertilizers	0.0000	0.0000	0.0000	0.0002	0.0003	0.0000	0.0015
32	Tanning/Dyeing Extracts/Ink	0.0004	0.0004	0.0005	0.0007	0.0008	0.0007	0.0007
33	Cosmetics	0.0021	0.0021	0.0013	0.0026	0.0019	0.0016	0.0025
34	Soap, Waxes, Pastes	0.0002	0.0002	0.0000	0.0001	0.0003	0.0003	0.0002
35	Glues	0.0000	0.0002	0.0001	0.0002	0.0001	0.0001	0.0000
36	Explosives	0.0001	0.0002	0.0002	0.0000	0.0000	0.0000	0.0000
37	Photographic Goods	0.0000	0.0001	0.0000	0.0001	0.0000	0.0000	0.0000
38	Misc. Chemical Products	0.0006	0.0011	0.0026	0.0048	0.0027	0.0039	0.0028
39	Plastics	0.0035	0.0045	0.0041	0.0049	0.0124	0.0133	0.0165
40	Rubber	0.1040	0.1567	0.0943	0.0834	0.0720	0.0536	0.0478
41	Raw Hides & Skins	0.0010	0.0004	0.0002	0.0003	0.0002	0.0002	0.0001
42	Articles of Leather	0.0202	0.0194	0.0123	0.0164	0.0225	0.0248	0.0277
43	Furskins	0.0000	0.0001	0.0000	0.0000	0.0000	0.0000	0.0000
44	Wood	0.1011	0.0679	0.0563	0.0542	0.0698	0.0474	0.0471
45	Cork	0.0000	0.0000	0.0000	0.0000	0.0000	0.0000	0.0000
46	Straw	0.0013	0.0015	0.0010	0.0004	0.0022	0.0020	0.0025
47	Wood Pulp	0.0000	0.0003	0.0003	0.0010	0.0002	0.0001	0.0003
48	Paper & Paper Board	0.0040	0.0047	0.0048	0.0144	0.0301	0.0184	0.0214
49	Books, Newspapers	0.0000	0.0001	0.0001	0.0004	0.0007	0.0007	0.0006
50	Silk	0.0000	0.0000	0.0000	0.0000	0.0000	0.0000	0.0000
51	Wool	0.0000	0.0000	0.0000	0.0000	0.0000	0.0000	0.0000
52	Cotton	0.0124	0.0117	0.0090	0.0098	0.0099	0.0108	0.0096
53	Paper Yarn	0.0000	0.0000	0.0000	0.0000	0.0000	0.0000	0.0000

APPENDIX TABLE 2.1 *(continued)*

Chapter	Sector	1993	1995	1996	1998	1999	2000	2001
54	Man-made Filaments	0.0061	0.0030	0.0034	0.0074	0.0062	0.0063	0.0068
55	Man-made Staple Fibers	0.0044	0.0025	0.0019	0.0036	0.0029	0.0031	0.0032
56	Wadding	0.0000	0.0000	0.0002	0.0004	0.0003	0.0003	0.0002
57	Carpets	0.0002	0.0000	0.0000	0.0000	0.0001	0.0001	0.0001
58	Special Woven Fabrics	0.0001	0.0000	0.0001	0.0001	0.0004	0.0005	0.0006
59	Laminated Textile Fabrics	0.0002	0.0000	0.0000	0.0005	0.0000	0.0005	0.0005
60	Knitted Fabrics	0.0001	0.0001	0.0000	0.0002	0.0004	0.0001	0.0002
61	Apparel, Knitted	0.0513	0.0451	0.0340	0.0407	0.0556	0.0626	0.0682
62	Apparel, not Knitted	0.1240	0.1160	0.0931	0.1179	0.1525	0.1631	0.1690
63	Other Textile Articles	0.0026	0.0030	0.0034	0.0022	0.0047	0.0074	0.0097
64	Footwear	0.1524	0.1375	0.1026	0.0761	0.0978	0.0817	0.0790
65	Headgear	0.0018	0.0012	0.0007	0.0006	0.0013	0.0013	0.0013
66	Umbrellas, Walking Sticks	0.0006	0.0008	0.0005	0.0010	0.0018	0.0015	0.0014
67	Prepared Feathers	0.0036	0.0037	0.0029	0.0034	0.0048	0.0050	0.0057
68	Stone/Plaster/Cement	0.0003	0.0004	0.0004	0.0003	0.0022	0.0013	0.0012
69	Ceramic Products	0.0060	0.0073	0.0055	0.0060	0.0091	0.0080	0.0078
70	Glass and Glassware	0.0031	0.0032	0.0026	0.0020	0.0032	0.0035	0.0031
71	Jewelry	0.0020	0.0023	0.0021	0.0040	0.0036	0.0029	0.0026
72	Iron and Steel	0.0014	0.0047	0.0035	0.0208	0.0142	0.0097	0.0028
73	Articles of Iron or Steel	0.0089	0.0075	0.0061	0.0070	0.0079	0.0116	0.0101
74	Copper	0.0012	0.0012	0.0010	0.0006	0.0007	0.0009	0.0006
75	Nickel	0.0000	0.0000	0.0000	0.0000	0.0000	0.0000	0.0000
76	Aluminum	0.0025	0.0034	0.0040	0.0052	0.0071	0.0072	0.0062
78	Lead	0.0000	0.0000	0.0000	0.0000	0.0000	0.0000	0.0000
79	Zinc	0.0000	0.0000	0.0000	0.0000	0.0000	0.0000	0.0000
80	Tin	0.0000	0.0000	0.0000	0.0000	0.0003	0.0000	0.0001
81	Other Base Metals	0.0000	0.0000	0.0000	0.0000	0.0000	0.0000	0.0000
82	Tools	0.0017	0.0017	0.0015	0.0023	0.0020	0.0030	0.0014
83	Miscellaneous Base Metals	0.0008	0.0005	0.0005	0.0006	0.0009	0.0012	0.0007
84	Computer/Machinery	0.0107	0.0331	0.0208	0.0155	0.0193	0.0532	0.0324
85	Electrical Equipment	0.0869	0.1085	0.1140	0.0793	0.0808	0.1317	0.1502
86	Railway	0.0049	0.0031	0.0014	0.0000	0.0000	0.0001	0.0005
87	Cars, Trucks, Autos	0.0012	0.0035	0.0029	0.0048	0.0047	0.0046	0.0055
88	Aircraft, Spacecraft	0.0009	0.0006	0.0004	0.0008	0.0006	0.0012	0.0001
89	Ships, Boats	0.0000	0.0000	0.0000	0.0000	0.0000	0.0000	0.0000
90	Optical/Medical Instruments	0.0037	0.0019	0.0053	0.0095	0.0120	0.0107	0.0099
91	Clocks	0.0001	0.0000	0.0000	0.0000	0.0000	0.0000	0.0000
92	Musical Instruments	0.0003	0.0015	0.0026	0.0039	0.0045	0.0056	0.0084
93	Arms & Ammunition	0.0000	0.0001	0.0000	0.0000	0.0000	0.0000	0.0000
94	Furniture	0.0263	0.0261	0.0205	0.0162	0.0468	0.0513	0.0576
95	Toys	0.0211	0.0154	0.0110	0.0037	0.0039	0.0141	0.0111
96	Misc. Manufactured Articles	0.0024	0.0026	0.0025	0.0029	0.0043	0.0039	0.0039
97	Works of Art	0.0000	0.0000	0.0000	0.0001	0.0001	0.0001	0.0001
98	Postal Packages & Special Trans	0.0000	0.0000	0.0000	0.1904	0.0276	0.0001	0.0001
99	Other	0.0000	0.0000	0.0000	0.0000	0.0000	0.0000	0.0000
	Total (US$ mil)	**5229.8**	**6321.7**	**6991.1**	**7031.0**	**6896.5**	**8475.4**	**7748.7**

APPENDIX TABLE 2.2
Disaggregated Malaysian Exports to U.S., 1993–2001

Chapter	Sector	1993	1995	1996	1998	1999	2000	2001
01	Live Animals	0.0000	0.0000	0.0000	0.0000	0.0000	0.0000	0.0000
02	Meat & Edible Meat Offal	0.0000	0.0000	0.0000	0.0000	0.0000	0.0000	0.0000
03	Fish	0.0002	0.0005	0.0023	0.0098	0.0022	0.0009	0.0012
04	Dairy Produce	0.0000	0.0000	0.0000	0.0000	0.0000	0.0000	0.0000
05	Other Animal Products	0.0000	0.0000	0.0000	0.0000	0.0000	0.0000	0.0000
06	Live Trees	0.0000	0.0000	0.0001	0.0001	0.0000	0.0002	0.0000
07	Edible Vegetables	0.0000	0.0000	0.0000	0.0000	0.0000	0.0000	0.0000
08	Edible Fruit & Nuts	0.0000	0.0000	0.0000	0.0000	0.0003	0.0000	0.0000
09	Coffee, Tea, Spices	0.0000	0.0000	0.0016	0.0037	0.0032	0.0002	0.0016
10	Cereals	0.0000	0.0000	0.0000	0.0000	0.0000	0.0000	0.0000
11	Malt & Wheat Gluten	0.0000	0.0000	0.0002	0.0000	0.0001	0.0000	0.0001
12	Seeds	0.0000	0.0000	0.0000	0.0000	0.0000	0.0000	0.0000
13	Lac, Gums & Resins	0.0000	0.0000	0.0000	0.0000	0.0000	0.0000	0.0000
14	Other Vegetable Products	0.0000	0.0000	0.0000	0.0000	0.0000	0.0000	0.0000
15	Fats & Oils	0.0200	0.0149	0.0102	0.0094	0.0080	0.0067	0.0070
16	Preparations Meat/Fish	0.0014	0.0007	0.0006	0.0009	0.0005	0.0007	0.0007
17	Sugars	0.0000	0.0006	0.0008	0.0025	0.0000	0.0001	0.0000
18	Cocoa	0.0038	0.0026	0.0022	0.0044	0.0030	0.0026	0.0032
19	Prep. Cereals/Flour/Milk	0.0002	0.0002	0.0002	0.0002	0.0002	0.0003	0.0004
20	Prep. Vegetables/Fruit/Nuts	0.0004	0.0007	0.0004	0.0005	0.0004	0.0004	0.0004
21	Misc. Edible Products	0.0001	0.0001	0.0002	0.0001	0.0003	0.0001	0.0001
22	Beverages	0.0000	0.0000	0.0000	0.0000	0.0002	0.0003	0.0004
23	Waste from Food Industry	0.0000	0.0000	0.0000	0.0000	0.0004	0.0000	0.0000
24	Tobacco	0.0000	0.0000	0.0006	0.0000	0.0019	0.0025	0.0000
25	Salt/Sulphur/Lime/Cement	0.0000	0.0000	0.0001	0.0000	0.0000	0.0000	0.0000
26	Ores	0.0000	0.0000	0.0000	0.0000	0.0000	0.0001	0.0003
27	Lubricants/Fuels/Oil	0.0061	0.0044	0.0088	0.0102	0.0187	0.0312	0.0301
28	Inorganic Chemicals	0.0004	0.0003	0.0003	0.0004	0.0003	0.0003	0.0001
29	Organic Chemicals	0.0018	0.0028	0.0041	0.0043	0.0046	0.0079	0.0086
30	Pharmaceutical Products	0.0000	0.0003	0.0002	0.0000	0.0001	0.0001	0.0001
31	Fertilizers	0.0005	0.0006	0.0006	0.0002	0.0000	0.0013	0.0021
32	Tanning/Dyeing Extracts/Ink	0.0002	0.0000	0.0000	0.0013	0.0001	0.0001	0.0013
33	Cosmetics	0.0003	0.0002	0.0002	0.0003	0.0002	0.0002	0.0003
34	Soap, Waxes, Pastes	0.0001	0.0015	0.0001	0.0014	0.0003	0.0005	0.0005
35	Glues	0.0000	0.0000	0.0000	0.0000	0.0000	0.0001	0.0000
36	Explosives	0.0000	0.0000	0.0000	0.0000	0.0000	0.0000	0.0000
37	Photographic Goods	0.0003	0.0001	0.0001	0.0002	0.0002	0.0003	0.0003
38	Misc. Chemical Products	0.0012	0.0062	0.0052	0.0045	0.0035	0.0047	0.0033
39	Plastics	0.0051	0.0038	0.0029	0.0039	0.0035	0.0060	0.0084
40	Rubber	0.0521	0.0504	0.0505	0.0516	0.0327	0.0385	0.0375
41	Raw Hides & Skins	0.0000	0.0000	0.0000	0.0000	0.0001	0.0000	0.0000
42	Articles of Leather	0.0010	0.0008	0.0008	0.0008	0.0005	0.0006	0.0007
43	Furskins	0.0000	0.0000	0.0000	0.0000	0.0000	0.0000	0.0000
44	Wood	0.0214	0.0117	0.0191	0.0094	0.0100	0.0090	0.0087
45	Cork	0.0000	0.0000	0.0000	0.0000	0.0000	0.0000	0.0000
46	Straw	0.0000	0.0000	0.0000	0.0000	0.0000	0.0000	0.0000
47	Wood Pulp	0.0000	0.0000	0.0000	0.0000	0.0000	0.0000	0.0000
48	Paper & Paper Board	0.0005	0.0004	0.0003	0.0006	0.0008	0.0030	0.0013
49	Books, Newspapers	0.0004	0.0003	0.0005	0.0005	0.0007	0.0009	0.0012
50	Silk	0.0000	0.0000	0.0000	0.0000	0.0000	0.0000	0.0000
51	Wool	0.0002	0.0001	0.0001	0.0001	0.0000	0.0001	0.0001
52	Cotton	0.0039	0.0024	0.0025	0.0009	0.0023	0.0010	0.0025
53	Paper Yarn	0.0000	0.0000	0.0000	0.0000	0.0000	0.0000	0.0000
54	Man-made Filaments	0.0001	0.0003	0.0008	0.0015	0.0010	0.0014	0.0009

APPENDIX TABLE 2.2 (*continued*)

Chapter	Sector	1993	1995	1996	1998	1999	2000	2001
55	Man-made Staple Fibers	0.0024	0.0013	0.0010	0.0007	0.0008	0.0010	0.0005
56	Wadding	0.0000	0.0000	0.0001	0.0001	0.0000	0.0002	0.0001
57	Carpets	0.0000	0.0000	0.0000	0.0000	0.0000	0.0000	0.0000
58	Special Woven Fabrics	0.0001	0.0000	0.0000	0.0000	0.0000	0.0001	0.0001
59	Laminated Textile Fabrics	0.0000	0.0000	0.0000	0.0001	0.0000	0.0000	0.0000
60	Knitted Fabrics	0.0000	0.0000	0.0000	0.0000	0.0000	0.0000	0.0000
61	Apparel, Knitted	0.0212	0.0162	0.0164	0.0241	0.0195	0.0282	0.0305
62	Apparel, not Knitted	0.0394	0.0236	0.0220	0.0246	0.0190	0.0257	0.0249
63	Other Textile Articles	0.0001	0.0000	0.0000	0.0000	0.0001	0.0001	0.0001
64	Footwear	0.0006	0.0004	0.0001	0.0001	0.0001	0.0001	0.0001
65	Headgear	0.0008	0.0004	0.0003	0.0001	0.0001	0.0001	0.0001
66	Umbrellas, Walking Sticks	0.0000	0.0001	0.0001	0.0000	0.0000	0.0000	0.0000
67	Prepared Feathers	0.0000	0.0000	0.0000	0.0000	0.0000	0.0000	0.0000
68	Stone/Plaster/Cement	0.0002	0.0001	0.0001	0.0002	0.0001	0.0001	0.0003
69	Ceramic Products	0.0043	0.0033	0.0024	0.0027	0.0018	0.0023	0.0024
70	Glass and Glassware	0.0003	0.0007	0.0003	0.0008	0.0008	0.0027	0.0035
71	Jewelry	0.0036	0.0040	0.0043	0.0048	0.0020	0.0023	0.0022
72	Iron and Steel	0.0001	0.0003	0.0005	0.0009	0.0008	0.0010	0.0028
73	Articles of Iron or Steel	0.0029	0.0027	0.0049	0.0064	0.0034	0.0035	0.0033
74	Copper	0.0010	0.0019	0.0015	0.0017	0.0014	0.0021	0.0016
75	Nickel	0.0000	0.0000	0.0000	0.0000	0.0000	0.0000	0.0000
76	Aluminum	0.0007	0.0019	0.0026	0.0060	0.0023	0.0005	0.0004
78	Lead	0.0000	0.0001	0.0000	0.0000	0.0000	0.0000	0.0000
79	Zinc	0.0002	0.0001	0.0001	0.0006	0.0000	0.0000	0.0000
80	Tin	0.0017	0.0010	0.0008	0.0008	0.0003	0.0003	0.0004
81	Other Base Metals	0.0000	0.0000	0.0000	0.0000	0.0000	0.0000	0.0000
82	Tools	0.0008	0.0005	0.0004	0.0007	0.0001	0.0004	0.0003
83	Miscellaneous Base Metals	0.0033	0.0008	0.0006	0.0015	0.0006	0.0008	0.0011
84	Computer/Machinery	0.1280	0.1867	0.2456	0.1864	0.2857	0.3047	0.2824
85	Electrical Equipment	0.5766	0.5310	0.4849	0.5324	0.4960	0.4085	0.4218
86	Railway	0.0000	0.0000	0.0000	0.0000	0.0005	0.0000	0.0002
87	Cars, Trucks, Autos	0.0008	0.0010	0.0013	0.0049	0.0011	0.0021	0.0011
88	Aircraft, Spacecraft	0.0316	0.0588	0.0271	0.0115	0.0058	0.0024	0.0030
89	Ships, Boats	0.0000	0.0004	0.0003	0.0007	0.0008	0.0016	0.0015
90	Optical/Medical Instruments	0.0154	0.0109	0.0148	0.0180	0.0172	0.0369	0.0412
91	Clocks	0.0004	0.0004	0.0007	0.0009	0.0004	0.0010	0.0005
92	Musical Instruments	0.0000	0.0001	0.0001	0.0008	0.0012	0.0021	0.0023
93	Arms & Ammunition	0.0001	0.0001	0.0001	0.0000	0.0000	0.0000	0.0008
94	Furniture	0.0219	0.0162	0.0259	0.0284	0.0264	0.0336	0.0333
95	Toys	0.0161	0.0171	0.0195	0.0115	0.0076	0.0092	0.0087
96	Misc. Manufactured Articles	0.0021	0.0020	0.0014	0.0011	0.0012	0.0012	0.0009
97	Works of Art	0.0000	0.0000	0.0000	0.0000	0.0000	0.0000	0.0000
98	Postal Packages & Trans	0.0012	0.0083	0.0027	0.0023	0.0020	0.0029	0.0041
99	Other	0.0000	0.0000	0.0000	0.0000	0.0000	0.0000	0.0000
	Total (US$ mil)	**9,407.3**	**13,697.5**	**14,984.3**	**14,306.6**	**17,489.3**	**14,177.4**	**12,695.6**

APPENDIX TABLE 2.3
Disaggregated Philippine Exports to U.S., 1993–2001

Chapter	Sector	1993	1995	1996	1998	1999	2000	2001
01	Live Animals	0.0002	0.0002	0.0001	0.0001	0.0001	0.0001	0.0001
02	Meat & Edible Meat Offal	0.0000	0.0000	0.0000	0.0000	0.0000	0.0000	0.0000
03	Fish	0.0112	0.0077	0.0066	0.0053	0.0067	0.0066	0.0065
04	Dairy Produce	0.0000	0.0000	0.0000	0.0000	0.0000	0.0000	0.0000
05	Other Animal Products	0.0001	0.0001	0.0001	0.0000	0.0001	0.0001	0.0001
06	Live Trees	0.0001	0.0001	0.0001	0.0000	0.0001	0.0000	0.0000
07	Edible Vegetables	0.0002	0.0001	0.0001	0.0001	0.0001	0.0000	0.0001
08	Edible Fruit & Nuts	0.0086	0.0051	0.0072	0.0035	0.0038	0.0032	0.0035
09	Coffee, Tea, Spices	0.0000	0.0001	0.0000	0.0000	0.0000	0.0000	0.0000
10	Cereals	0.0001	0.0001	0.0001	0.0002	0.0002	0.0002	0.0002
11	Malt & Wheat Gluten	0.0000	0.0000	0.0000	0.0000	0.0000	0.0000	0.0000
12	Seeds	0.0004	0.0008	0.0007	0.0004	0.0006	0.0006	0.0006
13	Lac, Gums & Resins	0.0014	0.0014	0.0011	0.0006	0.0005	0.0004	0.0003
14	Other Vegetable Products	0.0001	0.0000	0.0000	0.0000	0.0000	0.0000	0.0000
15	Fats & Oils	0.0437	0.0542	0.0503	0.0274	0.0168	0.0179	0.0143
16	Preparations Meat/Fish	0.0072	0.0061	0.0065	0.0038	0.0019	0.0018	0.0032
17	Sugars	0.0149	0.0111	0.0229	0.0080	0.0061	0.0048	0.0028
18	Cocoa	0.0011	0.0009	0.0009	0.0005	0.0002	0.0001	0.0002
19	Prep. Cereals/Flour/Milk	0.0013	0.0009	0.0014	0.0006	0.0007	0.0007	0.0009
20	Prep. Vegetables/Fruit/Nuts	0.0226	0.0148	0.0172	0.0086	0.0085	0.0089	0.0127
21	Misc. Edible Products	0.0014	0.0010	0.0012	0.0007	0.0008	0.0008	0.0011
22	Beverages	0.0004	0.0001	0.0002	0.0001	0.0003	0.0002	0.0003
23	Waste from Food Industry	0.0000	0.0001	0.0000	0.0000	0.0000	0.0001	0.0000
24	Tobacco	0.0009	0.0004	0.0007	0.0004	0.0007	0.0008	0.0012
25	Salt/Sulphur/Lime/Cement	0.0000	0.0000	0.0000	0.0000	0.0000	0.0003	0.0009
26	Ores	0.0004	0.0002	0.0003	0.0010	0.0000	0.0003	0.0001
27	Lubricants/Fuels/Oil	0.0013	0.0005	0.0010	0.0006	0.0009	0.0007	0.0005
28	Inorganic Chemicals	0.0003	0.0002	0.0002	0.0001	0.0001	0.0002	0.0003
29	Organic Chemicals	0.0000	0.0000	0.0001	0.0001	0.0001	0.0004	0.0002
30	Pharmaceutical Products	0.0000	0.0001	0.0002	0.0001	0.0001	0.0001	0.0002
31	Fertilizers	0.0000	0.0000	0.0000	0.0000	0.0000	0.0000	0.0000
32	Tanning/Dyeing Extracts/Ink	0.0000	0.0001	0.0001	0.0000	0.0001	0.0001	0.0001
33	Cosmetics	0.0001	0.0001	0.0001	0.0001	0.0001	0.0001	0.0001
34	Soap, Waxes, Pastes	0.0006	0.0004	0.0004	0.0006	0.0006	0.0007	0.0008
35	Glues	0.0000	0.0000	0.0000	0.0000	0.0000	0.0000	0.0000
36	Explosives	0.0000	0.0000	0.0000	0.0000	0.0000	0.0000	0.0000
37	Photographic Goods	0.0015	0.0010	0.0014	0.0005	0.0001	0.0000	0.0000
38	Misc. Chemical Products	0.0023	0.0017	0.0021	0.0014	0.0010	0.0015	0.0022
39	Plastics	0.0069	0.0055	0.0052	0.0028	0.0029	0.0025	0.0030
40	Rubber	0.0012	0.0007	0.0005	0.0003	0.0010	0.0016	0.0008
41	Raw Hides & Skins	0.0000	0.0000	0.0000	0.0000	0.0000	0.0000	0.0000
42	Articles of Leather	0.0346	0.0327	0.0322	0.0241	0.0226	0.0259	0.0323
43	Furskins	0.0000	0.0000	0.0000	0.0000	0.0000	0.0000	0.0000
44	Wood	0.0063	0.0057	0.0055	0.0034	0.0032	0.0022	0.0020
45	Cork	0.0000	0.0000	0.0000	0.0000	0.0000	0.0000	0.0000
46	Straw	0.0155	0.0114	0.0090	0.0050	0.0047	0.0052	0.0053
47	Wood Pulp	0.0004	0.0002	0.0004	0.0002	0.0001	0.0002	0.0001
48	Paper & Paper Board	0.0026	0.0020	0.0017	0.0015	0.0014	0.0014	0.0018
49	Books, Newspapers	0.0003	0.0003	0.0002	0.0003	0.0002	0.0001	0.0001
50	Silk	0.0000	0.0000	0.0000	0.0000	0.0000	0.0000	0.0000
51	Wool	0.0000	0.0000	0.0000	0.0001	0.0001	0.0006	0.0002
52	Cotton	0.0001	0.0001	0.0003	0.0002	0.0003	0.0001	0.0002
53	Paper Yarn	0.0012	0.0011	0.0011	0.0005	0.0006	0.0005	0.0003
54	Man-made Filaments	0.0004	0.0004	0.0003	0.0019	0.0017	0.0021	0.0021

APPENDIX TABLE 2.3 *(continued)*

Chapter	Sector	1993	1995	1996	1998	1999	2000	2001
55	Man-made Staple Fibers	0.0015	0.0016	0.0026	0.0015	0.0018	0.0011	0.0009
56	Wadding	0.0020	0.0014	0.0016	0.0011	0.0011	0.0011	0.0015
57	Carpets	0.0005	0.0004	0.0004	0.0003	0.0003	0.0004	0.0004
58	Special Woven Fabrics	0.0019	0.0008	0.0007	0.0003	0.0004	0.0002	0.0004
59	Laminated Textile Fabrics	0.0000	0.0000	0.0000	0.0000	0.0000	0.0000	0.0000
60	Knitted Fabrics	0.0000	0.0002	0.0001	0.0007	0.0001	0.0003	0.0011
61	Apparel, Knitted	0.0921	0.0846	0.0732	0.0526	0.0524	0.0501	0.0629
62	Apparel, not Knitted	0.2068	0.1735	0.1631	0.1127	0.1094	0.1161	0.1368
63	Other Textile Articles	0.0046	0.0045	0.0060	0.0032	0.0038	0.0035	0.0037
64	Footwear	0.0155	0.0115	0.0094	0.0062	0.0016	0.0015	0.0016
65	Headgear	0.0083	0.0102	0.0086	0.0027	0.0020	0.0024	0.0019
66	Umbrellas, Walking Sticks	0.0000	0.0000	0.0001	0.0000	0.0000	0.0000	0.0000
67	Prepared Feathers	0.0008	0.0007	0.0005	0.0004	0.0002	0.0002	0.0003
68	Stone/Plaster/Cement	0.0004	0.0003	0.0006	0.0004	0.0006	0.0004	0.0004
69	Ceramic Products	0.0046	0.0040	0.0037	0.0023	0.0026	0.0025	0.0027
70	Glass and Glassware	0.0001	0.0003	0.0004	0.0003	0.0003	0.0004	0.0009
71	Jewelry	0.0035	0.0012	0.0011	0.0009	0.0012	0.0015	0.0015
72	Iron and Steel	0.0005	0.0006	0.0012	0.0004	0.0001	0.0000	0.0000
73	Articles of Iron or Steel	0.0031	0.0056	0.0056	0.0011	0.0013	0.0019	0.0015
74	Copper	0.0001	0.0000	0.0000	0.0001	0.0000	0.0011	0.0000
75	Nickel	0.0000	0.0000	0.0000	0.0000	0.0000	0.0000	0.0000
76	Aluminum	0.0003	0.0002	0.0002	0.0003	0.0006	0.0003	0.0004
78	Lead	0.0000	0.0000	0.0001	0.0000	0.0000	0.0000	0.0000
79	Zinc	0.0000	0.0000	0.0000	0.0000	0.0000	0.0000	0.0000
80	Tin	0.0001	0.0000	0.0001	0.0001	0.0000	0.0000	0.0000
81	Other Base Metals	0.0001	0.0001	0.0003	0.0001	0.0000	0.0002	0.0047
82	Tools	0.0006	0.0001	0.0004	0.0002	0.0001	0.0001	0.0001
83	Miscellaneous Base Metals	0.0015	0.0022	0.0025	0.0020	0.0020	0.0017	0.0016
84	Computer/Machinery	0.0404	0.0577	0.1072	0.1285	0.1499	0.1516	0.1703
85	Electrical Equipment	0.3162	0.3775	0.3401	0.5227	0.5210	0.5091	0.4312
86	Railway	0.0000	0.0000	0.0000	0.0000	0.0000	0.0000	0.0000
87	Cars, Trucks, Autos	0.0104	0.0084	0.0086	0.0049	0.0063	0.0052	0.0073
88	Aircraft, Spacecraft	0.0001	0.0004	0.0009	0.0016	0.0010	0.0004	0.0041
89	Ships, Boats	0.0000	0.0001	0.0003	0.0001	0.0023	0.0000	0.0001
90	Optical/Medical Instruments	0.0126	0.0114	0.0143	0.0079	0.0081	0.0089	0.0141
91	Clocks	0.0250	0.0152	0.0147	0.0082	0.0075	0.0109	0.0123
92	Musical Instruments	0.0000	0.0002	0.0001	0.0000	0.0000	0.0000	0.0000
93	Arms & Ammunition	0.0001	0.0001	0.0002	0.0001	0.0003	0.0004	0.0003
94	Furniture	0.0278	0.0303	0.0296	0.0214	0.0225	0.0230	0.0237
95	Toys	0.0234	0.0215	0.0185	0.0088	0.0078	0.0078	0.0076
96	Misc. Manufactured Articles	0.0031	0.0029	0.0028	0.0010	0.0014	0.0014	0.0015
97	Works of Art	0.0001	0.0001	0.0001	0.0000	0.0000	0.0000	0.0001
98	Postal Packages & Trans	0.0000	0.0000	0.0000	0.0000	0.0000	0.0000	0.0000
99	Other	0.0000	0.0004	0.0000	0.0000	0.0000	0.0000	0.0000
	Total (US$ Mil)	**4230.7**	**5985.8**	**5963.1**	**10097.9**	**10445.5**	**11365.3**	**8979.0**

APPENDIX TABLE 2.4
Disaggregated Thai Exports to U.S., 1993-2001

Chapter	Sector	1993	1995	1996	1998	1999	2000	2001
01	Live Animals	0.0000	0.0000	0.0000	0.0000	0.0000	0.0000	0.0000
02	Meat & Edible Meat Offal	0.0000	0.0000	0.0000	0.0000	0.0000	0.0000	0.0000
03	Fish	0.0672	0.0599	0.0523	0.0448	0.0449	0.0592	0.0511
04	Dairy Produce	0.0000	0.0001	0.0001	0.0001	0.0001	0.0001	0.0003
05	Other Animal Products	0.0001	0.0001	0.0001	0.0001	0.0001	0.0001	0.0001
06	Live Trees	0.0005	0.0004	0.0004	0.0003	0.0005	0.0006	0.0007
07	Edible Vegetables	0.0008	0.0004	0.0006	0.0003	0.0005	0.0004	0.0005
08	Edible Fruit & Nuts	0.0008	0.0007	0.0009	0.0012	0.0010	0.0011	0.0008
09	Coffee, Tea, Spices	0.0031	0.0120	0.0065	0.0030	0.0013	0.0009	0.0007
10	Cereals	0.0112	0.0092	0.0115	0.0107	0.0094	0.0096	0.0078
11	Malt & Wheat Gluten	0.0009	0.0012	0.0015	0.0010	0.0010	0.0007	0.0008
12	Seeds	0.0007	0.0005	0.0009	0.0005	0.0010	0.0008	0.0004
13	Lac, Gums & Resins	0.0007	0.0004	0.0005	0.0003	0.0004	0.0005	0.0002
14	Other Vegetable Products	0.0001	0.0000	0.0001	0.0001	0.0000	0.0001	0.0001
15	Fats & Oils	0.0001	0.0001	0.0001	0.0001	0.0001	0.0001	0.0000
16	Preparations Meat/Fish	0.0543	0.0490	0.0537	0.0634	0.0678	0.0662	0.0594
17	Sugars	0.0010	0.0013	0.0016	0.0009	0.0008	0.0035	0.0013
18	Cocoa	0.0000	0.0001	0.0002	0.0005	0.0003	0.0001	0.0002
19	Prep. Cereals/Flour/Milk	0.0013	0.0012	0.0012	0.0010	0.0010	0.0013	0.0014
20	Prep. Vegetables/Fruit/Nuts	0.0277	0.0200	0.0183	0.0089	0.0151	0.0117	0.0143
21	Misc. Edible Products	0.0043	0.0038	0.0046	0.0033	0.0041	0.0043	0.0041
22	Beverages	0.0006	0.0006	0.0006	0.0004	0.0004	0.0005	0.0004
23	Waste from Food Industry	0.0031	0.0019	0.0022	0.0020	0.0015	0.0020	0.0015
24	Tobacco	0.0033	0.0005	0.0034	0.0016	0.0009	0.0003	0.0012
25	Salt/Sulphur/Lime/Cement	0.0000	0.0000	0.0001	0.0019	0.0098	0.0022	0.0077
26	Ores	0.0002	0.0000	0.0000	0.0001	0.0001	0.0002	0.0001
27	Lubricants/Fuels/Oil	0.0064	0.0001	0.0014	0.0001	0.0021	0.0074	0.0039
28	Inorganic Chemicals	0.0002	0.0004	0.0003	0.0001	0.0001	0.0000	0.0001
29	Organic Chemicals	0.0003	0.0000	0.0003	0.0003	0.0003	0.0028	0.0006
30	Pharmaceutical Products	0.0001	0.0000	0.0001	0.0001	0.0001	0.0002	0.0002
31	Fertilizers	0.0000	0.0000	0.0000	0.0000	0.0000	0.0000	0.0000
32	Tanning/Dyeing Extracts/Ink	0.0003	0.0009	0.0008	0.0003	0.0004	0.0005	0.0005
33	Cosmetics	0.0001	0.0003	0.0003	0.0002	0.0003	0.0004	0.0003
34	Soap, Waxes, Pastes	0.0006	0.0004	0.0003	0.0009	0.0013	0.0012	0.0012
35	Glues	0.0014	0.0014	0.0015	0.0010	0.0007	0.0007	0.0008
36	Explosives	0.0003	0.0003	0.0003	0.0003	0.0002	0.0002	0.0003
37	Photographic Goods	0.0001	0.0002	0.0002	0.0000	0.0000	0.0000	0.0000
38	Misc. Chemical Products	0.0001	0.0004	0.0004	0.0003	0.0002	0.0007	0.0002
39	Plastics	0.0109	0.0103	0.0085	0.0093	0.0105	0.0126	0.0152
40	Rubber	0.0353	0.0523	0.0495	0.0382	0.0315	0.0305	0.0378
41	Raw Hides & Skins	0.0037	0.0017	0.0007	0.0007	0.0007	0.0012	0.0011
42	Articles of Leather	0.0269	0.0295	0.0296	0.0281	0.0302	0.0269	0.0266
43	Furskins	0.0000	0.0001	0.0000	0.0000	0.0000	0.0000	0.0000
44	Wood	0.0107	0.0126	0.0126	0.0115	0.0113	0.0113	0.0107
45	Cork	0.0000	0.0000	0.0000	0.0000	0.0000	0.0000	0.0000
46	Straw	0.0001	0.0001	0.0000	0.0000	0.0000	0.0001	0.0001
47	Wood Pulp	0.0000	0.0000	0.0001	0.0004	0.0000	0.0003	0.0000
48	Paper & Paper Board	0.0004	0.0006	0.0004	0.0014	0.0019	0.0016	0.0026
49	Books, Newspapers	0.0012	0.0014	0.0013	0.0009	0.0011	0.0009	0.0012
50	Silk	0.0009	0.0007	0.0007	0.0006	0.0006	0.0006	0.0005
51	Wool	0.0000	0.0000	0.0001	0.0000	0.0000	0.0000	0.0000
52	Cotton	0.0087	0.0053	0.0057	0.0074	0.0065	0.0058	0.0051
53	Paper Yarn	0.0001	0.0000	0.0000	0.0000	0.0000	0.0000	0.0000
54	Man-made Filaments	0.0013	0.0015	0.0016	0.0026	0.0027	0.0035	0.0025

APPENDIX TABLE 2.4 (continued)

Chapter	Sector	1993	1995	1996	1998	1999	2000	2001
55	Man-made Staple Fibers	0.0079	0.0058	0.0045	0.0040	0.0037	0.0037	0.0039
56	Wadding	0.0007	0.0004	0.0004	0.0001	0.0004	0.0004	0.0005
57	Carpets	0.0006	0.0005	0.0005	0.0007	0.0007	0.0009	0.0008
58	Special Woven Fabrics	0.0007	0.0005	0.0006	0.0006	0.0007	0.0009	0.0008
59	Laminated Textile Fabrics	0.0009	0.0010	0.0011	0.0009	0.0005	0.0004	0.0004
60	Knitted Fabrics	0.0000	0.0000	0.0000	0.0000	0.0005	0.0008	0.0007
61	Apparel, Knitted	0.0528	0.0516	0.0575	0.0725	0.0689	0.0643	0.0715
62	Apparel, not Knitted	0.0612	0.0623	0.0611	0.0573	0.0558	0.0487	0.0591
63	Other Textile Articles	0.0051	0.0053	0.0051	0.0051	0.0059	0.0066	0.0081
64	Footwear	0.0461	0.0402	0.0364	0.0298	0.0260	0.0242	0.0233
65	Headgear	0.0013	0.0013	0.0013	0.0006	0.0005	0.0004	0.0004
66	Umbrellas, Walking Sticks	0.0013	0.0011	0.0010	0.0009	0.0006	0.0007	0.0004
67	Prepared Feathers	0.0096	0.0070	0.0050	0.0027	0.0025	0.0021	0.0021
68	Stone/Plaster/Cement	0.0004	0.0005	0.0004	0.0005	0.0021	0.0004	0.0005
69	Ceramic Products	0.0122	0.0101	0.0097	0.0085	0.0085	0.0070	0.0081
70	Glass and Glassware	0.0010	0.0009	0.0009	0.0008	0.0008	0.0009	0.0009
71	Jewelry	0.0603	0.0458	0.0468	0.0339	0.0383	0.0376	0.0433
72	Iron and Steel	0.0004	0.0023	0.0004	0.0067	0.0037	0.0095	0.0015
73	Articles of Iron or Steel	0.0091	0.0121	0.0135	0.0103	0.0122	0.0112	0.0128
74	Copper	0.0023	0.0029	0.0028	0.0022	0.0023	0.0020	0.0026
75	Nickel	0.0000	0.0000	0.0000	0.0000	0.0000	0.0000	0.0000
76	Aluminum	0.0020	0.0020	0.0046	0.0096	0.0071	0.0088	0.0084
78	Lead	0.0000	0.0000	0.0000	0.0000	0.0000	0.0000	0.0000
79	Zinc	0.0000	0.0000	0.0000	0.0000	0.0000	0.0000	0.0000
80	Tin	0.0002	0.0002	0.0006	0.0001	0.0001	0.0001	0.0001
81	Other Base Metals	0.0003	0.0013	0.0013	0.0006	0.0008	0.0010	0.0012
82	Tools	0.0016	0.0015	0.0013	0.0010	0.0007	0.0007	0.0005
83	Miscellaneous Base Metals	0.0019	0.0014	0.0012	0.0009	0.0010	0.0011	0.0015
84	Computer/Machinery	0.1144	0.1308	0.1420	0.2001	0.1815	0.1112	0.1468
85	Electrical Equipment	0.2150	0.2398	0.2339	0.2215	0.2298	0.2734	0.2244
86	Railway	0.0028	0.0019	0.0017	0.0000	0.0000	0.0000	0.0000
87	Cars, Trucks, Autos	0.0055	0.0040	0.0057	0.0056	0.0056	0.0214	0.0066
88	Aircraft, Spacecraft	0.0001	0.0025	0.0002	0.0010	0.0002	0.0015	0.0020
89	Ships, Boats	0.0001	0.0000	0.0001	0.0003	0.0003	0.0002	0.0001
90	Optical/Medical Instruments	0.0203	0.0222	0.0258	0.0222	0.0223	0.0164	0.0217
91	Clocks	0.0009	0.0008	0.0004	0.0004	0.0004	0.0005	0.0014
92	Musical Instruments	0.0007	0.0014	0.0008	0.0010	0.0010	0.0008	0.0005
93	Arms & Ammunition	0.0000	0.0000	0.0001	0.0000	0.0000	0.0001	0.0001
94	Furniture	0.0247	0.0183	0.0174	0.0165	0.0187	0.0197	0.0201
95	Toys	0.0302	0.0280	0.0236	0.0129	0.0136	0.0134	0.0163
96	Misc. Manufactured Articles	0.0058	0.0046	0.0040	0.0033	0.0035	0.0034	0.0033
97	Works of Art	0.0001	0.0000	0.0000	0.0000	0.0000	0.0000	0.0000
98	Postal Packages & Special Trans	0.0000	0.0000	0.0000	0.0000	0.0000	0.0000	0.0000
99	Other	0.0067	0.0035	0.0085	0.0135	0.0137	0.0279	0.0362
	Total (US$ Mil)	**8,089**	**9,928**	**10,012**	**11,194**	**12,773**	**13,386**	**13,230**

APPENDIX TABLE 2.5
Disaggregated Indonesian Imports from U.S. by Product Chapter,
1993–2001

Chapter	Sector	1993	1995	1996	1998	1999	2000	2001
01	Live Animals	0.0012	0.0014	0.0010	0.0005	0.0012	0.0008	0.0015
02	Meat & Edible Meat Offal	0.0015	0.0015	0.0014	0.0007	0.0015	0.0049	0.0022
03	Fish	0.0001	0.0003	0.0005	0.0001	0.0001	0.0002	0.0006
04	Dairy Produce	0.0006	0.0026	0.0010	0.0015	0.0042	0.0029	0.0099
05	Other Animal Products	0.0016	0.0010	0.0017	0.0003	0.0007	0.0000	0.0004
06	Live Trees	0.0000	0.0000	0.0000	0.0000	0.0000	0.0000	0.0000
07	Edible Vegetables	0.0010	0.0020	0.0024	0.0015	0.0019	0.0022	0.0027
08	Edible Fruit & Nuts	0.0055	0.0065	0.0058	0.0037	0.0057	0.0098	0.0102
09	Coffee, Tea, Spices	0.0001	0.0000	0.0004	0.0000	0.0001	0.0002	0.0002
10	Cereals	0.0040	0.0515	0.0630	0.0105	0.0531	0.0255	0.0696
11	Malt & Wheat Gluten	0.0003	0.0007	0.0011	0.0003	0.0006	0.0007	0.0006
12	Seeds	0.0433	0.0257	0.0517	0.0269	0.0948	0.0636	0.0670
13	Lac, Gums & Resins	0.0004	0.0006	0.0004	0.0007	0.0010	0.0011	0.0012
14	Other Vegetable Products	0.0001	0.0000	0.0003	0.0000	0.0000	0.0000	0.0000
15	Fats & Oils	0.0006	0.0006	0.0006	0.0005	0.0005	0.0006	0.0007
16	Preparations Meat/Fish	0.0001	0.0001	0.0001	0.0001	0.0001	0.0001	0.0002
17	Sugars	0.0003	0.0020	0.0006	0.0023	0.0018	0.0014	0.0013
18	Cocoa	0.0000	0.0000	0.0005	0.0001	0.0001	0.0001	0.0000
19	Prep. Cereals/Flour/Milk	0.0003	0.0004	0.0007	0.0003	0.0005	0.0004	0.0003
20	Prep. Vegetables/Fruit/Nuts	0.0005	0.0006	0.0005	0.0007	0.0008	0.0011	0.0011
21	Misc. Edible Products	0.0041	0.0044	0.0041	0.0018	0.0019	0.0017	0.0026
22	Beverages	0.0003	0.0001	0.0001	0.0001	0.0003	0.0001	0.0001
23	Waste from Food Industry	0.0099	0.0175	0.0162	0.0180	0.0124	0.0371	0.0954
24	Tobacco	0.0105	0.0112	0.0056	0.0027	0.0033	0.0033	0.0042
25	Salt/Sulphur/Lime/Cement	0.0064	0.0093	0.0088	0.0096	0.0089	0.0093	0.0079
26	Ores	0.0001	0.0007	0.0001	0.0001	0.0002	0.0001	0.0003
27	Lubricants/Fuels/Oil	0.0413	0.0145	0.0157	0.0118	0.0193	0.0104	0.0123
28	Inorganic Chemicals	0.0196	0.0200	0.0187	0.0231	0.0218	0.0221	0.0199
29	Organic Chemicals	0.0549	0.0634	0.0743	0.0326	0.0601	0.0630	0.0512
30	Pharmaceutical Products	0.0024	0.0030	0.0021	0.0022	0.0062	0.0032	0.0042
31	Fertilizers	0.0004	0.0008	0.0004	0.0003	0.0014	0.0012	0.0003
32	Tanning/Dyeing Extracts/Ink	0.0069	0.0055	0.0038	0.0061	0.0059	0.0072	0.0051
33	Cosmetics	0.0021	0.0023	0.0018	0.0033	0.0030	0.0034	0.0034
34	Soap, Waxes, Pastes	0.0056	0.0072	0.0069	0.0050	0.0074	0.0148	0.0160
35	Glues	0.0014	0.0022	0.0026	0.0017	0.0019	0.0026	0.0022
36	Explosives	0.0013	0.0009	0.0014	0.0012	0.0017	0.0019	0.0019
37	Photographic Goods	0.0028	0.0025	0.0028	0.0010	0.0012	0.0010	0.0011
38	Misc. Chemical Products	0.0330	0.0225	0.0229	0.0300	0.0497	0.0332	0.0288
39	Plastics	0.0432	0.0433	0.0350	0.0305	0.0280	0.0370	0.0259
40	Rubber	0.0044	0.0075	0.0063	0.0066	0.0141	0.0083	0.0089
41	Raw Hides & Skins	0.0065	0.0074	0.0063	0.0103	0.0108	0.0046	0.0018
42	Articles of Leather	0.0002	0.0001	0.0005	0.0002	0.0003	0.0002	0.0001
43	Furskins	0.0000	0.0000	0.0001	0.0000	0.0000	0.0000	0.0000
44	Wood	0.0070	0.0086	0.0076	0.0132	0.0160	0.0172	0.0160
45	Cork	0.0000	0.0000	0.0000	0.0000	0.0000	0.0000	0.0000
46	Straw	0.0000	0.0000	0.0000	0.0001	0.0001	0.0001	0.0000
47	Wood Pulp	0.0470	0.0538	0.0295	0.0412	0.0430	0.0635	0.0398
48	Paper & Paper Board	0.0078	0.0073	0.0105	0.0117	0.0151	0.0178	0.0168
49	Books, Newspapers	0.0021	0.0021	0.0019	0.0008	0.0007	0.0005	0.0011
50	Silk	0.0000	0.0000	0.0000	0.0000	0.0000	0.0001	0.0000
51	Wool	0.0001	0.0000	0.0002	0.0001	0.0002	0.0001	0.0000
52	Cotton	0.0411	0.0861	0.0408	0.0573	0.0367	0.0530	0.0985
53	Paper Yarn	0.0000	0.0001	0.0000	0.0000	0.0003	0.0000	0.0001

APPENDIX TABLE 2.5 *(continued)*

Chapter	Sector	1993	1995	1996	1998	1999	2000	2001
54	Man-made Filaments	0.0138	0.0135	0.0089	0.0143	0.0179	0.0101	0.0104
55	Man-made Staple Fibers	0.0010	0.0006	0.0026	0.0005	0.0004	0.0013	0.0018
56	Wadding	0.0004	0.0006	0.0005	0.0007	0.0007	0.0006	0.0005
57	Carpets	0.0005	0.0003	0.0003	0.0001	0.0000	0.0000	0.0000
58	Special Woven Fabrics	0.0007	0.0009	0.0011	0.0009	0.0008	0.0007	0.0005
59	Laminated Textile Fabrics	0.0009	0.0007	0.0018	0.0013	0.0012	0.0014	0.0009
60	Knitted Fabrics	0.0010	0.0008	0.0013	0.0009	0.0005	0.0003	0.0002
61	Apparel, Knitted	0.0000	0.0001	0.0001	0.0001	0.0001	0.0000	0.0000
62	Apparel, not Knitted	0.0001	0.0001	0.0004	0.0002	0.0002	0.0002	0.0001
63	Other Textile Articles	0.0013	0.0009	0.0012	0.0003	0.0002	0.0002	0.0003
64	Footwear	0.0017	0.0029	0.0044	0.0020	0.0023	0.0016	0.0017
65	Headgear	0.0000	0.0000	0.0000	0.0001	0.0000	0.0000	0.0001
66	Umbrellas, Walking Sticks	0.0000	0.0000	0.0000	0.0000	0.0000	0.0000	0.0000
67	Prepared Feathers	0.0000	0.0000	0.0000	0.0000	0.0000	0.0000	0.0000
68	Stone/Plaster/Cement	0.0021	0.0022	0.0019	0.0013	0.0014	0.0012	0.0014
69	Ceramic Products	0.0015	0.0031	0.0022	0.0005	0.0004	0.0011	0.0009
70	Glass and Glassware	0.0018	0.0017	0.0023	0.0035	0.0039	0.0020	0.0007
71	Jewelry	0.0002	0.0011	0.0022	0.0011	0.0002	0.0002	0.0002
72	Iron and Steel	0.0069	0.0069	0.0150	0.0055	0.0040	0.0035	0.0042
73	Articles of Iron or Steel	0.0281	0.0249	0.0284	0.0618	0.0240	0.0169	0.0205
74	Copper	0.0011	0.0031	0.0020	0.0012	0.0013	0.0008	0.0005
75	Nickel	0.0001	0.0001	0.0003	0.0000	0.0000	0.0000	0.0001
76	Aluminum	0.0028	0.0031	0.0042	0.0034	0.0023	0.0029	0.0040
78	Lead	0.0009	0.0002	0.0001	0.0003	0.0000	0.0000	0.0009
79	Zinc	0.0003	0.0003	0.0001	0.0004	0.0001	0.0001	0.0001
80	Tin	0.0000	0.0000	0.0000	0.0001	0.0002	0.0002	0.0001
81	Other Base Metals	0.0002	0.0031	0.0052	0.0008	0.0006	0.0005	0.0005
82	Tools	0.0039	0.0030	0.0028	0.0050	0.0042	0.0044	0.0046
83	Miscellaneous Base Metals	0.0010	0.0015	0.0016	0.0018	0.0023	0.0017	0.0015
84	Computer/Machinery	0.2801	0.2244	0.2609	0.3066	0.2752	0.2082	0.1938
85	Electrical Equipment	0.1048	0.1254	0.1054	0.0985	0.0411	0.0459	0.0360
86	Railway	0.0003	0.0021	0.0001	0.0022	0.0012	0.0016	0.0048
87	Cars, Trucks, Autos	0.0139	0.0235	0.0255	0.0617	0.0436	0.0469	0.0425
88	Aircraft, Spacecraft	0.0258	0.0069	0.0129	0.0091	0.0079	0.0065	0.0024
89	Ships, Boats	0.0294	0.0103	0.0173	0.0193	0.0051	0.0808	0.0111
90	Optical/Medical Instruments	0.0450	0.0238	0.0210	0.0182	0.0142	0.0218	0.0152
91	Clocks	0.0002	0.0001	0.0001	0.0001	0.0000	0.0002	0.0001
92	Musical Instruments	0.0001	0.0003	0.0006	0.0003	0.0003	0.0003	0.0002
93	Arms & Ammunition	0.0006	0.0004	0.0004	0.0000	0.0002	0.0000	0.0000
94	Furniture	0.0019	0.0037	0.0024	0.0018	0.0008	0.0005	0.0005
95	Toys	0.0011	0.0006	0.0006	0.0007	0.0002	0.0001	0.0002
96	Misc. Manufactured Articles	0.0008	0.0006	0.0006	0.0004	0.0004	0.0005	0.0006
97	Works of Art	0.0000	0.0000	0.0001	0.0000	0.0000	0.0007	0.0001
98	Postal Packages & Special Trans	0.0000	0.0000	0.0000	0.0000	0.0000	0.0000	0.0000
99	Other	0.0000	0.0000	0.0000	0.0000	0.0000	0.0000	0.0000
	Total (US$ mil)	**3254.5**	**4755.9**	**4549.8**	**3514.5**	**2839.0**	**3390.3**	**3207.5**

APPENDIX TABLE 2.6
Disaggregated Malaysian Imports from U.S., 1993–2001

Chapter	Sector	1993	1995	1996	1998	1999	2000	2001
01	Live Animals	0.0001	0.0002	0.0003	0.0002	0.0003	0.0003	0.0004
02	Meat & Edible Meat Offal	0.0002	0.0004	0.0005	0.0005	0.0002	0.0002	0.0003
03	Fish	0.0001	0.0002	0.0006	0.0017	0.0005	0.0009	0.0003
04	Dairy Produce	0.0000	0.0099	0.0061	0.0035	0.0009	0.0006	0.0008
05	Other Animal Products	0.0000	0.0002	0.0003	0.0001	0.0001	0.0001	0.0001
06	Live Trees	0.0000	0.0000	0.0000	0.0000	0.0000	0.0000	0.0000
07	Edible Vegetables	0.0003	0.0008	0.0012	0.0009	0.0011	0.0012	0.0015
08	Edible Fruit & Nuts	0.0013	0.0022	0.0030	0.0016	0.0017	0.0020	0.0024
09	Coffee, Tea, Spices	0.0000	0.0000	0.0000	0.0000	0.0003	0.0008	0.0005
10	Cereals	0.0014	0.0140	0.0119	0.0014	0.0048	0.0015	0.0027
11	Malt & Wheat Gluten	0.0006	0.0027	0.0022	0.0003	0.0002	0.0004	0.0010
12	Seeds	0.0048	0.0056	0.0066	0.0043	0.0069	0.0039	0.0050
13	Lac, Gums & Resins	0.0001	0.0002	0.0001	0.0002	0.0003	0.0001	0.0001
14	Other Vegetable Products	0.0000	0.0000	0.0000	0.0000	0.0000	0.0000	0.0000
15	Fats & Oils	0.0005	0.0020	0.0005	0.0013	0.0018	0.0002	0.0007
16	Preparations Meat/Fish	0.0002	0.0006	0.0005	0.0002	0.0003	0.0003	0.0002
17	Sugars	0.0001	0.0001	0.0001	0.0001	0.0002	0.0002	0.0004
18	Cocoa	0.0002	0.0001	0.0002	0.0001	0.0001	0.0003	0.0006
19	Prep. Cereals/Flour/Milk	0.0004	0.0003	0.0005	0.0003	0.0007	0.0006	0.0005
20	Prep. Vegetables/Fruit/Nuts	0.0009	0.0006	0.0007	0.0004	0.0008	0.0009	0.0010
21	Misc. Edible Products	0.0021	0.0019	0.0036	0.0029	0.0037	0.0030	0.0034
22	Beverages	0.0002	0.0001	0.0001	0.0004	0.0005	0.0004	0.0003
23	Waste from Food Industry	0.0017	0.0030	0.0045	0.0057	0.0042	0.0023	0.0043
24	Tobacco	0.0037	0.0045	0.0042	0.0041	0.0053	0.0054	0.0084
25	Salt/Sulphur/Lime/Cement	0.0016	0.0011	0.0014	0.0018	0.0025	0.0019	0.0026
26	Ores	0.0005	0.0004	0.0004	0.0003	0.0008	0.0011	0.0010
27	Lubricants/Fuels/Oil	0.0020	0.0018	0.0021	0.0039	0.0079	0.0058	0.0214
28	Inorganic Chemicals	0.0092	0.0089	0.0088	0.0051	0.0064	0.0061	0.0071
29	Organic Chemicals	0.0179	0.0215	0.0200	0.0151	0.0179	0.0221	0.0228
30	Pharmaceutical Products	0.0034	0.0023	0.0025	0.0020	0.0034	0.0025	0.0033
31	Fertilizers	0.0017	0.0053	0.0015	0.0039	0.0016	0.0015	0.0025
32	Tanning/Dyeing Extracts/Ink	0.0023	0.0039	0.0037	0.0028	0.0025	0.0022	0.0020
33	Cosmetics	0.0034	0.0048	0.0050	0.0036	0.0045	0.0037	0.0043
34	Soap, Waxes, Pastes	0.0022	0.0018	0.0020	0.0021	0.0023	0.0023	0.0018
35	Glues	0.0012	0.0018	0.0015	0.0012	0.0006	0.0006	0.0013
36	Explosives	0.0001	0.0001	0.0003	0.0001	0.0001	0.0002	0.0002
37	Photographic Goods	0.0016	0.0008	0.0011	0.0007	0.0015	0.0021	0.0016
38	Misc. Chemical Products	0.0059	0.0064	0.0073	0.0089	0.0122	0.0063	0.0145
39	Plastics	0.0192	0.0161	0.0179	0.0175	0.0236	0.0253	0.0263
40	Rubber	0.0020	0.0016	0.0017	0.0019	0.0027	0.0021	0.0032
41	Raw Hides & Skins	0.0003	0.0014	0.0004	0.0000	0.0003	0.0001	0.0001
42	Articles of Leather	0.0002	0.0001	0.0001	0.0001	0.0001	0.0001	0.0002
43	Furskins	0.0000	0.0000	0.0000	0.0000	0.0000	0.0000	0.0000
44	Wood	0.0034	0.0023	0.0034	0.0019	0.0021	0.0031	0.0018
45	Cork	0.0000	0.0000	0.0000	0.0000	0.0000	0.0000	0.0000
46	Straw	0.0000	0.0000	0.0000	0.0000	0.0000	0.0000	0.0000
47	Wood Pulp	0.0003	0.0005	0.0007	0.0009	0.0016	0.0022	0.0021
48	Paper & Paper Board	0.0177	0.0201	0.0160	0.0097	0.0093	0.0087	0.0080
49	Books, Newspapers	0.0024	0.0017	0.0020	0.0013	0.0013	0.0015	0.0021
50	Silk	0.0000	0.0000	0.0000	0.0000	0.0000	0.0000	0.0000
51	Wool	0.0000	0.0000	0.0000	0.0000	0.0000	0.0000	0.0000
52	Cotton	0.0017	0.0019	0.0026	0.0044	0.0019	0.0010	0.0025
53	Paper Yarn	0.0000	0.0000	0.0000	0.0000	0.0000	0.0000	0.0000

APPENDIX TABLE 2.6 *(continued)*

Chapter	Sector	1993	1995	1996	1998	1999	2000	2001
54	Man-made Filaments	0.0004	0.0006	0.0010	0.0006	0.0004	0.0002	0.0004
55	Man-made Staple Fibers	0.0016	0.0009	0.0009	0.0008	0.0011	0.0009	0.0010
56	Wadding	0.0005	0.0004	0.0003	0.0009	0.0006	0.0006	0.0002
57	Carpets	0.0004	0.0004	0.0003	0.0001	0.0001	0.0001	0.0001
58	Special Woven Fabrics	0.0004	0.0002	0.0002	0.0001	0.0002	0.0002	0.0001
59	Laminated Textile Fabrics	0.0004	0.0004	0.0005	0.0005	0.0004	0.0003	0.0004
60	Knitted Fabrics	0.0002	0.0001	0.0001	0.0000	0.0001	0.0000	0.0000
61	Apparel, Knitted	0.0001	0.0001	0.0001	0.0000	0.0000	0.0001	0.0001
62	Apparel, not Knitted	0.0003	0.0002	0.0003	0.0002	0.0001	0.0006	0.0002
63	Other Textile Articles	0.0012	0.0008	0.0008	0.0002	0.0007	0.0004	0.0004
64	Footwear	0.0001	0.0001	0.0001	0.0001	0.0003	0.0001	0.0001
65	Headgear	0.0001	0.0001	0.0000	0.0000	0.0000	0.0000	0.0000
66	Umbrellas, Walking Sticks	0.0000	0.0000	0.0000	0.0000	0.0000	0.0000	0.0000
67	Prepared Feathers	0.0000	0.0000	0.0000	0.0000	0.0000	0.0000	0.0000
68	Stone/Plaster/Cement	0.0007	0.0008	0.0008	0.0005	0.0008	0.0007	0.0012
69	Ceramic Products	0.0016	0.0011	0.0005	0.0005	0.0003	0.0003	0.0004
70	Glass and Glassware	0.0029	0.0019	0.0026	0.0024	0.0025	0.0032	0.0036
71	Jewelry	0.0070	0.0071	0.0027	0.0141	0.0371	0.0208	0.0008
72	Iron and Steel	0.0111	0.0233	0.0167	0.0071	0.0230	0.0060	0.0117
73	Articles of Iron or Steel	0.0080	0.0056	0.0113	0.0092	0.0067	0.0123	0.0102
74	Copper	0.0024	0.0093	0.0061	0.0045	0.0037	0.0031	0.0024
75	Nickel	0.0002	0.0002	0.0002	0.0002	0.0002	0.0002	0.0001
76	Aluminum	0.0030	0.0166	0.0106	0.0141	0.0092	0.0104	0.0107
78	Lead	0.0036	0.0005	0.0008	0.0002	0.0002	0.0000	0.0001
79	Zinc	0.0001	0.0001	0.0001	0.0001	0.0001	0.0001	0.0001
80	Tin	0.0001	0.0001	0.0001	0.0001	0.0001	0.0001	0.0002
81	Other Base Metals	0.0001	0.0001	0.0002	0.0002	0.0001	0.0001	0.0001
82	Tools	0.0028	0.0024	0.0020	0.0036	0.0040	0.0059	0.0061
83	Miscellaneous Base Metals	0.0011	0.0007	0.0009	0.0010	0.0010	0.0007	0.0007
84	Computer/Machinery	0.1584	0.1500	0.1985	0.1470	0.1510	0.1697	0.1416
85	Electrical Equipment	0.3892	0.4278	0.4532	0.4931	0.4678	0.5073	0.5095
86	Railway	0.0000	0.0001	0.0002	0.0001	0.0001	0.0000	0.0001
87	Cars, Trucks, Autos	0.0035	0.0060	0.0057	0.0010	0.0017	0.0047	0.0014
88	Aircraft, Spacecraft	0.2137	0.1086	0.0734	0.1095	0.0757	0.0283	0.0422
89	Ships, Boats	0.0139	0.0168	0.0032	0.0110	0.0114	0.0003	0.0001
90	Optical/Medical Instruments	0.0332	0.0314	0.0324	0.0430	0.0409	0.0763	0.0655
91	Clocks	0.0007	0.0003	0.0003	0.0001	0.0001	0.0001	0.0003
92	Musical Instruments	0.0001	0.0001	0.0001	0.0000	0.0000	0.0001	0.0000
93	Arms & Ammunition	0.0002	0.0003	0.0000	0.0000	0.0000	0.0000	0.0002
94	Furniture	0.0015	0.0009	0.0012	0.0008	0.0010	0.0009	0.0010
95	Toys	0.0022	0.0024	0.0029	0.0011	0.0014	0.0016	0.0017
96	Misc. Manufactured Articles	0.0011	0.0008	0.0008	0.0006	0.0006	0.0006	0.0004
97	Works of Art	0.0001	0.0000	0.0000	0.0000	0.0000	0.0000	0.0000
98	Postal Packages & Special Trans	0.0128	0.0244	0.0175	0.0115	0.0132	0.0146	0.0167
99	Other	0.0000	0.0000	0.0000	0.0000	0.0000	0.0000	0.0000
	Total (US$ mil)	**7665.1**	**12553.6**	**14499.0**	**16614.4**	**12348.7**	**12097.0**	**10930.8**

APPENDIX TABLE 2.7
Disaggregated Philippine Imports from U.S., 1993–2001

Chapter	Sector	1993	1995	1996	1998	1999	2000	2001
01	Live Animals	0.0011	0.0012	0.0015	0.0002	0.0005	0.0005	0.0006
02	Meat & Edible Meat Offal	0.0006	0.0007	0.0017	0.0010	0.0032	0.0015	0.0015
03	Fish	0.0001	0.0010	0.0007	0.0003	0.0007	0.0019	0.0011
04	Dairy Produce	0.0011	0.0068	0.0041	0.0023	0.0024	0.0033	0.0059
05	Other Animal Products	0.0002	0.0002	0.0003	0.0001	0.0001	0.0001	0.0001
06	Live Trees	0.0000	0.0000	0.0000	0.0000	0.0000	0.0000	0.0000
07	Edible Vegetables	0.0022	0.0020	0.0026	0.0015	0.0019	0.0015	0.0016
08	Edible Fruit & Nuts	0.0038	0.0028	0.0049	0.0019	0.0019	0.0014	0.0009
09	Coffee, Tea, Spices	0.0002	0.0001	0.0002	0.0001	0.0002	0.0003	0.0002
10	Cereals	0.0693	0.0612	0.0928	0.0408	0.0420	0.0546	0.0632
11	Malt & Wheat Gluten	0.0017	0.0032	0.0047	0.0006	0.0015	0.0007	0.0005
12	Seeds	0.0046	0.0044	0.0085	0.0069	0.0159	0.0087	0.0106
13	Lac, Gums & Resins	0.0020	0.0016	0.0013	0.0006	0.0006	0.0010	0.0008
14	Other Vegetable Products	0.0000	0.0000	0.0000	0.0000	0.0000	0.0000	0.0000
15	Fats & Oils	0.0020	0.0017	0.0015	0.0009	0.0010	0.0004	0.0005
16	Preparations Meat/Fish	0.0005	0.0007	0.0007	0.0003	0.0008	0.0005	0.0004
17	Sugars	0.0006	0.0008	0.0010	0.0007	0.0009	0.0008	0.0012
18	Cocoa	0.0025	0.0025	0.0027	0.0022	0.0029	0.0034	0.0028
19	Prep. Cereals/Flour/Milk	0.0011	0.0012	0.0024	0.0014	0.0011	0.0008	0.0009
20	Prep. Vegetables/Fruit/Nuts	0.0024	0.0013	0.0035	0.0025	0.0038	0.0043	0.0036
21	Misc. Edible Products	0.0020	0.0031	0.0055	0.0047	0.0057	0.0058	0.0066
22	Beverages	0.0007	0.0008	0.0012	0.0005	0.0005	0.0007	0.0008
23	Waste from Food Industry	0.0251	0.0249	0.0126	0.0287	0.0196	0.0310	0.0300
24	Tobacco	0.0067	0.0047	0.0043	0.0026	0.0046	0.0069	0.0047
25	Salt/Sulphur/Lime/Cement	0.0013	0.0027	0.0012	0.0008	0.0010	0.0009	0.0009
26	Ores	0.0055	0.0096	0.0000	0.0000	0.0000	0.0017	0.0022
27	Lubricants/Fuels/Oil	0.0262	0.0072	0.0029	0.0016	0.0015	0.0012	0.0015
28	Inorganic Chemicals	0.0062	0.0063	0.0090	0.0037	0.0041	0.0046	0.0044
29	Organic Chemicals	0.0187	0.0187	0.0165	0.0090	0.0088	0.0094	0.0072
30	Pharmaceutical Products	0.0048	0.0044	0.0054	0.0039	0.0056	0.0055	0.0062
31	Fertilizers	0.0052	0.0014	0.0023	0.0010	0.0011	0.0002	0.0013
32	Tanning/Dyeing Extracts/Ink	0.0045	0.0041	0.0046	0.0023	0.0032	0.0042	0.0025
33	Cosmetics	0.0079	0.0069	0.0060	0.0058	0.0064	0.0076	0.0074
34	Soap, Waxes, Pastes	0.0022	0.0023	0.0033	0.0020	0.0020	0.0022	0.0020
35	Glues	0.0023	0.0021	0.0030	0.0024	0.0027	0.0030	0.0029
36	Explosives	0.0003	0.0002	0.0002	0.0002	0.0002	0.0001	0.0001
37	Photographic Goods	0.0034	0.0023	0.0034	0.0019	0.0027	0.0042	0.0026
38	Misc. Chemical Products	0.0106	0.0103	0.0138	0.0091	0.0115	0.0083	0.0085
39	Plastics	0.0213	0.0243	0.0339	0.0138	0.0143	0.0170	0.0133
40	Rubber	0.0037	0.0033	0.0049	0.0018	0.0025	0.0025	0.0019
41	Raw Hides & Skins	0.0047	0.0023	0.0010	0.0009	0.0010	0.0013	0.0015
42	Articles of Leather	0.0003	0.0003	0.0002	0.0001	0.0001	0.0001	0.0002
43	Furskins	0.0000	0.0000	0.0000	0.0000	0.0000	0.0000	0.0000
44	Wood	0.0054	0.0037	0.0131	0.0040	0.0059	0.0059	0.0065
45	Cork	0.0000	0.0000	0.0000	0.0000	0.0000	0.0000	0.0000
46	Straw	0.0000	0.0000	0.0000	0.0000	0.0000	0.0000	0.0000
47	Wood Pulp	0.0052	0.0127	0.0067	0.0038	0.0067	0.0091	0.0069
48	Paper & Paper Board	0.0198	0.0257	0.0248	0.0124	0.0136	0.0154	0.0139
49	Books, Newspapers	0.0061	0.0068	0.0084	0.0032	0.0029	0.0038	0.0041
50	Silk	0.0001	0.0000	0.0000	0.0000	0.0000	0.0000	0.0001
51	Wool	0.0004	0.0007	0.0008	0.0005	0.0002	0.0002	0.0001
52	Cotton	0.0114	0.0156	0.0112	0.0049	0.0039	0.0038	0.0044
53	Paper Yarn	0.0000	0.0000	0.0000	0.0000	0.0000	0.0002	0.0001
54	Man-made Filaments	0.0036	0.0019	0.0012	0.0010	0.0010	0.0010	0.0010

APPENDIX TABLE 2.7 (*continued*)

Chapter	Sector	1993	1995	1996	1998	1999	2000	2001
55	Man-made Staple Fibres	0.0053	0.0040	0.0036	0.0023	0.0027	0.0024	0.0020
56	Wadding	0.0008	0.0005	0.0007	0.0006	0.0006	0.0004	0.0003
57	Carpets	0.0005	0.0005	0.0008	0.0003	0.0002	0.0003	0.0003
58	Special Woven Fabrics	0.0048	0.0035	0.0023	0.0013	0.0008	0.0009	0.0007
59	Laminated Textile Fabrics	0.0008	0.0006	0.0009	0.0003	0.0005	0.0004	0.0006
60	Knitted Fabrics	0.0016	0.0022	0.0012	0.0009	0.0014	0.0008	0.0014
61	Apparel, Knitted	0.0013	0.0003	0.0001	0.0002	0.0003	0.0004	0.0003
62	Apparel, not Knitted	0.0033	0.0029	0.0022	0.0006	0.0004	0.0004	0.0004
63	Other Textile Articles	0.0011	0.0004	0.0008	0.0005	0.0004	0.0008	0.0009
64	Footwear	0.0005	0.0002	0.0004	0.0002	0.0001	0.0002	0.0001
65	Headgear	0.0000	0.0000	0.0000	0.0000	0.0000	0.0000	0.0000
66	Umbrellas, Walking Sticks	0.0000	0.0000	0.0000	0.0000	0.0000	0.0000	0.0000
67	Prepared Feathers	0.0000	0.0000	0.0000	0.0000	0.0000	0.0000	0.0000
68	Stone/Plaster/Cement	0.0008	0.0012	0.0021	0.0009	0.0009	0.0007	0.0007
69	Ceramic Products	0.0007	0.0006	0.0013	0.0006	0.0006	0.0002	0.0002
70	Glass and Glassware	0.0017	0.0014	0.0022	0.0008	0.0011	0.0011	0.0011
71	Jewellery	0.0008	0.0006	0.0006	0.0003	0.0004	0.0004	0.0006
72	Iron and Steel	0.0025	0.0037	0.0078	0.0025	0.0021	0.0028	0.0024
73	Articles of Iron or Steel	0.0098	0.0048	0.0144	0.0072	0.0031	0.0030	0.0033
74	Copper	0.0006	0.0006	0.0009	0.0008	0.0005	0.0007	0.0003
75	Nickel	0.0000	0.0000	0.0000	0.0000	0.0000	0.0000	0.0000
76	Aluminum	0.0026	0.0032	0.0032	0.0026	0.0010	0.0014	0.0010
78	Lead	0.0000	0.0001	0.0002	0.0000	0.0000	0.0000	0.0000
79	Zinc	0.0002	0.0002	0.0001	0.0001	0.0002	0.0001	0.0001
80	Tin	0.0000	0.0001	0.0000	0.0000	0.0000	0.0001	0.0000
81	Other Base Metals	0.0000	0.0000	0.0000	0.0000	0.0001	0.0002	0.0001
82	Tools	0.0012	0.0019	0.0014	0.0010	0.0007	0.0010	0.0007
83	Miscellaneous Base Metals	0.0021	0.0016	0.0021	0.0010	0.0007	0.0010	0.0009
84	Computer/Machinery	0.1160	0.1133	0.1718	0.1092	0.0746	0.0861	0.0810
85	Electrical Equipment	0.3638	0.4654	0.2219	0.6275	0.6585	0.6028	0.6055
86	Railway	0.0000	0.0000	0.0002	0.0000	0.0001	0.0001	0.0002
87	Cars, Trucks, Autos	0.0113	0.0161	0.0194	0.0085	0.0083	0.0127	0.0116
88	Aircraft, Spacecraft	0.1346	0.0292	0.1608	0.0123	0.0055	0.0069	0.0132
89	Ships, Boats	0.0001	0.0003	0.0004	0.0001	0.0001	0.0001	0.0000
90	Optical/Medical Instruments	0.0134	0.0199	0.0258	0.0180	0.0122	0.0202	0.0219
91	Clocks	0.0005	0.0035	0.0043	0.0038	0.0027	0.0034	0.0022
92	Musical Instruments	0.0002	0.0002	0.0003	0.0001	0.0001	0.0001	0.0001
93	Arms & Ammunition	0.0005	0.0005	0.0011	0.0004	0.0006	0.0001	0.0001
94	Furniture	0.0013	0.0022	0.0038	0.0018	0.0021	0.0018	0.0012
95	Toys	0.0023	0.0025	0.0025	0.0010	0.0013	0.0018	0.0017
96	Misc. Manufactured Articles	0.0015	0.0010	0.0012	0.0008	0.0005	0.0007	0.0005
97	Works of Art	0.0000	0.0001	0.0004	0.0000	0.0000	0.0000	0.0000
98	Postal Packages & Special Trans	0.0000	0.0000	0.0000	0.0000	0.0000	0.0000	0.0000
99	Other	0.0000	0.0078	0.0000	0.0000	0.0000	0.0000	0.0000
	Total Value (US$ mil)	**3,507.9**	**3,885.6**	**4,354.4**	**6,560.0**	**6,365.1**	**5,323.3**	**4,989.3**

APPENDIX TABLE 2.8
Disaggregated Thai Imports from U.S., 1993–2001

Chapter	Sector	1993	1995	1996	1998	1999	2000	2001
01	Live Animals	0.0017	0.0008	0.0008	0.0007	0.0010	0.0001	0.0000
02	Meat & Edible Meat Offal	0.0006	0.0002	0.0002	0.0003	0.0003	0.0001	0.0001
03	Fish	0.0147	0.0024	0.0024	0.0021	0.0028	0.0028	0.0028
04	Dairy Produce	0.0005	0.0017	0.0011	0.0024	0.0023	0.0015	0.0020
05	Other Animal Products	0.0015	0.0036	0.0040	0.0024	0.0014	0.0020	0.0041
06	Live Trees	0.0000	0.0000	0.0000	0.0000	0.0000	0.0000	0.0000
07	Edible Vegetables	0.0005	0.0007	0.0007	0.0002	0.0002	0.0003	0.0001
08	Edible Fruit & Nuts	0.0088	0.0068	0.0059	0.0030	0.0038	0.0028	0.0033
09	Coffee, Tea, Spices	0.0000	0.0000	0.0000	0.0002	0.0002	0.0002	0.0002
10	Cereals	0.0123	0.0107	0.0133	0.0082	0.0114	0.0065	0.0081
11	Malt & Wheat Gluten	0.0002	0.0001	0.0001	0.0001	0.0002	0.0003	0.0004
12	Seeds	0.0026	0.0065	0.0138	0.0186	0.0269	0.0228	0.0168
13	Lac, Gums & Resins	0.0005	0.0003	0.0003	0.0005	0.0008	0.0007	0.0012
14	Other Vegetable Products	0.0001	0.0000	0.0001	0.0002	0.0002	0.0002	0.0000
15	Fats & Oils	0.0003	0.0007	0.0005	0.0004	0.0005	0.0003	0.0003
16	Preparations Meat/Fish	0.0000	0.0000	0.0000	0.0000	0.0000	0.0001	0.0001
17	Sugars	0.0002	0.0002	0.0002	0.0003	0.0004	0.0003	0.0003
18	Cocoa	0.0001	0.0001	0.0001	0.0002	0.0003	0.0003	0.0003
19	Prep. Cereals/Flour/Milk	0.0023	0.0005	0.0006	0.0005	0.0006	0.0004	0.0004
20	Prep. Vegetables/Fruit/Nuts	0.0005	0.0005	0.0006	0.0018	0.0027	0.0024	0.0022
21	Misc. Edible Products	0.0029	0.0022	0.0028	0.0032	0.0035	0.0031	0.0035
22	Beverages	0.0004	0.0004	0.0007	0.0002	0.0004	0.0004	0.0004
23	Waste from Food Industry	0.0088	0.0084	0.0142	0.0136	0.0185	0.0129	0.0164
24	Tobacco	0.0144	0.0099	0.0085	0.0117	0.0146	0.0071	0.0036
25	Salt/Sulphur/Lime/Cement	0.0022	0.0014	0.0016	0.0012	0.0024	0.0015	0.0014
26	Ores	0.0000	0.0000	0.0000	0.0001	0.0000	0.0000	0.0004
27	Lubricants/Fuels/Oil	0.0077	0.0149	0.0060	0.0077	0.0110	0.0116	0.0138
28	Inorganic Chemicals	0.0071	0.0071	0.0078	0.0065	0.0101	0.0066	0.0060
29	Organic Chemicals	0.0294	0.0356	0.0251	0.0248	0.0377	0.0373	0.0333
30	Pharmaceutical Products	0.0053	0.0048	0.0050	0.0071	0.0103	0.0081	0.0086
31	Fertilizers	0.0070	0.0085	0.0090	0.0142	0.0148	0.0109	0.0082
32	Tanning/Dyeing Extracts/Ink	0.0056	0.0041	0.0043	0.0046	0.0095	0.0070	0.0063
33	Cosmetics	0.0041	0.0031	0.0035	0.0045	0.0054	0.0059	0.0058
34	Soap, Waxes, Pastes	0.0061	0.0054	0.0062	0.0061	0.0077	0.0069	0.0065
35	Glues	0.0011	0.0012	0.0014	0.0014	0.0019	0.0016	0.0017
36	Explosives	0.0003	0.0003	0.0004	0.0003	0.0006	0.0000	0.0001
37	Photographic Goods	0.0057	0.0040	0.0041	0.0050	0.0071	0.0037	0.0033
38	Misc. Chemical Products	0.0172	0.0168	0.0158	0.0178	0.0203	0.0177	0.0191
39	Plastics	0.0324	0.0327	0.0325	0.0342	0.0440	0.0387	0.0373
40	Rubber	0.0048	0.0051	0.0051	0.0065	0.0072	0.0055	0.0058
41	Raw Hides & Skins	0.0105	0.0110	0.0090	0.0118	0.0131	0.0073	0.0108
42	Articles of Leather	0.0002	0.0002	0.0003	0.0002	0.0002	0.0002	0.0002
43	Furskins	0.0000	0.0000	0.0000	0.0000	0.0000	0.0000	0.0000
44	Wood	0.0064	0.0050	0.0047	0.0037	0.0047	0.0050	0.0042
45	Cork	0.0000	0.0000	0.0000	0.0000	0.0000	0.0000	0.0000
46	Straw	0.0000	0.0000	0.0000	0.0000	0.0000	0.0000	0.0000
47	Wood Pulp	0.0093	0.0181	0.0168	0.0128	0.0169	0.0183	0.0115
48	Paper & Paper Board	0.0105	0.0092	0.0112	0.0092	0.0125	0.0097	0.0096
49	Books, Newspapers	0.0024	0.0041	0.0027	0.0026	0.0028	0.0025	0.0030
50	Silk	0.0000	0.0000	0.0000	0.0000	0.0000	0.0000	0.0000
51	Wool	0.0005	0.0007	0.0004	0.0005	0.0004	0.0002	0.0003
52	Cotton	0.0120	0.0243	0.0126	0.0130	0.0073	0.0111	0.0146
53	Paper Yarn	0.0000	0.0001	0.0000	0.0000	0.0001	0.0000	0.0000
54	Man-made Filaments	0.0023	0.0018	0.0020	0.0020	0.0030	0.0032	0.0026

APPENDIX TABLE 2.8 *(continued)*

Chapter	Sector	1993	1995	1996	1998	1999	2000	2001
55	Man-made Staple Fibers	0.0022	0.0016	0.0020	0.0015	0.0016	0.0011	0.0011
56	Wadding	0.0007	0.0007	0.0007	0.0009	0.0012	0.0010	0.0013
57	Carpets	0.0004	0.0005	0.0006	0.0001	0.0002	0.0002	0.0001
58	Special Woven Fabrics	0.0006	0.0007	0.0006	0.0007	0.0007	0.0004	0.0004
59	Laminated Textile Fabrics	0.0013	0.0008	0.0008	0.0012	0.0012	0.0013	0.0010
60	Knitted Fabrics	0.0009	0.0007	0.0009	0.0016	0.0016	0.0008	0.0008
61	Apparel, Knitted	0.0001	0.0001	0.0001	0.0001	0.0001	0.0001	0.0001
62	Apparel, not Knitted	0.0005	0.0005	0.0005	0.0004	0.0003	0.0004	0.0003
63	Other Textile Articles	0.0009	0.0005	0.0006	0.0005	0.0004	0.0003	0.0004
64	Footwear	0.0009	0.0010	0.0009	0.0014	0.0016	0.0011	0.0008
65	Headgear	0.0003	0.0001	0.0000	0.0005	0.0000	0.0000	0.0000
66	Umbrellas, Walking Sticks	0.0000	0.0000	0.0000	0.0000	0.0000	0.0000	0.0000
67	Prepared Feathers	0.0000	0.0000	0.0000	0.0000	0.0000	0.0000	0.0000
68	Stone/Plaster/Cement	0.0016	0.0022	0.0018	0.0010	0.0009	0.0009	0.0011
69	Ceramic Products	0.0010	0.0006	0.0006	0.0006	0.0006	0.0004	0.0004
70	Glass and Glassware	0.0038	0.0026	0.0024	0.0027	0.0023	0.0021	0.0022
71	Jewelry	0.0214	0.0133	0.0113	0.0063	0.0117	0.0135	0.0170
72	Iron and Steel	0.0150	0.0164	0.0091	0.0023	0.0031	0.0044	0.0033
73	Articles of Iron or Steel	0.0174	0.0318	0.0231	0.0382	0.0329	0.0166	0.0202
74	Copper	0.0053	0.0129	0.0122	0.0038	0.0021	0.0011	0.0015
75	Nickel	0.0002	0.0001	0.0001	0.0006	0.0007	0.0016	0.0003
76	Aluminum	0.0085	0.0118	0.0069	0.0080	0.0079	0.0067	0.0078
78	Lead	0.0000	0.0000	0.0000	0.0000	0.0000	0.0000	0.0000
79	Zinc	0.0000	0.0001	0.0001	0.0000	0.0000	0.0000	0.0000
80	Tin	0.0000	0.0000	0.0000	0.0000	0.0001	0.0001	0.0000
81	Other Base Metals	0.0003	0.0002	0.0002	0.0002	0.0002	0.0002	0.0002
82	Tools	0.0034	0.0035	0.0039	0.0040	0.0044	0.0034	0.0040
83	Miscellaneous Base Metals	0.0016	0.0015	0.0014	0.0012	0.0013	0.0010	0.0011
84	Computer/Machinery	0.1788	0.1884	0.2147	0.1635	0.1842	0.1753	0.1784
85	Electrical Equipment	0.3212	0.3339	0.2995	0.3541	0.2840	0.3988	0.3160
86	Railway	0.0001	0.0003	0.0072	0.0010	0.0002	0.0000	0.0000
87	Cars, Trucks, Autos	0.0104	0.0106	0.0145	0.0135	0.0100	0.0070	0.0057
88	Aircraft, Spacecraft	0.0645	0.0372	0.0617	0.0716	0.0332	0.0287	0.1092
89	Ships, Boats	0.0012	0.0004	0.0075	0.0002	0.0001	0.0002	0.0015
90	Optical/Medical Instruments	0.0293	0.0297	0.0357	0.0327	0.0478	0.0338	0.0295
91	Clocks	0.0001	0.0002	0.0002	0.0002	0.0001	0.0001	0.0002
92	Musical Instruments	0.0004	0.0004	0.0004	0.0002	0.0002	0.0002	0.0002
93	Arms & Ammunition	0.0019	0.0032	0.0042	0.0026	0.0009	0.0006	0.0006
94	Furniture	0.0013	0.0019	0.0026	0.0016	0.0023	0.0014	0.0012
95	Toys	0.0014	0.0015	0.0016	0.0016	0.0013	0.0016	0.0016
96	Misc. Manufactured Articles	0.0015	0.0013	0.0014	0.0016	0.0017	0.0014	0.0016
97	Works of Art	0.0000	0.0000	0.0000	0.0000	0.0000	0.0000	0.0000
98	Postal Packages & Trans	0.0000	0.0000	0.0000	0.0000	0.0000	0.0000	0.0000
99	Other	0.0353	0.0105	0.0093	0.0091	0.0130	0.0038	0.0071
	Total (US$ mil)	**5,442**	**8,525**	**9,145**	**5,490**	**5,326**	**7,290**	**7,189**

APPENDIX TABLE 2.9
World Exports of Services by Selected Country and Region,
Selected Years, 1990–2001
(Percentage share of global trade)

	1990	1995	1999	2000	2001
World	100	100	100	100	100
North America	19.31	18.81	20.63	21.16	20.68
U.S.	16.97	16.68	18.17	18.67	18.27
Latin America	3.79	3.72	3.92	4.11	4
Argentina	0.29	0.3	0.31	0.3	0.28
Brazil	0.47	0.5	0.5	0.61	0.61
Mexico	0.92	0.8	0.84	0.93	0.87
Western Europe	53.06	47.57	47.97	45.95	46.54
France	8.46	6.98	5.94	5.57	5.49
Germany	6.59	6.31	6	5.52	5.54
Italy	6.2	5.14	4.22	3.81	4.13
UK	6.87	6.43	8.16	7.92	7.53
EU (15)	47.18	42.58	43.27	41.2	41.96
Africa	2.37	2.14	2.24	2.12	2.1
Algeria	0.06	0.06	0.08	...	...
Egypt	0.61	0.69	0.67	0.66	0.66
Kenya	0.1	0.07	0.05	0.05	...
Morocco	0.24	0.17	0.2	0.2	...
S.Africa	0.42	0.37	0.36	0.34	0.33
Middle East	...	...	...	...	...
Israel	0.58	0.65	0.79	0.98	0.78
Saudi Arabia	0.39	0.29	0.39	0.33	...
Asia	16.79	22	19.75	20.84	20.69
Indonesia	0.32	0.45	0.32	0.35	...
Malaysia	0.48	0.96	0.86	0.93	0.95
Philippines	0.37	0.78	0.35	0.28	0.23
Singapore	1.62	2.48	1.74	1.85	1.83
Thailand	0.8	1.23	1.06	0.95	0.89
Australia	1.26	1.32	1.24	1.23	1.1
China	0.73	1.55	1.9	2.07	2.15
HK	2.31	2.88	2.7	2.89	2.99
India	0.59	0.57	1.02	1.21	1.39
S.Korea	1.17	1.86	1.87	1.98	1.97
Japan	5.28	5.37	4.38	4.69	4.4

Source: World Trade Organization, http//:www.wto.org, June 2002, and Plummer (forthcoming).

3

Economics of U.S.-ASEAN Free-Trade Agreements

I.   Introduction

Recent trends in the global trading system present risks and opportunities for ASEAN and the United States. Major changes of particular relevance to the ASEAN countries include: (1) the accessions of China (and Taiwan) to the WTO; (2) the emergence of rapid economic growth in India and its penetration of many international niche markets and labour-intensive industries; (3) a process of multilateral liberalization under the WTO that has experienced significant difficulties, first at the Seattle Ministerial in 1999 and then in Cancun in 2003[1]; (3) and the dramatic increase in the number of preferential trade groupings (PTAs), such as free-trade areas (FTAs) and customs unions (CUs), and the expansion of existing ones, over the past 10 years.

These latter accords constitute the most significant trend in international commercial policy today. The WTO reports almost 300 PTAs of various sorts, most of which have been concluded since 1995. The EU recently expanded (1 May 2004) to 25 member-countries with the addition of 10 Central and Eastern European countries. Bulgaria and Romania are set to join the EU in 2007, and negotiations for the Turkish accession will begin in October 2005. Moreover, the EU has been negotiating FTAs with myriad developing countries of late, from

MERCOSUR to Africa.[2] It has also expanded its preferential treatment of least-developed countries under the "anything but arms" initiative. The United States itself, which eschewed FTAs until the early 1980s, has only recently used FTAs as a commercial policy tool; over the past two years alone it has signed FTAs with Chile, Jordan, Singapore, Morocco, Australia, and Central America (though CAFTA, as noted in Chapter 2, awaits ratification by the U.S. Congress). More are on the way. Finally, Japan and South Korea, who were the only countries in the OECD to have completely shunned PTAs until very recently, have each jumped on the FTA bandwagon: Japan negotiated an FTA with Singapore in November 2002 and completed negotiations for an FTA with Mexico in January 2004, and is currently at various stages of negotiations/discussions with six other nations (including ASEAN countries). South Korea recently completed an FTA with Chile and is studying various PTAs with many other countries (including ASEAN, China, and Japan).

Now, if the Doha Round were on course, this trend would be of less concern to protagonists of multilateral free trade. To the extent that the WTO can reduce international barriers to trade, the discriminatory effects of FTAs are less important. But with the Doha Round delayed and somewhat off-track and without a good idea of what, indeed, will ultimately be included, these FTAs are far more significant.

The regionalism trend can be both a threat and an opportunity to ASEAN and U.S. interests. As will be discussed below, from the point of view of economic theory—and, actually, common sense—in a perfect world it would make more sense to advocate liberalization based on a multilateral rather than a regional approach. This is why some of the best international economists deplore regional trading agreements: they are "second best" in the sense that, while they remove barriers to intra-regional trade, they create a system of preferential treatment which could actually harm the region's economies (and the world as a whole).

But, alas, we do not live in a perfect world. There are strong reasons why the GATT/WTO approach has fallen well short of global free trade. In fact, a general misconception in the anti-regionalism camp is that it tends to compare the welfare effects of regional approaches relative to free trade, whereas the appropriate comparison should be with the status quo. Even if ASEAN and the United States advocated complete and comprehensive multilateral free trade (their commitment to APEC's "open regionalism", however amorphous, is one indication of this), it is not their decision: it has to be negotiated with 140-plus WTO partners. But it *is* within their respective sovereign commercial policy capacities to form FTAs. We will argue that, if these FTAs are consistent with "open regionalism", they will be better than the *status quo*, even if they fall short of multilateral free trade.

Moreover, we will make the case that, particularly for developing countries, FTAs may actually be a stepping-stone to global liberalization and even could allow for greater market-consistent and efficient liberalization than what could be achieved at the current round of the WTO. We will deal at length with this point later; suffice to note here that countries like Italy, Portugal, Spain and Greece have been able to embrace far more liberal regimes by being part of the EU than they would ever have been able to do even if the GATT/WTO had achieved its goal of barrier-free international trade. This is because the EU, even in its more primitive form of economic cooperation as a CU, was able to adopt "deeper" integration policies that would have been impossible to achieve globally. And while in the case of the EU these policies have not always been open, this does not mean that regionalism policies need not be. In fact, the history of EU integration is full of lessons for the developing (and developed) world, both in terms of successes and mistakes.

In this chapter, we first consider the economics of regionalism from a theoretical point of view (Section II). We discuss the traditional effects of PTAs but place a greater weight on the "dynamics" of regionalism, at the economic and policy levels. Next, we consider direct estimates of the effects of the EAI (Section III). We begin with an econometric/ statistical analysis of the U.S.-EAI economic relationship, followed by some (partial equilibrium) projections of changes in trade through U.S.-ASEAN FTAs and a summary of economy-wide estimates of bilateral FTAs between the United States and ASEAN. We also develop our own approach to identifying the exact products that will be mostly affected by the U.S.-ASEAN FTAs for each country at a highly disaggregated level. Finally, we consider estimates of the effects on ASEAN countries of FTAs that exclude them. That is, if the ASEAN countries do not take an aggressive approach to regionalism, to what degree are they exposed to other regions that do? Section IV summarizes the main points of the chapter.

II. Overview of the Economics of Regional Integration

Before considering the empirical effects of the EAI, we must take into account what we would *anticipate* the ramifications of regionalism to be, that is, how FTAs and other forms of economic integration are expected to affect trade, investment, and other economic variables at least in theory. We first review the traditional (static) effects of FTAs/ CUs, which are fairly standard and frequently cited in trade-related discussions. But while most empirical analyses focus on an application of static theory, there are two other aspects that, though difficult to develop in economic models, are likely to be far more important to the integrating countries: (1) "dynamic" effects; and (2) the effects of FTAs and CUs on policy formation. These latter two effects are more important in the context of developing regions, such as ASEAN, and particularly in the context of developing–developed country accords, such as the proposed EAI FTAs.

A. Traditional or "Static" Effects

Prior to the seminal work by Jacob Viner, *The Customs Union Issue* (1950), it was believed that, if a PTA did not raise tariff and non-tariff barriers on non-member countries, it would constitute a movement toward free trade because it would involve a net reduction in (intra-regional) barriers. By reducing trade distortions a PTA would increase the gains from trade.

Viner was the first to demonstrate the shortcomings of this reasoning. He argued that if a PTA were to represent a step in the direction of free trade, then by definition it must be the case that post-PTA commodity purchases would come from lower cost sources than was the preunion case. Such an effect would occur if and when inefficient domestic (say, U.S.) production previously protected by tariffs, contracts as a result of a more efficient partner country (say, Malaysian) production. In Viner's terminology, this is "trade creation" and represents a movement toward free trade.[3] However, some protected commodities that were previously imported from a non-partner country (say, Japan)— the lowest-cost producer—will now be imported from the partner country (Malaysia), a higher-cost producer, because of the tariff discrimination against non-members. This is "trade diversion", and represents a movement away from free trade since it diverts imports away from the lowest-cost source.

Hence, even though the popular press will often characterize FTAs as being in the direction of "free trade", this is not necessarily the case: a net trade-diverting FTA would actually reduce global welfare (and could actually hurt economic prospects of the joining economies as well).

We should also note that this economic approach to the effects of a PTA conflicts with popular thinking. To an economist, trade creation is beneficial to a country because it leads to the contraction of inefficient industries, whose resources can be used more effectively elsewhere in the economy. On the other hand, trade diversion leads to greater inefficiency by enhancing production in the partner country in areas in which it has *intra-regional* comparative advantage but comparative disadvantage at the *global* level.[4] Yet, to many non-economists, contraction of domestic production (trade creation) is considered welfare reducing, for it means a loss of jobs. Trade diversion is viewed positively, as it suggests a gain to the union at the expense of non-partners. These sentiments were expressed forcefully during the NAFTA debate in the United States, in which the emphasis was on job loss to Mexico and on trying to keep the Japanese and the Europeans out of the North American market.

How can these views be reconciled? To the extent that they can be, reconciliation has to relate to basic assumptions. The Viner model and subsequent elaborations of it implicitly or explicitly assume that (*inter alia*): (1) markets are competitive; (2) there is full employment of economic resources at all times; (3) tariff revenues are redistributed to consumers; and (4) there are no externalities in production or consumption. If we lift these assumptions, we could obtain different results. For example, if there exists unemployed labour, then the contraction of domestic industry through the trade creation effect would lead to more unemployment and, hence, reduce welfare; trade diversion may be beneficial by putting resources back to work. *This "qualitative dependency" underscores the importance of overall policy reform as part and parcel of a regional integration approach if it is to be successful.*

Many of the new approaches to FTAs/CUs in international trade literature centre around locational advantages and the "natural" development of intra-regional trade before an agreement can be reached. Empirically, PTAs in the global economy are mostly geographically based. Also, it would appear that, *ceteris paribus*, the closer countries are to each other, the larger the percentage of trade that takes place between them. Hence, two-thirds of EU trade is intra-regional; Canada and the United States are each other's most important trading partners; and Mexico is heavily reliant on trade with the United States. The larger the volume of trade between countries within a regional bloc, the greater the potential for trade creation and the smaller the potential for trade diversion, making the agreement more likely to be efficiency-enhancing rather than efficiency-reducing. The exception might be between geographically-close developing countries whose trade tends to be inter-industry rather than intra-industry.

Thus, according to Krugman (1991) and others, "natural" economic integration takes place between geographically close countries due to lower transportation (and related) costs; hence forming a PTA between such countries would be consistent with the market and, therefore, would increase efficiency. As a rule of thumb, it is suggested that a PTA in which intra-regional trade is greater than, or equal to, 50 per cent of trade would increase efficiency.

Moreover, Frankel (1992, 1993) stresses that it is not enough merely to consider values of intra-regional trade. His "natural" economic bloc would be one in which the "bias" for trade within the region has been growing over time. Using the possible formation of a market-determined "natural" economic bloc in Asia, he suggests that the growth of intra-regional trade in Asia in the 1980s reflects mainly an economic growth effect rather than a "natural" increase in trade between countries of the region.

However, these approaches to the "natural" determinants of a trade bloc have several shortcomings. First, few economic blocs meet the 50 per cent criteria. While intra-regional trade in the EU exceeds that mark *today*, this occurs only after 36 years of a wide-reaching PTA. When the European Economic Community (EEC) was formed, the percentage of intra-regional trade was closer to one-third. Also, intra-regional flows as a percentage of total trade in NAFTA are close to forty per cent. The corresponding figure is about one-fourth in the case of ASEAN. Does this mean that all these blocs should be considered a priori "un-natural"? Moreover, such an approach says nothing about the degree of distortion involved in the other 50 per cent of trade. If discrimination against the extra-regional 50 per cent is high, can the group still be considered "natural"? If a PTA has only one-third intra-regional trade but its extra-regional trade is such that there would be little diverted trade, is this necessarily an "un-natural" bloc?

In sum, there is no easy test as to what is "natural"; the term will always be subjective. What it is important to note is that a PTA will not necessarily be efficient, or beneficial to the partner countries, or to global efficiency: it will very much depend on the agreement. We argue also that it will depend critically on the policy context within which reform is taking place.

B. Dynamic Effects

"Static" economic effects of PTAs generally refer to one-time changes in the allocation of resources (allocative efficiency). On the other hand, the "dynamic effects" of PTAs are long-term effects that tend to build up over time. Generally, economists tend to organize dynamic effects into at least three separate categories, though obviously each can be related and none is mutually exclusive: economies of scale, efficiency improvements, and changes in FDI flows.

Economies of Scale. The advantages derived from access to an expanded market have always been an attraction for countries to form PTAs. A main benefit is the possibility of reaping economies of scale in production. In industries where production technology is characterized by decreasing costs, the domestic market alone may be too small to permit production at an efficient level. If there are high tariff walls on these goods in foreign countries, international trade might be of little or no help in allowing these firms to expand output and increase competitiveness. With the formation of a PTA and the subsequent intra-union free trade, the expanded market could present the domestic decreasing-cost firms with adequate demand to produce more efficiently, a point which is particularly relevant for relatively advanced developing countries like those in ASEAN whose exports, as we noted in Chapter 2 and we will re-visit later in this chapter, are being increasingly concentrated in industries characterized by economies of scale (e.g., electronics).

Efficiency Improvement.[5] When countries integrate more fully with the international marketplace, through overall reductions in barriers to trade negotiated under the WTO or FTAs, their businesses are pushed to be more competitive in terms of the way they organize their operations, productive processes, work methods, incentive programmes, plant layout, management, and psychological environment at the workplace. In sum, they find it profitable to adopt "best practices".

In an FTA, if inefficient practices in the workplace of a protected industry are replaced by efficient methods due to competition from the partner country, it will improve productivity. This is called "forced efficiency"[6] and represents an improvement in welfare. In addition, there may be other benefits, such as improved technology and method sharing, new ideas to stimulate the atmosphere at the workplace, and increased standardization of quality and specification requirements allowing for longer production runs. When a PTA is formed of economic partners at diverse levels of economic development, the less-developed members stand to gain more from benefits inherent in efficiency-improving spillovers. *Hence, in this sense, greater competition that would be induced by the EAI bilateral FTAs could lead to gains in domestic productivity beyond just the trade sector. It could help push ASEAN up the development ladder.*

Investment Effects. A PTA may have several effects on the direction of investment flows. First, after a PTA is formed, domestic capital previously invested in partner countries in order to circumvent tariffs can now flow to where the return to capital is highest. This results in a more efficient allocation of investment funds. In addition, the formation of a PTA reduces the risk and uncertainty of investing in partner countries, as there is no longer risk of changes in foreign commercial policy, and the PTA itself may have investment provisions (all U.S. agreements have them).

However, there may also be an efficiency reduction associated with investment changes created by a preferential agreement. Investment funds that would be more efficiently invested in non-partner countries may be diverted to partner countries in the PTA. This investment diversion is caused by the "non-economic" attraction of investment funds to the FTA in order to evade its discriminatory tariff wall. For example, suppose Kia Motors wished to build an automobile assembly plant off shore for export to the U.S. market. Further, assume that it deems China to be the most efficient location. With the creation of a bilateral FTA between the U.S. and Indonesia, Kia could decide to build the plant in Indonesia instead. Thus, while this *investment diversion* effect reduces global efficiency, it constitutes an increased investment flow to Indonesia. While investment diversion is inefficient from a global perspective, the increased inflows of FDI to the EAI countries—from both the United States and non-partner countries—would likely be advantageous to the participating ASEAN countries.[7] Put another way, *if the EAI isn't pursued but the United States does reach FTAs with economies that compete directly with ASEAN for FDI flows, the region could be hurt by merely keeping the status quo.* This is one of the arguments associated with an FTA as a "defensive strategy", discussed below.

C. Policy Dynamics in the Context of Developing Countries

Free-trade areas are expressions of economic policy, and it is important to understand how FTAs can influence other policy-related areas, as well as how other policy areas can affect FTAs. These are complicated issues. Below, we consider briefly four salient policy areas that are affected by developed–developing country regional accords such as the EAI, from the developing country perspective.

i. *Macroeconomic Stability.* There is general consensus in economics that macroeconomic stability is critical to the continued success of any development strategy. Even short-term bouts of instability can haunt an economy for many years to come; Latin America's long struggle with inflation is only now beginning to be won, and this has been accomplished with considerable economic cost (through unemployment and foregone output) and social tension. Promoting macroeconomic stability tends to be difficult in developing countries, and external means to support this process are often a necessary part of the stabilization process.

Fortunately, developing Asia and ASEAN in particular have had less difficulty in keeping a stable macroeconomic environment, if by this we mean low inflation. It has also generally been fiscally conservative since economic reforms took off in the mid-late 1980s—indeed, prior to the Asia Crisis, all affected economies had budget surpluses. However, there continue to be a number of problems in terms of financial development, including regulation and supervision of the financial system, diversification away from a "one pillar" system based on banking finance, and associated moral hazard problems. Great progress has been made in the EAI countries in cleaning up the financial mess left by the Crisis; for example, only 9 per cent and 17 per cent of non-performing loans continue to exist in the Philippines' and Indonesian financial institutions, respectively, while Danaharta—the national asset-management company of Malaysia—expects to finish the clean-up in 2005 (Holland 2004). Nevertheless, some of the institutional problems that existed prior to the crisis in ASEAN continue to exist today. In particular, the lack of strong, effective international competition in domestic financial markets has hindered development.

Exchange-rate stability is also a vital area for the smooth functioning of the economy, particularly in the tradable sector. Developing countries tend to rely on variations of fixed exchange-rate regimes for a number of reasons, including vulnerability to inflation. The EAI countries currently have different exchange-rate regimes, from a US$-peg in Malaysia to generally managed-floating rates in Indonesia, the Philippines and Thailand (Brunei has a currency union with Singapore). But what became clear during the Asian Crisis is that the internationalization of these economies, though having many benefits, also exposes them more to "external shocks" originating abroad, and intra-regional interdependence, as well as the perception that ASEAN "performs" as a group[8], suggest that there exist strong policy externalities in the region. That is, macroeconomic instability created, say, by an asset bubble in one market, could have an important effect on the other markets. *Hence, closer integration at the real and policy levels imply the need for greater cooperation at the macroeconomic level as well.*

In this sense, the most important contribution that PTAs can make is to help support stable macroeconomic policies. It is possible to do this in the absence of a regional grouping, as Asia has done to some extent thus far.[9] But PTAs can help to encourage macroeconomic stability in a number of ways. *In particular, real-financial links endemic to PTAs require stable macroeconomic policies if the agreement is to function smoothly.* For example, a major push for monetary union in Europe came from the need to promote the Single Market, e.g., by abolishing the possibility of competitive depreciation and allowing for the removal of border controls. The NAFTA agreement was signed without any provision for exchange-rate cooperation (a very small currency stabilization fund was set up later), a decision that leaders came to regret by December 1994. From the U.S. government perspective, the Peso Crisis created problems not only because of the ensuing economic crisis in Mexico but also due to the effect of the steep fall in the Mexican peso, which turned a U.S. surplus into a deficit in a short period of time. MERCOSUR has experienced continual crises due to macroeconomic instability, beginning with the Brazilian devaluation in 1999 and followed by the Argentine meltdown beginning in December 2001.

Hence, in order to ensure a stable partnership, countries must share information, cooperate in advocating stable fiscal and monetary policies, and engage in strong "peer pressure" against unstable policies.

In advanced regional agreements, countries find that they must focus on non-traditional areas affecting trade and investment if they are to advance economic integration, including competition policy and government procurement. These "non-border" measures force a stronger market orientation, inject greater microeconomic competition by reducing the power of domestic monopolies and "rent seeking", and put constraints on government spending through, say, the abolition of export subsidies and restrictions on industrial policies. Thus, such "forced macroeconomic stability" could be highly beneficial to the economic development strategies of participating countries. *Moreover, these "deep" integration schemes tend to be far more difficult to achieve in multilateral negotiations.*

This aspect of economic cooperation could be the most important in the context of EAI-FTAs. Protection levels in terms of tariffs are not terribly high in the ASEAN countries, and the United States is one of the most open countries in the world. Hence, the static benefits of liberalization will not prove to be high, as we discuss below. However, modern FTAs, such as the U.S.-Singapore agreement, go well beyond tariffs and non-tariff barriers into non-border and other areas, with important implications for transparency, competitions policy, intellectual property rights, governance issues, and the like. While they will seem like major "concessions" of the ASEAN countries since they will be the ones that will have to make the changes, many of these policies will be highly salutary for stable growth and development in the region.

ii. *Technology Transfer and Foreign Direct Investment.* Although the link between FDI and technology transfer has been firmly established, the relationship between trade and technology transfer is less well known, or at least less well appreciated. Through trade liberalization, countries are also able to stimulate technological development. For example, trade leads to the adaptations of new technologies from abroad by increasing the potential for success in using these technologies to crack foreign markets; in addition, increased competition forces domestic firms to place a higher priority on creating their own or importing new technologies (Pissarides 1995). This implies a strong incentive for developing countries emphasizing technology transfer (such as ASEAN) to liberalize even unilaterally.

Moreover, to best take advantage of these new technologies, countries find that they must establish strong intellectual property protection laws and means of enforcement. Without an attractive, protective environment in which multinationals can operate and in which domestic firms can invest in new innovations, the process of technology transfer is significantly inhibited. Formal PTAs can help in creating a strong underlying framework for the protection of intellectual property and "peer pressure" in the implementation of associated laws.

In the area of technology transfer, using the above analysis might suggest that developing countries should seek partnerships with developed countries, a conclusion that seems counterintuitive to both traditional trade models as well as "import substitution industrialization" approaches. But it does present a powerful (though, perhaps, not over-riding) argument; McCleery (1992), for example, incorporates some aspects of investment and other dynamics into a regional model of NAFTA and finds much larger effects for Mexico than in a static model.

Moreover, when developing countries team up with developed countries in an FTA, they are able to encourage technology transfer specifically, either through internal promotional means (e.g., in terms of training facilities, regional research and academic institutes, research consortia) or in jointly devising means to bring in appropriate technologies from abroad. The U.S.-Singapore FTA, for example, tries to bring down barriers to greater cooperation in higher education and the establishment of foreign universities. This will no doubt be an important—though, obviously, controversial—aspect of the EAI negotiations.

iii. *Harmonization Issues.* The largest effects of the Single Market program in the EU were gauged to be in many of the "non-border areas" mentioned above, but, perhaps, one of the most important areas of cooperation can be classified under the rubric of "harmonization issues", such as product testing, professional certification, standards conformance, and so forth. ASEAN countries have greater divergence in these areas than the EU; hence, it may be argued that they stand more to gain from regional economic integration with a country like the United States. And for ASEAN, to the EU menu we can add such categories as investment codes, customs harmonization, and various legal impediments.

Further, gains in all of these areas would be maximized by adopting global harmonization standards. Nevertheless, doing so at the global level is much more difficult, particularly for developing countries who often feel threatened by such programmes. By conforming as a group to some global standards, the agreement clearly reinforces the global system. But even when they do not, such agreements will reduce the "stock of divergences", making global agreements much more feasible.

iv. *Political Economy Issues.*   All existing formal PTAs were either created as economic arrangements in support of political goals or at least were consistent with the diplomatic strategy of the founding countries. For example, the EEC was formed as a means to strengthen European economies in light of the Soviet threat, as were subsequent arrangements to develop association agreements with Greece and Turkey. ASEAN was created at a time of instability in Southeast Asia (the Cultural Revolution in China; war and the communist threat in Vietnam), and the first ASEAN summit was convened in 1975, when the communists unified Vietnam. NAFTA had as a special purpose the promotion of economic liberalization and (indirectly) stable political reform in Mexico, as are the cases of the proposal to create a Free Trade Area of the Americas (FTAA) and recent initiatives in Africa and the Middle East. Economic cooperation in these arrangements is seen as an important vehicle through which political goals can be pursued (which, in themselves, have important economic ramifications). The EU has been effective in using PTAs as diplomatic tools over the past 40 years, in part out of necessity: commercial policy was the only unified policy at the regional level (Messerlin 2001).

To the extent that these PTAs add to the political stability of the region, they do service to economic development in general and the goal of policy reform in particular, even if the arrangements have weak substance to them. This, of course, is an important part of the early success story of ASEAN, which we discuss more at length in Chapter 5. Although most ASEAN countries had only recently achieved independence and were struggling to create nation-states (complete with many territorial disputes), the arrangement established an important dialogue process that prevented overt hostilities between these countries.[10] Moreover, ASEAN created a united front in the face of any potential communist "domino" effect, which, interestingly, turned into a "reverse" domino effect with respect to market reform in the rest of Indochina.

The "constructive engagement" of the ASEAN countries vis-à-vis transitional economies of Southeast, though controversial in the West, has strong political intentions. ASEAN understands the critical need to use economic cooperation as an essential "carrot" when direct political dialogue is extremely sensitive. To say that the (intentionally) weak economic cooperation initiatives in ASEAN had nothing to do with the subsequent dynamic growth in the region is to seriously understate its role (Naya and Plummer 1991).

As some developing countries tend to have weaker political (and economic policy) traditions, instability is always a potential problem. This is not as true for developed countries. Hence, the beneficial economic effects of formal regional integration in, say, the Enlargement of the EU to include the EFTA countries might be estimated without regard to the indirect political stability factors without serious fear of underestimation. But this is not true of the Fifth Enlargement to include the Central and Eastern European countries, which are all transitional economies at various levels of market development. And it would not be true of ASEAN, where economic deepening at the regional level and a formal FTA with the United States could have an important stabilizing effect in certain countries.

Again, it would be difficult if not impossible to quantify the political economy effects of the EAI in a formal model, but they could easily prove to be even more important than any static effects.

III. Economic Effects of the U.S.-ASEAN FTAs: Direct Estimates

In our statistical review of Chapter 2, we noted that ASEAN countries compete with each other to varying degrees in the U.S. market. These results give some idea as to the stakes involved in the bilateral FTAs; the extent of export similarity will determine the degree to which the successful negotiation of one FTA within the framework of the EAI might potentially impact negatively the others. Indeed, the decision to form an FTA with the United States is no longer a matter of weighing the costs and benefits of the FTA itself in terms of greater margins of preference in the U.S. market, as might have been the case if FTAs were an "exception" (as in the past), but rather a question of preserving most-favoured nation status. In this section, we consider more directly the economic effects of this decision to form an FTA with the United States using three approaches: (a) a large gravity model; (b) a review of the results using a typical Computational General Equilibrium (CGE) Model; and (3) a disaggregated approach which, we would argue, is more useful in determining the economic effects of the EAI from the viewpoint of businesspeople.

A. An Applied Statistical Analysis of the U.S.-EAI Economic Relationship

In our Chapter 2 discussion, we gave a statistical overview of the relationship between the United States and ASEAN countries in a comparative context. But we were not able to say much about what drives that relationship, outside of certain references to policy change (such as liberalization policies in the ASEAN countries) and various shocks (such as the Asian Crisis). In this subsection, we attempt to evaluate the relationship from an econometric (or "applied statistical") perspective and ask the question: "to what extent is the U.S./EAI economic relationship 'special'?" In other words, is U.S.-EAI economic interaction in line with what one would expect from countries with the economic characteristics of the United States and EAI?

The question is more difficult to address than it appears at first, for in order to answer it, we need to control for a number of variables. For example, we know from international trade-related research that richer countries tend to trade more with each other. Hence, if bilateral trade between the United States and Canada is high, must it be true that they have a "special" relationship, in the sense that they have a bias in favour of trading with each other? No, not necessarily; it may be that they trade more because they are relatively rich. Moreover, the booming literature on "economic geography" suggests that geographically close countries engage in more bilateral trade, for a number of reasons (e.g., lower transportation costs, higher chance that they speak the same language and have similar cultures, institutions and histories); thus, perhaps they trade a great deal with each other because they are neighbours. *In order to determine if they have a truly "special" relationship, or a bias toward bilateral trade, we have to control for all of these "exogenous" variables, such as relative wealth, distance, size, etc., and focus on whether or not we can determine if there is evidence that, controlling for the usual variables that determine trade, they trade more with each other than would be predicted.* The answer is important: if, controlling for these variables, it turns out that, say, the United States and Thailand trade more with each other, this would suggest that their partnership—for some reason—is relatively strong and that exporters have taken advantage of the relationship. On the other hand, if we find that the two countries actually trade less with each other than we would have predicted, something might be wrong: for example, it could be that Thailand is suffering from trade diversion due to NAFTA, or that U.S. exporters are being inhibited by a Thai protective structure that particularly disadvantages U.S. exporters. Or it could just be that the United States and Thailand do not form a "natural" economic bloc.

We do this using a "gravity model" of international trade flows. This is an econometric procedure in which trade in a certain year is posited as a function of the GDP of the source and partner country (or their product) as a proxy for *size*, per capita income of the source and partner country (or their product) as a proxy for *wealth*,[11] distance between the two countries as a proxy for transportation and other "costs", and an "adjacency" binary ("dummy") variable to control for whether or not the trading countries have a common border. Some models, as we discuss below, use a number of other variables that might be "exogenous" factors relevant to trade flows. This is essentially the "benchmark" model, that is, it is what we would expect to determine trade flows if special relationships—say, in the form of an FTA, or just a heightened tendency to trade with one another—did not exist. In order to test the hypothesis that the region really makes a difference, we add a regional dummy variable. For example, if we are interested in whether or not ASEAN as a group is significant for bilateral trade flows globally, we would include a dummy variable which would take on the value one if the two countries trading with each other are both members of ASEAN, and zero otherwise. If the dummy variable is statistically significant and positive, then we conclude that there is, indeed, a special relationship (or favourable bias) between ASEAN member-states. If the estimated coefficient on the dummy variable is statistically insignificant, however, we conclude that ASEAN as a regional grouping made no difference, that is, being a member of ASEAN gives no additional explanatory power to the model in determining trade flows.

Below, we evaluate the U.S.-ASEAN relationship using two separate approaches. The first is a comprehensive model designed to capture the relationship that the United States has with ASEAN as a group and with individual partner countries. Second, we briefly summarize the results of DeRosa (2003), who uses a gravity model to project changes in trade between the United States and EAI countries in the context of an FTA.

i. The Unrestricted Global Trade Model and Restricted Scenarios

The database provided by Rose (2003)[12] includes international bilateral trade for almost the entire post-World War II period (1948–99) for 178 (IMF-delineated) trading entities, and encompasses the standard gravity variables we mention above along with some additional ones, that is (we give the expected sign of the estimated coefficient in parentheses): currency union (+), common language (+), common land border (+), if one of the countries is landlocked (–), if one of the countries is an island (+), and whether or not the two countries were recently colonies of the same country (+).[13] Regressions are first run using "pooled" (or panel) data, i.e., we model bilateral trade flows across countries and time. As the database features bilateral flows for 52 years between the 178 countries, this approach allows us to have almost a quarter of a million observations in the unrestricted (that is, the "full-blown") model.

We begin by running three benchmark-model regressions, in which we add to the traditional approach variables accounting for two specifications of ASEAN partnership: (1) Both trading partners for a given bilateral trade flow are in ASEAN (i.e., if so, the bilateral trade flow receives a "one", zero otherwise); and (2) One of the two trading partners is an ASEAN member. We do this in order to capture not only ASEAN membership in which both ASEAN countries have been members but also to understand how well ASEAN countries have performed in general. We use 1992 as the starting date for the original ASEAN countries, since no major regional trade initiative had been undertaken in ASEAN before AFTA.[14] Finally, we include a variable for participation in the Generalized System of Preferences (GSP) programme, in which developed countries give preferential treatment to developing countries[15] in certain manufactured and processed agricultural goods. We express the variables in logarithmic terms where possible (obviously, this is impossible with binary variables), which linearizes the equations and allows us to interpret the estimated coefficients as elasticities.

The results of these first gravity specifications are provided in Table 3.1.[16] The first column includes the results for the entire model, that is, all countries in the system (the "unrestricted" scenario). The model's "fit" (i.e., how well the independent or right-hand-side variables explain variance in the dependent variable, i.e., bilateral trade flows) is strong, explaining almost two-thirds of bilateral trade flows ($R^2=0.64$). All variables are of the expected sign (that is, they affect bilateral trade just as we thought they would), and all are statistically significant except the binary variable capturing whether or not countries had common colonizers. It is interesting to note that: (1) the largest effects are derived for the existence of a common currency. This supports the notion discussed above that groupings cannot pretend that macroeconomic and financial realities do not have an important bearing on the "real" sector (i.e., trade); extreme currency stability obviously has a very strong effect; and (2) distance is critical, supporting the literature on "economic geography" also discussed above.

With respect to our ASEAN binary variables, we note that being part of ASEAN as a regional grouping does indeed matter (the estimated coefficient on the ASEAN binary variable is 0.879); ASEAN countries do tend to trade more with each other, controlling for all other variables. This would suggest that both countries' being in ASEAN, *ceteris paribus*, increases bilateral trade by approximately 140 per cent ($\exp^{(.88)-1} = 140\%$) than what we would have expected otherwise. Moreover, just being an ASEAN country makes a difference (estimated coefficient=0.738), though this effect is somewhat less important than the "both in" effect. *Thus, at the global level, we have our first conclusion: ASEAN is special.*

Of greatest interest to us are the estimated coefficients on the two ASEAN-related binary variables. We note that the ASEAN "one-in" coefficient estimate is statistically significant in all regressions, but is especially large in the case of U.S. bilateral trade. This estimated coefficient (1.222) in the U.S. market is actually about two-thirds higher than for the unrestricted model (0.738) and about three-fourths higher than for the EU regressions (0.68–0.69). *Our second conclusion, therefore, is like the first: ASEAN countries as a group are also "special" to the United States and to the EU, but especially to the United States.*

This is also true of ASEAN country trade flows. As noted above, some scholars believe that ASEAN is not a "natural" trading bloc because intra-regional trade flows are only about one-fourth total trade

TABLE 3.1
Gravity Trade Regression Estimates: Benchmark Tests

	Baseline Model: All International Bilateral Trade	No Industrial Countries	Trade post 1970
Both in ASEAN	0.879 (3.68)**	0.577 (2.32)*	0.612 (2.58)**
One in ASEAN	0.738 (12.98)**	0.785 (10.86)**	0.773 (13.58)**
GSP	0.849 (26.22)**	0.015 (0.15)	0.838 (24.79)**
Log of Distance	−1.188 (53.80)**	−1.296 (40.91)**	−1.303 (53.81)**
Log of Product of Real GDPs	0.917 (96.28)**	0.934 (58.13)**	0.947 (92.26)**
Log of Product of Real GDPs per capita	0.316 (22.14)**	0.196 (8.30)**	0.320 (21.00)**
Strict Currency Union	1.543 (12.75)**	1.348 (9.44)**	1.507 (10.01)**
Common Language	0.536 (13.58)**	0.367 (6.35)**	0.574 (13.31)**
Land Border	0.502 (4.67)**	0.667 (5.41)**	0.663 (5.76)**
Landlocked	−0.288 (9.03)**	-0.281 (5.60)**	-0.325 (9.54)**
Islands	0.073 (1.98)*	−0.056 (0.92)	0.059 (1.49)
Log of Product of Land Areas	−0.108 (13.39)**	−0.179 (13.22)**	−0.111 (12.79)**
Same Nation/Perennial Colonies	1.744 (1.65)	0.000 (.)	1.677 (1.83)
Constant	−26.917 (73.55)**	−23.419 (38.77)**	−27.797 (68.86)**
Observations	234597	114615	183328
R-squared	0.64	0.47	0.64

Robust t statistics in parentheses
* significant at 5%; ** significant at 1%

flows, whereas the Krugman rule-of-thumb for a "natural" bloc is 50 per cent. However, we know from our econometric exercises that many variables can influence trade flows, including size. Common sense would also suggest this; an example might illustrate the point. According to Table 2.1 the United States accounted for 89 per cent of Mexican exports in 2002, thereby making it a "natural" market for Mexico. However, it could *never* be the case that, according to Krugman's 50 per cent, Mexico could be a "natural" market for the United States: 50 per cent of U.S. exports would come to US$346 billion, whereas *total* Mexican imports from *all* countries that year came to only half that figure (US$168 billion)!

Likewise, given that ASEAN markets are relatively small, it is logical that overall their bilateral trade would be dominated by major markets, which are much larger and richer. The gravity approach allows U.S. to control for these other effects—such as size and relative wealth—and focus on the question of whether or not being part of ASEAN really makes a difference in determining trade flows. And indeed it does: *the estimated coefficient on the "both in" ASEAN variable is statistically significant and, moreover, larger in magnitude than is the case in the unrestricted model.*

Our final series of tests regards how special ASEAN and the individual EAI countries in particular have been to the United States *over time*. To answer this question, we estimate our regressions on a yearly basis (rather than including all years at the same time, as in the regressions above) and then report our results for the relevant binary variables. We report the magnitude of the estimate coefficients in these regressions over time in the form of charts, in which the y-axis shows the magnitude of the estimated coefficients and the x-axis the year for which a specific regression was run (we include either the entire sample of 1948–99 for the ASEAN aggregates, and a somewhat shorter period for the individual countries), indicating whether the coefficient was statistically significant or not. We also do this for trade with the EU for comparison.

Figure 3.1 reports the estimated coefficients on the ASEAN binary variables for the United States and the EU. As expected (given the results of the pooled data above), the estimated coefficients are larger for the U.S. market than for the EU market. Moreover, prior to 1970, there were no statistically significant ASEAN binaries for Europe, whereas they were

FIGURE 3.1
ASEAN Gravity Regression, Original ASEAN Countries

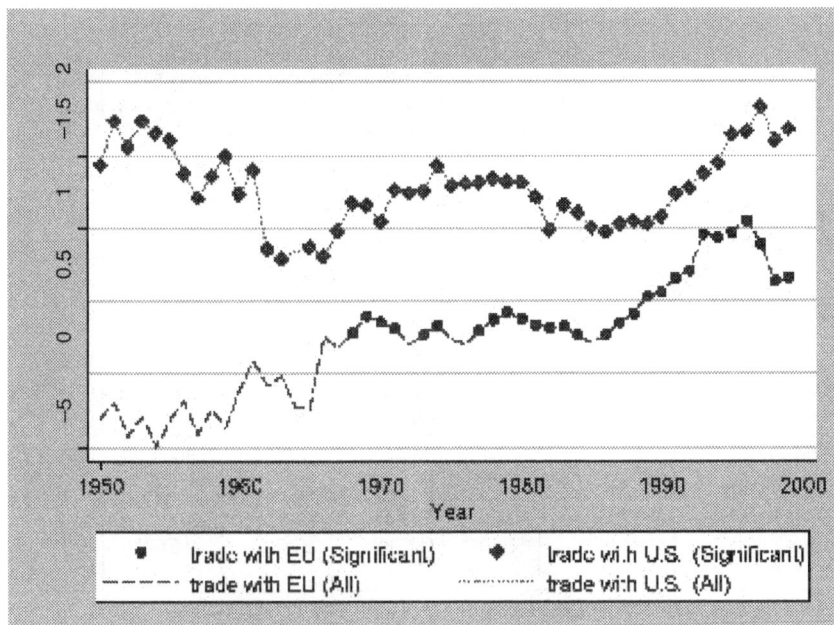

statistically significant for most of the period 1948–1970 for the United States, albeit with considerable volatility. Since the mid-1980s, i.e., when ASEAN countries began to embrace an aggressive outward-oriented development policy, the magnitudes of the ASEAN binary coefficients have been rising for both the United States and the EU, peaking just before the Asian Crisis. Estimated coefficients for the EU and the United States tend to move together over time.

Figure 3.2 performs the same exercise for the ASEAN countries *themselves*. We begin with the first year after the creation of AFTA, that is, 1993. We note a clear upward trend between 1993–95, followed by a great deal of fluctuation prior to and during the Asian Crisis.[17] The Crisis bottomed out in 1998 and we see a significant upward swing in the recovery-year of 1999, but with only one data point we cannot obviously delineate a trend.[18]

Figures 3.3–3.7 report the estimated coefficients for the Philippines, Malaysia, Indonesia, Thailand, and Singapore respectively. A few general

TABLE 3.2
Gravity Trade Regression Estimates: Selected Major Markets

	Benchmark: All Countries	Trade with US	Trade with NAFTA Countries	Trade with Countries of EU 15, Any Year	Trade with EU, limited by Accession date	ASEAN Trade
Both in ASEAN	0.879 (3.68)**	0.000 (.)	0.000 (.)	0.000 (.)	0.000 (.)	0.959 (4.12)**
One in ASEAN	0.738 (12.98)**	1.222 (4.12)**	1.165 (5.67)**	0.698 (8.40)**	0.683 (7.82)**	0.000 (.)
GSP	0.849 (26.22)**	0.260 (1.85)	0.756 (8.58)**	0.312 (7.22)**	0.199 (4.19)**	0.698 (5.38)**
Log Distance	−1.188 (53.80)**	−1.096 (7.82)**	−1.362 (12.37)**	−0.949 (28.63)**	−0.948 (26.17)**	−1.175 (11.77)**
Log Product of Real GDPs	0.917 (96.28)**	0.881 (16.94)**	0.944 (30.49)**	0.859 (55.89)**	0.860 (47.33)**	0.962 (21.97)**
Log Product of Real GDPs per capita	0.316 (22.14)**	0.392 (5.22)**	0.594 (11.90)**	0.385 (15.21)**	0.339 (12.25)**	0.287 (5.12)**
Strict Currency Union	1.543 (12.75)**	0.612 (2.29)*	0.854 (2.64)**	2.037 (7.75)**	1.795 (3.39)**	0.000 (.)
Common Language	0.536 (13.58)**	0.588 (5.23)**	0.875 (9.45)**	0.879 (11.86)**	0.909 (11.74)**	0.436 (3.48)**
Land Border	0.502 (4.67)**	−0.287 (0.72)	−0.235 (0.48)	−0.231 (1.50)	−0.244 (1.93)	0.013 (0.03)
Landlocked	−0.288 (9.03)**	−0.531 (2.84)**	−0.163 (1.29)	−0.440 (9.69)**	−0.575 (9.86)**	−1.015 (7.08)**
Islands	0.073 (1.98)*	0.128 (0.70)	0.434 (2.88)**	0.004 (0.05)	-0.035 (0.45)	−0.459 (4.44)**
Log Product of Land Areas	−0.108 (13.39)**	0.024 (0.50)	0.064 (2.13)*	−0.016 (1.11)	−0.017 (1.01)	20.218 (7.00)**
Same Nation/ Perennial Colonies	1.744 (1.65)	0.000 (.)	0.000 (.)	1.264 (1.47)	1.444 (1.68)	0.000 (.)
Constant	−26.917 (73.55)**	−29.934 (16.16)**	−36.347 (29.77)**	−28.843 (50.18)**	−28.136 (44.65)**	−25.570 (13.41)**
Observations	234597	6077	15781	71979	42627	5478
R-squared	0.64	0.83	0.79	0.79	0.82	0.68

Robust t statistics in parentheses
* significant at 5%; ** significant at 1%

FIGURE 3.2
ASEAN Gravity Regression, One ASEAN Member

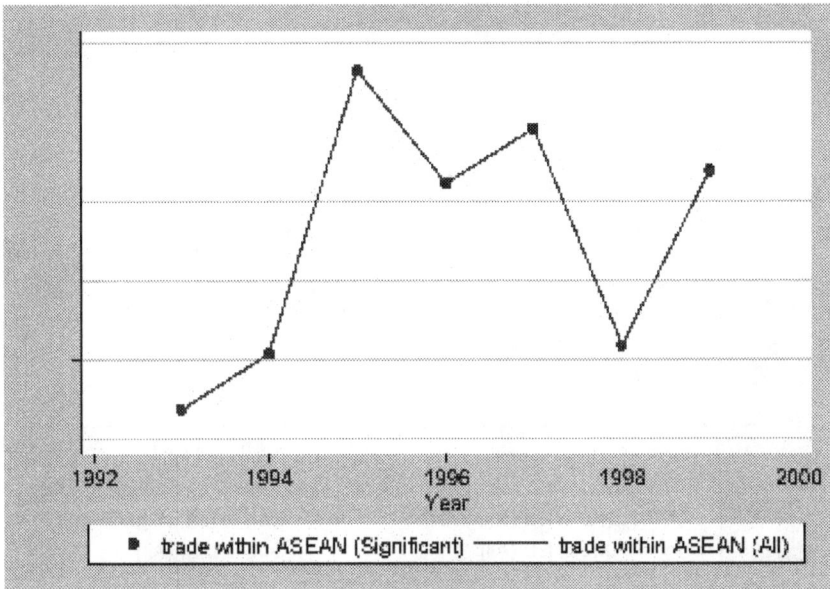

FIGURE 3.3
ASEAN Gravity Regression, Trade with Philippines

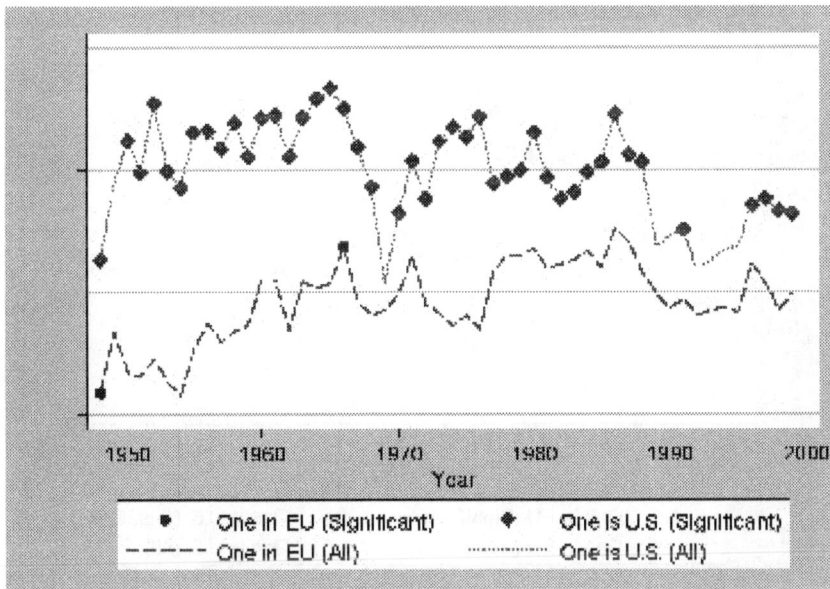

FIGURE 3.4
ASEAN Gravity Regression, Trade with Malaysia

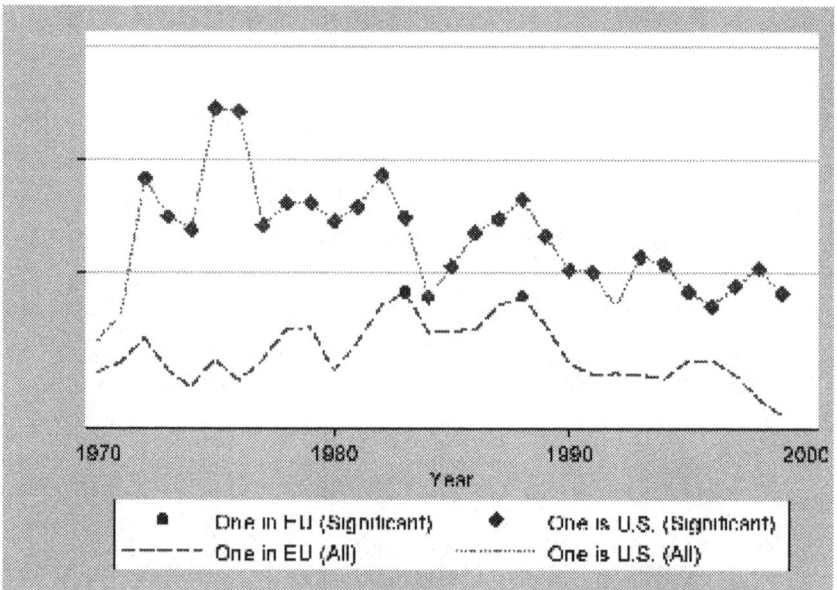

FIGURE 3.5
ASEAN Gravity Regression, Trade with Indonesia

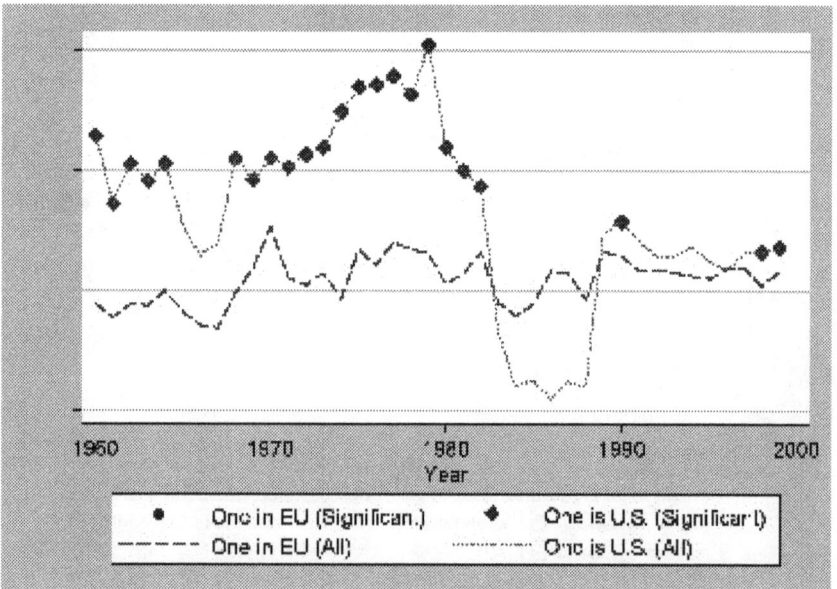

FIGURE 3.6
ASEAN Gravity Regression, Trade with Thailand

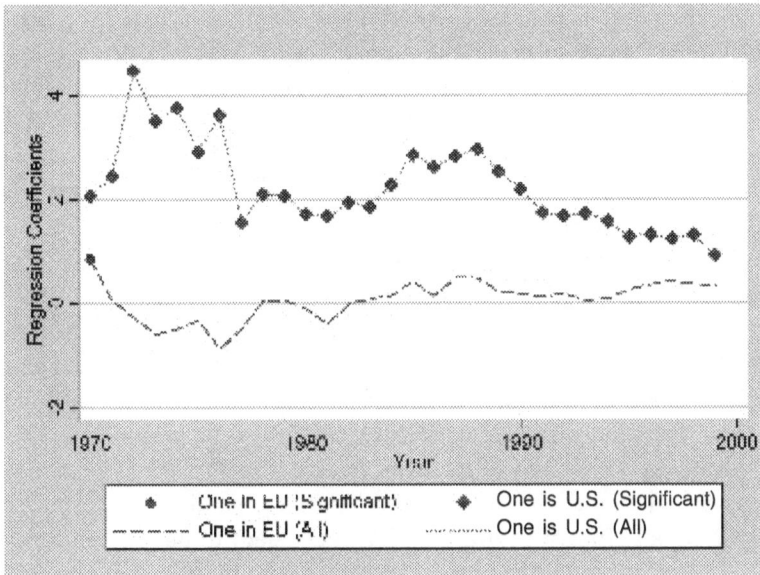

FIGURE 3.7
ASEAN Gravity Regression, Trade with Singapore

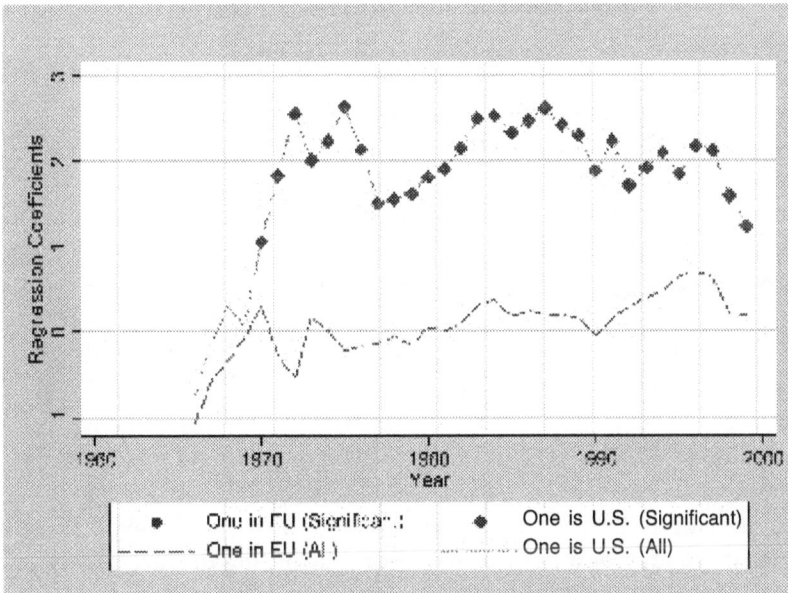

comments are in order. *First, U.S. trade with Singapore, the Philippines and Thailand are obviously the most "special" in the sense that they include the most statistically significant coefficients and they tend to be the highest in magnitude* (the time series for Malaysia and Indonesia were truncated, as there were no statistically-significant coefficients prior to 1970 and 1960, respectively). *The U.S.-Indonesia trade relationship, on the other hand, does not seem to be special at all,* at least since oil prices peaked in the early 1980s; from 1983 until the Asian Crisis, the estimated Indonesian binary variable coefficient was statistically significant only once (in 1990), though it became significant again as Indonesia began to emerge from the Asian Crisis in 1998–99. But the magnitudes are still low compared to the 1960s and 1970s. *Malaysia presents an intermediate case; however, the magnitudes of the estimated coefficients are clearly on a downward trend.*

Thus, the "special" role of ASEAN in U.S. trade may be significant and on an upward swing, but this is not true for all EAI countries: Singapore, Thailand, the Philippines and Malaysia do have positive and statistically significant coefficients but they seem to have a tendency to fall in importance over time, and the vast majority of Indonesian binary coefficients are statistically insignificant. Now, from an economics point of view, this is not necessarily a negative development. The problem with the gravity approach is that it does not tell us why things are happening. It may just be a result of market developments. On the other hand, it could be a reflection of trade diversion resulting from U.S. regional agreements with other countries; indeed, the relationship between these countries and the EU is in no way special (almost all binary coefficients are statistically insignificant), which could easily be a reflection of the myriad PTAs that the EU has negotiated with other developing countries (the so-called "Pyramid of Preferences"). *In any event, it may be the case that policy action, such as through the creation of bilateral FTAs under the rubric of the EAI, could help to reverse this trend, or, at least, allow the ASEAN countries to compete in the U.S. market on a level playing field.*

ii. Projections of Effects of U.S.-ASEAN FTAs using a Gravity Model

It is difficult to capture trade creation and trade diversion explicitly with a gravity model for a number of reasons, including the lack of any price variables, which makes estimation of explicit price elasticities impossible. In effect, when a regional dummy variable is statistically significant, it could reflect the effects of a regional trading agreement, but the results would be trade creation and trade diversion *combined*.

This restriction on gravity models renders them awkward tools in considering changes in economic efficiency with a PTA. However, this is not really our core interest: we would like to know if, given the fairly "disappointing" performance of U.S./EAI trade relations derived above, what would happen if any bilateral FTAs under the EAI were implemented? In the next section, we consider the results from a CGE model designed to address this question. In this subsection, we summarize the results from a simulation using gravity-generated parameters, as developed by DeRosa (2003), who borrows estimates of gravity coefficients undertaken by Rose (2003). DeRosa uses Rose's estimates to project what would essentially be maximum changes in trade flows with the EAI FTAs. Maximum, that is, from a static (price) point of view; he does not include the dynamic effects we discussed above.

DeRosa projects that bilateral FTAs between the United States and Indonesia, Malaysia, the Philippines and Thailand would yield increases in bilateral trade with the United States by 21.1 per cent, 31.3 per cent, 44.1 per cent, and 29.4 per cent, respectively. He also estimates that the increase of U.S. trade with the ASEAN-5 would yield an increase in its bilateral trade with the region by 15 per cent.

Hence, according to the results of DeRosa, the bilateral agreements under the EAI rubric could lead to a substantial increase in bilateral trade flows.

B. Aggregate Effects: CGE Models

Computable general equilibrium (CGE) models are a standard tool for analysing trade policy.[19] Their attraction is the inclusion of multi-country and multi-commodity dimensions, along with strong theoretical foundations, and a consistent interaction between economic variables. Revolutions in computing technologies have facilitated CGE modelling.[20] The Global Trade and Analysis Project (GTAP), which is used in the model applied in this section, is publicly available and is one of the most frequently used CGE models in the trade literature.

Computational General Equilibrium models are characterized by two common features. First, they employ a priori elasticity estimates. Elasticities are either derived from a literature search and logical approximations, or through independent estimation. Second, a system of equations that describes the actions of all agents in the economy at all stages of production and demand is specified.[21] By solving for profit and utility maximization of firms and consumers, respectively, a general equilibrium solution is derived using a special algorithm.

By changing economic variables, such as tariffs, one is able to solve for new equilibrium values of endogenous variables, called the "counterfactual equilibrium". It is possible to compare the values obtained for the endogenous variables from the counterfactual simulation with those in the benchmark simulation. From this comparison, one can deduce changes in output in different sectors, factor remuneration, economic efficiency (i.e., trade creation and trade diversion), the terms of trade, and the balance of payments.

CGE models tend to be static in nature, and the lack of more realistic assumptions, such as variety in market structure, economies of scale, and technological change, as well as the strong focus on trade, constrain the economic effects of any given policy change. These shortcomings become particularly limiting when developing countries are involved, because, as noted above, dynamic aspects of development are the most sensitive to policy change, and dynamic elements of economic integration tend to be more important.[22] These limitations may explain the alleged downward bias of the welfare effects of integration (e.g. Safadi and Laird 1996, Kreinin and Plummer 2002) obtained by this approach.

We summarize the results from (Gilbert 2003)'s GTAP-based CGE model, through which he estimates the effects of free-trade areas between the United States and ASEAN countries (2003). We want to stress that this model: (1) does not explicitly incorporate non-tariff barriers but does try to include them by estimating a tariff-equivalent effect of various non-tariff barriers; (2) includes only one services sector, a limitation given that it will be an important area in the EAI negotiations; (3) does not include any effects that we listed as "dynamic", that this, changes in investment flows, productivity spill-overs, economies of scale, and the like; and (4) as is the case with all CGE models, it cannot take into account the policy dynamics considered above. Hence, we would suggest that these effects have a strong downward bias, particularly in the case of the EAI.[23]

TABLE 3.3a
CGE Model Estimates of Effects of an Indonesia-U.S. FTA

Effects on:	Economy-Wide Effects:					Factor Returns:				
	Import Value (% change)	Export Value (% change)	Tariff Revenue (change, US$mill)	Nom GDP (% change)	Equiv. Var ($ mill)	Land	Unskill L	Skill L	Capital	Nat Res
United States	0.22	0.24	-1189	-0.02	-179	-0.02	0.01	0.02	0.02	0.21
Indonesia	4.95	4.29	-335	2.75	1313	0.61	1.03	0.79	0.94	-8.97
Other ASEAN	na	-0.03	na	na	-96					
China	na	-0.11	na	na	-295					
Korea	na	-0.01	na	na	-45					
Japan	na	-0.02	na	na	-278					
EU	na	-0.02	na	na	-286					
World	na	0.05	na	na	-200					

Source: Gilbert, John, "CGE Simulations of US Bilateral Free Trade Agreements" (Washington, D.C.: Institute for International Economics 2003), as cited in DeRosa 2003.

TABLE 3.3b
CGE Model Estimates of Effects of a Malaysia-U.S. FTA

Effects on:	Economy-Wide Effects:					Factor Returns:				
	Import Value (% change)	Export Value (% change)	Tariff Revenue (change, $mill)	Nom GDP (% change)	Equiv. Var ($ mill)	Land	Unskill L	Skill L	Capital	Nat Res
United States	0.15	0.15	-400	0.03	392	0.66	0.01	0.01	0.01	0.07
Malaysia	1.87	1.37	-658	0.46	248	-3.98	1.53	1.52	1.49	-3.05
Other ASEAN	na	-0.06	na	na	-91					
China	na	-0.04	na	na	-70					
Korea	na	-0.02	na	na	-30					
Japan	na	-0.01	na	na	-127					
EU	na	-0.01	na	na	-140					
World	na	0.03	na	na	-62					

Source: As for Table 3.3a.

TABLE 3.3c
CGE Model Estimates of Effects of a Philippines–U.S. FTA

Effects on:	Economy-Wide Effects:					Factor Returns:				
	Import Value (% change)	Export Value (% change)	Tariff Revenue (change, $mill)	Nom GDP (% change)	Equiv. Var ($ mill)	Land	Unskill L	Skill L	Capital	Nat Res
United States	0.19	0.22	-662	0.01	224	0.79	0.01	0.01	0.01	-0.07
Philippines	5.82	5.05	-504	3.06	907	-2.56	2.67	1.71	2.13	-0.75
Other ASEAN	na	-0.06	na	na	-75					
China	na	-0.06	na	na	-70					
Korea	na	-0.02	na	na	-30					
Japan	na	-0.01	na	na	-127					
EU	na	-0.01	na	na	-140					
World	na	0.03	na	na	-62					

Source: As for Table 3.3a.

TABLE 3.3d
CGE Model Estimates of Effects of a Thailand-U.S. FTA

Effects on:	Economy-Wide Effects:					Factor Returns:				
	Import Value (% change)	Export Value (% change)	Tariff Revenue (change, $mill)	Nom GDP (% change)	Equiv. Var ($ mill)	Land	Unskill L	Skill L	Capital	Nat Res
United States	0.38	0.40	-982	0.07	824	0.21	0.02	0.03	0.02	-0.17
Thailand	0.21	3.46	1.531	0.05	780	0.41	1.83	1.43	1.40	-2.56
Other ASEAN	na	-0.08	na	na	-196					
China	na	-0.10	na	na	-255					
Korea	na	-0.05	na	na	-56					
Japan	na	-0.05	na	na	-369					
EU	na	-0.02	na	na	-338					
World	na	0.06	na	na	-358					

Source: As for Table 3.3a

Table 3.3a–b summarize the CGE simulated aggregate effects on trade (exports and imports), tariff revenue (due to the reductions in intra-regional tariffs to zero), nominal GDP (per cent), equivalent variation (US$ millions),[24] and on factor returns for Indonesia, Malaysia, the Philippines and Thailand, respectively. The results are on the whole fairly unimpressive in nominal terms. But given the *caveats* noted above regarding the downward bias in this type of CGE model, it is perhaps best to consider them relative to other models, and in this sense, the results are fairly strong for the Philippines and Indonesia, whose respective GDPs rise by 3.06 per cent and 2.75 per cent, respectively. These magnitudes are generally on par with the CGE estimates of the effects of the Single Market Program in Europe in the mid-1980s. Malaysian and Thai GDP only increase by 0.46 per cent and 0.72 per cent, respectively. This is no doubt the result of the existing liberal trade regimes in Malaysia and the United States, as well as the low degree of discrimination in the Thai market in affected commodities.[25] The United States is only very marginally affected in the cases of all four FTAs (slightly negative in the case of the U.S.-Indonesia FTA, positive for the others), which is an intuitive result given the size of the U.S. economy. In all cases, the effect on bilateral exports and imports is far lower than what was projected in the gravity-model projections reviewed above.

We might point out that the estimated effects on the U.S. economy are always many times less than those calculated for the ASEAN partner (and, in the case of Indonesia, the U.S. actually loses while Indonesia gains considerably). *Such asymmetric gains result from the relative size of the U.S. economy, but underscore an important point in terms of policy: as the ASEAN countries have much more to gain in terms of trade-related market access, it is likely that the United States will push other areas of interest to its business community.* These are discussed more at length in Chapters 4–6.

Two additional points need to be made in the context of these aggregate calculations. First, regarding the implications for factor returns in ASEAN, *unskilled labour gains the most (sometimes, by far) due to the FTAs, and the owners of land (in most cases) and natural resource tend to be the losers.* Landowners gain (marginally) but natural resource owners are affected negatively in the cases of Indonesia and Thailand; however, they both lose in the cases of Malaysia and the Philippines. The returns to capital and skilled labour are positive and fairly high in all cases, though always lower than the return to unskilled labour. Hence, one would anticipate that opposition to the EAI would tend to come mostly from owners of natural resources and, in some cases, land. *Effects on factors in the United States are, of course, very small, but in no case does unskilled labour lose.* This should be reassuring to special interests in the United States who worry that FTAs with developing countries will ultimately hurt the most vulnerable in the labour force.

Second, *in the case of each bilateral FTA, the rest of ASEAN is negatively affected.* While the values are not high, as a percentage of the gains to the ASEAN member-state engaging in the agreement, they can be substantial, e.g., the loss to "other ASEAN" in the case of the U.S.-Malaysia FTA is over one-third the gains to Malaysia. This trade diversion effect, which is inherent in these agreements, is one motivation for FTAs as a "defensive strategy", as discussed in the next section.

In order to get a better idea of political economy issues in the EAI, it is important to consider sectoral effects. Table 3.4 shows the model's estimations of the effects of the bilateral FTAs on 18 different sectors, including the one service sector. As is evident from the table, while overall effects of the FTA on various sectors tend to be small (and, in the case of the United States, extremely small), the effect on *bilateral* trade can actually be very large. For example, the U.S. motor vehicle sector is not affected much overall by the ASEAN FTAs, with the possible exception of the U.S.-Thai FTA in which the sector would grow by 2 per cent. However, in terms of changes at the bilateral level, the percentage changes tend to be extremely large, i.e., 600 per cent, 1102 per cent, 537 per cent, and 1593 per cent for FTAs with Indonesia, Malaysia, the Philippines, and Thailand, respectively. This is one reason why motor vehicles will be a "sensitive area" when we discuss hurdles to overcome in the EAI in Chapter 4; motor vehicle protection continues to be a problem even in AFTA.

With respect to ASEAN country-level effects, winners tend to significantly outnumber the losers. Each EAI country has textiles and apparel and "other crops" as big winners, as U.S. protection is high in these areas and ASEAN tends to have a comparative advantage in these products. For the Philippines, processed food products also shows a hefty expansion. The losers are more varied, but in no case does a sector decline by more than eight per cent.

TABLE 3.4

Sectoral CGE Effects of U.S.–EAI Free Trade Areas

(Per cent Change in Value)

	U.S.-Indonesia				U.S.-Malaysia				U.S.-Philippines				U.S.-Thailand			
	United States		Indonesia		United States		Malaysia		United States		Philippines		United States		Thailand	
	Total	To IN	Total	To U.S.	Total	To MA	Total	To U.S.	Total	To PH	Total	To U.S.	Total	To TH	Total	To U.S.
Grains	0.0	19.6	-7.3	-5.7	-0.2	10.0	1.9	24.1	1.6	54.3	-3.9	0.2	-0.3	4.0	-4.5	7.7
Other Crops	1.0	34.4	21.4	104.9	2.8	210.0	11.4	143.2	0.3	66.0	-2.7	25.8	1.7	134.5	14.3	109.3
Animal Products	0.2	43.1	-10.7	-8.1	-0.2	103.4	0.1	6.1	0.1	132.9	-7.9	-4.9	1.1	111.4	-4.3	-2.0
Forestry & Fisheries	0.2	5.3	-4.3	-2.9	0.1	3.9	-1.9	-0.9	0.0	24.4	-10.4	-7.6	0.6	463.9	-4.6	-2.9
Processed Food Prod.	0.7	107.7	-1.4	40.1	0.2	67.8	4.7	49.6	0.8	99.5	25.5	70.5	1.4	289.0	8.8	55.3
Lumber	0.6	60.7	-4.6	14.1	0.3	76.5	-0.8	10.2	0.5	93.7	-3.9	2.5	0.1	77.1	-1.5	9.9
Pulp & Paper Products	0.2	20.7	-4.4	1.5	0.2	30.0	-1.6	2.4	0.2	28.4	-1.6	5.4	0.1	39.2	-2.1	1.4
Textiles & Apparel	1.1	137.4	34.8	123.7	0.3	170.3	27.3	145.1	1.2	208.0	76.4	126.9	1.2	290.1	38.4	132.2
Coal, Oil &Gas	0.3	32.1	-1.9	-0.4	0.0	9.9	-0.7	1.3	0.0	16.9	-4.1	-4.3	-0.2	18.7	-1.4	2.7
Petroleum & Coal Prods.	0.1	17.7	-1.5	7.7	0.1	90.5	-0.3	8.4	0.0	11.1	-0.2	-0.2	0.0	31.0	-0.8	8.7
Chemicals	0.3	42.9	-4.5	0.4	0.1	21.4	3.4	13.2	0.1	33.3	0.5	17.8	0.7	72.6	-1.8	8.1
Metals	0.2	62.1	-7.4	-1.8	0.3	48.4	-1.4	11.8	0.0	39.5	-5.6	19.4	0.1	52.9	-4.4	16.3
Metal Products	1.2	83.4	-1.6	11.8	0.5	70.8	-1.2	10.4	0.5	47.9	0.3	19.1	2.6	155.3	0.1	15.4
Electronic Equipment	0.3	58.8	-2.7	4.3	0.1	2.1	0.8	4.7	0.4	15.8	2.9	5.2	0.2	19.6	-2.2	3.4
Motor Vehicles	0.3	600.4	-13.1	0.5	0.6	1,101.5	-1.8	13.5	0.5	537.4	2.2	16.8	2.0	1,592.9	-0.2	15.1
Transportation Equip	0.0	2.6	-4.2	8.5	-0.2	1.5	-1.6	34.0	-0.1	45.0	-2.4	17.0	-0.2	10.5	-11.2	9.2
Machinery NEC	0.1	26.8	1.9	16.9	0.1	23.7	-0.4	11.1	0.1	30.5	4.8	17.4	0.4	72.4	-0.5	15.9
Manufactures NEC	0.5	200.2	-5.4	4.5	0.2	52.8	0.6	8.0	0.3	113.6	-4.4	0.8	0.1	108.6	2.4	20.0
Services	0.0	4.2	-6.8	-6.8	-0.1	1.4	-2.4	-2.3	0.0	4.8	-7.7	-7.7	-0.3	2.0	-3.7	-3.6

Source: Gilbert, John, "CGE Simulations of U.S. Bilateral Free Trade Agreements", (Institute for International Economics, Washington, D.C: 2003) as cited in DeRosa (2003).

Notes: IN, MA, PH and TH denote Indonesia, Malaysia, Philippines and Thailand, respectively. NEC denotes not elsewhere classified.

C. Product by Product Trade Expansion: A Disaggregated Approach

Although the estimated effects of the CGE model on U.S. and ASEAN aggregate welfare are low, the sectoral effects can be fairly substantial. As trade agreements are ultimately political agreements, it is useful to focus more specifically on the actual products that are being affected. After all, a U.S. businessperson is not so much interested in overall production in electronics in Indonesia; he or she is interested in exactly what the level of protection is for his or her electronics-related product. To arrive at this sort of detail, we need to work with the greatest degree of trade disaggregation possible.

In this section, we develop a disaggregated approach to the potential economic effects of the EAI that will be useful to especially businesspeople but also policy makers. The technique is fairly straightforward. We first gather SITC 5-digit data for the exports of the individual EAI countries to the United States, and from the United States to the EAI countries, for the latest year available (2001). As was noted in Chapter 2, this level of disaggregation gives us a maximum of approximately 3,000 commodities and is of the greatest detail available under the SITC system. We then rank these commodities by the value of exports to each market. This ranking system shows us clearly which individual products are the most important in bilateral trade.

Next, we have to consider levels of protection. The higher the value of an export and the higher the level of protection facing the proposed FTA partner, the greater is the potential for trade expansion. Hence, we need to calculate protection at these high levels of disaggregation, which is difficult for two reasons: first, tariff levels of the United States and the EAI countries are published under the Harmonized Coding (HS) system and include an even *higher* level of disaggregation than the SITC. Hence, we had to produce a weighted average of HS-based tariffs for each 5-digit SITC commodity, using a correspondence table that maps out the comparable commodities. These are called the "MFN-based" tariffs in our analysis. However, for U.S. protection, we also have to take into account the fact that the United States offers GSP and other forms of preferential treatment to Indonesia, the Philippines and Thailand), whereas Malaysia, Brunei, and Singapore do not qualify for this programme. Therefore we had to go into each tariff line and assign a zero tariff to any commodity receiving GSP treatment, and recalculate the average tariffs by commodity.[26]

Finally, we would like to estimate how much potential there is in each product for trade expansion under an FTA. We do this by multiplying the value of the product by the change in the tariff (which gives us our price change) and the elasticity of demand, using a rule-of-thumb estimate of –1.[27] Such an approach has a long tradition in the empirical PTA literature (under the "price-elasticities" approach), though it has not been done before at this level of aggregation and in this sort of framework. Using –1 as an elasticity for all commodities is obviously a generalization, but there exist no estimates of elasticity demand at the 2-digit level, let along the 5-digit level. Moreover, in many CGE models, elasticities seem to be very close to one for many commodities, though they tend to be somewhat smaller in agriculture and higher in manufactured goods. However, we are interested in merely a general idea of how much an individual export could possibly expand, and this seemed to be the easiest approach. One can easily adjust these estimates for higher (lower) elasticities by just multiplying through by another parametric value.

To give a concrete example of how this procedure works, let's consider an example from the Indonesian market. The most important Indonesian export to the U.S. market in 2001 was video recording or reproducing apparatus, with a value of US$588 million. How would a proposed FTA with the United States affect Indonesian exporters of this commodity? We first look at levels of protection. The United States does have certain tariffs in this area under the HS system, but they are obviously quite low, as the average tariff comes out to be less than one per cent (0.0035 per cent). Moreover, the products facing a tariff in the United States in this category are included under the U.S. GSP program, so we assign a zero to them when calculating the applied tariff on Indonesian exports. Hence, the estimated trade expansion in this area will be zero; an FTA would have no effect because Indonesia is already accorded free access to the U.S. market.

However, as was noted at length above, *this does not mean that exporters of this product should be indifferent to an FTA.* This procedure is useful in terms of supplying information, first in identifying which are the key sectors in bilateral trade (and now we know how important video recording or reproducing apparatus are in nominal and relative terms) and second in determining levels of protaretion. In addition, there could be many non-tariff and indirect aspects of the agreement that could benefit the sector. *The increased certainty, transparency, and assurances created by the agreement could make Indonesia a less risky place in which to invest, perhaps bringing more resources to this sector.* For example, better protection of intellectual property, which would likely be included in the agreement, would make multinationals less nervous about investing in high-tech areas in Indonesia, which may include video recording apparatus.

Thus, our discussion below focuses on tariffs, but it is important to keep in mind that there is much more to the EAI than mere tariff-based trade protection.

Our results for the top 40 ASEAN exports to the U.S. market are presented in Tables 3.5–3.10 for Indonesia, Malaysia, the Philippines, Thailand, Brunei, and Singapore, respectively, and for the top 40 U.S. exports to ASEAN (except Brunei and Singapore[28]) in Tables 3.11–3.13. We also include in Appendix Tables 3.4–3.9 all original ASEAN country exports to the United States, and U.S. exports to the EAI countries in Appendix Tables 3.11–3.14, for the top 100 products in terms of export value.[29] Hence, Appendix Tables 3.4–3.14 constitute an expanded version of the analysis for which Tables 3.5–3.10 and Tables 3.10–3.13 give a summary of the most important products and countries for this study.

i. *ASEAN Exports to the United States*

Table 3.5 shows that, while video recording or reproducing apparatus is the most important Indonesian export to the U.S. market, "other footwear" (SITC 85132) and "footwear" (SITC 85148) should be able to profit most from an Indonesian-U.S. FTA. This is due both to their relative value (US$203 million and US$420 million, respectively) and to the size of the U.S. tariff, which is relatively high in both cases (26.8 per cent and 7.4 per cent, respectively). These are excluded from the U.S. GSP. Trade expansion should be in the order of US$55 million and US$31 million, respectively. The next five items with trade expansion potential include cotton shirts for men (US$21 million), tennis shoes (US$19 million), brassieres (US$14 million), babies' garments (US$14 million), and plywood (US$10 million). Hence, while there are a number

TABLE 3.5

Indonesian Exports, U.S. Protection, and Potential for Expansion: Top 40 Products, 2001

(Ranked by Export Value)

	Exports 2001 (US$1000)	U.S. MFN Tariff (average)	Tariff on Indo (average)	Expansion (US$1000)
76381 Video recording or reproducing apparatus	588,254.7	0.0035	0	0
85148 Footwear, n.e.s., with outer soles of leather	419,353.1	0.0743333	0.0743333	31171.91
23125 Technically specified natural rubber	310,743	0	0	0
75997 Parts, accessories of the machines of group 752	206,470.7	0	0	0
85132 Other footwear, outer soles & uppers of rubber, pla.	203,452.6	0.2683257	0.2683257	54591.56
82159 Other wooden furniture	196,244.9	0	0	0
63431 Plywood, sheets of wood, ply of tropi. or non-conif.	182,181.5	0.0611	0.056	10202.16
84151 Shirts of cotton, for men	145,200.4	0.145	0.145	21054.06
03611 Shrimps and prawns, frozen	143,649.9	0	0	0
83199 Other holsters, cases, bags & containers, n.e.s.	139,643.2	0.0922308	0.0830769	11601.13
76289 Other radio-broadcast receivers, non-combined	135,062.2	0.03	0	0
76211 Radio, external source of power, vehicles, combined	134,524.2	0.01	0	0
77641 Digital monolithic integrated circuits	110,505.2	0	0	0
82155 Furniture, of wood, of a kind used in the bedroom	108,317.7	0	0	0
84551 Brassieres	104,837.7	0.13675	0.13675	14336.56
64248 Papers & paperboard, for graphic purposes	102,881.5	0.007	0	0
03721 Crustaceans, prepared or preserved, n.e.s.	96,740.3	0.03	0	0
82116 Seats, n.e.s., with wooden frames	96,200.4	0	0	0
89422 Dolls representing only human beings	88,633.8	0	0	0
84512 Babies' garments & clothing accessories, knitted	74,864	0.1841579	0.1841579	13786.8
84811 Articles of apparel, of leather	71,146.2	0.0535	0.03	2134.386
84119 Coats, capes & similar of other materials, for men	69,709.8	0.1107999	0.1107999	7723.84
88411 Contact lenses	65,054.8	0.02	0.02	1301.096
07511 Pepper, neither crushed nor ground	59,633.4	0	0	0

TABLE 3.5 (continued)

	Exports 2001 (US$1000)	U.S. MFN Tariff (average)	Tariff on Indo (average)	Expansion (US$1000)
77643 Non-digital monolithic integrated circuits	58,427.6	0	0	0
84511 Babies' garments & clothing accessor., not knitted	58,146.6	0.1550279	0.1550279	9014.343
85125 Tennis shoes, training shoes & the like, rubber, pla.	55,102	0.3465983	0.3465983	19098.26
89731 Articles of jewellery & parts, of precious metals	53,149	0.0628	0	0
77811 Primary cells & primary batteries	52,835.7	0.027	0	0
78439 Other parts & accessories of motor vehicles	52,273.7	0.0094444	0.0005556	29.04095
07111 Coffee, not roasted, not decaffeinated	51,969.2	0	0	0
89477 Gloves, mittens & mitts, for use in sports	49,980.9	0.0281667	0	0
77313 Ignit. wiring sets & the like used in vehicles, etc.	45,957.7	0.05	0	0
84219 Wind-jackets, anoraks & similar articles, for women	45,898.1	0.1101079	0.1101079	5053.744
57433 Polyethylene terephthalate	45,604.9	0.080576	0	0
89995 Wigs, false beards & simi.; art. of human hair, n.e.s.	44,135.3	0	0	0
69741 Household articles & parts, n.e.s, of iron or steel	42,136.9	0.0269	0	0
84822 Rubber gloves	41,046.9	0.0566667	0.0466667	1915.522
77261 Boards, panels for electric distribution <1000 volts	38,602.1	0.027	0	0
84589 Articles of apparel, women's or girls, n.e.s.	38,134.8	0.0972	0.0972	3706.702

Total Expansion Value for All Exports: US$301.1 million

Expansion as a Percentage of Total Included Exports: 3 per cent

Notes: [1] Difference between MFN and Applied Tariffs regards existing preferential treatment offered by the US (e.g., GSP).

[2] For addtional commodities, see Appendix Table 3.4.

TABLE 3.6
Malaysia Exports, US Protection, and Potential for Expansion: Top 40 Products
(Ranked by Export Value)

	Exports 2001 (US$1000)	US MFN Tariff (average)	Tariff (average)	Tariff on Malay Expansion (US$1000)
77641 Digital monolithic integrated circuits	3,408,248.9	0	0	0
75997 Parts, accessories of the machines of group 752	2,478,967.7	0	0	0
76432 Transmission apparatus with reception apparatus	1,098,085.7	0	0	0
76381 Video recording or reproducing apparatus	945,374.7	0.0035	0.0035	3308.811
77643 Non-digital monolithic integrated circuits	611,069	0	0	0
84822 Rubber gloves	447,353.3	0.0566667	0.0566667	25350.02
76411 Telephone sets	310,190.5	0	0	0
76281 Other radio receivers, combined with sound reprodu.	298,854	0.021	0.021	6275.934
76211 Radio, external source of power, vehicles, combined	186,365.9	0.01	0.01	1863.659
76289 Other radio-broad-cast receivers, non-combined	181,153.8	0.03	0.03	5434.614
77633 Transistors, dissipation rate > 1 w	170,438.2	0	0	0
82159 Other wooden furniture	163,805.7	0	0	0
76383 Other sound reproducing apparatus	159,363.3	0.00925	0.00925	1474.111
76431 Transmission apparatus	157,232	0.012	0.012	1886.784
76419 Other telephonic or telegraphic apparatus	154,787.2	0	0	0
82116 Seats, n.e.s., with wooden frames	120,042.8	0	0	0
76493 Parts & accessories of 761, 762, 7643, 7648	117,709.6	0.0217714	0.0217714	2562.706
77637 Photosensitive semi-conductor devices; light emitt.	111,409.8	0	0	0
84151 Shirts of cotton, for men	104,472	0.145	0.145	15148.44
77631 Diodes, not photosensiti. nor light emitting diodes	94,415.8	0	0	0
89429 Toys, n.e.s.	93,288.3	0	0	0
77121 Static converters	90,217.6	0.006	0.006	541.3056
77586 Ovens, cookers, cook. plates, boiling rings, roasters	85,287	0.0156667	0.0156667	1336.163
76491 Parts & accessories for apparatus of heading 7641	85,030.5	0	0	0

TABLE 3.6 (continued)

	Exports 2001 (US$1000)	US MFN Tariff (average)	Tariff on Malay (average)	Expansion (US$1000)
76221 Radio, without external source of power, combined	82,691.4	0	0	0
51616 Acycl., cyclan., cyclen., cyclo., arom ethers; derivat.	80,178.3	0.0589286	0.0589286	4724.792
63431 Plywood, sheets of wood, ply of tropi. or non-conif.	77,708.6	0.0611	0.0611	4747.995
88111 Photographic cameras	74,025.6	0.01775	0.01775	1313.954
84512 Babies' garments & clothing accessories, knitted	73,582.6	0.1841579	0.1841579	13550.82
76282 Other radio receivers, combined with a clock	70,579.4	0.015	0.015	13550.82
76422 Loudspeakers, mounted in their enclosures	66,579.2	0.049	0.049	1058.691
77632 Transistors, dissipation rate < 1 w	65,662.4	0	0	3262.381
76384 Sound recording apparatus	63,808.2	0	0	0
42249 Palm kernel, babassu oil & their fractions, refined	54,356.6	0	0	0
51217 Fatty alcohols, industrial	54,123.6	0.0316667	0.0316667	1713.914
75121 Electronic without external source of power	53,757.6	0	0	0
77261 Boards, panels for electric distribution<1000 volts	46,576	0.027	0.027	1257.552
42229 Palm oil and its fractions, refined	45,538	0	0	0
87477 Other instrum. & apparatus for telecommunications	45,367.5	0	0	0
51222 Glycerol (glycerine), glycerol waters & lyes	44,883.6	0.0025555	0.0025555	114.7

Total Expansion Value for All Exports: US$179.3 million
Expansion as a Percentage of Total Included Exports: 1%
Notes:
1. Difference between MFN and Applied Tariffs regards existing preferential treatment offered by the U.S. (e.g., GSP).
2. For additional commodities, see Appendix Table 3.5.

of electronic goods and other products that are more important than textile and clothing exports, the relatively elevated tariffs in this area in the United States, coupled with the fact that they are excluded from the U.S. GSP, suggest that they stand to gain the most from a U.S.-Indonesia FTA at the micro level.

As can be seen from Table 3.6, the top three Malaysian exports to the United States account for a large share of total Malaysia exports to the United States; out of the top 40 products' total of US$12.7 billion in exports, these three commodities account for about US$7 billion, or 55 per cent. Hence, Malaysian exports to the United States are fairly concentrated in a few commodities. However, the U.S. MFN tariff on these electronics-related items comes to zero in every case, suggesting that there will be no trade expansion in these areas, subject, of course, to the same caveat discussed above on the non-tariff benefits of an FTA. The fourth most important export is video recording or reproducing apparatus (SITC 76381), which it will be recalled was number one for Indonesia. However, as Malaysia does not benefit from the U.S. GSP anymore, there is the possibility of some trade expansion (US$3.3 million), though it is small as the U.S. MFN tariff is very low. The top potential beneficiaries in terms of trade expansion would be: rubber gloves (US$25 million), babies' garments (US$14 million), other radio receivers (US$6 million), and other radio broadcast receivers (US$5 million).

The Philippines export story (Table 3.7) is similar to that of Malaysia in that its top 4 exports are all electronics-related goods and constitute the lion's share of top 40 exports but face zero tariffs in the U.S. market, though in part this is due to the fact that the Philippines is able to profit from the U.S. GSP. By far the commodity that has the greatest potential for trade expansion is raw cane sugar, not because it is such an important Philippine export to the United States (US$37 million) but due to the high level of protection (87 per cent).[30] Potential trade expansion is calculated to be US$32 million. Note, however, that this will be one of the toughest products for the United States to include in a U.S.-Philippines FTA, as we discuss in Chapter 4. Indeed, in the recently-signed U.S.-Australia FTA, sugar was excluded all together. Other areas with significant trade expansion include: babies garments, knitted (US$16 million); other holsters, cases, bags and containers (US$15 million); shirts of cotton for men (US$15 million); and babies garments, not knitted (US$12 million).

TABLE 3.7

Philippine Exports, U.S. Protection, and Potential for Expansion: Top 40 Products
(Ranked by Export Value)

	Exports 2001 (US$1000)	US MFN Tariff (average)	Tariff on Phil (average)	Expansion (US$1000)
77643 Non-digital monolithics integrated circuits	855,309.8	0	0	0
75997 Parts, accessories of the machines of group 752	412,575.5	0	0	0
77313 Ignit. wiring sets & the like used in vehicl., etc.	288,219.3	0.05	0	0
77121 Static converters	222,464.6	0.006	0	0
83199 Other holsters, cases, bags & containers, n.e.s.	183,800.8	0.0922308	0.0830769	15269.6007
88541 Wrist watches, electrically powered	124,613.9	0	0	0
76431 Transmission apparatus	103,489.2	0.012	0.0045	465.7014
84151 Shirts of cotton, for men	100,841.4	0.145	0.145	14622.003
42231 Coconut oil, crude	99,113.5	0	0	0
83126 Satchels & simil., outer surface of plast. or text.	95,143.6	0.127	0.127	12083.2372
84512 Babies' garments & clothing accessories, knitted	88,994.9	0.1841579	0.1841579	16389.1139
76432 Transmission apparatus with reception apparatus	86,830.7	0	0	0
05893 Pineapples, prepared or preserved, n.e.s.	82,372.1	0.006215	0.006215	511.942602
84511 Babies' garments & clothing accessor., not knitted	79,139.1	0.1550279	0.1550279	12268.7685
82159 Other wooden furniture	78,184.6	0	0	0
77633 Transistors, dissipation rate > 1 w	75,553.4	0	0	0
84371 Shirts, of cotton, knitted or crocheted, for men	64,321.3	0.201	0.201	12928.5813
77637 Photosensitive semi-conductor devices; light emitt.	62,715	0	0	0
84119 Coats, capes & similar of other materials, for men	58,443.2	0.1107999	0.1107999	6475.50072
84551 Brassieres	52,066.3	0.13675	0.13675	7120.06653
05991 Pineapple juice	47,371.2	0.0671335	0.0671335	3180.19446
84219 Wind-jackets, anoraks & similar articles, for women	43,281.3	0.1101079	0.1101079	4765.61305
03713 Tunas, skipjack and Atlantic bonito, not minced	42,596.1	0.1011256	0.0925541	3942.4437
82179 Furniture of other materials (incl. bamboo)	42,433.9	0	0	0

TABLE 3.7 (continued)

	Exports 2001 (US$1000)	US MFN Tariff (average)	Tariff on Phil (average)	Expansion (US$1000)
88111 Photographic cameras	39,317.4	0.01775	0	0
42239 Coconut oil and its fractions, refined	38,837.9	0	0	0
77681 Piezo-electric crystals, mounted	38,445.1	0	0	0
89971 Articles made directly to shape from plaiting mat.	37,925.8	0.0483333	0.0246111	933.395656
77261 Boards, panels for electric distribution <1000 volts	36,606.2	0.027	0	0
06111 Cane sugar, raw	36,541	0.870787	0.870787	31819.4278
84589 Articles of apparel, women's or girls, n.e.s.	36,290	0.0972	0.0972	3527.388
76424 Headphones, earphones & combined microphone/speaker	33,771.2	0.0245	0	0
77315 Other elect. conductors, 80 volts <voltage< 1000 v	33,367	0.0236	0	0
76493 Parts & accessories of 761, 762, 7643, 7648	32,775.4	0.0217714	0.0108857	356.783172
77645 Hybrid integrated circuits	31,956	0	0	0
89477 Gloves, mittens & mitts, for use in sports	31,859	0.0281667	0	0
66491 Glass of headings 6643, 6644 or 6645, worked	31,569.1	0.067	0	0
84282 Nightdresses & pyjamas, for women	31,118.6	0.089	0.089	2769.5554
82139 Other furniture of metal	31,076.1	0	0	0

Total Expansion Value for All Exports: $212.4 million

Expansion as a Percentage of Total Included Exports: 3%

Notes: [1] Difference between MFN and Applied Tariffs regards existing preferential treatment offered by the US (e.g., GSP).
[2] For additional commodities, see Appendix Table 3.6.

TABLE 3.8
Thai Exports, U.S. Protection, and the Potential for Trade Expansion: Top 40 Products
(Ranked by Export Value)

Product	Exports 2001 (US$1000)	U.S. MFN Tariff (average)	Tariff on Thai (average)	Expansion (US$1000)
03611 Shrimps and prawns, frozen	799,810.1	0	0	0
89731 Articles of jewellery & parts, of precious metals	649,021.3	0.0628	0.0033333	2163.404
77641 Digital monolithic integrated circuits	530,565.7	0	0	0
03721 Crustaceans, prepared or preserved, n.e.s.	526,482.2	0.03	0	0
75997 Parts, accessories of the machines of group 752	309,631.3	0	0	0
84822 Rubber gloves	295,463.9	0.0566667	0.0466667	13788.32
84512 Babies' garments & clothing accessories, knitted	247,522.3	0.1841579	0.1841579	45583.18
77121 Static converters	233,668.7	0.006	0	0
83122 Satchels & simil., outer surface of plast. or text.	197,387.3	0.127	0.127	25068.19
77643 Non-digital monolithics integrated circuits	192,253.8	0	0	0
03713 Tunas, skipjack and Atlantic bonito, not minced	176,537.5	0.1011256	0.1011256	17852.46
85148 Footwear, n.e.s., with outer soles of leather	173,582.9	0.0743333	0.0743333	12903
76381 Video recording or reproducing apparatus	169,288.8	0.0035	0	0
74341 Fans with self-contained electr. motor, output<125w	162,552.4	0.047	0	0
82159 Other wooden furniture	148,056.1	0	0	0
66739 (semi-) precious stones, otherwise worked	140,689.6	0.035	0	0
83199 Other holsters, cases, bags & containers, n.e.s.	138,146.5	0.0922308	0.0830769	11476.79
77313 Ignit. wiring sets & the like used in vehicl., etc.	137,151.7	0.05	0.05	6857.585
75132 Electrostatic photo-copy. apparatus, indirect proc.	123,143.7	0.037	0.037	4556.317
76211 Radio, external source of power, vehicles, combined	122,067.2	0.01	0	0
77586 Ovens, cookers, cook. plates, boiling rings, roasters	119,543.3	0.0156667	0.0066667	796.9553
84551 Brassieres	117,282.2	0.13675	0.13675	16038.34
69743 Household articles & parts, n.e.s., of aluminum	107,192.4	0.031	0	0
76493 Parts & accessories of 761, 762, 7643, 7648	105,713.6	0.0217714	0.0108857	1150.768

TABLE 3.8 (continued)

	Exports 2001 (US$1000)	U.S. MFN Tariff (average)	Tariff on Thai (average)	Expansion (US$1000)
04231 Rice, semi-milled, wholly milled (excluding broken)	103,622.1	0.0738965	0.0178965	1854.473
23125 Technically specified natural rubber	100,692.9	0	0	0
66122 Portland cement	93,911.9	0	0	0
76419 Other telephonic or telegraphic apparatus	89,725.9	0	0	0
76383 Other sound reproducing apparatus	88,467.2	0.00925	0	0
89429 Toys, n.e.s.	82,794.6	0	0	0
84119 Coats, capes & similar of other materials, for men	82,250	0.1107999	0.1107999	9113.293
88541 Wrist watches, electrically powered	80,214.4	0	0	0
84371 Shirts, of cotton, knitted or crocheted, for men	78,879.9	0.201	0.201	15854.86
76411 Telephone sets	77,402.3	0	0	0
63541 Wooden frames for paintings, mirrors or similar	76,932.7	0.039	0	0
69741 Household articles & parts, n.e.s, of iron or steel	62,428.7	0.0269	0	0
84381 Underpants & briefs, knitted or crocheted, for men	59,913.3	0.07725	0.07725	4628.302
82116 Seats, n.e.s., with wooden frames	59,119.9	0	0	0
77884 Electric sound or visual signaling apparatus	57,515.7	0.0052	0	0
78439 Other parts & accessories of motor vehicles	54,901.7	0.0094444	0.0005556	30.50095

Total Expansion Value for All Included Exports: US$338 million

Expansion as a Percentage of Total Included Exports: 1.8%

Notes: [1] Difference between MFN and Applied Tariffs regards existing preferential treatment offered by the U.S. (e.g, GSP).

[2] For addtional commodities, see Appendix Table.

Analysis of Thai exports to the U.S. market also yields generally similar conclusions to those of the other ASEAN countries, with the exception of the fact that agricultural exports from Thailand to the U.S. market tend to be more important and, hence, there is more potential for trade expansion (Table 3.8). Given the greater degree of non-tariff barriers in agriculture (which will *not* be phased out in 2005 in the same way that the apparel, textiles, and clothing agreement will be[31]), the trade expansion in these static calculations may even be more promising in the case of Thailand.

Two of the top Thai exports to the United States were related to seafood, i.e., shrimps and prawns, which was the most important Thai export at US$800 million, and crustaceans (prepared or preserved), at US$526 million. These products had very low (or zero, in the case of the former) applied tariffs, and, hence, trade expansion is small. However, non-tariff barriers do exist, and the recent decision to place anti-dumping duties on Thai exports of shrimp to the United States in July 2004 suggest a much greater incentive for these sectors to advocate an FTA. Articles of jewellery (US$649 million) and digital integrated circuits (US$531 million) were number three and number four, respectively. The product line with the greatest potential for trade expansion (US$46 million) would be, once again, babies garments, mainly due to the relatively high tariff (18 per cent) in the U.S. market.

Table 3.9 underscores the relatively small amount of trade that Brunei does with the United States; total Brunei exports come to US$86 million, mainly because petroleum exports dominate Brunei's export regime and it exports very little in terms of energy-related projects to the United States. However, it is interesting to note that, since many of Brunei's exports fall in relatively protected areas in the U.S. markets (particularly textiles and clothing), the potential for trade expansion is actually quite high, at about 10 per cent of total exports (US$8 million).

Finally, low tariffs on electronics products in the United States ensure that trade expansion in the Singapore market will be small as well (Table 3.10). Twenty-five out of the top 40 products that Singapore exported to the United States faced zero tariffs in 2001. This is even more impressive if one recalls that Singapore does not benefit from the U.S. GSP programme. Singapore exports are also fairly concentrated; the top five Singaporean exports (parts and accessories of machines, digital integrated circuits, non-digital integrated circuits, "other" instruments for

TABLE 3.9
Brunei Exports, U.S. Protection, and the Potential for Trade Expansion: Top 40 Products
(Ranked by Export Value)

	Exports 2001 (US$1000)	U.S. MFN Tariff (average)	Tariff on Brunei (average)	Expansion (US$1000)
84371 Shirts, of cotton, knitted or crocheted, for men	18,600.6	0.201	0.201	3738.721
33542 Petroleum coke	17,220.2	0	0	0
84426 Trousers, bib & brace overalls, shorts, knitted, women	13,543.5	0.1525	0.1525	2065.384
33541 Petroleum bitumin, other residues; bitumin. mixtures	8,773.3	0	0	0
84512 Babies' garments & clothing accessories, knitted	5,286.1	0.1841579	0.1841579	973.4771
84324 Trousers, bib & brace overalls, shorts, knitted, men	5,149.3	0.1562107	0.1562107	804.3759
51127 Cumene	4,184.3	0	0	0
84599 Garments, knitted or crocheted, n.e.s.	2,982.6	0.1561428	0.1561428	465.7116
84489 Other night clothing or bodywear, knitted, women	2,058.4	0.0828	0.0828	170.4355
84483 Nightdresses & pyjamas, knitted or crocheted, women	1,764.8	0.0828	0.0828	146.1254
51122 Benzene, pure	1,591.1	0	0	0
84522 Men's garments of fabrics of 65732 through 65734	1,274.1	0.05675	0.05675	72.30518
51124 Xylenes, pure	988.6	0	0	0
84424 Dresses, knitted or crocheted, for women	750.7	0.1215	0.1215	91.21005
84591 Tracksuits	430.7	0.2086	0.2086	89.84402
84379 Shirts, of other textile materials, knitted, for men	308.7	0.142	0.142	43.8354
84169 Other vests, pyjamas & similar articles, for men	274.7	0.085625	0.085625	23.52118
84389 Other night clothing & bodywear, knitted, for men	274.7	0.092	0.092	25.2724
84382 Nightshirts & pyjamas, knitted or crocheted, men	214	0.089	0.089	19.046
84119 Coats, capes & similar of other materials, for men	194.1	0.1107999	0.1107999	21.50626
84425 Skirts & divided skirts, knitted, crochet, for women	193.1	0.1064286	0.1064286	20.55136
84511 Babies' garments & clothing accessor., not knitted	115.1	0.1550279	0.1550279	17.84371

TABLE 3.9 (continued)

	Exports 2001 (US$1000)	US MFN Tariff (average)	Tariff on Brunei (average)	Expansion (US$1000)
84162 Nightshirts & pyjamas, for men	71.7	0.089	0.089	6.3813
52239 Other inorganic oxygen compounds of non-metals	71	0.0185	0.0185	1.3135
84589 Articles of apparel, women's or girls, n.e.s.	69.3	0.0972	0.0972	6.73596
84482 Briefs & panties, knitted or crocheted, for women	67.5	0.1074	0.1074	7.2495
84151 Shirts of cotton, for men	60.6	0.145	0.145	8.787001
84159 Men's shirts of textile mater. other than cotton	30.3	0.1264022	0.1264022	3.829988

Total Expansion Value for All Included Exports: US$9 million
Expansion as a Percentage of Total Included Exports: 10 per cent

Notes: [1] Difference between MFN and Applied Tariffs regards existing preferential treatment offered by the U.S. (e.g., GSP).

TABLE 3.10

Singapore Exports, U.S. Protection, and Potential for Trade Expansion: Top 40 Products, 2001
(Ranked by Export Value)

Commodity		Exports (US$1000)	U.S. MFN Tariff	Trade Expansion
75997	Parts, accessories of the machines of group 752	214,4827.8	0	0
77641	Digital monolithic integrated circuits	1,307,038.6	0	0
77643	Non-digital monolithiques integrated circuits	347,783.2	0	0
87229	Other instruments, appli. for medical, etc., sciences	246,955.9	0	0
76281	Other radio receivers, combined with sound reprodu.	203,598.4	0.021	4275.566
76432	Transmission apparatus with reception apparatus	165,085.6	0	0
51577	Other heterocyclic comp. with nitrogen hetero-atom	130,652.9	0.0131	1711.553
51569	Heterocyclic compo. with ox. hetero-atom (s), n.e.s.	122,118.3	0.0313	3822.303
89219	Other books, brochures & simil., printed, excludingsheets	96,037.6	0	0
76493	Parts & accessories of 761, 762, 7643, 7648	95,010	0.0181714	1726.467
89961	Hearing aids	68,384.4	0	0
89969	Appliances, n.e.s., to compensate defect or disabil.	62,535.3	0	0
75124	Cash registers, incorporating a calculating device	62,042.4	0	0
79295	Other parts of aeroplanes or helicopters	61,712.5	0	0
89879	Recorded media, n.e.s.	59,346.9	0.003375	200.2958
87445	Other instruments & apparatus using optical radia.	51,871.6	0	0
77586	Ovens, cookers, cook. plates, boiling rings, roasters	51,638.7	0.0156667	809.0062
71491	Parts for turbo-jets or turbo-propellers	46,632.2	0	0
77637	Photosensitive semi-conductor devices; light emitt.	40,368.1	0	0
87425	Measuring or checking instruments, machines, n.e.s.	36,304.4	0.016125	585.4085
84426	Trousers, bib & brace overalls, shorts, knitted, women	36,213.6	0.1525	5522.574
76381	Video recording or reproducing apparatus	35,147.2	0.0035	123.0152
54131	Penicillins, deriv. with penicillan. acid structure	28,337.8	0	0

TABLE 3.10 (*continued*)

Commodity		Exports (US$1000)	U.S. MFN Tariff	Trade Expansion
87221	Syringes, catheters, needles, cannulae & the like	28,061	0	0
77258	Plugs & sockets, voltage < 1000 volts	26,076.5	0.0135	352.0327
77831	Starting equipm. for combustion engines; generators	25,081.1	0	0
87435	Instruments & apparatus for measuring the pressure	24,683.4	0	0
79319	Non-inflat. row. boats, vessels for pleasure, n.e.s.	22,061.6	0.0124	273.5638
78439	Other parts & accessories of motor vehicles	21,948.4	0.0094444	207.2905
88419	Optical fibres, bundles, cables; polarising material	21,703.6	0.0161429	350.3581
76483	Radar, radio-navigat. aid, -remote control apparatus	21,548.2	0	0
76211	Radio, external source of power, vehicles, combined	21,132	0.01	211.32
71899	Parts of headings 71449, 71891, 71892 & 71893	20,191.7	0	0
74315	Compressors of a kind used in refriger. equipment	18,048.6	0	0
77689	Parts of the articles of heading 7764	16,370.2	0	0
77645	Hybrid integrated circuits	15,989.5	0	0
89859	Prepared unrecorded media, n.e.s.	15,572.9	0	0
77121	Static converters	15,420.7	0	0
84151	Shirts of cotton, for men	14,686.1	0.145	2129.485
76383	Other sound reproducing apparatus	14,644.9	0.00925	135.4653
87456	Parts & accessoires for the instrument of 87455	14,149.4	0	0

Total Trade Expansion for ALL Included Products: US$44 million

Expansion as a Percentage of Total Exports: 0.7 per cent

medical and scientific purposes, and "other" radio receivers) constituted over 60 per cent of the included exports in the database. The top four exports faced zero tariffs in the U.S. markets. The largest increase in trade expansion is expected to come in the knitted trousers and shorts for women (SITC 84426), but this mainly due to the relatively high tariff in this sector (15 per cent) rather than the sheer value of exports, which came to only US$36 million in 2001. The "other" radio receivers sector, fifth in rankings in terms of exports, has a potential trade expansion of US$4.2 million, followed by cotton shirts for men, which once again is low on the export-rankings list (exports came to less than US$15 million) but relatively high in terms of trade expansion (US$2.1 million) due to the tariff regime (14.5 per cent). All in all, as in most of the EAI countries, Singaporean exports will not be affected much by *direct* tariff liberalization, though other aspects of the USSFTA could have major effects on economic integration with the United States.

Aggregating the value of trade expansion for all Indonesian, Malaysia, Philippine, Thai, Brunei and Singapore exports to the United States, we calculate a possible trade expansion of about US$300 million (3 per cent of total exports), US$179 million (1 per cent of total exports), US$212 million (3 per cent of total exports), US$340 million (3 per cent of total exports), US$8 million (10 per cent of total exports), and US$44 million (0.7 per cent of total exports), respectively. Hence, trade expansion in Thailand would be the greatest among the ASEAN countries in terms of value but Brunei would gain the most in terms of relative gains. While these values are not high in the aggregate, they are significant at the product level in many cases. Note, however, that this figure would be much larger if we had used higher trade elasticities and had included other trade-expanding aspects of FTAs discussed above. Indeed, out of the top 40 products for each of these countries, half or more than half faced zero tariffs in the U.S. market. This underscores the fact that the U.S. market is very open to ASEAN exports; however, this does not mean that the potential for trade expansion is limited. On the contrary, it could very well be that electronics, for example, will be a prime beneficiary of the bilateral FTAs, through the positive effect that they will have on FDI and other dynamic effects. The key role of U.S. FDI in the electronics sector in ASEAN is discussed in Chapter 2.

TABLE 3.11
U.S. Exports, Indonesian Protection, and Potential for Expansion:
Top 40 Products
(Ranked by Export Value)

Product	Exports (US$1000)	Indo Tariff (average, %)	Trade Expansion
08131 Oil-cakes of soya beans	166976.5	0	0
72399 Other parts for the machinery of 723 & 7443	78244.6	0	0
52372 Neutral sodium carbonate	57052.7	5	2852.635
72393 Parts for boring, sinking machinery of 72337, 72344	51564.9	0	0
77643 Non-digital monolithiques integrated circuits	36906.5	0	0
79295 Other parts of airplanes or helicopters	30025.6	0	0
76493 Parts & accessories of 761, 762, 7643, 7648	29603	0.7142857	211.45
59774 Lubricating preparations, excluding petroleum oils	28688.9	5	1434.445
08141 Flours, meals & pellets, meat, meat offal, non-edible	27175.7	0	0
26712 Artificial filament tow	23604.9	5	1180.245
72841 Machin. for assembling lamps, for hot working glass	19617.9	0	0
64211 Cartons, boxes & cases, of corrugated paper, paper.	18678.9	5	933.945
77641 Digital monolithic integrated circuits	18331.2	0	0
72849 Machinery having individual functions, n.e.s.	18225.2	2.777778	506.2556
25113 Waste of paper or paperboard, of mechanical pulp	17882	7.5	1341.15
61141 Other bovine, equine leathers, tanned or re-tanned	17745.7	0	0
59885 Other supported catalysts	17553.6	3.75	658.26
24752 Wood (excluding coniferous, tropical), rough, not treated	14932.1	0	0
59725 Additives for lubricating oils	14875.1	1.666667	247.91838
71499 Parts for the gas turbines of heading 71489	12835.3	0	0
08199 Preparations of a kind used for animal food, n.e.s.	12510.5	0	0
25151 Chemical wood pulp, coniferous, soda, sulph., bleached	12003.6	0	0
72322 Mechan. shovels, excavators, shovel-load. (360 deg.)	10652.4	10	1065.24
73721 Metal-rolling mills	10585.8	0	0
27826 Kaolin and other kaolinic clays, calcined or not	10485	5	524.25
08151 Residues of starch manufacture & similar residues	10328.7	3.333333	344.28997
75997 Parts, accessories of the machines of group 752	10327.2	0	0
76491 Parts & accessories for apparatus of heading 7641	9926.2	5	496.31
59889 Other catalysts and catalytic preparations	9683.9	5	484.195
78439 Other parts & accessories of motor vehicles	9680.8	15	1452.12
74291 Parts of the pumps of group 742	9282.5	0	0
76432 Transmission apparatus with reception apparatus	9187.5	3.333333	306.24997
25111 Waste of unbleached kraft paper or paperboard	8832.2	7.5	662.415
74411 Self-propelled trucks, electric., handling equipment	8784	5	439.2
74319 Other air or gas compressors	8596.6	0.8333333	71.63833
51131 Vinyl chloride (chloroethylene)	8535.6	5	426.78
74494 Parts of other machinery of heading 7448	8497.3	5	424.865
74414 Works trucks, elect., self-propel., no handling equi.	8486.9	15	1273.035
74412 Other self-propelled trucks, with handling equipm.	8473.9	5	423.695
02221 Milk, in solid form, of a fat content by weight<1, 5%	8416	5	420.8
09899 Other food preparations	8293.3	38	3151.454
59899 Other chemical products and preparations	8169.4	6.25	510.5875

TABLE 3.12
U.S. Exports, Malaysian Protection, and Potential for Expansion:
Top 40 Products (Ranked by Export Value)

Product	Exports (US$1000)	Mal Tariff (average, %)	Trade Expansion
77641 Digital monolithic integrated circuits	2784087	0	0
77643 Non-digital monolithiques integrated circuits	697854.4	0	0
75997 Parts, accessories of the machines of group 752	383547.5	0	0
77633 Transistors, dissipation rate > 1 w	155316.5	0	0
72849 Machinery having individual functions, n.e.s.	154634.8	0.8333333	1288.62328
87479 Parts & accessories for instr. & apparatus of 8747	149782.3	0	0
66399 Ceramic articles, n.e.s.	103544.1	5	5177.205
87478 Other apparatus for measuring electr. quantities	102113	0	0
72855 Parts, n.e.s., for 72348, 72721 & 72844 through 72849	91864.4	0	0
79295 Other parts of aeroplanes or helicopters	91558.5	0	0
71491 Parts for turbo-jets or turbo-propellers	85392.5	0	0
77689 Parts of the articles of heading 7764	83290.5	0	0
76493 Parts & accessories of 761, 762, 7643, 7648	77935.9	11.42857	8906.95889
77637 Photosensitive semi-conductor devices; light emitt.	57892.1	0	0
73114 Machine-tools operated by electro-chemical proces.	57091	0	0
77631 Diodes, not photosensiti. nor light emitting diodes	50065.3	0	0
77865 Ceramic dielectric fixed capacitors, multilayer	49568.9	0	0
89851 Magnetic discs	48847.1	0	0
77889 Electrical parts of machinery or apparatus, n.e.s.	47416.5	0	0
74174 Heat exchange units	46318.8	12.5	5789.85
76491 Parts & accessories for apparatus of heading 7641	44701.5	0	0
09899 Other food preparations	38975.2	12.08333	4709.50203
87425 Measuring or checking instruments, machines, n.e.s.	38443.7	0	0
05751 Grapes, fresh	36682	10	3668.2
77258 Plugs & sockets, voltage < 1000 volts	35303.8	17.5	6178.165
77688 Parts of the devices of 7763 & of item 77681	32813.6	0	0
89399 Other articles of plastics	31445.7	10	3144.57
77121 Static converters	30893.5	0	0
77639 Other semi-conductor devices	30362.2	0	0
08151 Residues of starch manufacture & similar residues	29116.2	0	0
77871 Particle accelerators	27671.4	0	0
28239 Ferrous waste and scrap, n.e.s.	26816.8	0	0
76492 Parts & accessories for apparatus of heading 7642	25949.7	0	0
76432 Transmission apparatus with reception apparatus	24857.9	20	4971.58
77649 Other electro. integrated circuits, micro-assemblies	23872.1	0	0
52372 Neutral sodium carbonate	20244.8	0	0
77632 Transistors, dissipation rate < 1 w	20165.5	0	0
68424 Aluminum plates, sheet & strip, thickness < 0, 20mm	19661	28.75	5652.5375
55421 Organic surface-active agents, retail sale or not	18693.2	0	0
77884 Electric sound or visual signaling apparatus	18666.2	0	0
64175 Kraft paper, coated with inorg. subs., blea., m2>150g	17906.3	0	0
25151 Chemical wood pulp, coniferous, soda, sulph., bleached	17461.2	0	0

TABLE 3.13
U.S. Exports, Philippines Protection, and Potential for Expansion:
Top 40 Products
(Ranked by Export Value)

Product	Exports (US$1000)	Phil Tariff (average%)	Trade Expansion
77641 Digital monolithic integrated circuits	3259659.3	1.5	48894.89
77643 Non-digital monolithic integrated circuits	834427.8	3	25032.834
08131 Oil-cakes of soya beans	138367.7	3	4151.031
75997 Parts, accessories of the machines of group 752	109462.7	0	0
77689 Parts of the articles of heading 7764	101514.3	0	0
77633 Transistors, dissipation rate > 1 w	82126.1	0	0
87478 Other apparatus for measuring electr. quantities	78530.9	2	1570.618
77632 Transistors, dissipation rate < 1 w	77510.4	0	0
87479 Parts & accessories for instr. & apparatus of 8747	71358.4	1.5	1070.376
77119 Other electric transformers	58792.1	6.5	3821.4865
77631 Diodes, not photosensiti. nor light emitting diodes	44556.7	0	0
69741 Household articles & parts, n.e.s., of iron or steel	43104.8	10	4310.48
79295 Other parts of airplanes or helicopters	37757.1	3	1132.713
89319 Articles for the conv., pack. of goods, n.e.s., plas.	37550.5	13	4881.565
72849 Machinery having individual functions, n.e.s.	34505.3	3	1035.159
76415 Telephonic or telegraphic switching apparatus	29112	0	0
04231 Rice, semi-milled, wholly milled (excluding broken)	28143.2	50	14071.6
77282 Other parts for apparatus of 7724, 7725 & 7726	27900.7	1.5	418.5105
77129 Parts of the electric power machinery of group 771	27031.4	3	810.942
64141 Kraft paper, uncoated, in rolls or sheets	25167.5	7	1761.725
77889 Electrical parts of machinery or apparatus, n.e.s.	22021.2	5	1101.06
88591 Watch cases & parts of watch cases	21719.8	3	651.594
87193 Other optical devices, appliances & instruments	21243.7	3	637.311
09899 Other food preparations	21194	5.222222	1106.7977
77259 Other apparatus for electrical circuits<1000 volts	20819.6	1.5	312.294
72855 Parts, n.e.s., for 72348, 72721 & 72844 through 72849	19749.1		0
06229 Other sugar confectionery	19465.5	8.5	1654.5675
76493 Parts & accessories of 761, 762, 7643, 7648	19344.3	1.833333	354.64544
76431 Transmission apparatus	18673.2	1.5	280.098
89219 Other books, brochures & simil., printed, excluding sheets	18149.4	4	725.976
05751 Grapes, fresh	17574.3	7	1230.201
89399 Other articles of plastics	17015.1	6.25	1063.4438
25151 Chemical wood pulp, coniferous, soda, sulph., bleached	16914.5	3	507.435
54139 Other antibiotics	16102.9	3	483.087
55141 Mixtures of odoriferous subst. for food industries	16017.4	3	480.522
77258 Plugs & sockets, voltage < 1000 volts	14161.9	2.5	354.0475
73513 Work-holders	13722.6	3	411.678
08199 Preparations of a kind used for animal food, n.e.s.	13383.8	12.25	1639.5155
87425 Measuring or checking instruments, machines, n.e.s.	13160.5	2.4	315.852
05661 Potatoes prepared or preserved (no vinegar), frozen	12807.3	7	896.511
59899 Other chemical products and preparations	12686.8	3	380.604
77688 Parts of the devices of 7763 & of item 77681	12639.7	0	0

Table 3.14
U.S. Exports, Thai Protection, and the Potential for Trade Expansion:
Top 40 Products
(Ranked by Export Value)

Product		Exports (US$1000)	Thai Tariff (average)	Trade Expansion
75997	Parts, accessories of the machines of group 752	317899.8	0	0
77631	Diodes, not photosensiti. nor light emitting diodes	165292.4	0	0
79295	Other parts of aeroplanes or helicopters	137780.1	5	6889.005
66491	Glass of headings 6643, 6644 or 6645, worked	122972.8	20	24594.56
78439	Other parts & accessories of motor vehicles	56521.1	42	23738.862
77633	Transistors, dissipation rate > 1 w	56410.9	0	0
74315	Compressors of a kind used in refriger. equipment	51687.9	20	10337.58
71499	Parts for the gas turbines of heading 71489	46503.9	3	1395.117
08131	Oil-cakes of soya beans	43946.3	6	2636.778
89731	Articles of jewellery & parts, of precious metals	38908	20	7781.6
66729	Diamonds (excludingindustrial), otherwise worked, not set	38707.2	0	0
72855	Parts, n.e.s., for 72348, 72721 & 72844 through 72849	36930.8	5	1846.54
59899	Other chemical products and preparations	35421.5	5	1771.075
51243	Other phenols et phenol-alcohols	35036.3	1.5	525.5445
77282	Other parts for apparatus of 7724, 7725 & 7726	33962.4	10	3396.24
33525	Oils, other products, n.e.s., from coal distillation	33569.6	1	335.696
72849	Machinery having individual functions, n.e.s.	31930.2	5	1596.51
68423	Aluminium plates, sheet & strip, thickness > 0, 20mm	28229.5	10	2822.95
72393	Parts for boring, sinking machinery of 72337, 72344	26821.3	5	1341.065
52372	Neutral sodium carbonate	22582.5	1	225.825
76493	Parts & accessories of 761, 762, 7643, 7648	22049.2	8.666667	1910.93074
08199	Preparations of a kind used for animal food, n.e.s.	21184.1	9.1	1927.7531
25151	Chemical wood pulp, coniferous, soda, sulph., bleached	20725.2	1	207.252
77259	Other apparatus for electrical circuits<1000 volts	19492	10	1949.2
76432	Transmission apparatus with reception apparatus	19344.1	0	0
87478	Other apparatus for measuring electr. quantities	17994.1	2	359.882
76491	Parts & accessories for apparatus of heading 7641	17843.6	3	535.308
87425	Measuring or checking instruments, machines, n.e.s.	17115.9	2.5	427.8975
77689	Parts of the articles of heading 7764	16595.8	0	0
74145	Other refrigerating, freezing equipment; heat pumps	16554.9	30	4966.47
77886	Battery carbons & other carbon articles, for elect.	16146.4	8.25	1332.078
08151	Residues of starch manufacture & similar residues	15021.1	9.1	1366.9201
54293	Medicaments, n.e.s., in forms for retail sale	14983.6	20	2996.72
25111	Waste of unbleached kraft paper or paperboard	14336.4	1	143.364
87229	Other instruments, appli. for medical, etc., sciences	13473.2	1	134.732
89399	Other articles of plastics	12983.4	30	3895.02
66739	(semi-) precious stones, otherwise worked	12921.1	0	0
54139	Other antibiotics	12714.9	1	127.149
55421	Organic surface-active agents, retail sale or not	12666.6	7	886.662
97101	Gold, non-monetary, unwrought, semi-manufactu., powder	12311.2	0	0

ii. U.S. Exports to ASEAN

Trade expansion analysis for the top 40 U.S. exports to the EAI can be found in Tables 3.11–3.14, and in Appendix Tables 3.9–3.12 for all U.S. exports (again, subject to the US$500,000 cut-off) to the ASEAN-4.[32] A first observation is that, although ASEAN countries do tend to have fairly low tariffs when compared to other developing countries, average tariffs in the Philippines, Thailand and Indonesia tend to be fairly high, especially in the case of the former. Malaysia, on the other hand, seems to be quite open even from the perspective of OECD countries: fully 32 out of the top 40 U.S. exports to Malaysia face zero duties, compared to 16 in the case of Indonesia, eight for Thailand, and only 7 for the Philippines. Of course, certain product lines in Malaysia do tend to be highly restricted (e.g., automobiles, in which tariffs can rise to 200 per cent and non-tariff barriers exist) and this would prevent major penetration in the protected areas, another reason why static projections are difficult to make (in terms of this methodology as well as CGE models, for that matter).

Hence, taking Malaysia first (Table 3.12), we note that while U.S. exports are large, trade expansion is low, due to the openness of the Malaysian market. Out of calculated exports of about US$11 billion, potential trade expansion comes to US$340 million, or a bit less than 2 per cent of total exports. Coupled with trade expansion estimates of only one per cent in the case of Malaysian exports to the United States, it is no wonder why the CGE estimates of a U.S.-Malaysia FTA were so low and gave the greater advantage to the United States (an estimated total gain of US$392 million and US$248 million to the United States and Malaysia, respectively). Again, in part this is a reflection of the static nature of this model as well as the downward biases inherent in the CGE model. The two most important U.S. exports to Malaysia, digital monolithic circuits (US$2.7 billion) and non-digital monolithic integrated circuits (US$700 million), comprise almost one-third of the total and each faces a zero tariff in Malaysia. The largest items for potential trade expansion are: parts and accessories (SITC 76493) at US$9 million, plugs and sockets (SITC 77258) at US$6.2 million, heat exchange units (SITC 74174) at US$5.8 million, and aluminum plates (SITC 68424) at US$5.7 million.

With respect to U.S. exports to Indonesia (Table 3.11), the top U.S. export is oil cakes of soya beans, reflecting the importance of U.S.

agricultural exports to Indonesia (as discussed in Chapter 2). But Indonesia applied zero tariffs to this category in 2001. The greatest potential for trade expansion is in another agricultural area, other food preparations (SITC 09899), which ranks 39th in terms of value but the high Indonesia tariff in this area (38 per cent) suggests the most room for trade expansion (US$3.1 million). Other products with considerable potential include: neutral sodium carbonate (US$2.9 million) and lubricating preparations (SITC 59774, US$1.4 million). Altogether, U.S. potential trade expansion comes to 3 per cent of total exports, approximately the same percentage as in the case of Indonesian exports to the United States.

Table 3.13 shows the top 40 U.S. exports to the Philippines. As was the case with exports to Malaysia, digital monolithic circuits and non-digital monolithic integrated circuits are the two most important export categories, coming to US$3.3 billion and US$834 million, respectively, about 60 per cent of all U.S. exports to the Philippines. Unlike the Malaysian case, however, the Philippine tariff is non-zero and potential trade expansion comes to US$49 million and US$29 million, respectively, given applied tariffs of 1.5 per cent and 3 per cent. This is about 40 per cent of our calculated total potential trade expansion (which, in turn, comes to 3 per cent of total U.S. exports to the Philippines). After these two, the potential for trade expansion drops off considerably, with articles for the packaging of goods (SITC 89319, US$4.8 million) and oilcakes of soybeans (US$4.2 million) being next in line.

U.S. exports to Thailand are actually quite different from those to the other ASEAN countries, as noted in Table 3.14. The top four exports are: parts and accessories of machines (SITC 75497, US$318 million), diodes (US$165 million), of airplane and helicopter parts (US$138 million), and glass headings (US$123 million). Combined these four account for 44 per cent of the top 40, suggesting that U.S. exports tend to be fairly concentrated, albeit less so than in the case of Malaysia. But, given that the two most important U.S. exports to Thailand faced zero tariffs, and number three only faced a five per cent tariff, the greatest potential for trade expansion were in the areas of glass, which faced a 20 per cent tariff and estimated trade potential of about US$25 million, and other parts and accessories of motor vehicles, which was only number five in terms of value rank (US$57 million) but together with its high 42 per cent tariff generates potential trade expansion of US$24 million.

Together these two commodities constitute 72 per cent of total trade expansion. As in the case of Malaysia, the relatively high tariffs on automobile production-related products will no doubt cause difficulties in the U.S.-Thai FTA negotiations.

D. EAI as a "Defensive Strategy": Trade Diversion Against ASEAN in the Regionalism Era

As a final point in this analysis of the economics of the EAI, we need to underscore ASEAN's exposure to trade diversion stemming from other PTAs negotiated by its major trading partners. Today, the costs associated with only adopting a multilateral commercial policy are obviously considered high, as no country is doing it anymore. *One reason for this is that Article XXIV of the GATT/WTO (allowing for FTAs and CUs under certain general conditions), which constitutes an exception to the principle of most-favoured nation treatment (MFN) enshrined in its Article I, works well if it is that: an exception, rather than the rule.* Once it becomes the rule, which it arguably already has, then MFN is no longer truly what it was meant to be. For example, approximately 80 per cent of EU trade takes place in the context of some PTA; for countries that do not have PTAs with the EU, e.g., the United States and ASEAN, trade certainly is not "most favoured".

There is evidence that ASEAN countries have been hurt in the past by trade diversion due to integration in the EU and in certain sectors under NAFTA.[33] Given the major increase in PTAs over the past few years, ASEAN does risk being disadvantaged in some of its most important markets and potential markets. And, as we discussed above, this is not merely a question of trade but also investment diversion, which in many ways is even more serious.

An example might illustrate the point. As we noted at length in Chapter 2, China has become a major competitor with ASEAN countries on international markets, a trend which appears to be intensifying over time. What would happen if China were to negotiate an FTA with its major markets? Lee et al. (forthcoming) uses a CGE model to estimate the effects of various Chinese commercial policy initiatives, including (1) an FTA with ASEAN; and (2) an FTA with Japan and the United States.[34] They calculate fairly large gains for ASEAN (US$34.8 billion, or an increase of 2.5 per cent of GDP) in the case of a China-ASEAN FTA, such as the one being currently negotiated with a goal of completion in 2010. However, a China-Japan-U.S. agreement would lead to a US$16.5 billion loss to ASEAN, or –1.6 per cent of GDP. Since Lee et al. exclude entirely any dynamic effects, this loss is probably an underestimate.

A second example would be Lee and van der Mensbrugghe (2004), who estimate the potential economic effects of the Fifth Enlargement of the EU in May 2004 on Asia, using a similar CGE model.[35] They estimate that the Fifth Enlargement will have a small but negative impact on ASEAN, to the tune of US$810 million to US$1.05 billion.

Hence, as discussed above, one incentive for a proactive approach to PTAs by ASEAN, either as a group or individually, is to be defensive: that is, in some ways to reclaim MFN and ensure that it will not be disadvantaged in the future.

IV. Summary of the Economics of the EAI

Below we highlight several of the key points from this chapter:

A. Introduction

1. The global economy is undergoing tremendous change, presenting challenges and opportunities to ASEAN and the United States.

2. One major feature of the new international trading system is the dramatic increase in the number and scope of preferential trading agreements (PTAs). The United States has recently been a very active participant in this process. ASEAN itself is a reflection of the new regionalism (e.g., AFTA) and ASEAN members have established or are negotiating FTAs with a number of non-partner countries and country groupings.

B. Main Points from the Theoretical Review

1. Free-trade areas and other forms of formal regional economic integration are "second-best" policies, that is, they have a positive effect (trade creation), which is also evident in non-discriminatory liberalization, but also a negative effect (trade diversion), which stems from the discrimination inherent in an FTA. These "static" or price-effects of PTAs have been the focus of the theoretical and empirical literature regarding PTAs.

2. However, studies have shown that the "dynamic" effects of PTAs (e.g., effects on FDI, efficiency, and economies of scale) are far more significant than the static effects, which constitute merely one price "shock" (i.e., the reduction of tariff and non-tariff barriers is a one-time event). Moreover, it is exactly these dynamic effects of regionalism that ASEAN and other developing countries find particularly attractive in PTAs.

3. But the effects of PTAs on overall policy formation are likely to be the most significant of all. If, for example, an FTA has the effect of creating a more inward-looking approach to economic development, regionalism would, indeed be a "stumbling bloc" to international trade. We argue, however, that there are reasons to believe that in the ASEAN context the implications of arrangements like the EAI actually reinforce policy reform by fostering greater policy efficiency, transparency, and the adoption of "best practices".

4. Moreover, closer macroeconomic and microeconomic cooperation between the ASEAN countries and between the United States and ASEAN through the EAI could have salutary implications for macroeconomic and financial stability, technology transfer and FDI, harmonization issues, and key political economy-related areas.

5. In fact, we argue that for PTAs to be effective, they have to be outward-oriented. This "qualitative dependency" can go a long way in reconciling the pro- and anti-regionalism camps, as well as underscoring the need to anticipate structural adjustments and balance short-run adjustment costs. It would appear that all parties in the EAI have an interest in keeping the agreement open and liberal, as was the case with the U.S.-Singapore FTA.

C. Highlights of the Quantitative Estimates of the Economic Effects of the EAI

1. We first develop a large econometric gravity model to assess closely the determinants of the U.S.-ASEAN economic relationship and whether or not the relationship is "special". We find that, indeed, the U.S.-ASEAN relationship is special in the sense that the ASEAN binary variable is statistically significant, relatively large in magnitude (e.g., compared to comparable EU regressions) and has a tendency to rise over time.

2. However, in separating out individual ASEAN member-states, this special relationship does not really materialize in the case of Indonesia (except in a few years); exists to some degree in the case of Malaysia but appears to be declining over time and with a good deal of volatility; and is most notable in the cases of the Philippines, Singapore, and Thailand, but, again, the significance decreases over time.

3. The results are difficult to explain, but certainly the PTAs that the United States has negotiated since the early 1980s have not helped. This effect is particularly evident in the EU case, which has long had a "pyramid" of regional preferences. We argue that a series of bilateral FTAs under the rubric of the EAI could remove any related biases (i.e., it might be used as a defensive strategy), and could actually help the EAI countries gain a competitive edge over key rivals such as China.

4. We summarize the results from the Glibert CGE model, which is explicitly designed to estimate the effects of U.S. bilateral FTAs with ASEAN countries. The aggregate effects tend to be small, with the GDP of the Philippines, Indonesia, Malaysia and Thailand rising by 3.1 per cent, 2.75 per cent, 0.46 per cent, and 0.72 per cent, respectively. The effects on the U.S. economy, given its size, are trivial. At least in relative terms, the ASEAN partner gains more than the United States in the case of every FTA, suggesting one reason why the United States will seek more than just market access in the EAI FTA negotiations (as they have in other bilaterals).

5. Despite the small overall effects of the bilateral FTAs, there are some very large effects at the sectoral level. Moreover, the factors of production that gain the most in ASEAN would be unskilled labour, and unskilled labour in the United States also gains in all cases (though marginally).

6. We stress that these fairly unimpressive results in the aggregate are the product of a strong downward-bias in the model. As this GTAP-based CGE model does not include the dynamic effects that U.S.-ASEAN FTA accords would produce, it misses what would likely be the most important economic effects of the agreement (and the very motivation for ASEAN's wishing to negotiate FTAs with the United States). Moreover, we stress that the policy reforms

that would have to take place in the context of EAI FTAs would be salutary to the economic development prospects of the region, an effect which of course, is also excluded from the CGE model.

7. In order to understand what the political economy of the EAI negotiations will entail, as well as to consider the potential benefits to the private sector, we note that it is critical to engage in as disaggregated trade analysis as possible. Businesspeople are interested in what the potential gains will be for their particular product, and policy-makers need to identify where potential problems and opportunities exist. Hence, we devise a disaggregated approach to "matching" 5-digit SITC commodities (up to a maximum of approximately 3,000 products) to protection applied export markets, and then assume a price elasticity parameter (of unity, as a rule-of-thumb) which allows us to project potential increases in trade at this highly disaggregated level. We do this both for exports from the EAI to the United States and for exports of the United States to the EAI. We find that such analysis is enlightening with respect to the key product groups that will be the major players in the EAI negotiations. Analysis of many of these sectors is taken up in Chapter 4.

8. Finally, we consider the EAI as a defensive strategy for the ASEAN countries. While the intellectual debate regarding whether or not PTAs constitute "building blocs" or "stumbling blocs" is not settled, it is an irrefutable reality that PTAs have recently been driving international commercial policy of late, rather than multilateral initiatives. *Regionalism has become the rule, rather than a special exception granted in Article XXIV of the WTO/GATT. Hence, in order for ASEAN to redeem its "MFN" status, it may have little choice but to join the regionalism bandwagon.*

9. For ASEAN, the decision to negotiate bilateral FTAs with the United States is complicated by the fact that the United States and its other key export markets are negotiating FTAs with its competitors. In this sense, it is losing MFN status in these markets. This serves as a powerful additional incentive to participate in the EAI. We summarize the results of a few CGE models showing how ASEAN would be negatively affected by an FTA between China and other markets as well as the Fifth Enlargement of the EU.

Notes

[1] An agreement as to the framework for the Doha negotiations was reached on 31 July 2004. However, it could easily take years before an actual accord will be negotiated.

[2] The EU is changing its current system of preferential arrangements with former colonies by establishing a series of FTAs under the "Coutonou Agreements". Its negotiations with MERCOSUR have been once again put on hold (March 2005).

[3] This subsection draws partially from Kreinin and Plummer (2002).

[4] Of course, it is possible for the partner country to have intra-regional and global comparative advantage in a certain product. But if this is the case, the home country would have been importing the product from that country before the union as well, meaning that there would be no trade diversion.

[5] This category is called "X-Efficiency" in the economics literature, both to differentiate it from allocative efficiency and to emphasize that it is a general concept (hence the "X").

[6] This term is from Lipsey (1981).

[7] In considering investment diversion at the firm level, we need to point out the underlying assumptions that: (1) there exists financing constraints; and (2) the investing company only requires one plant. Otherwise, there would be no investment diversion, only investment creation. In the example above, Kia motors would build plants both in China *and* Indonesia.

[8] What we mean here is that as ASEAN cooperation deepens, markets begin to view it as one entity. Besides, business cycles in the ASEAN countries have become more correlated (see., for example, Bayoumi and Eichengreen (1999) and Kim, Kose, and Plummer (2003).

[9] There are some regional organizations used to promote macroeconomic cooperation, such as under SEACEN, a group of Southeast Asian central banks, and under the auspices of the Asian Development Bank.

[10] See Sandhu and Siddique (1992), for a series of reflections on the political and economic evolution of ASEAN economic integration.

[11] Modern international trade theory suggests that *per capita* income between countries is correlated positively with trade.

[12] In order to exploit data on bilateral flows for as many countries as possible over as long as possible in order to construct our "benchmark" and tests for U.S.-EAI regional relationships, our primary data source is that constructed by Andrew Rose and available from his website as part of research for the article, "Do We Really Know that the WTO increases Trade?, " recently published in the *American Economic Review* (March 2004). The database is available at http://faculty.haas.berkeley.edu/arose/RecRes.htm#GATTWTO.

13 As Rose explains regarding his sources, the trade data come from the Direction of Trade Statistics CD-ROM data (IMF). Population and real GDP data (in constant American dollars) are obtained from the Penn World Table, the World Bank's *World Development Indicators*, and the IMF's *International Financial Statistics*. Rose uses the CIA's *World Factbook* for a number of country-specific variables, including: latitude and longitude, land area, landlocked and island status, physically contiguous neighbours, language, colonizers, and dates of independence. He also adds information on whether pairs of countries were involved in a currency union and from the WTO to create his indicator of regional trade agreements.

14 See Appendix Table 2.3 for details.

15 Some more advanced developing countries have been "graduated" from the GSP, e.g., the United States no longer grants GSP treatment to Malaysia.

16 For students of econometrics, we include a series of sensitivity tests regarding our unrestricted model in Appendix Table 3.1.

17 While 1996 was not technically a Crisis year, ASEAN export growth generally fell that year, in fact falling from double-digit rates in the late-1980s and early-1990s to less than one per cent in 1996 in the case of Thailand.

18 It will be useful to re-run this exercise through 2003 once data become available, as AFTA became effective in 2003 and most of the liberalization was "back loaded", that is, undertaken the last few years of AFTA.

19 For an early literature survey, see Shoven and Whalley (1984). Kreinin and Plummer (2002) give a more updated review.

20 This is true, for example, in the case of the Global Trade Analysis Project (GTAP) under the direction of Thomas Hertel at Purdue University. See Hertel (1997).

21 The functional forms of the economic agents include Leontief, CES, Cobb-Douglas, and LES production functions, depending on the model.

22 The "externalities" of economic openness, for example, have been extremely important in the case of developing Asian countries, as has been noted extensively in the economic literature (see, for example, Sachs and Warner 1995, World Bank 1993, and Dollar 1992).

23 In the interests of space, we do not review the results for Singapore, as: (1) the USSFTA is already in effect; and (2) the numbers are extremely small. The interested reader can refer to the original work for a summary of the results.

24 Equivalent variation proxies how much in financial terms by essentially calculating how much better off the country is after the FTA relative to before the agreement.

25 The lower the initial tariffs, the smaller will be the effects in such models, holding everything else constant. For example, if neither the United States

nor Malaysia had any pre-existing tariffs, the effects would be exactly zero. This was mainly the case with Singapore.

[26] We are unable to also include NTBs, as information is insufficiently detailed and quantitative estimates of their effects on price are very difficult. We also leave out anti-dumping duties and other administered actions. This poses a problem for agriculture exports of the EAI to the United States, though one might argue that the other area most affected in the U.S. market, textiles and clothing, will see its NTBs abolished in 2005 under its Uruguay Round commitments.

[27] We also make the implicit assumption that the exporting country will be able to supply additional products to the target market at no additional costs, i.e., we assume that the export supply curve is flat (infinitely elastic).

[28] As is noted in Chapter 4, Singapore tariffs are zero in every category except beverages, and Brunei tariffs are zero on most goods as well. Also, U.S. exports to Brunei are extremely small in value. Hence, the *direct* effect of trade liberalization on U.S. exports using this technique would be effectively zero.

[29] While a 100-commodity cut-off is arbitrary, we use it as a means of keeping the tables manageable. A full list of exports and trade expansion are available from the authors upon request.

[30] Of course, as we discuss in Chapter 3, one reason that it is not an important export to the United States is because the high level of protection in the U.S. market.

[31] In the WTO agreement reached in Geneva at the end of July 2004, which created a framework within which the Doha negotiations will take place, liberalization of agriculture was a main theme, including phasing out of export subsidies and lowering of various non-tariff barriers as well. It is not clear exactly how much liberalization will ultimately take place in agriculture, but it is certain that some non-tariff barriers will continue to exist, unlike in textiles and clothing.

[32] As was noted before, we do not include U.S. exports to Brunei or Singapore due to the fact that U.S. exports to the former are extremely small and face very low tariffs, and Singapore is essentially a free trade country.

[33] See Kreinin and Plummer (2002) for a survey of the literature in this regard and *ex post* estimates of the effects of the Single Market Program in the EU and NAFTA on ASEAN exports.

[34] Hiro Lee and Dominique van der Mensbrugghe (2004), with special reference to Table 3, p. 852.

[35] This differs slightly from the "ASEAN dummy" developed by Rose, where trade is flagged between two ASEAN members after 1992, with membership for Indonesia, Thailand, Philippines, Singapore, Malaysia in 1993, Burma and Laos in 1997, and Cambodia, Vietnam in 1998.

References

DeRosa, Dean. U.S. Free Trade Agreements with ASEAN. Washington D.C.: IIE, 23 April, 2003, mimeo.

Dollar, David. "Outward-oriented Developing Countries Really do Grow More Rapidly: Evidence from 95 LDCs". *Economic Development and Cultural Change*, 1992, pp. 523–44.

Frankel, Jeffrey, 1997. *Regional Trading Agreements in the World Economic System*. Washington, D.C.: Institute for International Economics.

Frankel, Jeffrey A. "Is Japan Creating a Yen Block in East Asia and the Pacific?", NBER Working Paper No. 4050, April 1992.

Hertel, Thomas W., ed. *Global Trade Analysis: Modeling and Appreciations*. Cambridge: Cambridge University Press.

Gilbert, John. "CGE Simulations of U.S. Bilateral Free Trade Agreements", mimeo, Washington, D.C.: IIE.

Holland, Tom, 1994. "Lessons from the Fall". *Far Eastern Economic Review*, 20 May 1994, p. 38.

Kim, Sunghyun H., M. Ayhan Kose and Michael G. Plummer. "Understanding the Asian Contagion". *Asian Economic Journal* 15, no. 2 (August 2001) pp. 111–38.

—————. "Dynamics of Business Cycles in Asia: Differences and Similarities". *Review of Development Economics* 7, no. 3 (August 2003).

Kreinin, Mordechai E. and Michael G. Plummer. "Effects of Regional Integration on DFI: An Empirical Approach", Paper presented at the American Economic Assocation meeting, Washington, D.C., 4 January 2003.

—————. *Economic Integration and Development: Has Regionalism Delivered for Developing Countries?* London: Edward Elgar, 2002.

Krugman, Paul. "Is Bilateralism Bad?" In Paul Krugman. *International Trade and Policy*, edited by Elhanan Helpman and Paul Krugman. Cambridge: MIT Press, 1991.

Lee, Hiro, David Roland-Holst, and Dominique van der Mensbrugghe. "China's Emergence and East Asian Trade under Alternative Trading Arrangements". *Journal of Asian Economics*, Table 1, forthcoming.

Lee, Hiro and Dominique van der Mensbrugghe, 2004. "EU Enlargement and Its Impact on East Asia". *Journal of Asian Economics* 14, no. 6 (2004): 843–60, with special reference to Table 3, p. 852.

Lipsey, Richard. "The Theory of Customs Unions: A General Survey." In *International Trade: Selected Readings*, edited by J. Bhagwati. Cambridge: MIT Press, 1981, p. 281.

McCleery, Robert. "An Intertemporal, Linked Macroeconomic CGE Model of the United States and Mexico Focusing on Demographic Change and Factor Flows", In *Economy Wide Modelling of the Economic Implications of a*

FTA with Mexico and a NAFTA with Canada and Mexico. Washington, D.C.: USITC, 1992.

Messerlin, Patrick. *The Costs of Protection in the EU*. Washington, D.C.: Institute for International Economics, 2001.

Petri, Peter. "East Asian Trade Integration: An Analytical History". In *Regionalism and Rivalry: Japan and the United States in Pacific Asia*, edited by Jeffrey Frankel and Miles Kahler. Chicago: University of Chicago Press, 1993.

Pissarides, Christopher A. "Learning by Trading and the Returns to Human Capital in Developing Countries". *World Bank Economic Review* 11 (January 1997): 17–32.

Rose, Andrew. "Do We Really Know that the WTO Increases Trade?" *American Economic Review* (March 2004).

Sachs, Jeffrey D. and Andrew Warner. "Economic Reform and the Process of Global Integration". Brookings Papers on Economic Activity 1 (1995): 1–95.

Safadi, Raed and Sam Laird. "The Uruguay Round Agreements: Impact on Developing Countries". *World Development* 24, no. 7 (1996): 1223–42.

Sandhu, Kernial and Sharon Siddique. *The ASEAN Reader*. Singapore: ISEAS, 1992.

Scollay, Robert and John P. Gilbert. *New Regional Trading Arrangements in the Asia Pacific?* Washington, D.C., Institute for International Economics, 2002.

Shoven, John and John Whalley. "Applied General Equilibrium Models of Taxation and International Trade: An Introduction and Survey". *Journal of Economic Literature* 22 no. 3 (September 1994): 1007–51.

Viner, Jacob. *The Customs Union Issue*. New York: Carnegie Endowment for International Peace, 1950.

World Bank. *East Asian Miracle: Economic Growth and Public Policy*. Washington, D.C.: IBRD, 1993.

Appendix Tables

APPENDIX TABLE 3.1
Sensitivity Tests of the Unrestricted Model

	Without Year Effects	Random Effects (GLS) Estimator	Fixed Effects (Within) Estimator	Weighted Least Squares
Both in ASEAN	0.969 (3.72)**	0.308 (2.02)*	0.297 (1.93)	0.901 (3.83)**
One in ASEAN	0.160 (2.84)**	0.699 (29.87)**	0.807 (34.16)**	0.731 (13.11)**
GSP	0.427 (13.68)**	0.049 (4.37)**	0.123 (10.82)**	0.831 (25.85)**
Log of Distance	−1.185 (50.70)**	−1.360 (48.45)**	0.000 (.)	−1.176 (53.83)**
Log of Product of Real GDPs	0.864 (86.77)**	0.405 (61.24)**	0.240 (30.26)**	0.920 (97.87)**
Log of Product of Real GDPs per capita	0.316 (20.71)**	0.236 (24.26)**	0.367 (31.49)**	0.323 (22.75)**
Strict Currency Union	1.582 (12.18)**	0.727 (15.18)**	0.684 (14.12)**	1.561 (12.81)**
Common Language	0.536 (12.62)**	0.237 (4.57)**	0.000 (.)	0.539 (13.79)**
Land Border	0.470 (4.58)**	0.675 (4.68)**	0.000 (.)	0.488 (4.52)**
Landlocked	−0.464 (13.24)**	−0.886 (23.45)**	0.000 (.)	−0.284 (8.97)**
Islands	0.061 (1.48)	−0.027 (0.57)	0.000 (.)	0.071 (1.93)
Log of Product of Land Areas	−0.047 (5.42)**	0.184 (22.50)**	0.000 (.)	−0.107 (13.39)**
Same Nation/Perennial Colonies	2.211 (2.21)*	4.867 (3.28)**	0.000 (.)	1.738 (1.66)
Constant	−25.751 (67.67)**	−7.123 (24.20)**	−7.371 (32.17)**	−27.299 (75.90)**
Observations	234597	234597	234597	234597
R-squared	0.58		0.11	0.65
Number of Unique Country-Pair Identifier		12150	12150	

Robust t statistics in parentheses
* significant at 5%; ** significant at 1%

APPENDIX TABLE 3.2
Additional Tests for Regional Effects

Region	Both In ASEAN	T Score	One In ASEAN	T Score
Southeast Asia	0	.	0.26	1.12
East Asia	0.31	1.29	0.27	3.12
Sub-Saharan Africa	0	.	0.92	6.07
Mediterranean, North Africa	0	.	1.26	5.78
Latin America	0	.	1.14	10.15
High Income	1.81	5.99	0.85	12.82
Middle Income	0.77	2.79	0.84	13.87
Low Income	0.3	0.95	0.65	7.02
Least Developed Countries	-0.24	-0.5	0.5	3.36

APPENDIX TABLE 3.3
Sample Sensitivity Analysis

Perturbation	Both in ASEAN	T Score	One In ASEAN	T Score
No Poorest Quartile GDP p/c	0.94	3.66	0.82	14.95
No Smallest Quartile of GDP	1.07	4.57	0.7	11.99
Without Outliers (3sd)	0.89	3.73	0.73	12.9
Trade with Canada only	0	.	0.98	4.14
Trade with US only	0	.	1.22	4.12
Trade with Britain only	0	.	0.79	3.08
Trade with France only	0	.	1.14	3.96
Trade with Italy only	0	.	0.58	2.4
Trade with Germany only	0	.	0.99	4.04
Trade with Japan only	0	.	1.34	5.7

APPENDIX TABLE 3.4
Notes on Dataset for Global Trade Gravity Model:

We make no fundamental changes to Rose's data set but nine additional dummy variables were added for:

1) A binary variable whereby one trade partner is an ASEAN Member ("one in"), limited by entry date. Where Indonesia, Malaysia Philippines, Thailand, Singapore are defined to enter in 1992 (as the effective date of trade barrier reductions; each officially entered in 1967 but no trade policies were in place), Vietnam in 1995, Burma and Laos in 1997, and Cambodia in 1999.[38]
2) Both trade partners are ASEAN members, limited by entry date ("both in").
3) One partner in an original ASEAN country, as defined by Indonesia, Malaysia Philippines, Thailand, and Singapore, regardless of year
4) One partner in an original ASEAN country or Vietnam, regardless of year
5) One partner is an ASEAN country, defined by Indonesia, Malaysia Philippines, Thailand, and Singapore, Vietnam, Burma, Laos, and Cambodia, regardless of year
6) Both partners are ASEAN countries, regardless of year
7) One partner is an EU 15 Member, where membership is defined by entrance for Belgium, France, Germany, Italy, Luxembourg and the Netherlands in 1957, Britain, Denmark and Ireland in 1973, Greece in 1981, Portugal and Spain in 1986, Austria, Finland and Sweden in 1995
8) One partner is an EU 15 country, regardless of year.
9) Both partners are EU 15 countries, regardless of year.

The Rose data set has trade information for the following periods relevant to this analysis (all other dates are missing):
1) Brunei: No trade information is provided
2) Burma 1950–97
3) Cambodia 1998–99
4) Indonesia 1960–99
5) Laos 1982–99
6) Malaysia 1966–99
7) Philippines 1948–99
8) Thailand 1950–99
9) Singapore 1958–99
10) Vietnam 1998–99

Indonesian Exports, U.S. Protection, and Potential for Expansion
Top 100 Products, 2001
(Ranked by Export Value)

Product	Exports 2001 (US$1000)	U.S. MFN Tariff (average)	Tariff on Indon (average)	Expansion (US$1000)
76381 Video recording or reproducing apparatus	588,254.7	0.0035	0	0
85148 Footwear, n.e.s., with outer soles of leather	419,353.1	0.0743333	0.0743333	31171.91
23125 Technically specified natural rubber	310,743	0	0	0
75997 Parts, accessories of the machines of group 752	206,470.7	0	0	0
85132 Other footwear, outer soles & uppers of rubber, pla.	203,452.6	0.2683257	0.2683257	54591.56
82159 Other wooden furniture	196,244.9	0	0	0
63431 Plywood, sheets of wood, ply of tropi. or non-conif.	182,181.5	0.0611	0.056	10202.16
84151 Shirts of cotton, for men	145,200.4	0.145	0.145	21054.06
03611 Shrimps and prawns, frozen	143,649.9	0	0	0
83199 Other holsters, cases, bags & containers, n.e.s.	139,643.2	0.0922308	0.0830769	11601.13
76289 Other radio-broadcast receivers, non-combined	135,062.2	0.03	0	0
76211 Radio, external source of power, vehicles, combined	134,524.2	0.01	0	0
77641 Digital monolithic integrated circuits	110,505.2	0	0	0
82155 Furniture, of wood, of a kind used in the bedroom	108,317.7	0	0	0
84551 Brassieres	104,837.7	0.13675	0.13675	14336.56
64248 Papers & paperboard, for graphic purposes	102,881.5	0.007	0	0
03721 Crustaceans, prepared or preserved, n.e.s.	96,740.3	0.03	0	082116
Seats, n.e.s., with wooden frames	96,200.4	0	0	0
89422 Dolls representing only human beings	88,633.8	0	0	0
84512 Babies' garments & clothing accessories, knitted	74,864	0.1841579	0.1841579	13786.8
84811 Articles of apparel, of leather	71,146.2	0.0535	0.03	2134.386
84119 Coats, capes & similar of other materials, for men	69,709.8	0.1107999	0.1107999	7723.84
88411 Contact lenses	65,054.8	0.02	0.02	1301.096
07511 Pepper, neither crushed nor ground	59,633.4	0	0	0

APPENDIX TABLE 3.5 *(continued)*

Product	Exports 2001 (US$1000)	U.S. MFN Tariff (average)	Tariff on Indon (average)	Expansion (US$1000)
77643 Non-digital monolithiques integrated circuits	58,427.6	0	0	0
84511 Babies' garments & clothing accessor., not knitted	58,146.6	0.1550279	0.1550279	9014.343
85125 Tennis shoes, training shoes & the like, rubber, pla.	55,102	0.3465983	0.3465983	19098.26
89731 Articles of jewellery & parts, of precious metals	53,149	0.0628	0	0
77811 Primary cells & primary batteries	52,835.7	0.027	0	0
78439 Other parts & accessories of motor vehicles	52,273.7	0.0094444	0.0005556	29.04095
07111 Coffee, not roasted, not decaffeinated	51,969.2	0	0	0
89477 Gloves, mittens & mitts, for use in sports	49,980.9	0.0281667	0	0
77313 Ignit. wiring sets & the like used in vehicl., etc.	45,957.7	0.05	0	0
84219 Wind-jackets, anoraks & similar articles, for women	45,898.1	0.1101079	0.1101079	5053.744
57433 Polyethylene terephthalate	45,604.9	0.080576	0	0
89995 Wigs, false beards & simi.; art. of human hair, n.e.s.	44,135.3	0	0	0
69741 Household articles & parts, n.e.s, of iron or steel	42,136.9	0.0269	0	0
84822 Rubber gloves	41,046.9	0.0566667	0.0466667	1915.522
77261 Boards, panels for electric distribution<1000 volts	38,602.1	0.027	0	0
84589 Articles of apparel, women's or girls, n.e.s.	38,134.8	0.0972	0.0972	3706.702
03713 Tunas, skipjack and Atlantic bonito, not minced	37,044.3	0.1011256	0.0925541	3428.604
76411 Telephone sets	36,559.3	0	0	0
76383 Other sound reproducing apparatus	36,156.8	0.00925	0	0
88111 Photographic cameras	35,286.3	0.01775	0	0
32121 Bituminous coal, not agglomerated	35,182.4	0	0	0
63539 Other builders' joinery & carpentry of wood	33,937.6	0.016	0	0
63599 Other articles of wood	33,801.5	0.0314288	0.0177859	601.1911
84161 Underpants & briefs, for men	31,036.7	0.0716667	0.0716667	2224.297
84324 Trousers, bib & brace overalls, shorts, knitted, men	30,499.3	0.1562107	0.1562107	4764.318
84371 Shirts, of cotton, knitted or crocheted, for men	30,320.8	0.201	0.201	6094.481

APPENDIX TABLE 3.5 (continued)

Product	Exports 2001 (US$1000)	U.S. MFN Tariff (average)	Tariff on Indon (average)	Expansion (US$1000)
07521 Vanilla	29,526.7	0	0	0
64157 Other paper & paperboard, uncoated, weight<150g/m²	29,113.2	0.0048333	0	0
85123 Other sports footwear, uppers of rubbers or plast.	29,015.8	0.1568215	0.1568215	4550.301
69743 Household articles & parts, n.e.s., of aluminium	28,879.3	0.031	0	0
89825 Keyboard instruments, sound electrically amplified	26,867	0.054	0	0
66613 Household & toilet articles of other ceramics	26,776.9	0.0891	0.0391	1046.977
84282 Nightdresses & pyjamas, for women	26,375.8	0.089	0.089	2347.446
83112 Handbags, with outer surface of plastics or textile	26,164.8	0.1015714	0.0895714	2343.618
05893 Pineapples, prepared or preserved, n.e.s.	25,835.2	0.006215	0.006215	160.5658
05674 Mushrooms & truffles prepared with no vinegar	25,356.3	0.058897	0.058897	1493.41
55132 Other essential oils	24,532.9	0.0078889	0	0
89826 Musical instruments, n.e.s., elec. amplified sound	23,660.7	0.05	0	0
76221 Radio, without external source of power, combined	23,497.1	0	0	0
76281 Other radio receivers, combined with sound reprodu.	23,471.5	0.021	0.0185	434.2227
82179 Furniture of other materials (incl. bamboo)	23,227.4	0	0	0
65221 Woven cotton fabrics>85%cotton, unb., weight<200g/m²	22,721.5	0.0875455	0.0875455	1989.164
88417 Spectacle lenses of other materials	20,941.2	0.02	0	0
52261 Ammonia, anhydrous or in aqueous solution	20,669.3	0	0	0
82113 Seats of cane, osier, bamboo or similar materials	20,595.2	0	0	0
74149 Parts of refrigerating or freezing equipment	20,337.7	0	0	0
84379 Shirts, of other textile materials, knitted, for men	20,254.4	0.142	0.142	2876.125
51211 Methanol (methyl alcohol)	19,846.9	0.046	0	0
76422 Loudspeakers, mounted in their enclosures	19,633.7	0.049	0	0
89971 Articles made directly to shape from plaiting mat.	18,345.7	0.0483333	0.0246111	451.5081
84564 Swimwear, women's & girls', knitted or crocheted	18,100.7	0.194	0.194	3511.536

APPENDIX TABLE 3.5 *(continued)*

Product	Exports 2001 (US$1000)	U.S. MFN Tariff (average)	Tariff on Indon (average)	Expansion (US$1000)
84483 Nightdresses & pyjamas, knitted or crocheted, women	17,697.1	0.0828	0.0828	1465.32
63541 Wooden frames for paintings, mirrors or similar	17,617.5	0.039	0	0
68711 Tin, not alloyed	17,535.3			0
66245 Glazed ceramic flags & paving, tiles; mosaic cubes	17,518.4	0.123	0.0905	1585.415
63549 Wood marquetry & inlaid wood; wooden arti., excluding 82	17,420.7	0.0214	0	0
84221 Suits, for women	17,232	0.161881	0.161881	2789.533
65813 Sacks & bags, of man-made textile materials	17,215.3	0.087	0.087	1497.731
84561 Swimwear, men's & boys', not knitted or crocheted	17,016.1	0.137	0.137	2331.206
89425 Toys representing non-humane creatures	16,097.3			0
77243 Other automatic circuit breakers, voltage > 1000 v	16,043.9	0.02	0	0
03423 Tunas, skipjack, bonito, frozen	15,608.1			0
84426 Trousers, bib & brace overalls, shorts, knitted, women	15,265.3	0.1525	0.1525	2327.958
56216 Urea, whether or not in aqueous solution)	15,102.8			0
77121 Static converters	14,901.8	0.006	0	0
42231 Coconut oil, crude	14,705.6			0
89813 Pianos; harpsichord; keyboard stringed instruments	14,622.9	0.043	0	0
89311 Sacks & bags (incl. cones), of plastics	14,485.9	0.03	0	0
64214 Other sacks & bags	14,472.6	0.016	0	0
76493 Parts & accessories of 761, 762, 7643, 7648	14,328.5	0.0217714	0.0108857	155.976
89941 Umbrellas & sun umbrellas	14,324.2	0.049	0	0
77253 Other apparatus for protecting electrical circuits	14,137.5	0.027	0	0
84159 Men's shirts of textile mater. other than cotton	13,973.2	0.1264022	0.1264022	1766.244
65842 Bed linen, not knitted nor crocheted, of cotton	13,834.9	0.121875	0.121875	1686.128
66611 Tableware & kitchen ware of porcelain or china	13,619.1	0.1350833	0.0536667	730.8917
84289 Other vests, night clothing, bodywear, women, n.e.s.	13,594.1	0.0851429	0.0851429	1157.441

APPENDIX TABLE 3.6

Malaysia Exports, U.S. Protection, and Potential for Expansion

Top 100 Products, 2001

(Ranked by Export Value)

Product	Exports 2001 (US$1000)	U.S. MFN Tariff (average)	Tariff on Malay (average)	Expansion (US$1000)
77641 Digital monolithic integrated circuits	3,408,248.9	0	0	0
75997 Parts, accessories of the machines of group 752	2,478,967.7	0	0	0
76432 Transmission apparatus with reception apparatus	1,098,085.7	0	0	0
76381 Video recording or reproducing apparatus	945,374.7	0.0035	0.0035	3308.811
77643 Non-digital monolithiques integrated circuits	611,069	0	0	0
84822 Rubber gloves	447,353.3	0.0566667	0.0566667	25350.02
76411 Telephone sets	310,190.5	0	0	0
76281 Other radio receivers, combined with sound reprod.	298,854	0.021	0.021	6275.934
76211 Radio, external source of power, vehicles, combined	186,365.9	0.01	0.01	1863.659
76289 Other radio-broad-cast receivers, non-combined	181,153.8	0.03	0.03	5434.614
77633 Transistors, dissipation rate > 1 w	170,438.2	0	0	0
82159 Other wooden furniture	163,805.7	0	0	0
76383 Other sound reproducing apparatus	159,363.3	0.00925	0.00925	1474.111
76431 Transmission apparatus	157,232	0.012	0.012	1886.784
76419 Other telephonic or telegraphic apparatus	154,787.2	0	0	0
82116 Seats, n.e.s., with wooden frames	120,042.8	0	0	0
76493 Parts & accessories of 761, 762, 7643, 7648	117,709.6	0.0217714	0.0217714	2562.706
77637 Photosensitive semi-conductor devices; light emitt.	111,409.8	0	0	0
84151 Shirts of cotton, for men	104,472	0.145	0.145	15148.44
77631 Diodes, not photosensiti. nor light emitting diodes	94,415.8	0	0	0
89429 Toys, n.e.s.	93,288.3	0	0	0
77121 Static converters	90,217.6	0.006	0.006	541.3056
77586 Ovens, cookers, cook. plates, boiling rings, roasters	85,287	0.0156667	0.0156667	1336.163
76491 Parts & accessories for apparatus of heading 7641	85,030.5	0	0	0

Product	Exports 2001 (US$1000)	U.S. MFN Tariff (average)	Tariff on Malay (average)	Expansion (US$1000)
76221 Radio, without external source of power, combined	82,691.4	0	0	0
51616 Acycl., cyclan., cyclen., cyclo., arom ethers; derivat.	80,178.3	0.0589286	0.0589286	4724.792
63431 Plywood, sheets of wood, ply of tropi. or non-conif.	77,708.6	0.0611	0.0611	4747.995
88111 Photographic cameras	74,025.6	0.01775	0.01775	1313.954
84512 Babies' garments & clothing accessories, knitted	73,582.6	0.1841579	0.1841579	13550.82
76282 Other radio receivers, combined with a clock	70,579.4	0.015	0.015	1058.691
76422 Loudspeakers, mounted in their enclosures	66,579.2	0.049	0.049	3262.381
77632 Transistors, dissipation rate < 1 w	65,662.4	0	0	0
76384 Sound recording apparatus	63,808.2	0	0	0
42249 Palm kernel, babassu oil & their fractions, refined	54,356.6	0	0	0
51217 Fatty alcohols, industrial	54,123.6	0.0316667	0.0316667	1713.914
75121 Electronic without external source of power	53,757.6	0	0	0
77261 Boards, panels for electric distribution<1000 volts	46,576	0.027	0.027	1257.552
42229 Palm oil and its fractions, refined	45,538	0	0	0
87477 Other instrum. & apparatus for telecommunications	45,367.5	0	0	0
51222 Glycerol (glycerine), glycerol waters & lyes	44,883.6	0.0025555	0.0025555	114.7
77878 Other electrical machines, having indivi. functions	42,273.7	0.0183636	0.0183636	776.2988
87479 Parts & accessories for instr. & apparatus of 8747	40,433.1	0.011	0.011	444.7641
84119 Coats, capes & similar of other materials, for men	38,495.1	0.1107999	0.1107999	4265.254
87478 Other apparatus for measuring electr. quantities	37,016.5	0.0113333	0.0113333	419.5204
82155 Furniture, of wood, of a kind used in the bedroom	36,558.8	0	0	0
77645 Hybrid integrated circuits	35,520.8	0	0	0
84371 Shirts, of cotton, knitted or crocheted, for men	35,234.9	0.201	0.201	7082.215
23125 Technically specified natural rubber	34,908.5	0	0	0
84426 Trousers, bib & brace overalls, shorts, knitted, women	34,494	0.1525	0.1525	5260.335
56216 Urea (whether or not in aqueous solution)	34,184.9	0	0	0

APPENDIX TABLE 3.6 (continued)

Product	Exports 2001 (US$1000)	U.S. MFN Tariff (average)	Tariff on Malay (average)	Expansion (US$1000)
77884 Electric sound or visual signalling apparatus	32,996.2	0.0052	0.0052	171.5802
66491 Glass of headings 6643, 6644 or 6645, worked	30,608.3	0.067	0.067	2050.756
89825 Keyboard instruments, sound electrically amplified	29,827.5	0.054	0.054	1610.685
69979 Articles of aluminium, n.e.s.	29,463.5	0.0166667	0.0166667	491.0583
74151 Air cond. mach., window or wall type, self-cont.	28,501.6	0	0	0
89594 Typewriter or similar ribbons, inked or prepared	28,026.7	0.039	0.039	1093.041
63532 Doors & their frames & thresholds, of wood	26,054	0.048	0.048	1250.592
84691 Gloves, knitted, coated, etc., with plastics or rubber	25,662.2	0.1207	0.1207	3097.427
82153 Furniture, of wood, of a kind used in the kitchen	25,338.4	0	0	0
89471 Articles for fishing sport; shooting requis., n.e.s.	24,248.2	0.0586693	0.0586693	1422.624
43131 Fatty acids; acid oils from refining	23,756.3	0.0444272	0.0444272	1055.426
77258 Plugs & sockets, voltage < 1000 volts	23,382.9	0.0135	0.0135	315.6692
89431 Video games of a kind used with televis. receiver	23,162.5	0	0	0
87221 Syringes, catheters, needles, cannulae & the like	21,871.5	0	0	0
84324 Trousers, bib & brace overalls, shorts, knitted, men	21,509.2	0.1562107	0.1562107	3359.968
77689 Parts of the articles of heading 7764	21,293.2	0	0	0
89851 Magnetic discs	21,198.2	0	0	0
84821 Articles of apparel & clothing access., of plastics	21,054.5	0.028	0.028	589.526
77315 Other elect. conductors, 80 volts <voltage< 1000 v	20,665.8	0.0236	0.0236	487.7129
87461 Thermostats	19,095	0.017	0.017	324.615
77681 Piezo-electric crystals, mounted	18,944.9	0	0	0
66613 Household & toilet articles of other ceramics	18,828.1	0.0891	0.0891	1677.584
76423 Loudspeakers, not mounted in their enclosures	17,545.3	0.0245	0.0245	429.8598
67621 Bar & rolls, iron, non-alloy steel, hot-rol., deforma.	17,511.5	0.015	0.015	262.6725
77811 Primary cells & primary batteries	16,845.3	0.027	0.027	454.8231
79319 Non-inflat. row. boats, vessels for pleasure, n.e.s.	16,661.2	0.0124	0.0124	206.5989

APPENDIX TABLE 3.6 *(continued)*

Product	Exports 2001 (US$1000)	U.S. MFN Tariff (average)	Tariff on Malay (average)	Expansion (US$1000)
87319 Parts & accessories of gas, liquid, electric. meters	15,596.3	0.032	0.032	499.0816
75122 Other calculating machines	15,504.2	0	0	0
63599 Other articles of wood	15,375.2	0.0314288	0.0314288	483.2239
63441 Other plywood, > one ply of non-coniferous wood	15,037.5	0.032	0.032	481.2
76483 Radar, radio-navigat. aid, -remote control apparatus	15,034.4	0.0163333	0.0163333	245.5618
03611 Shrimps and prawns, frozen	14,668.8	0	0	0
77129 Parts of the electric power machinery of group 771	14,518.7	0.0096	0.0096	139.3795
77863 Aluminium electrolytic fixed capacitors	14,442.2	0	0	0
81315 Electric lamps & lighting fittings, n.e.s.	14,167.1	0.0486667	0.0486667	689.4655
89311 Sacks & bags (incl. cones), of plastics	13,836.2	0.03	0.03	415.086
84424 Dresses, knitted or crocheted, for women	13,724.7	0.1215	0.1215	1667.551
76421 Microphones & stands	13,690.6	0.0245	0.0245	335.4197
74315 Compressors of a kind used in refriger. equipment	13,610	0	0	0
75124 Cash registers, incorporating a calculating device	13,579.8	0	0	0
75993 Parts, accessori. of the machines of sub-group 7519	13,469.8	0.0038	0.0038	51.18524
77812 Electric accumulators	13,371.4	0.0223846	0.0223846	299.3137
88541 Wrist watches, electrically powered	13,321.1	0	0	0
51376 Palmytic acid, stearic acid, their salts & esters	13,205.1	0.05	0.05	660.255
77232 Other fixed resistors	12,966.6	0	0	0
87475 Other apparatus for measuring electr., without rec.	12,945.9	0.017	0.017	220.0803
77235 Other variable resistors	12,888.6	0	0	0
69911 Padlocks & locks, of base metal; clasps, frames; keys	12,810.7	0.0426154	0.0426154	545.9329
59899 Other chemical products and preparations	12,295.1	0.0484868	0.0484868	596.1497
76424 Headphones, earphones & combined microphone/speaker	12,150.7	0.0245	0.0245	297.6921

Philippine Exports, U.S. Protection, and Potential for Expansion
Top 100 Products, 2001
(Ranked by Export Value)

Product	Exports 2001 (US$1000)	U.S. MFN Tariff (average)	Tariff on Phil (average)	Expansion (US$1000)
77641 Digital monolithic integrated circuits	2,413,508	0	0	0
77643 Non-digital monolithiques integrated circuits	855,309.8	0	0	0
75997 Parts, accessories of the machines of group 752	412,575.5	0	0	0
77313 Ignit. wiring sets & the like used in vehicl., etc.	288,219.3	0.05	0	0
77121 Static converters	222,464.6	0.006	0	0
83199 Other holsters, cases, bags & containers, n.e.s.	183,800.8	0.0922308	0.0830769	15269.60068
88541 Wrist watches, electrically powered	124,613.9	0	0	0
76431 Transmission apparatus	103,489.2	0.012	0.0045	465.7014
84151 Shirts of cotton, for men	100,841.4	0.145	0.145	14622.003
42231 Coconut oil, crude	99,113.5	0	0	0
83122 Satchels & simil., outer surface of plast. or text.	95,143.6	0.127	0.127	12083.2372
84512 Babies' garments & clothing accessories, knitted	88,994.9	0.1841579	0.1841579	16389.11389
76432 Transmission apparatus with reception apparatus	86,830.7	0	0	0
05893 Pineapples, prepared or preserved, n.e.s.	82,372.1	0.006215	0.006215	511.9426015
84511 Babies' garments & clothing accessor., not knitted	79,139.1	0.1550279	0.1550279	12268.76848
82159 Other wooden furniture	78,184.6	0	0	0
77633 Transistors, dissipation rate > 1 w	75,553.4	0	0	0
84371 Shirts, of cotton, knitted or crocheted, for men	64,321.3	0.201	0.201	12928.5813
77637 Photosensitive semi-conductor devices; light emitt.	62,715	0	0	0
84119 Coats, capes & similar of other materials, for men	58,443.2	0.1107999	0.1107999	6475.500716
84551 Brassieres	52,066.3	0.13675	0.13675	7120.066525
05991 Pineapple juice	47,371.2	0.0671335	0.0671335	3180.194455
84219 Wind-jackets, anoraks & similar articles, for women	43,281.3	0.1101079	0.1101079	4765.613052
03713 Tunas, skipjack and Atlantic bonito, not minced	42,596.1	0.1011256	0.0925541	3942.443699
82179 Furniture of other materials (incl. bamboo)	42,433.9	0	0	0

APPENDIX TABLE 3.7 (continued)

Product	Exports 2001 (US$1000)	U.S. MFN Tariff (average)	Tariff on Phil (average)	Expansion (US$1000)
88111 Photographic cameras	39,317.4	0.01775	0	0
42239 Coconut oil and its fractions, refined	38,837.9	0	0	0
77681 Piezo-electric crystals, mounted	38,445.1	0	0	0
89971 Articles made directly to shape from plaiting mat.	37,925.8	0.0483333	0.0246111	933.3956564
77261 Boards, panels for electric distribution<1000 volts	36,606.2	0.027	0	0
06111 Cane sugar, raw	36,541	0.870787	0.870787	31819.42777
84589 Articles of apparel, women's or girls, n.e.s.	36,290	0.0972	0.0972	3527.388
76424 Headphones, earphones & combined microphone/speaker	33,771.2	0.0245	0	0
77315 Other elect. conductors, 80 volts <voltage< 1000 v	33,367	0.0236	0	0
76493 Parts & accessories of 761, 762, 7643, 7648	32,775.4	0.0217714	0.0108857	356.7831718
77645 Hybrid integrated circuits	31,956	0	0	0
89477 Gloves, mittens & mitts, for use in sports	31,859	0.0281667	0	0
66491 Glass of headings 6643, 6644 or 6645, worked	31,569.1	0.067	0	0
84282 Nightdresses & pyjamas, for women	31,118.6	0.089	0.089	2769.5554
82139 Other furniture of metal	31,076.1	0	0	0
84221 Suits, for women	29,804	0.161881	0.161881	4824.701324
76381 Video recording or reproducing apparatus	29,332.1	0.0035	0	0
84426 Trousers, bib & brace overalls, shorts, knitted, women	28,427	0.1525	0.1525	4335.1175
05771 Coconuts	27,322	0	0	0
77884 Electric sound or visual signallimg apparatus	26,608.1	0.0052	0	0
82113 Seats of cane, osier, bamboo or similar materials	26,123.1	0	0	0
79295 Other parts of aeroplanes or helicopters	26,079.2	0	0	0
84424 Dresses, knitted or crocheted, for women	25,634.4	0.1215	0.1215	3114.5796
77632 Transistors, dissipation rate < 1 w	24,587.9	0	0	0
84483 Nightdresses & pyjamas, knitted or crocheted, women	22,348.4	0.0828	0.0828	1850.44752
78439 Other parts & accessories of motor vehicles	22,329.3	0.0094444	0.0005556	12.40615908

APPENDIX TABLE 3.7 (continued)

Product	Exports 2001 (US$1000)	U.S. MFN Tariff (average)	Tariff on Phil (average)	Expansion (US$1000)
87465 Other regulating or controlling instr. & apparatus	21,282.5	0.01525		0
84843 Hats & other headgear, of other textile fabric	20,997.6	0.0907398	0.0820125	1722.06567
88417 Spectacle lenses of other materials	20,173.8	0.02	0	0
89445 Other articles for christmas festivities	20,092	0	0	0
84482 Briefs & panties, knitted or crocheted, for women	19,710.2	0.1074	0.1074	2116.87548
03721 Crustaceans, prepared or preserved, n.e.s.	19,444.6	0.03	0	0
82155 Furniture, of wood, of a kind used in the bedroom	18,226.4	0	0	0
77878 Other electrical machines, having indivi. functions	17,870.6	0.0183636	0	0
03611 Shrimps and prawns, frozen	16,505.7	0	0	0
84692 Other gloves, mittens & mitts, knitted or crocheted	16,382.5	0.0970849	0.0914007	1497.371968
84289 Other vests, night clothing, bodywear, women, n.e.s.	16,334.7	0.0851429	0.0851429	1390.783729
77258 Plugs & sockets, voltage < 1000 volts	16,012.3	0.0135	0	0
84159 Men's shirts of textiles other than cotton	15,883.8	0.1264022	0.1264022	2007.747264
76622 Radio, without external source of power, non-combin.	15,414.8	0.015	0	0
77631 Diodes, not photosensiti. nor light emitting diodes	15,229.1	0	0	0
03637 Cuttlefish, octopus and squid, frozen, dried, salted	14,953.1	0	0	0
84324 Trousers, bib & brace overalls, shorts, knitted, men	14,459.5	0.1562107	0.1562107	2258.728617
77834 Electrical lighting or signalling equipment, vehic.	14,384.2	0.0181429	0	0
89399 Other articles of plastics	14,280	0.04516	0.00876	125.0928
29296 Mucilage and thickeners, from vegetable products	14,133.4	0.0106667	0.0106667	150.7567378
28929 Waste and scrap of precious metal, n.e.s.	13,961.6	0	0	0
81315 Electric lamps & lighting fittings, n.e.s.	13,928.3	0.0486667	0	0
84379 Shirts, of other textile materials, knitted, for men	13,614.9	0.142	0.142	1933.3158
84812 Gloves, mitts, not designed for sports, of leather	13,538.8	0.133	0.133	1800.6604
03414 Tunas, skipjack or striped bonito, fresh or chilled	13,177.4	0	0	0
84629 Other hosiery	13,041.2	0.1099091	0.1099091	1433.346555

APPENDIX TABLE 3.7 (continued)

Product	Exports 2001 (US$1000)	U.S. MFN Tariff (average)	Tariff on Phil (average)	Expansion (US$1000)
05897 Mixtures of fruits, parts of plants, prepared, n.e.s.	12,533.4	0.1025	0.1025	1284.6735
84524 Garments, knitted, croc., of fabrics of 65732 a 65734	12,148.9	0.0605	0.0605	735.00845
81317 Non-electrical lamps & lighting fittings	11,981.5	0.0486667	0	0
82116 Seats, n.e.s., with wooden frames	11,929.2	0	0	0
84211 Coats, raincoats, capes & similar articl., for women	11,838.7	0.1101955	0.1101955	1304.571466
87191 Telescopic sight for 7, 87, 881, 884, 8996	11,836	0.072	0	0
89479 Sport goods, n.e.s.	11,514.2	0.0220952	0.0013333	15.35188286
63549 Wood marquetry & inlaid wood; wooden arti., excluding 82	11,458.9	0.0214	0	0
68211 Unrefined copper; anodes for electrolytic refining	11,274.9	0	0	0
65842 Bed linen, not knitted nor crocheted, of cotton	10,971.2	0.121875	0.121875	1337.115
59864 Activated carbons	10,926.9	0.048	0	0
65315 Other woven fabrics>85% filam. of textured polyest	10,842.6	0.2031555	0.2031555	2202.733824
63532 Doors & their frames & thresholds, of wood	10,836.3	0.048	0	0
66629 Ornamental articles, of other ceramics	10,717.5	0.015	0	0
84489 Other night clothing or bopdywear, knitted, women	10,506.8	0.0828	0.0828	869.96304
85148 Footwear, n.e.s., with outer soles of leather	10,245.1	0.0743333	0.0743333	761.5520918
77649 Other electro. integrated circuits, microassemblies	10,047.2	0	0	0
77689 Parts of the articles of heading 7764	9,794.3	0	0	0
84169 Other vests, pyjamas & similar articles, for men	9,654.5	0.085625	0.085625	826.6665625
82117 Seats, n.e.s., with metal frames	9,379.6	0	0	0
65751 Twine, cordage, rope and cables	9,328.5	0.0536078	0.0427953	399.2159561
84161 Underpants & briefs, for men	9,319.5	0.0716667	0.0716667	667.8978107
84599 Garments, knitted or crocheted, n.e.s.	9,225.3	0.1561428	0.1561428	1440.464173

APPENDIX TABLE 3.8
Brunei Exports, U.S. Protection, and Potential for Expansion
Top 100 Products, 2001
(Ranked by Export Value)

Product	Exports 2001 (US$1000)	U.S. MFN Tariff (average)	Tariff on Brunei (average)	Expansion (US$1000)
84371 Shirts, of cotton, knitted or crocheted, for men	18,600.6	0.201	0.201	3738.721
33542 Petroleum coke	17,220.2	0	0	0
84426 Trousers, bib & brace overalls, shorts, knitted, women	13,543.5	0.1525	0.1525	2065.384
33541 Petroleum bitumen, other residues; bitumin. mixtures	8,773.3	0	0	0
84512 Babies' garments & clothing accessories, knitted	5,286.1	0.1841579	0.1841579	973.4771
84324 Trousers, bib & brace overalls, shorts, knitted, men	5,149.3	0.1562107	0.1562107	804.3759
51127 Cumene	4,184.3	0	0	0
84599 Garments, knitted or crocheted, n.e.s.	2,982.6	0.1561428	0.1561428	465.7116
84489 Other night clothing or bopdywear, knitted, women	2,058.4	0.0828	0.0828	170.4355
84483 Nightdresses & pyjamas, knitted or crocheted, women	1,764.8	0.0828	0.0828	146.1254
51122 Benzene, pure	1,591.1	0	0	0
84522 Men's garments of fabrics of 65732 through 65734	1,274.1	0.05675	0.05675	72.30518
51124 Xylenes, pure	988.6	0	0	0
84424 Dresses, knitted or crocheted, for women	750.7	0.1215	0.1215	91.21005
84591 Track suits	430.7	0.2086	0.2086	89.84402
84379 Shirts, of other textile materials, knitted, for men	308.7	0.142	0.142	43.8354
84169 Other vests, pyjamas & similar articles, for men	274.7	0.085625	0.085625	23.52118
84389 Other night clothing & bodywear, knitted, for men	274.7	0.092	0.092	25.2724
84382 Nightshirts & pyjamas, knitted or crocheted, men	214	0.089	0.089	19.046
84119 Coats, capes & similar of other materials, for men	194.1	0.1107999	0.1107999	21.50626
84425 Skirts & divided skirts, knitted, crochet, for women	193.1	0.1064286	0.1064286	20.55136
84511 Babies' garments & clothing accessor., not knitted	115.1	0.1550279	0.1550279	17.84371
84162 Nightshirts & pyjamas, for men	71.7	0.089	0.089	6.3813
52239 Other inorganic oxygen compounds of non-metals	71	0.0185	0.0185	1.3135
84589 Articles of apparel, women's or girls, n.e.s.	69.3	0.0972	0.0972	6.73596
84482 Brief & panties, knitted or crocheted, for women	67.5	0.1074	0.1074	7.2495
84151 Shirts of cotton, for men	60.6	0.145	0.145	8.787001
84159 Men's shirts of textiles other than cotton	30.3	0.1264022	0.1264022	3.829988

APPENDIX TABLE 3.9
Thai Exports, U.S. Protection, and Potential for Expansion
Top 100 Products, 2001
(Ranked by Export Value)

Product	Exports 2001 (US$1000)	U.S. MFN Tariff (average)	Tariff on Thai (average)	Expansion (US$1000)
03611 Shrimps and prawns, frozen	799,810.1	0	0	0
89731 Articles of jewellery & parts, of precious metals	649,021.3	0.0628	0.0033333	2163.404
77641 Digital monolithic integrated circuits	530,565.7	0	0	0
03721 Crustaceans, prepared or preserved, n.e.s.	526,482.2	0.03	0	0
75997 Parts, accessories of the machines of group 752	309,631.3	0	0	0
84822 Rubber gloves	295,463.9	0.0566667	0.0466667	13788.32
84512 Babies' garments & clothing accessories, knitted	247,522.3	0.1841579	0.1841579	45583.18
77121 Static converters	233,668.7	0.006	0	0
83122 Satchels & simil., outer surface of plast. or text.	197,387.3	0.127	0.127	25068.19
77643 Non-digital monolithiques integrated circuits	192,253.8	0	0	0
03713 Tunas, skipjack and Atlantic bonito, not minced	176,537.5	0.1011256	0.1011256	17852.46
85148 Footwear, n.e.s., with outer soles of leather	173,582.9	0.0743333	0.0743333	12903
76381 Video recording or reproducing apparatus	169,288.8	0.0035	0	0
74341 Fans with self-contained electr. motor, output<125w	162,552.4	0.047	0	0
82159 Other wooden furniture	148,056.1	0	0	0
66739 (semi-) precious stones, otherwise worked	140,689.6	0.035	0	0
83199 Other holsters, cases, bags & containers, n.e.s.	138,146.5	0.0922308	0.0830769	11476.79
77313 Ignit. wiring sets & the like used in vehicl., etc.	137,151.7	0.05	0.05	6857.585
75132 Electrostatic photocopy. apparatus, indirect proc.	123,143.7	0.037	0.037	4556.317
76211 Radio, external source of power, vehicles, combined	122,067.2	0.01	0	0
77586 Ovens, cookers, cook. plates, boiling rings, roasters	119,543.3	0.0156667	0.0066667	796.9553
84551 Brassieres	117,282.2	0.13675	0.13675	16038.34
69743 Household articles & parts, n.e.s., of aluminium	107,192.4	0.031	0	0
76493 Parts & accessories of 761, 762, 7643, 7648	105713.6	0.0217714	0.0108857	1150.768

APPENDIX TABLE 3.9 *(continued)*

Product	Exports 2001 (US$1000)	U.S. MFN Tariff (average)	Tariff on Thai (average)	Expansion (US$1000)
04231 Rice, semi-milled, wholly milled (excluding broken)	103,622.1	0.0738965	0.0178965	1854.473
23125 Technically specified natural rubber	100,692.9	0	0	0
66122 Portland cement	93,911.9	0	0	0
76419 Other telephonic or telegraphic apparatus	89,725.9	0	0	0
76383 Other sound reproducing apparatus	88,467.2	0.00925	0	0
89429 Toys, n.e.s.	82,794.6	0	0	0
84119 Coats, capes & similar of other materials, for men	82,250	0.1107999	0.1107999	9113.293
88541 Wrist watches, electrically powered	80,214.4	0	0	0
84371 Shirts, of cotton, knitted or crocheted, for men	78,879.9	0.201	0.201	15854.86
76411 Telephone sets	77,402.3	0	0	0
63541 Wooden frames for paintings, mirrors or similar	76,932.7	0.039	0	0
69741 Household articles & parts, n.e.s, of iron or steel	62,428.7	0.0269	0	0
84381 Underpants & briefs, knitted or crocheted, for men	59,913.3	0.07725	0.07725	4628.302
82116 Seats, n.e.s., with wooden frames	59,119.9	0	0	0
77884 Electric sound or visual signalling apparatus	57,515.7	0.0052	0	0
78439 Other parts & accessories of motor vehicles	54,901.7	0.0094444	0.0005556	30.50095
23121 Smoked sheets of rubber	49,821.6	0	0	0
74151 Air condit. machi., window or wall type, self-cont.	47,054.4	0	0	0
76432 Transmission apparatus with reception apparatus	46,802.8	0	0	0
89475 Golf equipment	45,750	0.031	0	0
84511 Babies' garments & clothing accessor., not knitted	45,562.1	0.1550279	0.1550279	7063.395
05893 Pineapples, prepared or preserved, n.e.s.	44,616.1	0.006215	0.006215	277.2891
85132 Other footwear, outer soles & uppers of rubber, pla.	42,652.3	0.2683257	0.2683257	11444.71
66491 Glass of headings 6643, 6644 or 6645, worked	42,554.9	0.067	0	0
85125 Tennis shoes, training shoes & the like, rubber, pla.	39,632.6	0.3465983	0.3465983	13736.59
88111 Photographic cameras	38,961.1	0.01775	0	0

Product	Exports 2001 (US$1000)	U.S. MFN Tariff (average)	Tariff on Thai (average)	Expansion (US$1000)
84219 Wind-jackets, anoraks & similar articles, for women	35,821.2	0.1101079	0.1101079	3944.198
09899 Other food preparations	35,241.8	0.1417564	0.1268193	4469.339
66613 Household & toilet articles of other ceramics	34,883.6	0.0891	0.0391	1363.949
89479 Sport goods, n.e.s.	34,183.6	0.0220952	0.0013333	45.57813
65847 Toilet & kitchen linen of cotton	33,623	0.0955	0.0955	3210.997
77878 Other electrical machines, having indivi. functions	33,546.3	0.0183636	0	0
65221 Woven cotton fabrics~85%cotton, unb., weight<200g/m2	33,422.2	0.0875455	0.0875455	2925.962
89445 Other articles for christmas festivities	33,230.6	0	0	0
77637 Photosensitive semi-conductor devices; light emitt.	32,377.3	0	0	0
87229 Other instruments, appli. for medical, etc., sciences	30,703.4	0	0	0
89332 Household articles & toilet articles, of plastics	30,077.9	0.041	0	0
65893 Life-jackets, life-belts & other made up articles	29,435.5	0.0500909	0.0353636	1040.946
84159 Men's shirts of textiles other than cotton	28,824.2	0.1264022	0.1264022	3643.444
89477 Gloves, mittens & mitts, for use in sports	28,025.3	0.0281667	0	0
89311 Sacks & bags (incl. cones), of plastics	27,856.8	0.03	0	0
84324 Trousers, bib & brace overalls, shorts, knitted, men	27,200.3	0.1562107	0.1562107	4248.979
87449 Microtomes; parts & accessories of articles of 8744	26,762.1	0.012	0	0
76491 Parts & accessories for apparatus of heading 7641	26,630.7	0	0	0
05896 Fruits or edible parts of plants, prepared, n.e.s.	26,582.1	0.0677104	0.0372412	989.9493
57433 Polyethylene terephthalate	25,966.2	0.080576	0	0
87221 Syringes, catheters, needles, cannulae & the like	25,462.7	0	0	0
63542 Tableware and kitchenware, of wood	24,872.3	0.0425	0	0
05897 Mixtures of fruits, parts of plants, prepared, n.e.s.	24,211.5	0.1025	0.1025	2481.679
84151 Shirts of cotton, for men	24,038	0.145	0.145	3485.51
67943 Other, welded, of circular cross-section	23,790.2	0.018875	0.013125	312.2464

APPENDIX TABLE 3.9 (continued)

Product	Exports 2001 (US$1000)	U.S. MFN Tariff (average)	Tariff on Thai (average)	Expansion (US$1000)
66729 Diamonds (exclud. industrial), otherwise worked, not set	23495.5	0	0	0
87439 Parts & accessories forthe articles of 8743	23,012.6	0	0	0
57112 Polyethylene having a specific gravity > 0, 94	22,970	0.083	0	0
62999 Articles of unhard. non-cell. vulca. rubber, n.e.s.	22,461.2	0.028	0	0
89472 Ice skates & roller skates	22,412.8	0.0096667	0	0
29199 Animal products, n.e.s.	22,360.3	0.0036667	0	0
82153 Furniture, of wood, of a kind used in the kitchen	22,192.9	0	0	0
84482 Brief & panties, knitted or crocheted, for women	22,158	0.1074	0.1074	2379.769
85151 Footwear, uppers of text., outer soles of plas., rub.	22,075	0.2993286	0.2993286	6607.679
63549 Wood marquetry & inlaid wood; wooden arti., excluding 82	21,696.3	0.0214	0	0
81221 Sanitary fixtures, of porcelain or china	21,688.7	0.058	0	0
65822 Tents	21,632.1	0.062	0.0585	1265.478
05991 Pineapple juice	21,391.5	0.0671335	0.0671335	1436.086
89841 Magnetic tapes for recording, width < 4 mm	21,355	0.04	0.04	854.2
08195 Dog or cat food, put up for retail sale	21,252.3	0	0	0
84522 Men's garments of fabrics of 65732 through 65734	20,868.7	0.05675	0.05675	1184.299
66611 Tableware & kitchenware of porcelain or china	20,772.3	0.1350833	0.0536667	1114.78
89929 Artificial flowers, foliage, fruits, excluding of plastics	20,623.8	0.1023333	0	0
88417 Spectacle lenses of other materials	20,493.9	0.02	0	0
06229 Other sugar confectionery	20,424.2	0.1266937	0.1216028	2483.64
76482 Television cameras	19,872.3	0.021	0	0
09849 Other sauces & preparations; seasonings, condiments	19,778.1	0.0733329	0.0290471	574.4973
84211 Coats, raincoats, capes & similar articl., for women	19,600.5	0.1101955	0.1101955	2159.887
69421 Screws & similar articles, threaded, iron or steel	19,546	0.0549167	0.02275	444.6715
77633 Transistors, dissipation rate > 1 w	19,432.8	0	0	0

APPENDIX TABLE 3.10
Singapore Exports, U.S. Protection, and Potential for Trade Expansion:
Top 100 Products, 2001
(Ranked by Export Value)

Product	Exports (US$1000)	U.S. MFN Tariff	Trade Expansion
75997 Parts, accessories of the machines of group 752	2144827.8	0	0
77641 Digital monolithic integrated circuits	1307038.6	0	0
77643 Non-digital monolithiques integrated circuits	347783.2	0	0
87229 Other instruments, appli. for medical, etc., sciences	246955.9	0	0
76281 Other radio receivers, combined with sound reprodu.	203598.4	0.021	4275.566
76432 Transmission apparatus with reception apparatus	165085.6	0	0
51577 Other heterocyclic comp. with nitrogen hetero-atom	130652.9	0.0131	1711.553
51569 Heterocyclic compo. with ox. hetero-atom (s), n.e.s.	122118.3	0.0313	3822.303
89219 Other books, brochures & simil., printed, excluding sheets	96037.6	0	0
76493 Parts & accessories of 761, 762, 7643, 7648	95010	0.0181714	1726.467
89961 Hearing aids	68384.4	0	0
89969 Appliances, n.e.s., to compensate defect or disability	62535.3	0	0
75124 Cash registers, incorporating a calculating device	62042.4	0	0
79295 Other parts of aeroplanes or helicopters	61712.5	0	0
89879 Recorded media, n.e.s.	59346.9	0.003375	200.2958
87445 Other instruments & apparatus using optical radia.	51871.6	0	0
77586 Ovens, cookers, cook. plates, boiling rings, roasters	51638.7	0.0156667	809.0062
71491 Parts for turbo-jets or turbo-propellers	46632.2	0	0
77637 Photosensitive semi-conductor devices; light emitt.	40368.1	0	0
87425 Measuring or checking instruments, machines, n.e.s.	36304.4	0.016125	585.4085
84426 Trousers, bib & brace overalls, shorts, knitted, women	36213.6	0.1525	5522.574
76381 Video recording or reproducing apparatus	35147.2	0.0035	123.0152
54131 Penicillins, deriv. with penicillan. acid structure	28337.8	0	0
87221 Syringes, catheters, needles, cannulae & the like	28061	0	0

Product	Exports (US$1000)	US MFN Tariff	Trade Expansion
77258 Plugs & sockets, voltage < 1000 volts	26,076.5	0.0135	352.0327
77831 Starting equip. for combustion engines; generators	25,081.1	0	0
87435 Instruments & apparatus for measuring the pressure	24,683.4	0	0
79319 Non-inflat. row boats, vessels for pleasure, n.e.s.	22,061.6	0.0124	273.5638
78439 Other parts & accessories of motor vehicles	21,948.4	0.0094444	207.2905
88419 Optical fibres, bundles, cables; polarizing material	21,703.6	0.0161429	350.3581
76483 Radar, radio-navigat. aid, -remote control apparatus	21,548.2	0	0
76211 Radio, external source of power, vehicles, combined	21,132	0.01	211.32
71899 Parts of headings 71449, 71891, 71892 & 71893	20,191.7	0	0
74315 Compressors of a kind used in refrig. equipment	18,048.6	0	0
77689 Parts of the articles of heading 7764	16,370.2	0	0
77645 Hybrid integrated circuits	15,989.5	0	0
89859 Prepared unrecorded media, n.e.s.	15,572.9	0	0
77121 Static converters	15,420.7	0	0
84151 Shirts of cotton, for men	14,686.1	0.145	2129.485
76383 Other sound reproducing apparatus	14,644.9	0.00925	135.4653
87456 Parts & accessories for the instrument of 87455	14,149.4	0	0
89212 Children's picture, drawing or colouring books	14,129.5	0	0
87449 Microtomes; parts & accessories of articles of 8744	12,974.7	0.012	155.6964
75991 Parts, accessories for sub-group 7511	12,405.3	0.015	186.0795
77125 Other inductors	12,330.4	0	0
88432 Other objective lenses	12,290.5	0.023	282.6815
62999 Articles of unhard. non-cell. vulca. rubber, n.e.s.	12,019.7	0.0246667	296.4859
77261 Boards, panels for electric distribution<1000 volts	11,687.9	0.027	315.5733
77255 Other switches, voltage < 1000 volts	11,344.2	0.018	204.1956
84371 Shirts, of cotton, knitted or crocheted, for men	11,210.7	0.201	2253.351

APPENDIX TABLE 3.10 *(continued)*

Product	Exports (US$1000)	U.S. MFN Tariff	Trade Expansion
51616 Acycl., cyclan., cyclen., cyclo., arom ethers; derivat.	10,639.3	0.0300714	319.9389
74291 Parts of the pumps of group 742	10,290.4	0	0
76482 Television cameras	10,023.2	0.021	210.4872
33411 Motor spirit (gasolene) including aviation spirit	9,643.6	0.0229113	220.9472
79293 Under-carriages & parts thereof	9,559.4	0	0
77649 Other electro. integrated circuits, microassemblies	9,555.9	0	0
77884 Electric sound or visual signalling apparatus	9,366.9	0	0
74918 Injection, compres. types of moulds for rub., plast.	8,951.9	0.0103333	92.50297
66729 Diamonds (exc. industrial), otherwise worked, not set	8,934.4	0	0
72849 Machinery having individual functions, n.e.s.	8,876.3	0.00675	59.91503
77681 Piezo-electric crystals, mounted	8,867.7	0	0
84324 Trousers, bib & brace overalls, shorts, knitted, men	8,532	0.1562107	1332.79
03411 Fish, live	8,425.9	0	0
51389 Polycarboxylic acids, n.e.s.; derivatives	8,386.4	0.0423466	355.1352
84483 Nightdresses & pyjamas, knitted or crocheted, women	8,338	0.0828	690.3864
76491 Parts & accessories for apparatus of heading 7641	8,023.6	0	0
97101 Gold, non-monetary, unwrought, semi-manufactu., powder	7,922.1	0.0117143	92.80175
72842 Machinery for working rubber or plastics, n.e.s.	7,758.8	0.0180833	140.305
89284 Calendars of all kind, printed	7,465.7	0.00413	30.83334
77863 Aluminium electrolytic fixed capacitors	7,397.8	0	0
57419 Other polyethers	7,114.3	0	0
77259 Other apparatus for electrical circuits<1000 volts	6,965.6	0.0135	94.0356
84512 Babies' garments & clothing accessories, knitted	6,863.2	0.1841579	1263.912
53311 Pigments & preparations based on titanium dioxide	6,830.1	0.06	409.806
87413 Surveying, hydrological, etc., instruments & appliances	6,806.6	0.0129091	87.86702
87479 Parts & accessories for instr. & apparatus of 8747	6,761	0	0

Product	Exports (US$1000)	U.S. MFN Tariff	Trade Expansion
88417 Spectacle lenses of other materials	6,741.9	0.02	134.838
89399 Other articles of plastics	6,554.1	0.04164	272.9127
87443 Spectrometers, spectrographs using optical radiat.	6,480.7	0	0
77833 Parts of the equipment of heading 77831	6,390.7	0.0186667	119.2931
74151 Air condit. mach., window or wall type, self-cont.	6,384	0	0
77429 Other apparatus for examination or treatment	6,238.5	0.0101429	63.27621
04849 Other bakers' ware	6,141.3	0.0225	138.1793
84424 Dresses, knitted or crocheted, for women	5,901.6	0.1215	717.0444
67621 Bar & rolls, iron, non-alloy steel, hot-rol., deforma.	5,789.9	0.015	86.8485
77129 Parts of the electric power machinery of group 771	5,716.1	0.0096	54.87456
77282 Other parts for apparatus of 7724, 7725 & 7726	5,707.9	0.028	159.8212
59725 Additives for lubricating oils	5,698.9	0.0735	418.8691
51574 Heterocyc. comp., nitrogen hetero-atom, pyridine ri.	5,663.8	0.0352264	199.5154
87477 Other instrum. & apparatus for telecommunications	5,565.8	0	0
03428 Other fish, frozen (excluding livers and roe)	5,547	0.0001184	0.656923
77252 Automatic circuit breakers, voltage < 1000 volts	5,277.6	0.027	142.4952
77412 Other electro-diagnostic apparatus	5,090	0	0
54153 Adrenal cortical hormones and their derivatives	4,823.8	0	0
87149 Parts & accessories of microscopes	4,759.1	0.057	271.2687
76411 Telephone sets	4,521.6	0	0
87446 Apparatus for physical or chemical analysis, n.e.s.	4,517.2	0	0
88541 Wrist watches, electrically powered	4,510.7	0	0
61172 Leather of reptiles, without hair	4,497.4	0.0166667	74.95667
54293 Medicaments, n.e.s., in forms for retail sale	4,431.5	0	0

US Exports, Indonesian Protection, and Potential for Expansion
Top 100 Products, 2001

Product	Exports (US$1000)	Indo Tariff (average)	Trade Expansion
08131 Soya beans oil-cakes	166976.5	0	0
72399 Other parts for the machinery of 723 & 7443	78244.6	0	0
52372 Neutral sodium carbonate	57052.7	5	2852.635
72393 Parts for boring, sinking machinery of 72337, 72344	51564.9	0	0
77643 Non-digital monolithiques integrated circuits	36906.5	0	0
79295 Other parts of aeroplanes or helicopters	30025.6	0	0
76493 Parts & accessories of 761, 762, 7643, 7648	29603	0.7142857	211.449996
59774 Lubricating preparations, excluding petroleum oils	28688.9	5	1434.445
08141 Flours, meals & pellets, meat, meat offal, non-edible	27175.7	0	0
26712 Artificial filament tow	23604.9	5	1180.245
72841 Machin. for assembling lamps, for hot working glass	19617.9	0	0
64211 Cartons, boxes & cases, of corrugated paper, paperb.	18678.9	5	933.945
77641 Digital monolithic integrated circuits	18331.2	0	0
72849 Machinery having individual functions, n.e.s.	18225.2	2.777778	506.255596
25113 Waste of paper or paperboard, of mechanical pulp	17882	7.5	1341.15
61141 Other bovine, equine leathers, tanned or retanned	17745.7	0	0
59885 Other supported catalysts	17553.6	3.75	658.26
24752 Wood (excluding coniferous, tropical), rough, not treated	14932.1	0	0
59725 Additives for lubricating oils	14875.1	1.666667	247.918383
71499 Parts for the gas turbines of heading 71489	12835.3	0	0
08199 Preparations of a kind used for animal food, n.e.s.	12510.5	0	0
25151 Chemical wood pulp, coniferous, soda, sulph., bleached	12003.6	0	0
72322 Mechan. shovels, excavators, shovel-load. (360 deg.)	10652.4	10	1065.24
73721 Metal-rolling mills	10585.8	0	0

APPENDIX TABLE 3.11 *(continued)*

Product	Exports (US$1000)	Indo Tariff (average)	Trade Expansion
27826 Kaolin and other kaolinic clays, calcined or not	10,485	5	524.25
08151 Residues of starch manufacture & similar residues	10,328.7	3.333333	344.289966
75997 Parts, accessories of the machines of group 752	10,327.2	0	0
76491 Parts & accessories for apparatus of heading 7641	9,926.2	5	496.31
59889 Other catalysts and catalytic preparations	9,683.9	5	484.195
78439 Other parts & accessories of motor vehicles	9,680.8	15	1452.12
74291 Parts of the pumps of group 742	9,282.5	0	0
76432 Transmission apparatus with reception apparatus	9,187.5	3.333333	306.249969
25111 Waste of unbleached kraft paper or paperboard	8,832.2	7.5	662.415
74411 Self-propelled trucks, electric., handling equipment	8,784	5	439.2
74319 Other air or gas compressors	8,596.6	0.8333333	71.6383305
51131 Vinyl chloride (chloroethylene)	8,535.6	5	426.78
74494 Parts of other machinery of heading 7448	8,497.3	5	424.865
74414 Works trucks, elect., self-propel., no handling equi.	8,486.9	15	1273.035
74412 Other self-propelled trucks, with handling equipm.	8,473.9	5	423.695
02221 Milk, in solid form, of a fat content by weight<1, 5%	8,416	5	420.8
09899 Other food preparations	8,293.3	38	3151.454
59899 Other chemical products and preparations	8,169.4	6.25	510.5875
68423 Aluminium plates, sheet & strip, thickness > 0, 20mm	8,096.2	12.75	1032.2655
33525 Oils, other products, n.e.s., from coal distillation	8,065.8	4.166667	336.075027
77282 Other parts for apparatus of 7724, 7725 & 7726	8,044.1	5	402.205
51569 Heterocyclic compo. with ox. hetero-atom (s), n.e.s.	7,958.6	3.5	278.551
05751 Grapes, fresh	7,770.9	5	388.545
71631 Ac motors (incl. universal (ac/dc) motors, >37, 5w)	7,745.7	10	774.57
71481 Turbo-propellers	7,641.2	0	0
51489 Compounds with other nitrogen functions	6,951.9	3.75	260.69625

Product	Exports (US$1000)	Indo Tariff (average)	Trade Expansion
89399 Other articles of plastics	6,749.5	13.75	928.05625
51372 Esters of acetic acid	6,618.6	5	330.93
29195 Skin & other parts of birds simply prepared; waste	6,304.8	5	315.24
54139 Other antibiotics	6,160.7	4.166667	256.695854
51614 Methyloxirane (propylene oxide)	6,062.2	0	0
33542 Petroleum coke	6,054.1	5	302.705
51617 Ethers-alcohols, ethers phenols; peroxides; deriv.	5,866.9	4.285714	251.438555
77259 Other apparatus for electrical circuits<1000 volts	5,832.3	6	349.938
64163 Paper for household purposes, width > 36cm	5,669.2	5	283.46
01252 Edible offal of bovine animals, frozen	5,446.7	5	272.335
25112 Waste of other paper, of bleached chemical pulp	5,338.6	7.5	400.395
57111 Polyethylene having a specific gravity < 0, 94	5,158.7	7	361.109
51112 Propene (propylene)	5,045.1	5	252.255
25162 Chemical wood pulp, sulphite, bleached	5,009.7	0	0
69554 Chain saw blades	4,900.6	5	245.03
75199 Office machines, n.e.s.	4,854.2	2.5	121.355
59812 Residual lyes, from the manufacture of wood pulp	4,826.6	5	241.33
71441 Turbo-jets	4,799	0	0
79291 Propellers & rotors & parts thereof	4,696.4	0	0
55141 Mixtures of odoriferous subst. for food industries	4,686.1	87.5	4100.3375
88111 Photographic cameras	4,620.9	6.666667	308.060015
53342 Paints, varn. based on polymers, excluding aqueous medi.	4,607.6	8.333333	383.966651
25152 Chemical wood pulp, non-coniferous, soda, bleached	4,597	0	0
04721 Groats and meal of maize	4,529.1	5	226.455
57531 Polyamide-6, -12, -6, 6, -6, 9, -6, 10, or -6, 12	4,387.7	3	131.631
76431 Transmission apparatus	4,334.1	10	433.41

Product	Exports (US$1000)	Indo Tariff (average)	Trade Expansion
88415 Spectacle lenses of glass	4,242.7	5	212.135
55421 Organic surface-active agents, retail sale or not	4,190.1	5.833333	244.422486
51213 Butanols	4,179.9	2.5	104.4975
78219 Motor vehicles for the transport of goods, n.e.s.	3,917.9	24	940.296
64142 Sack kraft paper, uncoated, in rolls or sheets	3,913.5	5	195.675
57529 Other acrylic polymeres	3,829.4	7.5	287.205
06191 Lactose and lactose syrup	3,662.6	5	183.13
28239 Ferrous waste and scrap, n.e.s.	3,568.7	0	0
05661 Potatoes prepared or preserved (no vinegar), frozen	3,556.4	5	177.82
74315 Compressors of a kind used in refriger. equipment	3,554.1	0	0
00141 Poultry, weighing not more than 185 grammes	3,474.5	2.5	86.8625
51479 Other cyclic amides and their derivatives; salts	3,420.3	7	239.421
72443 Textile spinning, twisting, winding, reeling machines	3,384.5	0	0
72852 Parts for the machines of heading 72842	3,324.1	0	0
63412 Sheets, wood sawn lengthwise, non-coniferous, < 6 mm	3,294.6	5	164.73
64141 Kraft paper, uncoated, in rolls or sheets	3,197.7	5	159.885
72391 Buckets, shovels, grabs and grips	3,195.9	0	0
01122 Meat of bovine animals, frozen, boneless	3,167	5	158.35
71652 Other generating sets	3,150	10	315
51561 Lactams	3,111.1	0	0
72344 Other boring & sinking machinery, not self-propell.	3,077.9	0	0
05612 Onions, dried, whole, cut, sliced, broken or powdered	3,069	5	153.45
87437 Other instruments & apparatus for measuring, check.	3,029.9	0	0
64241 Cigarette paper, cut to size	2,987.2	5	149.36

APPENDIX TABLE 3.12

U.S. Exports, Malaysian Protection, and Potential for Expansion

Top 100 Products, 2001

Product	Exports (US$1000)	Mal Tariff (average)	Trade Expansion
77641 Digital monolithic integrated circuits	2,784,086.7	0	0
77643 Non-digital monolithiques integrated circuits	697,854.4	0	0
75997 Parts, accessories of the machines of group 752	383,547.5	0	0
77633 Transistors, dissipation rate > 1 w	155,316.5	0	0
72849 Machinery having individual functions, n.e.s.	154,634.8	0.8333333	1288.6233
87479 Parts & accessories for instr. & apparatus of 8747	149,782.3	0	0
66399 Ceramic articles, n.e.s.	103,544.1	5	5177.205
87478 Other apparatus for measuring electr. quantities	102,113	0	0
72855 Parts, n.e.s., for 72348, 72721 & 72844 through 72849	91,864.4	0	0
79295 Other parts of aeroplanes or helicopters	91,558.5	0	0
71491 Parts for turbo-jets or turbo-propellers	85,392.5	0	0
77689 Parts of the articles of heading 7764	83,290.5	0	0
76493 Parts & accessories of 761, 762, 7643, 7648	77,935.9	11.42857	8906.9589
77637 Photosensitive semi-conductor devices; light emitt.	57,892.1	0	0
73114 Machine-tools operated by electro-chemical proces.	57,091	0	0
77631 Diodes, not photosensiti. nor light emitting diodes	50,065.3	0	0
77865 Ceramic dielectric fixed capacitors, multilayer	49,568.9	0	0
89851 Magnetic discs	48,847.1	0	0
77889 Electrical parts of machinery or apparatus, n.e.s.	47,416.5	0	0
74174 Heat exchange units	46,318.8	12.5	5789.85
76491 Parts & accessories for apparatus of heading 7641	44,701.5	0	0
09899 Other food preparations	38,975.2	12.08333	4709.502
87425 Measuring or checking instruments, machines, n.e.s.	38,443.7	0	0
05751 Grapes, fresh	36,682	10	3668.2

APPENDIX TABLE 3.12 (continued)

Product	Exports (US$1000)	Mal Tariff (average)	Trade Expansion
77258 Plugs & sockets, voltage < 1000 volts	35,303.8	17.5	6178.165
77688 Parts of the devices of 7763 & of item 77681	32,813.6	0	0
89399 Other articles of plastics	31,445.7	10	3144.57
77121 Static converters	30,893.5	0	0
77639 Other semi-conductor devices	30,362.2	0	0
08151 Residues of starch manufacture & similar residues	29,116.2	0	0
77871 Particle accelerators	27,671.4	0	0
28239 Ferrous waste and scrap, n.e.s.	26,816.8	0	0
76492 Parts & accessories for apparatus of heading 7642	25,949.7	0	0
76432 Transmission apparatus with reception apparatus	24,857.9	20	4971.58
77649 Other electro. integrated circuits, microassemblies	23,872.1	0	0
52372 Neutral sodium carbonate	20,244.8	0	0
77632 Transistors, dissipation rate < 1 w	20,165.5	0	0
68424 Aluminium plates, sheet & strip, thickness < 0, 20mm	19,661	28.75	5652.5375
55421 Organic surface-active agents, retail sale or not	18,693.2	0	0
77884 Electric sound or visual signalliimg apparatus	18,666.2	0	0
64175 Kraft paper, coated with inorg. subs., blea., m2>150g	17,906.3	0	0
25151 Chemical wood pulp, coniferous, soda, sulph., bleached	17,461.2	0	0
02221 Milk, in solid form, of a fat content by weight<1, 5%	17,360.3	0	0
59883 Supportes catalysts with precious metal, compounds	16,420.3	0	0
87426 Parts & accessories for the articles of 87425	16,205.2	0	0
77645 Hybrid integrated circuits	15,435.5	0	0
74369 Filters & purifying machinery for gases, n.e.s.	15,175.2	10	1517.52
51213 Butanols	14,948.4	0	0
77412 Other electro-diagnostic apparatus	14,636.1	0	0
89879 Recorded media, n.e.s.	14,567.6	11.81818	1721.6252

APPENDIX TABLE 3.12 (continued)

Product	Exports (US$1000)	Mal Tariff (average)	Trade Expansion
71499 Parts for the gas turbines of heading 71489	14,460.9	0	0
57431 Polycarbonates	14,280.4	0	0
77421 Apparatus based on the use of x-rays	14,034.2	0	0
74133 Other industrial or laboratory furnaces or ovens	13,779.8	0	0
89319 Articles for the conv., pack. of goods, n.e.s., plas.	13,582.7	25.83333	3508.8637
87477 Other instrum. & apparatus for telecommunications	13,570.3	0	0
74918 Injection, compres. types of moulds for rub., plast.	13,437.8	0	0
33525 Oils, other products, n.e.s., from coal distillation	13,329	0	0
87229 Other instruments, appli. for medical, etc., sciences	12,999.5	0	0
05711 Oranges, fresh or dried	12,974.9	10	1297.49
74395 Parts of filtering or purifying machinery & appar.	12,663.4	8.333333	1055.2833
59899 Other chemical products and preparations	12,449.5	4.615385	574.59236
72393 Parts for boring, sinking machinery of 72337, 72344	12,284.5	10	1228.45
74315 Compressors of a kind used in refriger. equipment	12,007	0	0
73167 Honing or lapping machines	11,620.4	0	0
71652 Other generating sets	11,615.5	0	0
08131 Oil-cakes of soya beans	11,610.6	0	0
77878 Other electrical machines, having indivi. functions	11,507.5	1	115.075
77282 Other parts for apparatus of 7724, 7725 & 7726	11,177.4	13.75	1536.8925
71441 Turbo-jets	11,007.5	0	0
77812 Electric accumulators	10,735.3	14.7619	1584.7343
83122 Satchels & simil., outer surface of plast. or text.	10,715.7	0	0
77879 Parts of the electrical machines of sub-group 7787	10,661	0	0
51574 Heterocyc. comp., nitrogen hetero-atom, pyridine ri.	10,365.4	2.5	259.135
52223 Silicon	10,231.8	0	0
51124 Xylenes, pure	10,157.9	0	0

Product	Exports (US$1000)	Mal Tariff (average)	Trade Expansion
89475 Golf equipment	10,157.5	6.666667	677.1667
87475 Other apparatus for measuring electr., without rec.	10,142	0	0
12239 Manufactured tobacco, extracts & essences, n.e.s.	10,084.5		0
71489 Other gas-turbines (excluding turbo-propellers)	10,078.9	0	0
64141 Kraft paper, uncoated, in rolls or sheets	10,007.1	10	1000.71
77235 Other variable resistors	9,923.6	0	0
66523 Glassware for table or kitchen purposes, excluding 66522	9,849.1	30	2954.73
23215 Acrylonitrile-butadiene rubber (nbr)	9,805.9	12.5	1225.7375
72852 Parts for the machines of heading 72842	9,753.8	0	0
74359 Other centrifuges	9,618.8	0	0
54292 Medicaments with vitamins or 5411, for retail sale	9,373.3	0	0
72811 Machine-tool for working mineral materials	9,326.2	0	0
59885 Other supported catalysts	9,065.5	0	0
76419 Other telephonic or telegraphic apparatus	9,011.7	10	901.17
57545 Polyurethanes	8,877.5	0	0
53311 Pigments & preparations based on titanium dioxide	8,608.4	15	1291.26
73591 Parts, n.e.s., & accessories for machines of 731	8,544.5	0	0
74494 Parts of other machinery of heading 7448	8,529.7	0	0
87221 Syringes, catheters, needles, cannulae & the like	8,490.2	0	0
69955 Wire, rods, similar, of base metal, for soldering, etc.	8,468.4	30	2540.52
51231 Cyclanic, cyclenic, cycloterpenic alcohols & deriva.	8,396.4	0	0
76415 Telephonic or telegraphic switching apparatus	8,385.6	12.5	1048.2
87465 Other regulating or controlling instr. & apparatus	8,331.1	0	0
26712 Artificial filament tow	8,182.8	0	0

APPENDIX TABLE 3.13
U.S. Exports, Philippines Protection, and Potential for Expansion
Top 100 Products, 2001

Product	Exports (US$1000)	Phil Tariff (average)	Trade Expansion
77641 Digital monolithic integrated circuits	3,259,659.3	1.5	48894.89
77643 Non-digital monolithiques integrated circuits	834,427.8	3	25032.834
08131 Oil-cakes of soya beans	138,367.7	3	4151.031
75997 Parts, accessories of the machines of group 752	109,462.7	0	0
77689 Parts of the articles of heading 7764	101,514.3	0	0
77633 Transistors, dissipation rate > 1 w	82,126.1	0	0
87478 Other apparatus for measuring electr. quantities	78,530.9	2	1570.618
77632 Transistors, dissipation rate < 1 w	77,510.4	0	0
87479 Parts & accessories for instr. & apparatus of 8747	71,358.4	1.5	1070.376
77119 Other electric transformers	58,792.1	6.5	3821.4865
77631 Diodes, not photosensiti. nor light emitting diodes	44,556.7	0	0
69741 Household articles & parts, n.e.s, of iron or steel	43,104.8	10	4310.48
79295 Other parts of aeroplanes or helicopters	37,757.1	3	1132.713
89319 Articles for the conv., pack. of goods, n.e.s., plas.	37,550.5	13	4881.565
72849 Machinery having individual functions, n.e.s.	34,505.3	3	1035.159
76415 Telephonic or telegraphic switching apparatus	29,112	0	0
04231 Rice, semi-milled, wholly milled (excluding broken)	28,143.2	50	14071.6
77282 Other parts for apparatus of 7724, 7725 & 7726	27,900.7	1.5	418.5105
77129 Parts of the electric power machinery of group 771	27,031.4	3	810.942
64141 Kraft paper, uncoated, in rolls or sheets	25,167.5	7	1761.725
77889 Electrical parts of machinery or apparatus, n.e.s.	22,021.2	5	1101.06
88591 Watch cases & parts of watch cases	21,719.8	3	651.594
87193 Other optical devices, appliances & instruments	21,243.7	3	637.311
09899 Other food preparations	21,194	5.222222	1106.7977

Product	Exports (US$1000)	Phil Tariff (average)	Trade Expansion
77259 Other apparatus for electrical circuits<1000 volts	20,819.6	1.5	312.294
72855 Parts, n.e.s., for 72348, 72721 & 72844 through 72849	19,749.1		0
06229 Other sugar confectionery	19,465.5	8.5	1654.5675
76493 Parts & accessories of 761, 762, 7643, 7648	19,344.3	1.833333	354.64544
76431 Transmission apparatus	18,673.2	1.5	280.098
89219 Other books, brochures & simil., printed, exc. sheets	18,149.4	4	725.976
05751 Grapes, fresh	17,574.3	7	1230.201
89399 Other articles of plastics	17,015.1	6.25	1063.4438
25151 Chemical wood pulp, coniferous, soda, sulph., bleached	16,914.5	3	507.435
54139 Other antibiotics	16,102.9	3	483.087
55141 Mixtures of odoriferous subst. for food industries	16,017.4	3	480.522
77258 Plugs & sockets, voltage < 1000 volts	14,161.9	2.5	354.0475
73513 Work-holders	13,722.6	3	411.678
08199 Preparations of a kind used for animal food, n.e.s.	13,383.8	12.25	1639.5155
87425 Measuring or checking instruments, machines, n.e.s.	13,160.5	2.4	315.852
05661 Potatoes prepared or preserved (no vinegar), frozen	12,807.3	7	896.511
59899 Other chemical products and preparations	12,686.8	3	380.604
77688 Parts of the devices of 7763 & of item 77681	12,639.7	0	0
77121 Static converters	12,463.3	3.5	436.2155
03637 Cuttlefish, octopus and squid, frozen, dried, salted	12,166	3	364.98
76432 Transmission apparatus with reception apparatus	11,951.2	0	0
02221 Milk, in solid form, of a fat content by weight<1, 5%	11,504.7	3	345.141
02241 Whey	9,829.9	3	294.897
55149 Mixtures of odoriferous subst., excluding food industr.	9,470.3	3	284.109
52372 Neutral sodium carbonate	9,411.4	3	282.342
75993 Parts, accessori. of the machines of sub-group 7519	9,337.4	1	93.374

APPENDIX TABLE 3.13 *(continued)*

Product	Exports (US$1000)	Phil Tariff (average)	Trade Expansion
87475 Other apparatus for measuring electr., without rec.	9,292.9	5.333333	495.6213
74145 Other refrigerating, freezing equipment; heat pumps	8,593	5.75	494.0975
77637 Photosensitive semi-conductor devices; light emitt.	8,539.1	0	0
54293 Medicaments, n.e.s., in forms for retail sale	8,187.8	3.666667	300.21936
77252 Automatic circuit breakers, voltage < 1000 volts	8,145.9	4	325.836
72393 Parts for boring, sinking machinery of 72337, 72344	7,999.6	3	239.988
55423 Surface-active preparations, n.e.s., excluding retail	7,951.1	5	397.555
71631 Ac motors (incl. universal (ac/dc) motors, >37, 5w)	7,943.1	3	238.293
74511 Tools for working in the hand, pneumatic	7,877.7	3	236.331
89879 Recorded media, n.e.s.	7,679.6	3.25	249.587
77812 Electric accumulators	7,635.4	6.285714	479.93941
77249 Other apparatus for electrical circuits>1000 volts	7,587.8	3	227.634
74361 Machinery for filtering & purifying waters	7,515.7	7	526.099
28231 Waste and scrape of tinned iron or steel	7,513	3	225.39
76491 Parts & accessories for apparatus of heading 7641	7,384.3	0	0
54163 Antisera or other blood fractions; vaccines	7,293.5	3	218.805
57596 Petrole. resins, coumaro-indene, other resins, n.e.s.	7,196.2	3	215.886
25113 Waste of paper or paperboard, of mechanical pulp	7,152.8	3	214.584
77111 Liquid dielectric transformers	6,971.6	6.5	453.154
77313 Ignit. wiring sets & the like used in vehicl., etc.	6,773	11	745.03
89851 Magnetic discs	6,744.3	3.5	236.0505
04849 Other bakers' ware	6,721.3	10	672.13
59885 Other supported catalysts	6,509.9	3	195.297
77822 Discharge lamps	6,442.2	8	515.376
64175 Kraft paper, coated with inorg. subs., blea., m2>150g	6,258	3	187.74
55352 Personal deodorants and anti-perspirants	6,256	5	312.8

APPENDIX TABLE 3.13 (continued)

Product	Exports (US$1000)	Phil Tariff (average)	Trade Expansion
82139 Other furniture of metal	6,137.1	15	920.565
78229 Other special purpose vehicles	6,135.6	3	184.068
51617 Ethers-alcohols, ethers-phenols; peroxides; deriv.	6,089	3	182.67
05676 Potatoes prepared with no vinegar, not frozen	6,087.9	7	426.153
25112 Waste of other paper, of bleached chemical pulp	6,059.8	3	181.794
26712 Artificial filament tow	6,037.6	3	181.128
77639 Other semi-conductor devices	6,011.2	0	0
73162 Non-num. cont. flat-surface grind. mach., (>0, 01mm)	6,009.6	3	180.288
58211 Plates, films	5,971.4	15	895.71
61142 Other bovine, equine leathers, tanned & prepared	5,656.8	5	282.84
77312 Co-axial cable & other co-axial conductors	5,589	7	391.23
77879 Parts of the electrical machines of sub-group 7787	5,561.2	2	111.224
77884 Electric sound or visual signalling apparatus	5,421.3	1.5	81.3195
09849 Other sauces & preparations; seasonings, condiments	5,396.8	7	377.776
77421 Apparatus based on the use of x-rays	5,364.5	3	160.935
79215 Helicopters, of an unladen weight > 2000 kg	5,336.3	3	160.089
05421 Peas, dried, shelled	5,325.5	3	159.765
74395 Parts of filtering or purifying machinery & appar.	5,205.9	3	156.177
89332 Household articles & toilet articles, of plastics	5,122.5	15	768.375
26901 Worn textile articl. (excluding6589, 6592, 6596, 821), bulk	4,984.4	15	747.66
87229 Other instruments, appli. for medical, etc., sciences	4,979.8	3	149.394
74315 Compressors of a kind used in refriger. equipment	4,952.1	3	148.563
77412 Other electro-diagnostic apparatus	4,868.5	3	146.055
71651 Electric generating sets, internal combust. engines	4,706.5	3	141.195

APPENDIX TABLE 3.14
US Exports, Thai Protection, and Potential for Expansion
Top 100 Products, 2001

Product	Exports (US$1000)	Thai Tariff (average)	Trade Expansion
75997 Parts, accessories of the machines of group 752	317,899.8	0	0
77631 Diodes, not photosensiti. nor light emitting diodes	165,292.4	0	0
79295 Other parts of aeroplanes or helicopters	137,780.1	5	6889.005
66491 Glass of headings 6643, 6644 or 6645, worked	122,972.8	20	24594.56
78439 Other parts & accessories of motor vehicles	56,521.1	42	23738.862
77633 Transistors, dissipation rate > 1 w	56,410.9	0	0
74315 Compressors of a kind used in refriger. equipment	51,687.9	20	10337.58
71499 Parts for the gas turbines of heading 71489	46,503.9	3	1395.117
08131 Oil-cakes of soya beans	43,946.3	6	2636.778
89731 Articles of jewellery & parts, of precious metals	38,908	20	7781.6
66729 Diamonds (excludingindustrial), otherwise worked, not set	38,707.2	0	0
72855 Parts, n.e.s., for 72348, 72721 & 72844 through 72849	36,930.8	5	1846.54
59899 Other chemical products and preparations	35,421.5	5	1771.075
51243 Other phenols, eg. phenol-alcohols	35,036.3	1.5	525.5445
77282 Other parts for apparatus of 7724, 7725 & 7726	33,962.4	10	3396.24
33525 Oils, other products, n.e.s., from coal distillation	33,569.6	1	335.696
72849 Machinery having individual functions, n.e.s.	31,930.2	5	1596.51
68423 Aluminium plates, sheet & strip, thickness > 0, 20mm	28,229.5	10	2822.95
72393 Parts for boring, sinking machinery of 72337, 72344	26,821.3	5	1341.065
52372 Neutral sodium carbonate	22,582.5	1	225.825
76493 Parts & accessories of 761, 762, 7643, 7648	22,049.2	8.666667	1910.9307
08199 Preparations of a kind used for animal food, n.e.s.	21,184.1	9.1	1927.7531
25151 Chemical wood pulp, coniferous, soda, sulph., bleached	20,725.2	1	207.252
77259 Other apparatus for electrical circuits<1000 volts	19,492	10	1949.2

APPENDIX TABLE 3.14 (continued)

Product	Exports (US$1000)	Thai Tariff (average)	Trade Expansion
76432 Transmission apparatus with reception apparatus	19,344.1	0	0
87478 Other apparatus for measuring elect. quantities	17,994.1	2	359.882
76491 Parts & accessories for apparatus of heading 7641	17,843.6	3	535.308
87425 Measuring or checking instruments, machines, n.e.s.	17,115.9	2.5	427.8975
77689 Parts of the articles of heading 7764	16,595.8	0	0
74145 Other refrigerating, freezing equipment; heat pumps	16,554.9	30	4966.47
77886 Battery carbons & other carbon articles, for elect.	16,146.4	8.25	1332.078
08151 Residues of starch manufacture & similar residues	15,021.1	9.1	1366.9201
54293 Medicaments, n.e.s., in forms for retail sale	14,983.6	20	2996.72
25111 Waste of unbleached kraft paper or paperboard	14,336.4	1	143.364
87229 Other instruments, appli. for medical, etc., sciences	13,473.2	1	134.732
89399 Other plastic articles	12,983.4	30	3895.02
66739 (semi-) precious stones, otherwise worked	12,921.1	0	0
54139 Other antibiotics	12,714.9	1	127.149
55421 Organic surface-active agents, retail sale or not	12,666.6	7	886.662
97101 Gold, non-monetary, unwrought, semi-manufactu., powder	12,311.2	0	0
51481 Quaterna. ammonium salt, hydrox.; phosphoaminolipids	12,284.5	1	122.845
78219 Motor vehicles for the transport of goods, n.e.s.	11,927.3	46.66667	5566.0737
77639 Other semi-conductor devices	11,585.4	0	0
77878 Other electrical machines, having indivi. functions	11,456.7	9.2	1054.0164
89319 Articles for the conv., pack. of goods, n.e.s., plas.	10,656.6	25	2664.15
79191 Signalling, safety, control equipm. for railway, etc.	10,483.5	12.5	1310.4375
57431 Polycarbonates	10,367.6	20	2073.52
77258 Plugs & sockets, voltage < 1000 volts	10,366.7	10	1036.67
54163 Antisera or other blood fractions; vaccines	10,252.7	0.25	25.63175
03721 Crustaceans, prepared or preserved, n.e.s.	10,092.2	20	2018.44

APPENDIX TABLE 3.14 (continued)

Product	Exports (US$1000)	Thai Tariff (average)	Trade Expansion
88136 Parts & accessories for the equipment of 88135	10,037.8	20	2007.56
87426 Parts & accessories for the articles of 87425	9,989.5	3	299.685
59869 Composite diagnostics or laboratory reagents	9,877.1	5	493.855
89879 Recorded media, n.e.s.	9,707.3	20	1941.46
74918 Injection, compres. types of moulds for rub., plast.	9,598.9	5	479.945
71489 Other gas-turbines (excluding turbo-propellers)	9,503.7	3	285.111
87477 Other instrum. & apparatus for telecommunications	8,866.6	0	0
74395 Parts of filtering or purifying machinery & appar.	8,683.1	5	434.155
09899 Other food preparations	8,659.6	27.85	2411.6986
59885 Other supported catalysts	8,545.7	5	427.285
77412 Other electro-diagnostic apparatus	8,543.5	1	85.435
51574 Heterocyc. comp., nitrogen hetero-atom, pyridine ri.	8,484.4	1	84.844
51617 Ethers-alcohols, ethers-phenols; peroxides; deriv.	8,404	3.285714	276.1314
58221 Plates, sheets, of polymers of ethylene, non-combined	8,161.8	30	2448.54
74527 Other packing or wrapping machinery	8,078	5	403.9
08141 Flours, meals & pellets, meat, meat offal, non-edible	7,858.8	1	78.588
51549 Other organo-sulphur compounds	7,846.2	1	78.462
57593 Silicones in primary forms	7,747.3	10	774.73
54291 Medicaments n.e.s., not in forms for retail sale	7,519	10	751.9
58229 Plates, sheets, of other plastics, non-combined	7,451	15	1117.65
72842 Machinery for working rubber or plastics, n.e.s.	7,438.9	4.428571	329.43697
87446 Apparatus for physical or chemical analysis, n.e.s.	7,131.9	0	0
74361 Machinery for filtering & purifying waters	7,092.1	5	354.605
57419 Other polyethers	6,876.8	20	1375.36
27826 Kaolin and other kaolinic clays, calcined or not	6,822.8	1	68.228
87465 Other regulating or controlling instr. & apparatus	6,733.3	10	673.33

APPENDIX TABLE 3.14 (continued)

Product	Exports (US$1000)	Thai Tariff (average)	Trade Expansion
87431 Apparatus for measuring the flow or level of liqu.	6,637.3	0	0
64163 Paper for household purposes, width > 36cm	6,600.1	15	990.015
71491 Parts for turbo-jets or turbo-propellers	6,567.8	3	197.034
77313 Ignit. wiring sets & the like used in vehicl., etc.	6,441.8	20	1288.36
74494 Parts of other machinery of heading 7448	6,342.4	5	317.12
53311 Pigments & preparations based on titanium dioxide	6,221.7	3	186.651
87233 Therapeutic respiration apparatus	6,138.8	1	61.388
87479 Parts & accessories for instr. & apparatus of 8747	6,094.4	3	182.832
55132 Other essential oils	6,070	5	303.5
75199 Office machines, n.e.s.	6,044.2	20	1208.84
74369 Filters & purifying machinery for gases, n.e.s.	6,031.6	5	301.58
57531 Polyamide-6, -12, -6, 6, -6, 9, -6, 10, or -6, 12	5,932.6	20	1186.52
57529 Other acrylic polymeres	5,903.6	20	1180.72
87475 Other apparatus for measuring electr., without rec.	5,824.8	3	174.744
59889 Other catalysts and catalytic preparations	5,816	5	290.8
89475 Golf equipment	5,787.7	10	578.77
88419 Optical fibres, bundles, cables; polarising material	5,785.9	6.666667	385.72669
55141 Mixtures of odoriferous subst. for food industries	5,749.9	5	287.495
52363 Other phosphates	5,694.2	1	56.942
72729 Parts for the food-processing machinery of 72722	5,584.6	5	279.23
74155 Other air conditioning machines	5,543	30	1662.9
58211 Plates, films	5,479.1	30	1643.73
87221 Syringes, catheters, needles, cannulae & the like	5,475.9	5	273.795
57511 Polypropylene	5,440.4	20	1088.08

4

Special Issues in the EAI Bilateral FTAs

I.   Introduction

Chapters 2 and 3 analysed the U.S.-EAI economic relationship in a comparative framework, as well as the economic and policy-economy effects of possible bilateral FTAs. However, we did not concentrate specifically on the existing policy environment within which the U.S.-EAI FTAs will be negotiated. We do this in Chapters 4 and 5. In the current chapter, we focus specifically on the bilateral policy relationships between Indonesia, Malaysia, the Philippines, Brunei Darussalam, and Thailand, identifying in particular key areas in these relationships and salient issues that will no doubt emerge in the FTA discussions. We begin, however, with an *ex-post* review of the Singapore-U.S. negotiations, as an example of how such bilateral negotiations unfold in practice. Chapter 5 will review the EAI in the context of a rapidly changing global economy.

The following review of these special issues in the EAI bilateral FTAs has been undertaken in collaboration with regional researchers based at the Center for Strategic and International Studies (CSIS), Jakarta; the Malaysian Institute for Economic Research (MIER), Kuala Lumpur; the Asian Institute of Management (AIM), Manila; and the National Institute of Development Administration (NIDA), Bangkok.

Professor Chia Siow Yue of the Global Development Network undertook the Singapore review. After the USSFTA overview, the contributors consider the major bilateral issues, identify salient problem areas and opportunities, and offer some recommendations as to how any obstacles to a given bilateral FTA might be overcome. Our approach is mainly from the ASEAN-country perspective but we also include U.S. considerations as well. The goal is to understand better and analyse from a political economy approach where key problems will likely emerge in the negotiations.[1] The researchers use the areas covered in the USSFTA as a framework of analysis, including which issues will likely be on the table in FTA discussions and how they will play out in the bilateral negotiations.

II. Singapore

by Chia Siow Yue

A. Introduction

Singapore is an island-city state of only 650 sq meters and 4 million people. It has always relied on open trade and investment for economic growth and prosperity. Its trade in goods and services is more than three times its GDP. It practices free trade in goods but is less open in terms of services. For goods, the average applied MFN tariff level on imports is only 0.4 per cent, as there are just 6 tariff lines (imposed on alcoholic products). However, it has bound only 69 per cent of its MFN tariffs with an overall simple average rate of 7.5 per cent. The higher bound rates provide the government some flexibility to raise tariffs in case of future need. The few import and export restrictions are imposed primarily for health, security and environmental reasons. There are no production or export subsidies.

In the services sector, trade and regulatory liberalization has accelerated in recent years, in line with the objective of consolidating and enhancing Singapore's position as a regional services hub. The Monetary Authority of Singapore (MAS) has been progressively liberalizing financial services to further develop Singapore as a financial centre. The insurance and securities industries are fully open to foreign investment and competition. Wholesale and offshore banking are also fully open to foreign banks. The main remaining banking restriction is the access to domestic retail banking. The telecommunications services sector was liberalized in 2000, two years ahead of original schedule and in anticipation of the liberalization required under the WTO. Since then, there has been a considerable increase in the number of service providers and a sharp drop in telecommunications charges. On health services, Singapore is liberalizing to become a health services hub. It has increased its recognition of foreign qualifications, although the registration of foreign-trained medical personnel remains regulated. On legal services, restrictions on foreigners practicing Singapore law remain, although some reforms have taken place. Education services are also increasingly open to foreign participation, particularly at the tertiary level.

Singapore is one of the largest recipients of foreign direct investment (FDI) in the world, on aggregate, per capita and ratio-to-GDP bases. Traditionally, FDI in manufacturing has been unrestricted. FDI in services is rapidly being liberalized. In 1999 a 40 per cent foreign shareholding restriction on local banks and a 70 per cent limit on foreign ownership of the Stock Exchange of Singapore was removed. In 2000, all foreign investment restrictions in the telecommunications sector were removed. However, foreign investment limits continue to be maintained in the mass media (broadcasting and newspaper services).

B. Rationale for an FTA with the United States

For the United States, the FTA with Singapore was the first to be concluded with a major trading partner since NAFTA, the first with an Asian country, and the first since the lapse of "Fast Track" under the Clinton administration and its replacement with the "Trade Promotion Authority". For Singapore, the USSFTA followed on bilateral FTAs signed with New Zealand, Japan, the European Free Trade Area, and Australia and is the most complex and comprehensive bilateral FTA to which it has acceded to date.

i. Singapore's 3-tiered Trade Strategy

Singapore practices a 3-tiered trade strategy. First, Singapore has always been a strong supporter of the multilateral trading system (GATTS/WTO), as global free trade and investment and MFN treatment are crucial to its economic survival. Singapore is also active in the current Doha Round negotiations. The latest WTO Trade Policy Review on Singapore (2004) praises Singapore's trade regime. Second, Singapore is a strong supporter of the APEC and ASEAN trade and investment liberalization agenda and its economic integration goals and programmes. Singapore has entered into bilateral FTAs with several APEC economies (New Zealand, Australia, Japan, the United States) in part to give a push to the APEC liberalization momentum. Singapore has been pushing for faster and deeper economic integration of ASEAN and for the establishment of the ASEAN Economic Community (discussed in Chapter 5). It has already fulfilled all its liberalization commitments under the AFTA, ASEAN Framework Agreement on Services, and the ASEAN Investment Area, ahead of other ASEAN members.

Third, the Singapore government views FTAs as building blocs for a stronger multilateral trade liberalization framework. The strong government interest in bilateral FTAs in recent years has been spurred by the slow and uncertain progress in global and regional trade and investment liberalization under the WTO, APEC and ASEAN. Singapore has not only signed bilateral FTAs with New Zealand, Japan, EFTA, Australia and the United States, but is also engaged in bilateral negotiations with Canada, India, Jordan, Mexico, Korea, and Sri Lanka, and in trilateral negotiations with Chile and New Zealand (Pacific-3), and under the ASEAN umbrella with China (See Table 4.1).

In negotiating bilateral FTAs, Singapore is committed to the provisions of GATT Article XXIV, rather than sheltering under the GATT "enabling clause" for developing countries. This means its FTAs cover substantially all trade; achieve zero tariffs within a 10-year time frame; and do not raise trade barriers against non-FTA partners. Singapore's bilateral FTAs are generally "WTO-plus": encompassing free trade in goods, including agriculture (not difficult in the case of Singapore, whose agricultural sector is extremely small); liberalizing services beyond GATS; liberalizing investments beyond TRIMS; enforcing protection of intellectual property beyond TRIPS; and sometimes including commitments on labour and environmental standards. Singapore's bilateral FTA strategy initially raised many concerns and criticisms in ASEAN and beyond. Many trade economists are against all RTAs, be it NAFTA, AFTA, or bilateral, as these are seen to be discriminatory and resource distorting, undermine the WTO, and create a messy "spaghetti bowl" rules of origin.[2] Some ASEAN economists have also expressed opposition to Singapore's bilateral FTAs, arguing that these undermine ASEAN solidarity; can be used as a backdoor entry to ASEAN markets; and set a bad example by

TABLE 4.1
Singapore's Bilateral FTAs

Bilateral partner	Start of negotiations	Date concluded	Date in force
Concluded FTAs:			
New Zealand	Sep 1999	Nov 2000	Jan 2001
Japan	Oct 2000	Jan 2002	Nov 2002
EFTA	May 2001	April 2002	Jan 2003
Australia	Nov 2000	Feb 2003	Jul 2003
USA	Dec 2000	Aug 2003	Jan 2004
Jordan	Dec 2003	May 2004	
Negotiations ongoing:			
ASEAN-China			
Republic of Korea	Feb 2004		
India	May 2003		
Sri Lanka	Oct 2003		
Bahrain	Feb 2004		
Egypt	Feb 2004		
Canada	Oct 2001		
Mexico	Jul 2000		
Panama	May 2004		
Peru	Nov 2004		
Pacific 3 (with NZ and Chile)	Sep 2003		

Source: Singapore Ministry of Trade and Industry website *http://www.mti.gov.sg.*

allowing a big power (Japan) to exclude the agricultural sector.[3] Some of these criticisms have become muted as more ASEAN countries embark on bilateral FTA negotiations.

C. Why the Singapore-U.S. Partnership?

Countries enter into FTAs for both economic and political-strategic reasons. The same is true of the USSFTA.

On economic grounds, Singapore is keen on bilateral FTAs with the economic superpowers of the United States, Japan, EU, as they have large markets, and large investment and technological resources.[4]

As was noted in Chapter 2, the United States is Singapore's second largest trading partner, as well as its largest foreign investor and most important source of technology and management know-how. Singapore is also the second largest Asian investor in the United States, after Japan (and

U.S. investments in Singapore reached US$58 billion in 2001, as noted in Table 2.11). There are about 1,300 U.S. companies and 15,000 U.S. citizens in Singapore. Many U.S. multinational companies use Singapore as a base to export to the region, the world and the United States. Singapore also views the United States as playing an important strategic role in regional peace and stability and hence the importance of securing a continuing U.S. presence through the FTA.

For the United States, the FTA with Singapore is one of a string of plurilateral and bilateral FTAs spanning North America, Latin America, Africa and the Middle East. The USSFTA was initiated during the Clinton administration and concluded under the Bush administration. Singapore is a close political and strategic friend (not treaty ally) of the United States. The USSFTA is an important political statement of serious U.S. interest in Singapore and Southeast Asia; an FTA with Singapore could provide the momentum for trade and investment liberalization in the region.[5] Singapore is also not an insignificant economic partner of the United States, being its eleventh largest trading partner in the world and the largest in Southeast Asia. Moreover, it is the sixth largest service market for the United States in Asia and the largest in Southeast Asia. There is a high degree of economic complementarity and, unlike in the case of other EAI countries, import-sensitive industries in the United States need not fear competition from Singapore suppliers. In fact, Singapore is one of the few countries in the world that has a more open merchandise trade regime than the United States. Although Singapore has free trade in goods, U.S. businesses can gain from opening up the Singapore services market and from securing better protection of investments and of intellectual property rights. The FTA with Singapore could serve as a template for the United States in its negotiations with other Asian economies, as discussed at length in this Chapter.

D. Negotiating the USSFTA

President Bill Clinton and Prime Minister Goh Chok Tong agreed to enter into a bilateral FTA on 16 November 2000 on the sidelines of the APEC Leaders' Meeting. There followed 11 rounds of negotiations over the next two years, straddling the Clinton and Bush administrations. Negotiations concluded in January 2003 with resolution of the outstanding capital control issue. There were 21 negotiating groups, one for each chapter of the USSFTA agreement. President Bush and Prime Minister Goh signed the Agreement on 6 May 2003. The U.S. Congress passed implementation legislation in July 2003 by a sizeable majority, with the House voting 272–155 and Senate voting 66–32 in favour. The USSFTA came into force on 1 January 2004, except for the chapter on intellectual property rights that came into force six months later.

Singapore already had some experience in negotiating bilateral FTAs by the time it embarked on the USSFTA. It proved to be the toughest negotiations to date, as the United States had very demanding requirements of Singapore and an elaborate process of reaching domestic consensus. Initially, the Clinton administration had opted for an agreement modelled on the U.S.-Jordan FTA and to be completed before the end of the second Clinton administration. The Bush administration wanted a comprehensive and ambitious "world class" agreement which required two full years of negotiations. Delays became inevitable when the U.S. negotiators waited for new guidelines. For services liberalization, negotiations switched from a "positive list" approach to a more ambitious "negative list" approach that required detailed and careful analysis of all the service sectors. Negotiations on intellectual property protection were protracted to accommodate associated stakeholders. The various interested sectors in the United States had reached a difficult domestic compromise under the Digital Millennium Copyright Act (DMCA), and the U.S. negotiators wanted to embed its basic provisions in the USSFTA.

The Singapore negotiators were surprised by the complex and time-consuming process of decision-making and checks and balances in the United States and the powerful role of U.S. business (Ong 2004). The U.S. negotiators held public hearings and consulted frequently with Congress and various stakeholders, including more than 100 meetings with some 700 advisers from business, farm groups, labour unions, environmental groups, consumer organizations and state governments. The U.S. business community sought regular briefings and actively lobbied the two governments. As Singapore tariffs on U.S. products were already zero (except for alcoholic beverages), the U.S. business community lobbied for better access to Singapore's services market, especially financial and professional services, and for strengthening of Singapore policies on intellectual property protection, transparency and competition. Proposed texts of the Agreement were cleared with Congressional staff and advisers. The final draft was sent to Congress and advisers for review in early January 2003. Of 31 chartered advisery committees, all endorsed the final agreement except the Labor Advisory Committee.

Singapore found it had to negotiate with both the executive and legislative branches of the U.S. government as well as with business, industry and civil society. The Singapore Mission in Washington worked hard to meet with government and business representatives that influence the U.S. negotiating positions. The U.S.-Singapore FTA Business Coalition is a group of about 100 leading U.S. companies and trade associations that helped to lobby for the USSFTA. The Singapore National Trades Union Congress (NTUC) dialogued with the AFL-CIO to gain support for the USSFTA.

In contrast to the United States, the Singapore domestic consultative process was much less encompassing. Mainly, the Singapore negotiators convened meetings of stakeholders from government statutory boards and government-linked-companies to brief them on developments in the negotiations and to seek their help. The Singapore chief negotiator, Tommy Koh, coordinated the efforts of 21 negotiating groups comprising team members drawn from various government ministries and agencies. There were also meetings to brief the private sector on the negotiations and to solicit their views and cooperation (Koh 2004, p. 18). However, as with past bilateral FTAs, the USSFTA was very much a Singapore government initiative and the Singaporean private business sector did not play a very active role, preferring to adopt the "government knows best" approach (Ithnian 2004, p. 73).[6]

E. Coverage and Key Features of the USSFTA

The USSFTA contains over 1,400 pages, with about 250 pages of text and about 1,200 pages of annexes. It contains 21 chapters (see Table 2) It is not only comprehensive in scope but breaks new ground in several areas.

i. Trade in Goods

Trade in Goods covers tariffs, non-tariff measures (trade restrictions and customs), and rules of origin.

ii. Tariffs and Import Restrictions

Singapore has zero applied tariffs on imports, except for alcoholic

TABLE 4.2
U.S.-Singapore Free Trade Agreement Contents

Chapters:	Title
1	Establishment of Free Trade Area and Definitions
2	National Treatment and Market Access for Goods
3	Rules of Origin
4	Customs Administration
5	Textiles and Apparel
6	Technical Barriers to Trade
7	Safeguards
8	Cross-Border Trade in Services
9	Telecommunications
10	Financial Services
11	Temporary Entry of Business Persons
12	Anticompetitive Business Conduct, Designated Monopolies, and Government Enterprises
13	Government Procurement
14	Electronic Commerce
15	Investment
16	Intellectual Property Rights
17	Labor
18	Environment
19	Transparency
20	Administration and Dispute Settlement
21	General and Final Provisions
Annexes:	
2A	US tariff schedule and head notes
2B	Singapore tariff schedule
2C	Definitions
3A	Product specific rules of origin
3B	Integrated Sourcing Initiative
8A	US: existing non-conforming measures
8B	US: other non-conforming measures
8C	Singapore: existing non-conforming measures
8D	Singapore: other non-conforming measures
10A	US: existing non-conforming measures
10B	US: other non-conforming measures
10C	Singapore: existing non-conforming measures
10D	Singapore: other non-conforming measures
13A	Covered entities
13B	Covered products and services
13C	Indexation and conversion of thresholds
Side letters:	
6 May 2003	Singapore government commitment to recognize degrees from four US law schools
6 May 2003	Singapore government commitment to the privatization of Singtel and ST Telemedia
Source: http://www.mti.gov.sg	

beverages. Hence it is no "give away" for Singapore to commit to immediate zero tariffs on all U.S. goods, including alcoholic beverages under the USSFTA. However, unlike Singapore's MFN tariffs in the WTO, these zero tariffs are binding.

A crucial objective for Singapore is to gain preferential zero-tariff access into the U.S. market. U.S. tariffs are phased out in stages, with 92 per cent of products enjoying immediate zero tariffs, and the remaining 8 per cent of tariffs phased out over a 10-year period. Sectorally, major beneficiaries in Singapore are chemicals, petrochemicals, electronics, instrumentation equipment, processed foods, and mineral products. Across sectors, the major beneficiaries are the U.S. multinational corpoerations (MNCs) in Singapore, as they accounted for over 60 per cent of Singapore's merchandise exports to the U.S. in 2000. A clear Singapore objective is to anchor U.S. MNCs in Singapore. Singapore exports will also benefit from U.S. waiver of the 0.21 per cent *ad valorem* Merchandising Processing Fee that U.S. customs levy on all merchandise imports. Another benefit for Singapore is the waiver of the 50 per cent *ad valorem* Vessel Repair Duty that the U.S. levies on the cost of equipment and repairs obtained by U.S.-flagged vessels outside the U.S.

One of Singapore's high-profiled import restrictions is the 1992 ban on chewing gum. Singapore agreed only to a partial lifting of the ban, to allow imports of U.S. gums sold for therapeutic purposes.

iii. Customs

The U.S. import declaration will be the only document necessary to prove origin at point of entry into the United States. The USSFTA applies the provision of the WTO Agreement on Customs Valuation, which provides access to businesses to a review and appeal mechanism.

A key issue in the customs negotiations pertains to transparency and risk management (Lim 2004). Singapore and the United States already practice transparent customs procedures, either through the use of the Internet or other media, in accordance with Article X of GATT. Both customs authorities also practice risk management, that is, a systematic framework to assess the risk on goods imported which target limited resources on high risk goods and high risk traders while facilitating the clearance of legitimate cargoes through the checkpoints. In the USSFTA, both pledged to adopt risk management in their daily work.[7] A major concern of the United States was trade enforcement of transshipments.

Singapore is a major transshipment hub, a port of call for some 400 shipping lines linking 600 ports around the world. The volume of transshipment cargo made physical inspection impossible. The United States was therefore concerned about illegal mixing of goods and free riding on the USSFTA concessions. Singapore assured the United States that illegal mixing of goods in Singapore ports was not possible with its highly secured facilities in place. Nonetheless, the two customs authorities agreed to strengthen trade enforcement through cooperation and information sharing.

iv. Rules of origin and the Integrated Sourcing Initiative (ISI)

The USSFTA uses a product-specific approach, with each product having a separate and distinct rule of origin. There are three general origin rules, i.e., change in tariff classification, local or regional value content and process rules. The most commonly used is the product transformation at the 6-digit level. Manufacturing in Singapore makes heavy use of outward processing. For example, parts and components are shipped from Singapore to another country for assembly and the final product is returned to Singapore for testing before export to the United States and other destinations. The process rule recognizes outward processing and so both the value of parts and components made in Singapore as well as value of testing count towards Singapore origin. This facilitates modern fragmented production and distribution of the production chain to take advantage of the comparative advantage of different production locations.

Singapore proposed the "Integrated Sourcing Initiative" (ISI) under which certain products that are not made in Singapore, but exported through Singapore, are deemed as of Singapore origin and entitled to preferential treatment when exported to the United States. ISI was intended to encourage investments in the neighbouring Indonesian islands of Batam and Bintan, as goods could be exported to the United States through Singapore. This would help consolidate Singapore as a manufacturing hub. The ISI covers 266 IT products and some medical/ precision equipment. These products already enter the U.S. duty-free under the 1996 WTO Information Technology Agreement (ITA). The preferential treatment accorded under the USSFTA is the waiver of the 0.21 per cent Merchandise Processing Fee. There would also be savings in administrative cost as the importer does not need to meet detailed rules of origin tests. However, the ISI proposal ran into criticism in the U.S. Congress from those who believed it might create a backdoor entry for imports from low-wage countries like Indonesia (Lavin 2004, p. 49). There was also concern that the ISI sectoral list could be expanded without Congressional approval. As a result of this concern, the benefits originally proposed in the ISI were substantially reduced and new products could be added to the ISI list only by express approval of U.S. Congress.

v. Textiles and Apparel

A whole chapter in the USSFTA Agreement is devoted to the textiles and apparel industry. It is a highly politically sensitive industry in the United States, as it is a labour-intensive industry employing large numbers of workers and concentrated in a few politically influential states. U.S. imports are subject to tariffs as well as bilateral quotas under the Multi-Fibre Agreement (MFA) that expires on 31 December 2004. Singapore is not a major exporter of textiles and apparel to the world market or to the United States, but the industry had annual exports of some S$500 million and employed some 10,000 workers. The Singapore industry is concerned over its international competitiveness when the MFA quotas are abolished, as Singapore is a high-wage country.

The USSFTA negotiations cover market access, enforcement and cooperation, and safeguards. For immediate duty-free entry into the U.S. market, Singapore textiles and apparel must satisfy the "yarn forward" rule of origin (made from U.S. or Singapore yarn), with limited exceptions. All other assembly processes must be carried out in Singapore. While the requirement is intended to help the U.S. textile industry, the higher priced U.S. yarn would handicap the Singapore apparel industry. The United States offered a "Tariff Preference Level" allowing some amount of Singapore apparel exports to be exempted from the yarn forward rule for 8 years and with tariffs to be phased out over 5 years. As Singapore exports were facing U.S. MFN import tariffs of 10–33 per cent, the Singapore negotiators calculated that the preferential zero tariff would absorb part of the increased cost of using U.S. yarn and still give Singapore exporters a price edge of 5–15 per cent vis-à-vis competitors facing U.S. MFN tariffs, with total tariff savings estimated at S$140 million a year (Ng 2004, p. 91). The FTA has necessitated the Singapore apparel industry to source from a high-cost partner in place of cheaper suppliers in the region, suggesting a negative effect on global efficiency but a boon to Singapore.

The United States was concerned about possible quota circumvention and emphasized the need for enforcement and cooperation.[8] First, Singapore has to establish and maintain a register of all enterprises engaged in production and export of Singapore textiles and apparel to the U.S. market and has to establish a system to monitor, inspect and verify import, export and production of Singapore textiles and apparel destined for the United States. Second, Singapore has to amend its laws and regulations to allow for the sharing of information and cooperating with the United States in investigating circumvention and allow onsite visits to enterprises engaged in textiles and apparel manufacturing and trade with the United States. Exporters and traders are required to maintain records and documents for five years. Another U.S. concern was safeguard action that will enable it to suspend or reverse its tariff reduction and elimination obligations. Singapore agreed to the safeguard action to be undertaken only after due investigation of serious injury caused to the U.S. industry by increased imports from Singapore, as provided under the WTO Safeguard Agreement.

F. Trade in Services

Services are a major segment of the U.S. and Singapore economies. The USSFTA provides for wide-ranging services trade liberalization by adopting the "negative list" approach, that is, both countries are committed to provide substantial access for all types of services, subject to explicit exceptions, and grant national treatment and MFN treatment to each other's services suppliers. Unlike trade in goods, which is already very free and open in Singapore, some services sectors are fairly restricted. Under the USSFTA, Singapore is committed to market access beyond the levels it committed in GATS. The market access provisions are supplemented by strong regulatory disciplines that also go beyond those mandated in GATS. In addition, the USSFTA provides for mutual recognition of qualifications, and certification and licensing requirements.

i. Financial Services

This sector merited a full chapter in the USSFTA and took two full years to negotiate. The United States sought to fully pry open Singapore's financial services while Singapore sought to retain some prudential measures. First, the Monetary Authority of Singapore (MAS) has to exempt U.S. banks from the quota of 6 Qualifying Full Bank (QFB) licences and 20 new Wholesale Bank (WB) licences; these quotas are to be lifted for U.S. banks in 1.5 years and 3 years, respectively, after entry into force of the Agreement. Second, MAS has to double the quota of not more than 15 service locations for QFBs to 30 locations for U.S. QFBs, and remove the quota in 2 years. Third, MAS has hitherto restricted foreign banks from having access to the local banks' much larger ATM networks, but under the USSFTA locally incorporated U.S. QFBs would be permitted to negotiate access to the local banks' ATM networks after 2.5 years, and QFBs operating as branches after 4 years. The local banks are bracing themselves for intensified competition from U.S. banks operating in Singapore. We discuss this area more at length below in the context of Malaysia.

Singapore retained the right to prohibit foreign control of local banks (Menon 2004). Singapore's banking industry already had one of the world's highest foreign penetration rates and the government is concerned that further erosion of the local banks' market share would expose the economy to increased financial instability. The United States agreed to drop its demand provided that Singapore agreed to review the issue within 3 years. Singapore also retained the right of local incorporation of foreign banks. As a financial centre, Singapore allowed foreign banks to operate in the retail banking sector as branches of their head offices instead of locally incorporating as subsidiaries, in line with the practice of other international financial centres but in contrast to U.S. practice. While Singapore had no plans in the near term to impose such local incorporation, it wanted the flexibility to do so if necessary at some future date. The United States was concerned that this would represent a serious departure from the liberalization objective and finally agreed to allow Singapore to retain the right of local incorporation provided that it was exercised in a reasonably objective and impartial manner and the banks concerned were given 6 months notice.

Singapore also safeguarded its right to modify its schedule of restrictions under specified circumstances. The negative list approach in the USSFTA means no new discriminatory measures could be introduced in the future. However, MAS wanted flexibility to put in place new safeguards as it continued to liberalize the banking industry. Eventually, the United States allowed Singapore this flexibility provided that such modification was made in the context of an overall banking liberalization program, did not derogate from the timeframes for removal of quotas on licenses, and allowed affected banks to opt out of the liberalization measures.

ii. Capital Controls

The United States had insisted on the free transfer of capital in the USSFTA, in line with other U.S. bilateral trade and investment agreements. Singapore is also committed to the free flow of capital and had never imposed capital controls before, not even during the Asian financial crisis, as it regards an open capital account to be crucial to underpin its economic growth and its reputation as an international financial centre. Nonetheless, it wanted the ability to impose capital controls as a safeguard measure in the event of a serious balance of payments crisis. In the end it was agreed that Singapore would not impose restrictions on current payments and transfers such as debt servicing, profit repatriation, dividend payments and proceeds from sale of FDI, but could restrict "hot money" or short-term capital flows in the event of a crisis. Restrictions that lasted for less than one year and did not "substantially impede transfers" would not be liable for any claims for damages by affected investors. And even if the measures were to "substantially impede transfers" Singapore's liability would be limited.[9]

iii. Telecommunications and E-Commerce

Both the U.S. and Singapore already have open ICT markets and sought to build on the existing WTO disciplines. The telecommunications chapter achieves significant advances over the work undertaken in the WTO, covering a wide range of telecommunications issues, including reasonable and non-discriminatory access to networks, transparent rule-making by independent regulators, and adherence to the principles of deregulation and operator choice of technology.

The Singapore negotiating team sought to put in place strong disciplines that address the issue of dominant incumbents, so as to provide Singapore telecommunications companies meaningful access to the huge U.S. market.[10] The size of the U.S. government procurement market for telecommunications equipment was about US$4.8 billion in

2001. Singapore companies would enjoy better access to U.S. government tenders with the guaranteed non-discriminatory treatment for such contracts. Singapore companies would also find it easier to test and certify telecommunications equipment for sale in U.S. market, which would lower testing costs and provide faster market access.

The e-commerce chapter breaks new ground. It is the first of its kind in a bilateral FTA, putting in place trade commitments covering digital products. Both countries agreed on a permanent moratorium on the application of customs duties to e-transmissions and agreed that any customs duty imposed in the future would apply only to the physical medium and not to the content.

iv. Professional Services

Singapore has a large foreign workforce spanning the whole skills spectrum from the highly-skilled to the unskilled, and accounting for 25 per cent of the total workforce. In recent years the government has been proactive in recruiting "foreign talents" to supplement and complement the domestic talent pool. Nonetheless, like most countries, for some professions Singapore maintained restrictions on free inflow through immigration restrictions and professional licensing and certification criteria and standards. The United States wanted its professionals, including lawyers, architects, and engineers, to be able to practice freely in Singapore but made limited progress in the negotiations. The USSFTA provides for mutual consultation on acceptable standards and criteria for licensing and certification of professional service providers. Singapore agreed to ease conditions on U.S. firms creating joint law ventures to practice Singapore law and to recognize degrees from four U.S. law schools for admission to the Singapore bar. Singapore also agreed to reduce board of director requirements for architectural and engineering firms and phase out capital ownership requirements for land surveying services.

Singapore asked for improved visa treatment for its professionals, similar to that granted by the United States to Canada and Mexico under NAFTA. The United States agreed to provide a special enhanced visa category for a limited quota of professionals. Some members of Congress were unhappy that a trade agreement dealt directly with immigration (Lavin 2004, p. 48). In the end, the visa provisions stayed in, with a Congressional warning to USTR not to negotiate immigration issues again.

G. Other Features
i. Investment

As Singapore has a highly liberal FDI regime, negotiations in this chapter did not present a serious problem. The USSFTA obliges both countries to accord national treatment, MFN, and fair and equitable treatment to each other's investments. Both countries undertake not to impose any unfair performance requirements. The Agreement provides for an investor-versus-state dispute mechanism. Investors can take disputes with the host government directly to an international arbitration tribunal for resolution.

ii. Intellectual Property

The Singapore economy is moving rapidly towards a knowledge-based economy in both its manufacturing and services operations. Government policy has been focusing on promoting domestic R&D and inflows of knowledge-intensive investments and R&D personnel, particularly in biomedical sciences and information-communications. Given these goals, improving the protection of intellectual property (IP) is imperative. As a trade-dependent economy, Singapore also needs to assure its trading partners that their intellectual property rights are safeguarded.

Both Singapore and the United States are members of the WTO Trade-Related Aspects of Intellectual Property (TRIPS) agreement.[11] The USSFTA builds on TRIPS, providing strong protection for new and emerging technologies, and containing stronger provisions on enforcement of IP rights. The USSFTA also incorporates obligations in the WIPO Copyright Treaty and the WIPO Performance and Phonograms Treaty. The IP chapter covers a broad range of areas, including trademarks; domain names on the Internet; copyright obligations; pharmaceutical patents; plant protection; IP enforcement; and anti-piracy.

The U.S. gives top priority to ensuring IP protection of U.S. goods and services and to promoting adequate and effective IP protection on a global basis. The USSFTA is intended to be a model for future U.S. FTAs with Asian countries, as many of them are not TRIPS-compliant and are still developing their IP regimes. In the IP negotiations, the

U.S. pharmaceutical industry lobbied strongly for a longer term of patent protection, while the U.S. media and entertainment industries sought strong action against piracy and online distributors. Singapore agreed to implement legislation making it unlawful to: (1) knowingly circumvent effective technological measures that control access to use the protected copyright works; and (2) manufacture, provide or deal in technologies that are primarily designed, or marketed for the purpose of circumvention, or which have no other significant purpose than to circumvent the effective technological measures. The IP chapter provides for criminal penalties for manufacture, distribution or sale of infringed articles. Surveillance and enforcement of IP provisions is of concern for Singapore, in view of technological developments that made such infringements hard to track and detect. There was also concern over the impact of stringent protection on access to products by local consumers and businesses.

Another IP issue in the negotiations concerned parallel imports. In some industries it is common for suppliers to practice market segmentation, supplying products at different prices to different countries and enforced through exclusive licensing arrangements. Such arrangements are undermined by parallel imports. Singapore has rapidly growing biomedical science and pharmaceutical industries and the government is keen to promote Singapore as a choice location for value-added activities such as R&D, clinical development, and HQ activities. Singapore allows the IP owner to sue a parallel importer who knowingly and intentionally induces a breach of contract between the IP owner and his licenced distributor. This was insufficient for the United States. The Agreement allows the prevention of the purchase of any patented pharmaceutical product that the purchaser knows has been distributed in breach of a licence agreement.

iii. Competition and Government Enterprises

Trade and investment liberalization is not confined to cross-border measures but encompasses the domestic competitive environment. At the time of the USSFTA negotiations, Singapore did not have a comprehensive competition policy or competition law, but had already implemented sector-specific competition legislation in utilities and telecommunications services and the government had indicated its intention of enacting a general competition law. In the USSFTA, Singapore committed to enact a general competition law by 2005.

Of particular concern to U.S. negotiators was the behaviour of Singapore's government-linked-companies (GLCs).[12] The U.S. perception was that GLCs played a significant part in the country's economy and enjoyed an unfair advantage over other companies. The Singapore government explained that its GLCs receive no special advantages, are registered under the Companies Act and subject to the same laws and regulations and accounting and reporting requirements as other companies. The government is not involved in the day-to-day operations or commercial decision-making. In the USSFTA, Singapore commits to maintain its existing policy of not interfering with the commercial decisions of GLCs, and commits to an annual public disclosure of the government's stake in the GLCs. Singapore further commits to continue with divesting its ownership of GLCs. In particular, the divestment commitment pertaining to GLCs in the telecommunications industry was stated in a side letter to the USSFTA, wherein the Singapore government "is committed to the privatization of Singtel and ST Telemedia and to the objective of reducing its existing stakes in these companies to zero, subject to the state of capital markets and the interest of other shareholders". In pursuance of this commitment, in January 2004 Temasek divested US$1.25 billion worth of its holdings in Singtel and reduced its stake from 67.18 per cent to 64.98 per cent (and up to 61.49 per cent when the exchangeable notes are converted by 2009).[13]

iv. Government Procurement

Both Singapore and the United States are members of the WTO Agreement on Government Procurement (GPA). The USSFTA offers additional market access concessions. Both countries commit to allow market access by service suppliers of the other country, unless specifically reserved in the negative list. The commitment applies to all procurement contracts for goods and services worth more than US$56,190 and for construction procurement contracts worth more than US$6,481,000.

v. Temporary Entry of Business Persons

The USSFTA has separate categories of entry for citizens of each country to conduct business and investment activities on temporary basis. The United States extends the E1 and E2 visas to Singapore — E1 visa is available to traders with enterprises engaged in trade with the U.S.; E2 visa is available to investors who have invested or are actively in the process of investing a substantial amount of capital in the U.S.. The U.S. also grants Singapore a special quota of 5,400 visas (H1B1) a year. This category applies to professionals such as IT personnel. Employers of such visa holders need not satisfy the market test, that is, they do not have to show that there is no American who can do the job. The visa is renewable on an annual basis.

vi. Transparency

Enhanced transparency is another important feature of the USSFTA, with an entire chapter devoted to notice and comment procedures. In addition, many of the other chapters contain specific provisions to ensure regulatory transparency. Improved transparency is an effective deterrent against corrupt business practices. The two countries expressly affirmed their strong commitments to effective measures against bribery and corruption in international business transactions.

vii. Labour and Environment

The Trade Promotion Act mandates the inclusion of provisions on labour and environmental standards in U.S. trade agreements. With obvious differences between the labour regimes of Singapore and the United States, the Singapore negotiators had initial apprehensions on negotiating the labour chapter (Ong 2004, p. 135). At the outset, U.S. civil society groups and labour unions, especially the AFL-CIO, had called for strong measures to be included in the USSFTA to ensure that the rights of workers are not compromised in the process of trade liberalization.

Actually there was much common ground between the two countries, notwithstanding differences in systems and practices. Both had the same objective to promote labour standards and safeguard and enhance worker interests. Both already have high labour standards and effective enforcement of domestic labour laws.[14] Both countries agreed to the following: (1) reaffirm the commitment to observe the labour principles and rights embodied in the ILO Declaration on Fundamental Principles and Rights at Work;[15] (2) recognize that labour standards should not be used for trade protection; and (3) commit to ensure that their respective domestic laws are effectively enforced to safeguard workers' interests and rights. Both recognize that cooperation provides enhanced opportunities to improve labour standards and well-being and incorporated a comprehensive Labor Cooperation Mechanism including joint cooperative activities to strengthen bilateral ties in labour in the USSFTA.

One difficult issue in the labour negotiations pertained to the minimum wage. The United States has legally binding minimum wages while Singapore has none. Singapore relies on a tripartite approach of consensus-building and annual wage guidelines by the tripartite National Wages Council. It was finally agreed that Singapore need not adopt the minimum wage but would continue with its tripartite approach to achieve the same objective of ensuring that workers are fairly rewarded.

At the close of the USSFTA negotiations, the AFL-CIO and the Singapore trade union movement (NTUC) issued a joint statement urging the two governments to affirm and implement their commitment to creating greater and better employment opportunities, and improving the standard of living and quality of life for all workers and honour their commitment towards the fulfilment of international labour standards and the effective enforcement of domestic labour legislation. The joint statement also called for both governments to subscribe to principles of transparency and accountability in the process of bilateral trade and investment agreement negotiations.

As with labour, the environment chapter in the USSFTA also reflects the high standards already achieved in Singapore and the United States and the common objective of environmental standards and protection for sustainable development. Over the past three decades, Singapore has developed a robust environmental regime even as economic and industrial growth has taken off, in the firm belief that the objectives of environmental protection and economic development are equally important and mutually enhancing for the small city-state.

Both countries agreed that each has the right to exercise discretion in the development and execution of its environmental laws and regulations, and the right to exploit own resources in accordance with its own level of domestic environmental protection and its own development policies. Both are committed to enforce actively and rigorously their respective domestic laws relating to environment as well as not to compromise the protection afforded by these laws when promoting bilateral trade and investment. In addition, the environmental chapter encourages both countries to consult and cooperate closely on environmental issues of mutual interest and concern, including the setting up of a working subcommittee and channels and mechanisms for public participation in the implementation of environment commitments. Both also agreed to sign a Memorandum of Intent on Cooperation in Environmental Matters.

viii. Dispute Settlement

Dispute settlement provisions in the USSFTA encourage resolution of disputes in a cooperative manner and provide an effective settlement mechanism. If a Party is found to be in breach of the Agreement, it will be asked to bring its offending measure into compliance, failing which the party has to pay compensation. If compensation is not possible, the injured party may resort to other actions without formal approval of a dispute settlement body.

H. Summary and Conclusions

i. Summing up Singapore's Gains

It is difficult to have a level playing field when a small country engages in negotiating a bilateral FTA with an economic superpower. The resulting outcome depends on many factors, but primarily on the importance each party places on pushing further the bilateral economic and political relations and on the cost–benefit calculus of what constitutes a "win–win" agreement that each party can live with and implement. Increasingly the term "free trade agreement" has become a misnomer as the negotiating agenda extends beyond free trade and market access in goods and services to trade-related issues of investment, competition policy, intellectual property rights, government procurement, transparency, and labour and environmental standards. The USSFTA covers all these grounds.

As was discussed at length in Chapter 3, econometric studies on the benefits and costs of FTAs for participating countries centre on the trade creation and trade diversion effects of zero-tariff market access. There are difficulties in quantifying the effects of removal of various non-tariff barriers on trade and investment flows, and on employment and productivity growth. It is also difficult to quantify the systemic effects on policy regimes and business practices in areas such as business competition, intellectual property protection, regulatory transparency, and improving labour and environmental standards. Tariff elimination is not a primary feature of the USSFTA, since Singapore had very few applied tariffs and U.S. MFN tariff levels were generally low. The main intent of the USSFTA, from the Singapore perspective, is to encourage Singapore traders and investors to venture more boldly into the U.S. market and to encourage U.S. businesses to regard Singapore as a manufacturing and trading base.

The Singapore negotiators in the USSFTA (Koh 2004, pp. 18–20) summarized the following benefits for Singapore:

(1) Improved market access and tariff savings with the removal of U.S. import tariffs on exports originating from Singapore: Estimated tariff savings of $200–300 million annually. For non-textile products, largest savings go to chemical sector (S$178 million or 60 per cent), followed by mineral product sector (S$54 million or 18 per cent). Tariff savings in electrical and electronics, processed food and metal products constitute the remaining 22 per cent of total tariff savings for non-textile products. The largest beneficiary of this improved market access are U.S. MNCs in Singapore, as they already accounted for over 60 per cent of Singapore's exports to the United States in 2000.

(2) Savings from the waiver of the Merchandise Processing Fee of 0.21 per cent *ad valorem* imposed by U.S. Customs on imports into the United States. Estimated saving of S$51 million annually.

(3) The Integrated Sourcing Initiative means Singapore-based companies can source widely for components in ICT and medical equipment industries.

(4) The textile and apparel industry will enjoy price advantage of 5–15 per cent if Singapore manufacturers can restructure their input sourcing to comply with the yarn forward rule of sourcing yarn from the United States or Singapore. Synthetic fabrics can be produced by Singapore's chemical industry.

(5) Waiver of the vessel repair duty imposed on repair work on U.S. ships outside the U.S.. Estimated saving of S$7.7 million annually.

(6) Singapore service suppliers guaranteed access and national treatment in the U.S. market, including in ICT and financial services.

(7) Professional bodies in Singapore to consult with those in the U.S., especially in architecture and engineering, in order to develop

mutually acceptable standards and criteria for licencing and certification of professional service providers.

(8) Companies in both Singapore and the U.S. will enjoy increased protection of IP. Singapore will amend its IP laws in line with technological changes and international developments and will accede to WIPO treaties on copyright and implement anti-circumvention measures. The improved IP regime in Singapore will attract more FDI, especially in knowledge-intensive industries.

(9) Singapore investors in the United States will enjoy strong protection. For breaches in the FTA obligations, the aggrieved Singaporean investor can take the U.S. government to an international arbitration tribunal.

(10) The U.S. visa system will make changes in favour of Singapore business visitors.

Singapore's manufacturing sector is the main beneficiary of the USSFTA through the market access provisions, while its service sectors have to prepare themselves for intensified competition from U.S. service suppliers. While Singapore's manufactured exports have a global reach, including into the United States, Singapore's services exports are still very much oriented to the region and have to reach out to the U.S. market. Singapore has made numerous concessions, ranging from the opening up of its services sectors to U.S. competition, to enhanced IP protection, enhanced transparency, and enhanced domestic competitive environment. It bears noting, however, that all these concessions are in areas to which Singapore is already unilaterally committed to change. The USSFTA serves to strengthen Singapore's resolve and hastened the process but does not change its direction. *The utility of a bilateral FTA with the United States in expediting policy and structural reform in ASEAN resonates also in the bilateral reviews below.*

ii. Template for ASEAN?

The United States has indicated that the USSFTA can serve as a useful template for future U.S. negotiations with other Asian economies, particularly for FTAs under the Enterprise for ASEAN Initiative (EAI).[16]

In assessing whether the USSFTA can serve as a template for U.S. negotiations with the rest of ASEAN, several features of the Singapore economy have to be borne in mind, as these were crucial in contributing to the successful outcome of USSFTA from the perspective of both countries. First, Singapore is the most advanced of the ASEAN economies, and has already attained high domestic standards in IP protection, labour rights and welfare, and environmental protection and maintenance. The USSFTA notwithstanding, Singapore is already unilaterally committed to further improvements in these areas. Second, Singapore is a long-standing strong advocate and practitioner of free trade. It has already achieved free trade in goods and is rapidly opening up its services sectors to international competition. It has no sensitive domestic agricultural sector to protect and no large agricultural exports to compete and threaten the U.S. farm sector. It is rapidly restructuring its economy out of labour-intensive industries and into activities in accordance with its dynamic comparative advantage. It has no massive labour-intensive exports to threaten the employment of American workers. It has a highly efficient and transparent customs administration and is internationally acknowledged as one of the least corrupt economies and governments in the world.

All of these factors suggest that bilateral negotiations with other countries under the EAI rubric will be more difficult.

II. Indonesia

by Hadi Soesastro

A. Introduction

Bilateral free trade agreements constitute a major element of Indonesia's trade diplomacy and policy. Indonesia has thus far promoted bilateral trade relations through efforts other than forming FTAs. It is only rather recently that Indonesia has begun to contemplate more seriously the role of bilateral FTAs in promoting trade and economic cooperation with a number of countries. On 23 October 2003 the Ministry of Industry and Trade formed a FTA Team to undertake studies on a number of possible bilateral FTAs.

It may be useful to categorize Indonesia's possible FTA partners into two groups of countries. The first group consists of developing countries such as Pakistan, Bangladesh, Iran, Chile and South Africa. Indonesia's trade relations with these countries are insignificant. Therefore, the economic impact of FTAs with these countries are likely to be insignificant as well. However, they are being contemplated for one or more of the following reasons: (a) developing new markets for Indonesian exports; (b) strengthening political and overall relations; and (c) as a training ground for negotiating FTAs with other countries. In early May 2004, Indonesia and Iran agreed to form an FTA as part of a comprehensive economic and trade partnership.

The second group consists of advanced industrial countries such as Japan and the United States. As noted in Chapter 2, Japan and the United States are Indonesia's two most important trade and economic partners. We also noted in Chapter 3 that a U.S.-Indonesia FTA could have a fairly significant effect at the aggregate level and particularly in certain key sectors. We also demonstrated that the U.S.-Indonesia economic relationship, for various reasons, is not what it could be. An FTA with the United States could have an important impact on bilateral economic interaction, both through the positive effects of opening markets as well as a defensive strategy given the increase in U.S. FTAs in recent years (and more in plans for the future).

In fact, to some degree, as Indonesia is a newcomer in forming bilateral FTAs, it may now be exploring the FTA route more seriously largely in response to offers by other countries. It will definitely give priority to FTAs with countries that it regards as politically and economically important, namely Japan and the United States. These two countries have made approaches to Indonesia at the highest level. President Bush launched the Enterprise for ASEAN Initiative (EAI) at the APEC Summit in Mexico (November 2002). This was followed up by a visit by U.S. Trade Representative Robert Zoellich to the region, including Indonesia. A Japan-Indonesia FTA was proposed during President Megawati's official visit to Japan in 2003.

But FTAs with developed countries like the United States are inevitably complicated, as they include myriad border- and "non-border-" related policy changes. Indonesia can intuit what to expect from negotiations with the United States from FTAs concluded by the United States with Singapore (2002) and Australia (ratified in July 2004), as well as from the ongoing negotiations with Thailand, for these will no doubt give a good indication as to which issues the United States will want to include. However, it is also cognizant of the fact that each country is special in this regard, and the size and characteristics of the Indonesian economy—as well as that of the United States—will bring to the fore a number of controversial areas.

In this section, we consider these issues in the context of the proposed U.S.-Indonesia FTA, using the U.S.-Singapore agreement as a reference as to what areas might be included in the agreement.

B. Special Problems in Indonesia-United States Trade Relationship

In Chapter 2, we reviewed the U.S.-Indonesia trade and investment relationship in terms of changing trends in flows and structure, followed by an applied statistical approach to the U.S.-Indonesian relationship. But we did not review in-depth policy regimes, outside of a careful delineation of bilateral tariffs at a highly disaggregated level. In this subsection, we consider these policies in more detail.

The textiles and apparel sector has faced significant problems associated with U.S. quota restrictions. Indonesia in the past requested regularly higher quotas for some product categories for which orders have been high. U.S. quotas will be removed as of 1 January, 2005 as part of the final phase of Uruguay Round liberalization; Indonesian exporters of textiles and apparel will, therefore, face greater competition in maintaining market shares. Hence, Indonesian exporters definitely see some advantages in gaining preferential access to the U.S. market.[17] They may constitute a strong constituency for an FTA.[18]

A number of primary commodity exports face restrictions upon entering the U.S. market. Standards constitute the main problem. Many fisheries products, cocoa and spices experienced Detention Without Examination (DWE) for failure to meet the FDA's standards. The United States is the largest market for Indonesian cocoa, but it has imposed "automatic detention" of its imports from Indonesia due to concerns about pests. Shrimp and tuna exports also face many problems. Shrimp exporters currently have *uncertified* status. In addition, Indonesia and a number of countries have been accused by the Southern Shrimp Alliance in the United States of dumping cultivated shrimp.[19] Processed food also faces hurdles. Exports of instant coffee fall under a quota regime because they include sugar. Since 1 January 2004, exports of juices to the United States require certification.[20]

To overcome these problems the Indonesian side has raised the possibility of mutual recognition agreements (MRAs), as well as technical assistance to increase quality, strengthen standards, and improve sanitary and phytosanitary (SPS) measures. In addition, security concerns have penalized the exportation of agricultural products and processed food. The Bioterrorism Act and the Container Security Initiative increase costs to Indonesian exporters. Due to the Act, exporting food and feedstuff has become more difficult and complicated. All agricultural products from Indonesia must undergo security inspection in Singapore.

In terms of the Indonesian import regime, there also exist problems related to agricultural products. The United States has raised concerns regarding its exports of chicken parts to Indonesia. The Indonesian government has imposed de facto quantitative restrictions on the import of meat and poultry products by requiring a special certification. The other issue is a policy of allowing the government to maintain a ban on the import of chicken parts for not meeting the *halal* certification requirement.[21] In fact, pressures to protect the domestic poultry industry in Indonesia are strong. Imports of chicken parts are still small but have increased rapidly in the past few years. Indonesian producers have been alarmed by this especially because the U.S. export price of CLQ (chicken leg quarters) is much lower than the cost of domestic production. The Indonesian Chamber of Commerce (Kadin Indonesia), represented by Soy Pardede, stated that "the Government needs to admit that many of the existing trade policies are too complicated and should be replaced by simpler ones".[22]

On the importation of chicken parts, for instance, it was pointed out that under the existing regulations, the authority to issue the certificate lies with the Indonesian Ulemas Council (MUI), the Ministry of Religious Affairs and the Food and Drug Monitoring Agency. Instead, Kadin suggested that the policy should be executed by the Ministry of Industry and Trade. The other bodies should only issue the *halal* criteria (*Jakarta Post*, 5 April 2004).

Soybean imports are another sensitive issue. According to the Institute of Agriculture and Trade Policy in Minnesota, there is dumping of wheat, soybean, corn, cotton and rice to Indonesia. Even if this is true, the fact that soya-related products constitute some of the top exports items from the United States suggests that this will continue to be a controversial sector.

Additional areas that have been cited by the U.S. government regarding Indonesian protection include (*Jakarta Post*, 5 April 2004):

1.   High rice import tariffs. At present the tariff is only 430 rupiah (five U.S. cents) per kilogram, but the Ministry of Agriculture

keeps proposing to raise it.

2. The customs service uses arbitrary "check prices" on food imports rather than actual transaction prices on importation documents.
3. The government restricts the importation of and requires special licencing for the importation of alcoholic beverages, explosives and certain dangerous chemicals in a way that violates WTO rules.
4. The requirement for food product producers to register their products at the Agency for Drug and Food Control (BPOM).
5. The requirement for all consumer products to have labels written in Indonesian.
6. Weak enforcement of intellectual property rights (IPRs).

Intellectual property protection is a major sticking point in the relationship. The following statement is contained in the USTR's *2004 Trade Policy Agenda and 2003 Annual Report of the President of the United States on the Trade Agreements Program*:

> The U.S. Government has continued to urge Indonesia to take steps to strengthen its IPR regime. USTR placed Indonesia on the Special 301 Priority Watch List in 2003 due to concerns over continued optical media piracy and weaknesses in Indonesia's IPR enforcement. Indonesia took some noteworthy steps to strengthen its IPR regime over the past year, but significant problems remain. The Indonesian government enacted an extensive revision of its copyright law in July 2002 that came into effect in July 2003 and addressed a number of the United States' concerns. Over the last year it initiated public awareness campaigns and began addressing problems of interagency coordination. In addition, in November 2003 it submitted new draft regulations governing optical media production for Presidential approval. However, these proposed regulations, if signed, still would not firmly commit Indonesia to seize and destroy machinery and materials used in piracy. Overall, protection of intellectual property rights remains weak and U.S. industry continues to report increases in illegal optical media production lines for both domestic consumption and export. U.S. industry also raised serious concerns about counterfeiting and trademark violations of a wide range of products. While a limited number of raids against retail outlets for pirated optical media products have occurred, long delays remain in prosecuting intellectual property cases. Sentences continue to be light and insufficient to deter intellectual property piracy, further undermining the criminal penalties established by the new copyright law.

The above issues have been the subject of discussions and consultation between officials of the two countries for a number of years. Progress in overcoming them has been slow. The forum for discussion has been provided by the Trade and Investment Facilitation Agreement (TIFA), signed between Indonesia and the United States in October 1997. There is now a Trade and Investment Council between Indonesia and the United States constituted through TIFA. The first meeting of this bilateral forum took place in Jakarta in October 1998, the second in September 2001, and the third in Bali in November 2002. Under the TIFA the United States provided an IPR action plan to Indonesia in May 2002. The implementation of the specific recommendations in the IPR action plan, including steps to improve the legal framework and enforcement mechanisms to protect IPR, has proven to be unsatisfactory to the U.S. government.

Issues related to IPR are illustrative of the difficulties that will be encountered in creating an Indonesia-U.S. FTA, namely: (1) insufficient policies in place to protect IPR; (2) weak capacity to implement commitments; and (3) lack of transparency. This is in part caused by a serious problem of inter-agency coordination. It may well be that the process of forming an FTA with United States will help focus the attention on the main issues to be covered under the FTA and to organize the bureaucracy to develop coherent policies on the various sectors included in the FTA. The exercise was initiated a few years ago by the Ministry of Industry and Trade to draft a hypothetical FTA (with Chile) has contributed to intensified exchanges among various government agencies.[23]

However, it appears that some groundwork will need to be prepared by the Indonesian side. There is only so much "learning by doing" that can be accommodated by the process. Most likely the USTR will not be willing to be dragged into a protected process of negotiations, and many of the issues discussed above (and below) will have to be resolved satisfactorily before the process of negotiating the FTA can actually begin.[24]

For Indonesia, it is critically important that the creation of an FTA with the United States be seen as a national project, and not merely a matter of trade diplomacy. Therefore, the formulation of an overall strategic framework is required. Broad-based exchanges of views within the country are essential. Perhaps a national commission of sorts should be established to formulate this framework.

On the U.S. side, the possibility of an FTA was briefly discussed in the *Report of the National Commission on U.S.-Indonesian Relations* (2003). The National Commission was co-chaired by the George Schultz, Lee Hamilton, and George Russell. It stated that an FTA would go a long way to underscore the special Indonesia-U.S. relationship. In addition to helping deal with certain interest groups in the United States that advocate restrictions on imports of tuna, shrimp, steel, and possibly coffee from Indonesia, it might overcome export restrictions in the United States in areas where Indonesia has a competitive advantage, e.g., textile and apparel, footwear and agriculture (see Chapter 3). But perhaps most importantly, it can contribute to consistent U.S. engagement with Indonesia (USINDO 2003).

From the Indonesian perspective, the major perceived benefit from an FTA with the United States is the improvement of allocative efficiency as it helps lock in major domestic economic policy reforms that go with the FTA, as discussed in a general context in Chapter 2 and in Soesastro (2003) in the specific Indonesian context. Moreover, as was also discussed in the earlier chapters, an FTA is as much about investment expansion as it is about trade expansion. The United States has traditionally been a major source of FDI for Indonesia. Since the crisis, followed by political transition, Indonesia's investment climate has become less attractive as the economic recovery remained sluggish and the policy and legal environment continued to deteriorate.[25] While Japanese investors have focused more on investment incentives and tax administration and customs, U.S. investors have placed a high premium on investment protection (Maidir and Atje 2004). "Reliability" is important for all investors as production activities in Indonesia are becoming an integral part of the regional production networks. An FTA could help a great deal in this regard.

But, as noted above, forming an FTA with the United States is not an easy proposition for Indonesia. As the Report of the National Commission indicates, the "Indonesian side favors expanding trade but is concerned about the political costs of market-opening commitments". (USINDO 2003). The Report also suggests that the immediate hurdle for Indonesia to overcome relates to the issue of IPR protection. This was also explicitly stated in the Report by the U.S.-ASEAN Business Council. The Council additionally proposed that the two sides revive the bilateral energy dialogue that was suspended during the Asian Crisis. The importance to U.S. business is that their involvement in the energy sector in Indonesia is particularly concerned with contract sanctity.

C. The Likely Main Elements of a U.S.-Indonesia FTA

Indonesia does not need to start from scratch in designing and formulating a FTA with the United States. It can draw on some of the elements in the U.S.-Singapore FTA (USSFTA), for example. It is clear that adjustments will need to be made since the structure, nature and level of development of the two economies are significantly different. It is possible that Thailand, which is currently negotiating its FTA with the United States, will also make use of the USSFTA. Perhaps the U.S.-Thailand FTA, when concluded, will provide a better model for Indonesia than the USSFTA, given that Thailand is more comparable to Indonesia in terms of factor endowments. In preparation for the talks which began in the end of June 2004, a U.S.-Thailand Business Coalition was formed in March 2004. It is made up of approximately 100 U.S. companies interested in supporting the negotiation, passage, and implementation of the U.S.-Thailand FTA. They have pledged to work for a "world-class" agreement.[26]

As can be seen from Table 4.2 above, which lists the principal elements of the USSFTA, the agreement is comprehensive in scope and covers aspects of trade in goods, services, investment, government procurement, protection of intellectual property, competition policy, and the relationship between trade and labour and environment. The following is a brief discussion on aspects of the main elements that are of relevance to Indonesia in designing an FTA with the United States. This discussion is limited to general principles. In the manufacturing sector it is easy to identify the sensitive sectors. They are limited to foods, beverages and tobacco, chemical products, and the automotive sector, where peak tariffs in Indonesia are found. But in agriculture there are many sensitive sectors. While applied tariffs have also come down, the use of non-tariff measures is still fairly pervasive. In services, many sectors are considered to be sensitive sectors. However, there have been significant developments in terms of reform in a number of these sectors, including financial services and telecommunications, largely because of increased involvement by foreign investors through acquisitions.

The principle of *National Treatment* (Chapter 2) prevents discrimination against foreign products once they have entered the domestic market. Excise duties and value-added taxes must apply equally to imported and domestic products. A thorough investigation needs to be made to see whether Indonesia has made some violation of this principle.

Rules of Origin (Chapter 3): Indonesia does not have the capacity to deal with complicated methods. Rules of origin should be kept as simple as possible and as liberal as possible. Transparency is most important. The USSFTA uses a product-specific approach based on a change in tariff classification. The USSFTA tends to be more liberal than, for instance the Japan-Singapore Economic Partnership Agreement (JSEPA). The USSFTA mostly requires a lesser degree of product transformation at the 6-digit or sub-heading level; the JSEPA requires a change at the 4-digit or heading level.

The Integrated Sourcing Initiative (ISI), perhaps, will not be applied to Indonesia. It has been said that this Initiative was originally proposed as a way of showing appreciation to Singapore for its support in the war against terrorism. An ISI product is considered to originate from Singapore as long as it is imported into the United States from Singapore. In other words, it does not matter where the ISI product is manufactured provided there is a Singapore consignee involved. The ISI list contains 266 electronic (products covered under the WTO Information Technology Agreement) and medical/precision instruments. However, these products already enter the United States and Singapore duty-free. Thus, the ISI will not have much of a liberalizing effect on bilateral trade. It will only tend to benefit companies that procure such products regionally or globally through Singapore.

With respect to *Customs Administration* (Chapter 4), the USSFTA is most comprehensive in terms of customs cooperation. This is an area in which Indonesia needs a great deal of capacity building, facilitation and cooperation. The USSFTA applies the provisions of the WTO Agreement on Customs Valuation. Under the article on Review and Appeal, it provides access to businesses to a review and appeal mechanism that is applicable to all determinations relating to customs matters. Administrative rulings must be made public. The USSFTA has an expansive section on customs cooperation. This could be an important area in which the U.S.-Indonesia FTA could actually be an important stepping-stone toward "best practices", which would be greatly facilitated by U.S. technical assistance (not an issue in the USSFTA).

Textiles and Apparel (Chapter 5) is clearly a "sensitive" industry in the United States. As noted above, it is also an important export sector for Indonesia and will no doubt be a key element of the FTA. The enforcement and cooperation regime instituted in the textiles and apparel chapter in the USSFTA is much more strict than that provided for under the general customs administration chapter. The United States is concerned about Singapore's status as a transshipment hub. Therefore, Singapore must track the movement of all textile trade, including activities between partners with which it has an FTA, and is obliged to turn over all information obtained to the U.S.. Singapore must also facilitate site visits by U.S. "jump" teams.

Technical Barriers to Trade, "TBTs" (Chapter 6) is also an important area for the FTA, for TBTs create serious distortions in the domestic economy. While it has made considerable progress in reforming this area since the late 1980s, Indonesia still has in place a number of licencing requirements, such as in sugar trade, that tend to be inefficient and create considerable "dead-weight loss" in the economy. Reform in this area may be one of the more salutary ones in the FTA in that it will be used as a means to lock in more efficient domestic economic reforms.

Safeguards (Chapter 7): the USSFTA does not impose any additional obligations or rights with regard to *global* safeguard measures. The Agreement specifically permits either party to exclude the other party from such measures. With respect to *bilateral* safeguard measures, the USSFTA allows one FTA partner to suspend preferential import duty reductions or increase import duties for goods from the other FTA partner during the 10-year transition period following the effective date of the USSFTA. The parties can impose a bilateral safeguard measure only after an investigation conducted according to the WTO Safeguards Agreement provisions, namely, that there must be an increase in imports, a finding of serious injury, and a causal link between the injury and imports. Safeguards will be an important element in a U.S.-Indonesia FTA. It is seen as an "insurance policy" and provides some level of comfort to pursue further liberalization from the perspective of both countries.

Cross-border Services (Chapter 8): the USSFTA contains obligations and disciplines provided for under the GATS, but it makes significant improvements as compared to the transparency requirements outlined in the GATS. Singapore will provide substantial access for all types of services, subject to a few exceptions. U.S. services suppliers are granted non-discrimination and national treatment. Singapore's services market access commitments include: financial services (banking and insurance); construction and engineering; computer and related services; telecommunications services; tourism; professional services (architects, accountants, lawyers); express delivery; and energy services. In many of these areas, Singapore agreed to bind its market access commitments at levels that provide substantially better access than that which it currently offers other WTO members (GATS plus). The USSFTA uses a "negative list" approach.

While the extensive liberalization of services in the USSFTA is impressive by any measure, the fact that the United States and Singapore are both advanced, open economies made such negotiations much easier. This will be a far more difficult task in the context of Indonesia, whose services market is far more closed, segmented, and underdeveloped.

The USSFTA also provides for bilateral negotiations on mutual recognition of qualifications, certification and licencing requirements. For instance, Singapore commits to recognize law degrees from specific U.S. law schools for admission to the Singapore Bar. In the field of educational services, Singapore guarantees unrestricted access for U.S. suppliers to provide primary education services to non-Singapore citizens. Singapore's commitments in secondary education are rather limited, but on higher education, Singapore only limits U.S. education service suppliers in relation to the training of doctors in Singapore. Indonesia has yet to liberalize its educational system. It lags behind its neighbours, Malaysia and Thailand, in this regard. There are increased pressures from within the country to liberalize this field. Hence, while this will be a difficult sector in negotiations with the United States, it may prove to be one of the more fruitful.

Telecommunications (Chapter 9) and *Financial Services* (Chapter 10) are likely to be included in the Agreement as these two sectors are of great interest to the United States. Within these sectors there are many areas of activities that Indonesia is prepared to open up. However, Indonesia must have a clearer picture as to how it wants to develop the telecommunications industry in Indonesia. (It also needs to have a firm implementation plan to realize the recently drafted changes in the country's financial architecture, but this is a separate issue). Telecommunications market-opening measures include reasonable and non-discriminatory access to networks, transparent rule making by an independent regulator, and adherence to the principles of deregulation and operator choice of technology. But the USSFTA recognizes the United States' and Singapore's respective rights to regulate these sectors.

Temporary Entry of Business Persons (Chapter 11) is not as sensitive an issue for Indonesia as it appears. Its inclusion in the Agreement will be seen as favourable to Indonesia, particularly in that it will facilitate FDI inflows.

A provision on *Competition Policy*, as in the USSFTA Chapter 12 (Anticompetitive Business Conduct, Designated Monopolies, and Government Enterprises), is an element that is now common to most FTAs. Indonesia has a competition law, but it continues to seal off its state enterprises. This is an area ripe for reform, but the government lacks determination to implement reforms of its state enterprises. The Agreement provides protection for U.S. firms relating to sales to and purchases from Government Linked Companies (GLCs). It also ensures that GLCs do not discriminate against U.S. goods, services and investments, and do not engage in anti-competitive practices. Singapore will enact laws that will proscribe anticompetitive business conduct and establish an authority to enforce such laws.

Government Procurement (Chapter 13): Indonesia is unlikely to agree to an inclusion of this provision. It is not a signatory to the WTO Government Procurement Agreement (GPA), which opens government contracts to foreign bidders on a non-discriminatory basis when the value of a government contract exceeds a designated threshold. Under the USSFTA, Singapore has agreed not to exercise any governmental control or influence over the procurement decisions of its GLCs. Singapore is one of the 27 GPA countries. It also reduced each country's GPA thresholds for federal/national government procurement by over two-thirds.

Electronic Commerce (Chapter 14) is a new area for Indonesia. There are no strong feelings in the country as to whether to include or exclude this subject in an FTA. The USSFTA commits to the non-discriminatory and duty-free treatment of all digital goods, whether they are classified as goods or services. It establishes (for the first time) an explicit guarantee that the principle of non-discrimination applies to digital products delivered electronically. It also creates the first binding prohibition on customs duties being levied on digital products delivered electronically.

Investment (Chapter 15) will be another key element in a U.S.-Indonesia FTA, especially given the U.S. private-sector preferences for investment protection and predictability. Like its ASEAN partners, Indonesia's investment regime is already quite open, but the problem is the overall investment climate which suffers from legal uncertainty, inconsistent policies in general, discretionary policies of local governments, as well as the lack of many business-friendly labour policies. The draft law on investment provides for national treatment (NT), but the law has been pending agreement by the Parliament for many years.

On investors' protection, the USSFTA ensures a secure and predictable legal framework. The investment provisions draw from U.S. legal principles and practices, including due process and transparency. The investor rights are backed by effective and impartial procedures for dispute settlement. The USSFTA obliges Singapore and the U.S. to accord NT, MFN and fair and equitable treatment. It does not make MFN exceptions for situations involving other FTAs. This implies that any deals Singapore offers on investment issues in future FTAs may be extended to the U.S. ("unconditional MFN"). This holds for the U.S. as well.

As discussed above, *Intellectual Property Rights* (Chapter 16) is an area that is of great importance to the United States and of considerable difficulty in Indonesia. Indonesia must strengthen its legal system to make any commitment on IPR protection credible. This could be a sticking point in the negotiations. Protection of IPR builds upon the TRIPS agreement, and provides strong protection for new and emerging technologies and reflects standards of protection similar to those in U.S. laws.

The USSFTA vastly expands protection for and enforcements of IPR, including protections for patents, trademarks, copyrights and digital copyrights, and trade secrets. It represents the highest standards of protection and enforcement for intellectual property achieved to date anywhere in the world in any bilateral or multilateral agreements, treaty or convention.

The Agreement stipulates the following:

1. Full NT and non-discrimination obligations that are as broad as possible, apply to all types of IP, and permit no exceptions.
2. The parties agreed to accede to a number of international treaties,

agreements and conventions that establish IPR protection and enforcement standards.

3. Increased copyright protection.
4. Enhanced trademark protection.
5. Greater patent protection.
6. Other Internet-related provisions.
7. Restrictions on use of compulsory licensing that are stricter than those in the WTO TRIPS Agreement.
8. Singapore agreed to apply its IPR laws to transshipments through its territory.
9. Strengthened enforcement of IPR rights.

Labour (Chapter 17) and *Environment* (Chapter 18) will be areas of controversy in the FTA discussions between Indonesia and the United States. The labour and environment chapters of the USSFTA include commitments by the FTA partners regarding effective enforcement of their respective labour and environmental laws, high levels of worker rights and environmental protections, and a pledge not to weaken existing labour and environmental laws to attract investment or encourage trade. These areas are controversial in Indonesia and, given the diversity in policies between the two countries—in part related to the differences in economic development—will no doubt be difficult to negotiate.

The USSFTA is the first trade agreement subject to review under the terms of the Trade Promotion Act (TPA), whereby the U.S. Congress is mandated to evaluate all aspects of a trade agreement, including provisions on labor and environment standards.

Transparency (Chapter 19) should be promoted. The Agreement includes provisions to ensure regulatory transparency. This is an effective deterrent to combat corrupt business practices. It constitutes another area where "best practices" adopted in the FTA will be to Indonesia's own interest, especially with technical assistance from the United States.

Dispute Resolution (Chapter 20): the USSFTA allows for some involvement by the private sector. Developing such a dispute resolution system will also be in Indonesia's own interest.

As a final note in this regard, it is useful to point out that the coverage of the Australia-Thailand FTA is similar to that of the USSFTA. Unlike the Australia-Thailand FTA, the USSFTA has separate chapters on Textiles and Apparel, Telecommunications, and Financial Services, as well as provisions on Labor and Environment, while the Australia-Thailand

FTA has provisions on anti-dumping and subsidies and countervailing duties that are included in its first chapter, Trade in Goods (Annex). In contrast, the USSFTA has avoided inclusion of anti-dumping measures because any suggested changes in the U.S. anti-dumping law would be politically controversial, particularly for frequent users of the law, such as the steel industry. The USSFTA contains no specific provision for dealing with subsidies and countervailing duties, most likely for the same reasons.

Indonesia will certainly be interested to include a clause on anti-dumping. As noted by DeRosa (2003), Indonesia has been affected heavily by recent U.S. administered protection activities, with 13 anti-dumping investigations and 4 countervailing investigations initiated between January 1995 and June 2002 against U.S. imports from Indonesia, and with duties ultimately being applied in 50 per cent of the cases for which investigations were started (7 out of 13 and 2 out of 4, for anti-dumping and countervailing duties, respectively). Indonesia will have to see whether Thailand is able to negotiate an anti-dumping clause included in its FTA with the United States. If it does not, it is unlikely that Indonesia will be successful. In that case it should not even attempt to do so and should direct its energies to other areas of great concern.

III. Malaysia

by Mohamed Ariff

A. Introduction

As was noted in earlier chapters, the economies of the United States and Malaysia are quite different in many obvious ways, and it is precisely these differences that render the U.S.-Malaysia economic relations mutually rewarding. However, the underlying common denominator is that both are market economies that have been ardent supporters of the liberal trading system. The United States has long championed the cause of free trade. Although it succumbs occasionally to domestic protectionist pressures in certain sectors (particularly in recent years), especially in the form of anti-dumping duties and countervailing duties in textiles/clothing and agriculture, the U.S. trade regime remains one of the most liberal in the WTO. However, protectionist pressures are, of course, of concern to Malaysia, which depends heavily on trade and whose top export market is the United States.

Viewed in this light, a linkup between the United States and Malaysia is by any measure an enticing proposition. For the United States, it is mainly a question of extending to Malaysia the special bilateral relations that it already has with NAFTA, and nations such as Israel, Chile and Singapore. For Malaysia, it is essentially a matter of taking a bold step towards putting more "candies on the table". Despite many lingering questions, a U.S.-Malaysia FTA might be in the cards in the not-so-distant future and this interesting policy option merits serious consideration. In this section, we consider the salient issues that would be included in the agreement, as well as an analytical perspective as to how salient issues will likely play out during the negotiations.

The first subsection (B) provides an overview of the political economy environment underpinning the willingness of Malaysia to adopt FTAs in general, and with the United States in particular. Subsection C analyses the possible changes in issues of governance, the regulatory environment and policy transparency in the creation of an FTA with the U.S., while Subsection D uses the USSFTA as a possible guideline in drafting a U.S.-Malaysia FTA, along the lines of the approach to the U.S.-Indonesia FTA. Subsection E reviews the details concerning several key sectors that need to be taken into consideration in the drafting of such an agreement between the two countries, and what the ramifications of liberalizing these sectors would be. The last subsection gives some concluding remarks.

B. The Political Economy Environment

i. Policy Orientation

By any economic measure, Malaysia is an open economy. Trade is the lifeblood and FDI the backbone of the Malaysian economy. Exports and imports account for roughly 200 per cent of the country's GDP, while FDI constitutes about 10 per cent of total investment in the country.[27] The manufacturing sector, which constitutes 30 per cent of the country's GDP, is highly export-oriented. Manufactured exports comprise about 80 per cent of total exports. As noted in Chapter 2, electronic and electrical (E&E) goods account for about 60 per cent of total exports.

Nearly all the major multinational corporations (MNCs) have production bases in Malaysia. These MNCs are rooted, and not footloose, for they are strongly linked to local ancillary industries, which provide components, parts and intermediate inputs. The MNCs with similar operations in neighbouring countries engage extensively in intra-firm trade, contributing to Malaysia's growing intra-regional as well as intra-industry trade. Production networking among the MNCs has strengthened Malaysia's regional linkages.

As noted in Chapter 3, Malaysia has a fairly liberal trading regime, with generally low tariffs. The trade-weighted average tariff is only about 8 per cent, although this low average conceals high tariff protection accorded to heavy industries. Malaysia has been lowering its tariffs both regionally and multilaterally. Under the ASEAN Free Trade Area (AFTA), Malaysia has offered extensive tariff concessions, most of which have been subsequently extended to outsiders as well. Malaysia plays an active role in the AFTA process, although it was criticized for postponing tariff cuts on automobiles from 2003 to 2005, to protect its national cars (the Philippines has done the same). The Malaysian government started to cut back tariffs on automobiles from January 2004, replacing tariffs with excise duties for revenue purposes, and resisting pressure from the industry to postpone liberalization to 2008.

As noted earlier, trade and investment are interlinked, with MNCs importing components and parts from their home countries and exporting their finished products back home, although this pattern is changing with MNCs importing their inputs from, and exporting their output to, third countries as well. Thus, Malaysia's main trading partners are also the major sources of FDI for the country. Malaysia has been actively attracting FDI through investment missions and investment incentives of sorts. It is important to underline that the Malaysian government has been quite pragmatic in this regard. It is not averse to temporarily shelving even the politically charged affirmative action plans, designed to correct racial imbalances, in times of crises, as was indeed the case in the mid-1980s and late-1990s, paving the way for 100 per cent foreign ownership.

Malaysia's understanding of the concerns of foreign investors has improved since its own MNCs have increased FDI to other countries within the region and beyond. Such "reverse investments" complement FDI inflows in bringing about industrial restructuring in the country, as was well borne out, for example, in the Japanese and Korean cases. Consequently, policy approaches towards FDI have become more liberal over the years.

ii. Policy Responses

An important hallmark of Malaysian policy-making is the political will to bring about changes warranted by changing circumstances. It is important to stress that Malaysia has always been pragmatic—rather than dogmatic—over various policy stances. Despite rhetoric in the face of trying times, the Malaysian government has always stood by its commitment to the policy of economic openness, notwithstanding certain sectoral exceptions. It is indeed remarkable that the Malaysian economy has become more—rather than less—open after every economic crisis. Table 4.3 shows this with respect to increasing trends in trade-to-GDP ratios over time.[28] It also shows just how open the Malaysian economy has become, with its trade-to-GDP ratio now being one of the highest in the world. In short, the fact that economic openness increases the vulnerability of the domestic economy to external fluctuations has not deterred the government, as it has learned to cope with such fluctuations through appropriate macroeconomic policy intervention.

Malaysia's reputation for policy consistency, coherence and predictability was somewhat tarnished when the government imposed capital controls and the currency peg in September 1998 in the wake of the financial crisis. What was not understood well by foreign investors was that these so-called "unorthodox measures" were meant to be (and turned out to be) temporary and directed at speculative capital flows. It is indeed unfortunate that these measures have, perhaps, given the wrong impression that Malaysia's commitment to openness has changed, when it has not.

iii. Trade Initiatives

To be sure, the political economy environment in Malaysia is conducive to multilateral, regional and bilateral trading arrangements, even though it has not negotiated any FTAs outside of ASEAN yet. Under the Uruguay Round, Malaysia liberalized trade in thousands of items. Malaysia subscribes fully to the WTO process through its active involvement in the Doha Development Agenda. As mentioned earlier, Malaysia is also firmly wedded to ASEAN and is strongly committed to the AFTA process. Malaysia sees no contradiction between multilateral and regional approaches; they are viewed as two sides of the same coin. As noted in the case of Indonesia, PTAs can serve as training grounds for liberalization and be used as stepping-stones toward global arrangements, along the lines outlined in Chapter 3. What cannot be accomplished at the multilateral level in the near term can be experimented on in a more expeditious fashion in a regional context.

Although ASEAN has a population of over 500 million, it is still small as a market in terms of purchasing power. This is one reason why ASEAN member-states have been forging wider trading arrangements with major trading nations. The main motivation for this actually is the quest for greater market access, as well as a defensive strategy in light of growing regionalism in its key markets. It was in this context that Malaysia supported the idea of an ASEAN-Japan FTA at the ASEAN Summit in Bali in 2003. The framework for ASEAN-Japan Comprehensive Economic Cooperation (CEP) was signed by ASEAN leaders on 8 October 2003. The CEP framework aims at strengthening ASEAN-Japan economic links by progressively liberalizing and facilitating trade in

TABLE 4.3
Trade Openness Measure for Malaysia, 1990–2003*

Year	Export (X)	Import (M)	GDP	(X + M) / GDP
1990	46,840.5	79,119	119,081	1.06
1991	61,319.4	100,831	135,124	1.20
1992	71,457.6	101,441	150,682	1.15
1993	89,694.2	117,405	172,194	1.20
1994	120,294.4	155,921	195,461	1.41
1995	147,253.0	194,345	222,473	1.54
1996	158,540.2	197,280	253,732	1.40
1997	178,945.1	220,984	281,795	1.42
1998	237,648.9	228,124	283,243	1.64
1999	271,730.2	248,477	300,764	1.73
2000	317,908.3	311,459	342,612	1.84
2001	285,316.2	280,229	334,309	1.69
2002	298,671.2	302,589	360,658	1.67
2003	310,433.1	307,266	392,012	1.58

*Figures in RM millions according to current prices
Source: Economic Reports, various years.

goods and services and creating a transparent and liberal investment regime. ASEAN-Japan FTA is expected to be completed by 2012 (with an additional five years for Cambodia, Laos, Myanmar, and Vietnam [CLMV] countries). It is noteworthy that consultations on the ASEAN-Japan FTA began in February 2004. Initially, Malaysia was in favour of ASEAN collectively entering into a PTA with Japan and was against Singapore signing a bilateral FTA with Japan. But that position has changed subsequently.

Malaysia's primary objection to the Singapore-Japan FTA was that it would weaken the solidarity of ASEAN as an entity. There were other concerns as well. For one thing, it would be extremely unwieldy for 10 ASEAN countries to sign 10 separate agreements with Japan. For another, not all ASEAN countries possess the capabilities to negotiate effectively bilateral deals with third countries. It would be a lot simpler if ASEAN as a group could enter into a trade pact with Japan or any other country.

Hence, upon careful rethinking, Malaysia changed its stance with respect to bilateral FTAs. Malaysia has recognized that there are merits in going it alone rather than collectively. What is more, the danger this would pose to ASEAN unity can be minimized, if PTAs are developed simultaneously in a two-track mode. As noted above, the main advantage of a bilateral deal is that it can go further and deeper than a collective one. In the latter case, the deal would go only as far as the lowest common denominator, which is a major constraint considering the vast heterogeneity that exists among ASEAN member countries. Thus, a collective PTA would not necessarily render a bilateral FTA redundant.

Malaysia is thus favourably inclined towards both approaches being pursued in a parallel fashion. ASEAN-Japan, ASEAN-China, and ASEAN-India FTAs are underway with the goal of realization within 10–12 years. At the same time, Malaysia is also actively working on bilateral trade agreements with all three. ASEAN-China FTA should be in place by 2010 for the six original members and 2015 for the new members, but details are still in the works. The Framework Agreement on Comprehensive Economic Cooperation was signed in 2002 in Cambodia. The Protocol to amend the Framework Agreement was signed in October 2003 in Bali. The ASEAN-China Early Harvest Program covering 590 products came into effect on 1 January 2004. An Early Harvest Program for the

ASEAN-India FTA is due to begin November 2004. Meanwhile, Malaysia is negotiating bilateral FTAs with China, Japan, India and Korea, as well as the Closer Economic Partnership with Australia and New Zealand.

However, the EAI is somewhat different. Under the EAI approach, the U.S. interest lies in forging bilateral FTAs with individual ASEAN countries, with the ultimate goal of having a network of bilateral FTAs between ASEAN and the United States. The pace at which the bilateral FTAs will be developed will obviously depend on the willingness and capacity of individual ASEAN countries.

Our research would suggest that all indications are that Malaysia is keen on a bilateral FTA with the United States. For example, references have been made in a positive way to the EAI in the Malaysia International Trade and Industry Report 2002 released by the Ministry of International Trade and Industry (MITI) in July 2003, stating that a bilateral FTA with the United States "will be developed at a pace agreeable to the parties concerned" (p. 189). To pave the way, Malaysia signed a bilateral trade and investment framework agreement (TIFA) with the United States on 10 May 2004.

The fact that Singapore has already signed a bilateral FTA with the United States might have given some impetus to the idea, although Malaysia would nonetheless find this attractive on its own, given the strong trade and investment linkages between the two countries discussed in earlier chapters.

A bilateral FTA with the United States will also give Malaysia a platform to address many thorny issues that cannot be resolved adequately through the WTO process. Non-tariff measures such as labelling requirements and certifications, stringent sanitary and phytosanitary (SPS) procedures and mandatory recycling, as well as restrictive trade practices, have tended to retard trade flows. Most exports of textiles and apparel from Malaysia are still subject to quantitative restrictions in the form of quotas in the United States (though these will be phased out by 2005), while exports of some steel products have been affected by safeguard measures through a Presidential Proclamation in March 2002 (withdrawn in 2003, after a WTO ruling and EU retaliatory threats). Malaysia's exports of wood and wood products to the United States have been affected by the ruling that the wood used in government buildings must be from "sustainably-managed" forests. All such issues can be addressed and, hopefully, resolved within a bilateral framework.

However, it is pertinent to note that policy friction will continue; the U.S.-Canada FTA, for example, has not prevented fierce policy disputes between the United States and Canada. But this is a natural product of closer relations.

Finally, we underscore that FTAs are viewed positively in Malaysia as useful tools to help the nation achieve its long-term goals. Malaysia's Vision 2020, which aims at developed country status by the year 2020, cannot be achieved in isolation, particularly in the context of a country that is so open. Policy-makers recognize that FTAs serve to not only improve market access but also enhance competitiveness. Needless to say, market access is a good thing only if exporters are ready to compete.

C. Governance, Regulatory Environment, and Transparency

i. Governance

The *World Development Report Survey 1997* measured the quality of governance on the basis of perceptions of 4,000 firms in 67 countries using a variety of indicators. These indicators included the protection of property rights, judicial reliability, the predictability of rules and the control of corruption. Scholars suggest that improving governance requires actions along four dimensions. These areas include the structure of government, civil society voice and participation, public sector management, political accountability, and ensuring a competitive private sector. The report suggested that the quality of governance improved with improvements in the suggested areas.

One area of inadequacy in Malaysia as far as governance is concerned has to do with the nature of government involvement in privatization. The declared objective of privatization has been to bring about a shift in policy from public sector-led growth to private sector-led growth. It is also the purpose of the privatization policy that was launched in 1983 to promote competition, efficiency and productivity. Yet another objective of the move was to reduce the size of the public sector and its participation in the marketplace.

Nevertheless, the Malaysian government has retained its hold on privatized projects. Three glaring examples are Petronas, Tenaga National Berhad and Telekom Malaysia. In each case, the government has a legal right to participate in the running of the companies. This is done by appointing representatives, who have to be approved by the government, on the board of directors. A significant number of directors appointed need to have the approval of the Ministry of Finance and the Economic Planning Unit. Further, a substantial number of the shares of these companies are held by the Ministry of Finance or by companies that represent the government (e.g., Petronas). The government also ensures that these companies retain a high degree of monopoly. For instance, only Tenaga Nasional Bhd (TNB) is permitted to supply electricity throughout the country. There are independent power producers (IPPs), but they are not permitted to supply electricity directly to end-users. The IPPs are allowed to supply electricity only to TNB. In this manner a more competitive environment is not permitted to emerge.

Corruption remains an important issue in Malaysia. The Prime Minister has stated that he plans to take a serious view of corruption. This is not surprising given that Malaysia received a disappointing score in the Corruption Perceptions Index (CPI) 2003. Although this put Malaysia in the 37th position, ahead of countries like South Korea, China, Thailand and Indonesia, there is much room for improvement. The 2001 CPI placed Malaysia in 36th position, lagging behind Singapore which was ranked 4th, Hong Kong (14th), Japan (21st), and Taiwan (27th).

In sum, Malaysia has a long way to go in improving governance, an area in which progress is rather restricted. A more robust system of governance could be obtained if there were less intervention from the government in the functioning of the economy, particularly in the private sector. The case of privatization is a striking example, since privatized projects still support government interference, as mentioned earlier, albeit less visibly. The proposed U.S.-Malaysia FTA can address shortcomings in this area by pressing for less interference by the government in the private sector, indirect as this involvement might now be. An agreement that places governance in proper perspective will reduce rent seeking and barriers to trade and promote trade that is mutually beneficial.

ii. Transparency

There has been much concern in Malaysia about the question of transparency of the government, especially when it comes to the conduct of business. Tunku Abdul Aziz, President of Transparency International, Malaysia notes that:

> We have to ensure that the systems and procedures that regulate the way the government, in particular, conducts its affairs are open, transparent and that they put accountability in the driving seat (*Corruption Perceptions*

Index, 2003, http://www.transparency.org.my).

The government has been criticized for not exercising transparency in public procurement, military purchases and in relation to engineering and construction contracts. Tunku Abdul Aziz addresses this point in the same publication:

> Rightly or wrongly, Malaysia is viewed as a country that is not as transparent as it should be. Many large infrastructure projects are apparently awarded on the basis of closed-door negotiations, a practice that must be changed if we want to gain and retain public confidence in our system. We ignore the call for greater transparency and accountability at our peril. We are sending the wrong signal to the international business community by persisting with some of our questionable practices (*Corruption Perceptions Index, 2003,* http://www.transparency.org.com).

Tunku Abdul Aziz's observations are extremely pertinent in the context of any future U.S.-Malaysia FTA. The lack of transparency creates obstacles to the free functioning of markets since the success of any FTA depends on the removal of obstacles and hindrances to trade. It would run against the rationale of subscribing to an FTA if awards for projects were to be based on non-transparent negotiations. Indeed, the threshold levels for access to information need to be lowered so that all stakeholders in the business community have equal access to information. If access to information is denied or restricted, this would be tantamount to discrimination against agents wanting to do business in Malaysia. Transparency also has implications on government procurement, an issue that we shall discuss below.

iii. Regulatory Environment

Malaysia's privatization policy places limits on foreign equity participation. Foreign-equity participation is allowed up to 30 per cent of share capital as a general rule (larger foreign-equity participation is permitted under special circumstances[29]) Thus, the regulatory framework is such that foreign equity participation is not readily encouraged. This adds a constraint to the free flow of equity funds into the country.

In order to offset in part negative perceptions among foreign investors due to the institution of capital controls during the Asian Crisis, Malaysia took some measures to encourage foreign investment. Profit remittances and the repatriation of capital connected with FDI were never subject to control. But new incentives were offered, and these included:

- Allowing 100 per cent foreign ownership of new investment made before 31 December 2000 in domestic manufacturing.
- Allowing an increase in the foreign ownership share in telecommunications projects from 30 per cent to 69 per cent, with the understanding that the ownership share would be brought down to 49 per cent by 2005.
- Allowing an increase in foreign ownership in stockbroking and insurance companies.
- Relaxing restrictions on foreign investment in landed property to allow foreigners to purchase all types of properties above RM 250,000 in new projects or projects which are less than 50 per cent completed.

The Malaysian government has progressively permitted more foreign participation in local businesses. Over the years, the limits to foreign participation have been relaxed. But much more remains to be done in order to provide a truly open environment. A larger margin of participation by foreign firms is still possible and should be included explicitly within the U.S.-Malaysia FTA.

iv. Other Issues

a. Competition policy

Competition policy is likely to be a thorny issue in any FTA between the United States and Malaysia. Malaysia has been trying to introduce elements of competition law within its legal framework. At present the effort is piecemeal, with only select sectors having competition regulations. The communications and multimedia sector is one such sector, having elements of competition within the Communications and Multimedia Act (CMA) 1998. The CMA 1998 expressly states that anticompetitive behaviour such as rate fixing, market sharing, and the boycotting of competitors are prohibited. Similarly, the Energy Commission Act (ECA) 2001, declares that one of its functions is to "promote and safeguard competition and fair and efficient market conduct" (ECA 2001, p. 14). It also seeks to "prevent the misuse of monopoly power or market power in respect of the generation, production, transmission, distribution and supply of electricity and the supply of gas through pipelines" (ECA 2001, p. 14). Notwithstanding these attempts, the government has been reluctant to enact general competition legislation. Neither has the government made any concerted attempt to set up a competition authority.

The absence of a competition law and authority will be a stumbling block to the smooth conclusion of an FTA. It is worth mentioning that MITI has held a strong stance on the Singapore Issues. Minister Rafidah Aziz has made it clear that Malaysia does not agree to a launching of negotiations on the Singapore issues since there is "no explicit consensus and there is a need for further clarification of these issues" (Third World Network, 2003). Further, she has remarked that the proponents of the new issues have "kept demanding things that others couldn't deliver" (Kaur 2003). More specifically, the government fears that a multilateral competition policy could impinge on Malaysia's development-related policies and hinder the growth of domestic industries.

Admittedly, there is no consensus to begin negotiations on competitions policy under the umbrella of the WTO, but active debate on the issue may even delay work at the level of instituting domestic competition law. If the USSFTA is any benchmark, the United States will likely insist upon both parties proscribing anti-competitive business conduct and promoting competition, including specific laws against anti-competitive behavior as well as the establishment of national authorities to implement and enforce such policies fairly.

While an FTA with the United States will not deprive Malaysia of the right to establish government enterprises, there will be restrictions on how the Malaysian government can establish or maintain its enterprises. There are three constraints that may apply to government enterprises. First, these enterprises will have to extend non-discriminatory treatment to investments and goods and services supplied from the United States. Second, government enterprises will be required to act in accordance with commercial considerations in their operations and transactions (but the Malaysian government may lay claim that its national policies will be at stake if its enterprises act solely on the basis of commercial considerations since some of their considerations are non-economic). And third, these enterprises will be restrained from acting in a manner that is anti-competitive and to the detriment of the welfare of consumers.

The USSFTA takes competition issues quite seriously. The decision to introduce competition law and policy explicitly in the agreement is a sign of this seriousness. Another striking point is the willingness on the part of the Singapore government to permit U.S. banks to open branches in the island state. The banking sector in Malaysia, by contrast, is not likely to take an easy line on competition in banking services (discussed below). As it stands the operations of foreign banks are limited in Malaysia. They do not have the liberty to open branches in response to the demand for their services. There are strict controls on the number of ATM machines that they can open. This situation protects local banks and discriminates against foreign banks, a condition that will likely be untenable in an FTA.

The automobile sector is another area where monopoly power is vested in the hands of domestic car producers. The heavily protected automotive sector is not accommodating to foreign firms, and is another area that will show resistance from the Malaysian government (also discussed below).

A third area of resistance will come from the utilities (water and electricity) sector. This, again, is a sector that has a significant government presence. The rationale for government presence is based on the grounds that these are public goods. However, it is doubtful that the government will loosen its grip over this sector even if it can be demonstrated that a competitive market will result in lower prices and larger output due to greater competition and innovation.

b. Government procurement

In the case of the USSFTA, the entire chapter on Government Procurement was built on the foundation of the Agreement on Government Procurement (GPA) of the WTO. As was the case with Indonesia (as well as the Philippines in Section IV), Malaysia is not a signatory to the GPA although it is on the working group. However, Section 1 of Article 13.1 of this chapter in USSFTA unequivocally states: "The Parties reaffirm their rights and obligations under the GPA and their interest in further expanding bilateral trading opportunities in each Party's government procurement market." The next section of Article 13.1 includes an agreement to cooperate actively in working towards a multilateral agreement on transparency in government procurement.

The question of government procurement is likely to be a sensitive point. If the USSFTA is any guide, the United States is likely to demand greater transparency from Malaysia on the issue of government procurement. Malaysia, on the other hand, has made its stand quite clear by not being a signatory to the GPA. It is possible that Malaysia might agree to a phased approach to transparency in government procurement, however.

c. Rules of origin

Malaysia abides by the rules of origin of products as established under the Agreement on the Common Effective Preferential Tariff (CEPT) of AFTA. Under these rules, products under the CEPT imported from one ASEAN state into another are eligible for preferential concessions if they are wholly produced or obtained in the exporting member state. Alternatively, if the goods are not wholly produced or obtained in a member state, they are deemed to be originating from a member ASEAN state if at least 40 per cent of its content originates from that state. Where inputs are used for a finished product eligible for preferential treatment in another ASEAN state, the cumulative rule of origin requires that not less than 40 per cent of the aggregate content be ASEAN in origin.

Technically, the rules of origin for the CEPT are at variance with U.S. customs law where the concept of "substantial transformation" is invoked. The U.S. customs authorities look at the location at which the manufacturing process constituted a "substantial transformation" of the materials and components into the finished product. The site at which substantial transformation occurs determines origin for U.S. tariff purposes. However, in substance one can see some convergence between the two approaches. Once the necessary technical specifications are spelt out as to what can be considered "substantial transformation" in the U.S.-Malaysia context, agreement on the rules of origin can be envisaged. This approach will no doubt be useful across all ASEAN countries under the EAI.

One can think of two issues that will arise in the course of negotiations in this context. First, Malaysia perceives the rules of origin that the U.S. secured under NAFTA as being overly complicated. This is particularly true in the automotive, textiles and clothing and agricultural sectors, where rules of origin can be highly restrictive. It therefore follows that Malaysia will strive to obtain a more simple set of origin rules than applied in NAFTA. Second, the Malaysian government may try to negotiate for a position whereby preferential treatment under rules of origin developed under a U.S.-Malaysia FTA will qualify for preferential treatment under NAFTA. The USSFTA states that both parties shall consult to review the rules in the light of increasing global competition and in harmony with the WTO Agreement on the Rules of Origin. It does not mention whether or not a product that satisfies the origin rules under the USSFTA would also satisfy NAFTA requirements. This is a possibility that the Malaysian government might want to pursue.

D. The U.S.-Singapore FTA as a Guideline for the U.S.-Malaysia FTA

As one of the most comprehensive FTAs in the world, the USSFTA includes an impressive array of trade- and investment-related areas. With respect to the U.S.-Malaysia FTA negotiations using the USSFTA as a model, anecdotal evidence suggests that there exist apprehensions in Malaysia about the adverse effects of such an FTA on the domestic economy, given the experiences drawn from other regional or bilateral arrangements. Moreover, a problem with bilateral FTAs is that they tend to advantage the larger partner, and given the sheer size differential between the United States and Malaysia, this asymmetry could disadvantage Malaysia in the negotiations.

Comparing notes with the USSFTA, we suspect that a U.S.-Malaysia FTA would likely involve a scaled-down agreement, particularly in relation to the investment rules and related matters as well as market access for services. The USSFTA will accord substantial market access to U.S. firms across the entire spectrum of services, subject to very few exceptions. It is, however, unlikely for the U.S.-Malaysia FTA to include such breadth and depth of the services commitments seen in the U.S.-Singapore agreement.

Malaysia's stance in the realm of services is consistent with the Doha Development Agenda, which emphasizes continued flexibility for developing countries provided by the GATS. Nonetheless, Malaysia has undertaken numerous voluntary liberalization measures in services, for example, opening up the distribution and consultancy services to foreign providers although they have yet to be committed under the GATS. Furthermore, Malaysia, being a signatory to the ASEAN Framework Agreement on Trade in Services[30] (AFAS), is currently discussing issues such as harmonization of professional standards, acceptable levels of accreditation between member countries, movement of labour in relation to the provision of services, and licensing and certification of service suppliers with the ASEAN member countries, which serve as possible avenues for discussion with the United States.

The USSFTA also contains provisions to protect U.S. companies against possible anti-competitive behaviour but, as noted above, Malaysia has yet to formulate its own domestic competition policy. Perhaps more importantly, the Malaysian government procurement policy is intended to encourage greater business participation of *bumiputera* (Malays), promotion of local industries, and the transfer of technology and expertise. Government procurement in Malaysia is basically categorized into three classes: supplies, services (including engagement of manpower, expertise and consultants, research, designing, and repairs), and works (including construction and engineering activities). No threshold value is specified for international tender, which is only called when the goods are not locally available. However, all procurement above RM 200,000 will be undertaken through an open tender process, in which all bidders must be registered with the government.

No doubt, an area that should be included in the U.S.-Malaysia FTA is the e-commerce segment, an area in which the United States and Malaysia are of like-minds. The United States and Singapore agreed to provisions on e-commerce that reflect the issue's importance in global trade, which affirms that any commitments made related to services will also be extended to the electronic delivery of such services, such as financial services delivered over the Internet. Such inclusion is deemed important due to the fact that the Malaysian online market is expected to grow.

Custom procedures, dispute settlement mechanism and rules of origin provisions in the U.S.-Singapore agreement should be able to serve as a useful guide for the U.S.-Malaysia agreement in these areas. There will inevitably be labour and environment provisions in the U.S.-Malaysia FTA as well, which may be difficult but easier than in case of Indonesia discussed above. In the area of labour provisions, Malaysia has ratified five of the eight ILO Fundamental Conventions. What concerns Malaysia or issues that may need to be ironed out in the future agreement are mainly the issues of trade union rights and migrant workers while child labour and forced labour, though they exist, are generally insignificant in Malaysia.[31] In the context of the environment, both parties might choose to follow the USSFTA such that it involves cooperation to protect the environment as well as effectively enforcing their own domestic environmental laws. Since the 1970s, sustainable development goals have always been embodied in the Malaysian government's policies as reflected in the Five-Year Development Plans, Industrial Master Plan (1986–95), the Second Industrial Master Plan

(IMP2), the Outline Perspectives Plans and Vision 2020.[32] Despite some hiccups, environmental resource management practices in the country have been relatively successful in certain areas.

Another debate that might surface is the issue of genetically modified organisms (GMO). Although this will not be an important area in the negotiations, the issue basically centres around the growing sensitivity of Malaysia towards gene-altered soybeans and other foodstuff which are increasingly causing concern among the U.S. soy trade as well as the palm oil.

E. Sectoral Analysis

Free-trade areas can have varying effects on the goods and services sectors of participating countries. We reviewed the estimated effects on Malaysia of an FTA with the United States, using a CGE model, gravity model, and disaggregated matching approach in Chapter 3, where we estimated that, even if the aggregate effects of integration will not be great, they could be significant in a number of sectors. In this section, we consider sectoral effects from a *policy* perspective.

i. Agriculture

At the Uruguay Round and Doha WTO negotiations, Malaysia has argued for more aggressive tariff-reduction formulae than those proposed in agriculture.[33] Malaysia's position takes into account the need to balance its interest as a major exporter of palm oil, as well as the developmental objectives of its agricultural sector. Malaysia will continue to seek an outcome that will discipline the use of most trade-distorting subsidies that palm oil currently has to contend with in third country markets. This will be an important issue in the U.S.-Malaysia agreement, as well as various policies on the Malaysian side that seek to maintain the flexibility to utilize non-trade measures in pursuing the goals set out in its National Agricultural Policy.

a. Palm oil

In general, Malaysia maintains a non-interventionist policy for palm oil. Crude palm oil (CPO), like rubber, pepper, and some timber products, is subject to export taxes. Other direct policy measures are insignificant. Palm oil has been subject to export taxes throughout its commercial history in Malaysia. The export tax in the 1950s and 1960s was a flat 5 to

7.5 per cent of the value of the export, but in the 1970s the government changed the tax structure to favour the development of downstream processing. It put a high tax on exports of CPO while reducing the tax levied at each level of processing. The imposition of such export taxes is a point of contention in the Uruguay Round of Agriculture Agreement (URAA) negotiations because it has the effects of restricting exports of cheaper commodities to the detriment of importers. The government also supports the production of palm oil by allowing the use of rubber-replanting grants for planting oil palm.

In addition to the above, institutional support from the government for the production, promotion, research and development, and marketing of palm oil is generally strong. Export credits are not directly given to palm oil but there are some support measures that implicitly contain subsidy elements. For example, the export credit re-financing (ECR) is available for palm oil exporters, while export credit insurance and guarantee (ECIG) has been introduced to protect banks and financial institutions against non-payment of loans and advances made by them to exporters and importers.

Liberalization in the palm oil industry would impact the industry in several ways. First, the protective action of developed countries through the Blue Box[34] provisions has resulted in over-production of soybean oil that is dumped on world markets. Being a close substitute to palm oil, this disadvantages exports of Malaysian palm oil and causes its price to fall drastically, with the eventual adverse impact on the domestic palm oil industry. Second, such a shift in the trade regime will affect different groups of producers — estates, organized smallholdings in government land development schemes, and unorganized smallholdings. The estates, mainly owned by large corporations with their relatively advanced management, marketing and technological capabilities, could be able to meet the challenges posed by the vagaries of international edible oils market but this is certainly not the case for the smallholdings, organized or not.

b. Paddy and Rice

Liberalization of this sector in the context of the U.S.-Malaysia FTA would impact the rice industry, particularly the smallholders, by depressing farm prices, which could then lead to lower farmers' income, the displacement of the farming population and a severe contraction of the industry. As

Jegatheesan (2001) notes,

> the future of the country's rice farming industry, given its present
> structure, isolation from external competition, excessive dependence on
> direct domestic support for viability and a historical policy environment
> that has spawned a dependency syndrome amongst farmers, is faced
> with more risk than promise as the inexorable drive towards complying
> with our international trade liberalization obligations nears fulfillment.

In view of the potential negative impact, the Ministry of Agriculture is
formulating detailed and focused plans and courses of action to respond
positively in the direction of complying with WTO and AFTA. However,
there are constraints in the range and type of options available due to
the socio-political realities surrounding Malaysian rice production and the
farming community. The government's stand on these issues is reflected
in the Third National Agricultural Policy (NAP3, 1998–2010), which
aims to make Malaysia a net food exporter by 2010. Besides continuing
with regulated imports of rice to achieve the self-sufficiency target of
a minimum domestic production of 65 per cent for food security,[35] the
NAP3 is focused on increasing domestic production to substitute food
imports by encouraging the production of cost-competitive products,
reducing labour requirements, strengthening rural infrastructure and
improving market efficiency. The NAP3 acknowledges the basic WTO
non-compliance of these direct industry supports and proposes that they
be "repackaged" into forms that do not violate WTO rules, and that
farmers would still continue somehow to enjoy the equivalent monetary
benefit, though in a different, WTO-compliant, form.[36]

ii. Services

The Malaysian services sector has been earmarked as a sector to propel
further growth of the economy. We might divide this sector into six
sub-sectors, namely:

- Finance, insurance, real estate and business services
- Transport, storage and communication
- Government services
- Wholesale and retail trade, hotels and restaurants
- Electricity, gas and water
- Other services

The overall share of the Malaysian services sector relative to GDP
has remained steady at about 40–45 per cent for some time,[37] although

there has been a shift in the relative importance of the various sub-sectors over time. During the 1960s and 1970s, policies directed at the services sector focused on basic infrastructure facilities such as utilities, transportation and government services. Since late 1980s, the government has emphasized financial services, wholesale and retail trade, tourism and telecommunications.

Today, developments in trade liberalization, emergence of new markets such as China and the East European countries and the proliferation of the information and communication industry (ICT) have spurred the consumption of services, particularly in finance, transport and telecommunications. Furthermore, the government's policy of maximizing the sector's potential, initially to mitigate the services deficit in the balance of payments and later to develop new growth areas, has also contributed to the stronger growth of the sector. Given its strong performance, the share of the services sector in GDP growth has been rising gradually from 46.8 per cent in 1990 to nearly 57 per cent in 2003. As a result, the services sector hovers generally between 60–70 per cent of GDP now (Ministry of Finance 2003), on par with some developed economies.

Since the Uruguay Round agreement, Malaysia has undertaken numerous voluntary liberalization measures such as the distribution and consultancy services which have been opened to foreign providers although the sectors have not been committed under GATS. Traditionally, shipping, tourism and education were the primary industries that were actively promoted by the government. While these sectors continue to be the star performers of the services sector in Malaysia, some new industries are also being promoted, particularly knowledge-based industries that specialize in ICT-based services, professional and technical services, banking and insurance, and modern health care. Nevertheless, as Malaysia has been widely acknowledged to be facing an acute shortage of skilled labour, this particular strategy requires the development of a critical mass of highly-skilled knowledge-workers in the country, as well as the need to foster other supporting institutions.

a. Higher education
Hence, human capital development presents an important challenge to economic and social development in Malaysia; reform of higher education will be an important protagonist in this process. The growing

demand for higher education and the limited number of places in public institutions spurred a growing number of private higher learning institutions to develop split-site degree arrangements such as twinning degree programmes, credit transfer programmes and advanced standing entry programmes with foreign universities. Under such programmes, private colleges are in a position to offer various types of degree courses and professional qualification in affiliation with foreign higher-learning institutions, which serves as an alternative for students embarking on their university education.

The development of private higher education in Malaysia has witnessed new players, including large corporations, into this area. For example, the Sunway Group, a large public-listed corporation, operates the Sunway College to offer academic programmes for higher learning, and also provide infrastructure and administrative support to the Monash University Malaysia. The Multimedia University operates under Telekom Malaysia, another large corporation, to conduct a spectrum of information technology and multimedia-based courses at the undergraduate and postgraduate level. Although it is possible to assume that these large corporations engage in the higher education business to earn "normal" profits or to channel profits to obtain tax breaks, nonetheless, the primary driving force behind the set up of private colleges and universities appears to be the desire to provide alternative avenues for higher learning.[38]

Also, apart from providing increased opportunities for university education to local students, these programmes have helped save millions of ringgit in foreign exchange for the country, based on the escalating cost of overseas education. In addition, the presence of such programmes has also helped the country to achieve its objective to develop and promote the country as a regional centre of educational excellence,[39] thereby attracting foreign students to embark on their higher learning in Malaysia.

The various study options between Malaysia and the United States that are currently in place include internal award certificate and diploma programmes, and the split-site arrangement bachelor degree programme.[40] The latter covers twinning degree programmes, credit transfer programmes and advanced standing entry programme. Of the three study methods, the American Degree Transfer Programme is considered very popular among students as it allows students to continue their degree programme at various American universities. For example, RIMA College offers the American Degree Programme (ADP)[41] to allow students to transfer credits to over 39 American universities in various fields of study, e.g., business, computer science, engineering, applied science, liberal arts and social science.

The U.S.-Malaysia FTA could help American universities facilitate other education arrangements with Malaysia such as setting up offshore branches or campuses. At present, the establishment of an offshore branch or campus in Malaysia is only allowed by invitation from the government. Currently, there are four foreign university branch campuses, two each from Australia and the United Kingdom, operating in the country. Other possible arrangements could include partnership or collaboration with a local private institution to conduct an entire franchised university degree programme such as the "3+0 degree programme".

Most programmes offered by local private institutions are usually limited to lower capital-investment courses like business, commerce and applied arts. However, progress is being made to provide more science and technology courses that are vital to the country's human resource development. As such, with the United States being one of the leading providers of higher learning services in these areas, more courses and programmes related to science and technology like pure sciences, engineering and technology-related areas could be made accessible to local students via such programmes. This will be in line with the Malaysian government's policy thrusts for the development of human resources.

Modern technology has brought changes to the structure of the education market, including "borderless learning". As a result of the development of new information and communication technologies such as cable and satellite transmissions, audio and video conferencing, distance and lifelong learning has become a new, important phenomenon. Thus, another positive outcome that could result from the U.S.-Malaysia FTA would be a promotion of further development in distance education courses between the United States and Malaysia.

The following are some issues that may be of concern to the United States based on the types of regulations and legislation imposed by Malaysia on foreign higher learning providers:

- Requirements to form a partnership/joint-venture programs with a local education institution, subject to approval from the Ministry of Education, to offer higher learning programs;

- Degree of access to establishment of local branch campuses by American universities; and
- Immigration measures on the entry or stay of foreign permanent education staff.

While the liberalization of education services may bring benefits to higher learning to Malaysia, local authorities are concerned that the opening of the education services will pose problems related to quality and accountability. Therefore, to ensure quality education as well as to safeguard the interests of students, foreign educational institutions have to be approved by the Ministry of Education before they are allowed to conduct any academic courses and degree programs. In particular, U.S. education providers will be concerned that the government will require local partnerships or joint ventures. Such arrangements can be tedious, as regulations pertaining to the participation of *bumiputera* partners must be followed. This may be an issue in the U.S.-Malaysia FTA negotiations, as such regulations could be perceived as trade and investment restrictions. It may also be that the government will want to restrict U.S. institutions to the provision of education in the technology-related areas noted above, which may not necessarily be the most profitable.

Moreover, although the government has placed more liberal rules for the recruitment of foreign teachers and educators, the immigration measures in place may impose controls on the entry or stay of foreign academic staff. U.S. citizens are not required to have a visa for the purpose of social or business visits for not more than three months, but the Malaysian government could impose quotas on the number of foreign *permanent* academic staff. Such a policy would be designed to encourage foreign education providers to source for local talent, but will likely be an issue in the U.S.-Malaysia negotiations, as will be possible restrictions on the mobility of foreign permanent academic staff.

b. Tourism and travel

The tourism sector is one of the fastest growing in the Malaysian services industry. For the whole of 2003, Malaysia recorded almost 11 million inbound travellers, making the tourism industry the second largest income generator for the national economy for four consecutive years.[42] Pertinent to this area, a U.S.-Malaysia agreement could address, *inter alia*, important issues relating to areas of immigration, air services liberalization, market access to tourism services, and safety and security for Malaysian and American tourists. Since the main mode of supply for tourism comprises mainly consumption abroad, the U.S.-Malaysia FTA may benefit the Malaysian tourism and travel industry in terms of generating higher tourist traffic from the United States. Similarly, Malaysia, with 25 million people boasting a relatively high per capita income for a developing country (roughly US$4,000), could also be an important potential market for the United States.

In particular, a U.S.-Malaysia FTA could facilitate tourism through the removal of certain direct and indirect barriers to tourism. For example, a mutual agreement on immigration regulations that allows favourable visa arrangements for Malaysian travellers destined to the United States.[43] Other specific arrangements could include forming alliances among Malaysian and U.S. airlines, which will help to increase passenger air-service by removing the limitations on routing, type of service or aircraft type.[45] This will also help increase long-haul travel[44] and increase the frequency of flights between the two countries. In addition, the U.S.-Malaysia FTA would represent an opportunity to form strategic alliances and "smart partnerships", e.g., in terms of hotels and restaurants, travel agencies and tour operators, and tour guide services.

Facilitating the setting up of hotels, restaurants, travel and tour services and the like will be an important market-access goal of the U.S. negotiators. However, the Malaysian authorities, while allowing the entry of foreign enterprises, have set the following regulations for hotel and hotel services, tourism projects, and tour services:[45]

1. Hotel and hotel services, and tourism projects, i.e., theme parks, recreational camps, convention centres: *Requirement for foreign hotels, and tourism projects to be established as a locally incorporated joint venture with Malaysian individuals or Malaysian controlled firms.*

2. Tour services, including ticketing and reservations: *(a) Licences must be obtained from the Ministry of Culture, Arts and Tourism (MOCAT), and renewed annually; (b) Joint ventures must be made only with Malaysian individuals or Malaysian controlled firms, and locally incorporated; (c) General aggregate foreign shareholding is limited to 30 per cent; (d) Separate licences must be obtained before operating an additional branch, also to be renewed annually; and (d)*

There exists a quota of personnel applied to inter-company transfers.

Based on the government's policy for foreign investment in tourism and hospitality, it would seem that the government has placed an important emphasis on joint-ventures and the formation of partnerships, to allow provisions for local content and knowledge transfer for capability and capacity building in preparation for full liberalization. To encourage foreign investment in tourism, foreign investors for hotel and hotel services and tourism projects are allowed 100 per cent foreign equity but only for the first five years from the date of incorporation. For the subsequent years, aggregate foreign equity is limited to 51 per cent. The remaining equity is to be held by a Malaysian, and at least 30 per cent allocated to *bumiputeras*. These will all be important areas that the United States will have to address in its negotiations with Malaysia.

This is not to exaggerate the restrictions on foreign participation in Malaysian tourism. At present, there are many foreign players in the hospitality industry in the country. To name some of the major foreign players, they are Shangri-La Hotels and Resorts, Mandarin Oriental Hotel Group, and Marriott International, which operate hotels like the Ritz Carlton, J.W. Marriott and Renaissance. On the local front, the Berjaya Group is one of Malaysia's major conglomerates in the development and management of hotels and resorts, both domestic and international. From a list obtained from the American Hotel and Lodging Association (AH&LA), some of the top 50 hotel companies in the United States, like Hilton Hotels Corporation, Marriott International, Hyatt Hotel Corporation, have already gained market presence in the Malaysian hospitality industry. However, there are still ample investment opportunities for other American hotel chains to enter the Malaysian hospitality industry, and existing firms could benefit from greater liberalization in this important sector.

c. Financial services

Although the Malaysian financial sector has not yet undergone full-scale liberalization, foreign participation is already dominant in the banking and insurance sectors. Some are even pioneers in their own sectors, e.g., the Standard Chartered Bank, one of the first banks to operate in Malaysia, and in insurance, the American International Assurance and Great Eastern Life Assurance companies. As the financial market is still under-developed and opportunities abound for mutual fund and insurance industries to grow, foreign firms are eager to offer their services to Malaysian consumers. On the banking side, there is a growing need for sophisticated products as business expands. As such, foreign experts can complement the services of domestic service-providers.

Permission to own more than 50 per cent of common stocks in domestic institutions undoubtedly will attract foreign investors who are interested in penetrating the Malaysian financial sector. In principle, applications to provide any financial services require the approval of the central bank, Bank Negara Malaysia (BNM). In the banking sector, the government has allowed the existing 13 foreign banks in the country to maintain their 100 per cent equity ownership, but were required to be locally incorporated. It has also bound foreign presence at an aggregate maximum of 30 per cent of the total equity of a previously established *domestic* banking institution. In the insurance sector, existing foreign shareholders were allowed to increase their ownership subject to a maximum of 51 per cent of total equity. New entry of foreign insurance companies was also allowed through participation of up to 30 per cent of total equity of a locally incorporated insurance company.

The capital market has been progressively opened up, with gradual increases in foreign-equity participation in stockbroking, fund management and entry of managers, specialists, experts and professionals. Malaysia is committed to 49 per cent foreign equity in stockbroking companies. Under appropriate circumstances, Malaysia allows full foreign ownership, such as in fund management.

At the end of 2002, apart from the 13 wholly foreign-owned banks noted above, foreigners also owned an average 23 per cent of total equity in four domestically-owned banks. On an aggregate basis, foreigners account for about 33 per cent of total commercial bank assets. In the insurance sector, 23 out of a total of 54 insurance companies are majority foreign-owned. Foreign market share in the insurance industry remains high, accounting for 77 per cent of life insurance premiums and 40 per cent of general insurance premiums. In the capital market, 5 out of 79 licenced fund managers are majority or wholly foreign-owned, while in the investment advisory sector, close to half of the licenced advisers are majority or wholly foreign-owned. Besides equity participation, foreign participation has also taken other forms, such as participation through strategic alliances with local entities. In the insurance sector, there are 10 bank assurance arrangements involving locally incorporated foreign-owned banks, of which nine were established with domestically owned insurance companies (Ministry of Finance 2003).

At present, however, further liberalization of the government's policy vis à vis foreign-equity ownership is unlikely. Some foreign banks have chosen to reduce their ownership to below 51 per cent in order to receive the same treatment as domestic banks. And as domestic banks, their applications to open new branches are facilitated. Foreign-controlled banks in Malaysia are prohibited from opening new branches and they are not allowed to join local automated teller machines (ATM) networks. This applies to all non-resident controlled companies (NRCCs), which, therefore, includes 100 per cent foreign-owned subsidiaries (companies with more than 50 per cent foreign ownership are classified as NRCCs). Their commercial lending is capped by limiting the share of funding that may be obtained by foreign-owned firms or NRCCs from foreign-controlled banks to 50 per cent. This limit on lending activities and exclusion from the local ATM network has contributed to the foreign banks' declining market share. Another disadvantage that they have over their domestic counterparts is that they can only employ up to two foreign managers or specialists. On the other hand, there is no limit on the issuance of credit cards, which is considered to be the most liberal financial market.

Insofar as liberalization of Malaysia's financial services is concerned, the government's position is that for the benefits of liberalization to be fully realized, the pace of liberalization has to be in tandem with the capacity and the ability of the system to absorb these changes without undermining financial stability. It is imperative that liberalization does not marginalize domestic financial institutions; the government is, therefore, unprepared to open its doors fully to foreign financial institutions, as their presence could jeopardize smaller-sized domestic institutions. Even though the number of foreign banks in Malaysia is low, their presence is still significant.[46]

There are several factors that attract foreign firms to invest in Malaysia, and some are given below. In the case of commercial banks, the initial role of these foreign interests was to provide foreign exchange facilities to foreign business traders specifically to those of the same nationalities. But today, foreign banks operate very much like any domestic bank, offering an extensive range of products and services to cater to both retail and corporate clients. Thus, in general, foreign banks are engaged in both retail banking and wholesale banking services. Nevertheless, some may concentrate more on wholesale rather than retail banking services such as the case of the Bank of America.[47] This reduced emphasis on retail banking is due to the prohibition on foreign banks from opening new branches and joining local ATM networks. Some concentrate on providing foreign currency loans to local businessmen, particularly to those investing outside Malaysia, and providing bank guarantees. Therefore, while foreign banks do not enjoy the same privileges as those given to domestic banks, they make up for this setback through greater product/service innovation and efficiency, well ahead of their domestic counterparts.

Nevertheless, the private sector recognizes that greater participation from foreign producers of services in the Malaysian services sector is imperative for the sector to progress further. Alliances between Malaysian firms and foreign players will also greatly benefit both users and domestic firms. This is because foreign entrants can bring about promotion of competition, management skills, sophisticated products and technological know-how that make for effective transfer of financial technology. They also tend to promote greater transparency in supervision, as well as adequate regulatory, policy and legal frameworks. These are imperative in creating a stable, efficient, and creative financial system.

The above discussion would be useful as points of consideration in the drafting of an FTA between Malaysia and the United States. In the following analysis, we will once again use the USSFTA as reference for what might be expected in these negotiations, in particular as a menu for what the United States would like.

The financial services chapter under the USSFTA includes core obligations of non-discrimination, MFN treatment, and additional market-access obligations. Singapore's ban on new licences for full-service banks will be lifted within 18 months, and within three years for "wholesale" banks. Once the agreement is in effect, licensed full-service banks will be able to offer all their services in Singapore at an unlimited number of locations within two years. Locally incorporated subsidiaries of U.S. banks can apply for access to the local ATM network within two-and-a half years, and branches of U.S. banks will have access to the ATM network in four years.

In the area of insurance, under the USSFTA, U.S. insurance firms will be able to establish subsidiaries, branches or joint ventures. U.S. firms will be able to sell marine, aviation and transport insurance, reinsurance, and insurance auxiliary services. In addition, prior regulatory product approval will not be required for all insurance products other than life insurance, Central Provident Fund (CPF)-related products, and investment-linked products sold to the business community.

In the realm of securities and related financial services, the USSFTA specifies that U.S. firms may provide asset/portfolio management and securities services in Singapore through the establishment of a local office, or by acquisition of local firms. In essence, under the USSFTA, Singapore will treat U.S. firms the same as local firms for the cross-border supply of financial information, advisory and data processing services. Hence, national treatment will rule.

d. Professional and business services

The government of Malaysia has made commitments in favour of progressive liberalization in professional and business services under the General Agreement of Trade in Services (GATS). Nonetheless, the government has undertaken several measures to regulate the presence of foreign professional and business services, particularly legal services, in the country. While allowing foreign participation in the services industry, the level of market access offered is subject to conditions. These regulations and restrictions are in place to ensure that local professionals are given priority and local firms are protected from foreign competition. The key services sectors that are subject to conditional market access include business services such as architectural, engineering, accounting and taxation services.

At present, foreign architectural, engineering and accounting firms in Malaysia are generally limited to partnership or joint-venture participation with Malaysian partners with no more than 30 per cent of foreign equity ownership. For architectural firms, these partnerships and joint ventures are usually confined to specific projects, hence the licences are temporary. In addition, Malaysian architectural firms may not engage foreign architectural firms as registered partners. Thus, foreign architecture firms are only allowed to operate as affiliates of Malaysian companies, which is also subject to the approval from the Board of Architects. Although foreign architects can be temporarily registered as architects under the Architect Rules 1996, the strict criteria imposed—such as no less than 15 years of practice, or no less than 5 years of work experience in any specific project currently being undertaken—may be an issue for the United States. This is due to the Malaysian government's policy not to encourage direct appointment of foreign consultants in implementing local projects unless local talent cannot be sourced, another issue which may be taken up in the U.S.-Malaysia FTA.

The general regulations applied to foreign engineering services are more or less similar to those applied to foreign architectural services, as are accounting and taxation services. Additionally, a person undertaking public practices in the accountancy profession must be registered with the Malaysian Institute of Accountants (MIA) as a member. In addition, citizenship or permanent residency is required for registration with the MIA.

Foreign presence is, by and large, closed in the legal services and is heavily regulated by the Bar Council. The Malaysian legal bar council does not allow foreign lawyers to practice Malaysian law or even to operate as foreign legal consultants, except on a limited basis in the Federal Territory of Labuan. The practice of Malaysian law is only permitted for citizens and permanent residents. However, preparations are now being made to allow foreign lawyers to practice in Malaysia. The Legal Profession Committee of the Bar Council has drafted proposed amendments to the Legal Profession Act, as well as Rules of the Admission of Foreign Lawyers.[48] Once adopted, foreign law firms will be able to practice in Malaysia in permitted areas of practice as a partner in a Joint Law Venture (JLV) between a local and a foreign law firm or serve as an employee in a local law firm.[49]

While this may be a positive step in liberalizing legal services in Malaysia, some obstacles may continue to exist due to differences in the Malaysian legal system and, in this case, the American legal system. One of the main obstacles may involve the lack of recognition in foreign qualifications by Malaysian authorities, unless the foreign lawyer possesses a law degree accredited by the British Barristers at Law. Second, the use of the national language, Bahasa Malaysia, in formal proceedings creates a language barrier since the foreign lawyer will be required to have a competent understanding of the language.

According to information provided by the U.S. International Trade Commission, architectural, engineering and accounting firms from the United States are highly competitive and maintain strong presence in the global marketplace. As such, these industries will no doubt push for a stronger foothold in the Malaysian market through an FTA and will lobby for the removal of the above regulations to the greatest extent possible.

The following are some possible issues for concern for the United States based on the following reservations on foreign professional and business services set by Malaysia[50]: (a) Commercial presence limited to partnership/joint ventures; (b) Access restrictions involving foreign shareholding; (c) Quota of personnel applied to inter-company transfers; (d) Hiring of foreign professionals subjected to economic needs test; and (d) Residency requirements for foreign professionals.

One of the primary concerns in liberalizing foreign business and professional services in Malaysia is that the interests of the local professionals will be affected as a result of increased competition by foreign talent. The United States may, in the FTA with Malaysia, address the issue on the quota imposed on intra-corporate transferees and, thus, may seek for a relaxation in intra-corporate transferees and temporary licensing since this prevents foreign talent from competing effectively with local professionals.

There will also be benefits to Malaysia of liberalization in this area through the U.S.-Malaysia FTA. For example, Malaysia will stand to benefit from the transfer of know-how by foreign architectural, engineering, accountancy and legal services. This will equip local professionals with added skills and knowledge through practical training, transfer of technology and secondment, allowing them to become more competitive locally and globally.

iii. The Automotive Market

Malaysia has frequently been involved in controversy due to its protection of the automotive sector, especially in the context of AFTA. Malaysia's automotive market is protected both by tariffs and non-tariff measures. Tariffs on automobiles were raised in October 1997; currently, they range from 42 per cent to 80 per cent on completely knocked down (CKD) cars, and from 140 to 300 per cent on completely built up (CBU) cars.[51] Most automobile parts and components, except tractor parts (duty free), are subject to 25–30 per cent tariffs.

Under AFTA, ASEAN countries were committed to cut import duties on automobiles to 0–5 per cent by 2003. Malaysia asked for a two-year extension to meet this deadline covering 218 tariff lines on CKD and

CBU automotive products, and ASEAN Trade Ministers approved the request on 1 May 2000. Recently, import duties on imported cars within AFTA have been reduced to 20 per cent beginning in 2004. However in order to compensate for the loss in revenue, the government has decided to increase the levy on the excise duties for imported cars, that is, an excise duty ranging from 60–100 per cent was imposed. Hence, it would appear that price discrimination between national and non-national cars will persist. Automotive protection will no doubt be high on the U.S. agenda in the U.S.-Malaysia negotiations.

Despite the government's heavy-handed interventionist policy instruments in this sector, the national automobile projects have not met expectations. Apparently, none of the national automobile projects has reached the expected economies of scale, although all of them have been important growth engines for over 250 local small and medium component and accessory manufacturers. Another worrying issue is that the increase in the annual production volume has surprisingly failed to translate into lower prices per unit. On the contrary, the prices of all the local makes have been edging up over the years. If we were to benchmark against other world automobile producers, the existing 300,000 units or so of annual production is far below the minimum economically efficient production size of at least 1 million per year. Also, lack of competition as a result of government's intervention has caused some inefficiencies in the product value chain and distortions in the market mechanism. This is not surprising as the vendors of the national automobile makers are appointed through a single-sourcing system, which allows them to enjoy undue advantages of direct and protected relationships with the manufacturers. Mostly likely due to self-complacency and the moral hazard problem, this kind of system can hardly encourage vendors to be innovative and cost competitive.

Inevitably, in the post-AFTA regime, the national car projects will have to compete directly with imported CBU automobiles from other ASEAN member countries. Motor vehicles are subject to only 5 per cent import duty as long as they satisfy the 40 per cent local content rule. Ironically, with Proton's plan to re-enter the one-litre compact car segment in 2004, Proton and Perodua will have to compete among themselves from 2005 onwards. Of course, in AFTA the local automobile makers are not competing with other ASEAN member countries, but with international giants that use countries such as Thailand as their production base.

To date, it is not certain whether the local automobile makers are able to compete head-on in a highly competitive environment in the wake of the unprecedented liberalization of regional and international trade regimes. Their market share and profitability, especially of the passenger car segment, are likely to be gradually eroded by the impact of AFTA. The recent entry of China into the WTO will likely create a totally different playing field for the world automobile producing countries. Despite all these imminent threats, it is believed that the onslaught of cheaper imported brands will not be able to wipe the national automobile makers out of the market, as they still have the most extensive network of sales and service centres in Malaysia.

Given the above circumstances, it will be difficult for the U.S.-Malaysia FTA to go beyond what has been offered under the automobile sector in AFTA, which could be a key point of contention in the negotiations.

F. Final Comments on the U.S.-Malaysia FTA

A U.S.-Malaysia FTA would go a long way in helping Malaysia become more competitive, not merely in the market of its most important trading partner but also in the global marketplace. It would also be a useful insurance mechanism, as the United States is concluding FTAs with many of Malaysia's competitors. The estimated economic effects of a U.S.-Malaysia FTA are uniformly positive, albeit small, with fairly large potential changes at the sectoral level.

But the road to the conclusion of a U.S.-Malaysia FTA will most likely neither be smooth nor without compromises. Judging from the U.S.-Singapore and U.S.-Chile FTAs, it is clear that there will be several areas in which Malaysia will have to take hard decisions. There is no doubt that an U.S.-Malaysia FTA will be based on such principles as non-discrimination, most-favoured nation treatment and market access obligations. In effect this will mean that U.S. firms will have as much access to Malaysian markets as Malaysian firms will have to U.S. markets. The Malaysian position may be more vulnerable in the sense that Malaysia's trade regime, though liberal, is less liberal that that of the United States.

The Malaysian services sector will have to liberalize and will be forced into being more competitive, in particular with respect to banking, insurance, and securities services. So will express delivery and professional services. While the field of competition will be more intense for Malaysian firms in this area, consumers—both households and businesses—can expect to gain from such competition.

Though far less important than in the case of Indonesia (discussed above) and the Philippines (discussed below), another difficult area may lie in the area of IPR. Malaysia has made important strides in ensuring IPR protection, but far more will be required if a bilateral FTA is to be negotiated with the United States. The same is true for government procurement and competition policy.

In sum, a U.S.-Malaysia FTA will demand strong obligations from Malaysia and will push it toward greater openness and global competitiveness. Though some will argue that the demands that will be made by the United States are heavy-handed and exaggerated, it will be more a question of sequencing than direction, as Malaysia is embracing policy reform at all levels. As summed up by the U.S.-ASEAN Business Council President Ernest Bower on the signing of the TIFA (May 2004):

> This framework is important strategically for both the United States and for Malaysia. For the U.S., it moves us closer to an FTA with Malaysia, which would be a foundational building block in our goal of a broader free trade agreement linking ASEAN and the U.S.. For Malaysia, this move is fundamental to its competitiveness. Its most competitive neighbors to the north and south, Thailand and Singapore, have begun or completed free trade agreements with the United States. Malaysia will now be making its way to that level of competitiveness with regard to U.S. companies.

IV. The Philippines

by Federico Macaranas[52]

A. Introduction

Statistical analysis in Chapters 2 and 3 underscored that the Philippines arguably has the closest economic (and political) relationship with the United States of the ASEAN countries. The United States is by far its most important trading partner; the econometric work applied in Chapter 3 demonstrated the "special" relationship between the two countries, particularly relative to Indonesia and Malaysia (and also in comparison to the Philippines' relationship with the EU); and aggregate and disaggregate economic analysis, showed that the Philippines probably has the most to gain from an FTA with the United States.

But that research also emphasized that the Philippines is increasingly competing with its ASEAN partners and China in OECD markets generally and the U.S. market in particular. Because the United States is so important to the Philippines economically, perhaps more than any other EAI country the Philippines is exposed to possible trade diversion caused by U.S. agreements with other trading partners. For example, Avila, Manzano and Lynch (2003) suggest that in particular 18 key products from the Philippines are vulnerable to trade diversion once the U.S. signs separate FTAs with other Asian countries that export similar products to those of the Philippines.[53]

Thus, there will be much at stake for the Philippines in the U.S.-Philippines FTA discussions. As in the cases of Indonesia and Malaysia above, in this section we focus on the policy aspects of the U.S.-Philippines economic partnership, in particular the opportunities and challenges that an FTA will entail.

B. Overview of Sectoral and Trade Related Issues

In this subsection, various issues will be identified and discussed across a wide range of sectors pertinent as background to the U.S.-Philippines FTA discussions, from tariff policy in the manufacturing and agricultural sectors to the tradable services. Other trade-related issues are also included, such as IPR, government procurement, labour and environment, electronic commerce, customs administration and corruption.

i. Background Statistical Review

Manufacturing, agriculture and services accounted for 32 per cent, 15 per cent and 53 per cent, respectively, of the Philippines' Gross Domestic Product in 2002. Over time, the Philippine agriculture sector has declined in relative importance in terms of its share in GDP, in favour of the services sector (the manufacturing sector's share has remained relatively flat). Structural change in the Philippines has been rapid: in 1985, the agriculture sector accounted for a significant 25 per cent share of the Philippine economy. With regard to export breakdown by sector, industrial exports dominate (86 per cent of the total in 2001), followed by services and agriculture (9 per cent and 6 per cent), respectively.

The rising importance of international trade to the Philippine economy is clearly evident from the substantial share of exports and imports of goods and services in the country's GDP. In 1985, exports of goods and services amounted only to about 24 per cent of GDP. In 2002, exports had better than doubled to 49 per cent. Correspondingly, the share of imports of goods and services in GDP increased by 126 per cent from a 22 per cent share of GDP in 1985 to 49 per cent in 2002.

The U.S. trade deficit with the Philippines reached US$2.1 billion in 2003, a decrease of US$1.6 billion from 2002 levels of US$3.7 billion. In 2003, the U.S. registered US$8.0 billion in exports of goods to the Philippines, a growth of 9.8 per cent from 2002 levels. U.S. imports from the Philippines, meanwhile, were at $10.1 billion, an 8.4 per cent decrease from 2002 figures.[54]

U.S. exports of private commercial services to the Philippines were US$1.5 billion in 2002, while imports of the same were placed at US$1.3 billion. Sales of services in the Philippines by U.S.-owned affiliates were US$1.2 billion in 2001, while sales of services in the United States by majority Philippine-owned firms were US$18 million.[55]

As was noted at length in Chapter 2, the United States is the top trade partner of the Philippines. Total trade in 2003 amounted to US$14 billion. The Philippines is currently the 19th largest export market for U.S. goods and the 20th largest merchandise import market of the United States. In terms of total trade, the Philippines is the 22nd trading partner of the U.S. in 2002. Singapore (12th), which recently signed a bilateral free trade agreement with the U.S., joins Malaysia (11th) and Thailand (18th) as the only ASEAN countries ranking higher than the Philippines in total trade with the United States. Moreover, the United States is the top export market of the Philippines and the second most important import source based on 2003 figures. The United States had a 20 per cent share of total Philippine exports and a 20 per cent share of total imports in 2003 (DTI).[56]

ii. Philippine Tariff Policy

The Philippines' Tariff Reform Program incorporates WTO and AFTA-CEPT commitments, as well as APEC voluntary commitments. AFTA-CEPT commitments are already in full force, falling in the range of 0–5 per cent, though for sensitive agricultural products there will be a delayed implementation to a maximum 5 per cent tariff by 2010.

The United States has been monitoring the Philippines' implementation of its WTO commitments, and the USTR notes only that, in the area of tariffs, the Philippine government in January 2003 undertook a comprehensive review of all tariff lines in reaction to global and domestic developments. This review led to the issuance of Executive Orders 241 and 264 by President Arroyo during the latter part of 2003, which effectively raised tariff rates on more than 1,000 product lines and maintained 2003 rates for more than 1,000 others. Tariff rates on products such as industrial goods, chemical fertilizers, cement, consumer products like apparel and footwear, and raw materials, were increased from previous rates of between 3 per cent and 10 per cent to between 5 per cent and 20 per cent.[57] However, the increases were well below the WTO bound rates, even if it did signal a reversal in the systematic programme to reduce applied tariffs.[58]

The move by President Arroyo, which included the temporary suspension of the AFTA tariff reduction schedule on petrochemical resins and certain plastic products, brought about tangible repercussions in ASEAN as Singapore demanded (and received) compensation from the Philippines, by way of AFTA procedures, for its failure to implement agreed reductions and non-compliance with the agreement.[59]

The average tariffs for the agriculture sector are significantly higher than the mining and manufacturing averages due to higher tariffs for sensitive agriculture products. The tariffs for the agriculture sector currently range from 0–65 per cent; for mining, 1–5 per cent; and for manufacturing, 0–30 per cent. Average tariffs are low due to the distribution of tariff rates. More than half of tariff lines are dutiable at 0–3 per cent (Table 4.4).

Except for the issue of bound vs. applied rates, tariffs—particularly on manufactures—are not as central an issue of bilateral concern as non-tariff measures (NTMs) that include the Philippine's quantitative import restrictions on rice and import licensing for minimum access volumes (MAVs) on sensitive agricultural products (on the U.S. side, these NTMs include U.S. quotas for sugar and textiles and garments). There are also the areas of technical barriers to trade (TBTs) that include safeguards and standards, customs procedures and trade-related investment measures (TRIMs). Finally and perhaps most importantly for a prospective bilateral U.S.-Philippines free trade agreement, are barriers to investment that particularly affect trade in services and regulatory

TABLE 4.4
Average Philippine Tariff Rates, 2000–2005

Sector	Year	Simple Average Tariff (%)	Trade-Weighted Average Tariff (%)
Agriculture	2000	14.40	15.74
	2001	14.20	11.39
	2002	12.18	10.26
	2003	11.04	10.32
	2004–2005	12.19	10.57
Mining	2000	3.27	3.07
	2001	3.25	3.31
	2002	2.84	2.91
	2003	2.84	2.91
	2004–2005	2.56	2.79
Manufactures	2000	6.92	3.85
	2001	6.68	3.56
	2002	5.04	2.90
	2003	5.43	2.97
	2004–2005	5.60	3.12
Overall	2000	7.96	4.95
	2001	7.70	4.24
	2002	6.03	3.56
	2003	6.19	3.64
	2004–2005	6.49	3.79

Source: Philippine Tariff Commission

issues such as competition policy. These are all discussed below.

C. Trade in Manufactures

i. Electronics

As noted in Chapters 2 and 3, the electronics industry had the biggest total exports to and imports from the United States, accounting for 47 per cent of the total Philippine merchandise exports and 36 per cent of imports in 2003. The semiconductors (microelectronics) sub-sector is the biggest in the industry with a total export value of US$1.8 billion and import value of US$2.5 billion. It involves manufacturers of integrated circuits (ICs), transistors, diodes, resistors, capacitors, coils, transformers, PCBs and other components. Philippine subsidiaries of Intel, Texas Instruments, Philips, Amkor, and Fairchild Semiconductors are some of the major players in the market.

Electronic data processing (EDP) equipment, composed of computer, peripheral storage and input/output manufacturers, is the next biggest sub-sector with export sales of US$1.2 billion and import amount of US$112 million. This sector is generally controlled by Japanese companies such as Toshiba, Acer, Epson, Fujitsu, Ionics, and Sampo Technology.

Dominated by multinational firms, the electronics industry employs about 335,000 workers. Out of the 715 electronic firms, 72 per cent are foreign-owned while 28 per cent are locally owned.

A perennial concern for the industry is that the value-added of semiconductor exports is low. A World Bank survey in the late 1990s showed that local content produced in the Philippines amounted to only 20 per cent of semiconductors, 25 per cent of printed circuit boards and 15 per cent of central processing units. Further, the Philippines have a small domestic market unlike China and India. Thus, a *maquiladora*-style of trade exists where the country is used mainly for outsourced production with the product being re-exported back to the United States or to other countries.

ii. Textiles and Garments

Philippine garments exports to the United States in 2003 reached US$1.64 billion accounting for 23 per cent of total exports to the United States or 4.6 per cent of total Philippine exports. The garments industry is, thus, the second largest export category to the U.S. in 2003 after electronics. As was noted in our discussions of Indonesia and Malaysia, Chapter 5 of the USSFTA is wholly devoted to this sector, which is a politically sensitive one in the United States as well as in the Philippines. Indeed, the net benefit to the Philippine garments industry within a bilateral FTA is ambiguous due to the following factors:

- Competition from other countries offering lower labour costs will be intensified especially when the quota system on apparel exports is dismantled in 2005 (i.e. U.S. or European Union buyers may now source garments from any country-supplier. China, Bangladesh, India, Sri Lanka, Eastern European countries, Caribbean countries and Mexico pose as threats to the country in terms of cost).

- Raw materials and intermediate goods for Philippine garment exports are almost wholly imported. The lack of a strong textile sector is expected to become an even bigger handicap as the world market moves away from the quota system for garments. Large import requirements may also give rise to rules of origin complications under a future regime.
- Given a quota-less regime, a bilateral agreement will eliminate tariffs of 15 per cent on goods entering the U.S. market and facilitate import and export procedures. This will greatly assist local players in competing with other foreign suppliers on the basis of quality and prices.
- Low productivity continues to characterize textile production due to outdated technology and lack of investment.

iii. Automobiles and Automotive Parts

Transport equipment accounted for a 5 per cent share in total Philippine exports to the United States in 2003 with US$348 million in export sales. Automotive parts are the most significant sub-sector with 98 per cent of total transport equipment or US$340 million in export sales. In an effort to transform the Philippines into a regional hub for automotive production, the administration of President Arroyo, under the Commercial Vehicle Development Program, lowered tariffs on automotive vehicle components from 10 per cent to 3 per cent in April 2001.

Consequently, to encourage local assembly under the Philippine Motor Vehicle Development Program, imports of completely built-up units (CBUs) and motorcycles have been subject to 30 per cent tariff duty extended until 2007 by Executive Order 241.[60] In addition, Executive Order 156 effected last October 2003, provided an incentive of US$400 per vehicle exported by auto manufacturers from the Philippines.[61] The Board of Investment (BOI)-imposed industry-wide local content requirements under the Motor Vehicle Development Program were eliminated in July 2003. Tariffs for completely knocked-down automobile units imported under the Motor Vehicle Development Program have been scheduled to decrease from the current 10 per cent to 5 per cent in 2004.

The automotive excise tax was restructured in August 2003 to allow for a shift from an engine displacement-based tax system — which discriminated against importing vehicles with larger displacement, including those originating from the United States – to a vehicle value-based system. Most types of manufactured vehicles are covered by the new law, which also eliminated the tax exemption of vehicles under the 10-seater rule.[62]

iv. Distilled Spirits

It has been noted by the USTR that the Philippines protects its domestically-produced distilled spirits to some extent by way of a tax structure providing for lower taxation of domestically-produced distilled spirits relative to imports. An example cited is that of the country's excise tax regime, which subjects distilled spirits produced from indigenous materials to a specific tax of 8.96 pesos per proof litre versus the 84–336 pesos per litre tax imposed on spirits originating from other raw materials. As locally produced spirits are usually sourced from coconut palm, cane, and root crops and imported ones are not, locally-manufactured spirits enjoy the benefit of lower taxes.[63] Even though the very fact of domestic production using local raw materials distinguishes the Philippine spirits industry from that of Singapore, the protection inherent in the tax regime may well be an issue in prospective FTA negotiations, given that distilled spirits are featured within Chapter 2 of the USSFTA.

Some exporters to the Philippines have been looking forward to a Congressional bill which would adopt indexation (for cigarettes as well as spirits) and revert tax rates to more equitable levels. However, this bill has been deferred since 2002 and is not expected to be given renewed attention until a new congress assembles in the second half of 2004 at the earliest.[64]

v. Standards for Industrial Goods

The USTR has identified a range of issues on standards, testing labelling and certification that it considers as effective TBTs. Mandatory inspections for standards compliance on 75 products (including cosmetics, medical equipment, lighting fixtures, electrical wires and cables, cement, pneumatic tires, sanitary wares, and household appliances) were cited, as well as mandatory labelling of fabrics and garments and garments accessories. The removal, rationalization or simplification of these procedures, or their monitoring by a joint committee (a common feature within the U.S.-Singapore FTA) may be raised by the United States in bilateral negotiations.

D. Trade in Agriculture

The Philippines, a major exporter of fruit and marine products is, as a whole, a net agricultural importer.[65] In 2001, the balance of trade deficit in agriculture increased by 27 per cent to US$1 billion. This resulted mainly from the slow growth in agricultural productivity, which in turn may be attributed primarily to the very low degree of agricultural mechanization and investment in infrastructure. Top agricultural imports include wheat, rice, milk and cream products.

The United States is the world's top exporter of food. Last year, American farmers exported more than US$52 billion worth of goods, far more than any other country in the world. One out of every three crop acres planted in the United States is exported.[66] The Philippines is the 13th largest export market for U.S. agricultural products in 2002 with an export value of US$778 million. The only ASEAN country ranking higher than the Philippines is Indonesia at 12th place with U.S. exports amounting to US$815 million.

Bilateral issues in agriculture are more numerous than in manufacturing, and two points must be remembered: first, the USSFTA did not include agriculture, for the obvious reason of Singapore having no agricultural sector; and second, over a third of Filipinos are employed in agriculture.

i. U.S. Agricultural Subsidies

Within the context of a bilateral FTA, the problem of agricultural subsidies is of vital concern to the Philippines, as competition with subsidized American agriculture is asymmetrical and may have detrimental effects on Philippine agriculture. On the production side, the Philippines may only gain marginally in opening agricultural trade with the United States due to its relatively low production capacity and lack of relative competitiveness in many areas. In addition, like other developing countries, compliance with strict sanitary and phytosanitary standards of the United States is also an important market access concern, as in some cases they can be considered NTMs. In this scenario, gains to U.S. agriculture will be much larger through greater access to the Philippine market because of better quality and lower priced agricultural products.

The highly subsidized U.S. agricultural sector is at the centre of this debate. The Philippine rice, corn and livestock industries—sensitive sectors relevant to Philippine food security as well as rural economies—will be ill-equipped to compete. U.S. rice subsidies reached US$1.07 billion in 2002. The U.S. corn industry is the top recipient of agricultural subsidies, with total subsidies in corn reaching US$1.98 billion in 2002, albeit a 64 per cent decline from US$5.49 billion subsidies the industry received in 2001. Meanwhile, U.S. livestock subsidies have experienced phenomenal increases over time, from US$63 million in 1995 to US$976 million in 2002.

On 13 May 2002, President Bush signed into law the *U.S. Farm Security and Rural Investment Act of 2002*, giving U.S. farming interests US$180 billion in subsidies over the next ten years concurrently increasing certain subsidies by 80 per cent. Increasing farm subsidies will further distort farm prices in the U.S. and will depress world prices since the U.S. is a major exporter of agricultural goods. Controlling these subsidies will obviously be an important consideration in the EAI negotiations in general and for the U.S.-Philippines FTA in particular.

ii. Sugar

The Philippines continues to be a major recipient of the U.S. sugar quota. As of year 2000, the Philippines is the third major supplier of raw sugar to the U.S. after the Dominican Republic and Brazil, with prospects of greater growth as American sugar needs are likely to increase over time. We also estimated in Chapter 3 that, while sugar is not a major export to the U.S. market, it is one of the most promising sectors for trade expansion. The U.S. market provides much-needed revenue for the sugar industry which in turn provides for over 500,000 jobs.

While liberalization of this sector in a U.S.-Philippines FTA could, therefore, be highly significant to the Philippines, it will be a difficult item in negotiations. For example, the U.S.-Australia FTA, which was ratified by the United States Congress in July 2004, excludes sugar completely.

iii. Tuna Fisheries

Based on national trade figures, the fishing industry contributed 3.9 per cent to the country's GDP in 2001. The importance of this sector is reflected in the fact that about 10 per cent of the active labour force in agriculture is employed in this sector. In terms of its sub-sectors, the tuna industry reportedly employs at least 18,000 workers inclusive of allied and support industries. Those engaged in municipal operations number 773,000 while 51,000 are in commercial fisheries.

Philippine marine exports to the United States have increased through the years from US$82 million in 1995 to US$117 Million in 2003, or a 43 per cent increase in eight years. Tuna exports to the United States in 2003 at US$53 million have enjoyed 47 per cent growth since 1995, where export value stood at US$36 million.

In 1999, the United States was the largest market for Philippine yellow fin tuna with a 52 per cent share of total exports while Japan, with a 33 per cent share, was the second largest market. The United States has duty-free rates for most fresh, chilled or frozen fish (including tuna) but maintains peak rates for canned tuna and skipjack dutiable from 15–35 per cent. The Philippines is pushing for zero tariffs on canned tuna exports to the United States in relation to the United States' move to grant zero tariffs on tuna exports coming from countries belonging to the Andean Trade Preferences Expansion Act. Indeed, the U.S. government is considering duty-free access of a number of products in this area, including tuna in pouches, for the Andean countries to discourage narcotics-related activities. In October 2003, the *Fair Trade in Pouch Tuna Act of 2003* was introduced in the U.S. Senate. Specifically, the Act seeks to eliminate tariffs on pouch tuna imported from the ASEAN countries in a quantity equal to the quantity imported from Andean countries.

iv. *Philippine Treatment of "Sensitive" Agricultural Products*

The Philippines maintains high levels of protection on certain sensitive agricultural products such as: grains, livestock and meat products, sugar, frozen and processed potatoes, onions, coffee, and fresh citrus fruits including oranges, lemons and grapefruit. Executive Order 164 set tariff rates for most agricultural products at 2002 levels with the exception of pork, poultry, processed meats, corn, coffee and vegetables. Tariffs on other less-sensitive goods were maintained at 7 per cent in 2003 while tariffs for several vegetables such as lettuce, broccoli and cauliflower were raised from 7 per cent to between 20 per cent and 25 per cent. Some sensitive products subject to MAV and tariff-rate quotas (TRQs) are as follows:[67]

- Corn: in-quota tariff rate of 35 per cent and out-quota tariff rate of 65 per cent.
- Poultry meat: in-quota and out-quota tariff rate at 40 per cent.
- Pork: in-quota tariff rate of 30 per cent and out-quota tariff rate at 40 per cent.[68]
- Rice: in-quota and out-quota tariff rates at 50 per cent.[69]

The unpredictability and seeming unfairness of the administration of the TRQs for pork and poultry meat was eventually raised by the United States, which insists that domestic producers who showed no interest in importing pork and poultry meat received the majority of the import licences. To ensure the smooth implementation of the tariff rate quotas, the two governments entered into a Memorandum of Agreement on February 1998, and since then, the United States has been closely monitoring the progress in this area. Despite these initiatives, however, and despite improvements in other areas, there continues to be a feeling that permit issuance continues to be unpredictable, thereby discouraging many importers from even applying. Some even point out that this unpredictability seems to take on the form of discretionary licencing which is a violation of WTO rules.

The highly sensitive and protected Philippine rice and corn industries may pose as one of the most serious challenges in negotiating an FTA with the United States. Rice is the staple food of about 85 per cent of the total population of the Philippines. Eleven per cent of the expenses of most households is allocated for purchasing rice. In terms of inputs, labour comprises 40 per cent of all expenses in rice production.

The Philippine government considers rice as vital in its goal of food and national security. As such, it insists on national rice self-sufficiency as opposed to suggestions, consistent with comparative advantage, on sourcing through cheaper imports. It continues to take this protective stance even as demand for rice imports is expected to grow given the erratic local production and the continuously growing Philippine population. Some progress was made in 2003 when the Philippine Department of Agriculture opened up the importation of rice to the private sector, taking away the sole privilege of importing rice from the National Food Authority. Although this is seen as a positive step toward liberalization of the agriculture sector, the United States government is disturbed by the plan to move import rights to domestic rice farmers, which could lead to a discriminatory treatment against imports.[70]

v. Standards on Agricultural Products

The Philippine Department of Agriculture (DA) has followed strict measures in the importation of agricultural products. Although the importation of U.S. produce — apples, grapes, oranges, potatoes, onions, and garlic — is allowed, the 1995 plant health regulations indicate that when necessary, said products must undergo a specified cold treatment to control targeted pests. In March 2000, a protocol between the Philippines and the United States eventually allowed for the importation of Florida grapefruit, oranges and tangerines into the Philippines.

The United States government has repeatedly raised issues with regard to the Philippine agriculture system and procedures, which the United States observes as contrary to Philippine WTO obligations, specifically in the area of sanitary and phytosanitary measures. One such measure being contested is the DA's continued use of veterinary quarantine certificates (VQCs) which are issued after as long as one month, and the limiting of the issuance of VQCs to holders of MAV licences.

Another issue which caught the attention of the United States government is the DA's announcement in September 2002 of its plans to introduce mandatory third-party Hazard Analysis and Critical Control Point (HACCP) inspections for all meat and dairy plants exporting to the Philippines as of April 1, 2003. This meant that all foreign meat and milk plants exporting to the Philippines would be required to undergo a third-party quarterly audit to ensure compliance with international standards. The United States aired its concerns citing that this would result to losses of US$55 million or roughly the value of U.S. trade to the Philippines in the affected commodities.

E. Services Trade

As noted above, the USSFTA devotes several chapters to services, explicitly including professional services, financial services, telecommunications and government procurement. Many other services that by the first mode of delivery under GATS (cross-border trade, as opposed to consumption abroad, commercial presence and movement of natural persons) is implicitly included in Ch. 8 of the agreement.

The Philippines is cognizant of the fact that its relative abundance and quality of human capital and skilled labour represents one of its foremost competitive economic strengths, and that liberalization of services presents great opportunities. However, this is an area that presents particular difficulties, not least because the government is yet to develop a comprehensive policy on how to approach services liberalization, particularly in sectors that involve constitutional and statutory investment barriers that effectively restrict foreign delivery of services by way of commercial presence.

The best framework for analysing bilateral concerns within the broad area of services is to adopt the four modes by which services can be traded, pursuant to the WTO General Agreement on Trade in Services (GATS). These were delineated in Chapter 2, i.e., cross-border trade, consumption abroad, commercial presence and presence of natural persons. This is necessary because Philippine and American interests within the services sector differ widely. It will be seen that Philippine interests can be categorized mainly under consumption abroad (particularly tourism) and presence of natural persons (temporary entry of Filipino labour) as well as cross-border trade in the area of information technology (IT) and IT-enabled services. American concerns regard mainly restrictions on commercial presence, particularly in banking and financial services, public utilities (which include telecommunications, power, transportation), retail and professional services. There are also some cross-border services trade concerns in telecommunications, but most notably perhaps in air transportation.

i. Cross-Border Trade in Services

a. Information Technology and IT-Enabled Services

Filipino labour is recognized as well equipped with information technology skills, a prerequisite for success in the new knowledge based economy. The 2002 Global New Economy Index (GNEI), a study conducted by the Connecticut-based META Group, ranked the country 4th overall worldwide on the basis of the quality and availability of IT professionals behind India, Israel and Iceland and ahead of developed countries such as the United States, Australia, Canada and France. The study stated that the Philippines excelled in meeting the requirements of the ideal work force for the New Economy. Reinforcing its position as an ICT hub in Asia, the country was notably ahead of its Asian neighbours for "excellent availability" of skilled workers.

In the same study, the Philippines ranked first in the availability of competent senior management, second in the availability of information technology (IT) skills, and fourth in the availability of qualified engineers. Filipino ICT workers were cited for their proficiency in mainframes, minicomputers, and microcomputers as well as their technical and business skills for ICT projects. They were also noted for their experience in providing "e-enabling" services such as business outsourcing and human resources, customer interaction, finance and accounting, and website services. Along with India, the Philippines, because of widespread facility in English and familiarity with Western culture, has been touted as a natural leading player in this emerging industry of business outsourcing made possible by advances in ICT. Indeed, the country has, with the influx of foreign and local investment in call centres, become a major business outsourcing destination for U.S. firms.

A controversial area of concern to the Philippines relates to international business outsourcing. Currently, there is proposed legislation in California which would prohibit firms located in the state to outsource medical transcription services internationally. This may be due at least in part to political manoeuvrings in time for the U.S. elections in 2004. Indeed, Democratic presidential candidate Senator John Kerry introduced a bill which effectively discourages U.S. corporations and subsidiaries from operating call centres overseas or from engaging in offshore outsourcing.

The Philippine government has sought assurances from the United States that the outcome of the proposed measures on outsourcing will not be contrary to market trends. Efforts to ensure the continued expansion of this trade on the part of the Philippines can be expected to feature in FTA discussions. Particularly given the involvement of U.S. investment in the industry to date, difficulties may not arise in what is clearly an area for lucrative bilateral trade, unless the subject of business outsourcing becomes increasingly politicized.

b. Air Transportation Services

The U.S.-Singapore FTA explicitly does not cover air services, presumably because these are governed by an "open skies" agreement signed in 1997 that provides for unrestricted "Fifth Freedom" rights.[71] Malaysia also entered into such an agreement with the United States in the same year. However, the Philippines, together with Thailand and Indonesia, permit only limited Fifth-Freedom access for passenger traffic. Though the country signed the first international open skies agreement with the United States in 1980, the effectiveness of the agreement has been continually deferred at the request of the Philippines.

Cargo services, however, do enjoy an open skies regime that even incorporates seventh freedom rights.[72] But these are limited to the economic zones and airports at Clark and Subic. Further, foreign air express couriers and airfreight forwarding firms must either contract with a 100 per cent Filipino-owned firm or establish a domestic company with a minimum of 60 per cent Filipino equity participation.

In principle both the Philippine and U.S. governments are in favour of liberalization of the aviation industry. But the degree of openness of the skies is a critical issue, especially if both countries are to rationalize how the agreement can boost their respective economies without contradicting their respective laws. The Philippine panel to the bilateral air agreement requested another 12-year deferment of the open skies implementation. The government also asked for Philippine passenger airlines to be given new routes within the United States, but the U.S. did not agree because, like the Philippines, its laws prohibit "cabotage" or the transportation of persons, property, or mail between points within the United States in a foreign aircraft.

The United States wanted code-sharing rights for both combination and cargo services between non-designated bilateral carriers, between U.S. carriers, and between U.S. carriers and Asian airlines. It also requested expanded Seventh-Freedom rights including passenger traffic. The Philippines rejected these demands, saying that seventh freedom rights, which would of course enable U.S. passenger and cargo planes to mount more flights to, from and within the Philippines, in effect operating like local carriers, would violate the constitutional 40 per cent foreign ownership cap.

Philippine Airlines asked the Philippine Senate to renegotiate the provisions of the bilateral air accord and to hold its implementation until the local airline completes its ongoing rehabilitation programme. Philippine Airlines and other players in the local aviation industry need to make significant investments in product enhancements, technology, and networks in order to compete with American airlines. Of course, there is also the issue of tourism infrastructure, which remains underdeveloped in the Philippines. Capacity and quality of transportation infrastructure is an issue that significantly affects integrators' operations. The tightness of on-airport space for customs clearance and sorting has been cited as a potential problem.

c. Maritime Transportation Services

The Philippines, being an archipelago of 7,107 islands with a very long coastline measuring about 235,973 km (longer than that of the U.S.), considers the maritime industry to be strategic, and cabotage restrictions reserve domestic shipping exclusively to Filipino vessels, which in turn, as the USTR noted, must be crewed by Filipinos.[73] Foreign equity participation is again restricted to a maximum of 40 per cent, and because the *Public Service Act of 1936* defined shipping as a public utility, the restrictions for this category of industries apply.

In the United States, cabotage restrictions in effect similar to the Philippines are applied to domestic coastal shipping, for similar strategic reasons, and so it is likely that a U.S.-Philippines FTA will exclude this issue. Even so, indicators for international shipping further point to the likely relative unimportance of this sector as far as FTA negotiations are concerned (and the corresponding likely importance of air services), as Philippine exports by value are overwhelmingly delivered by air (and those by ship mostly travel on foreign-registered vessels).

ii. Consumption Abroad

Concerns under this mode of services delivery are reserved to domestic Philippine efforts to promote tourism, health and retirement services, and educational services.[74] Tourism and health and retirement services are particularly suitable for promotion in the United States, as well as Japan. However, these areas will probably not be a central feature of an FTA with the United States (unless the Philippines opts to promote tourism through an expanded air agreement), except in the area of cooperation and assistance in order to help mitigate (at the Philippines' request) the mode of presence of natural persons as Filipino nurses and teachers continue to travel to the United States to work. Here, the United States can help by facilitating the accreditation of Philippine services in the health insurance, retirement and education plans of Americans.

iii. Commercial Presence

Barriers to commercial presence will be central to American efforts to expand services trade with the Philippines, particularly in banking and financial services, telecommunications and other public utilities, retail trade services, advertising, and professional and consulting services.

a. Financial Services

The U.S.-Singapore FTA defines financial services including "all insurance and insurance-related services, and all banking and other financial services (excluding insurance), as well as services incidental or auxiliary to a service of a financial nature."[75] Auxiliary and incidental services include all the functions of a full-service investment bank, as well as settlement and clearing, custody, trust, advisory, guarantees, underwriting, etc. The Agreement mandates national treatment and most-favoured nation treatment in all the above areas. In the Philippines, however, broad restrictions exist.

With respect to banking services, the *General Banking Law of 2000* allowed for a seven-year window in which foreign banks could wholly acquire one locally incorporated commercial or thrift bank, and that during the first three years of the law's effectiveness, such foreign investments must be made only in existing banks. Current regulations require that majority Filipino-owned domestic banks control at least 70 per cent of total banking system assets at all times, a policy similar to the one existing in Malaysia (see Section III). Rural banks are closed to foreign participation. The United States can be expected to urge the removal of restrictions, such as an economic needs assessment, on the granting of licences to American banks.

Productivity Commission data show that, relative to counterparts in ASEAN, the Philippine banking sector is not unduly discriminatory against foreign banks, particularly after entry and establishment of operations. The main barriers are in obtaining a licence and in investment restrictions. However, the price effects are considerable, with discriminatory barriers towards foreign banks alone representing a 47.36 per cent tax on Filipino consumers of banking services. The total price effect of both domestic and foreign restrictions is 58.35 per cent, second only among the selected ASEAN countries to Malaysia.

Regarding insurance, total foreign ownership has been permitted since 1994. Entry is allowed by way of ownership of the voting stock of an existing domestic insurance or reinsurance company or intermediary, investment in a new insurance or reinsurance company or intermediary incorporated in the Philippines, or establishment of a branch. However, minimum capitalization requirements differ depending on the line of business, the degree of foreign equity, and the mode of entry. For government-funded projects, only the state-owned government insurance system may provide coverage.

Securities underwriting firms not established under Philippine laws may only underwrite Philippine issues for foreign markets. Those established in the Philippines are subject to the 60 per cent foreign equity limit for securities underwriting companies pursuant to Republic Act No. 8366 or the Investment Houses Law of 1997; as the Securities Industry of America (SIA) noted however, this limit is above the bound GATS commitment of 51 per cent.[76]

"Technical barriers" that have been highlighted regarding foreign-controlled stock brokerages include the fact that foreign brokers and dealers are limited to underwriting on a best-efforts basis, and that foreign portfolio investment in domestic stocks is restricted. Both these points reflect the constitutional provision that foreign ownership in Philippine firms is generally limited to 40 per cent.

Other concerns relate to the level of regulatory transparency in the domestic securities industry and the issue of processing financial information, for which there is no binding Philippine commitment in GATS. Indeed, the Philippines has yet to ratify the Fifth Protocol to GATS, which embodies its commitments under the WTO Financial Services Agreement.

The Philippine position on lifting restrictions on foreign involvement in this area were noted by the USTR, which explained that the country "took an MFN exemption on foreign equity participation in securities firms, stating that Philippine regulators would approve applications for foreign equity only if Philippine companies enjoy similar rights in the foreign investor's country of origin". Hence, reciprocity would be expected to be the key principle for negotiations here, suggesting that this could be a lucrative area for the U.S.-Philippine FTA.

b. Telecommunications Services
An entire chapter (Chapter 9) of the U.S.-Singapore FTA is devoted to telecommunications and dwells on non-discrimination, competitive

safeguards, unbundling of network elements and co-interconnection and network access, and independent regulation and privatization, among many others. It can consequently be expected to feature prominently in FTA discussions with the Philippines.

Concerns expressed by the USTR include, once again, the fact that there are constitutional limits of 40 per cent foreign ownership in telecommunications firms. More important, however, are the proposed regulatory commitments the Philippines made on basic telecommunications services under the GATS. These deal with competitive safeguards, nondiscriminatory interconnection, competitively neutral universal service obligations, regulatory independence and competitive resource use and allocation. However, the Philippine government is yet to ratify the Fourth Protocol to the GATS that embodies these proposed commitments despite, as the USTR notes, the urging of the United States.[77]

Restrictiveness data suggest that the Philippines has the least restrictive and discriminatory telecommunications sector among the EAI countries, but the price effects of these restrictions are significant, representing a price wedge of almost 100 per cent. The extent of discrimination towards foreign providers, apart from establishment restrictions, is composed of restrictions on ongoing international operations in such areas as collection rates and termination fees.

Certainly, FTA discussions in this area will focus on competition and independent regulation, which is the responsibility of the National Telecommunications Commission (NTC).

c. Other Public Utilities

As in the case of telecommunications, the Philippine Constitution limits foreign participation in all other sectors considered public utilities to 40 per cent. All executive and managing officers of these enterprises must be Philippine citizens. Included here are water and sewage, power generation, transmission and distribution, public transportation, radio and television broadcasting and cable television.

The United States has been expressing its interest particularly in the power generation and transmission sector.[78] Again, regulation and transparency issues will be central to this area.

d. Advertising and Mass Media Services

The Philippine constitution limits foreign ownership of advertising agencies to 30 per cent. However, all executive and managing officers of advertising agencies must be Philippine citizens. The local industry is characterized by partnerships with the major international U.S. and European agencies, particularly where the management of multinational accounts is concerned. While Filipino advertising professionals are highly regarded, the very fact that no less than a constitutional amendment is required renders the liberalization of barriers to greater foreign participation in advertising, considered "impressed with the public interest", problematic.

This is also the case with mass media (radio, television, print media and film), the ownership and management of which the constitution (Article XVI, Section 11) wholly reserves to Filipinos.

e. Professional Services

As a general policy, the Philippine constitution (Article XII, Section 14) reserves the practice of licenced professions for Filipinos. In the case of foreigners, *Republic Act No. 5181 of 1967* prescribed a three-year residency requirement and nationality of a country which allows Filipinos to practice the relevant profession (unless a law limits a particular profession to Filipinos). Liberalization can, therefore, be legislated, but this has yet to be done with respect to any profession, and there are currently no pending bills in the legislature that seek to do so.

The Australian Productivity Commission data on trade restrictiveness presented by Duc (2000) have quantified restrictions in several professional fields: Engineering, Architectural, Accountancy and Legal Services. This shows the Philippines to be more restrictive than Thailand and far more so than the United States, though the range of restrictiveness narrows for the legal and accounting professions. These are typically subject to higher barriers to entry than the architecture or engineering professions. The high levels in the foreign indices for the Philippines are in large part generally due to nationality and residency requirements.

Reciprocity and related cooperation arrangements to help accredit Filipino professionals in the United States would significantly assist in the liberalization of this sector. Further, there are valid arguments for opening up the practice of professions to former Philippine nationals who have become American citizens but have not yet opted for dual citizenship. Such liberalization makes possible the transfer of technology which improves the quality of potential U.S.-bound Filipino professionals (particularly in the medical and IT-related professions, where upgrading of skills needs to be continuous in light of rapid developments in these fields). The United States may find it easier to have these U.S.-based professionals lobby for opening up the Philippine market in the wider context of long-term human resource imbalances globally, which is seeing the movement of younger professionals from developing countries to aging Western countries (mainly European countries and Japan).

iv. Presence of Natural Persons

This area mainly represents a Philippine concern, as the government is pursuing a policy to ensure that overseas employment remains a legitimate option for Filipinos. Indeed, the country continues to be among the top labour-sending countries in the world. It is estimated that an average of 2,500 Filipinos are deployed overseas daily. At present, there are about 7.4 million Filipinos working temporarily or living permanently in 200 countries all over the world. Since the year 2000, out of every 10 newly hired workers deployed overseas, 7 are women. Although Filipino professionals and workers in the United States are relatively few compared to those in the Middle East or other Asian countries, remittances from overseas Filipinos mostly come from Filipinos in the United States. In 2003 alone, U.S.-based Filipinos remitted to the Philippines more than half of such remittances received by the country. Hence, a bilateral FTA would be expected to include provisions allowing for the movement of Filipinos into the United States, particularly in these areas.

F. Trade-Related Issues

i. Intellectual Property Rights

Intellectual property rights protection is a major area of concern for the United States, as reflected by the Philippines' being included on the "Special 301 Priority Watch List" since 2001. The intellectual property rights (IPR) regime in the Philippines is considered weak, despite legislation in the form of the *Intellectual Property Code of 1997*, due mainly to inadequate enforcement, insufficient punishment for violations and a lack of judicial remedies. In fact, the Philippines is a signatory to the major IPR conventions (WTO-TRIPS, Paris Convention, the Berne Convention, the Bern Treaty, Patent Cooperation Treaty, the Rome International Convention for the Protection of Performers, Producers of Phonograms and Broadcasting Organization, WIPO Performances and Phonograms

Treaty, the WIPO Copyright Treaty, and the Budapest Treaty).

Efforts to increase awareness for a better appreciation of and respect for IPR, and to train and strengthen the enforcement capabilities within the institutions underlying the Philippine IPR regime (the Intellectual Property Office, Department of Justice, National Bureau of Investigation, the new Videogram Regulatory Board, Bureau of Customs and National Telecommunications Commission), have been an active area of cooperation and assistance with the United States.

Nonetheless, and notwithstanding the fact that the Philippine government believes that the significant strides made in the area of IPR protection warrant removal from the watch list, the United States reports widespread IPR infringements in the Philippines in a variety of areas.[79] In negotiations for a prospective FTA, the United States would definitely insist on including Philippine commitments under the various existing treaties, as well as a monitoring mechanism, with the Philippines in return requesting further technical cooperation. Given the fact of an existing policy and operational framework under international agreements, this should not be a problematic area in the sense that no further commitments other than the more effective enforcement of prevailing ones will be sought from the Philippines.[80]

ii. Government Procurement

The U.S.-Singapore FTA in Chapter 13 affirms the provisions of the WTO Agreement on Government Procurement, to which the Philippines has yet to become party. Urging the Philippines to sign can be expected to feature in bilateral negotiations.

The Philippine government provides preferential treatment to local suppliers and domestically produced materials for use in government projects, although consulting services and infrastructure projects are exempted from this requirement, particularly when funded by foreign assistance. With regard to the latter, the USTR noted that potential discrimination against foreign contracts still effectively exists as contractors located in the province where the project will take place are allowed to match the lowest offer made by a bidder based outside the province.

The United States has expressed additional concerns on corruption in government procurement, and is monitoring the implementation of counter-trade requirements for government procurement.

iii. Labour and the Environment

Linking trade with traditionally non-economic issues such as labour and environmental protection are explicit U.S. policy decisions—based on the *Trade Promotion Act of 2002* and found in the U.S.-Singapore FTA—that are likely to remain or become yet more forceful in the event of negotiations with developing countries like the Philippines. The U.S. government appears to be steadily moving towards requiring adequate workers' rights as a determinant of market access. The Philippines sees the question of labour relations and workers' rights as very complicated, maintaining that the countries involved, rather than overseas inspectors, are the best judges of the ideal balance between union rights and the welfare of the workers and industries.

As far as bilateral negotiations are concerned, these issues may not be problematic. The U.S.-Singapore FTA in Chapter 18 and 19 dwells on shared commitments to principles, the application and enforcement of existing laws (which the Philippines also has) and institutional arrangements and cooperation.

iv. Customs Administration

Covered in Chapter 4 of the U.S.-Singapore FTA, this area was noted by the USTR as presenting effective barriers to trade.[81] The Philippine government has been devoting time, effort and resources to the improvement of its customs systems and procedures, in compliance with its WTO obligations. Progress has been achieved in the past years. In legislation, Republic Acts 8181 and 9135 were enacted in 1996 and 2001 respectively to provide the legal context for the Philippines' WTO agreement on customs valuation. These new laws allowed for the implementation of reforms in the Philippine custom schedule including the discontinuation of the home consumption value and the adoption of the transaction value in calculating *ad valorem* rates of duty.

Despite marked improvements in the Philippines' customs regime and the apparent effort of the Philippine government to comply with its WTO obligations, the U.S. government and exporters continue to raise some concerns. For example, the United States has been concerned following reports that private-sector involvement in the valuation process has not been completely eliminated especially in activities of the import specialist team in charge of reviewing all green lane entries for possible valuation-related offences.

Irregularities in the valuation system and inconsistencies in the application of customs rules and procedures, undue and costly processing delays, and corruption are issues that have been repeatedly raised by the U.S. government in its bilateral talks with the Philippines. The U.S. government has been urging the Philippine government constantly to improve the administration of its customs regime, and has in fact extended technical support to the country (through the USAID and donor agencies) in improving its customs systems and procedures. The United States has urged the Philippines to look into the improvement of the classification of entries, and the provision of precise descriptions of imported articles to reduce discretionary authority of customs officials as important "first steps" in enhancing the Philippine customs regime.

v. Corruption

The issue of corruption is actually addressed in the General and Final Provisions (Chapter 21) of the USSFTA. However, corruption is perceived as being a far more entrenched and serious problem in the Philippines than in Singapore, and so can be expected to be given more prominence in a U.S.-Philippines FTA.

It has been noted that anti-corruption efforts have been inconsistent and only limited in effectiveness, and that despite the harsh penalties for both offering and accepting bribes, the Philippines fares very poorly in terms of prevalence of corruption in Asia. This is, needless to say, a potential area for intensified cooperation.

G. Summary of Sectoral and Trade-related Issues

The following table gives a very brief summary of the concerns of both countries that would likely appear in prospective negotiations to a bilateral FTA, in line with the discussion given in this section across the various sectors within manufactures, agriculture, and services, as well as additional areas.

H. Concluding Remarks

In addition to the direct economic gains discussed and estimated in earlier chapters, the U.S.-Philippines FTA will generate a variety of

Table 4.5

Philippines-U.S. FTA: Issues and Concerns

Sector	Philippine Concerns	U.S. Concerns
Goods — Manufactures		
Electronics	Market access secondary to trade expansion from further investment.	Large parts of the Philippine export sector (i.e. semiconductors) are dominated by U.S. multinationals within special export zones; so only housekeeping and investment-protection measures are likely to figure.
Textiles and Garments	Lack of competitiveness under an anticipated future quota-less regime; scope for enhanced trade-facilitation through simplification of procedures.	Within an FTA framework, rules of origin (which signified largely in the Singapore FTA); these however can be carried over from the existing bilateral agreement on trade in textiles.
Furniture and Houseware	Strengthening of small and medium enterprises (finance, training, technology); potential issues concerning rules of origin	No issues identified
Automobiles and Automotive Parts	Further investments for employment-generation and technology transfer under the Philippine Motor Vehicle Development Program	Maintenance of adjustments (local content requirements) to the Program and applicable excise tax which had discriminated against U.S. exports of vehicles and parts.
Distilled Spirits	Further development of domestic industry using local raw materials	The discriminatory tax against spirits derived from raw materials other than those indigenous to the Philippines has been noted and may be raised as an issue.

Cellular Phone Units	Planning and development considerations; equipment standards	The import permit required by the National Telecommunications Commission for telecommunications equipment including cellular phone units has been noted as a potential technical trade barrier
Standards for Industrial Goods	Consumer protection considerations	Mandatory inspections on a wide range of items were noted as effective TBTs; therefore the idea of subjecting these to the monitoring of a joint committee (particularly where they cannot be removed, simplified or rationalized) may be raised.
Goods – Agriculture		
Doha Developing vs. Developed Country Issues	Elimination of protection; preferential treatment for developing countries in terms of market access	Protection of farmers; market access
General System of Preferences	Predictability of access to encourage investment; expansion to include tuna and tropical fruit products, as well as fatty acids	Limiting GSP coverage extensions
Tuna Fisheries	Lower tariffs on canned tuna, particularly in line with proposed U.S. concessions to Andean countries.	Protecting local producers
Shrimp	Simplify or remove certification procedures	Environmental protection
Tropical Fruit	Technical cooperation and further preferential access	Prevention of disease and pests; protection of local producers

Sensitive Goods – Pork and Poultry	Protect local producers and employment	Reform of unfair and unpredictable administration, which amounts to illegal discretionary licensing
Sensitive Goods – Rice and Corn	Food security, employment	Liberalization of import restrictions
Sensitive Goods – Fisheries	Protection of domestic industry, employment	Liberalization of import restrictions
Standards on Agricultural Products	SPS cooperation on mangoes	Reform of unfair SPS, licensing and inspections measures
Genetically Modified Organisms	No issues identified, but may want to sign the Cartegena Protocol as a safeguard	Expanded market access, though no issues identified
Goods – Mining and Natural Resources Extraction		
Mining and Natural Resources Extraction	Protection of the integrity of national resources; environmental and ancestral lands concerns; enhancing employment and investment	No concerns identified, but probably will urge for liberalization of (constitutional) restrictions to foreign mining
Services		
IT and IT-Enabled Services (Cross Border Trade in Services)	Market access and investment	Protecting employment
Telecommunications (Cross Border Trade in Services)	No issues identified	Collection rates and termination fees regime
Air Transport (Cross Border Trade in Services)	Protection of local airlines	More liberal access
Tourism (Consumption Abroad)	Cooperation and assistance	No concerns identified

Health, Retirement and Education Services (Consumption Abroad)	Accreditation of Philippines service providers to American health and retirement and education plans; cooperation and assistance to mitigate brain drain of doctors, nurses and teachers	No concerns identified
Financial Services (Commercial Presence)	Responsiveness to development needs, protection of local banks, reciprocity	Further liberalization of licensing regime for foreign banks; more effective regulation and increased transparency; Philippines has yet to ratify the Fifth Protocol to GATS
Telecommunications (Commercial Presence)	No concerns identified; overall, protection of public interest	Philippine ratification of fourth protocol to GATS; removal of equity limits (constitutional barrier on public utilities); safeguarding competition and improving regulation and transparency
Other Public Utilities (Commercial Presence)	No concerns identified; overall, protection of public interest	Removal of equity limits (constitutional barrier on public utilities); safeguarding competition and improving regulation and transparency
Retail Trade (Commercial Presence)	Protection of local retailers, particularly small retailers	Capital and local content requirements
Advertising and Mass Media (Commercial Presence)	No concerns identified; overall, protection of public interest	Removal of (constitutional) equity limits

Professional Services (Commercial Presence)	No concerns identified; overall, preferential treatment of Filipinos; will likely insist on reciprocity and technical cooperation for U.S. accreditations in FTA negotiations	Removal of nationality requirements
Consulting Services (Commercial Presence and Cross-Border Trade in Services)	No concerns identified	No concerns identified, except for potential barriers under government project rules
Other Issues		
Intellectual Property Rights	Further technical cooperation and assistance	Overall lack of consistent, effective and sustained IPR protection
Government Procurement	No concerns identified; overall, preferential treatment of Filipinos	Philippines not signatory to WTO Agreement on Government Procurement; corruption in government projects; countertrade requirements
Labour and Environment	Overall, should not be a trade-related issue	No concerns identified, but probably will urge strengthened enforcement of environmental laws
E-Commerce	No concerns identified, but will likely insist on reciprocity in FTA negotiations	No concerns identified, but Philippine statutory reciprocity requirement for extension of e-commerce provisions was noted
Customs Administration	Further technical assistance and cooperation	Irregularities in the valuation system; inconsistencies in the application of customs rules and procedures; undue and costly processing delays; corruption

Corruption	A general concern; may request technical cooperation and assistance in FTA discussions	A concern particularly in the administration of licences, government procurement, customs, etc.

positive policy outcomes that will enhance the future efficiency of the Philippine economy. It will encourage crucial gains in the quality of governance (government effectiveness, rule of law, regulatory quality, policy transparency) that will reinforce the efforts of domestic industry and business to be more efficient, productive and competitive. Indeed, Intal (2003) believes that an FTA with the United States can be justified only if the Philippines uses the opportunity "to further its development and international competitiveness objectives and strategies".

The benefits from the necessary policy changes could be expected in the form of improved institutions, policies and regulations, but issues of productivity and investment may be most important, being as they are key to sustained growth, employment generation and poverty reduction through enhanced competitiveness. Again, according to Intal (2003), benefits from a U.S.-Philippines FTA are best derived if a prospective agreement is viewed "primarily from the investment perspective, rather than largely from an efficiency or market access perspective". If investment is taken to include the strengthening of institutions and human capital as well as infrastructure and machines, then the effects on labour as well as agricultural productivity (better education, lower cost of doing business, improved access and facilities) could be profound. Competitiveness could also be expected to improve because the very fact of a U.S.-Philippines FTA in the offing will force industries to review themselves and undergo adjustment and upgrading in anticipation of increased competition with the United States.

The United States is an especially appropriate FTA partner for the Philippines in that, as Avila (2002) stresses:

We want to partner with a stable country with a fairly robust economy. If a particular partner is not very stable, then that could have contagion effects. The size also matters — the larger the market, the better. We also have to look at the complementarity with our export sector — whether it is competitive — and if trade between our countries would be beneficial to both parties. Potential for trade expansion is also an important factor, as well as the sources of FDI. Finally, we also have to consider the prospects of retaliation. It is important to partner with a country that could have immense retaliatory effects should we decide to renege on the agreement — so we would lock in our commitment to the FTA.

On all these counts — stable macroeconomic conditions, large market, complementary export structure, trade balance, potential source of FDI, tendency towards protectionism and capability of retaliation — the United States figures better than the other feasible alternatives of Japan and China. All three have a large market and strong capability for retaliating. However, Japan's economy has long been sluggish, China's export structure is similar to that of the Philippines and therefore competitive, the Philippines has a trade deficit with both Japan and China but a surplus with the U.S. and China is at this time a weak source of FDI. It only remains that the United States has a marked tendency towards protectionism, but this is also arguably true with Japan and China.

In the FTA negotiations, the United States can be expected to be especially interested in issues such as regulatory effectiveness, competition and investment policy, corruption and good governance. Happily, the Philippines acknowledges these same points to be vital to its own overall development objectives, for which there are also large reform constituencies.

On matters of further liberalizing sensitive areas — not so much in manufactures as in agriculture (pork and poultry, rice and corn, fisheries) and in services (retail trade and possibly professional services)—the Philippines must consider the impact on employment and the vulnerability of the less prosperous sectors of society. Obviously, the United States and the Philippines each have political economy issues to consider in the negotiations. The sectoral matrix above showed that lucrative areas for U.S. assistance and cooperation include those very areas of American interest such as IPR enforcement, enhanced customs administration and combating corruption — and may also include regulatory strengthening and governance-enhancing initiatives.

In agriculture, the question of American (and, especially, EU) subsidies to agriculture and their effects on developing countries such as the Philippines is already being tackled at the WTO in the Doha Development Agenda, and it is in the interest of most individual developing countries to keep it in that particular multilateral forum, rather than to raise it in bilateral discussions. This seems already to be the Philippine approach:

to participate in building a developing-country coalition at the WTO on agricultural issues, and bilaterally to focus rather on issues concerning the U.S. GSP, where the Philippines is seeking to institutionalize its access under the GSP in an FTA as a means of reducing uncertainty and attracting investment in areas which will then enjoy predictable access to U.S. market.

Preferential market issues might be raised by the Philippines on tuna fisheries, tropical fruits and fruit products (fresh mangoes and pineapple juice) and coconut products, as well as guarded liberalization of sensitive sectors over which the Philippines will want to maintain a measure of protection (rice and corn, pork and poultry). A key consideration within agriculture is, again, the prospect of trade diversion. Important agricultural exports compete with those of Indonesia and Thailand, and so might suffer from trade diversion should FTAs with the U.S. be concluded with those countries ahead of the Philippines.

Liberalization of mining, which the Philippines must achieve if it is to have a mining sector that contributes significantly to growth, requires statutory amendments and, above all, constitutional amendment. This is also true for the liberalization of restrictions in services and investment. The simple fact of the need for constitutional amendment guarantees that, unlike perhaps for Thailand and maybe Indonesia, there is no chance of prospective U.S.-Philippine FTA discussions being dispassionately viewed — not that there is much chance of this in the first place, for it must always be remembered that matters involving the U.S. provoke more political emotion in the Philippines than those concerning, for example, Japan or China. This is precisely the flip side of the important bilateral relations and the historic ties that the two countries have experienced and certainly not always as equal partners.

Allowing FTA negotiations to be framed in terms of whether or not Philippine sovereignty is being eroded may well be fatal. The sharp national divisions and debates over whether to renew America's leases over the military bases at Subic Bay and Clark Field are especially demonstrative. Rejecting evident economic gains, the treaty to extend the leases was rejected by the Senate in the cause of asserting total sovereignty, and these massive bases were closed in 1992. Those Senators who voted to reject are still counted as heroes by many Filipinos.

Clear reciprocity and careful sequencing are certainly of the essence if advocates of an FTA are not to be put on the defensive. The substance of the FTA negotiations should be prominently advertised in those areas that individual Filipinos across the country would most appreciate: agriculture and services.[82] This should be complemented with other crucial considerations:

- If the greatest benefits of the FTA will arise from investments attracted by a more liberal regime, which in turn can only come about by what would surely be the most contentious element of the negotiations — amendment of the Philippine Constitution — then a Catch-22 may arise: to amend up-front and realize the greater benefits sooner rather than later, but risk opposition that may well derail the whole process; or amend later with the possibility that the FTA may be seen in the intervening years as having benefited only a few at the expense of many, eroding further the chance that amendments would pass (and risking the termination of the agreement). Viewed alone, amending the Constitution later rather than sooner would seem to be more advisable, but careful sequencing must be devised to ensure that benefits from earlier liberalizations are broad and real, so as to increase the number and influence of those with a stake in the agreement's success through its various phases.
- Wherever possible, liberalization should be matched with investment or technical assistance and cooperation. The Philippine government must take a proactive stance and encourage or take the lead on programmes of review and adjustment. This is particularly relevant in the areas where transfer of technology and the building of research capabilities is crucial. It has already been mentioned how Philippine science and technology contributes very little to overall productivity and economic growth, and how linkages between government and the private and academic sectors are inadequate.
- Stressing market access for goods will energize a natural ally in the Philippine exporters and importers, whom should be encouraged to organize more effectively as lobbies to counter the non-export/import lobby.
- Stressing lower prices and higher quality as a result of liberalization and, ultimately, of competition should give rise to consumer support. The notoriously fragmented consumer groups are (ever) potentially a key lobby that should finally be properly organized.

Success in doing so will be critical to a bilateral initiative achieving the broad support required to overcome entrenched lobbies and vested interests. The considerations discussed in Part One above are some of the most important offered in this section.

- Advocating higher labour and environmental standards, if only in compliance with existing laws and agreements (as done with Singapore), may — if framed in fair trade approaches — encourage the support of trade unions and environmentalists, who with farmers' groups form the core of the influential and very vocal "left" that is traditionally hostile to liberalization.

- Liberalization of services must be undertaken to win the support of Philippine professionals, who are drawn mainly from the influential (though relatively small) middle class. The United States may choose to make some initial concessions in favour of the Philippines (rapidly-expanding quotas for practice in the U.S.), while maintaining high standards and accreditation requirements, and cognizant of long-term sustainable development of qualified Filipino professional migrants. An area of technical cooperation would be to assist in the strengthening and accrediting of university and training courses in the professions, and the retention of faculty in key areas to assure the future quality of locally-educated and trained emigrants.

- Liberalization of agriculture must also be framed to favour clearly Filipino farmers in key areas such as tropical fruits, fisheries and marine products, and U.S. interests in areas where subsidy elements have been threshed out (again, fair trade issues). Rice, corn, pork and poultry are probable contentious areas.

- Issues such as IPR are matters of enforcement and adherence to existing agreements, and not further concessions.

- Anti-trust legislation is already being debated in the Philippines and is recognized for the domestic imperative that it is.

Moreover, as noted above, there must be measures for capacity building and competitiveness-enhancement on the one hand, and coalition building among actual and prospective beneficiaries of liberalization on the other. Achieving this requires clear leadership from the Philippine government, which must be seen in this matter to be acting at its own behest while at the same time drawing on American technical assistance and cooperation. This is a delicate act that needs to be carried out not only by the President but also by Congress; a combined and coherent purpose and determination in the exercise of their leadership will ultimately be the decisive factor.

VI. Brunei Darussalam[83]

by Seiji F. Naya and Michael G. Plummer

A. Introduction

Brunei Darussalam (hereafter "Brunei") joined ASEAN soon after independence in 1984. It is a small, open economy, in which petroleum and natural gas play a key role in overall output (together, they constitute over one-third of GDP), source of government revenue, and foreign-exchange income (approximately 90 per cent of its exports are attributable to the energy sector). Hence, Brunei has always been cognizant of the need to exploit the international marketplace, and prepare for its considerable volatility. Brunei was a member of the GATT and is a founding member of the WTO. It is also an active member of APEC and ASEM. It places a strong emphasis on economic liberalization and has launched numerous initiatives in recent years in order to promote further domestic reform as well as a more liberal foreign commercial policy regime.

The government estimates that it will run out of petroleum in approximately 20 years (production peaked in 1979); hence, it has attempted to diversify its domestic economy away from such a strong dependence on energy in favour of greater diversification. As we noted in Chapters 2 and 3, it has been fairly successful in increasing exports of textiles and clothing, particularly to the U.S. market, and the government would especially like to increase the competitiveness of its services sector, which currently accounts for approximately 50 per cent of GDP (2000 numbers).[84]

While the United States is not as important a market to Brunei as in the case of the other ASEAN countries, Brunei's exports of various manufactures to the U.S. market have been rising; hence, it could be an increasingly important market to Brunei in the future. As mentioned in Chapter 3, the potential for trade expansion, in relative terms, may be greater for Brunei than for any other EAI country. Moreover, while Brunei is a small market for the United States by any measure, it demands an important political priority as a member of APEC and ASEAN and as a political ally in the region. In addition, one of the key sectors that Brunei would like to develop is the financial sector; given that the United States has a strong comparative advantage in this area, there may be many niche opportunities for U.S. companies.

Given the scarcity of information available on Brunei's commercial policy regime, we restrict ourselves to a brief review of its basic characteristics.

B. The Brunei Tariff Structure

As can be seen in Table 4.6, which summarizes disaggregated bound and applied tariff lines, Brunei's commercial policy regime is even more liberal than its ASEAN partners (with the exception of Singapore). Its average tariff applied to all imports—which accounted for 37 per cent of GDP in 1998—came to only 3.1 per cent, which is lower than the corresponding average tariff rate in the United States and the EU. Average tariffs on agriculture, forestry, and fisheries were essentially zero, with a few minor exceptions (especially in logging). It also has no import quotas for these products, though there is some monitoring of imports of meat and poultry in order to stabilize market prices. It does have export restrictions on a limited number of commodities, including timber, oil palm, rice and sugar, but these are applied mainly to ensure adequate domestic supplies, rather than having a trade-distortionary goal (e.g., in order to encourage downstream processing for export, as was the case for Indonesian timber products).

Hence, unlike the other EAI countries, in which various agriculture sectors will no doubt be a major negotiating obstacle for both the United States and its EAI partners, this area should pose few problems in the case of the U.S.-Brunei FTA.

Tariffs on manufactures also tend to be low, but are characterized by a large range, from zero to 200 per cent. The highest tariffs are in the transportation sector, where they average 20 per cent and rise to up to 200 per cent. This sector accounts for 13 per cent of manufactured imports and the value of related imports comes to 4.4 per cent of GDP. Hence, as in the case of other EAI countries, this will be one area in which FTA negotiations could imply considerable adjustment in the Brunei tariff regime. However, according to the WTO (2002), the high tariff on motor vehicles is not intended to protect domestic production and/or raise tariff revenue but rather to reduce traffic congestion and pollution. These goals can be easily obtained through other sorts of taxation; after all, the key to an FTA will be national treatment for foreign producers.

Although average tariffs are low, there is a problem of tariff escalation in Brunei. The WTO estimates that this is particularly a problem in the wood and furniture, fabricated metal products and machinery, and chemicals sectors. Tariff escalation is problematic in that it distorts the difference between *nominal* protection and the *effective rate* of protection. The latter calculates the amount of protection accorded value-added in a particular industry and, hence, is a much better gauge of the actual distortionary effects of any given nominal tariff.

As a founding member of AFTA, Brunei has had to meet the same requirements of the other ASEAN-6 countries. Brunei included 6,263 tariff lines in its CEPT tariff schedule, which, as was noted earlier, will range from 0–5 per cent. Given the open nature of the Brunei regime, this was not a difficult task to complete. Regarding its temporary exclusion list products, Brunei originally included coffee and tea, tobacco, alcohol, and motor vehicles.

In sum, despite certain potential problems, it is unlikely that the trade in goods sector will be highly contentious from the Brunei point of view in the U.S.-Brunei FTA negotiations. More likely, difficulties will arise on the U.S. side, particularly with respect to textiles and clothing. However, as Brunei is such a small economy, liberalization of this sector should not be a major issue, though rules of origin requirements will likely be very stringent, as they were in the case of NAFTA. This is because of Brunei's proximity to potentially major exports of textiles and clothing, particularly China.

With respect to services, Brunei has only committed itself to four (out of twelve) areas under the GATS, that is, communication services business services, financial services (discussed below), and transport services.

C. Investment Regime and Initiatives

Brunei is encouraging FDI in much the same way as its ASEAN partners have. It is hoping to use FDI as a means of diversifying its economy. It is an active participant in AICO and the AIA (see Chapter 4), as well as having a cooperative arrangement in the form of the "East Asian Growth Area", which includes Brunei and regions of Indonesia,

TABLE 4.6
Tariff Regime of Brunei Darussalam, 1998 and 2000
(units and per cent)

Products	No. of lines	Applied tariffs 2000		Bound rates		Imports 1998 (% of GDP)
		Simple avg	Range	Simple avg	Range	
Total	**6,503**	**3.1**	**0–200**	**24.8**	**0–50**	**37.1**
Agriculture, forestry and fishing	**363**	**0.4**	**0–20**	**25.5**	**20–50**	**1.7**
Agriculture and livestock production	268	0.0	0–0	26.4	20–50	1.6
Forestry	20	0.0	0–0	20.0	20–20	0.0
Logging	8	17.5	0–20	37.5	20–40	0.0
Fish and shellfish, live, fresh or frozen	67	0.1	0–5	21.9	20–30	0.1
Mining and quarrying	**112**	**0.3**	**0–0**	**20.6**	**20–30**	**0.6**
Coal mining	4	0.0	0–0	20.0	20–20	0.0
Crude petroleum and natural gas production	4	0.0	0–0	20.0	20–20	0.0
Metal ore mining	27	0.0	0–0	20.0	20–20	0.0
Other mining	77	0.5	0–0	20.9	20–30	0.6
Manufacturing	**6,027**	**3.3**	**0–200**	**24.8**	**20–50**	**34.8**
Food products	508	0.0	0–0	23.0	20–50	2.7
Other food products and animal feed	89	0.2	0–5	23.1	20–50	0.9
Beverages	49	0.0	0–0	20.0	20–20	0.6
Tobacco products	14	0.0	0–0	20.0	20–20	0.4
Textiles	895	0.5	0–10	27.3	20–30	2.3
Clothing, except footwear	136	1.0	0–10	29.9	20–30	0.4
Leather and leather products, except footwear and wearing apparel	54	1.1	0–10	21.1	20–30	0.1
Footwear, except rubber or plastic footwear	19	4.5	0–10	20.0	20–20	0.1
Wood products, except furniture	75	10.9	0–20	30.9	20–40	0.2
Wooden furniture	29	4.1	0–5	36.8	20–40	0.7
Paper and product products	131	0.0	0–0	20.0	20–20	0.4
Printing and publishing	32	0.0	0–0	20.0	20–20	0.7
Industrial chemicals	859	0.1	0–20	20.1	20–40	0.9
Chemical products and pharmaceuticals	380	1.6	0–30	24.0	20–50	1.5
Petroleum refineries	32	0.0	0–0	20.0	20–20	0.1
Petroleum and coal products	16	0.0	0–0	20.0	20–20	0.0
Rubber products	126	5.7	0–20	25.8	20–40	0.3
Plastic products, n.e.s.	31	1.3	0–20	21.3	20–40	0.5
Pottery, china and earthenware	15	1.3	0–20	22.7	20–40	0.2
Glass and glass products	73	1.4	0–20	21.2	20–40	0.2
Other non-metallic mineral products	84	0.0	0–0	20.0	20–20	1.1
Iron and steel products	205	0.0	0–0	20.0	20–20	1.8
Non-ferrous basic metals	166	0.0	0–0	20.0	20–20	0.2
Metal products, except machinery and equipment	233	0.8	0–20	20.9	20–40	3.4
Non-electrical machinery and equipment	750	7.3	0–20	29.2	20–40	5.2
Electrical machinery	313	12.4	0–20	39.0	20–40	3.4
Transport equipment	211	20.3	0–200	26.6	20–40	4.4
Professional and scientific equipment	270	6.8	0–20	22.7	20–40	1.0

Source: WTO Secretariat calculations, based on data provided by the authorities of Brunei Darussalam; and UNSD, Comtrade database, as cited in WTO, *Trade Policy Review: Brunei Darussalam*, 2002, WT/TPR/S/84.

Malaysia, and the Philippines.[85] As of 2002, it had very few bilateral investment treaties (BITs), having signed accords only with Germany, Oman, Korea, and China.

Foreign investment in Brunei is regulated under the 1975 Investment Incentives Act and allows foreigners to hold up to 100 per cent equity in certain promoted industries. The government also provides special incentives, particularly tax breaks, in areas which the government would like to develop.

As noted above, Brunei has expressed its desire to become a financial centre. It has embraced liberal banking regulations, except along prudential-requirement lines. However, the WTO laments that much more needs to be done in terms of improving transparency in the financial system. Moreover, it has a long way to go in developing its capital markets. For example, the bond market has yet to get off the ground.

In this sense, *the EAI could present an important opportunity for Brunei to improve its financial-services sector, adopt "best practices", and become more open. As was noted at length above, financial services was a key area in the USSFTA and will likely be a priority in the EAI FTAs as well.*

D. Conclusions

To conclude, while there will no doubt be some difficult areas to negotiate, the U.S.-Brunei FTA will probably be the easiest of the EAI FTAs, for the most important obstacles noted in the case of the other EAI countries (e.g., with respect to agriculture, labour-intensive products, etc.) are far less problematic in the context of the Brunei-U.S. negotiation framework. Moreover, Brunei's small size, commercial-policy openness, and high per capita income, as well as its role as an important strategic ally to the United States, will make it a relatively uncontroversial trade pact.

The U.S.-Brunei FTA could help Brunei reach its overriding goal of greater economic diversification away from the energy sector into other areas of comparative advantage. While the agreement will not do a great deal in terms of promoting structural adjustment in trade in goods—non-tariff barriers are very few and average tariffs are low—it could be very beneficial in the area of services, in particular financial services, which is a government priority.

V.   The U.S.-Thailand FTA from the Thai Perspective[86]

by Wisarn Pupphavesa, Yuthana Sethapramote and
Niramol Ariyaarpakamol

A. Introduction

Thailand and the United States have traditionally had strong political and economic relations, particularly since the 1960s with the Treaty of Amity and Economic Relations (1966). In June 2004, Thailand and the United States began negotiations on a bilateral FTA, technically making Thailand the first country to be a candidate under the EAI framework. Given that the FTA with Singapore is *sui generis* in many ways (for the many reasons stated in this chapter), negotiations with Thailand constitute a major test case for the EAI in that Thailand is a resource-rich ASEAN-4 country par excellence. Many of the sensitive sectors that were predicted to be difficult in Indonesia, Malaysia and the Philippines will no doubt manifest themselves in the U.S.-Thai negotiations as well.

As was discussed at length in Chapters 1–3, the U.S.-Thai economic relationship is strong and growing, though the relationship has experienced considerable volatility in the wake of the Asian Crisis. Details of the U.S.-Thai economic relationship can be found in these chapters. Suffice to note here that the United States ranks as Thailand's number one export market; in 2002 the United States took in 19.6 per cent of Thailand's total exports, compared to the EU's and Japan's 14.8 per cent and 14.5 per cent shares, respectively (Table 2.1). The United States accounts, however, for only 9.6 per cent of Thailand's imports, placing it behind Japan (23 per cent), ASEAN (16 per cent), and the EU (11 per cent). While Thailand accounts for less than 1 per cent of U.S. exports (and less than ⅛ of all U.S. exports to ASEAN as a whole), its share of imports is almost double that figure (1.3 per cent) and constitutes one-third of U.S. imports from ASEAN (Table 2.2). Almost two-thirds of U.S. exports are geared to the electronics and electrical machinery sector (Table 2.4), whereas Thailand's exports to the United States are quite diversified, especially relative to its ASEAN partner countries. Forty-five per cent of exports fall under the category of electrical machinery and equipment, 27 per cent fall under "miscellaneous manufactures", and 14 per cent under food (Table 2.3). Moreover, the United States' stock of FDI came to US$7.39 billion in 2003, down from US$7.61 billion in 2002 but up considerably from US$6.2 billion in 2001 (Table 1.5). This ranks it fourth in terms of U.S. FDI stock in ASEAN, behind Singapore, Indonesia, and (marginally) Malaysia.

Using several techniques, Chapter 3 also concluded that Thailand could potentially be one of the biggest winners in ASEAN with a bilateral FTA. In addition, that chapter argued that the dynamic effects of the FTA could be many times as important as the static effects. However, how much Thailand and the United States will eventually gain from an FTA will depend critically on the contents of the agreement. The goal of this section, similar to the ones above, is to identify and analyse the key "special issues" or sensitive areas that will emerge in these negotiations. This is done first by reviewing briefly the Thai commercial policy regime, using the WTO's most recent *Trade Policy Review* (October 2003) as the primary source. This is followed by a delineation of the main issues of contention from the U.S. perspective, as articulated in the USTR's *2005 Foreign Barriers to U.S. Exports*, and then from a Thai perspective, using the USSFTA as a guide to which areas will most likely be put on the table during the negotiations.

B. Overview of the Thai Commercial Policy Regime

Thai tariffs at a highly disaggregated level and applied to U.S. exports can be found in Chapter 3, i.e., Table 3.13 and Appendix Table 3.14. However, Table 4.7 below gives us an overview of the aggregate structure of Thai MFN tariffs and how they have evolved since 1999, based on WTO data. The simple Thai average tariff of 14.7 per cent is relatively low by the standards of developing countries, but high in the context of East Asia. Tariffs have come down marginally since 1999, when they averaged 17 per cent. But it is important to note that tariffs had been raised—in some cases fairly substantially, such as in the automotive sector—during the Asian Crisis.

As is the case for many OECD and ASEAN countries, average tariffs on agricultural products (25 per cent) tend to be substantially higher than for industrial products (13 per cent). Over two-fifths of Thai tariff lines exceed 15 per cent. Tariff spikes—defined as tariffs that exceed three times the simple average applied tariff rate—come to 1.6 per cent of all tariff lines, which is substantially down from 1999 when it was more than twice that figure. The standard deviation of tariff rates has also fallen over this period. Hence, while tariffs on average continue to be relatively high, there is evidence that they are becoming more evenly distributed.

Nevertheless, it is clear that Thailand has a strong comparative advantage in many agricultural products, such as rice. While it may be true that tariffs are high in the Thai context, Thailand faces even more formidable barriers to its agricultural exports in global markets, particularly the OECD. In addition to significant market access issues in these markets, Thailand must also compete with the myriad agricultural export subsidies that result from OECD agricultural policies.[87] In fact, the WTO *Trade Policy Review* notes that agriculture is the main, or perhaps even the *only*, reason that Thailand has entered enthusiastically into the most recent trade negotiations (WTO 2003, p. 22).

Another aspect of the Thai tariff regime that the WTO cites as problematic regards its use of the 7-digit HS system, resulting in 5,505 tariff lines. It stresses that this leads to the system's being overly complex. Moreover, non-*ad valorem* duties, which tend to be less transparent and

TABLE 4.7
Overall Structure of Thai Tariffs: 1999, 2002, 2003
(percentages)

	1999	2002	2003
Simple average applied rate	17.0	15.0	14.7
Agricultural products (HS01-24)	32.7	26.0	25.4
Industrial products (HS25-97)	14.6	13.1	12.9
WTO agricultural products	33.1	26.3	25.7
WTO non-agricultural products	14.7	13.1	13.0
Textiles and clothing	24.7	22.5	21.7
Domestic tariff "spikes" (% of all tariff lines)[a]	3.6	1.6	1.6
International tariff "spikes" (% of all tariff lines)[b]	45.5	43.6	43.5
Overall standard deviation (SD) of tariff rates	16.3	13.6	13.2
"Nuisance" applied rates (% of all tariff lines)[c]	7.1	16.1	16.2

Notes: a. Domestic tariff spikes are defined as those exceeding three times the overall simple applied rate (indicator 8).

    b. International tariff spikes are defined as those exceeding 15 per cent.

    c. "Nuisance" rates are those greater than zero, but less than or equal to 2 per cent.

Source: WTO Secretariat calculations, based on data provided by the Thai authorities, as cited in WTO Trade Policy Review, Thailand, November 2003, Table III.1.

can be more complicated to liberalize, account for 23 per cent of Thai tariff lines. Finally, Thailand applies tariff-quotas on 1 per cent of its tariff lines (AFTA beneficiaries are excluded from this system). The in-quota average tariff rate is approximately 23 per cent, but the average out-of-quota tariff rate comes to 40 per cent. Import licences are required in order to apply for tariff quotas.

With respect to investment, the WTO notes that Thailand has a generally liberal foreign investment regime. This is consistent with the traditionally high importance that Thailand has placed on attracting FDI, particularly in the wake of the Asian Crisis. For example, no investment project that met the legislative criteria for FDI has been rejected, and only approximately 11 per cent were rejected as having not met the criteria, with most of these projects being related to the services sector (WTO 2003, p. 30). However, the WTO does fault the Thai FDI regime as being non-transparent in certain respects, characterized by an application process that can be "time-consuming and unpredictable" (WTO 2003 p. 30). Interesting from the point of view of this study, the WTO notes that, due to the Treaty of Amity and Economic Relations with the United States, Thailand is required to grant national treatment to U.S. investors, except in a number of politically-sensitive areas, mostly in services (e.g., communications, transport, banking, and agricultural trade).

C. U.S. Concerns Regarding Thai Commercial Policy

In its 2005 Report, the USTR identifies eight salient areas in which there exist impediments to U.S. exports. Below, the USTR's main arguments are summarized under each of these topics, namely: (1) general import policies; (2) standards, testing, labelling and certification; (3) government procurement; (4) export subsidies; (5) intellectual property protection (IPR); (6) trade in services; (7) investment barriers; and (8) electronic commerce.

1. Thai Import Policies.

The U.S. government maintains that Thailand's relatively high tariffs are an important impediment to U.S. exports. It also deems the Thai import regime to be "complicated" (with 46 different rates) and begs to be streamlined. It notes progress in these areas as of 2005 but stresses that more needs to be done in meeting both its commitments under the WTO and AFTA, mainly in the area of agricultural products. The USTR Report is most critical with respect to protection of agriculture in Thailand, which as noted above features relatively high tariffs, quantitative restrictions, and various additional impediments to U.S. exports.

Other areas that are cited in the Report include: *Taxation*, which it considers too "complicated and non-transparent", in particular with respect to price controls on some products, quantitative restrictions (such as the tariff-rate quotas mentioned above) that affect market access, and import license fees for various agricultural imports; *Automotive protection*, which it says is among the most restrictive in ASEAN, having deteriorated with tariff increases applied during the Asian Crisis; *Textiles tariffs*, which it claims are high (20–30 per cent for most exports of U.S. fabrics and 30 per cent for most clothing); *Quantitative restrictions and import licensing*; and *Customs barriers* (particularly in terms of transparency and efficiency of the customs bureaucracy), which the USTR notes has been making process since 2004 from discussions under the U.S.-Thai TIFL.

2. Standards, Testing, Labelling and Certification

Based on input from the U.S. private sector, the USTR cites a number of specific areas in which standards and testing tend to be costly, often stringent, and overly complex. Moreover, the U.S. private sector has complained that, as part of the certification process, they have been asked to give proprietary information that could compromise trade secrets. Certain regulations, such as on motorcycle emissions, can be extremely strict and costly.

3. Government Procurement

Thailand is not a signatory to the WTO Agreement on Government Procurement, though it has indicated support for a WTO Agreement on Transparency in Government Procurement. While the Thai government's own regulations are technically non-discriminatory, state enterprises tend to have their own rules. Preferential treatment is usually accorded to domestic suppliers (including, the USTR notes, Thai affiliates of U.S. multinationals), who receive a 15 per cent advantage in the initial bid-round evaluations.

4. Export Subsidies

While the Report emphasizes that Thailand has made progress with respect to eliminating its subsidies for exports, it notes that it still maintains a number of direct and/or indirect export subsidies in favour of manufactured products and processed agricultural goods. The types of export subsidies applied take on several forms, including tax benefits, import duty reductions, credit benefits, and other types of preferential financing.

5. Intellectual Property Protection

The USTR Report features a long section criticizing IPR policies in Thailand, as it does for some other ASEAN countries. It maintains that piracy and counterfeiting continue to be at "high levels" and that enforcement efforts have been "inconsistent". Copyright industries estimate that the loss to U.S. industries due to IPR infringement came to approximately $166 million in 2003. Since November 2004 Thailand has been on the U.S. Special 301 Watch List. The United States has held extensive negotiations regarding IPR protection with Thailand under the TIFA and in the first FTA discussions, but it is clear that the U.S. government continues to be disappointed at the lack of sufficient progress in this area. The IPR sector will be discussed more at length in the next subsection, as it promises to continue to be one of the most controversial in the U.S.-Thailand FTA negotiations.

6. Trade in Services

As was the case with other EAI countries, services is another area in which FTA negotiations will be difficult. A number of sectors are mentioned in the USTR Report, namely, telecommunications; legal services; financial services; construction, architecture and engineering; accounting services; express-delivery services; health care services; retail services; and advertising. The first three appear to be the most significant. The most salient complaint regarding telecommunications services is that, while foreign entry has been allowed since 1989, state-owned enterprises still dominate the market. Thailand is committed under the WTO to liberalize the market fully by January 2006 but USTR doubts that it will happen. It also complains that state-owned entities are taking too long to be privatized. With respect to legal services, U.S. investors continue to receive special benefits (relative to other foreign entities) and actually can own law firms in Thailand, whereas other nationals can own a maximum of 49 per cent of a law firm. However, it is still the case that U.S. nationals cannot provide legal services in Thailand. Finally, regarding financial services, the USTR acknowledges that Thailand did liberalize significantly this sector in the aftermath of the Asian Crisis. But the sector remains at least partially closed in a number of respects. For example, foreign participation in Thai banks continues to be limited to 25 per cent, though there are plans to raise that limit to 49 per cent. Moreover, the USTR notes that foreign banks are at a clear disadvantage in many respects, e.g., in only being able to have one branch, and not being able to provide off-site ATM machines (which would be considered additional branches). There are also significant limitations on expatriate bank-management personnel.

7. Investment Barriers

The USTR does underscore the important advantages that U.S. entities have in Thailand due to the Treaty of Amity and Economic Relations. As noted above, the national treatment accorded U.S. firms in all but a few explicitly-named sectors gives it an advantage over other foreign affiliates. It would appear that the only complaints that the United States has in this sector regards these few sectors, as well as the fact that national treatment under the Treaty does not extend to "the practice of professions, or callings reserved for [Thai] nationals." (USTR 2005, p. 15). It duly notes that Thailand has met its obligations in areas that previously may have been controversial, e.g., local-content requirements.

8. Electronic Commerce

The USTR stresses that, while the Thai government has made e-commerce an important priority, the related legal framework tends to be underdeveloped, and relatively limited internet penetration has negatively affected growth prospects. Key legislation has been delayed. It also notes that the problems noted above with respect to telecommunications overall tend to spill over into electronic commerce as well.

In sum, the U.S. government acknowledges that Thailand has made a good deal of progress in terms of trade and investment liberalization and transparency, and relative to many other developing countries it has a liberal regime. Moreover, two facts may mitigate in favor of a U.S.-

Thai accord from the U.S. perspective: (1) while the U.S. trade deficit with Thailand is fairly significant (the Thai merchandise trade surplus came to US$11 billion in 2004) it is less important if one considers the relatively large trade in services surplus that the United States enjoys with Thailand. Further, the Thai trade surplus is nowhere near as large as it is with certain other Asian countries, in particular China and Japan, which have received the most political attention in recent years. And (2) the United States' long, special relationship with Thailand through the Treaty of Amity and Economic Relations suggests that a trade deal could have some natural political "momentum". However, as is clear from the above discussion, the U.S. government is bringing to the negotiations a number of issues that will have to be resolved before an FTA can be reached. Many of these areas will be sensitive in the Thai context as well. In addition, Thailand itself will have a number of demands that the United States will have to meet, particularly in the area of agriculture, before it will be ready to enter into an FTA. We turn to these issues in the next subsection.

D. The U.S.-Thai FTA from the Thai Perspective

The authors of this section, like those of this Study, are convinced that a successful conclusion to the bilateral FTA negotiations between the United States and Thailand, initiated on 19 October, 2003 by President Bush and Prime Minister Thaksin, is in the interest of each country. This viewpoint is obviously shared by both governments. In President Bush's letter to the Senate regarding the government's intent to negotiate an FTA with Thailand, he stresses the potential commercial and foreign policy gains that could be derived from such an agreement as the main motivation for the United States. Moreover, the letter underscores the usefulness of an FTA in strengthening cooperation with Thailand in bilateral, regional and multilateral forums.

As for Thailand, its interest in negotiating bilateral FTAs in general has increased recently to become one of its key external policy tools to stimulate economic growth. The Thaksin Government views FTAs as a strategic channel to promote exports to its major trading partners. Since 2004, Thailand has signed FTAs with Australia (2004) and New Zealand (2005). Moreover, it is in the process of negotiations with the other countries, such as Japan, China, India and, of course, the United States.

Thailand's over-riding incentive for these negotiations is to use the FTA as a means to maintain or enhance its competitive stance in the U.S. market by reducing U.S. tariff and non-tariff barriers (NTBs) against Thai exports. While the United States is one of Thailand's most important trading partners, Thai exports have been experiencing intense competition in the U.S. market from a variety of sources, such as China and Mexico, which have experienced rapid increases in their trade shares over the past decade (Mexico having gained a preferential edge through NAFTA). Therefore, the Thai government views an FTA with the United States as a vehicle to increase competitiveness and market share, or at least to maintain its position *vis à vis* its many competitors, some of which have recently formalized FTAs with the United States, e.g., Chile and Singapore.

In addition, Thailand expects benefits from a potential surge in FDI from the United States, which could derive from enhanced protection of investors, sector-specific agreements, and general investment measures inherent in modern FTAs. Improvement in efficiency, higher levels of technology, better managerial skills, and other favourable "dynamic" effects that should derive from greater inflows of U.S. FDI are essential to enhance the competitiveness of the Thai economy and improve its competitive advantage.

1. Issues of Interest in the FTA Negotiations: The Thai perspective

Conventionally, FTAs are established to enhance market access in goods between trading partners by eliminating tariffs and NTBs on mutual goods and services. However, as noted at length in this and earlier chapters, the recent U.S. FTA negotiations are far more comprehensive than a mere textbook accord. These include, for example, the so-called "Singapore issues", IPR-related areas, and trade in services. Issues of specific interest and concern that will demand careful attention in the negotiations from the Thai perspective are analysed below under the following headings: trade in goods; trade in services (generally); financial services; telecommunications; investment; IPR; competition policy; and labour and environmental standards.

a. Trade in Goods

Thailand expects that the elimination of tariffs and NTBs in the context of an FTA with the United States will strengthen the competitive ability of Thai exports in the U.S. market. Of course, the average U.S. tariff rate imposed on Thai non-agricultural exports is currently low, i.e., in the range of 2–3 per cent (see Chapter 3). As can be seen from Table 4.8, which compares levels of tariffs in Thailand to those of the United States in 20 sectors, U.S. tariffs range from 0–3 per cent in all sectors save crops, dairy products, and textiles and apparel.

In addition, many of Thai export items receive tariff exemptions under the U.S. Generalized System of Preferences (GSP) scheme. However, the average tariff rate of 13 per cent in the textiles and clothing sector is high. Therefore, according to the study of Pupphavesa et al. (2005), the advantage derived from the reduction of tariffs under an FTA framework would be concentrated on only some specific sectors, such as textiles, processed foods and agricultural products where the current tariff rates are still significant. Moreover, additional benefits for Thailand would flow

TABLE 4.8
Average import tariffs between Thailand and the U.S. by commodity (percentages)

Sectors	Thai tariffs on U.S. imports	U.S. tariffs on Thai imports
Grains	20.29	1.60
Crops	16.16	6.23
Animal products	1.87	0.35
Forestry and fishing	15.70	0.00
Coal, Oil and Gas	1.30	0.00
Processed food products	25.80	2.18
Dairy products	13.43	18.73
Textiles and apparel	15.36	12.58
Wood products	7.67	0.05
Paper products and publishing	8.77	0.00
Petroleum and coal products	3.33	0.38
Chemical, rubber and plastic	11.22	1.09
Mineral products	18.01	1.42
Ferrous metals and metals	7.00	0.76
Metal products	17.91	0.42
Motor vehicles and parts	38.62	0.16
Transportation equipment	2.27	0.04
Electronic equipment	1.67	0.30
Machinery and equipment	7.62	1.12
Manufactures	10.34	0.30

Source: GTAP 6 Data Package

from the reduction of Thai import tariffs, which would reduce import costs for some industries that rely on machinery and intermediate-good imports, such as the automobiles and auto parts industries.

In addition to tariff reduction, the competitiveness of Thai exports should also be enhanced. TDRI (2003) uses calculations of revealed comparative advantage (RCA) as a proxy of a country's competitiveness. The results show that 1,157 products of Thai exports with RCA greater than one and increasing over time are expected to benefit from the tariff reduction scheme resulting from an FTA with the United States. Using the same technique, TDRI (2003) derives for U.S. exports a similar range (955 items) in terms of products gaining competitiveness in the Thai market. Therefore, the U.S.-Thailand FTA would be expected to help increase the advantage of Thai goods in the U.S. market and vice versa.

Another interesting issue from the analysis of the RCA in TDRI (2003) is that the United States is a complementary trading partner with Thailand in the automotive sector, especially in spare-parts markets. Therefore, the U.S.-Thailand FTA is likely to benefit both countries from mutual tariff reductions, given their respective comparative advantages (and especially relatively high tariffs in Thailand). In addition, Thailand also expects that the potential trade creation would attract more FDI from U.S. major automobile and auto-parts companies, which is already one of the most rapidly-growing industries in Thailand.

Although tariffs constitute the traditional type of barriers to trade in goods, NTBs also play a significant role in the protection of the domestic market from foreign competition. These could be far more substantial in limiting Thai exports to the U.S. market and, hence, will offer greater gains in relevant sectors. For example, the higher product standards and procedures required to enter the U.S. market for a variety of goods pose difficulties for Thai exporters—especially small- and medium-sized enterprises (SMEs)—to enter the U.S. market. While some of these standards reflect legitimate concerns, others may not; they may merely be another form of protectionism.[88] Therefore, while the U.S. market is reasonably open to Thai exports, it is in Thailand's interest to seek improvements in market access through the reduction of both tariff and NTB restrictions in key export areas. Thailand also should seek technical cooperation from the United States in the areas of technical regulations, product standards, and conformity assessment procedures to provide Thai exporters with a better understanding and awareness of measures required to meet the U.S. standards, and efficient means to meet them.

In addition, Thai concerns also arise in the context of certain U.S. trade remedy measures, such as the use of anti-dumping (AD) and countervailing (CV) measures to protect domestic industries. The United States had initiated nine AD and two CV investigations against Thailand. Some of the AD-affected producers are SMEs in, for example, canned pineapple, shrimp, and plastic bags. Other AD-affected products are steel-related and petrochemical products. Thailand has not applied any AD measures against U.S. products (See Terdudomtham 2005). The conflict in shrimp between Thailand and the United States is just one (*albeit* an important) case in this regard. Thai shrimp exporters are threatened by the AD investigations filed by the United States shrimp producers for selling shrimp in the U.S. market below their cost of production. Moreover, the United States also banned imports of shrimp and shrimp products based on the justification that the catching method was harmful to sea turtles. Therefore, it is Thailand's interest in the FTA negotiations to demand clear and better disciplines regarding mechanisms for dispute settlements, especially for the use of AD and CV duties.

b. Trade in Services
The General Agreement on Trade in Services (GATS) provides a framework to liberalize trade in the service sector (see Chapters 1–2). The cross-border mode of supply is considered the traditional approach to selling services abroad. In addition, trade in services includes the "commercial-presence" mode, which involves domestic sales by local affiliates of foreign multinationals, and the "presence of natural persons" mode, which involves the temporary entry of a businessperson(s) to supply a service. Issues in liberalizing market access in trade in services have been pushed by the United States in FTA negotiations as a means of seeking better access for U.S. service providers. As noted above, the sectors of specific interests for the United States in the FTA negotiations with Thailand include financial services, telecommunications, and professional services. From the Thai perspective, liberalizing services will induce greater competition from U.S. service providers via both cross-border and commercial presence modes of supply, which will in turn provide benefits in terms of improvements in quality of services and lower prices. Moreover, investment and technological know-how

received from the United States is also viewed as an important channel to improve performance in the domestic services market. However, there are some sensitive service sectors including financial services and telecommunications, in which the regulatory capacity is still lacking.

i. Financial Services

Financial services liberalization is a definite priority for the United States in the FTA negotiations. The United States has a strong comparative advantage in financial services, given the depth, liquidity, sophistication and experience of its financial markets, resulting in lower costs of capital and a wide range of financial instruments.

Since the 1990s and particularly since the Asian Crisis, Thailand has increasingly deregulated its national financial markets. However, bank, security, asset management and insurance companies are still regulated intensively by government authorities. In the early 1990s, market openness had been increased through offshore banking facilities, resulting in a surge of short-run capital inflows. Consequently, debts of domestic companies in foreign currencies increased considerably. The problems associated with such large foreign-debt exposure became evident with the Asian Crisis, which began in Thailand on 2 July, 1997, with the formal floating of the *baht*. After 1997, the increased market access granted to foreign firms, which allowed them to hold higher percentages of equity and gain corporate control, was used as a measure to prevent bankruptcy and liquidation of financial companies that suffered severely from the effects of the financial crisis.

Recently, Thailand has further liberalized its financial markets. In January 2004, the Bank of Thailand (BoT) announced its financial sector "master plan", allowing, *inter alia*, for increased participation for branches and subsidiaries of foreign banks in the domestic market. Existing foreign banks are allowed to perform similar transactions as local banks, with a limited number of branches and small restrictions on specific services, such as ATM services. A three-year period of transition has been imposed in order to facilitate liberalizing and new licence applications.

Despite a series of financial-market liberalization measures, Thailand is still reluctant to commit to further openness of the financial sector in the FTA negotiations with the United States. Harsh memories and experiences of the 1997 Crisis have raised concerns that the further deregulation of the financial system without adequate preparation of domestic institutions may expose or exacerbate problems in periods of economic fluctuation, and increase the systematic risk of financial crisis.

Another key hurdle to negotiations regards the "negative list" approach employed by the United States in negotiations of FTA for financial services. This approach defines an area of liberalization on the premise that all service sectors are completely open unless a specific reservation is taken. The lists of areas in which countries wish to take reservation, called "Non-Conforming Measures" (NCMs), are then drawn up. This approach ensures comprehensive coverage and continuously enlarges the liberalized areas to include new services. From Thailand's point of view, this negative list basis is unacceptable in financial services negotiations. Concerns about the ability to cope with the impact of capital movements are exacerbated by the fact that new financial instruments in the U.S. financial markets are constantly being introduced. Under the negative-list approach, such services would be automatically open. Hence, Thailand needs to maintain reservations about the negative-list approach, even though this position may well result in one of the major obstacles in the FTA negotiations with the United States.

The political economy aspect of financial services also plays a significant role in the Thai reluctance to accelerate the liberalization process. The potential benefits of the FTA to the financial sector are likely to include increasing competitiveness of the market, the development of higher quality financial services, and increased diversification of products (see, for example, Levine 1996). In addition, improvements in financial services efficiency would lead to more effective resource allocation and risk management for the whole economy and increase the country's access to international capital. However, the competition and diversification in the financial market may not improve equitable access for all domestic borrowers. Competition may concentrate in the modern sectors and central areas. Foreign financial services companies may continue to have a strong interest in big corporate customers, but this might be to the disadvantage of SMEs, especially in the rural areas.

ii. Telecommunications

The telecommunications issue is of interest to both Thailand and the United States in the ongoing FTA negotiations. This section will stipulate in detail rights to the use of and connection to public telecommunication networks, which provide the technical framework to liberalize the market, ensure adequate supply of communication services to foreign companies, and offer greater opportunities to participate in the networks without technical barriers. The ability to access public telecommunication networks is key to cost-saving and further development of new telecommunication services. For example, the high-speed Internet service providers and interactive TV services are required to use the local cable network as a channel to supply their services to customers. In addition, adequate supply of telecommunications is also crucial to the operation of other important businesses, such as financial services, information technology (IT), and educational services.

The primary concern of Thailand with respect to this issue regards the commitment to liberalize the telecommunications market, which is characterized by limited competition and relatively high prices (see, for example, TDRI 2003). The market is dominated by two state enterprises: the CAT telecom and the TOT corporation. Any telecommunications chapter in an FTA would stipulate a requirement for partners to notify any intention to eliminate an ownership interest in a supplier of public telecommunications services. Currently, the privatization framework for the CAT and TOT still allows the Thai government to hold the majority stake (70 per cents) in these companies. Given that the establishment of a National Telecommunications Commission (NTC) to serve as an independent regulator has been delayed, deregulation and liberalization of the telecommunications market is still likely to be problematic.

Regarding the U.S. market, the satellite services sector may provide an important opportunity for Thai satellite companies. In the U.S. satellite services sector, the spectrum allocation and licencing are still discriminatory *vis à vis* foreign companies. Therefore, Thailand's mobile or satellite companies could expect the FTA negotiations to provide greater access and help overcome technical difficulties in increasing participation in the U.S. market (See Hunton &Williams LLP 2003).

c. Investment

As noted above, Thailand has in place an investment agreement with the United States under the Treaty of Amity and Economic Relations. The national treatment accorded to U.S. companies via the

Treaty applies to all but a few (sensitive) sectors as well as professional services. However, the Treaty, which provides special privileges to U.S. investors over other countries, is considered by some to be in violation of WTO/MFN obligations. It has stayed in place due to an allowance by the WTO. Hence, the incorporation of investment-related protection and other benefits under an FTA would perpetuate national treatment, which would be of interest both to the United States and Thailand.

However, the investment issue in the FTA negotiations also enlarges the coverage of the investment protections beyond the existing Treaty of Amity. Free- trade agreements formalized by the United States with other trading partners, such as Singapore, Chile and Australia, grant extremely broad investment protection coverage. "Covered investment" in these agreements has been defined to include equity participation in enterprises, loans, bond and other debt instruments, futures, options and other derivatives, contracts, licences, permits, other tangible or intangible property, and related IPRs. In addition, a special dispute settlement mechanism is included in the FTA agreement on investment to provide fair and acceptable standards of treatment in resolving disputes involving foreign investors and the host country. The broad coverage of the investment definition raises concerns for Thailand regarding certain sensitive issues; in particular, foreigners' landholding, short-run loans and portfolio investments, and derivatives, as well as the provisions regarding the ability of the government to regulate in some areas, such as imposing restrictions on all transfers relating to covered investment (particularly short-term portfolio investments).

Nevertheless, despite these concerns, Thailand expects that the investment agreement in the context of an FTA will generate potential benefits in the form of greater FDI from U.S. multinationals, and greater protection for U.S. investors could be a channel for more technology transfer and cooperation in research on science and technology. In addition, it is interesting to note that the rights and coverage of the investor protections in the U.S.-Thailand FTA could be extended to other foreign investors on the MFN basis, which would also be in Thailand's interest.

d. Intellectual Property Rights

As noted in the summary of the USTR Report above, the United States has been concerned about deficiencies in the protection of IPRs in Thailand. Although a variety of measures to improve IPRs has been adopted, the

United States is still concerned that Thailand has not implemented a rigorous regime to overcome various problems, such as the manufacture of pirated media products, pirated optical discs and their exports.

There are a number of issues regarding IPRs that the United States and Thailand are discussing at the moment in the FTA negotiations. These include: (1) trademarks and geographical indications; (2) domain names on the Internet; (3) copyright and related rights; and (4) patents.

To begin with trademarks and geographical indications, the United States strongly encourages Thailand to provide sufficient protection for registered trademarks and geographical indication owners. The registration should not be limited to only visually perceptible trademarks; the protection should cover scent marks and sound marks as well. This requirement is not addressed in the agreements on the Trade-Related aspects of Intellectual Property Rights (TRIPs) in the WTO. It is also possible that FTAs will impose rules and regulations for management of domain names on the internet that require dispute resolution mechanisms to prevent trademark cyber-piracy.

Another main concern regarding IPRs is that of drug patents. Even though this issue has not been formally discussed, it is likely that the U.S. proposed agreements would mirror those of the U.S.-Singapore FTA that obligate both parties to provide five-year protection for a pharmaceutical product in the case that its marketing approval requires the submission of undisclosed information concerning the safety and efficacy of the pharmaceutical product. During this period of protection, both parties would not allow third parties to market the same or similar products. If this particular agreement is to be adopted, it will result in higher prices of medicines and make them unaffordable to the poor. Therefore, the main concern regarding this issue is that it is essential to ensure that the patent law will not limit access to medicine; otherwise, the costs, especially to the poor, in the short-term could be considerable.

With regards to copyright issues, the United States is particularly concerned about the deficiencies in copyright law and its enforcement in Thailand. Prevention and enforcement against the illegal manufacture, export and import of pirated products, including CDs, VCDs and DVDs as well as pirated optical discs, will be an important part of the U.S. agenda in the FTA negotiations. Hence strong measures against the distribution of pirated goods within and across Thailand's borders are necessary.

In addition to optical media products and optical discs, the unauthorized reception and re-distribution of encrypted programme-carrying satellite signals are of concern to the United States. Although copyright protection may be considered beneficial to both parties, from the perspective of Thailand, the copyright law could potentially prevent access to useful educational material as well as information technology. Thus, the government will want to ensure that the ultimate copyright law under the FTA does not inhibit Thailand's development goals, and the scope of the agreement should not be beyond the IPR principle discussed in the WTO.

e. Competition Policy

Thai competition policy, law and enforcement are rather weak in comparison to U.S. standards. As a result, U.S. industry is seeking to remedy any competitive disadvantages in the Thai market through the FTA. The focus of competition policy chapters in U.S.-related FTAs involves strengthening antitrust (monopoly power, anticompetitive mergers and acquisitions, etc.) and fair trade, as well as consumer protection to guarantee fair treatment for both partners in each other's markets.

Seeking the establishment of an independent competition law enforcement agency in Thailand will be one of the priorities for the United States in the FTA negotiations. At the moment, the Thai Competitive Commission is under the supervision of the Ministry of Commerce and Cabinet. Transformation and removal of the competitive commission from the auspices of this government body into an independent office ensuring the effective enforcement of competition law without political interferences is of particular interest to the United States. In addition, the United States will seek an amendment to the Trade Competition Act to include state-owned and state-linked enterprises relevant to anti-competitive practices to ensure fair competition with these state enterprises.

The primary concern of Thailand regarding competition-policy law is that, without protection, it will be difficult for Thai industries, especially state enterprises and SMEs, to compete with large U.S. firms that are possibly endowed with higher investment and sophisticated technology (TDRI 2003). Therefore, in the negotiations it would be wise to take into account the need for essential adjustment on the Thai side;

a suitable transitional period should be provided before enforcing any new competition law.

f. Labour and Environment Standards

Like its peers in the OECD, the United States has high standards regarding labour rights and environment protection. Both of these areas will be controversial from the Thai perspective in the FTA negotiations. Past experiences with the United States, such as the threat to suspend the GSP for Thai exports due to lack of progress on labor reform and the Shrimp-Turtle and Tuna-Dolphin disputes, provide reasons to be anxious about labour and environment issues in the negotiations. According to the report by TDRI (2003), sectors of interest for Thailand in these areas include especially shrimp, canned seafood, electrical circuits, computer parts, clothing and footwear. Trade conflicts in these sectors, which as we know from Chapter 3 constitute some of the most important Thai exports to the United States, could easily emerge, especially given the political economy of protectionism in the United States and Thai competitiveness.

However, the recent U.S. FTAs with Singapore and Chile reaffirm the principle that each country would be committed to improve its standards and effectively enforce its own domestic labour laws and environment standards. Partners are not required to apply the higher labour and environment standards legislated in the United States. Therefore, it is of interest to Thailand to ensure that coverage of these issues would be similar to those of Chile and Singapore, in which partners have agreed to merely enforce their existing laws without applying additional obligations. In addition, Thailand should also seek for the technical cooperation to improve labour and environmental standards for Thai exporters, which should be of mutual benefit to Thailand and the United States. In fact, the FTA could be very positive for Thailand in this regard, as it would put in place protection from anti-dumping duties and threats of GSP withdrawal that have arisen in the past without any agreement.

2. Concluding Perspective and Suggestion on Negotiations

In conclusion, an FTA between Thailand and the United States should prove to be mutually beneficial in terms of increased trade and investment by reducing barriers to economic interaction, improving transparency, and facilitating structural adjustment in favour of more competitive industries. As was noted in this and earlier chapters, there is expected to be a considerable increase in the volume of trade in goods and services through the elimination of tariffs and NTBs. In addition, greater FDI from the United States in goods and service sectors will be advantageous to all parties. The improvement in the regulatory systems in key economic activities such as financial services and telecommunications and the strengthening investor protection measures would also increase inflows of FDI, as would greater enforcement of IPR protection, labour and environment standards, and other policy changes that would improve the business climate. Cooperation in science and technology, technical assistance to improve the ability of Thailand's enterprises to overcome the U.S. domestic restrictions and technical barriers, and related areas could also be important advantages that would emerge out of an FTA with the United States from the Thai (and U.S.) perspective.

However, the sensitive areas reviewed above will need to be addressed carefully in the negotiations in order to achieve coverage that is appropriate to both sides. From the Thai perspective, negotiations on financial services will be a primary concern, especially given prominent role of this sector in the 1997–98 Crisis. The potential costs of an overly-liberalized financial sector, including systematic risk due to the inadequate preparation of domestic institutions for rapid adjustment, may offset the potential benefits derived from increased trade and investment, if not handled correctly. Suitable transition periods must be allowed in order to prepare the sector for the level of openness that the United States has come to expect from its FTAs. In addition, the Thai authorities will prefer a "positive list" approach, or at least one that is less open-ended than the "negative list" approach the United States has preferred, in order to limit the scope of openness in financial services and ensure that the liberalized sectors will not induce greater fluctuations in the domestic market or increase the risk of financial crisis. Concerns regarding economic stability also extend to the investment issue, in which open-ended coverage of investment provisions may hold similar risks to those of financial services.

Moreover, considering the advantages that could be derived from FTAs, the United States is unlikely to be the first priority for Thailand in negotiating FTAs. The study by Pupphavesa et al. (2005) shows that the Japan-Thailand and China-Thailand FTAs are expected to generate more potential benefits than the U.S.-Thailand FTA in terms of improvement in social welfare of Thailand.

In sum, an FTA with the United States is in Thailand's interest, subject to prudent liberalization in certain sensitive areas such as financial services and short-run investment. This will no doubt make for difficult negotiations in these areas. But an FTA without difficulties would either be unimportant (e.g., in the case of two completely open economies) or superficial (e.g., in the case of an agreement that left out all sectors that required liberalization). Even the U.S.-Singapore FTA was difficult. Ultimately, the FTA that will be hammered out will be worth it.

Notes

[1] These are in effect edited and abridged versions of more detailed studies carried out by Professor Chia, CSIS, MIER, AIM, and NDA for this project. The section on Brunei Darussalam was written by Seiji Naya and Michael Plummer.

[2] See, for example, Jagdish Bhagwati's Testimony to the U.S. Subcommittee on Domestic and International Policy, Trade and Technology on 1 April 2003.

[3] Some of these criticisms and concerns are unfounded. The strict rules of origin in the various bilateral agreements are designed to prevent "backdoor entry" both into the markets of Singapore's ASEAN partners and vice versa into the markets of Singapore's bilateral FTA partners. The Singapore-Japan FTA does include most of agriculture, although a positive list approach was adopted. Singapore wanted to be a pathfinder, going first and paving the way for other ASEAN countries to enter into similar agreements when they are ready.

[4] Singapore entered into a bilateral FTA with Japan in 2002, and has been actively seeking an FTA with the EU, so far without success, as the EU is not keen on bilateral FTAs.

[5] See, Franklin Lavin, "The USSFTA: Socio-Political Context". Lavin was the U.S. Ambassador to Singapore during the period of the USSFTA negotiations.

[6] To help the business community become savvy about FTAs and the opportunities they offer, the Singapore Ministry of Trade and Industry launched a dedicated FTA website and mounted briefing seminars for the business community.

[7] Singapore uses a computerized system to first pre-clear cargo consignments, using permit information submitted to customs prior to the physical arrival of the consignments. Customs selects cargo for physical inspection at the checkpoints , relying on risk profiling techniques and a good intelligence system

to effectively target high-risk cargo consignments. Singapore customs also has in place a post-importation clearance audit system to eliminate the need for detailed scrutiny of clearance documents at checkpoints. Post-importation audit relies on risk assessment and intelligence to target and select firms for back-end checks.

8   Circumvention is a problem as some quotas would still be in place after the entry into force of USSFTA, notwithstanding the expiry of the MFA.

9   A measure was presumed not to "substantially impede transfers" if it was non-confiscatory, non-discriminatory, price-based, did not interfere with an investor's ability to earn a market rate of return in Singapore, and did not prevent a reasonable investor from taking his money out of Singapore. Investors could only claim for losses in the value of investments in Singapore dollars as a result of the capital restrictions after taking account of the returns they could earn in Singapore. No liability could be claimed for opportunity costs from foregoing alternative investments outside of Singapore.

10   With the high capital entry barrier, free market access alone will not be enough to prevent dominant incumbents from acting to prevent foreign operators from offering viable services. The dominant incumbent could refuse to enter into interconnection arrangements with the new operator or unfairly price essential services like co-location of equipment or access to poles and conduits owned by the dominant incumbent.

11   TRIPS cover five broad issues: how basic principles of the trading system and other international IP agreements should be applied; how to give adequate protection to IP rights; how countries should enforce those rights adequately in their own territories; how to settle disputes in IP between WTO members; and special transitional arrangements during the period when the new system is being introduced. Areas covered under TRIPS are copyright and related rights; trademarks including service marks; geographical indications; industrial designs; patents; layout designs of ICs; and undisclosed information including trade secrets.

12   GLCs are owned by the Singapore government holding company, Temasek, and are active in a wide range of sectors, including finance, telecommunications and media, transport and logistics, and utilities, and account (along with statutory board companies) for about 13 per cent of GDP. The Temasek Charter of July 2002 states that Temasek will exercise its shareholder rights to influence the strategic direction of its companies, but will not involve itself in their day-to-day commercial decisions.

13   Temasek denied the divestment was related to the USSFTA, linking it instead to fund raising for its active acquisition of regional and international businesses and capital deployment in 2003.

14   Singapore has its Employment Act and Industrial Relations Act and since

the early 1970s has carefully nurtured a tripartite cooperative relationship among labour, management and government that has resulted in decades of industrial harmony.

[15] These cover freedom of association and collective bargaining; abolition of forced and child labour; and ensure acceptable conditions of work including minimum age and elimination of employment discrimination.

[16] According to the White House website: Fact Sheet on Enterprise for ASEAN Initiative dated 26 October 2002, FTA negotiations with ASEAN countries will be based on the high standards set in the USSFTA.

[17] As part of this study, CSIS interviewed many members of the respective industrial associations dealing with textiles and clothing in Indonesia.

[18] However, it is also true that a U.S.-Indonesia FTA will require removal of the licencing of imports of textile as inputs into other products to "producer-importers" (importer produsen), affecting 18 items at the four-digit SITC. This is seen as a trade barrier by U.S. Textile Manufacturers Association.

[19] They were successful in levying duties of up to 112 per cent on Chinese and Vietnamese shrimp imports in July 2004 (Wall Street Journal, "Bubba Gump Protectionism", 19 July 2004).

[20] Interview with Industrial Association.

[21] The halal certification requirement is regarded by some quarters as a form of disguised protectionism.

[22] Personal interview conducted by CSIS.

[23] CSIS interview with a responsible government official.

[24] CSIS interview with a U.S. Embassy official in Jakarta.

[25] This may be changing in 2004, with economic growth at 4.5 per cent in the first quarter and the successful electoral process in 2004.

[26] Thailand has recently finalized its FTA negotiations with Australia, which could also be used as a reference for Indonesia.

[27] Data cited in this paragraph were obtained from the Economic Report 2002/2003.

[28] This figure, however, contracts in 2001 possibly due to the pump priming activities by the Government.

[29] There are several grounds on which it is possible for foreign equity participation to exceed the normal limit of 30 per cent: it is thought that foreign expertise, which is not available locally, is needed to upgrade efficiency; if foreign participation is necessary to promote export of the product; the supply of local capital is insufficient, and global linkages are required.

[30] The AFAS is an agreement made within the auspices of the GATS.

[31] The Trade Unions Act of 1959 and the Industrial Relations Act of 1967 and subsequent amendments not only restrict the right to organize but also allow for wide-ranging interference in trade union affairs. Migrant workers,

on the other hand, fill in the workforce gaps left by local workers where generally inferior working conditions and lower wages prevail, which may still be better than those in their country of origin. This may very well be a problem, given the position of U.S. trade unions.

[32] The results of the Rio process generally, and of Agenda 21 particularly, were incorporated and where appropriate, were integrated into the national planning process when the Sixth Malaysia Plan (1991–95) was reviewed in 1993, and was also used as inputs to subsequent plans. Specifically, the government has put in place various environment-related policies such as the *Environmental Quality Act (EQA) 1974*, National Environment Policy, National Policy on Biological Diversity 1998, National Mineral Policy 1998, and the NAP3 (1998–2010), to attain sustainable development goals.

[33] By virtue of being a member of the group.

[34] The types of subsidies in the Blue Box supposedly do not distort trade or production, and are thus excluded from any reduction commitments. What about the developing nations, particularly those of Asia? Governments of developing countries have proposed a "Development" Box such that domestic support measures to develop the agriculture sector should not be subjected to reduction commitments. They also suggested a "Food" Box to exempt measures that are taken to ensure domestic food security from reduction commitments. This is where negotiation power and skills are important to obtain exclusions for these boxes from the URAA.

[35] But the self-sufficiency ratio for rice in 1995 is already 75.3. See Mohayidin and Samdin, undated.

[36] The Blue and Green Boxes are tied to the Peace Clause of the Agreement on Agriculture, which shielded nations involved from reduction commitments for as long as the Uruguay Round itself. Any extension beyond the Round would serve the U.S. and EU agribusiness.

[37] This contribution is comparable to that of Indonesia, the Philippines and Thailand (ranging from 40–50 per cent), although it is still significantly lower than Singapore (1994: 65 per cent).

[38] Noran Fauziah Yaakub and Ahmad Mahdzan Ayob, "Business of Higher Education In Malaysia: Development and Prospects in the New Millennium", Paper presented at the Association of Southeast Asian Institute of Higher Learning (ASAIHL), Hong Kong, 27–29 May 1999.

[39] Under the Eighth Malaysia Plan 2001–2005, the government of Malaysia aims to develop education as an export industry and promote the growth of local tertiary education.

[40] http://www.studymalaysia.com/is/education11.shtml.

[41] The ADP is a study arrangement designed to link up a local private college with a range of American universities, Department of Private Education: http://www.studymalaysia.com.

[42] This brought in nearly RM22 billion in foreign exchange earnings. *New Straits Times*, "Tourism Industry Remains Second Highest Forex Earner", 18 March 2004.

[43] This could be accomplished by including Malaysia in the Visa Waiver Program, which currently only includes three Asian countries, namely Brunei, Japan and Singapore.

[44] Similar to the "open skies" deal agreement between Malaysia and Hong Kong, http://news.airwise.com, 12 March 2004.

[45] ASEAN Secretariat; *ASEAN Tourism Investment Guide*, http://www.aseansec.org/tourism/malaysia.htm.

[46] For example, as of end-1996, foreign banks like the Hong Kong and Shanghai Banking Corporation (HSBC), the Overseas Chinese Banking Corporation (OCBC), and the Standard Chartered Bank ranked fifth, seventh and tenth in terms of total assets; fourth, seventh and ninth in terms of total loans; fifth, eighth and tenth in terms of deposits; and third, ninth and sixth in terms of profits before taxes, respectively (Bankers Directory 1996).

[47] Bank of America has been in Malaysia since 1959. From a subsidiary in Kuala Lumpur, they offer wholesale banking services to corporations and financial institutions. They also have an International Offshore Financial Senter (IOFC) branch in Labuan.

[48] Bar Council Malaysia: "WTO and its Impact on Malaysia and the Legal Profession", Mah Weng Kwai, January/February 2004, http://www.malaysianbar.org.my/resources/infoline.asp.

[49] Bar Council Malaysia, "Is Liberalisation and the Advent of Foreign Lawyers Inevitable?", Yeo Yang Poh, January/February 2004, http://www.malaysianbar.org.my/resources/infoline.asp

[50] Ministry of International Trade and Industry: Malaysia and the WTO, October 2003.

[51] Similarly, import tariffs on vans range from 5 per cent to 40 per cent for CKD vans and from 42 per cent to 140 per cent for CBU vans. Tariffs on multi-purpose vehicles are 10–40 per cent on CKD vehicles and 60–200 per cent on CBU vehicles. Motorcycles are subject to import tariffs of 30 per cent on CKDs and 80–120 per cent CBU. Imports of tractors for agriculture purposes are duty-free, and tariffs on road tractors and buses are zero for CKD and 30 per cent for CBU vehicles.

[52] The author would like to acknowledge the research assistance of Jeremy Morales Barns, Sophia Noreen Castillo-Plaza, Royce Escolar and Alain Manilon.

[53] These products are: fresh, preserved, tinned or prepared fish, preserved fruits, honey and sugar, crude vegetable materials, fixed vegetable oil, wood, pottery, office machines, electric power machine switches, electrical machinery, telecommunications equipment, furniture, travel goods and handbags, clothes,

watches and clocks, and other manufactured goods. The study noted that of the 18 products vulnerable to trade diversion, the Philippines competes in 16 products with Thailand, 10 with Indonesia and 6 with Singapore.

[54] *National Trade Estimate Report on Foreign Trade Barriers*, p. 378.

[55] Ibid.

[56] The second largest export market is Japan with a 16.1 per cent share. Japan is also the top source of Philippine imports garnering a 20.4 per cent share of total imports for 2003.

[57] The new rates are expected to remain in effect until 2007.

[58] Sixty-five per cent of the Philippines' total tariff lines are bound under the WTO. Tariffs on industrial products, except textiles, reached their bound levels in 1999, tariffs on agricultural products in 2003 and textile products will reach their bound levels and 2004.

[59] *National Trade Estimate Report on Foreign Trade Barriers*, p. 378.

[60] A 30 per cent tariff is the highest duty rate applied to non-agricultural products. Executive Order 241 reversed a previous order that scheduled a drop of tariffs to 5 per cent in 2004.

[61] The $400 per vehicle benefit is provided through reduced tariff rates on finished vehicles the manufacturer imports into the Philippines. MFN rates of 30 per cent to 20 per cent will be reduced to 10% and the ASEAN CEPT rate of 5 per cent will be reduced to 1 per cent for imports from other ASEAN countries.

[62] *National Trade Estimate Report on Foreign Trade Barriers*, pp. 380–81. The new excise tax scheme divides vehicles into four brackets based on their price, as follows: (1) for vehicles with a manufacturer's price of PHP600,000 and below, the tax will be only 2 per cent; (2) those priced over PHP600,000 to PHP1.1 million, the tax will be PHP12,000 plus 20 per cent of the amount in excess of PHP600,000; (3) those priced over PHP1.1 million to PHP2.1 million, the tax will be PHP112,000 plus 40 per cent of the amount in excess of PHP1.1 million; and (4) those over PHP2.1 million, the tax will be PHP512,000 plus 60 per cent of the amount in excess of PHP2.1 million. This is currently being reviewed by the Secretary of Finance who is contemplating indexing the brackets to reflect the manufacturer's net price every two years.

[63] Ibid.

[64] Ibid.

[65] Based on the 2002 Census of Agriculture conducted by the Philippine National Statistics Office (NSO), the number of farms in the country contracted by 2.36 per cent, from 4.61 million in 1991 to 4.50 million in 2002. Average farm size was placed at 2.04 hectares, a decrease from 1991 average levels of 2.16 hectares. Total farm area in 2002 reached 9.19 million hectares, a decrease from 9.97 million hectares reported in 1991. Farm is defined as land used

for raising crops, fruit trees, livestock, poultry or in any other agricultural activity.

66 Griswald (2002).

67 Other sensitive agricultural items subject to MAVs and TRQs are: chevon (in-quota: 30 per cent; out-quota: 35 per cent), potatoes (in-quota/out-quota: 30 per cent), coffee beans (in-quota/out-quota: 30 per cent), coffee extracts (in-quota/out-quota: 30 per cent), and sugar (in-quota/out-quota: 50 per cent).

68 The Tariff Commission has temporarily lowered the tariff on imported pork to 10 per cent under the MAV for a one-time importation of 10,000 metric tons. This is expected to reduce pork prices by 14 per cent. The imports would be allocated directly to hog raisers, traders and processors. There is a current temporary shortage of 4,000 heads a day in the National Capital Region (NCR) alone. The pork shortage was caused by consumers' shift to pork due to the avian flu virus that struck some neighbouring countries in Asia.

69 The Philippines has formally notified the WTO of its intent to extend the quantitative restriction (QR) on rice imports. The rice QR was set to be removed in 2005. The National Food Authority (NFA) imports around 600,000 to 1.2 million MT of milled rice from China, Thailand, Vietnam, the U.S. and other countries annually. Despite being slapped with a 50 per cent tariff, imported rice reportedly remains cheaper by 25 per cent to 38 per cent compared to locally produced rice.

70 *National Trade Estimate Report on Foreign Trade Barriers,* p. 381.

71 The Fifth Freedom of the Air is the right of an airline of one country to carry traffic between two countries outside of its own country of registration as long as the flight originates or terminates in its own country of registration.

72 The Seventh Freedom of the Air is the right of an airline of one country to operate flights between two other countries without the flight originating or terminating in its own country of registration.

73 *National Trade Estimate Report on Foreign Trade Barriers,* p. 388.

74 Tullao and Cortez (2004) has recently suggested that educational services (tuition and training as opposed to teachers) "may present complementary values" to both the Philippines and the United States, arising from an "English milieu" and somewhat similar educational systems, although liberalization in this area may encounter opposition from Filipino institutions.

75 Article 10.19, paragraph 6.

76 Securities Industry Association, "Opening Capital Markets, Financing Growth: The Treatment of U.S. Securities Firms Abroad," Memorandum to U.S. Financial Service Sector Negotiators, April 2002.

77 *National Trade Estimate Report on Foreign Trade Barriers,* p. 386.

78 On 13 January, 2004, U.S. Secretary of Energy Spencer Abraham made an
    official visit to Manila and signed a Memorandum of Understanding with
    his counterpart Energy Secretary Vincent Perez. Both agreed to strengthen
    the Sustainable Energy Development Program which is a US$5 million
    project sponsored by the U.S. and Philippine Departments of Energy and
    the USAID. The Philippines and the USAID will work together to promote
    private investments in the use of clean and indigenous fuels such as natural
    gas and renewable energy.

79 These points are provided in June 2004 by the Bureau of International Trade
    Relations, Department of Trade and Industry.

80 IPR protection concerns are not all one-way. The Bureau of International Trade
    Relations disclosed the information that Profood International Corporation,
    a Philippine firm, is pursuing a case in the United States against the
    counterfeiter of Philippine Brand Dried Mangoes. Profood is now working on
    the registration of its trademark in the U.S., which is a requirement before a
    trade alert on the infringement of Profood's label and trademark can be issued.

81 *National Trade Estimate Report on Foreign Trade Barriers*, p. 381.

82 The offer of an "early harvest" of benefits to ASEAN by China is a case in
    point. Clearly a shrewd move, it overwhelmed the region, adjusting as it is
    to the supposed inevitability of China's economic dominance in East Asia.

83 This brief survey of Brunei's commercial policy regime mainly draws from
    the WTO's *Trade Policy Review* (various years), and certain government on-
    line resources. The USTR does not include Brunei in its annual survey of
    foreign barriers to U.S. exports.

84 The contributions of the various subsectors of services are social and personal
    services (54 per cent), wholesale and retail trade (20 per cent), banking and
    insurance (13 per cent) and transport and communications (ten per cent).

85 The East Asian Growth Area was created in March 1994 and includes all of
    Brunei, ten provinces of Indonesia (on Sulawesi, Maluku, and Irian Jaya);
    the Malaysian states of Sabah and Sarawak, and the federal territory of
    Labuan; and in the Philippines, Mindanao and Palawan. Like other "growth
    triangles", its goal is to pool resources, provide infrastructure, and offer special
    incentives in order to lure particularly foreign businesses to these areas.

86 The authors of this section are at the Center for International Economics and
    Development Studies, School of Development Economics, National Institute
    of Development Administration (NIDA). Seiji Naya and Mike Plummer
    contributed to parts of subsections A-C.

87 The EU is the most significant user of agricultural export subsidies. However,
    the United States also provides export subsidies to certain sectors, particularly
    cotton.

88 The United States had also frequently made this argument at the GATT/WTO,

e.g., with respect to the EU ban on various genetically-modified-organism (GMO) food imports.

References

Singapore

Koh, Tommy and Chang Li Lin, eds. *The United States-Singapore Free Trade Agreement: Highlights and Insights*. Singapore: Institute of Policy Studies and World Scientific, 2004. Particularly the following chapters:
- Koh, Tommy. "The USSFTA: A Personal Perspective". (Singapore Chief Negotiator)
- Ives, Ralph. "The USSFTA: Personal Perspectives on the Process". (U.S. Chief Negotiator)
- Ong Ye Kung. "Lessons from the USSFTA Negotiations".
- Lavin, Franklin L. "The USSFTA: Socio-Political Context". (U.S. Ambassador to Singapore).
- Ithnain, Rossman. "The Goods Package".
- Lim Teck Leong. "Customs Administration".
- Ng Kim Neo. "Textiles and Apparel".
- D'Costa, Valerie. "Telecommunications and Electronic Commerce".
- Menon, Ravi. "Financial Services and Capital Controls".
- Minn Naing Oo. "Competition Policy".
- Liew Woon Yin. "Intellectual Property Rights".
- Ong Yen Her. "Labour".
- Loh Ah Tuan et al. "Environment".

Singapore Ministry of Trade and Industry website: *FTA with the United States*
United States Trade Representative (USTR) website: *Quick Facts on U.S.-Singapore Free Trade Agreement*.
World Trade Organisation (WTO). *Trade Policy Review, Singapore*. Geneva: WTO, 2004.

Indonesia

Aswicahyono, Haryo. "De-Industrialization?" In *Challenges of the New Government*. Jakarta: CSIS, May 2004.
DeRosa, Dean A. "U.S. Free Trade Agreements with ASEAN". Paper prepared for presentation at the Conference on Free Trade Agreements and U.S. Trade Policy, organized by the Institute for International Economics (IIE), Washington, D.C., 7–8 May 2003.
Gilbert, John P. "CGE Simulation of U.S. Bilateral Free Trade Agreements". Background paper prepared for the Conference on Free Trade Agreements

and U.S. Trade Policy, organized by IIE, Washington, D.C., May 7–8; In DeRosa (2003).

Maidir, Imelda and Raymond Atje. "Investment". In *Challenges of the New Government*. Jakarta: CSIS, May 2004.

Pangestu, Mari. "The External Environment". In *Challenges of the New Government*, Jakarta: CSIS, May 2004.

Soesastro, Hadi. "Aspek Ekonomi dan Perdagangan dalam Hubungan R.I.-A.S". (Indonesia-U.S. Trade and Economic Relations). *Jurnal Studi Amerika* [Journal of American Studies], 9, no.1 (January-June 2003) pp. 22–31.

USINDO. *Report of the National Commission on U.S.-Indonesian Relations*. USINDO, Washington, D.C.: 2003.

U.S.-ASEAN Business Council, *U.S.-ASEAN Relationship: Building on a Framework of Success*. Washington, D.C., February 2004.

Malaysia

Asia-Pacific Economic Cooperation (APEC). "Measures Affecting Trade And Investment in Education Services in the Asia-Pacific Region". A Report to the APEC Group On Services, 2000.

Ariff, Mohamed and Lim Chze Cheen. "Regional Integration for Growth and Development in ASEAN". Paper presented at the Seventh Sasakawa Peace Foundation Issyk-Kul Forum, Kuala Lumpur, Malaysia. 18–20 October 2001.

Ariff, Mohamed and Lim Chze Cheen. "ASEAN-India FTA: Issues and Prospects". Paper presented at the Institute of Southeast Asian Studies (ISEAS) ASEAN-India Forum, Singapore, 9–10 February 2004.

Bank Negara Malaysia. *Annual Report*, various years, Kuala Lumpur.

Bank Negara Malaysia. *Monthly Statistical Bulletin*, various issues, Kuala Lumpur.

Bar Council Malaysia. http://www.malaysianbar.org.my.

Board of Architects. Malaysia, http://www.lam.gov.my.

Board of Engineers. Malaysia, http://www.bem.org.my.

Brewer, D. "Raid Silences Malaysian news Web site". http://edition.cnn.com/2003/WORLD/asiapcf/southeast/01/20/malaysia.raid/.

Economic Planning Unit. Eighth Malaysia Plan 2001–2005, Kuala Lumpur: Golden Printers 2001.

The Edge. "Interview with Dr Tun Mahathir on Proton". 3 May 2004.

Goolam Mohamedbhai. "Globalization and Its Implications on Universities in Developing Countries". Paper presented at the Conference for Globalization: What Issues are at Stake for Universities, Université Laval, Canada, 19 September 2004.

Jegatheesan, S. "Perils of Levelling the Rice Field". *New Straits Times*, 26 April 2001.

Jose L. Tongzon. "U.S.-Singapore Free Trade Agreement: Implications for ASEAN". *ASEAN Economic Bulletin* 20, no. 2 (2003): 174–78.

Kaufmann, D., A. Kraay and M. Mastruzzi. "Governance Matters III: Governance Indicators for 1996–2002". The World Bank, draft. http://www.worldbank.org/wbi/governance/wp-governance.html.

Kaufmann, D., A. Kraay and P. Zoido-Lobaton. "Governance Matters: From Measurement to Action". *Finance and Development* 37, no. 2 (June 2000).

Kaur, H. "West to be Blamed for Collapse of Cancun," *New Straits Times* online, 16 September 2003. http://www.mindfully.org/WTO/2003/Cancun-West-Blamed16sep03.htm.

Lim, Chze Cheen and Shankaran Nambiar. "Regional Cooperation Towards Multi-lateral Arrangements on Agriculture, Labour and Environment in the Context of Globalisation: The Case of Malaysia" Paper presented at RIS, New Delhi, India, March 2003.

Mah Weng Kwai. WTO and Its Impact on Malaysia and the Legal Profession. Paper presented at the 12th Malaysian Law Conference organised by the Bar Council Malaysia, Hotel Nikko, Kuala Lumpur, 10–12 December 2004.

Malaysian Institute of Accountants (MIA) "Globalisation and Liberalisation of Trade in Services: Challenges and Direction for the Malaysian Accountancy Services Sector", MIA, 4 March 2004. http://www.mia.org.my/dept/sprd/updates/Globalisation%20And%20Liberalisation.pdf, 2004.

Malaysian Ministry of Finance. *Economic Report*, various years.

Malaysian Ministry of International Trade and Industry. *Second Industrial Master Plan (1996–2005)*. Kuala Lumpur.

Mohayidin, M.G. and Z. Samdin. Food Availability and Consumption Pattern in Malaysia. mimeo, undated.

Noran Fauziah Yaakub and Ahmad Mahdzan Ayob. "Development of Graduate Education in Malaysia: Prospects for Internationalisation". Paper presented at the 2000 ASAIHL Seminar on University and Society: New Dimensions for the Next Century, Naresuan University, Phitsanulok, Thailand, 19–21 May 2000.

_____. "Higher Education and Socioeconomic Development in Malaysia: A Human Resource Development Perspective". Paper presented at the ASAIHL Conference on The New Millennium: Business and Higher Education in the Asia-Pacific, Auckland Institute of Technology, New Zealand, 6–8 December 1999.

_____. "Business Of Higher Education in Malaysia: Development and Prospects in the New Millennium". Paper presented at the Association of Southeast Asian Institute of Higher Learning (ASAIHL) Seminar on 'Liberal Arts Education and Socio-economic Development in the Next Century', Lingnan College, Hong Kong, 27–29 May 1999.

Raja Zainal Abidin, Raja Zaharaton bte. "Service Industries as Source of Economic

Growth". Paper presented at the 1996 National Outlook Conference organised by the Malaysian Institute of Economic Research, Shangri-La Hotel, Kuala Lumpur, 3–4 December, 1996.

Singh Previndran. "My Space: Opportunities in Hotel Investment". *TheEdgeDaily*, 23 March 2004.

Study Malaysia Online. "The Education System of Malaysia, Types of Institutions and Study Options Available". Study in Malaysia Handbook (International) 3rd Edition, Challenger Concept (M) Sendirian Berhad. http://www. studymalaysia.com/is/education11.shtml.

_____. "Private Education—The Development and Progress of Private Education in Malaysia". Education Guide Malaysia 8th Edition. Challenger Concept (M) Sendirian Berhad. http://www.studymalaysia.com/is/ education12.shtml.

Syarisa Yanti Abubakar. "The Services Sector: Malaysia's Next Engine of Growth?" In *Globalization and the Knowledge Economy: Perspectives for Malaysia*, edited by Mohd. Ariff and Frank Flatters. Kuala Lumpur: Malaysian Institute of Economic Research, 2001.

Transparency International. *Corruption Perceptions Index 2003*. http://www. transparency.org.my.

Third World Network (2003). "Singapore Issues: No Negotiations, say 70 Developing Countries", 12 September, Third World Network, available at www.twnside.org.sg, 2003.

U.S.-Singapore Free Trade Agreement. http://www.ustr.gov/new/fta/Singapore/ final/2004-01-15-final.pdf.

Vishwanath, T. and D. Kaufmann. "Towards Transparency in Finance and Governance". World Bank: Policy Research Working Paper. Washington D.C., 1999.

Yeo Yang Poh. "Is Liberalisation and the Advent of Foreign Lawyers Inevitable?". Paper presented at the 12th Malaysian Law Conference organized by the Bar Council Malaysia, Hotel Nikko, Kuala Lumpur, 10–12 December 2004.

The Philippines

3M Philippines. "The Sun is Shining on the Philippine Furniture Industry", at www.3m.com/int/ph/about3M/newsroom/3M_furniture.html, 2003.

Araneta, S. *America's Double Cross of the Philippines*, Manila: Sahara Heritage Foundation, 1999.

Asia Pacific Economic Cooperation Economic Committee. *The Benefits of Trade and Investment Liberalization and Facilitation in APEC*. Singapore: APEC Secretariat, 2002.

Asian Development Bank (ADB), *Key Development Indicators*. Manila: ADB,

2003.

Asian Institute of Management. Consumer Policy Strategy: Philippines 2004–2010, 23 September 2003 mimeo.

Avila, J. "The Philippines and Free Trade Areas". In *International Trade and Integration: Global Views and Philippine Implications*. Asian Institute of Management Policy Center, December 2002.

Avila, J., G. Manzano and M. Lynch, "Aftermath of WTO in Cancun: Bilateral Free Trade Areas". Manila: University of Asia and the Pacific, 2003.

Bello, W. "The AOA: Institutionalizing Monopolistic Competition". *Philippine Daily Inquirer*, 30 August 2003.

Board of Investments, Republic of the Philippines, various documents.

Brandenburger, A. and B. Nalebuff. *Competition*. New York, 1996.

Bureau of Census, United States of America, various statistics.

Bureau of International Trade Relations, Department of Trade and Industry, Republic of the Philippines, various documents including a brief note, prepared in June 2004, on the trade concerns of key Philippine government agencies.

The Chamber of Furniture Industries of the Philippines, position papers.

Commonwealth Act No. 733 (Bell Trade Act or Philippine Trade Act of 1946).

Conde, C. "Tuna Bill could Worsen Terrorism in RP, say U.S. Solons", MindaNews, June 2002. http://www.mindanews.com/2002/06/2nd/nws07tuna.html.

De Ocampo, R., F. Macaranas and S. Butocan. "The State of Philippine Competitiveness 2003. In *The State of Philippine Competitiveness 2003*. Manila: Asian Institute of Management Policy Center, December, 2003.

Dela Cruz, R. "RP Formally Notifies WTO of Intent to Extend Rice QR", *Manila Times*, 5 April 2004.

_____. "RP Paves Way for GM Imports". *Manila Times*, 20 April 2004.

_____. "Economists Push for RP-U.S. Free Trade Agreement". *Manila Times*, 3 December, 2003.

Department of Agriculture, Republic of the Philippines, various documents.

Department of Foreign Affairs, Republic of the Philippines, various documents.

Department of Trade and Industry, Republic of the Philippines, various documents.

Dixit, A. *The Making of Economic Policy: A Transaction-Cost Politics Perspective*, Cambridge: MIT Press, 1999.

Domingo, R. "RP Seeks Zero Tariff on Electronics by 2005". *Philippine Daily Inquirer*, 22 April 2004.

Duc, N.H. "Restrictions on Trade in Professional Services", Staff Research Paper. Productivity Commission, Australia, August 2000.

Embassy of the United States in Manila, Bilateral Press Conference on the U.S.-RP Trade and Investment Council, 20 November, 2002, at http://usembassy.

state.gov/posts/rp1/wwwhtrn2.html.

Environmental Working Group. Farm Subsidy Database. http://www.ewg. org/farm.

Felix, R. "Anti-GMO Groups Seek Review of RP Policy on Bt Corn". *Philippine Star*, 7 March, 2004.

Fibre2Fashion.Com. "FTA With U.S. Will Benefit Garment Sector". 6 November, 2003. http://fibre2fashion.com/news/NewsDetails.asp?News_id=5028.

Findlay, C. "Services Sector Reform and Development Strategies: Issues and Research Priorities," *Policy Issues in International Trade and Commodities Study Series*, No. 8, Geneva: UNCTAD, 2001.

Foreign Services Institute, Republic of the Philippines. *Philippine External Relations: A Centennial Vista*, 1998.

Van den Geest, W. "Sharing Benefits of Globalisation through an EU-ASEAN FTA?" Brussels: European Institute for Asian Studies, 2003.

Golay, F.H. *Face of Empire: United States-Philippine Relations, 1898–1946*. Quezon City: de Manila University Press,: Ateneo, 1998.

Global IT Economy Index. White Paper. http://www.tech-economy.org/gitei. html.

Global New Economy Index. http://www.e-servicesphils.com/mediaroom. php/mrid=7.

Government of the Philippines, Executive Order No. 139, Promulgating the Fifth Regular Foreign Investment Negative List, 22 October, 2002.

Griswold, G. "Farm Bill Follies". Presented during the Cato Institute Policy Forum. Washington D.C., 6 June 2002.

Hill, H. "Industry". In *The Philippine Economy: Development, Policies and Challenges*, edited by A. Balisacan and H. Hill Manila: Ateneo de Manila University Press, 2003.

Hutchcroft, P.D. *Booty Capitalism: The Politics of Banking in the Philippines*. Quezon City: Ateneo de Manila Press, 1998.

Institute for International Management and Development. *World Competitiveness Yearbook*. Lausanne: IIMD, 2003.

Intal, P. "Towards a Framework for an RP-US Free Trade Agreement". Paper presented at the Conference on Free Trade Areas, Dusit Hotel, 27 October, 2003.

Kalirajan, K. "Restrictions on Trade in Distribution Services". *Staff Research Paper*, Productivity Commission, Australia, August 2000.

Lantican, S. and J. Silva, "The Mindanao Tuna Industry: Breaking Into Deep Waters". AIM Policy Center Mindanao Development Series, no. 2, 2002.

Macaranas, F, ed. *APEC and the Philippines: Catching the Next*. Department of Foreign Affairs, Manila, 1996.

Macaranas, F. and J. Barns. "Poor Governance as a Constraint to Philippine Competitiveness: "It's the Politics, Stupid!". In *The State of Philippine*

Competitiveness 2003. Manila: Asian Institute of Management Policy Center, December, 2003.

Mani, S. "Moving Up or Going back the Value Chain". Discussion Paper, UNU INTECH, 2002.

Medalla, E., ed. *Toward a National Competition Policy for the Philippines*. Manila: Philippine APEC Study Center Network, and Philippine Institute for Development Studies, 2002.

Memorandum Order No. 136, Approving the 2004 Investment Priorities Plan, February 18, 2004.

Messerlin, P. *Trade Policy Indices*. Geneva: World Trade Organization, 2002.

Mitra, S. "U.S. Farm Bill 2002: Its Implications for World Agricultural Markets". International Development Economics Associates, 2002. http://www. networkideas.org/themes/ agriculture/May2002/ag17_U.S._Farm_Bill_2002. htm.

Monsod, T. "ICT: Flagship for the Services Sector". Paper presented during the annual meeting of the Philippine Economic Society, 14 March 2002.

National Economic and Development Authority, Republic of the Philippines, *The Medium-Term Philippine Development Plan 2001–2004*, 2001.

National Statistics Office, Republic of the Philippines. *Census of Agriculture*, 2002.

New York Times. "The Rigged Trade Game: The WTO in the Philippines". July 20, 2003. http://www.nytimes.com20003/07/20/opinion/20SUN1.html.

Office of the United States Trade Representative, United States of America. *National Trade Estimate Report on Foreign Trade Barriers*, 2004, at http://www. ustr.gov.

Office of the United States Trade Representative. "Quick Facts: U.S.-Singapore Free Trade Agreement", 6 May 2003, http://www.ustr.gov.

Oliva, E. "Politics Seen Behind U.S. Bid versus RP Medical Transcription". *Philippine Daily Inquirer*, 15 March 2004.

Oxfam International. "Rigged Rules and Double Standards: Trade, Globalisation and the Fight Against Poverty", 2002. http://www.oxfam.org.au/campaigns/polliewatch/.

Philippine Daily Inquirer. "Rice Self-sufficiency is National Security". 2 January, 2004.

PhilMaize. http://philmaize.norminet.org.ph/preserving.htm

PhilRice. http://www.philrice.gov.ph/prorice/Philippine_rice.industry.htm.

Poso, N. "The Philippines' Stake in the Global e-Economy," December 2003, at http://itmatters.com.ph/news/news_07282000a.html.

Productivity Commission, Australia. Data on trade restrictiveness and related price impacts.

Remo, M. "NEDA Pushing for Further Liberalization of Local Industries". *Philippine Daily Inquirer*, 22 April, 2004.

Republic Act No. 1355 (Laurel-Langley Agreement or the Revised Philippine Trade Act of 1955).

De Rosa, D. "U.S. Free Trade Agreements with ASEAN". Revised version of a conference paper presented at the Conference on Free Trade Agreements and U.S. Trade Policy, Institute of International Economics, Washington D.C., May 7–8, 2003.

Del Rosario, A. "The Philippines and the United States: A New Partnership for Peace and Development". Speech before the Grand Decisions Forum of the World Affairs Council at Hampton Roads, Virginia, 31 January, 2004.

Rubin, H. "The Global New e-Economy Index: Cybergeography and the Digital Divide", 2000. http://members.nyas.org/events/policy/pol_00_1205.html.

Schwarz, A. and R. Villinger. "Integrating Southeast Asia's Economies". *McKinsey Quarterly*, no.1, 2004.

Social Weather Stations. *The Philippine Round of the WEF Poll on Globalization*, 25 November, 2003.

Soesastro, H. "Dynamics of Competitive Liberalization in RTA Negotiations: East Asian Perspectives". Paper presented at the PECC Trade Forum, Washington, D.C., 22–23 April, 2003.

Tariff Commission, Republic of the Philippines.

Tullao, T. and M. Cortez, "Collaborative mechanisms at bilateral and regional levels: Impact on education in the Philippines". Paper presented at the Ambassador Alfonso Yuchengo Inaugural Policy Conference, "After Cancun, What's Next? Policy Implications for Developing Countries in Asia". Manila, January 2004.

UK Trade and Investment. "Agriculture, Horticulture & Fisheries Market in the Philippines", February, 2002, at http://www.uktradeinvest.gov.uk/agriculture/philippines/profile/overview.html.

Villacorta, W., T. Tullao and A. Unite. "The Political Economy of Philippine Commitments to APEC: The Legislative Record". In *Coalition-Building and APEC*, edited by W. Villacorta. Philippine APEC Study Center Network et al., Makati, 2001.

The White House, United States of America, "Enterprise for ASEAN Initiative", 26 October, 2002, at http://www.whitehouse.gov/infocus/internationaltrade/aseaninitiative.html.

Xinhua Net. "Philippines to Export Corn for the First Time in History". 5 April, 2004, at http://www.chinaview.cn.

Brunei Darussalam

ASEAN Secretariat, homepage: www.aseansec.org

World Trade Organization, 2002. *Trade Policy Review: Brunei Darussalam*, WT/TPR/S/84.

Thailand

Levine, Ross. "Foreign Banks, Financial Development, and Economic Growth". In *International Financial Markets*, edited by Claude E. Barfield. Washington, D.C.: AEI Press.

Hunton & Williams, LLP. *Thailand-U.S. FTA: A Road Map to Negotiations*. http://www.dtn.moc.go.th/web/147/650/roadmap.pdf.

Pupphavesa, Wisan et al. *A Study on the Potential Impacts of Thailand's Bilateral Free Trade Agreements*, A Study Report Submitted to National Economic and Social Development Board, Center for International Economics and Development Studies, School of Development Economics, National Institute of Development Administration (in Thai), 2005.

TDRI. *A Study on the Impacts of Thailand-U.S. Free Trade Agreement*. TDRI: Bangkok, 2003.

Terdudomtham, Thammavit. "*Anti-Dumping Measure: Agreement and Experience*". Research Paper No. 6, WTO Watch Project (in Thai), 2005.

USTR. *2005 Foreign Barriers to U.S. Exports*. Washington, D.C.: USTR, 2005.

WTO. *Trade Policy Review Thailand*. http://www.wto.org, 15 October.

5

EAI in a Dynamic Policy Context

I.   Introduction

Until very recently, Asian countries eschewed regionalism and rather
focused on unilateral and multilateral liberalization approaches. The
large increases in intra-regional trade noted in Chapter 2 resulted from
regionalization, rather than *regionalism*, in the sense that this integration
was fostered by the market and not by a preferential trade agreement
(PTA). ASEAN itself, in existence since 1967, did not really embrace
any significant formal economic integration policies until 1992, when
it created AFTA.

But even after the Singapore Declaration created AFTA, ASEAN
countries still insisted on keeping an outward-looking approach to
international trade liberalization, that is, to minimize discrimination
against non-partner countries. In this sense, ASEAN was ahead of its
time; the creation of the EEC certainly did not place an emphasis on
"open regionalism" (quite the contrary) and to some degree the same
might be said of NAFTA. In ASEAN, there was even an early proposal
(tabled by the Philippines) to multilateralize any AFTA cuts so as to
make the agreement completely liberal and non-discriminatory. Since
the Asian Crisis, this proposal has been scrapped, but it is clear from

various initiatives coming from ASEAN leaders that their goal is to embrace regionalism *not* to create a "bloc", which after all would be nonsensical given the small size of the ASEAN economies, their dependence on trade with and investment from non-members, and their overall outward-oriented trade strategies, *but rather* to use "deeper" integration as a means to build a more unified and competitive region. The goal was to increase trade with—and inflows of FDI from—all countries, not merely between ASEAN member-states.

The importance of this instinctive outward-orientation of ASEAN external commercial policy should not be underestimated. Many regional groupings between developing countries today list increasing intra-regional trade and investment as a key objective of the trade and/or investment agreement. This underscores the fact that most of these agreements are being undertaken for political, not economic, reasons. *In the case of ASEAN, the objective is to increase competitiveness overall, not merely at a sub-regional level.* Success is defined by greater economic growth and prosperity in the region, which in turn are a function of global performance in terms of trade and investment. As we noted in Chapter 3, AFTA in a certain sense was more of an investment than a trade agreement, in that its objective was to reduce intra-regional barriers to trade and thereby facilitate the creation of an integrated production base that could be exploited by ASEAN-based and foreign companies alike. Hence, if AFTA were successful in achieving this goal, it is not at all clear whether or not this would lead to an increase in intra-regional trade. In fact, it could actually lead to a decrease in intra-regional trade, if multinational corporations add only a small amount of value in ASEAN, importing to and exporting from the region with respect to the rest.

A heuristic example may help illustrate the point. Suppose that AFTA succeeds in luring a Japanese auto company to produce two parts of a car in ASEAN, a labour-intensive part in Indonesia and a capital-intensive part in Singapore. After this firm establishes its production facilities in Indonesia and Singapore (thereby increasing FDI from outside the region and, hence, decreasing intra-regional FDI, *ceteris paribus*), it may just add a small percentage of the total value-added of the car in Indonesia and Singapore. Therefore, Japanese exports to the region (of original components) will increase, as will the exports of the region to

Japan (or elsewhere) when the process is completed. These are extra-regional trade flows and will, therefore, tend to reduce intra-regional trade. Whether or not the trade in components within the region is great enough to compensate for this increase in external flows will depend on initial parameters: it may increase or decrease intra-regional trade in ASEAN. But the point is that FDI has increased, trade has increased, employment has increased, the potential for technological spillovers has increased, and so on.

As expounded at length in Chapter 4 in the context of bilateral U.S.-ASEAN relations, from an economic perspective the new regional approach to external trade and investment relations emerging in ASEAN is designed to increase global market access (or at least to avoid losing out in key markets due to trade diversion from other PTAs) while at the same time promoting domestic market reform. Technically, the same objectives could be obtained through a successful WTO Doha Development Agenda accord. But as we mentioned in Chapter 3, the Doha Development Agenda is currently experiencing difficulties, though the July 2004 agreement on a framework for discussions offers some hope for an accord over the medium term. But it has not reached its original goal of completing a deal by the end of 2004 (in part a result of its having been an election year in the United States). *Nevertheless, even if in an optimistic scenario an accord could be reached within a reasonable period of time, the problem is that compromises required in an organization with 148 member-states—not all of whom are wedded to economic liberalism—will no doubt prevent the agreement from approaching anywhere near the type of "deep" integration that can be created in a bilateral FTA.* The non-traditional areas of FTAs that are apparent in modern accords—and the U.S.-Singapore FTA is a classic case—go well beyond what the WTO can hope for in terms of market access, harmonization issues, transparency, competition policy, national treatment of foreign investors, labour policies, certain services (e.g., finance, air and marine transport, education), and, of course, agricultural goods. Indeed, some believe that the WTO has already gone just about as far as it can in terms of a "Single Undertaking", i.e., traditional trade GATT/WTO rounds. Moreover, many of these modern FTAs explicitly cite adherence to global rules, e.g., GATS "Plus" and WTO rules on government procurement, as a condition in the agreement.

Thus, in many ways the regionalism route makes a great deal of sense for the ASEAN countries in the context of the global status quo. Economists who denounce regionalism tend to due so in fears that PTAs can: (1) result in significant trade diversion, which is costly to the home market as well as to non-partners; (2) potentially lead to the creation of a "fortress" in the sense of using regionalism as a means of promoting import substitution; and (3) lead member-states to turn their backs on the more logical multilateral approach under the WTO, which in theory should generate even greater gains than under any regional approach. In the case of certain FTAs and in specific historical periods, these arguments would be valid. *But they are unconvincing in the case of ASEAN today regarding its overall PTA approach and the proposed FTA with the United States in particular.* As we stressed in Chapter 3, a U.S.-ASEAN FTA would be: (1) net-trade creating, with far greater positive implications for efficiency and competitiveness likely in terms of "dynamic changes" not incorporated in the models surveyed (as we shall see in this chapter, one study calculates that an ASEAN+3 FTA would actually generate more gains to ASEAN than global free trade); (2) there is no indication that ASEAN has any intention to create a "fortress"; its words, deeds, and entire policy thrust have been outward-looking, including myriad unilateral-liberalization policies of the member states over the past 10 years; and (3) it is not clear where the WTO is going and, in fact, liberalization in the WTO is highly constrained by a large membership with divergent views on liberalization.

The FTA approach will allow ASEAN countries to increase market access in key markets that will likely prove to be "untouchable" at Doha and facilitate the implementation of the required "non-border" measures that will be necessary as part of any accord with the United States (or other developed countries). This will help them promote and/or expedite their own domestic policy agenda.

In this chapter, we consider some additional key emerging regionalism-related issues at the subregional, regional, and global levels pertinent to this policy agenda and the decision to enter into these FTAs, particularly in the context of U.S.-ASEAN. These include: (1) PTAs in the global economy (Section II); PTAs and economic cooperation at the Asia-Pacific level (Section III); (3) economic "deepening" issues in ASEAN (Section IV); and (4) the "Chinese threat" and its implications for ASEAN commercial policy (Section V).

II. Implications of Regionalism in Japan, the EU and the United States

A. Japan

Chapter 2 emphasized that the United States was the number one export market in the case of several EAI countries, and where it was not, Japan was the leader. Japan completely eschewed a PTA approach to commercial policy in favour of multilateralism until two years ago, when it formed an FTA with Singapore. It now has formal negotiations or is informally studying FTAs with a host of potential competitors to ASEAN (as well as possible accords with ASEAN as a region and bilaterally with individual member-states), including countries such as China, South Korea, and even a recently completed accord with Mexico. To the extent that Japan succeeds in concluding these PTAs, excluded ASEAN countries will suffer from trade and investment diversion, potentially significantly so at the sectoral level.

Studies of the potential effects of these Japanese accords and various configurations with other Asia-Pacific economies are few. One such study, Scollay and Gilbert (May 2001), offers a fairly typical model that is especially useful in the context of analysing the trade diverting effects of various PTAs on ASEAN member states. They use a GTAP-based CGE model similar to the one we discussed at length in Chapter 3. The results for the following potential FTAs are summarized in Table 5.1: Japan-Mexico; South Korea-Mexico; Singapore-United States; a group of open Asia-Pacific economies, the "Pacific 5" (Australia, New Zealand, Chile, Singapore, and the United States); Japan-Singapore; Japan-South Korea; and a Northeast Asian FTA (Japan-South Korea-China).

Several observations are worth noting. First, we spoke at length about the U.S.-Singapore FTA in Chapter 4, frequently noting that Singapore's economy differs considerably from those of the other ASEAN countries. This was due to the fact that Singapore is an advanced, open economy without an agriculture sector. However, we see that in the case of Singapore-U.S., net trade diversion to the detriment of other ASEAN countries does show up in all cases. And while the aggregate effect on the economy is always small (ranging from –0.01 in the case of Thailand to –0.05 in the case of the Philippines), *we must recall the strong downward bias inherent in this type of modelling technique*. In relative terms, the

TABLE 5.1
Effects of Various FTAs on EAI Countries
(Equivalent variation basis; per cent of GDP)

	Indonesia	Malaysia	Philippines	Thailand
FTAs:				
Japan-Mexico	0.00	−0.03	0.01	0.00
South Korea-Mexico	0.00	−0.02	−0.01	0.00
Singapore-United States	−0.02	−0.04	−0.05	−0.01
Pacific 5[1]	−0.02	−0.13	−0.06	−0.02
Japan-Singapore	−0.02	−0.35	−0.08	−0.09
Japan-South Korea	−0.01	−0.07	−0.05	−0.03
Japan-SK-China	0.15	−0.70	−0.35	−0.21
Global Free Trade	1.31	6.05	3.42	2.57

Notes: [1] Pacific 5= FTA between Australia, Chile, New Zealand, Singapore, and the United States.

Source: Scollay, Robert and John P. Gilbert, *New Regional Trading Arrangements in the Asia-Pacific?* (Washington, D.C.: IIE, May 2001).

negative effect on the ASEAN economies is in every case greater in the case of U.S.-Singapore than Japan-Mexico, for example.

Second, with respect to arrangements involving Japan, the Japan-Singapore FTA is even more significant and negative for the other ASEAN countries than is the case of U.S.-Singapore, ranging from −0.02 (Indonesia) to −0.35 (Malaysia) of GDP. The greatest blow in relative terms comes from the Northeast Asian FTA, with negative effects ranging from −0.15 (Indonesia) to −0.70 (Malaysia) of GDP. In fact, Malaysia seems to be the most vulnerable among the ASEAN countries to Japanese FTAs, as it always receives the largest negative effects.

Third, as a related point to the discussion of multilateralism, we have included the overall effects of global free trade on the EAI economies calculated by Scollay and Gilbert. Malaysia gains considerably (at least in relative terms) from global free trade, with a positive effect equivalent to over 6 per cent of GDP; the Philippines comes in at a distant second (3.42 per cent) followed by Thailand (2.57 per cent) and Indonesia (1.31 per cent). Thus, with the possible exception of Malaysia, global liberalization does not seem to have a large effect on the ASEAN economies, a result that is counterintuitive. However, once again, it is to be recalled that the model leaves out all dynamic effects of liberalization, "non-border" and some border-related policy changes that would be necessary with global free trade, and the effects on domestic policy formation. All economies do better (and, in the case of Malaysia, much better) within the context of global free trade than APEC liberalization (figures not shown[1]), either in terms of a non-discriminatory accord or a preferential agreement (discussed below), with the exception of the Philippines, which, interestingly, does better with APEC.

Given that the Japan-Singapore Economic Partnership Agreement (JSEPA) will be significant in terms of the need for a "defensive" strategy for the EAI countries, it behooves us to consider the nature of the agreement.[2] As noted above, the JSEPA constitutes the first FTA that Japan has negotiated and signed, and perhaps certain features can serve as a model for Japanese pacts in the future, in much the same way that the U.S.-Singapore (USSFTA) arrangement may serve as a model for the EAI. Like the USSFTA, the JSEPA is a comprehensive agreement, involving not only trade and investment liberalization but also investment and business facilitation, as well as the use of information technology, a Mutual Recognition Agreement (MRA), entry visa relaxation, and other notable features such as intellectual property rights, competition policies, and government procurements.

Briefly, under this agreement, 98 per cent of traded items from Singapore will enter Japan duty-free, and Singapore, in the context of generally low trade barriers to all countries, will eliminate several tariffs on Japanese imports of particular interest to Japan, such as beer on which Singapore levies a 10 per cent tariff. In the area of services, in contrast to the trade sector, Singapore has more barriers than Japan. Under the WTO's General Agreement on Trade and Services (GATS), services are divided into 155 items. Japan already liberalized 102 under the GATS, and under JSEPA an additional 32 were liberalized. So instead of 66 per cent of the total items, 86 per cent will be liberalized together. In the case of Singapore, there were already 62 items liberalized; this agreement saw restrictions lifted on 77 more, to a total of 139. Expanding from 40 per cent to 90 per cent signalled a great compromise on Singapore's part. For Japan, finance, the medical profession, and social work rules were relaxed. For Singapore, electronics communication, education, *and environment limits were reduced.*

Thus, while the JSEPA goes well beyond a traditional FTA, it falls well short of the substance of the USSFTA surveyed at length in Chapter 4. It was also an easy FTA in that Singapore is an advanced economy without an agricultural sector. Nevertheless, the JSEPA appears to be only the first of many PTAs that Japan would like to conclude within the decade. Agriculture and certain politically sensitive services have always been difficult areas for Japan in GATT/WTO negotiations and are proving to be stumbling blocs to FTAs as well. Still, there seems to be political determination to move forward on these FTA pacts, and ultimately this will mean compromising on the sensitive areas as well. Given the comparative advantage in certain sensitive agricultural products in the ASEAN countries, this may suggest that concrete negotiations as part of bilateral, regional (Japan-ASEAN) or "ASEAN+3" will be difficult, but not impossible, particularly since a dozen years of economic stagnation has convinced Japan of the need to boost competitiveness and expedite necessary structural change. It still has a long way to go; but compromises in agriculture during the Uruguay Round, the "Big Bang" liberalization of financial services in the late 1990s, and recent liberalization plans (e.g., privatization of postal savings) would have been unthinkable in Japan 20 years ago.

Clearly, the regionalism approach is being pursued by Japan as a means of not only enhancing market access but also exerting diplomatic influence at a delicate time. In fact, while Japan is used to competing with the United States for influence in the region, it is only recently that China has become a major concern. The ASEAN-China FTA accord in December 2004 underscores this competition. Hence, it could very well be that Japan perceives FTAs with Asian partners as a necessary economic and political vehicle, providing sufficient incentives to overcome domestic obstacles to structural change.

B. European Union

ASEAN countries have always benefited from the EC's Generalized System of Preferences (GSP) scheme, which allows for the duty-free entry (up to a certain point) of ASEAN manufactured exports and processed agricultural products, with a number of exceptions. Like in the case of other GSP programmes, areas in which the resource-rich ASEAN countries have had comparative advantage (e.g., textiles and clothing, agricultural products) have been generally excluded from the EU GSP. According to Messerlin (2001), who surveys the EU's GSP scheme, the limited preferential margin implied small gains to developing countries. Moreover, ASEAN countries have had to deal with the EU's "pyramid of preferences" in exporting to the EU market, that is, with the ACP countries for agriculture and labour-intensive items,[3] and with the customs union or FTAs in the case of (intra- and extra-EU) European countries. Messerlin (2001) calculates that, for agricultural (non-agricultural) products, the average applied MFN tariff rate was 17.3 per cent (4.6 per cent), whereas the GSP+MFN rate—which would generally correspond to the ASEAN countries—came to 15.7 per cent (2.3 per cent) and the Lome+GSP+MFN rate was 10.3 per cent (0.0 per cent).

The simple (bound) mean of tariffs in manufactures and agriculture is 4.1 per cent and 19.5 per cent, respectively.[4] The most heavily protected sectors are footwear and textiles for manufactures, and live animals and prepared foods in the area of agriculture. Commodities with actual tariffs over 100 per cent are only found in the live animals and animal products categories; in fact, there are 22 such commodities at the 6-digit HS level (most of which fall under the general HS 02, 04, 10, and 23), with bovine products reaching up to 252 per cent.[5]

Moreover, the EU has used fairly extensive non-tariff barriers as a means of protecting its market. The Common Agricultural Policy (CAP) is, perhaps, the most notorious example. The multi-fibre arrangement is an orderly-marketing arrangement that has limited trade in textiles (though, as noted earlier, this will be phased out completely in 2005); the EU has periodically used voluntary export restraints to restrict imports for specific sources; and it has applied fairly extensively anti-dumping measures, affecting 336 tariff lines in 2000 and 141 in textiles alone, having the equivalent of a 22 per cent (simple average) *ad valorem* tariff on affected products (Messerlin 2001, p. 23).[6]

ASEAN does engage with the EU in an ongoing dialogue known as the Asia-Europe Meeting (ASEM). An ASEM-wide preferential trade agreement has not developed in ASEM, nor has some sort of concerted regional liberalization been developed, such as in the case of the Asia-Pacific Economic Cooperation (APEC) organization's 1994 "Bogor Vision", in which member-states committed themselves to a region of "open trade and investment" by 2010 (2020 for developing countries).

However, there have been trade-related agreements under ASEM that support WTO conventions and generally fall under the rubric of trade and investment facilitation.[6]

Over the past ten years, there have been essentially three major changes in Europe regarding intra-regional economic integration of relevance to the EAI countries: (1) the Single Market Program (EC-1992)—creating a European common market in which goods, services, capital and labour flows—was essentially completed in 1994, though there continue to be certain areas that have not been completely freed (e.g., financial services); (2) the introduction of the euro on 1 January, 1999 (with the "hard euro" being introduced 1 January, 2002); and (3) the membership expansion of the EU to include 10 new Central and Eastern European countries on 1 May 2004 (the Fifth Enlargement), to be followed by two more (Bulgaria and Romania) in 2007 (in December 2004, the EU also agreed to formally begin accession negotiations with Turkey in October 2005). We noted in Chapter 3 that the Fifth Enlargement would not have a large impact on ASEAN but that the effect will be negative: Lee and van der Mensbrugghe (2004) estimate that the Fifth Enlargement will cost ASEAN countries in the range of US$810 million to US$1.05 billion. Moreover, the introduction of the euro had no direct effect on Asia and, in fact, the indirect effects will likely be positive, as the U.S. dollar now has greater competition in international markets.

Thus, the most significant EU programme having an effect on Asia would be EC-1992. A major report estimating the positive effects of dismantling trade barriers within Europe, called the Cecchini Report (*The Costs of Non-Europe*) claimed that the internal growth effect of the EC 1992 programme would be so strong as to swamp static diversionary effects on non-members countries. However, *ex post*, it turns out that this is not the case. A number of studies have postulated what might be the effects of EC 1992 on third country exports, with the results being generally mixed *ex ante* but negative *ex post*. Bleaney, Greenaway, and Hine (1995) delineate a number of possible changes stemming from the EC 1992 programme that might serve to reduce non-partner country penetration of EC markets: improved competitiveness of EC firms in EC and non-EC markets; trade diversion induced by internal liberalization; market exclusion due to discriminatory harmonization of technical barriers; market exclusion due to discriminatory government procurement; market exclusion due to "reciprocity" requirements;

protection induced by eliminating national quotas; and protection induced by adjustment pressures (p. 86). Because these effects go well beyond the traditional price-related effects of a FTA or customs union, empirical trade models are not well equipped to estimate their ultimate effect on trade. Nevertheless, Verbiest and Tang (1992) use a macroeconomic simulation model to estimate the effects of the completion of the internal market in the EC on Asian developing countries. While the paper suggests that "protectionist temptations" may increase as a result of EC 1992, it estimates a positive impact on developing Asia over the medium- to long-run, assuming the Cecchini growth estimates are in the correct range (2–6 per cent increase in GDP).

However, these studies were *ex ante*; *ex post* it would seem that the effect was negative. Certainly, the relatively slow growth of the European economies over the 1987–94 period (when EC 1992 was being implemented) and since then do not seem to support the assumptions of great dividends that the Single Market Program was supposed to create. Indeed, Kreinin and Plummer (2002) look at the *ex post* effects of EC 1992, focusing on developing countries. They use an import growth approach (called the "standard normalized approach") in which the "counterfactual" (that is, what EC imports would have been in the absence of the Single Market Program) is estimated by using the commodity growth rates of two control countries, the United States and Canada.[7] The counterfactual estimates are compared to the actual changes in commodity trade to calculate the implicit trade creation/trade diversion values. Net trade diversion for ASEAN is obtained for both agricultural commodities (US$997 million) and manufactures (US$9.8 billion). These numbers are many times the estimated effects of the Fifth Enlargement cited above. Thailand and the Philippines experienced the largest negative effects. At the sectoral level, the biggest losers were, for agriculture, Thai fish exports (with net trade diversion coming to US$808 million), and for manufactures, telecommunications and electronic machinery (net trade diversion of about US$6 billion). These latter two sectors accounted for the bulk of net trade diversion and are also two priority areas for ASEAN exports.

While the EU has not been active in negotiating FTAs with Asian countries, it has been with just about all other regions. For example, the EU has been negotiating a series of FTAs with its former colonies to replace the ACP "Lomé Accords". It is currently negotiating an FTA with MERCOSUR, though bottlenecks emerged during negotiations—particularly with respect to agriculture-related issues—and in March 2005 was put on hold.

As the United States, Japan, and China move forward in negotiating FTAs with various Asian countries, particularly in ASEAN, it is highly likely that the EU, too, will begin to place a priority on negotiating bilateral agreements with the region. *Hence, in a sense, the fact that ASEAN has been engaging in the FTAs with other OECD countries will likely make it a more likely target for EU initiatives.* However, it is unclear when this will begin to happen. In the meantime, ASEAN countries are facing greater competition from China in Europe (see Chapter 2) and are being shut out to some degree in European markets due to the EU expansion and Pyramid of Preferences. Hence, the prospects for increasing market share in Europe without a PTA are probably not bright.

C. United States

As noted earlier, relative to its predecessors, the Bush administration has been aggressive in developing regional agreements in all parts of the world. In fact, prior to the U.S.-Israel Free Trade Agreement (in manufactures) signed in 1985, U.S. trade policy was strictly multilateral under the auspices of the GATT. Shortly after that, the United States negotiated a number of free trade and special-trading agreements, most notably with Canada (1989) and Mexico (NAFTA, 1994) but also with other groups.

The Bush administration has made it very clear that it intends to pursue the regionalism route as a key economic and diplomatic policy. Even as far back as his presidential campaign, President Bush was a strong protagonist of the Free Trade Area of the Americas (FTAA), to include the entire Western Hemisphere (save Cuba). True to his word, he has actively pursued agreements in Latin America (e.g., an FTA with Chile and FTAA negotiations) but has also been aggressive in other regions. In the Asia-Pacific, these have been in the form of "normal" FTAs (e.g., the USSFTA in 2003 and the U.S.-Australia in 2004) and special trading agreements (e.g., U.S.-Vietnam, U.S.-Laos Bilateral Trade Agreements); in Africa, the Bush administration has added to the Clinton-era "African Growth and Opportunities Act" well-publicized proposals for U.S.-African FTAs; and in the Middle East, it has offered up the possibility of FTAs with Middle Eastern countries, building on the U.S.-Jordan free-trade area (2000) and the U.S.-Israel agreement.

While the economics of these integration agreements are controversial, it is clear that this jump to the regionalism bandwagon is a strong departure from traditional U.S. policy, with likely far-reaching ramifications. Moreover, the nature of these agreements and the way they are being prioritized suggest that most of these agreements are being used toward diplomatic ends. This is most evident in the case of the free-trade area with Jordan and the push towards agreements in Africa and the Middle East. The United States seems to be emulating the EU approach: given the lack of any other policy levers, the EU has always used PTAs as a means of diplomacy.

D. NAFTA and the FTAA

The largest and, in many ways, "deepest" FTA that the United States has is NAFTA. The NAFTA agreement, which features the world's first trading accord between developed countries (Canada and the United States) and a major developing country (Mexico), began in January 1994. All tariff and most non-tariff barriers were to be eliminated in four rounds, the first having taken place immediately, and the remaining three to unfold in successive 5-year phases. Virtual free trade between the United States and Canada was achieved in 1998, and free trade between all three countries should be complete by 2008. In large part NAFTA is an expanded version of the Canada-U.S. Free Trade Area (initiated in 1989) which commits Mexico to implement a similar degree of trade and investment liberalization, while also addressing a number of additional "non-traditional" issues, including trade in services, investment, protection of international property rights, labour and environmental standards, and government procurement. NAFTA's treatment of trade in services and intra-regional investment is considerably more thorough than that found in the Uruguay Round's GATS and TRIMS. Many of these issues were duplicated in the USSFTA.

Moreover, NAFTA's tackling of issues like labour and environmental standards goes well beyond the scope of current multilateral talks (and would be controversial in the context of the EAI, as discussed at length in Chapter 4). These innovations should promote significant dynamic gains in the Mexican economy over the next few years.

The effect of NAFTA on the ASEAN economies is still not clear, given the fact that the accord is still being implemented and the most recent comprehensive available trade data are for 2002. Few studies have analysed *ex post* the effects of NAFTA on the ASEAN countries in particular. An exception is Kreinin and Plummer (2002), which, unlike its estimates for the Single Market Program, actually calculates a positive effect on ASEAN to the tune of US$13 billion in 1996, or 4 per cent of total ASEAN exports to North America. Over a third of this net external trade creation is accounted for by Malaysia, and in all countries the greatest effect occurs in SITC 75 and SITC 77, which would be expected given the orientation of Malaysian exports. However, it should be stressed that these are tentative results, as the data only reflected a few years of NAFTA. *Still, as a basically outward-oriented agreement, one would expect that external countries could ultimately benefit in terms of trade, particularly given the positive policy reform that Mexico has had to embrace in order to take part in NAFTA.* The sectoral exceptions would be automobiles and textiles and clothing, whose very high rules of origin requirements (62.5 per cent and essential 100 per cent, respectively) would make trade and investment diversion highly likely. Mexico has recently been courted by many countries (from the EU to Japan) to form bilateral FTAs, no doubt due to the privileged position Mexico enjoys in NAFTA. Also, there are some restrictions on agricultural trade that have emerged since the signing of the agreement (e.g., in the area of tomatoes).

The positive effects of NAFTA are also consistent with the gravity-model regressions we reported in Chapter 3, at least at the ASEAN *regional* level. In that section, we saw no substantial decline in the ASEAN binary variable at all. In fact, the opposite was true. However, we did see a general tendency for the coefficient estimates on the individual EAI country regressions to fall (or, in the case of Indonesia, continue to be fairly insignificant). However, this trend was in evidence well before the creation of NAFTA. Moreover, relative to the EU country regressions—if we might use the EU as a "control country"—the U.S. regression estimates were actually superior.

The proposed FTAA, however, could potentially be more harmful to ASEAN, given its size and the fact that it would include countries with highly diverse factor endowments, overlapping with ASEAN member-states (from the poorest to the richest). There is also the fear that the

FTAA would be a policy diversion (away from Asia) for the United States, though this fear does not seem to have been realized.

As we noted earlier, ultimately, the degree to which an FTA like FTAA will affect ASEAN depends critically, *inter alia*, on the similarity of export structure of these countries, as well as the share of trade with integrating markets. SRCC calculations (not reported) would suggest that there is considerable overlap between the export structure of a number of ASEAN and Latin American countries, even though the degree of similarity can differ significantly. For example, the export structure of Chile, which has been aggressive in seeking out PTAs in Latin America, North America, and the Asia-Pacific (including South Korea), has a low degree of similarity with both ASEAN and Latin American countries, whereas Brazil has a fairly high similarity index. This would suggest that, for the major countries anyway, they are sufficiently similar to each other to be characterized as "competitive" economies.

As a final point in this regard, the FTAA talks did not go particularly well in 2004. The United States would like to make the FTAA as comprehensive as possible—similar in scope to NAFTA in coverage would be ideal, though not particularly realistic—but MERCOSUR and Brazil in particular have resisted this approach, preferring a much more limited agreement. The traditional inward-looking instincts in many Latin American countries vis-à-vis the United States, combined with history, have contributed to the lack of progress in the talks. *Hence, the FTAA may end up being a reality, but it will likely be a distant reality.* In the meantime, the United States continues to negotiate bilateral and plurilateral agreements with Latin American countries, most recently the Central America Free Trade Area (CAFTA). This sort of approach is important for U.S. policy goals but, given the fact that it is the big countries like Brazil and Argentina that might be threats to ASEAN, it should not have any significant negative implications for ASEAN.

E. Africa and the Middle East

The current wave of U.S. FTA proposals in Africa and the Middle East will likely have little effect on the ASEAN countries. These countries tend to have quite different trade structures than ASEAN, with the exception of certain SITC 7 (electronics and electrical machinery) exports from North Africa and Israel. But North African exports of these—and other products—tend to be overwhelmingly geared to the European market. An FTA with the United States might change this to some degree, but it is unlikely to have much impact, especially since the United States almost has a completely open market in SITC 7 anyway. And Israel already has an FTA with the United States in manufactures for two decades.

Hence, proposals for FTAs in Africa and the Middle East are highly politically determined and their economic impact on ASEAN will likely be extremely small. *To the extent that they create greater stability in the region, they actually could end up benefiting ASEAN considerably.* The fact that Mexico had to undergo extensive economic reform as part of NAFTA—and continued to do so once NAFTA was created—makes that market even more attractive to ASEAN exporters through both income and price effects. This needs to be balanced against any trade and investment diversion effects.

Thus, the challenge for ASEAN is to keep the United States engaged in the region, which is what the EAI is all about. We discuss East Asian regionalism and the United States in the next section.

III. ASEAN Economic Integration: From the PTA to the AEC

It has become a cliché to say that ASEAN is at a crossroads. Indeed, Richard Pomfret, in criticizing ASEAN economic integration in the 1990s, wrote an article entitled, "ASEAN: Always at a Crossroads?" Without a doubt, ASEAN adopted a cautious, slow approach to regional cooperation from its creation with the Bangkok Declaration in 1967 until arguably AFTA in 1992, proceeding at the pace of the "slowest common denominator" member state in terms of cooperative policies. While it may appear that the pace of ASEAN integration has been slow, in fact, such an approach may have been advisable at the time. In the mid-1970s, had ASEAN forged ahead with regional integration in an ambitious manner, the inward-looking orientation of ASEAN governments at that time probably would have led the region to adopt regional economic cooperation programs that were popular in Latin America. These accords were used as a means of furthering inward-looking paradigms. They failed. If ASEAN had moved too quickly, it is likely that economic cooperation in Southeast Asia would have met the same fate. And given the key political underpinning of the organization, the consequences could have been highly problematic.

Another important characteristic of ASEAN is its willingness to add members into the group in the interests of pursuing regional issues. At the time of its inception, ASEAN consisted of five countries—Indonesia, Malaysia, the Philippines, Singapore and Thailand. Since then, Brunei, Cambodia, Laos, Myanmar and Vietnam have joined the group. Indeed, few would dispute the fact that ASEAN has been a great success in terms of its diplomatic mission from the late 1960s through the 1980s, where it was a great protagonist of peace and stability in the region. This peace and stability constituted a *quid pro quo* for the impressive economic growth performance that began in the late 1980s. Hence, while regional cooperation during this period can only be considered marginal in terms of its economic effects (see below), the stability created and perpetuated by ASEAN cooperation had pervasive indirect effects on economic growth and development in the region.

From the statistical review of earlier chapters, it is clear that in terms of trade and investment links, ASEAN does not represent a "natural" economic bloc, at least in terms of trade shares (see Chapter 3). *Nevertheless, the goal of ASEAN economic integration was not necessarily to increase intra-regional trade and investment—even though this could be a logical result—but to enhance competitiveness of the ASEAN region globally.* This continues to be its most important challenge.

Hence, judging from the perspective of the ASEAN member-states themselves and in light of the analysis of this study, we note that there need not be any contradiction between closer intra-ASEAN economic cooperation and commitments to the WTO. Moreover, there exists a strong economic argument to proceed with closer intra-regional cooperation while at the same time cementing closer relations globally, as proactive and defensive strategies. We have argued that the EAI should be an important part of this policy strategy, given the importance to ASEAN of the U.S. market.

Below we provide a review of the evolution of ASEAN economic cooperation, from humble beginnings to the ASEAN Economic Community and ASEAN+3 initiatives. The process of economic integration in the region has become increasingly complicated; only those scholars who follow it closely are able to keep up with recent significant developments. Hence, we summarize in Table 5.2 the chronological progression of cooperation and integration in the region.

TABLE 5.2
Chronology of ASEAN Integration

Main Points	ASEAN Summit	Year	APT Summits	Main Points
ASEAN Concord • Established ASEAN Secretariat • Treaty of Amity: mutual respect for independence, sovereignty, equality, territorial integrity and identity of nations, i.e. non-interference • Establishment of Zone of Peace, freedom, and neutrality	1st — Bali	1976		
• ASEAN Industrial Project agreed upon • Preferential Trading Agreement (PTA)	2nd — Kuala Lumpur	1977		
• Accelerate PTA • Accelerate and make more flexible ASEAN Industrial Joint Venture (AIJV)	3rd — Manila	1987		
• ASEAN Free Trade Area (AFTA) • Common Effective Preferential Tariff (CEPT)	4th — Singapore	1992		
	5th — Bangkok	1995		
• Proposal for ASEAN Vision 2020	1st informal — Jakarta	1996		
• ASEAN 2020 presented, a broad long-term vision for ASEAN in 2020 (with ASEAN Economic Community in mind)	2nd informal — Kuala Lumpur	1997	1st — Kuala Lumpur	1st ASEAN+3 (China, Korea and Japan)
Hanoi Plan of Action adopted to move towards Vision 2020: 1. Advance AFTA to 2002, 90% intra-trade subject to 0–5% tariff 2. ASEAN Investment Area (AIA)-goal investment liberalization within by ASEAN 2010, outside ASEAN by 2020 3. Increase Secretariat Staff from 64 to 99 4. ASEAN Surveillance (revolutionary idea) 5. Eminent Persons Group (EPG) proposed to come up with plan for ASEAN Vision 2020	6th — Hanoi	1998	2nd — Hanoi	East Asian Vision Group (EAVG) proposed by Kim Dae Jung, President of Korea, to look into East Asian Integration
EPG develops plan for Vision 2020: • Concern that ASEAN not effective in responding to Asian Crisis, so proposed financial cooperation. • Speed up AFTA • Accelerate AIA • To respond to surge of China, need to become more competitive, attract investment, faster integration, and promote IT	3rd informal — Manila	1999	3rd — Manila	

TABLE 5.2 (*continued*)

Adopted Initiative for ASEAN Integration (IAI): • Framework for more developed ASEAN members to assist those less-developed members in need • Focus on factors to enhance competitiveness for new economy: education, skills development, and work training	4th informal — Singapore	2000	4th — Singapore	• East Asian Study Group (EASG) to consider EAFTA and agree to hold East Asian Summit • Two big ideas: 1) Development of institutional link between Southeast Asia and East Asia 2) Study group for merit of an East Asian Free Trade Area (EAFTA) and investment area • Begin financial cooperation, ex. Chiang Mai Initiative May 2000 • Propose Expert Group Study on ASEAN-China FTA
• Challenges facing ASEAN: Declining FDI, erosion of competitiveness. • Road map for Integration for ASEAN to achieve 2020 • Go beyond AFTA and AIA by deepening market liberalization for both trade and investment	7th — Brunei	2001	5th — Brunei	• Endorse EAVG recommendation for EAFTA but overshadowed by China-ASEAN Free Trade Agreement proposal within 10 years, with the adoption Early Harvest Provision to speed up FTA • Prompted by China-ASEAN FTA proposal, Prime Minister Koizumi proposed Japan-ASEAN Economic Partnership in reaction to China-ASEAN proposal • Japan-Singapore Agreement for a New Age Partnership signed January 2002 and enforced Summer 2002
• AEC end goal of Vision 2020	8th — Phnom Penh	2002	6th — Phnom Penh	Adopt EASG recommendations of deepening and broadening of East Asian integration
	9th — Bali	2003	9th — Bali	
• Vientiane Action Plan • Australia attends for 1st time	10th — Vietianne	2004	10th — Vietianne	China speed up FTA with ASEAN from 2015 to 2010

Notes: In 1998, 1999 and 2000 China's speeches always contained advice to ASEAN. It is difficult to imagine this from leaders of other countries, like Japan and Korea.

A. The Evolution of ASEAN[8]

ASEAN economic cooperation began modestly in the mid-1970s with the first two ASEAN summits. Initially, political instability was the driving force behind ASEAN and it has been argued that ASEAN's goal of regional economic integration was simply a "cover" for political cooperation, particularly in light of the instability in Indochina and China's Cultural Revolution at that time. First attempts at cooperation in trade—through the Preferential Trading Arrangement—were piecemeal and voluntary; they began with a product-by-product approach to integration that allowed for the exclusion of almost all items that would be important in stimulating trade.

ASEAN also established programmes to promote industrial cooperation among its members. The ASEAN Industrial Projects (AIP), the ASEAN Industrial Complementation (AIC) scheme, the Brand-to-Brand Complementation (BBC) scheme and the ASEAN Industrial Joint Ventures (AIJVs) are examples of these efforts. While these initial agreements were modest, they were nevertheless essential to the creation of a strong base on which to build deeper ASEAN economic integration.

In 1992, ASEAN made the significant leap in the direction of economic integration with the formation of AFTA. With the exception of the JSEPA, which began implementation over ten years later, AFTA is the only example of cooperation in Asia that is similar in concept to NAFTA.[9] However, in true ASEAN fashion, rather than overly commit to regional integration in sensitive areas, the specifics of AFTA were purposefully left somewhat ambiguous with the agreement basically committing the ASEAN members to free trade in a 15-year timeframe. Also, the definition of "free trade" is somewhat loose, as it includes tariffs in the range of 0–5 per cent, rather than the traditional zero per cent.[10] After the original agreement, ASEAN broadened the scope of goods covered by AFTA and the period of implementation has been shortened such that AFTA was technically in full effect at the beginning of 2004 for the original ASEAN countries and Brunei, though there are transitional periods for inclusion of products on the temporary exclusion lists (e.g., sensitive products such as rice and automobiles in some cases) and some problems in implementation in specific areas of some countries (as noted in Chapter 4). The target for full implementation is 2006 for Vietnam, 2008 for Laos and Myanmar, and 2010 for Cambodia.

ASEAN has also made important strides in the area of investment cooperation, e.g., in the form of ASEAN "one-stop investment centres" and the ASEAN Investment Area (AIA). An important component of the AIA is the ASEAN Industrial Cooperation (AICO) Scheme, which offers more in terms of tariff (0–5 per cent) and non-tariff incentives than the traditional industrial cooperation programmes.[11] The AICO is designed to promote inward investment in technology-based industries, and was essentially an intermediate step giving favoured industries a "head start" in attracting FDI before the full implementation of AFTA. Moreover, the ASEAN countries created the ASEAN Agreement for the Promotion and Protection of Investments (September 1996), which includes simplification of investment procedures and approval processes, as well as enhanced transparency and predictability of FDI laws.

These efforts at industrial cooperation have been designed with essentially the same goal in mind as AFTA: reduce transactions costs associated with intra-regional economic interaction. The AIA and ancillary investment agreements create common policies vis-à-vis FDI and provide greater stability, certainty and transparency to investing in ASEAN. Other agreements related to the goal of creating a regional market for integrated production processes include framework agreements in the areas of services, especially financial cooperation (discussed below), and intellectual property.

As noted earlier, while intra-regional trade within ASEAN has grown over the years, the impact on intra-regional trade flows does not appear at first glance to have been large. Intra-ASEAN exports tend to be on the order of one-fourth of total exports. But if one controls for the size of the ASEAN countries in international trade and other variables—as we did in our econometric gravity model of Chapter 3—one gets a very different picture as to how strong the propensity to engage in intra-regional trade actually is. The problem is simple. ASEAN countries will naturally have a tendency to trade disproportionately with developed countries, because these markets are by far the largest. If intra-regional trade shares are small in ASEAN, in part this is because ASEAN is not a major player in international markets. Our econometric estimates summarized in Chapter 3 suggested that, controlling for other variables, being part of ASEAN does significantly make a difference in the determination of intra-regional trade flows. Also, we demonstrated that other countries have a disproportionate tendency to trade with ASEAN, a result no doubt of the successful outward-oriented development strategy of ASEAN economies.

It should also be noted that the economies of the ASEAN member-states have become more "symmetrical" over time, in the sense that their business cycles have become increasingly correlated. *The degree of economic symmetry is an important question in considering issues related to the extent of economic integration: the more symmetrical economies are, the more that they are hit in the same way by global economic "shocks" and, hence, joint strategies begin to make more sense.* This is especially important in the context of monetary union, for example: a common monetary policy requires symmetric economies in order to be effective. An example will illustrate the point. If economies are completely symmetric, then they will tend to experience inflation (unemployment) at the same time and the monetary response is clear, i.e., contractionary policy (expansionary policy). However, suppose that the economies are asymmetrical: then it could be that some economies are experiencing inflation while others are in an economic downturn with high unemployment. Monetary policy becomes difficult in such an environment. This problem is in evidence in the EU, where countries such as Ireland have been booming, whereas Germany is stuck in an economic slump.

In the run-up to the introduction of the euro, the European Commission always stressed that monetary union made sense, as it would generate considerable gains to the member-states and the economies were sufficiently "symmetric" to allow for a rational monetary policy. Moreover, it insisted that, as barriers to interchange across Europe fell to zero, the economies would eventually become more symmetric. Bayoumi and Mauro (2001) consider how close ASEAN economies have become in terms of the correlation of their business cycles. The extent to which they have become more symmetric would imply that problems facing the region would be increasingly common and, hence, the incentive for a joint response would be greater. This would also be an important consideration in the case that ASEAN/Asia ever wanted to move toward monetary union, for the same reason as it was key in the EU context. Bayoumi and Mauro (2001) correlate the ASEAN business cycles over time, and compare their results to the same methodology applied to the EU context. The results are summarized in Table 5.3.

It is actually striking how strong ASEAN business cycles are correlated compared to the EU. In fact, while the German-French correlation is highest among all countries, it is only a hair's breadth above that of Malaysia-Indonesia (0.49). Moreover, the ASEAN countries are on average more correlated with each other than the EU countries in the sample. Hence, if the EU constituted an "optimal currency area", then so does

ASEAN. Kim, Kose and Plummer (2003) use a similar technology to show that business cycles in ASEAN are not only fairly correlated but that the correlation has been *increasing* over time.

The conclusion from this discussion is that, while intra-ASEAN trade is not large, it is greater than one would expect given the size of the economies. In addition, even if economic cooperation initiatives have not been as ambitious as in the case of the EU, the economies have been "converging" in the sense that they have been developing fairly rapidly and their economic structures have become more similar. This suggests that common approaches to external "shocks" and commercial policies could be important.

TABLE 5.3:
Correlations of Aggregate Supply Shocks from
Bayoumi and Eichengreen

ASEAN-5[1]

	Malaysia	Indonesia	Singapore	Philippines	Thailand
Malaysia	1				
Indonesia	0.49	1			
Singapore	0.4	0.32	1		
Philippines	0.05	0.16	0.01	1	
Thailand	0.02	0.16	0.33	0.14	1

Selected EU[2]

	Germany	France	Italy	Spain	Portugal	Ireland	Finland
Germany	1						
France	0.52	1					
Italy	0.21	0.28	1				
Spain	0.33	0.21	0.2	1			
Portugal	0.21	0.33	0.22	0.51	1		
Ireland	0	-0.21	0.14	-0.15	0.01	1	
Finland	0.22	0.12	-0.32	0.07	-0.13	-0.23	1

Source: Bayoumi, T. and P. Mauro. "The Suitability of ASEAN for a Regional Currency Agreement", *World Economy*, 24, no. 7 (July 2001): p. 944, Table 3

The concept of the "public good" nature of economic cooperation in the region was driven home during the Asian Crisis. Although real and financial links across the ASEAN countries were relatively weak, it became apparent that policies in one ASEAN country will ultimately affect other ASEAN member-states. Hence, internalizing this policy "externality" has become a salient goal of ASEAN economic cooperation. The AIA itself also underscores the "public good" nature of investment laws in the region, and recognizes that the extent to and facility with which foreign investment is allowed into one ASEAN country will affect other ASEAN members as well.

The Asian Crisis also underscored the need to advance financial cooperation. There are obvious complementarities between trade and finance, and most businesspeople would not dare separate them. However, this has not stopped policy-makers and economists from doing so, which has created significant problems in most economic integration accords (e.g., the Single Market Program and the EMS Crisis of 1992; NAFTA and the Mexican Peso Crisis of 1994; the Brazilian devaluation of 1999 and the Crisis in MERCOSUR, further compounded by the Argentine financial meltdown in December 2001). Thus, the ASEAN countries have been exploring means to strengthen regional cooperation by bringing in the financial sector. The *Ministerial Understanding on ASEAN Cooperation in Finance* (March 1997) sets out the broad goals of cooperation in diverse areas of finance and macroeconomics, including banking, capital markets, insurance matters, taxation and public finance, as well as exchanging information on developments affecting ASEAN countries in various multilateral and regional organizations.

For example, although the degree of sophistication of debt markets in the ASEAN countries varies widely, all countries recognize the need to offer an attractive menu of financing options to companies and the government, as well as diverse instruments through which savers can invest. The Asian currency crisis underscored the need to build better and more diversified financial institutions and markets (currently, finance is dominated by banks). Hence, the ASEAN finance ministers are seeking ways to develop new markets in the ASEAN countries. One such proposal is the creation of an ASEAN Bond Market, which would not only help the development of national bond markets but would also include a regional "anchor" with respect to the legal and institutional characteristics of bond markets.[12] The financial area will be an important aspect of the ASEAN Economic Community (AEC), to which we now turn.

B. The ASEAN Economic Community

In November 2002, shortly after the EAI was launched, it was proposed at the ASEAN Heads of Government meeting in Phnom Penh that the region should consider the possibility of creating an "ASEAN Economic Community" (AEC) by 2020. The name is significant, for an "Economic Community" brings to mind the European experience. In fact, when APEC was "re-inventing" itself, it was proposed that the words behind the acronym for "Asia-Pacific Economic Cooperation" should be replaced with "Asia-Pacific Economic Community." This idea was rejected explicitly because it would give the impression that APEC was intending to move in the direction of the EC model, which was thought to be too controversial.

That the ASEAN Heads of Government should consider an AEC, even with the baggage the term brings, is in some sense nothing new. ASEAN has always studied carefully European economic integration and has seen it as a sort of "role model", though certainly to be adapted to the Southeast Asian development context. However, the fact that the ASEAN leaders would actually agree, at the Bali ASEAN Summit in October 2003, to create a region in which goods, services, capital and skilled labour would flow freely is a giant step in regional cooperation and certainly creates a plethora of challenges to the region.

The reasons behind the decision to create the AEC are many, including: (1) desire to create a post-AFTA agenda that would be comprehensive; (2) perceived need to deepen economic integration in ASEAN in light of the new international commercial environment, especially the dominance of FTAs; (3) given (2), the possibility that bilateral FTAs could actually jeopardize ASEAN integration since all member-states were free to pursue their own commercial-policy agenda; and (4) the recognition since the Asian Crisis that cooperation in the real and financial sectors must be extended concomitantly, and that free flows of skilled labour will be necessary to do this.[13]

But how will ASEAN be able to create its own "customs union plus", even by 2020? As noted in earlier chapters, tariff dispersion rates across ASEAN countries are, indeed, impressive: while ASEAN members tend to have fairly low tariffs and NTBs relative to other developing countries (except for the transitional ASEAN economies), they still vary considerably across the region. Moreover, Singapore is unique: it essentially has no tariffs. The EEC did not face this problem. Given the openness of its economy (over 300 per cent of GDP), Singapore cannot raise tariff rates to accept an ASEAN Common External Tariff that is not equal to zero. Likely options here would include a complete free-trade zone in ASEAN, perhaps with some external tariff harmonization, or a "10-X" customs union, in which the Common External Tariff would be determined through negotiations similar to those of the EEC but not all ASEAN countries would join.

Thus, the AEC will be a complicated endeavour and will require considerable political will to accomplish. While some might fear that the region could end up creating a "Fortress ASEAN" in the same way that the world feared the Single Market Program would create a "Fortress Europe", this result would be highly unlikely, given the outward-oriented policy stances of the ASEAN countries.

Of course, the transitional economies pose unique problems here. Cambodia, for example, received until only recently about 70 per cent of its government income from import-related taxes. However, it is reducing reliance on international-trade-based taxes as part of its membership in the WTO[14] with technical assistance from developed countries. Vietnam has made tremendous progress in its transition programme and should be in line with AFTA in 2006. Allowing the logical progression of this reform programme to continue to 2020 will not be easy but would be quite desirable from an economic development perspective. Again, 2020 is a long way off and much can happen. But Vietnam has reinvented itself from a non-market, closed, and state-directed economy into an increasingly outward-looking, market-oriented economy in less time than it will have for the AEC. As noted above, Laos has recently followed in the footsteps of Vietnam by signing a bilateral trade agreement with the United States, similar to the U.S.-Vietnam BTA, in September 2003, which will go into effect with the U.S. Congress' granting normal trade relations with Laos in 2005. It may even be possible for ASEAN to allow for a longer-term transition period for Cambodia, Myanmar, and Laos, especially since there remain political uncertainties in each of these countries.

Even the free-flow of skilled labour will not be an easy proposition. It certainly was difficult in the context of the EU Single Market Program.

Mutual recognition of professional qualifications, university and technical education preparation, and the like will require a great deal of effort and political support. Yet, this process actually presents a good opportunity for the region, and especially for the CMLV countries, to embrace "best practices". It may well be that the process will be easier for ASEAN than it was for the EU, as fewer entrenched special interests and general resistance to reform in this area are present. Many would welcome this approach. Moreover, these types of policies are already showing up in modern bilateral FTAs, as we saw at length in Chapter 4.

The idea of adopting "best practices" also extends to other areas that were important in the creation of the European Single Market, e.g., product testing, technical standards, food/health-related standards, etc. Mutual recognition will be necessary in these areas and, hence, harmonization of at least minimum acceptable standards will have to be developed. Codes should borrow from internationally accepted standards wherever possible.

Moreover, the free-flow of services will also be essential, especially since services constitute a growing sector in all ASEAN countries (see Chapter 2), a process that will continue as development proceeds apace. The ASEAN Framework Agreement on Services (AFAS), which takes a "GATS-plus" approach, is a significant step forward in creating an integrated market. However, for the AEC, ASEAN has a long way to go, even though services in the AEC will not require a radical change in policy: The third round of AFAS negotiations, which began in 2001, should at least in theory cover all sectors and "modes" of service provisions defined by the OECD, that is, (1) cross-border supply, in which a company exports the service from home; (2) consumption abroad, in which the user of the service consumes it outside his/her home country, e.g., tourism; (3) commercial presence, in which a company directly supplies the service to foreign customers (this involves establishment of an affiliate abroad and constitutes over three-fourths of all trade in services); and (4) presence of natural persons, in which the service-exporting country sends personnel abroad to supply services (these were discussed in Chapter 4). The AEC will ultimately have to ensure a generally open market in services, including no policy-induced discriminatory restrictions (including trade taxes), national treatment, mutual recognition, and related harmonization. This was a difficult process in the EU, as some of these sectors remain quite sensitive.

For example, the financial services sector in the EU continues to be segmented, even within the confines of the euro-zone.

Lastly, developing appropriate institutions under which the AEC can evolve will be necessary. The ASEAN Secretariat has been significantly strengthened but is still extremely small compared to the tasks that will be required by the AEC. Perhaps this is not such a bad thing: the European bureaucracy is widely-criticized as being far too large, non-transparent and expensive, with approximately one-third of the civil servants being merely translators of sorts. The drain on human capital in a large bureaucracy would be something that ASEAN could ill-afford. However, many of the directorates of the EU could be emulated in the ASEAN context. The executive component of ASEAN integration will have to be enhanced considerably, but this could arguably be done by adapting and expanding current institutions. Certainly, all ASEAN Secretariat staff will have to be recruited on a competitive basis, rather than being on secundment from a member-state government, in order to ensure a technically strong unit with a regional vision. This approach has been essential in the EU context. On the other hand, the creation of some sort of judicial authority to "enforce" (hitherto a bad word in ASEAN) AEC rules will be necessary. No doubt this will be difficult, as it is in the EU. As we learned in Chapter 4, many ASEAN countries do not have any competition policies in place, which will be a problem in the context of bilateral agreements with the United States, and will be even a bigger problem in the context of the AEC.

In short, the AEC is extremely ambitious and, if successful, could go a long way in creating a truly economically integrated region. Skeptics of ASEAN's ability to do this abound, but this was also the case with AFTA: many pundits believed that an FTA in ASEAN would be impossible, as the organization was serious only regarding political—not economic—affairs. However, the ASEAN leaders proved them wrong.

But even if the AEC does face challenges along the way, the process of integration will likely be salutary for domestic economic reform, for many of the reasons noted above. Moreover, as economic deepening proceeds in ASEAN, it will become easier to negotiate positions at various regional forums as a group, thereby augmenting significantly its clout (as the Europeans have been able to do). The same will be true for FTAs; Chapter 1 stressed that one reason why the U.S.-ASEAN FTAs will be best undertaken on a bilateral basis rather than regionally with ASEAN is that ASEAN continues to be far too diverse in terms of international commercial policy and economic interests. The creation of, for example, a "10-X" Common External Tariff and policy harmonization between ASEAN member-states will remove this disincentive.

IV. Asia-Pacific Economic Cooperation (APEC)

A. A Brief Review of the Evolution of Cooperation in the Pacific

Academics, governments, and research institutions have debated how to pursue regional cooperation among countries in the Asia-Pacific for at least half of the 20th century. Early discussions were perhaps stimulated by the growth and progress of the EU, but with the growing debate on the appropriate role of multilateral development institutions, the issue has assumed greater urgency in recent years.

Unlike the more formal diplomatic negotiation process leading to the formation of the EU and other multilateral institutions, it is noteworthy that the drive for Asian regional cooperation was led by academics on the one hand and businessmen on the other. Governments showed interest, but institutional arrangements which emerged from the discussions, the Pacific Trade and Development Conferences (PAFTAD) and the Pacific Basin Economic Council (PBEC), reflected academic and business interests, respectively.[15]

It was not until the discussions led to the formation of the Pacific Economic Cooperation Council (PECC) that states became more formally involved, but as just one part of tripartite delegations representing each country (the others being from academic and business sectors). It was not until the formation of APEC that governments were to deliberate more formally on regional cooperation issues.

The PAFTAD process entailed the development of an extensive network of leading economists and policy advisers from both developing and more developed countries and from market-oriented and centrally planned economies. It has received financial support from the Japanese government, other regional state agencies, multilateral organizations, and private foundations, but has remained largely free from state influence. It established an international secretariat at the Australian National University; has sponsored both regional and globally oriented conferences and symposiums; and has introduced and developed a variety of conceptual frameworks and analytical approaches for a closer evaluation of the problems and potentials of Asia-Pacific regional development.

On the private sector side, PBEC was officially established in Tokyo in 1967 with private sector representation from Australia, New Zealand, and Japan. Since then, its membership has expanded to include corporate representation from practically all developed countries and a large number of developing countries around the globe.

PBEC's original charge was to increase the flow of capital and goods among industrialized nations of the Pacific, accelerate joint ventures in resource development in the region, and enable advanced nations to cooperate with each other in expanding economic and technical assistance to lesser-developed countries. With its expanding and more diverse membership, PBEC can be regarded as the principal private sector institutional participant in overall development in the Asia-Pacific. Indeed, along with PAFTAD, PBEC helped lay the groundwork for wider-based regional cooperation.

By the early 1980's, PAFTAD had established itself as a forum for a policy-oriented, scholarly approach to regional economic issues, whereas PBEC's mandate was primarily business. The role of government was recognized, and official observers attended meetings of the two regional organizations. However, the overall diplomatic climate was not considered ripe for official representation.

A major step was taken in 1980, when academics, business leaders, and state officials (technically participating in a *private* capacity) attended a Pacific Community Seminar held in Canberra under the sponsorship of the prime ministers of Japan and Australia. The participants were organized on the basis of tripartite national delegations to ensure balanced sectoral input. The tripartite format of this gathering has become a prominent feature of what is known as the Pacific Economic Cooperation Council (PECC). PECC has proven to be an enduring instrument for regional cooperation, even after the creation of APEC; its Trade Policy Forum (TPF), an active group of academics holding regular conferences, addresses cutting-edge economic-integration issues facing the Asia-Pacific region and its research is commonly used in the policy-making process.

Ultimately, formal regional cooperation is developed at the official level, meaning that PAFTAD, PBEC, and PECC could only be limited in their ultimate ability to influence policy. Australia's Prime Minister,

Bob Hawke, during a visit to South Korea in 1980, proposed a meeting of senior ministers from economies in the region with high levels of common trade, to establish a framework for regional economic cooperation. Over time this process came to be known as Asia Pacific Economic Cooperation (APEC) and the first ministerial-level meeting took place in Canberra in November 1989.

B. Asia-Pacific Economic Cooperation

Since its creation in 1989, APEC has received a great deal of attention as the first post-Cold War international organization. While it was originally conceived as a forum for economic dialogue, APEC quickly gained stature in 1993 when President Clinton invited APEC heads-of-state and raised the level of the APEC talks to a ministerial level with annual Summit meetings.

APEC is a different kind of organization altogether. It is the only inter-governmental organization that brings together the countries of Asia and North America including the United States, Canada, Australia, New Zealand, ASEAN, Japan, Korea, China and now even Peru and Russia. *In a way, the establishment of APEC reflects the recognition by the Asia-Pacific countries of the importance of the United States as a major market for their goods and as a source of investment; because of this, the United States cannot be left out of any meaningful cooperation effort in the region.* In fact, originally Bob Hawke launched his idea as a means of making sure that Australia would not be locked out of East Asian economic cooperation. He originally intended on excluding countries on the Eastern side of the Pacific, in particular the United States. Strong pressure from Japan, along with support from other key trading partners with the United States in Asia, changed this.

A second reason why APEC is different is that, rather than being a tightly-knit regional grouping, APEC embraces "open regionalism" whereby whatever preferences are negotiated among the APEC members are also extended to a third party so that there is no trade diversion effect. In practically all APEC declarations, the association commits itself to shunning an inward orientation and, instead, advocates "open regionalism". Although there are differences between countries regarding the means to promote cooperation within APEC, the overriding goal is ostensibly shared by all: to create an Asia-Pacific region in which transactions costs of international interchange are as low as possible.

The main difference in the interpretation of "open regionalism" regards reciprocity. In its "purest" form, open regionalism would suggest concerted liberalization among APEC member states, and the lower barriers to trade would be automatically extended to third parties. While such an approach would suggest that some countries would get "something for nothing" and could, in fact, affect negatively WTO negotiations by taking away regional bargaining chips, economists that support this strategy note that APEC is large enough to make the endeavour still worthwhile for all participating economies. Moreover, as protectionism also tends to hurt local economies the most, this approach would be beneficial to member states even without commitments from outside. Finally, these economists would warn that APEC is so huge that a discriminatory PTA would end up splitting the global trading system in half, to everyone's detriment. Some have argued that President Clinton's motivation for increasing the profile of APEC was a warning to the Europeans that they need to compromise at the GATT Uruguay Round negotiations or else the United States would lead a trade bloc in the Asia-Pacific, which included the most dynamic economies in the world. The EU seemed to cave into this threat, which is why some would argue that APEC has revealed itself to be a "building bloc" to multilateralism: it allowed the Uruguay Round to succeed. But, according to the "purists", this was a very high stakes and reckless threat, potentially jeopardizing the integrity of the global trading system.

Advocates of reciprocal "open regionalism" believe that APEC liberalization should be made available to outsiders, provided that non-regional partners also join the liberalization process. This would avoid the problem of doing away with "bargaining chips", and would not be discriminatory per se, at least in the European sense: any country could participate. While in this approach there would continue to be the threat of a divided global marketplace, protagonists would suggest that the "purists" interpretation of open regionalism is unworkable politically. The U.S. Congress, for example, would not agree to extend open markets, say, to the EU in exchange for nothing (particularly in the current transatlantic environment). Their argument, therefore, is that APEC will either embrace a reciprocal version of open regionalism, or APEC will go nowhere.

A third reason why APEC is different from other initiatives is that it does not negotiate formal reductions in trade and investment barriers. All liberalization within APEC is voluntary; no sanctions or penalties exist for countries that miss agreed-upon targets. While extensive "Individual Action Plans" are submitted each year by member-states, countries can include commitments implemented under other accords, e.g., the Uruguay Round, as part of their steps toward reaching the Bogor Vision. Hence, in terms of actual implementation of trade liberalization, APEC's "value-added" is quite minimal for most countries to date.

Nevertheless, APEC does play a role in trade and investment facilitation in the region by providing a forum for discussions, urging trade and investment liberalization, and developing region-wide practical ways of reducing transactions costs. For example, extensive work is being undertaken by APEC working groups on improving customs clearance procedures, including the creation of a businessperson's "smart card", APEC investment agreements, exploration of means to facilitate technology transfer, cooperation in infrastructure, standards and conformance, harmonization of product standards, enhanced dialogue on trade and investment facilitation and development cooperation (ECOTECH), and means toward improving other areas generally classified under "deep integration".

Following the Asian currency crisis, APEC has been compelled to deal with financial issues. APEC cooperation was not initially intended to include finance as a principal area of cooperation; the emphasis has been on facilitating and liberalizing trade and FDI, as well as ancillary "nuts-and-bolts" issues that are useful for improving business interaction and lowering transactions costs in the region. Because of the 1997 crisis, APEC officials now agree that the region should be actively involved in supporting regional financial stability, but there does not yet seem to be a consensus on what should be done. Moreover, the work that *has* been done within APEC regarding financial stability concerns is not well known and, hence, APEC has thus far had little effect to date in promoting financial cooperation (Feinberg 2001).

Nevertheless, one can argue that the APEC experience is unique in that it includes major developed countries and major developing countries, highly sophisticated financial systems and underdeveloped ones, and substantial capital exporters and importers. *Such diversity might change the "natural" balance of the regional organization in favour of closer cooperation in financial areas.* And given the close relationship between trade and finance and the rising degree of interdependence due to policy liberalization, inclusion of financial issues not only seems logical, but is perhaps necessary.

C. East Asian Regionalism and the United States

Despite the progress that has been made hitherto under APEC, there is a general impression that APEC lags far behind the implementation of its ambitious agenda (after all, 2010 is less than five years away). Given the new international and regional zeal for regionalism, it would appear that most countries have put APEC on the back burner and are considering other options. As noted throughout this Report, some of these are bilateral but others are regional. Indirectly, the idea of creating an East-Asia only economic grouping seems to be attracting new interest in the form of the ASEAN+3-related initiatives.

In addition to the "APEC ebb", there were a couple of events that shifted the focus to East Asia. First, even with the successful APEC Summits at Blake Island and Bogor, East Asian Economic Grouping (EAEG) concept never faded away.[16] On the contrary, it began to grow in substance. Strangely, the initiative came from ASEAN's effort to expand economic cooperation with the EU, but the EU's desire to deal with all of East Asia led to ASEAN's asking China, South Korea, and Japan to participate. The first Asia-Europe Meeting (ASEM) was held in Bangkok in March of 1996, and officials from ASEAN and the rest of East Asia met with EU representatives—a format which was regularized and has continued twice a year since. Even though the initial impetus for these meetings was economic cooperation with the EU, the significance for East Asian regionalism lies in that these meetings brought officials from ASEAN, China, South Korea, and Japan together, to discuss issues of economic cooperation. In 1997, these meetings culminated in an informal summit of ASEAN+3 Heads of State in Kuala Lumpur.

Even more significantly, the Asian Financial Crisis of 1997 and 1998 strengthened the move toward East Asian economic integration. As was noted earlier, in addition to underscoring how closely interlinked East Asian economies were—as borne out painfully through the "contagion effect" that began with the crisis in Thailand on 2 July, 1997—most Asian countries also believed that the IMF's solution to the Asian Financial Crisis was not the most appropriate. The IMF recognized that the nature of government spending and macroeconomic policies was different from that which took place in Latin America. For example, many Asian countries had a budget surplus when the Crisis occurred, which is unlike what has happened in various Latin American economic crises. However, Asian governments complained that the IMF insisted upon solutions which were more or less the same as those applied in the Latin American case, e.g., that the currency collapse and capital flight could be combated by keeping interest rates high and shoring up budget surpluses to be used to recapitalize banks later on. Also, Asian countries were disappointed when the United States was not more forthcoming with assistance especially to Thailand (which had a special Treaty of Amity with it), even though it was aggressive in assisting Mexico during the Peso Crisis of December 1994. It is arguably this absence of swift support from the United States and even the IMF that caused Asian countries to begin looking for alternative means of defence from international crises.

As noted above, APEC was neither effective in managing the crisis nor in preventing it from happening. Moreover, while it was the Asia-Pacific *Economic* Cooperation organization, its focus had been on the real side of the economy, not finance. Yet dissatisfaction with the external response to the crisis touched off many discussions in the various formal and informal regional forums.

The original Miyazawa plan initiated by Japan to create an Asian Monetary Fund to supplement the IMF, which was opposed by the IMF and the United States, eventually led to the establishment of a currency swap arrangement among East Asian countries (basically bilateral swaps between Japan and individual countries) during the annual meeting of the Asian Development Bank in May 2000. It would be known as the Chiang Mai Agreement.

However, financial integration in general is a complicated process. Usually it occurs well into the process of regional integration, as suggested by the experiences of the EU and the creation of the euro, which was only possible after decades of a customs union and a common market. Because the benefits of monetary cooperation are less clear— particularly in the Asian case, since exchange rate stability among Asian countries is of limited value for the many countries that trade heavily outside the region—and the political benefits no doubt are far less than in the EU case, countries have begun to focus more on FTAs, at least as a first step.

The lack of influence of APEC in the Asian Financial Crisis has served to solidify East Asia's move towards the establishment of the ASEAN+3. The current spates of agreements however, have not been extended to the entire ASEAN+3, but have come more from ASEAN to individual countries. For example, the completion of the China-ASEAN joint FTA study in the summer of 2001 prompted Japan to quickly initiate a study of its own with ASEAN. One month later, at the 2001 ASEAN+3 meeting in November, ASEAN and China announced their intention to negotiate a free trade area within 10 years (the agreement was formalized in December 2004).

However the ASEAN+3 evolves, there is little reason to fear that the grouping would ever become an inward-looking trade bloc. Such an approach would contradict the word and deed of economic reform and international commercial policy of just about every prospective member-state. But it is likely that the grouping will continue to intensify cooperation at all levels, a process that will be pushed by national and regional considerations but also international developments, such as regionalism in Europe-Africa and the Americas. *Hence, it would behove the United States to continue to be significantly engaged in the region in terms of its own commercial policy objectives. It is unclear where APEC will go; hence, initiatives such as the EAI will take on increasing economic, political economy, and strategic importance.*

V. ASEAN and the "Chinese Competitive Threat"

In our statistical review of Chapter 2, the increasing presence of China in the international marketplace was evident. Moreover, our applied analysis showed that Chinese and EAI-country exports are not only highly correlated but are becoming more so over time, both in the U.S. market and in the OECD overall. In fact, it would appear that China is, indeed, presenting a key economic challenge to the global economy. Developed countries have become so nervous about Chinese success in international markets that they took years to work out adequate safeguard measures before accepting China in the WTO in 2002. It has become a frequent target for anti-dumping duties administered by the United States, the EU, and Japan. More recently, developed countries have been applying strong pressure to the Chinese government to revalue its currency in order to reduce its export competitiveness on international markets. In anticipation of the expiration of the Agreement on Textiles and Clothing in January 2005, developed countries have already been pressuring to restrain exports. In late December 2004, the Chinese government was even reported to be considering export *taxes* on popular clothing exports in partial response to this pressure.[17]

These concerns are due to both the large increase in the bilateral trade surplus with the United States—at a time when the expenditure-switching effects of a changing U.S. dollar seem to be generating considerable volatility both for the U.S. and international markets—and the surprising resilience of Chinese economic growth, even throughout the Asian Crisis of 1997–98 and the most recent global slowdown, suggesting that China can "afford" a revaluation. For example, Chinese economic growth came to about 9.5 per cent in 2004. An overheating of the Chinese economy would lead to a real appreciation of the exchange rate anyway; Chinese inflation is, indeed, on the rise, prompting the Chinese government in spring 2004 to try to cut credit expansion. The government itself has targeted 8 per cent growth in the medium-term, rather than its traditionally-higher targets. There have even been some suggestions within China that the country should move to a basket-peg—rather than an exclusive U.S. dollar-peg—which would allow the Chinese to revalue to some degree. But in any event, the perception of "threat" remains.

If the emergence of China is a key issue for developed countries, one can easily imagine the challenge that ASEAN countries perceive. Export growth was a central factor in the "Asian economic miracle" and, as China begins to move up the development ladder, it will continue to compete in areas in which ASEAN has comparative advantage, a trend that is already clear from the data (Chapter 2).

Perhaps even more important than competition in the area of trade, the huge increase in FDI flows to China is feared to be even more problematic for developing Asia. As noted earlier, in addition to bringing in new non-debt-creating capital and foreign exchange, FDI has been actively courted as a means of stimulating technology transfer, increasing efficiency in the economy, and providing ready-made markets for a country's exports. Indeed, mounting empirical evidence, including that which is presented in this Report, suggests that trade and investment are intricately linked, with larger FDI flows being associated with robust exports. Moreover, the Asian Crisis was a result in part of a maturity mismatch in which the ratio of footloose capital flows to long-term flows (i.e., FDI) rose prior to the Crisis, thereby leaving the country open to capital flight. Hence, attracting greater FDI inflows became a more pressing priority after the Asian Crisis, as evidenced by the creation of the AIA and other ambitious "deepening" programmes. The perceived Chinese threat has no doubt been a main protagonist in the process.

Chapter 2 showed that the Chinese economy has "internationalized" rapidly over the past decade, with exports growing at a far more rapid clip than imports until very recently. Moreover, the structure of trade is changing such that China appears to be competing increasingly in higher-end markets, especially in the electric machinery and transport category. This is why there is such a high correlation between Chinese exports and the exports of some ASEAN countries to third markets. To sum up, three important conclusions emerge from Chapter 2 and in other research[18] in the area regarding China and its competition with ASEAN: (1) China has become a major competitor on international markets and to ASEAN in particular both in terms of trade and FDI inflows; (2) the structure of Chinese trade has been changing rapidly in the direction of more sophisticated exports, thereby increasingly competing with ASEAN countries; and (3) the literature (and our statistical results below) would suggest that there is a clear trade-investment link in the process of Chinese internationalization.

Moreover, it turns out that, despite what the popular press would suggest, China in no way seems to be a "special" case, defining "special" along the lines of Chapter 3, that is, if one controls for size, wealth, distance, *and* trade, FDI inflows into China, as well as Chinese trade with OECD countries, one obtains essentially what one would expect (there is no "China effect"). We show this by running a gravity regression on the determinants of FDI in major OECD markets (for a detailed description and analysis of the gravity approach, see Chapter 3). We posit FDI to be a function of trade, the product of per capita income, the product of GDP, and distance (the standard "benchmark" variables), as well as a binary variable for China to capture the country effect. A statistically significant estimate coefficient on the Chinese binary variable would suggest that, controlling for all other variables, China is, indeed, a special case at the global level. Otherwise, we reject the hypothesis. We use FDI data from 1982–99[19] and include trading partners for which we were able to obtain FDI data (using the OECD's *International Direct Investment Statistics*). Given the strong evidence of the trade-investment link in the literature, we also run the gravity model for the determinants of trade flows, using FDI as an explanatory variable (and keeping the Chinese binary). The results are presented in Table 5.4.

Several interesting results emerge from these regressions. *First, the only estimated coefficients that are consistently statistically significant and of the expected sign across all countries relate to the "trade-investment nexus", that is, trade in the FDI regressions and FDI in the trade regressions.* Hence, ASEAN is correct to look at the issue "holistically", that is, from both the trade and investment perspectives. Second, the statistical fit of the regressions as calculated by the adjusted R^2s—i.e., the degree to which the explanatory variables explain the variance in the dependent variable—are generally on par (and in some cases, higher) than in other gravity models, and they are higher in the case of trade than FDI, which is to be expected given the complicated nature and myriad motivations of FDI. Third, in no regression does it appear that China is "special"; in all regressions, the Chinese binary variable is statistically insignificant. This would imply that the world has no greater tendency to trade with or invest in China that wouldn't be predicted by its economic characteristics (i.e., its size, relative wealth, and location).

Hence, the Chinese "threat" may be real in the sense that China's emergence on the international scene is creating greater competition for ASEAN countries in their own and third markets. *However, this is not just a "Chinese" threat; it is the threat of the global marketplace, in which China is becoming an increasing important force.* Efforts to "restrain China" are therefore likely to be misplaced; the ASEAN policy direction needs to be in the direction of enhancing competitiveness through domestic policy reform at the national level and greater engagement at the regional and international levels.

Several key issues might be addressed in this regard, including:

1. *FDI diversion toward China.* While it may very well be true that FDI is being "diverted" to China away from, say, the ASEAN countries, this may reflect deficiencies in local markets rather than Chinese competition per se. Ultimately, multinationals will invest where they believe they will make money; if China promises very high returns and ASEAN merely high returns, a rational multinational—at least one that is not financially constrained, and at least as a group they are not—will invest in

TABLE 5.4
Determinants of Selected OECD Trade and Investment with China

Ind. Var:	C	Trade/FDI	GDPiGDPj	PCi*PCj	Distance	China	R2
Dep. Var:							
a. US FDI:	1044**	0.06**	0.00006**	0.32	−0.07**	−442	0.21
b. US Trade:	15322**	1.67**	0.001**	−1.09	−1.19**	−847	0.36
c. Germ FDI:	−370	0.14**	0.0009**	−1.56*	0.01	−673	0.32
d. Germ Trade:	9294**	0.59**	0.001**	9.50**	−0.92**	−154	0.49
e. France FDI:	−2696*	0.77**	0.01	2.48	0.18*	−328	0.28
f. France Trade:	3643**	0.29**	0.02*	5.47**	−0.49**	500	0.42
g. Japan FDI:	−796**	0.16**	0.00007*	−0.37	0.07**	−227	0.78
e. Japan Trade:	7253**	2.5**	0.002**	−1.96*	−0.57**	−538	0.87

Note: [1] Years: 1982–99 for all countries save Japan; Japan: 1982–95
Source: FDI Data: OECD, *International Investment Statistics, 2002*.

both markets. Even before China's huge increase in FDI inflows ASEAN countries were facing bottlenecks in the attraction of FDI (as noted above, short-term capital inflows boomed while FDI inflows ebbed). Moreover, the Chinese emergence as a major player in a way has shifted at the margin the regional focus of multinationals, which could also have positive spillover effects for other Asian countries.

2. *China as an import market*. China does have a large trade surplus, and its massive accumulation of foreign exchange reserves reveals that China has been keeping its exchange rate at an artificially low level. However, most Asian developing countries also have a trade surplus. Moreover, as noted above, the Chinese economy appears to be overheating, suggesting that its real exchange rate will appreciate even if it does not revalue. The focus on China in the media has been on its role as a competitor; however, the Chinese market is huge and presents many opportunities for developing Asian exports, especially since China is now a member of the WTO. Clearly, Chinese competition will speed-up structural adjustment in its Asian neighbors but this is not necessarily a bad thing, as the country will offer tremendous opportunities as an export market.

3. *China as a partner*. There is no doubt that Chinese economic growth

has increased the profile of China at the economic-diplomacy level in various regional and international forums. But most Asian countries feel that its role has been generally constructive. For example, during the Asian Crisis, it was feared that China would devalue its currency in order to maintain competitiveness in light of the tremendous depreciations of Crisis-affected currencies. It did not. It has also been proactive in APEC. Moreover, China has been entering into regional discussions, e.g., with ASEAN, to increase regional cooperation at various levels. The ASEAN-China FTA is indicative of this process.

As was noted in Chapter 3, Lee, et al. (2004) calculate what the effects of various Chinese commercial policy initiatives would be on a number of countries and country groupings, including the United States and ASEAN. The results are summarized in Table 5.5. The effects of an ASEAN-China FTA are actually quite high (an increase of 2.5 per cent of GDP, or US$26 billion), only slightly less than an ASEAN-Japan FTA. Trade diversion from the United States is trivial (approximately US$800 million) for an ASEAN-China FTA, whereas it would be considerably higher in the case of ASEAN-Japan. However, a China-Japan-U.S.

TABLE 5.5
Welfare Effects of Various Chinese Commercial Policy Initiatives

Region	China Unilat	ASEAN-China	ASEAN-Japan	ASEAN plus 3	ASEAN-China-EU	China-Japan-U.S.	GTL[a]
(A) Absolute deviations (US$1997 billions)							
ASEAN[b]	5.4	26.0	28.4	41.8	43.0	−16.5	38.1
United States	13.8	0.8	−1.4	−0.9	−2.9	60.6	70.9
World	142.4	61.8	37.7	231.1	223.4	198.1	732.2
(B) Per cent deviations							
ASEAN	0.5	2.5	2.7	4.0	4.2	−1.6	3.7
United States	0.1	0.0	0.0	0.0	0.0	0.6	0.7
World	0.4	0.2	0.1	0.7	0.6	0.6	2.1

Notes: [a] GTL denotes "global trade liberalization" (free trade).
   [b] Only Indonesia, Malaysia, the Philippines, Singapore, Thailand, and Vietnam are included in ASEAN. In the GTAP database, Brunei, Cambodia, Laos, and Myanmar are aggregated into the rest of the world.
Source: Lee, Hiro, David Roland-Holst, and Dominique van der Mensbrugghe. "China's Emergence and East Asian Trade under Alternative Trading Arrangements", *Journal of Asian Economics.* 15, no. 4: (August 2004): 697–712; Table 1.

agreement would have a significant negative effect on ASEAN (to the tune of US$16.5 billion, or 1.6 per cent of GDP), whereas this is the best scenario for the United States (it gains US$60.6 billion). It is to be recalled that, given the nature of this type of CGE model, the effects are most likely strong underestimates (global free trade, for example, only increases U.S. GDP by considerably less than one per cent). Hence, it is clearly in ASEAN's (and the U.S.) interest to stay actively engaged with China from a commercial policy perspective.

As a final point, we can apply the Lee et al. results to our above discussion regarding the United States and East Asian regionalism. We noted that, while it is unlikely that the ASEAN+3 grouping will become an inward-looking bloc, we also know from our theoretical discussion of Chapter 3 that FTAs are discriminatory even if they do not become inward-looking, that is, through the traditional (vinerian) trade diversion effect. In fact, as the numbers in Table 5.5 suggest, the United States does not lose much in terms of trade diversion (US$900 million), subject to the usual caveat of a downward bias. However, an ASEAN+3 scenario would generate large benefits to the ASEAN countries, coming to US$43 billion or 4.2 per cent of GDP. *These numbers are greater than what ASEAN would reap in the case of global free trade.* This supports our conclusion above that it is important that the United States continue to be actively engaged in the Asian region, as the incentives for an East Asian grouping may be fairly strong.

VI. Summary: EAI and the U.S.-ASEAN Interest

We summarize below some of the most important points of this chapter:

A. Introduction:

1. While the United States continues to be a key market for ASEAN countries, intra-regional economic integration in East Asia has been increasing substantially. Moreover, this trend is market-driven, rather than policy-driven, as was arguably the case in the early years of EU integration. Hence, regional initiatives such as AFTA tend to be of the "flag following trade" variety.

2. ASEAN economic cooperation, though in the form of a PTA, has unambiguously embraced an outward-oriented approach

to trade and investment with other countries and regions. This "open regionalism" will tend to be welfare enhancing and meets the "qualitative dependency" criteria referred to in Chapter 3.

3.   In fact, intra-ASEAN economic integration is being driven by a desire to increase regional economic efficiency in order to increase efficiency and competitiveness at the *global* level, rather than to increase intra-regional trade as a goal in and of itself (as is the case with many other PTAs in the developing world, which are driven more by politics than economics).

4.   Economic integration within ASEAN—and with the world in general—is also being used as a means of promoting needed domestic economic reform, in much the same way as regional initiatives enabled countries in the EU and NAFTA to undertake reforms that would otherwise have been difficult or impossible.

5.   Many of the initiatives that are being developed within ASEAN and between ASEAN member-states and other partners, such as the United States, could also have been accomplished under the WTO, at least in theory. However, the WTO process is currently experiencing considerable difficulties and, besides, in some areas much more can be done within a regional framework.

B. Implications of regionalism in Japan, the EU, and the United States

1.   Japan has made an important and obvious shift toward embracing PTAs only over the past few years. Its first PTA was with Singapore, finalized in November 2002.

2.   The estimated (*ex ante*) effects of Japan's existing and regional initiatives are almost uniformly negative for the ASEAN countries (when they are excluded). Malaysia is the most vulnerable to these accords. While the effects are not estimated to be large relative to GDP, the downward bias of CGE models, plus the usual disproportionate sectoral effects, suggest that the real implications for the respective ASEAN countries could be more drastic.

3.   Hence, given the importance of Japan as a trading partner and source of FDI, ASEAN countries have a strong incentive to link up with Japan. However, PTA will be more difficult than in the

case of the EAI, mainly due to agriculture.

4.   The EU is a less important economic partner and, relative to Japan and the United States, has not done much in terms of promoting economic cooperation accords with the region. Its most important initiative to date is ASEM. But unlike, say, APEC, ASEM has no specific economic agenda or liberalization vision.

5.   ASEAN countries suffer from the loss of most-favoured nation status created by the EU's complicated "pyramid of preferences", in which all (original) ASEAN countries find themselves among the lowest preferential rankings (along with other WTO members). ASEAN has also been negatively affected by the Single Market Program, which created a common market in Europe, and will be hurt (though marginally) by the Fifth Enlargement of the EU, which began on 1 May 2004.

6.   Hence, ASEAN countries do have an incentive to develop closer economic ties with the EU. However, no such initiatives are in the offing. Moreover, the agricultural question will be an important one once the EU and ASEAN sit down at the negotiating table, given the highly protectionist Common Agricultural Policy of the EU. For example, agriculture is the reason why the EU-MERCOSUR agreement has not yet been concluded. Labour-intensive sectors like textiles and clothing will also cause difficulties, as they will within the EAI context.

7.   Nevertheless, it is likely that the EU will soon realize its strong interest in staying engaged in East Asia, particularly as the EAI and Japanese initiatives develop, given the fact that Asia is the most exciting region in the world. After all, the EU is the most unrepentant regionalist in the world.

8.   With respect to the United States, the Bush administration has been far more aggressive than its predecessors in pursuing PTAs. Many of these are already being undertaken with EAI-country competitors, including Singapore. The EAI is an important part of this process and will likely receive a priority in the near future; the USTR is already in the first phase of negotiations with Thailand over a bilateral FTA.

9.   The most significant PTA that the United States currently has is NAFTA, and it is a bit too early to gauge just how much trade

diversion the region has suffered due to preferential treatment in favour of Mexico. One study actually has estimated a positive effect. However, certain key sectors are no doubt being negatively affected, and there is strong anecdotal evidence that ASEAN is suffering from investment diversion in favour of Mexico. *The EAI would allow ASEAN to redeem its most-favoured-nation treatment in the U.S. market and could give it a competitive edge over other competitors, most notably China.*

10. Regarding proposed initiatives, the biggest threat to ASEAN would be the FTAA. While the FTAA is currently stalled, the United States has been negotiating PTAs with the more outward-oriented countries in the region, including completed accords with Chile and Central America. These should not be too problematic for ASEAN, except if an accord could be reached with Brazil, which is the largest of the South American economies and appears to have the greatest degree of overlap with ASEAN exports to the U.S. market. But such an accord is unlikely (Brazil's cautious stance regarding liberalization actually constitutes the greatest obstacle to a successful FTAA).

11. Actual and potential accords with other regions, such as in Africa and the Middle East, actually pose little threat to ASEAN. They actually could be positive for the region to the extent that these bilateral and regional accords lead to greater stability in this volatile region.

C. ASEAN Economic Integration: From the PTA to the AEC

1. The creation of AFTA was a major step forward in terms of regional economic integration in ASEAN. Prior efforts at creating a PTA were marginal at best. Since the launching of AFTA, ASEAN has embraced various economic deepening programs, from the investment-related cooperation (e.g., the AICO, AIA) to trade in services, intellectual property protection, and even finance. The decision in October 2003 to create an ASEAN Economic Community is the most ambitious programme to date and will likely focus ASEAN integration initiatives for the near, medium, and long terms.

2. The decision to create a region within which goods, services, capital, and skilled labour would flow freely stems from:

(1) the desire to create a post-AFTA agenda that would be comprehensive; (2) the perceived need to deepen economic integration in ASEAN in light of the new international commercial environment, especially the dominance of FTAs; (3) the possibility that bilateral FTAs could actually jeopardize ASEAN integration since all member states were free to pursue their own commercial-policy agenda; and (4) the recognition since the Asian Crisis that cooperation in the real and financial sectors must be extended concomitantly, and that free flows of skilled labour will be necessary to do this.

3. The regional integration process in ASEAN is mainly designed as a means of lowering transactions costs and increasing efficiency at the global level, rather than merely to increase intra-regional trade and investment. This is at the core of its outward-oriented, "open regionalism" approach to commercial policy.

4. From an economic perspective, ASEAN is not a "natural economic bloc" by some definitions, which is why some pundits are critical of ASEAN. However, by other definitions, including our econometric gravity-model estimates, it would be considered a "natural bloc". Still, given that ASEAN integration is outward oriented, from an economic perspective this question is not particularly important.

5. The economies of the ASEAN member-states have become more "symmetrical" over time, in the sense that their business cycles have become increasingly correlated. This suggests that greater economic cooperation at the macroeconomic level is becoming more important, and emphasizes the "public good" nature of appropriate policies in the region. The Asian Crisis demonstrated clearly that ASEAN economies are jointly dependent on economic shocks, as evidenced by the contagion effect, even though these countries are not that closely integrated in terms of real economic integration. Macroeconomic cooperation may be one way to internalize this policy externality.

D. Asia-Pacific Economic Cooperation

1. There is actually a long history of cooperation at the Asia-Pacific level, including PAFTAD, PBEC, and PECC. However, APEC,

launched in 1989, was the first government-related form of cooperation initiated at the regional level.

2. In a way, the establishment of APEC reflects the recognition by the Asia-Pacific countries of the importance of the United States as a major market for their goods and as a source for investment. Because of this, many countries believe that the United States cannot be left out of any meaningful cooperation effort in the region.

3. APEC is unique internationally for a variety of regions. For example, rather than being a tightly knit regional grouping, APEC embraces "open regionalism" whereby whatever preferences are negotiated among the APEC members are also given to a third party so that there is no trade diversion effect (though it is not clear if countries outside the region would have to reciprocate or not). Moreover, it does not negotiate formal reductions in trade and investment barriers. All liberalization within APEC is voluntary; no sanctions or penalties exist for countries that miss agreed-upon targets.

4. By just about any measure, the "value-added" of APEC is quite low. However, some progress is being made. For example, extensive work is being undertaken by APEC working groups on improving customs clearance procedures, including the creation of a businessperson's "smart card", investment agreements, exploration of means to facilitate technology transfer, cooperation in infrastructure, standards and conformance, harmonization of product standards, enhanced dialogue on trade and investment facilitation, and development cooperation.

5. The "ASEAN+3" initiatives, which range from finance to trade, are essentially a re-packaging of the East Asian Economic Group proposed by former Malaysian prime minister Mahathir. It is likely that economic integration along the lines of the ASEAN+3 will continue, particularly since the gains to the member-states would be large (though, obviously, negotiations will continue to be difficult in sensitive sectors). While there is little reason to believe that ASEAN+3 initiatives will end up being inward-looking—quite the contrary—the United States will still suffer from a loss of competitiveness in these markets if it is locked out

of the ASEAN-3 accords. Hence, it is in the U.S. interest, as well as those of the EAI countries, to keep the United States actively engaged in the region.

E. ASEAN and the "Chinese Competitive Threat"

1. As China has become a major international powerhouse, it has been perceived as a threat by both developed and developing countries. This is particularly true of the ASEAN countries, whose exports are increasingly similar to China's in the U.S. and other OECD markets.

2. Moreover, there is a perception in ASEAN that FDI has been diverted to China. The fact that FDI inflows to the EAI countries have been generally disappointing while Chinese inflows have been booming has been used to support this argument.

3. However, our statistical work shows that China is not necessarily "special"; as the world becomes more closely integrated, competition rises. China is just an important part of this process.

4. Hence, while the Chinese threat is real in this sense, the policy prescriptions for ASEAN are essentially the same as they would have been without the spectacular emergence of China in the international marketplace: ASEAN countries need to concentrate on lowering the costs of doing business, improving productivity, and facilitating market-consistent structural change.

5. In addition, China will likely be a key economic partner, as well as competitor, in the future. China does have a huge trade surplus but its import growth has been extremely strong. This will likely continue as the economy continues to overheat. Regional initiatives with China might be embraced with this goal in mind: China is, after all, an important part of the ASEAN+3.

6. ASEAN is currently working on creating an FTA with China and fruits of these discussions are already being reaped (e.g., the "early harvest" liberalization launched at the beginning of 2004). This is important, especially since ASEAN will have a great deal to lose if China were to negotiate PTAs with its key markets.

7. Finally, the Chinese Threat strengthens the case for the EAI. The ASEAN countries have the incentive to obtain a competitive edge

over China in the U.S. market, and the United States needs to avoid being locked out of the East Asian integration process, of which China will ultimately be a key protagonist.

Notes

1   See Scollay and Gilbert (2001), Table 3.2e, p. 70.
2   This and the following paragraph draws from Naya (2004).
3   In 2000, the Lome IV Convention expired and the EU and the 78 ACP countries accepted the Cotonou Partnership Agreements, which will, for eight years, extend non-reciprocal Lome preferences (except for bananas, which fall under a different protocol) (Messerlin 2001, p. 207).
4   Messerlin (2001, p. 23) calculates a measure of tariff and non-tariff barriers, called the "rate of overall protection," for the EU in 1999, which comes to 7.7 per cent and 31.7 per cent for manufactures and agriculture, respectively.
5   The actual HS heading is 020610, "edible offal of bovine".
6   Agreements include: adoption of international standards regarding sanitary and phytosanitary measures; adoption of international standards and conformance measures; simplification of customs procedures; reduction in differences in intellectual property protection and enforcement standards; provision of greater transparency in government procurement procedures; continued services liberalization; and the consideration of the issuance of an ASEM travel card for businesspeople.
7   They use the United States and Canada for lack of any better candidates. They exclude from the calculations U.S.-Canadian trade, which may have been distorted due to the Canada-U.S. Free-Trade Area, and correct for any differences in inflation, exchange rate, and GDP growth rates. For more details, see Kreinin and Plummer (2002).
8   For more details on the history and development of ASEAN, see Naya and Plummer (1997) and Plummer (forthcoming 2005). This survey borrows from both. The contributions to Kumar (2005) consider this evolution in the context of Asian economic integration.
9   The Closer Economic Relations (CER) FTA between Australia and New Zealand is also an exception if we define Asia more broadly to include them.
10 In fact, this range of tariffs probably contradicts the requirements spelled out in Article 24 of the GATT/WTO, which provides for possibility of RTAs. However, as developing countries, ASEAN benefits from the Enabling Clause, which has always freed it from the constraints of Article 24 (obviously the PTA was even a more egregious violation).

[11] Operationalized in November 1996, AICO is based on commodities under CEPT. The CEPT programme, launched at the 1992 ASEAN Summit meeting, was the main mechanism by which AFTA was to be initiated. Products under the CEPT programme included only manufactured goods, including capital goods and processed agricultural products.

[12] For updated reports on developments in intra-regional cooperation in the area of fixed-income securities, see the Asian Development Bank's Asian Regional Information Centre, www.aric.adb.org, and in particular "Asian Bonds Online", http://asianbondsonline.adb.org/regional/regional.php.

[13] The free flow of all labour, including unskilled labour, was deemed too politically difficult to consider in the AEC.

[14] The WTO accepted Cambodia's application to join in 2003, though its formal accession, which followed after approval by the Cambodian parliament, came in September 2004.

[15] This section draws in part from Naya (2003).

[16] Parts of this subsection draw from Naya (2004).

[17] *Wall Street Journal online*, www.wsj.com, 20 December 2004.

[18] For example, see Lee and Plummer (forthcoming) for an in-depth analysis of these issues.

[19] The Japanese regression only runs from 1982–95, due to problems associated with the FDI data.

References

Bayoumi, Tamim, Barry Eichengreen, and Paolo Mauro. *On Regional Monetary Arrangements for ASEAN*, Prepared for the ADB/CEPII/KIEP Conference on Exchange Rate Regimes in Emerging Economies, Tokyo, 17–19 December, 1999.

Bleaney, M.F., D. Greenaway and R.C. Hine. "The Impact of the 1992 Programme on Non-EC European Countries: An Overview". In *Economic Integration in Europe and North America*, edited by M. Panic and A. Vacic. New York: United Nations, 1995.

Feinberg, Richard E. and Ye Zhao, eds. *Assessing APEC's Progress: Trade, Ecotech and Institutions*. Singapore: ISEAS, 2001.

Kim, Sunghyun H., M. Ayhan Kose, and Michael G. Plummer. "Dynamics of Business Cycles in Asia: Differences and Similarities," *Review of Development Economics* 7, no. 3 (August 2003).

Kreinin, Mordechai E. and Michael G. Plummer. *Economic Integration and Development: Has Regionalism Delivered for Developing Countries?* London: Edward Elgar, 2002.

Kumar, Nagesh, ed. *Towards an Asian Economic Community*. Singapore: ISEAS, 2005.

Lee, Chung H. and Michael G. Plummer. "Economic Development in China and Its Implications for East Asia". In *Miracle and Mirages in East Asian Economic Development*, edited by LaCroix, Imada-Iboshi, and Togashi, forthcoming.

Lee, Hiro, David Roland-Holst, and Dominique van der Mensbrugghe. "China's Emergence and East Asian Trade under Alternative Trading Arrangements". *Journal of Asian Economics* 15, no. 4 (August 2004): 697–712.

Lee, Hiro and Dominique van der Mensbrugghe. "EU Enlargement and Its Impact on East Asia". *Journal of Asian Economics* 14, no. 6 (2004): 843–60, with special reference to Table 3, p. 852.

Messerlin, Patrick. *The Costs of Protection in the EU*. Washington, D.C.: IIE, 2001.

Naya, Seiji F. "Japan in Emerging East Asian Regionalism". Forthcoming.

Naya, Seiji F. and Michael G. Plummer. "Economic Cooperation after 30 Years of ASEAN". *ASEAN Economic Bulletin*, 14, no. 2 (November 1997): 117–26.

Plummer, Michael G. "On the Creation of an ASEAN Economic Community: Lessons from the EU and Reflections on the Roadmap". In *Roadmap for the ASEAN Economic Community*, edited by Denis Hew, forthcoming.

Scollay, Robert and John P. Gilbert. *New Regional Trading Arrangements in the Asia Pacific?* Washington, D.C.: IIE, 2002.

6

The Economic Case for U.S.-ASEAN Bilateral Free-Trade Areas

I.   Introduction

Throughout this study, we have stressed that the U.S.-ASEAN trade and investment relationship is important to all parties. But we have also stressed that the relationship is not what it could be. There is plenty of statistical evidence that the U.S.-ASEAN economic relationship could be improved through policy action, at the national (e.g., through domestic policy reform), regional (e.g., closer economic cooperation within ASEAN and with the United States), and international (e.g., the WTO) levels. Free-trade areas between the United States and ASEAN were also shown to create positive welfare effects for all countries. Moreover, given changes in the contemporary international commercial policy environment, including the new regionalism trend and the emergence of India and especially China as major players in international markets, failure to take a proactive approach to the U.S.-ASEAN bilateral relationship could risk a progressive deterioration in bilateral links. In addition, the considerable increase in intra-regional trade in Asia, driven by the market in the past but no doubt to be pushed by new FTAs in the future, presents a strong incentive to the United States to remain engaged in the region.

In the late 1980s, when the United States and ASEAN were contemplating closer economic relations through the "ASEAN-U.S. Initiative", both parties had the option of either embracing closer formal economic integration or maintaining the status quo (Naya et al. 1989). They generally opted for the latter. However, in the mid-2000s, there is arguably no turning back: the choice may well be either to move forward or backward by default.

Thus, in this study we have emphasized that U.S.-ASEAN bilateral FTAs under the rubric of the EAI would be both timely and advantageous to the United States and ASEAN, for a variety of reasons. These include:

- the traditional economic effects of FTAs;
- the dynamic economic effects of FTAs;
- the EAI as a "defensive" policy strategy;
- the positive effects these accords would imply for structural change and policy reform in both ASEAN and the United States; and
- the non-economic implications of developing stronger relations.

In this chapter, we essentially make the case for the EAI, primarily based on the results of the previous chapters. We begin in Section II with a basic statistical and analytical review of the U.S.-ASEAN economic relationship, followed in Section III by a summary of the economic effects of the proposed U.S.-ASEAN FTAs for the United States and ASEAN, including the likely "traditional" (static) effects and dynamic effects of the EAI, as well as its implications for policy reform in the EAI. Section IV considers associated policy variables, such as ASEAN integration and the EAI, bilateral FTAs as a defensive policy strategy for ASEAN and the United States, and a brief review of a few key non-economic variables.

II. The Economic Realities behind the U.S.-EAI Economic Relationship

1. The trade review in Chapter 2 (Table 2.1) clearly demonstrates that the United States is the most important export market for Thailand, Malaysia and the Philippines, and is a key market for Indonesia, Singapore and Brunei. However, aggregate bilateral trade flows can be deceiving; in addition to many data-related

issues involved in a region with considerable entrepôt trade (e.g., double-counting problems), the *composition* of these flows is in many ways more important. After all, in summer 2004, the price of oil increased to over US$50 a barrel and remained above US$40 for the rest of the year; this will no doubt cause a decrease in the U.S. share of Brunei's exports, as Brunei's exports most of its oil to Asia. But this would hardly be an indication of a deterioration of the importance of the United States to Brunei.

2.   In fact, we were able to show that the United States is emerging as an important market for many of the areas that Brunei is trying to develop in order to diversify its over-reliance on energy-related products, e.g., textiles and clothing. We estimated that it is the country with the greatest trade expansion potential of the EAI countries (as a percentage of total exports). Moreover, as the United States is a world leader in financial services trade, it could be an increasingly important partner as Brunei endeavours to establish itself as a financial centre.

3.   For all other EAI countries, the data are even more conspicuous: electronics and electronic machinery has emerged as the dominant sector for the exports of Singapore, Malaysia, the Philippines, and Thailand, and it is the most dynamic area in Indonesia. The United States has been the most important market for these exports. Moreover, our research (and that of others) shows that FDI—and particularly U.S. FDI—has been the key protagonist of electronics exports for all of these countries. Hence, the U.S. market will likely be more important in the future as ASEAN countries develop and diversify.

4.   The ASEAN countries do constitute an important market for certain U.S. exports, though obviously the relatively small size of the ASEAN markets and the fact that the U.S. trade structure is fairly evenly split between Europe, the Americas, and Asia naturally produce relatively low trade shares. Nevertheless, rapid growth in ASEAN (pre- and post-Crisis) has provided myriad new market opportunities for U.S. exports and investors abroad. ASEAN countries have not yet reverted to the pre-Crisis growth trend, but the economic expansion over the past five years has been far greater than the global average, and future prospects are bright. These trends would suggest that ASEAN will become

increasingly important to the United States. Moreover, as ASEAN lies in the heart of the most exciting region of the world, it will continue to be an attractive place for U.S. multinationals.

5. In addition to this potential "growth effect", we would argue that ASEAN could easily become an even more attractive destination for U.S. FDI in the short- and medium-term for other reasons, such as: (a) AFTA, which reduces considerably transaction costs associated with using ASEAN as a production hub, has now come into effect. It will be a few more years before the "bugs" are worked out of the agreement, particularly in terms of information dissemination to the private sector and practical matters as to how it can benefit from the 0–5 per cent CEPT tariffs (according to the *Economist* magazine of July 2004, there have been reports of numerous bureaucratic problems and ignorance of potential benefits/procedures); and (b) the huge increase in FDI inflows to China will likely subside over the next few years, as (i) the government's attempt to reduce economic activity in the country by reducing investment begins to "bite"; (ii) underlying problems in China's spectacular growth of recent years, particularly in—but not limited to—the financial sector will increase uncertainty as to growth prospects; and (iii) the low rate of return on multinational investment in China starts to have its obvious effect.[1]

6. The United States has a merchandise trade deficit with the EAI countries. However, it is important to stress that the United States has a significant trade surplus with ASEAN in the area of services. The growth rate of U.S. exports of services to the EAI countries was higher than the global average for all save the Philippines (which is the United States' most important EAI market).

7. The surplus on services is not sufficient to balance the deficit on the merchandise account, but, as we noted in Chapter 2, the origins of the trade deficit in the United States—or any country for that matter—are macroeconomic in nature: the United States had a US$509 billion dollar overall merchandise trade deficit in 2002, essentially because of insufficient net private savings in the United States to cover the huge increase in the U.S. government's need to borrow (i.e., the budget deficit).

8. In Chapter 3, we use a large econometric gravity model to assess closely the determinants of the U.S.-ASEAN economic relationship and assess whether or not the relationship is "special", i.e., if, controlling for all factors, there exists a bias in U.S.-ASEAN trade patterns. If such a trade bias does exist, we stressed that it would be consistent with at least one definition of a "natural" economic bloc. We find that, indeed, the U.S.-ASEAN relationship is special in the sense that the ASEAN binary variable is statistically significant, relatively large in magnitude (e.g., compared to comparable EU regressions) and has a tendency to rise over time. However, in separating out individual EAI countries, this special relationship does not really materialize in the case of Indonesia (except in a few years); exists to some degree in the case of Malaysia, but appears to be declining over time and with a good deal of volatility; and is most notable in the cases of Singapore, Thailand and the Philippines but, again, the magnitudes and, in the case of the Philippines, statistical significance, decreases over time. The reason for this decline in trade bias is unclear from the econometric model used, but we note several policy variables, including preferential treatment under NAFTA and in other accords, may have played a role.

9. Our statistical analysis of Chapters 2 and 3 show that the EAI countries increasingly compete with each other (and China) in the U.S. and other OECD markets. The overlap would suggest that an FTA between the United States and one ASEAN country to the exclusion of the others would have an important negative effect on ASEAN partners. CGE-model results confirm this potential trade diversion problem. *This is why the EAI as a joint initiative makes sense: (a) the agreements should be related, such that they do not cause discrimination/imbalances in the accords, and, hence, a regional rubric is warranted; but (b) as Chapter 4 clearly demonstrated, the ASEAN countries are diverse in many respects, in terms of economic and non-economic characteristics, and a bilateral approach will make it much easier to accommodate these special needs.* Indeed, while some in ASEAN have lamented the fact that the United States first worked out an FTA with Singapore, it is important to note that Singapore is very different from any other ASEAN country

particularly in areas that will be the most sensitive in the FTA
process (most notably agriculture).

III. The Economics of the EAI

1. What will be the likely economic effects of the U.S.-ASEAN
    FTAs? We devote a considerable part of Chapter 3 to the analysis
    of the possible implications of the regionalism trend in general
    and the potential economic effects of bilateral FTAs between the
    United States and ASEAN in particular. Our main conclusions
    follow.
2. Free-trade areas and other forms of formal regional economic
    integration are "second-best" policies in that they are characterized
    by both positive (trade creation) and negative (trade diversion)
    effects. We noted that this is why many economists are against
    FTAs; multilateral liberalization provides for the positive effects
    without any negative ones, that is, initiatives under the WTO
    are "first best" in that they unambiguously improve efficiency.
3. While true in theory, we stressed that the WTO is currently off-
    track and the Doha Development Agenda will take a considerable
    amount of time to conclude. Moreover, its results will likely be
    quite limited relative to what can be accomplished within the
    framework of an FTA, as it is difficult to work out compromises
    between its 148 member states, some of which are not particularly
    pro-liberalization. This is one reason why the new regionalism
    movement has become so popular. As the ASEAN member-states
    and the United States are enthusiastic in their outward-oriented
    policy stances, they make strong candidates for an FTA in this
    regard.
4. A major shortcoming with economic modelling in this area is
    that it fails to take policy-related issues sufficiently seriously.
    These models generally focus on the one-time effect of a price
    change induced by an FTA; such a scenario *a priori* would no
    doubt have limited long-run effects on associated economies.
    However, policy changes (and dynamic effects, discussed below)
    have long-run effects that build up over time and tend to be
    "path dependent". This could be either positive or negative
    for economic efficiency; an FTA, for example, that is used to

create an inward-looking "fortress" could be detrimental to the member-states themselves (Latin American FTA initiatives in the past have been of this type and have all ended in failure) and to global trade. This possibility is another reason why some economists fear the FTA trend.

5. In this study we made the case that U.S.-ASEAN FTAs will no doubt be outward-oriented in substance, as only this sort of approach would be consistent with the overall direction of commercial policies of the parties involved and, by the way, would be the only approach that would make sense. *The United States is arguably the most open large economy in the developed world, and ASEAN initiatives have demonstrated an instinctive outward-orientation at the regional level, a natural result of its member-states having embraced external liberalization at the national level over the past two decades.* Hence, it would only make sense that the FTAs under the rubric of the EAI would be outward-oriented. Certainly the U.S.-Singapore agreement is of this type.

A. Static Efficiency Effects of the EAI

6. Of course, FTAs are inherently discriminatory and there will be trade diversion effects. Also, the United States has created FTAs, such as NAFTA, with certain inward-oriented characteristics (e.g, rules of origin in automobiles and textiles and clothing). However, these tend to be the exception rather than the rule. And it is important to emphasize that these sectors were closed in the U.S. market anyway. In other words, if we ask the question as to whether or not NAFTA made these sectors more protectionist, it is not clear. What is clear is that the textiles and clothing sector would have remained highly protected without NAFTA and there would have been less competition in the U.S. market from labour-abundant Mexico. It is inappropriate to compare NAFTA with global free trade; we must compare NAFTA with the status quo, and in this light it looks far more open.

7. With respect to the actual effects of bilateral FTAs between the United States and individual ASEAN countries, we concluded that, in general, the overall economic effects would be fairly small, but this is in part due to the "static" nature of the models

used. If we include dynamic and/or policy changes, the overall effects could potentially be many times larger. Having said that, we found that: (a) CGE modelling suggests that the GDP of the Philippines, Indonesia, Malaysia and Thailand should rise by 3.1 per cent, 2.75 per cent, 0.46 per cent, and 0.72 per cent, respectively; (b) the effects on the U.S. economy, given its size, are trivial. At least in relative terms, the ASEAN partners gain more than the United States in the case of every FTA, suggesting one reason why the United States will seek more than just market access in the EAI FTA negotiations (as they have in other bilaterals, including the USSFTA); (c) despite the small overall effects of the bilateral FTAs, there are some very large effects at the sectoral level. *Moreover, the factors of production that gain the most in ASEAN would be unskilled labour, and unskilled labour in the United States also gains in all cases (though marginally)*; (d) we devise a highly-disaggregated approach to "matching" 5-digit SITC commodities to protection-applied export markets and then estimate potential trade expansion, which allows us to underscore the key product groups that would be affected (in both the United States and ASEAN). We find that the top few exports of every EAI country (with the possible exceptions of Thailand and Brunei) tend to dominate exports to the United States. Moreover, as would be expected, these commodities generally fall in the electronics-related category, with some exception. However, protection tends to be low in electronics in the United States; therefore, the estimated trade expansion potential is limited (in many cases, the U.S. MFN-applied or GSP-applied tariff is even zero, implying zero trade potential). But it is important to note that these estimates are merely extrapolations based on a partial, static methodology: we stress that the dynamic effects of the EAI could actually make these sectors by far the chief benefactors. Other top product groups where protection is high would not only generate the greatest degree of trade but also would help facilitate structural change in partner countries.

8. We did not do similar estimates for the services sector, due to the lack of disaggregated trade in services data and, of course, difficulties associated with quantifying estimates of protection.

However, given the growing importance of trade in services to the U.S. and EAI economies, it will likely be heavily influenced by the EAI. As is noted in Chapter 4, services will be a key negotiating area in all bilateral FTAs. *Our analysis in this chapter also strongly suggests that an FTA with the United States could also go a long way in helping the ASEAN countries push their own economic reform agenda in these areas.*

B. Dynamic Effects of the EAI

9. The fairly unimpressive results estimated using the GTAP-based CGE models are derived in part because the U.S. and ASEAN economies are already so open. Hence, if the driving force behind policy change is merely reducing tariffs to zero, and tariffs are already fairly close to zero, the net effect cannot be large. The ASEAN countries have advocated economic deepening initiatives in the region as a means of lowering transactions costs and stimulating FDI inflows, particularly from outside the region. Increasing FDI inflows from the United States—and from other countries wishing to have duty-free access to the U.S. market—is a key incentive for the ASEAN countries, particularly given the fairly disappointing inflows of FDI to ASEAN—from the United States and the rest of world. Excluding FDI is therefore a key problem in capturing the true effects of the U.S.-ASEAN FTAs.

10. When the EU went about creating a common market—through the Single Market Program, which set the groundwork for economic union—the economic effects calculated by a standard CGE model would have been trivial: a customs union already existed in the EU. The only change driving the model would have been the integration of a few non-tariff barriers. Instead, the EC Commission set out to estimate many of the dynamic effects that would be forthcoming through the creation of a truly integrated market in Europe. In order to do this, it undertook a major study to try to quantify the benefits of a common market by estimating the costs associated with *not* having a common market (indeed, the title of the study is *The Costs of Non-Europe* [Cecchini 1998]). Rather than producing marginal results, the study estimated that the benefits of the Single Market Program

could be as much as 6.25 per cent of the entire EC GDP. In addition to the above-mentioned investment effects and the other dynamic effects discussed below, a key area that stood out in the study regarded the harmonization of product standards, mutual recognition of product testing, mutual recognition of professional certifications and qualifications, and the like. These ended up being very difficult to integrate, particularly in the context of a region like the EU where there are deeply-entrenched traditions. Many of these areas are covered in the U.S.-Singapore agreement and, as we noted in Chapter 4, will likely be an important part of other bilateral FTAs with the United States. Now, it is important to underscore that these areas generally imply the adoption of "best practices", reducing unnecessary costs, and bolstering competition, rather than creating a "fortress". The United States, which was suspicious that the Single Market Program would be used as means of creating a "fortress Europe", was fairly quickly convinced that the EU construction project was generally outward-oriented in nature. The same will likely be true for the EAI.

11. Economies of scale is another area that is excluded from economic modelling but yet could lead to substantial gains for ASEAN exports. As ASEAN countries move up the development ladder, they will be competing increasingly in areas in which economies of scale matter, including electronics, chemicals, and auto-related production. They are currently restricted by the small size of each ASEAN market. As ASEAN integration proceeds apace, exports will have duty-free (or close to duty-free) access to a regional market, but once again, the combined ASEAN market is not large relative to the domestic markets of the United States, Japan, and the EU. Hence, the EAI—as well as ASEAN+3 initiatives—could help competitiveness in related areas.

12. *More significantly, the "forced efficiency" effect that will be created by the EAI could improve productivity in the ASEAN countries and facilitate structural change in key sectors.* In particular, the non-border areas that the U.S.-Singapore agreement included involve the need to adopt "best practices", create an effective competitions policy (currently lacking in many ASEAN countries), reduce investment distortions by

providing national treatment to foreign investors, promote the effective implementation of existing intellectual property protection legislation, and improve corporate and government transparency. These changes could lead to considerable gains in efficiency and productivity in the EAI, as well as provide for the necessary groundwork to facilitate technology transfer. Also, as we discovered in Chapter 4, most of these areas are already priorities of the various ASEAN governments. The EAI should, therefore, expedite and facilitate the implementation of this policy framework.

13. It is important to note that, while a successful multilateral liberalization process would do as much (or more) for the investment- and economies-of-scale-related dynamic effects, this is not necessarily so in the case of "forced efficiency". Many of the areas covered under the U.S.-Singapore agreement, particularly with respect to the non-border issues mentioned above, would be extremely difficult—if not impossible—to negotiate realistically in the context of the WTO. The grouping is just too diverse. Even the "Singapore Issues", which are modest compared to the comprehensiveness of the U.S.-Singapore accord, were sufficient to sink the Cancun WTO Ministerial meeting.

14. Finally, the non-border issues that are covered in the agreement tend to make frequent reference to WTO protocols, disciplines and agreements, e.g., in the area of services, government procurement, and intellectual property. In this sense, the forced-efficiency related areas are clearly "building blocs" to multilateral cooperation.

IV. Other Policy Considerations

A. ASEAN Integration and the EAI

1. ASEAN economic integration has been proceeding at a rather rapid clip in the early 2000s (at least relative to the past), with the advent of AFTA and the agreement to create an ASEAN Economic Community (AEC). We have argued here that closer macroeconomic and microeconomic cooperation between the ASEAN countries and between the United States and ASEAN through the EAI will have salutary implications for

macroeconomic and financial stability, as well as generating static and dynamic benefits through integration.

2. From an economic perspective, ASEAN is not a "natural economic bloc" by some definitions, which is why some pundits are critical of ASEAN. However, by other definitions, including our econometric gravity-model estimates, it *would* be considered a "natural bloc". Still, given that ASEAN integration is outward-oriented, from an economics perspective this question is not particularly important in considering economic efficiency effects of regionalism.

3. The decision to create a region within which goods, services, capital, and skilled labour would flow freely within the context of the AEC stems from: (a) the desire to create a post-AFTA agenda that would be comprehensive; (b) the perceived need to deepen economic integration in ASEAN in light of the new international commercial environment; (c) the possibility that bilateral FTAs could actually jeopardize ASEAN integration because all member-states were free to pursue their own commercial policy agenda; and (d) the recognition since the Asian Crisis that cooperation in the real and financial sectors must be extended concomitantly, and that free flows of skilled labour will be necessary to do this. *We argue in this study that deeper economic integration between ASEAN countries will actually facilitate accords with non-member countries, such as the United States.* In fact, the "ASEAN-U.S. Initiative" mentioned above did not produce substantive results for two main reasons: (a) the ASEAN economic reform process was still in its infancy; and, especially, (b) regional economic integration within ASEAN had not yet been sufficiently developed. Since then, ASEAN countries have reformed their external commercial policy to earn them the right to be included among the most liberal in the developing world, and the ASEAN leaders have succeeded in creating AFTA, the AIA, and developing a blueprint for the AEC. These would have been thought impossible in the late 1980s. *We argue here that this new policy regime in ASEAN, coupled with the U.S. government's recent regionalism approach to commercial policy, suggest that the time is ripe for the EAI.*

5. The economies of the ASEAN member-states have become more

"symmetric" over time, in the sense that their business cycles have become increasingly correlated. This suggests that greater economic cooperation at the macroeconomic level is becoming more important, and emphasizes the "public good" nature of appropriate policies in the region. The Asian Crisis demonstrated clearly that ASEAN economies are jointly affected by economic shocks, as evidenced by the contagion effect, even though they are not that closely integrated in terms of real economic integration. Macroeconomic cooperation may be one way to internalize this policy externality.

6. Economic integration within ASEAN is also being used as a means of promoting needed domestic economic reform, in much the same as regional initiatives enabled countries in the EU and NAFTA to undertake reforms that would otherwise have been difficult or impossible. This will also be true of the EAI. Many of the initiatives that are being developed within ASEAN and between ASEAN member-states and other partners, such as the United States, could also have been accomplished under the WTO, at least in theory. However, the WTO process is currently experiencing considerable difficulties and, besides, in some areas much more can be done within a regional framework.

B. The EAI as a Defensive Strategy for ASEAN

7. An additional motivation for ASEAN in pursuing the EAI regards the need for a "defensive" strategy in the current international economic environment. While the intellectual debate regarding whether or not FTAs constitute "building blocs" or "stumbling blocs" is not settled, it is an irrefutable reality that FTAs and other forms of economic integration have recently been driving international commercial policy of late, rather than multilateral initiatives. *Regionalism has become the rule, rather than a special exception granted in Article XXIV of the WTO/GATT. In order for ASEAN to redeem its "MFN" status, it may have little choice but to join the regionalism bandwagon.*

8. Hence, for ASEAN the decision to negotiate bilateral FTAs with the United States must be viewed in light of the current global race toward creating preferential trading arrangements: the United States, Japan and the EU—the most important markets

for the ASEAN countries—have negotiated various FTAs with ASEAN's competitors, and many more are in the works. In this sense, it is losing MFN status in these markets. This serves as a powerful additional incentive to participate in the EAI. We noted that estimates in the literature of associated trade diversion effects would not be large (except possibly in the case of bilateral FTAs with China), but the models suffer from the downward-biases of CGE modelling discussed above. Also, sectoral effects can be considerable.

9. Japan has made an important and obvious shift toward embracing preferential trading arrangements only over the past few years. Its first FTA was with Singapore, finalized in November 2002. The estimated effects of Japan's existing and regional initiatives are almost uniformly negative for the ASEAN countries (when they are excluded). Malaysia is the most vulnerable to these accords. Hence, given the importance of Japan as a trading partner and source of FDI, ASEAN countries have a strong incentive to link up with Japan.

11. The EU is a less important economic partner and, relative to Japan and the United States, has not done much in terms of promoting economic cooperation accords with the region. Its most important initiative to date is ASEM. But unlike, say, APEC, ASEM has no specific economic agenda or liberalization vision. ASEAN countries suffer from the loss of MFN status created by the EU's complicated "pyramid of preferences", in which all (original) ASEAN countries find themselves among the lowest preferential rankings (along with other WTO members). ASEAN has also been negatively affected by the Single Market Program and will be hurt (though marginally) by the Fifth Enlargement of the EU, which began on 1 May 2004. Hence, ASEAN countries do have an incentive to develop closer economic ties with the EU. But no such initiatives are in the offing. Moreover, the agricultural question will be an important one once the EU and ASEAN sit down at the negotiating table, given the highly-protectionist Common Agricultural Policy of the EU. Nevertheless, it is likely that the EU will soon realize its strong interest in staying engaged in East Asia, particularly as the EAI and Japanese initiatives develop, given the fact that

Asia is the most exciting region in the world. After all, the EU is the world's most unrepentant regionalist.

13. With respect to U.S.-related accords, the Bush administration has been far more aggressive than its predecessors in pursuing FTAs and other preferential arrangements. Many of these are already being undertaken with EAI-country competitors, including Singapore. The EAI is an important part of this process and will likely receive a priority in the near future; the USTR is already in the first phase of negotiations with Thailand over a bilateral FTA. The most significant FTA that the United States currently has is NAFTA. While it is too early to gauge just how much trade diversion the region has suffered due to preferential treatment in favour of Mexico, some sectors are no doubt being negatively affected, and there is strong anecdotal evidence that ASEAN is suffering from investment diversion to Mexico. The EAI would allow ASEAN to redeem its MFN status in the U.S. market and could give it a competitive edge over other competitors, most notably China.

14. Regarding initiatives in the works, the biggest threat to ASEAN would be the FTAA. While the FTAA is currently stalled, the United States has been negotiating FTAs with the more outward-oriented countries in the region, including completed accords with Chile and Central America. These should not be too problematic for ASEAN, except if an accord could be reached with Brazil, which is the largest of the South American economies and appears to have the greatest degree of overlap with ASEAN exports to the U.S. market. But such an accord is unlikely (Brazil's cautious stance regarding liberalization actually constitutes the greatest obstacle to a successful FTAA). Actual and potential accords with other regions, such as in Africa and the Middle East, actually pose little threat to ASEAN. They actually could be positive for the region to the extent that these bilateral and regional accords lead to greater stability in this volatile region.

15. In this study, we stress the unique role of China. While the economic growth unleashed by Deng's Four Modernizations in the late 1970s has stimulated tremendous progress in terms of reducing poverty levels and promoting development and prosperity in the world's most populous country and (until

recently) one of its poorest, it also creates a competitive threat, particularly to ASEAN. Our statistical work noted that Chinese exports increasingly compete with ASEAN in the U.S. and other OECD markets, and the trend is likely to continue. Moreover, ASEAN countries do compete in many ways for the same type of FDI that has been flowing so richly to China. We argue that the "Chinese threat" presents a challenge, but no more of a challenge than would otherwise be launched by an increasingly integrated *global* economy. The policy prescriptions to meet the Chinese threat are the same as they would be to meet the generic "threat" of the global marketplace, e.g., macroeconomic stability; liberalization of external commercial policies; greater microeconomic competition; and more ambitious, market-friendly policy reform at the national level, as well as more ambitious integration at the regional level. *But the EAI will no doubt give the ASEAN countries an important edge in competing with the Chinese in the U.S. market.* It would also be effective in ensuring that ASEAN does not lose out in the case of a China-U.S. accord, even if this is neither a realistic short- nor medium-term possibility.

C. The EAI as a Proactive Strategy for the United States

16. While the United States continues to be a key market for ASEAN countries, intra-regional economic integration in East Asia has been increasing substantially. Moreover, this trend is market-driven, rather than policy-driven, as was arguably the case in the early years of EU integration. The many new FTAs being proposed in the region, if implemented, could compound the existing trend. This would suggest that the United States could find itself losing market share in the world's fastest growing market.

17. In the past, the United States did not have to compete with other Asian powerhouses for policy influence in the region. Japan and South Korea were committed multilateralists, and China had not yet emerged as a major economic player. In the 2000s, however, the policy situation has changed considerably. Japan (and, to a lesser extent, South Korea) has become active in proposing new FTAs in Asia, either bilaterally or under the

ASEAN+3 umbrella. China is now a regional powerhouse and is doing the same. Both have launched negotiations with ASEAN regarding eventual FTAs, with China and ASEAN agreeing to an "early harvest programme" as a sort of down payment in the FTA negotiation process in 2004 and, finally, an FTA accord at the end of the year.

18. Thus, the United States is finding that major powers are now competing with it for influence in some of its most lucrative and promising markets. In fact, we have argued here that in many ways the ASEAN+3 is merely a repackaging of the East Asian Economic Bloc proposal articulated by Prime Minister Mahathir in December 1990. Fearing that a bloc that excluded the United States in Asia could have severe consequences for U.S. competitiveness in the region, the (first) Bush administration voiced forcefully its disapproval of such an arrangement publicly, upset that it was suggested at a time when APEC was getting off the ground. The proposal was also criticized by Malaysia's ASEAN partners; in the Singapore Declaration of 1992, which established AFTA, ASEAN agreed to a watered-down and non-threatening version of the proposal, i.e., the East Asian Economic Caucus.

19. If the ASEAN+3 succeeds in advancing regional integration, through FTAs and/or closer financial cooperation, it is likely that these accords will be open, for the reasons noted above. The United States does not need to fear Fortress Asia. Still, the United States could be affected negatively by trade diversion and could find itself losing influence if it, too, does not create an FTA with the ASEAN countries, which, after all, form the core of the ASEAN+3. Thus, the EAI can be useful as a defensive strategy to the United States as well.

20. Finally, it may be useful to discuss the role of APEC. After all, if APEC were to be successful in achieving the Bogor Vision of "open trade and investment" in the region by 2010 (for developed countries, 2020 for developing countries), these defensive strategies really would not be necessary. However, in this study we have argued that the "open regionalism" approach of APEC in its purest form, while preferred from an economic perspective is likely to be politically unworkable. Moreover, its voluntary

nature could ultimately be problematic. (Perhaps predictably, by just about any measure, the "value added" of APEC is quite low, even though some progress has been made especially in terms of trade and investment faciliation). Hence, while the United States should continue to take a proactive stance at APEC, it should be wary as to what really can be ulimately accomplished.

D. The Strategic Imperative

1.   Although we have focused this study on the economic effects of the EAI, it is of the essence to appreciate the close connection between political stability and economic growth and development. Africa and Latin America have often suffered due to bad economic policies, but it has been war—in the case of Africa—and political instability—in the case of both—that have been the great obstacles to economic progress in these regions.

2.   ASEAN's greatest success in Southeast Asia has been to bring peace and stability, without which the ASEAN economic "miracle" would not have been possible. Many critics of the slow progress of economic integration in ASEAN and its marginal effects on real economic interaction would best recall that without this peace and political stability in the region, successful development would have been impossible.

3.   The motivations behind ASEAN's enlargements in the 1990s were certainly not exclusively nor even primarily economic in nature: they were attempts to bring former adversaries (e.g., Vietnam) and countries with economic, political, and political-economy problems into the ASEAN fold. This was a controversial decision, and the United States and various ASEAN member-states are not in agreement as to whether or not "constructive engagement" or economic isolation is the best approach to sow change in Myanmar, for example. But this does not make the goal any less noble.

4.   After the Cold War, there was a great deal of excitement as to what the future held. It was widely anticipated that a new era of global peace was dawning. The world would finally be able to disarm after a very costly and nerve-wrenching post-World War II period. A large "peace dividend" was expected in terms of the ability for countries to now reduce drastically

military expenditures. Francis Fukuyama, in *The End of History*, hypothesized that the world was now converging toward common values of democracy, respect for human rights, and market-driven capitalism.

5. Such a world does not seem to be in evidence in the 2000s. Objective indicators would suggest that it is as dangerous as it ever was. The United States and ASEAN are close allies in on-going efforts to thwart global terrorism and reduce potentially devastating risks on the Korean peninsula and in the Taiwan Strait, as well as reduce tensions throughout the world. Clearly, it is in the interest of all parties to perpetuate and deepen these strong relations.

6. ASEAN and the United States do not need a series of bilateral FTAs under the EAI in order to accomplish this task. However, by building closer economic cooperation, political cooperation can become easier. This was certainly true in the case of ASEAN, as well as the EU. Moreover, we must stress that global exigencies have removed the option of either going forward or staying still: relations either go forward or they go backward. It is in the interest of all parties that the United States stay engaged in the region and the EAI can help accomplish this goal.

Note

[1] See Hsiao and Hsiao (2004) for an in-depth critique of FDI in China and an evaluation of its FDI "bubble".

References

Cecchini, Paolo, 1988. *The Costs of Non-Europe*. Brussels: Commission of the European Communities.

Hsiao, Frank and Mei-chu Hsiao. "The Chaotic Attractor of Foreign Direct Investment: Why China? A Panel Data Analysis". *Journal of Asian Economics* 15, no. 4 (August 2004): 641–70.

Naya, S., N. Akransee, M. Plummer and K. Sandhu, 1989. *The ASEAN-US Initiative*. Singapore: Institute of Southeast Asian Studies.

Index

About the Authors

Seiji Naya currently serves as a Distinguished Visiting Senior Fellow at the East-West Center and Emeritus Professor at the University of Hawaii.

He has worked in the field of international economics and Asian Development for over 40 years. He has served as Rockefeller Foundation Visiting Professor at Thammasat University in Thailand; as Chief Economist of the Asian Development Bank (ADB); Professor of Economics at the University of Hawaii, in the cabinet of the State of Hawaii. His publications include articles in *American Economic Review* and *Economic Development and Cultural Change*. His research on ASEAN has included the *US-ASEAN Initiative* in 1989, where he served as main author, and his latest publications include the *Asian Development Experience*, published by the ADB in 2002. He holds a BA from the University of Hawaii, PhD from the University of Wisconsin, and is a two-time U.S. featherweight boxing champion.

Michael G. Plummer is Professor of International Economics at Johns Hopkins University SAIS-Bologna.

He has published extensively on regional economic integration and development issues, in particular in the Asian context and in relation to ASEAN, and has consulted for numerous international organizations and government agencies. Professor Plummer was previously a professor at Brandeis University and a fellow at the East-West Center, with which he continues to collaborate regularly. He has also been a visiting professor/scholar at many universities and research institutes throughout the world, including Kobe University, the Monterey Institute of International Studies, the Institute of Southeast Asian Studies, and the Institut d'Etudes Politiques (Paris), as well as having been a Pew Fellow at Harvard University (1994–95). He is on the editorial boards of the *Journal of Asian Economics* and *World Development*.

He holds a BA from the University of Michigan and a Ph.D. from Michigan State University.